UNDERSTANDING PERFORMANCE APPRAISAL

UNDERSTANDING PERFORMANCE APPRAISAL

Social, Organizational, and Goal-Based Perspectives

Kevin R. Murphy
Jeanette N. Cleveland

SAGE Publications
International Educational and Professional Publisher
Thousand Oaks London New Delhi

For information address:

SAGE Publications, Inc.
2455 Teller Road
Thousand Oaks, California 91320

SAGE Publications Ltd.
6 Bonhill Street
London EC2A 4PU
United Kingdom

SAGE Publications India Pvt. Ltd.
M-32 Market
Greater Kailash I
New Delhi 110 048 India

Printed in the United States of America

Library of Congress Cataloging-in-Publication Data

Murphy, Kevin R., 1952-
    Understanding performance apprasial: Social, organizational, and goal-based perspectives / Kevin R. Murphy, Jeanette N. Cleveland.
        p.   cm.
    Includes bibliographical references and index.
    ISBN 0-8039-5474-3—ISBN 0-8039-5475-1 (pbk.)
    1. Employees—Rating of.   2. Performance standards.
I. Cleveland, Jeanette.   II. Title.
HF5549.5.R3M863   1995
658.3'125—dc20   94-23537

95 96 97 98 99 10 9 8 7 6 5 4 3 2 1

Sage Production Editor: Astrid Virding

Contents

Preface

This book began on the back of a cocktail napkin. At a conference, over drinks with Cris Banks and Janet Barnes-Farrell, we debated the state of the art of performance appraisal, bemoaning the lack of progress in several areas. Jan Cleveland suggested that a simpler model of the appraisal process was needed and sketched it out on the napkin. This model, with several modifications and elaborations, became the four-component model of the appraisal process in organizations that is used to organize this book.

In our first book on performance appraisal (Murphy & Cleveland, 1991) we presented a perspective that emphasized the role of the goals pursued by raters, ratees, and the various users of performance appraisal in understanding and improving the appraisal process. This book takes those ideas further and suggests ways this goal-oriented perspective might be applied in developing, implementing, and evaluating performance appraisal systems.

Our perspective emphasizes the context in which appraisal occurs and takes as a starting point the assumption that many of the apparent shortcomings of performance are in fact perfectly sensible adaptations to the various pressures, demands, and requirements of that context. We will present a substantial amount of research that supports this assumption. As a result of this perspective, we will suggest some new avenues for analyzing and improving appraisals in organizations.

Chapter 1 introduces the four-component model. Chapters 2 through 4 examine the ways in which the rating context affects performance appraisal processes and outcomes. Chapter 2 deals with the external environment, and Chapters 3 and 4 deal with the internal environments of organizations. Chapters 5 through 7 deal with the judgments raters make about ratees' performance. Chapter 5 examines methods by which raters obtain the information needed to assess performance. Chapter 6 examines the formation and application of standards for evaluating performance. Chapter 7 reviews the cognitive and affective processes involved in evaluating performance.

Chapters 8 and 9 examine a wide range of factors that lead raters to distort their ratings (usually upward). Chapter 8 suggests that this distortion is not simply a rater error, but rather an effect of the wide range of goals pursued by raters, ratees, and others. Chapter 9 examines in greater detail the forces in an organization that often motivate raters to inflate their performance appraisals.

Chapters 10 and 11 examine the criteria that are used to evaluate appraisal systems. These chapters suggest frameworks for choosing criteria that are relevant and useful for determining the contribution of performance appraisals to the organization. Chapter 12 considers the question of whether the gain outweighs the pain—that is, whether performance appraisal does more good than harm to an organization.

Chapter 13 considers the implications of ongoing changes in the nature and function of organizations, the units of production (i.e., individual vs. group), the place and time for work, and the workforce for performance appraisal, and suggests future directions for performance appraisal development.

Chapter 14 builds on ideas presented in several preceding chapters and outlines the rationale, and the design, implementation, and evaluation of a goal-oriented performance appraisal system. This type of system is designed to take advantage of the fact that the many users of performance appraisal are pursuing a complex set of goals, and tailors the system to those goals rather than designing an appraisal system that does not fit with the important goals of key constituencies.

Finally, Chapter 15 considers 53 suggestions for future research and practice in the area of performance appraisal. Research and practice suggestions relevant to understanding and improving performance judgments, ratings, the rating context, and the evaluation of performance appraisal systems are offered.

Acknowledgments

W e want to thank the many colleagues whose input or whose generosity in sharing research information helped to shape this book; especially Bill Balzer, Cris Banks, Janet Barnes-Farrell, Wally Borman, Bob Cardy, Angelo DeNisi, Greg Dobbins, Gerry Ferris, Clint Longenecker, Bob Morrison, Ray Noe, Joyce Russell, Hank Sims, and Kevin Williams. Special thanks to Rich Arvey, whose help, and encouragement, in developing our first book on performance appraisal is greatly appreciated. Finally we want to acknowledge the insightful comments of all of the graduate students in our 1992 seminar on performance appraisal (Rebecca Anhalt, Julie Chen, Janet Hollenshead, John Howes, Melinda Kerst, Chris Lovato, Sandra Lee, Joan Ratz, Taaj Suri, Lucy Wenzel, Kristie Wright); this seminar helped crystallize our thinking about the main theme of this book—the role of goals in performance appraisal.

1

Introduction

Performance appraisal (PA) has traditionally been viewed by industrial/organizational psychologists as a measurement problem. Indeed, a quick review of its historical roots shows that early research on PA has focused on such issues as scale development, scale formats, reducing test and rater bias, and the like (Austin & Villanova, 1992; Edwards, 1957; Guilford, 1954; Landy & Farr, 1980, 1983). To date, much of the research on performance appraisal can be described as a search for better, more accurate, and more cost-effective techniques for measuring job performance. In this book, we will depart from the traditional measurement orientation and, instead, approach PA from an applied social-psychological perspective. That is, we view PA primarily as a social and communication process rather than primarily as a measurement tool.

Viewing performance appraisal as a social-psychological process is not unique (Ilgen & Favero, 1985). We will argue strongly, however, that the nearly exclusive treatment of PA by researchers as a measurement instrument is unrealistic. The assumption has led researchers to focus on questions that may not yield significant understanding or improvement in the practice of performance appraisals in organizations (Banks & Murphy, 1985). Researchers currently know a great deal about the measurement problems involved in appraisals. The measurement perspective has enhanced our understanding of the mechanics of appraisal with, however, little consideration of the context of performance appraisal in organizations. Even the recent cognitive research on appraisal has attempted to improve appraisals as measurement tools with less application to their role as a communication or decision-making tool.

One advantage in considering appraisals from a social-psychological perspective is that the role of context receives greater attention. Further, this perspective provides psychologists with more opportunity to explore psychological and social-psychological problems associated with the appraisal process. For example, it leads to questions about what role the social climate and norms of the organization play in the appraisal process or what role socialization processes play in the development of performance norms and standards.

Given our perspective, we have two general goals for this book. First, we hope that our treatment of performance appraisal, from a social-psychological perspective rather than the traditional measurement approach, will stimulate readers to think about performance appraisal in a different or a more macro way. Second, we hope that, given a different way of viewing PA, future research in this area will enhance the practice of performance appraisal in organizations.

This chapter presents a four-part conceptual model of performance appraisal in organizations. We will treat appraisal as a communication process in which the rater attempts to convey information to the organization about subordinates' performance. The model is based on three assumptions: (a) rater behavior is goal directed, (b) performance appraisals are social interactions, and (c) performance appraisals in organizations function primarily as a tool for effective management rather than as a measurement instrument. The elements of the model include the rating context, the performance judgment, the performance rating, and the evaluation; these four components provide the general outline of the book. Before the model is introduced, however, we will review the history of PA research to identify the trends and events influencing our current research and practice.

PERFORMANCE APPRAISAL: EARLY HISTORY

Although the interest in and use of performance appraisal have increased over the past 30 years, the practice of formally evaluating employees has existed for centuries. As early as the third century A.D., Sin Yu, an early Chinese philosopher, criticized a biased rater employed by the Wei dynasty on the grounds that "the Imperial Rater of Nine Grades seldom rates men according to their merits but always according to his likes and dislikes" (Patten, 1977, p. 352). In 1648, the *Dublin* (Ireland) *Evening Post* allegedly rated legislators using a rating scale based on personal qualities (Hackett, 1928). According to Heilbroner (1953), the first industrial application of merit rating was probably made by Robert Owen at his cotton mills in New Lanark, Scotland, in the early 1800s. Wooden cubes of different colors indicating different degrees of merit were hung over each employee's work station. As employee performance changed, so did the appropriate wooden cube. The merit rating or efficiency rating in the Federal Civil Service has been in place since at least 1887 (Petrie, 1950) and perhaps as early as 1842 (Lopez, 1968).

One impetus to the development of performance appraisal in U.S. industry (Patten, 1977) can be traced to the work of industrial psychologists at Carnegie-Mellon University and their early work in salesman selection and "man-to-man" rating forms based on trait psychology (Scott, Clothier, & Spriegel, 1941). The man-to-man rating form was later used by the army in World War I to assess the performance of officers (Scott et al., 1941), although formal PA probably began in the United States in 1813 (Bellows & Estep, 1954) when army General Lewis Cass submitted to the War Department an evaluation of each of his men using such terms as "a good-natured man" or "knave despised by all."

Although the man-to-man ranking by department is not frequently used in industry or in appraising performance, it can be an effective method for determining the order of layoffs. In fact, in the late 1960s it was used by many companies that experienced cutbacks in government contracts to make layoff and retention decisions (Patten, 1977). This technique was known as the "totem approach" to personnel cutbacks. After World War I, many of the individuals associated with the work of the man-to-man appraisal secured positions in industry, in part because business leaders were impressed by the contribution of industrial psychologists to army research. Despite early criticisms (Rudd, 1921), the graphic rating scale increased in popularity and remains predominant today. Just prior to and during World War II, the army again sought assistance from psychologists to improve its rating system. The outcome of these research efforts included the forced-choice technique and the critical-incident approach to merit rating (Flanagan, 1949; Sisson, 1948). Appraisal of industry employees became popular only after World War I, and appraisal of managers was not widely practiced until after World War II.

By the early 1950s, appraisal was an accepted practice in many organizations. In 1962, performance appraisal was conducted in 61% of the organizations surveyed (Spriegel, 1962) and typically top management was exempt from such ratings (Whisler & Harper, 1962). After the passage of the 1964 Civil Rights Act and the 1966 and 1970 Equal Employment Opportunity Commission (EEOC) guidelines for regulation of selection procedures, legal considerations exerted strong pressure on organizations to formalize their appraisal systems (DeVries, Morrison, Shullman, & Gerlach, 1986). Federal legislation and the civil rights and women's movements of the 1960s and 1970s created the need for rapid improvements in organizational appraisal practices.

Several surveys of business organizations have indicated that between 74% and 89% of those surveyed have a formal performance appraisal system (Bretz & Milkovich, 1989; Feild & Holley, 1982; Lacho, Stearns, & Villere, 1979; Lazer & Wilkstrom, 1977). Further, surveys concerning the prevalence of formal appraisal systems indicated that approximately 76% of the city governments and 100% of the state governments sampled had appraisal systems. Large organizations were more likely to have performance appraisal than smaller organizations (95% and 84%, respectively), and lower (74%) to middle (71%) management levels were more likely to have formal appraisals than top management (55%) (Lazer & Wilkstrom, 1977). Finally, in a recent study, approximately 96% of the organizations surveyed that had an industrial/organizational psychologist on staff also had at least one formal performance appraisal system (Cleveland, Murphy, & Williams, 1989). In general, then, performance appraisal appears to be nearly universal (Bretz & Milkovich, 1989; Cleveland et al., 1989; DeVries et al., 1986), and the apparent importance of performance appraisal as a tool for managing human resources has increased (Latham, Skarlick, Irvine, & Siegel, 1993).

DeVries and colleagues (1986) point out two particular trends in the practice of PA during the past 30 years. First, appraisal methods have evolved from traits and essay approaches to such behavioral and results-oriented methods as Behaviorally Anchored Rating Scales (BARS) and Management by Objectives (MBO). DeVries and colleagues note, however, that although newer methods have evolved, the older trait-rating scales are still prevalent. A second trend is that the number of uses of PA in organizations has increased during the past 30 years (Cleveland et al., 1989; DeVries et al., 1986). As Figure 1.1 indicates, the earliest use of performance appraisal was as a basis for administrative decisions such as promotions, salary increases, and so on. Throughout the 1960s and 1970s, however, performance appraisals were increasingly used for employee development and feedback, corporate planning, legal documentation (DeVries et al., 1986), systems maintenance, and research (Cleveland et al., 1989).

Finally, performance appraisal represents one of the least popular aspects of human resource management. As Meyer (1991) notes, performance appraisal is one of the most frequent sources of dissatisfaction in the entire human resource system; neither supervisors nor subordinates look forward to appraisal, and neither is likely to be totally satisfied with the appraisal systems in their organization. George (1986) refers to the appraisal systems in many organizations as "sterile paper chases." One possible reason for the widespread dissatisfaction with performance appraisal in organizations is that the systems used by organizations do not help them or their employees meet important goals. This theme will be fleshed out in several of the chapters that follow.

PERFORMANCE APPRAISAL RESEARCH:
HISTORICAL TRENDS

The research on performance appraisal parallels the events and trends in industry and the military and can be categorized into a number of key content areas.

Objective Versus Subjective
Measures of Performance

There are many ways to measure performance. In general, performance data can be categorized into two groups: judgmental or subjective measures and nonjudgmental or objective measures (Landy & Farr, 1983). Although

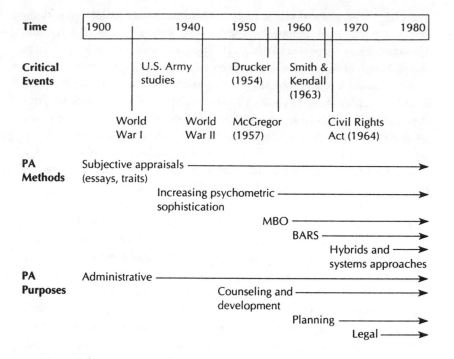

Figure 1.1. Historical Trends in Performance Appraisal Research and Practice

SOURCE: D. L. DeVries, A. M. Morrison, S. L. Shullman, & M. L. Gerlach, *Performance Appraisal on the Line* (Greensboro, NC: Center for Creative Leadership, 1986), p. 12. Reproduced by permission of the Center for Creative Leadership, Greensboro, NC, copyright 1986. All rights reserved.

judgmental measures are more widely used, objective performance indices (e.g., production output, scrap rates, and time to complete a task) have been useful measures of performance for routine, manual jobs since the 1940s (Rothe, 1946a, 1946b, 1947, 1949, 1951; Rothe & Nye, 1958, 1959, 1961) and have received renewed attention more recently (Bass & Turner, 1973; Bassett, 1979; Goldstein & Mobley, 1971; Hackman & Porter, 1968; Kidd & Christy, 1961; Yukl & Latham, 1975). Further, other nonjudgmental measures that do not directly measure performance but would provide information on the general health of the organization (e.g., absenteeism, turnover, grievances, and accidents) have received renewed research attention (Campbell et al., 1990; Chadwick-Jones, Nicholson, & Brown, 1982; Fitzgibbons & Moch, 1980; Hunter, Schmidt, & Judiesch, 1990; Mowday, Porter, & Steers, 1981; Muchinsky, 1977; Steers & Rhodes, 1978).

Specific objective measures are not without their unique problems, however. Although it is not possible here to discuss these measures exhaustively (see Landy & Farr [1983] for a detailed discussion), each has specific limitations. For example, absence measures (a) do not apply to many jobs, (b) are frequently inaccurate, (c) have a variety of causes depending on the definition of absence, (d) vary in the length of observation, and most important, (e) do not correlate with each other. A major drawback of using turnover as a criterion is that it is difficult to distinguish between voluntary and involuntary turnover. Grievances are limited in scope and generalizability because often they are not available for nonunion employees. The major problem with accidents is that there is confusion about whether they are the result of people or of their environments, which calls into question the validity of such measures. Finally, rate of advancement or salary increases are poor criteria; the rate may be controlled by a quota, or salary adjustments may reflect organizational health (economic) but not individual performance.

Landy and Farr (1983) have identified several problems with objective measures and possible reasons why psychologists have pursued judgmental measures, especially for evaluating managerial behavior. First, objective indices tend to have low reliability. One reason for the low reliability in absence measures, for example, is that the observation period may be not stable across measures. That is, assessing absence during a one-week period and then correlating it with another week may yield a low correlation because a longer period is required for a reliable measure (Chadwick-Jones, Brown, Nicholson, & Sheppard, 1971; Farr, O'Leary, & Bartlett, 1971-1977; Ilgen & Hollenbeck, 1977; Latham & Pursell, 1975). Further, factors external to the individual—such as the organization's sick-leave policies—may influence the reliability of absence measures.

Second, objective measures tend to be available for only a limited number of jobs. For example, it would not be sensible to collect tardiness or absence measures from sales representatives or from corporate managers who may not have a predetermined or fixed 8-hour workday. Finally, Landy and Farr (1983) cite the changing nature of skilled and semi-skilled work as a final limitation to objective performance measures. For example, because operators are being replaced by machine tenders, productivity measures such as output are more dependent on machine functions than on individual performance. The changing nature of work suggests that objective measures may be increasingly less appropriate for evaluating worker performance, and subjective measures may continue to experience popularity.

Management by Objectives. Evaluations of managerial and executive performance often involve the use of Management by Objectives (MBO) to define and measure job performance, with a particular emphasis on the individual's contribution to organizational goals and outcomes (Drucker, 1954; Milkovich & Wigdor, 1991; Odiorne, 1965). MBO programs take a number of forms, but there are several components common to most MBO applications. First, MBO involves participation in goal-setting. In particular, MBO programs involve joint supervisor-subordinate determination of specific goals and performance indicators. In particular, supervisors and subordinates jointly set performance goals by agreeing on what needs to be accomplished and how accomplishments will be measured (usually in terms of output or some objective indicator). Second, MBO requires objective feedback concerning progress toward goal accomplishment. There is evidence that MBO can contribute to organizational productivity, but that the effectiveness of MBO depends strongly on the degree of top management support for the process (Rogers & Hunter, 1991).

Although the title "Management by Objectives" might lead you to conclude that performance appraisal under MBO systems is done solely on the basis of objective measures, this is not really the case. It is true that "performance" is likely in an MBO system to be defined in terms of countable outcomes. The process of setting goals, targets, and objectives is a very subjective one, however, involving negotiation between the supervisor and subordinate. Furthermore, if a good-performing subordinate fail to meet his or her objectives, it is not unusual for the supervisor to renegotiate objectives. This way, the supervisor can be reasonably sure that a good performer will obtain "objective" results that are interpreted as "good performance."

Rating Scale Formats

The most voluminous area of research on PA deals with the format of appraisal scales. These issues include between-person comparisons (norm-referenced criteria) versus comparison to a standard (criterion-referenced formats), use of trait versus behavioral anchors, the optimal number of anchors, identification of formats conducive to the fewest rater errors, scaling of anchors, and comparison of format validity. An example of each of the scale formats discussed below is provided in the Appendix.

Landy and Farr (1983) classify judgmental measures of performance into two general groups: norm-referenced criteria and criterion-referenced criteria. Examples of norm-referenced criteria include simple rankings and paired comparisons. Most research, however, has been devoted to the development of psychometrically sophisticated criterion-referenced scales. Since 1922, when Paterson introduced the *graphic rating scale,* an extensive amount of research has been conducted on scale format, with the goal of improving the measurement quality and the "numbers" that such scales yield (cited in Landy & Farr, 1983). As many psychologists indicate (Guion, 1965; Landy, 1987; Landy & Farr, 1983), early graphic rating scales consisted of trait labels and unbroken lines with varying types and numbers of adjectives below. Raters were asked to rate each employee on each trait or statement by circling a number or box that represented how much of that characteristic was present. Research on the graphic scale attempted to determine the meanings of the response categories (i.e., scaling) or anchors, the types of anchors (trait, behavior, adjective, number, etc.), and the number of anchors that resulted in discernible ratings and that raters found acceptable.

One systematic attempt to enhance the graphic scale was the result of work conducted by Smith and Kendall (1963) that led to the development of the *Behaviorally Anchored Rating Scales (BARS).* Smith and Kendall attempted to replace numerical or adjective anchors with behavioral examples of actual work behaviors. Using scaling procedures borrowed from psychophysics and attitude measurement, BARS were designed to have improved psychometric properties (Landy & Farr, 1983). Raters read a number of behavioral statements and then circle the number that corresponds to the statement that best describes the employee's behavior.

The *Behavioral Observation Scales (BOS)* were developed as an attempt to improve BARS (Latham & Wexley, 1977). Raters evaluate the frequency of specific employee behaviors or critical incidents that have been observed. A decade or so after the introduction of BARS, Blanz and Ghiselli (1972) designed the *Mixed Standard Rating Scale,* which disguised the nature of the performance dimension and the levels of performance described by the behavioral examples. This derived scale, where the employee's score is later calculated on the basis of the pattern of rater responses to three items comprising a particular dimension, was again intended to reduce rating errors. Raters respond to behavioral statements that reflect high, average, and low performance. For each statement, raters simply respond by indicating whether the employee's performance is better than (+), equal to (=), or worse than (–) the behavior reflected in each item. The *Forced-Choice Rating Scale,* similar to the mixed standard scale, also disguises the rating scale outcome (Zavala, 1965) with the intent of reducing rating errors.

Kane and Lawler (1979) introduced the *distributional measurement model (DMM)* to performance measurement. In this approach, an attempt is made to obtain ratings in terms of the frequency or rate at which a person has exhibited a given performance dimension at a series of performance levels or benchmarks (Landy & Farr, 1983). Although the DMM is rather complicated and cumbersome, its proponents (Bernardin & Beatty, 1984; Kane, 1981; Kane & Lawler, 1979) indicate that it addresses three problems that beset all other appraisal methods:

1. DMM considers performance as the distribution of occurrence rates over the range of possible achievement levels (on each performance area/dimension).
2. DMM considers the extraneous factors such as machine failure or late delivery of supplies that may influence the performance of individuals.
3. DMM places a minimum of cognitive demands on the raters.

As Landy and Farr (1983) point out, however, more research is needed to determine the applicability of this model. Jako and Murphy's (1990) study provides one of the few empirical evaluations of distributional measurement systems. Although far from definitive, this study does not support claims that this measurement method captures aspects of performance not captured by other scale formats.

Much of the research on scale formats has attempted to determine what formats are superior measurement instruments (fewest rater errors) (Bernardin, 1977; Bernardin, Alvares, & Cranny, 1976; Borman & Dunnette, 1975; Borman & Vallon, 1974; Burnaska & Hollman, 1974; Friedman & Cornelius, 1976; Jacobs, Kafry, & Zedeck, 1980). Extensive research has also been conducted on the characteristics of rating scales, such as the number of response categories (Bendig, 1952a, 1952b, 1953, 1954a, 1954b; Bernardin, LaShells, Smith, & Alvares, 1976; Finn, 1972; Lissitz & Green, 1975), the advantages of the type of anchor (numerical, adjectival, or behavioral) (Barrett, Taylor, Parker, & Martens, 1958; Bendig,

1952a, 1952b, 1953; Shapira & Shirom, 1980; Smith & Kendall, 1963), and the process of assigning scale values to the anchor (Barnes & Landy, 1979; Bendig, 1952a, 1952b).

Performance Appraisal and the Legal System

The single greatest influence on development and use of performance assessment in the United States has been the Uniform Guidelines on Employment Selection (1978) established by the EEOC. The guidelines apply to "tests and other procedures which are used as a basis for any employee decisions" (1978). In a key case, *Brito v. Zia* (1973), the Tenth Circuit Court of Appeals ruled that evaluations are, in fact, tests and are subject to guidelines enforced by the EEOC. Although recent cases may relax the application of these guidelines, it is probably best for employers to continue to regard performance evaluations as tests. Therefore, PA becomes an important legal issue when it is used in making any type of personnel decision. As we indicated earlier in the chapter, the oldest and most predominant purpose of appraisal is for making administrative decisions. More recently it has been used as an employee development and feedback tool (DeVries et al., 1986).

In *Albemarle Paper Company v. Moody* (1975), the Court indicated that the accuracy or validity of PA could be examined in a validation study. In this decision, the Supreme Court discredited an empirical validation study because the criteria used were vague and open to many errors (Bernardin & Beatty, 1984). Therefore, performance appraisals are subject to court action or consideration on at least two grounds: (a) the accuracy or validity of ratings to predict future performance or promotability and (b) the validity or accuracy of ratings to assess past behavior. In addition, as a result of EEOC guidelines and interpretation of the Age Discrimination in Employment Act in 1981, performance appraisal has emerged as particularly relevant for establishing a Bona Fide Occupation Qualification (BFOQ) such as a maximum age limit. In order to assert a BFOQ, the organization must demonstrate, usually through performance data, that an age limit is justified by business necessity or for public safety.

We do not intend here to review the legal cases concerning appraisal or issue of adverse impact. There are many excellent reviews of case law (see Arvey & Faley, 1988; Cascio, 1987; Cascio & Bernardin, 1980, 1981). Further, based on a review of 66 cases by Feild and Holley (1982),

Bernardin and Beatty (1984) outline a set of guidelines or standards for developing legally sound appraisals. These guidelines suggest that legally defensible appraisals must reflect standards that are based on job requirements, and the standards should reflect specific dimensions of job performance rather than an overall rating (Bernardin & Beatty, 1984; Cascio & Bernardin, 1981). The performance dimensions should be defined in behavioral terms and must be communicated to employees. A defensible appraisal system requires high-quality ratings. Whenever possible, there should be multiple raters rather than a single rater. Each individual rater should have the validity of his or her ratings assessed. Extreme ratings should be accompanied with documentation, including such things as a critical incident, date, and location. Finally, a sound performance appraisal system has a formal appeal process (Bernardin & Beatty, 1984).

With the Court's interpretations of the guidelines, the historical view of appraisal as a measurement device has been reinforced and given enhanced importance and visibility. This legal scrutiny may be one reason why appraisal research has focused on measurement issues while largely ignoring (until recently) the social and organizational goals of the appraisal process. The heightened awareness that appraisals are subject to legal action emphasizes the importance of the measurement qualities of appraisal, but it also may have obscured the decision-making and communication roles of PA in organizations.

Criteria for Assessing Appraisal Effectiveness

Numerous criteria exist for assessing the effectiveness of performance appraisal outcomes. In the 1950s, representatives of the American Psychological Association defined a test as "nothing more than careful observation of actual performance under standard conditions" (Bernardin & Beatty, 1984; Mullins & Ratliff, 1979). Therefore, it is not surprising that the many criteria used to assess predictor effectiveness would also apply to appraisals. Frequently, the uses of PA as a criterion and as a predictor are interchangeable. One illustration of this was provided by the case of *Washington v. Davis* (1976). At one point in the court process, performance in a training program served as the criterion in an empirical validation study; at another point in the same case, evidence was presented to assess whether training performance predicted on-the-job performance (Bernardin & Beatty, 1984).

In addition to numerous criteria for evaluating appraisal effectiveness, there is an additional problem in that there has been little attempt to refine definitions or operational definitions of criteria. That is, it is often not clear or agreed upon as to what constitutes error in ratings. In Chapter 10 the criteria for assessing appraisal effectiveness will be explored more fully. For the purposes of this chapter, however, research on rater errors can be categorized into three areas: (a) criteria for assessing appraisal effectiveness, including the utilization criteria of PA (i.e., utilization criteria, qualitative criteria, and quantitative criteria); (b) rating source (i.e., peer, supervisor, and subordinate) as it relates to appraisal errors and effectiveness; and (c) rater training.

Jacobs and colleagues (1980) provide a meaningful framework for describing the numerous types of appraisal criteria. They describe three categories against which any PA system should be evaluated; this framework nicely captures the type of research that has been conducted in appraisal effectiveness. The most basic are the *utilization criteria,* which address the purposes for which appraisal are conducted, including administrative decisions (i.e., promotion, disciplinary, selection, etc.) and employee development (i.e., feedback, training, diagnosis, etc.). The most frequent distinction is whether performance appraisal will serve individual or organizational goals and needs.

A related issue that has received much research attention is whether performance is best described by using multiple criterion measures or composite criteria (Schmidt & Kaplan, 1971). Except for the issue of multiple and composite criteria, the utilization criteria have received less attention in the empirical literature than in trade or practitioner journals. One reason for this may be that practitioners are concerned more with quantitative criteria of appraisal effectiveness than qualitative criteria.

Qualitative criteria include the relevance of the appraisal to job performance, data availability, equivalence, interpretability, and practicality (Jacobs et al., 1980). Wexley (1987) has urged psychologists to use employee attitudes toward performance appraisal more frequently as a useful way of assessing appraisal effectiveness. Specifically, Wexley (1987) stated that the highly researched criterion of rating accuracy is an overused and less useful measure of effectiveness and instead suggested more practical qualitative measures.

The third criterion area, *quantitative measures of effectiveness,* has received extensive attention in the empirical literature. Definitions of rating errors have evolved throughout the history of performance appraisal. Kingsbury (1933) was perhaps first to list the three most frequently mentioned psychometric errors in the literature: halo, leniency, and central tendency. Halo refers to the tendency to rate the same on all dimensions, leniency to the tendency to give extreme ratings, and central tendency to the overreliance on the middle of the scale. Since then, many other criteria have been added, including reliability, interrater reliability, and validity (content, construct, predictive, concurrent; discriminant and convergent validity; etc.).

Bernardin and Beatty (1984) and others (Carroll & Schneier, 1982; Landy & Farr, 1983) describe in some detail the vast amount of research using these criteria to compare the effectiveness of various appraisal formats and systems (we review this literature in Chapter 10). Given that appraisals have been viewed primarily as measurement tools, and considering the legal constraints imposed on appraisals, the extensive research devoted to the psychometric properties and accuracy of appraisal processes is understandable and warranted.

Another general consideration within the domain of appraisal concerns the appropriate source of ratings. Much research attention has compared peer, supervisory, and subordinate ratings (Mount, 1984a) using the criteria described by Jacobs and colleagues (1980). In general, the intent of this research is to determine what source or sources provide the most psychometrically sound and accurate ratings.

Rater training in PA—specifically Rater Error Training (RET), Rater Accuracy Training (RAT) (Bernardin & Pence, 1980), or frame of reference training (Bernardin & Beatty, 1984)—are all designed with similar objectives: to improve the psychometric properties of appraisals. The research literature on training is devoted to assessing the effectiveness of such training and the longevity of training effects.

Cognitive Research in Performance Appraisal

Reviews on performance appraisal have generated considerable research on the way in which raters mentally process information about ratees or the cognitive processes involved in evaluation. As we will discuss in Chapter 7, the growth of research in cognitive process and appraisal can be traced to Wherry's seminal work (Wherry & Bartlett, 1982) as well as works by DeCotiis and Petit (1978) and Landy and Farr (1980). Other reviews by

Feldman (1981), Ilgen and Feldman (1983), and DeNisi and Williams (1988) also have called attention to the importance of considering the rater's capacity to evaluate. Current cognitive research draws on two models for hypotheses and for interpretations of experimental findings: one by Feldman and colleagues (Feldman, 1981; Ilgen & Feldman, 1983) and the second by DeNisi and colleagues (DeNisi, Cafferty, & Meglino, 1984; DeNisi & Williams, 1988).

The research in this area has focused on four major cognitive processes. The first process is *information acquisition,* which involves what behaviors and characteristics the rater selectively attends to and those ratee features and behaviors to which the rater devotes little attention. Research on information acquisition has focused on two influences: the context of observation (McArthur, 1980; Taylor & Fiske, 1978) and the purpose of observation (Balzer, 1986; Cafferty, DeNisi, & Williams, 1986; Murphy, Philbin, & Adams, 1989). The second process in the general cognitive model is *encoding and mental representation.* This research has focused on such issues as the categories, prototypes, and schema involved at this stage. Research on the *storage and retrieval* of information focuses on how memory works, how many types of memory exist (i.e., short-term vs. long-term memory), and so on. Specifically, memory research in the area of social cognition and person perception has been primarily concerned with the effects of categorization on memory (Cantor & Mischel, 1977; Wyer & Srull, 1986). A fourth area of cognitive research on evaluation concerns the *integration of different pieces or types of information* (Cooper, 1981b; DeNisi & Williams, 1988; Feldman, 1981).

Although the cognitive influence in PA research has enhanced understanding of the capabilities and limitation of raters as information processors and as evaluators, such research has not been without critics. These criticisms are reviewed in Chapter 7.

Models of Performance Appraisal

Prior to 1975, few published or comprehensive models of performance appraisal were devoted to the identification of factors that influence rating outcomes. Instead, the literature reflected a concern with criterion measurement and understanding what (construct) is measured by criteria (James, 1973) in general and not with PA ratings specifically.

The debate on the usefulness of the *ultimate criterion model* (Blum & Naylor, 1968; Nagle, 1953; Thorndike, 1949) versus the *multiple criterion model* (Ghiselli, 1964; Guion, 1961, 1965) was waged during the 1960s and resolved more or less by Schmidt and Kaplan (1971). The major issue was whether criteria should be combined or interpreted separately. Little consideration was given to the various types of measures obtained or to other factors that may influence performance.

The model of managerial effectiveness proposed by Campbell, Dunnette, Lawler, and Weick (1970) and labeled the *general criterion model* by James (1973) progressed beyond the issue of one versus many indicators of performance by viewing managerial performance as a function of individual abilities, motivation, and organizational situation or opportunity. Although the Campbell and associates (1970) general criterion model is not a PA rating model per se, it is important because it (a) distinguishes motivation from ability and performance and (b) considers situational variables as they might influence job performance and organizational outcomes. The difference between the general criterion model and subsequent rating models (e.g., Landy & Farr, 1980) is that the unit of analysis is much broader; the model by Campbell and colleagues was concerned with understanding managerial performance and organizational effectiveness.

James (1973) proposed a fourth criterion model, called the *integrated criterion model,* that integrates the multiple and the general criterion model and construct-validation procedures. As with each of the other three models, the integrated model was intended to guide future criterion research by applying a rationale and a set of procedures to assess the underlying nature (construct) of criteria.

In the 1950s, Wherry developed a sophisticated psychometric model of rating (Wherry & Bartlett, 1982). Unfortunately, the model was described in unpublished technical reports and did not come to most researchers' or practitioners' attention until the 1980s. This model used the theory of reliability to derive a number of unique theorems about rating bias, the process, and so on.

In 1978, the first widely cited model of the PA process was published in the *Academy of Management Review* by DeCotiis and Petit. They proposed a model of the determinants of the accuracy of appraisal ratings and suggested several propositions and directions for future research. DeCotiis and Petit (1978) stated that rating accuracy was determined by rater motivation, rater ability, and the availability of appropriate judgmental norms. Although their work is similar to the subsequent Landy and Farr (1980) study (published in *Psychological Bulletin*), the DeCotiis and Petit model distinguishes itself in at least two ways: (a) there is an explicit distinction made between rater ability (i.e., rater skills in interpreting ratee behavior) and rater motivation (i.e., what energizes, directs, and sustains behavior) and (b) more emphasis is placed on organizational or situational characteristics that may influence and shape rating outcomes.

The Landy and Farr (1980) model reached a wider audience. Their process model of appraisal, although recognizing the influence of situational variables on ratings, most specifically addresses the rater's cognitive process. The model includes components such as rating process, observation and storage of performance information, retrieval of such information from memory, the actual judgment, and the performance description.

A MODEL FOR RESEARCH AND PRACTICE IN APPRAISAL

Reviews, such as DeCotiis and Petit (1978) and Landy and Farr (1980), have stimulated a significant body of research on PA but, to date, this research has made few contributions to the practice of performance appraisal in organizations (Latham, 1986). We believe that the conceptual models that guide current research on PA (examples include process models developed by DeNisi et al. [1984], Ilgen & Feldman [1983], and Landy & Farr [1980]) are partly to blame.

Although these models have helped to clarify research (especially cognitive research) in performance appraisal, they have (a) paid insufficient attention to the organizational context in which appraisals occur, (b) failed to identify issues of concern to both researchers and practitioners, and (c) failed to illustrate the links between the concerns of current performance researchers (e.g., research on the cognitive and affective bases of appraisal) and the practice of performance appraisal. A different type of conceptual model is needed in order to make progress in both research and application.

In this book we present a conceptual model of PA in organizations (Cleveland, Murphy, Barnes-Farrell, & Banks, 1988). Performance appraisal research has traditionally treated appraisal as a measurement process and has treated context factors (to the extent that they are considered at all) as nuisance variables that interfere with accurate appraisal. We treat appraisal as a communication and social process. The rater is not a passive measurement instrument but rather an active agent pursuing specific goals. The central assumption is that appraisal outcomes are the result of a rater's goal-directed behavior, which is shaped by the organizational context in which rating occurs. This assumption, together with our analysis of the academic and applied literature dealing with PA, leads to the four-component model illustrated in Figure 1.2.

Before introducing the four elements of the model, we will explain how this model is different from earlier models of the appraisal process (e.g., DeCotiis & Petit, 1978; Ilgen & Feldman, 1983; Landy & Farr, 1980). First, previous models tended to focus on a specific aspect of the appraisal process (e.g., judgment) without explicitly recognizing that the variables identified in the model operated in a larger, dynamic context. Our model identifies the context of performance appraisal, especially the organizational context, as the starting point from which other components should be examined. Second, previous models generated many "boxes and arrows." That is, they attempted to identify all possible variables or characteristics within a given box. As a result, the models provided detailed information about narrow portions of the question, yet many times lost sight of how the information fits into the larger understanding of performance. Further, it is difficult to determine from previous models which elements are and are not critical to understanding effective performance appraisal. The proposed model is intended to highlight a limited number of variables that we believe are critical in performance appraisal research and practice.

Our four-component model takes a more holistic approach than previous models. Therefore, we do not provide an exhaustive review of all of the variables that may play a part within each of our major components. Rather, our intent is to highlight the critical elements in this domain. We think that the critical questions in appraisal research have been confused or ignored among the myriad boxes and arrows of previous models. The proposed model is suggested as one approach for organizing PA research efforts. It may also provide a mechanism for posing research questions that will address PA problems that are encountered in organizations. The four-component performance appraisal model includes the following elements: the rating context, the performance judgment, the performance rating, and the evaluation of the appraisal system.

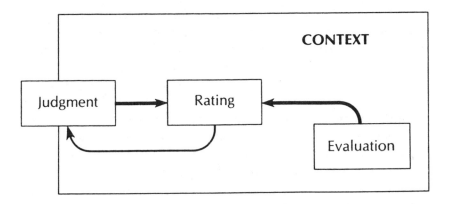

Figure 1.2. Performance Appraisal in Context: A Four-Component Model

Rating Context

The organizational context in which ratings are collected influences the judgment process, the rating process, the evaluation process, and the eventual uses of the rating data. Performance appraisal research has traditionally followed a microanalytic approach, focusing on such things as scale construction, scale format, or rater biases (Ilgen & Feldman, 1983). Research on the rating context can also profit from the consideration of two sets of macrolevel issues: (a) *intraorganizational factors,* such as organizational values, climate or culture within the organization, competition among departments or functions, status differences among functions, effect of downsizing on the PA system, and the like (Cleveland, Morrison, & Bjerke, 1986; Duncan, 1972; Duncan & Weiss, 1979); and (b) *organization-environment issues,* such as organizational performance within a specific industry, extent of competition within an industry, general economic/political conditions regarding the organization's products, and so on (Duncan & Weiss, 1979). For example, some departments of the organization are likely to contain fast-track employees, whereas others will not; the purpose, tone, and focus of appraisal may vary accordingly (Cleveland et al., 1989).

Consideration of the context within which performance appraisals are conducted, especially at the macro-organizational level, has been largely ignored by researchers (Ilgen & Feldman, 1983). An understanding of the context within which the appraisal system operates, however, may enhance the implementation, utilization, or change of PA systems.

Cleveland and colleagues (1986) categorized contextual variables into two groups: proximal and distal variables (Brunswick, 1952). According to these authors, *proximal variables* are those that directly impinge upon or influence the rater. They include the interaction between supervisor and employee, the nature of the rated task or job, consequences of ratings (Lawler, 1972), and rater time constraints (Wright, 1974). For example, the established interaction patterns between a supervisor and an employee are determined by the day-to-day interactions over time (Dansereau, Graen, & Haga, 1975). If a supervisor has a close, informal relationship as opposed to a more formal, distant relationship with his or her employee, it is reasonable to assume that this will have an impact on ratings used for salary increases or promotion recommendations.

Distal variables are those intra- and extraorganizational characteristics that influence judgments, ratings, and assessments indirectly. Distal contextual variables include organizational structure, organizational climate or culture, the value system within the organization, and so on. The status of the specific function or unit and external/legal entrance standards to a functional unit or job type (i.e., lawyer, nurse, engineer) are also examples of distal cues.

For example, Cleveland and associates (1989) found that organizational complexity and organizational coordination were correlated with ways in which organizations use performance appraisals in making decisions. Organizations high in complexity and coordination were more likely to use appraisal for within-person uses (i.e., feedback and identifying strengths and weaknesses in employees) and systems maintenance than other organizations. In addition, Cleveland and colleagues (1986) found anecdotal support for the influence of an organization's value system upon ratings. Specifically, employees whose jobs or activities were perceived as more closely linked with the organization's mission or purpose (i.e., what was valued) were rated systematically higher than employees in jobs that were perceived as less central to the organization's mission.

Cleveland and colleagues (1989) surveyed over 100 organizations on their uses of PA. More than 70% of those surveyed indicated that ratings had a moderate to substantial impact on two or more decisions or goals. The most frequently cited uses within an organization were administrative decisions (promotion, etc.) and employee feedback and development. There is research evidence (Meyer, Kay, & French, 1965; Sharon & Bartlett, 1969; Williams, DeNisi, Blencoe, & Cafferty, 1985) and anecdotal evidence from raters (Cleveland et al., 1986) suggesting that organizations may convey multiple and conflicting messages to raters when appraisal is used to achieve both individual goals (i.e., employee feedback) and organizational goals (i.e., administrative or between-person decisions) (DeCotiis & Petit, 1978). Furthermore, an appraisal system within such an organization may invoke different rater cognitive processes, yield different rating outcomes, and establish different criteria for evaluating the goodness of ratings than in an organization that conveys a unitary message to raters regarding the purpose of performance appraisal.

Context effects are not limited to those that determine the purpose of ratings. Additional evidence shows that contextual factors can affect effort or motivation and performance (Peters & O'Connor, 1980), differentially affect high- and low-ability individuals in organizations (Peters, Fisher, & O'Connor, 1982), influence organizational learning and intellectual flexibility (Kohn & Schooner, 1978; Medin & Schaffer, 1978), impact safety effectiveness (Zohar, 1980), and affect updating activities (Kozlowski & Hults, 1987).

Duncan (1972) and Schein (1971) suggest groupings of organizational characteristics that may be useful for defining the context of performance appraisal. Duncan (1972) suggests that contextual variables can be categorized into those that affect the internal environment or the external environment. The internal environment includes organizational personnel, organizational function and staff units, and organizational level. The external environment includes customers, suppliers, competitors, sociopolitical environment, and technological environment. Duncan and Weiss (1979) suggest that the components of the internal and the external organizational environments may be used by individuals through the process of enactment (Weick, 1977) to define or give meaning to the organizational situation.

Another way of looking at organizational context is through the three dimensions that Schein (1971) uses to describe an organization's defined role. The three dimensions in Schein's model of organizations are (a) functional—various tasks performed by members of the organization (i.e., finance, marketing, staff, etc.), (b) hierarchical—the distribution of rank within an organization (i.e., decentralized, centralized, etc.), and (c) the person's inclusion within the organization—an interactional dimension (i.e., newcomers vs. a key or central figure).

In a report on performance appraisal practice in organizations, McCall and DeVries (1977) identify five contextual factors of organizations that appear to conflict directly with the requirements of an effective PA system. First, a manager's job includes activities short in duration, ad hoc contacts, tasks that are nonroutine, and a preference for current information (Mintzberg, 1980); whereas current PA systems require preparation, formal interviews, a focus on past behavior, and action as a result of the appraisal.

Second, organizations have limited resources, are hierarchical in structure, and decision making is subjective; whereas PA systems require administrative or development programs (with costs associated with them), require mutual problem solving, and there is an attempt for objective appraisals. Next, appraising individual performance assumes that performance varies, a person's performance is relatively independent of the performance of others, there is some consensus on what is good or bad, and performance can be changed via enhanced motivation and development; whereas the organizational reality may be that there is little variability in performance, performance is interdependent (on the group or the leader), there is a lack of agreement on what is good or poor performance, and performance is difficult to change.

Fourth, external environmental demands placed on the organization may clash with effective performance appraisals (DeVries et al., 1986). For example, unions favor the seniority system, whereas appraisals attempt to reward individual performance. Further, EEOC guidelines require appraisal validity, whereas the users of appraisal attempt to set mutual goals between the individual and the supervisor or the organization. Last, the day-to-day relationships that typify organizations are another source of potential problems (McCall & DeVries, 1977). For example, the authority relationship reflected in an organization may be inconsistent with the goal-setting interview of the appraisal; alternately, the goal of preserving the relationship may clash with the possibility of uncovering an insoluble performance problem in the appraisal interview.

Organizations send both formal and informal messages to raters about performance standards, norms for ratings, the immediate purpose of ratings, and the ways in which information regarding performance will be used. Much of the variance in ratings dismissed as rater error may be, in fact, an adaptive rater reaction to multiple, competing, and conflicting organizational forces. Rater behavior is an active, goal-directed process (Mohrman & Lawler, 1983). As such, goals may be a key concept in understanding how managers structure their performance appraisals.

Performance Judgment

Laboratory research on performance appraisal has focused primarily on judgments of raters who have observed or obtained information about the performance of workers (see DeNisi & Williams [1988] for a review of cognitive research in performance evaluation). Judgments are part of the rating process, but judgments and ratings are not identical. *Judgments* represent private evaluations; *ratings* represent public statements about ratees' performance (Mohrman & Lawler, 1983).

Judgments are, in part, context free. Extensive research shows that global evaluative judgments are made in practically every context and that efforts to remove this component are likely to be fruitless (Hastie & Park, 1986; Murphy, 1982b; Osgood, 1962). Judgments are also context bound. The job context determines the specific judgments that must be made as well as the relative emphasis on discriminating between persons versus identifying individual strengths and weaknesses. Judgments are subject to a wide variety of biases, almost all of which are likely to be unconscious.

Context-free aspects of judgment consist of those that lie within the cognitive schema and evaluation criteria of the individual, regardless of job-specific context. These would include the appraiser's cognitive capacities, personal biases and decision heuristics, and prior experience with appraisal tasks. Clearly, appraisers differ along these attributes, and research is needed that delineates how each might be involved in generating accurate performance judgments.

Recent research suggests that the content of an appraiser's PA schema, independent of the data collected on a particular ratee or perhaps even independent of knowledge of the job in question, will influence how a ratee will be evaluated (Borman, 1987; Feldman, 1981, 1986). This means that appraisers will evaluate a ratee in part based on their own conceptualizations and implicit theories about people and only partially utilize the criteria supplied by researchers or by the organization. These internal evaluation criteria need to be acknowledged and explored in order to determine how accuracy of judgments may be increased.

Context-bound judgments consist of those aspects that rely on job- or organization-specific information to define performance levels. For example, performance evaluation cannot proceed without knowledge of the tasks, duties, and responsibilities involved in the job performed by the ratee. In addition, judgments must also include guidelines defining effective and ineffective performance (i.e., performance standards).

Judgments are also bound by the appraiser's opportunity to collect performance-related information and his or her ability to sort out to what extent job behavior is under the control of the ratee (Banks & Murphy, 1985). Finally, the structure of the appraisal system can affect how well appraisers can generate accurate judgments—for example, by the amount of structure in the appraisal, the amount of time that can be devoted to the judgment process, the comprehensiveness and representativeness of the performance dimensions included on the appraisal form, and the presence of mechanisms for recalling performance-related information accurately.

Much of the recent cognitive research in performance appraisal has focused on aspects of the judgment process. For the most part, this research has dealt with two issues: (a) how information about performance is acquired and (b) how this information is processed to form judgments. Research on information acquisition is consistent with our distinction between context-bound and context-free judgment. Some behaviors carry strong evaluative implications (e.g., yelling at a customer) and will be relevant in almost any context (Murphy, 1982b). Other behaviors become salient as a result of the observational goals of the rater (Murphy et al., 1989; Williams et al., 1985). These goals may be driven by such things as the purpose of the appraisal task, organizational norms, and individual theories of good or poor performance (Borman, 1983, 1987).

Judgments are not determined solely by the behaviors observed by raters. Several other forms of information about ratee performance influence judgments, such as previous impressions of the ratee (Murphy, Balzer, Lockhart, & Eisenman, 1985), observation of the results of behavior (Smith, 1976), and indirect reports concerning ratee behavior (e.g., complaints or praise from customers). A final source of information that will drive judgments is the rater's affective reaction to each ratee. Until recently, affect has not been included in PA models. There is evidence that performance evaluations are influenced by the degree to which the supervisor likes the subordinate (Cardy & Dobbins, 1986; Dobbins & Russell, 1986). There is also evidence that the rater's mood and temperament influence judgments (Clark & Isen, 1982; Isen & Daubman, 1984; Tsui & Barry, 1986).

Research on information processing in performance evaluation has focused on encoding and retrieval processes (DeNisi & Williams, 1988; Wyer & Srull, 1986). As is true in other areas of cognitive research, PA researchers have focused more on errors in information processing than on understanding what raters do well (Funder, 1987). It is thus apparent that biases in encoding and retrieval can lead to a variety of errors (Higgins & King, 1981; Ilgen & Feldman, 1983; Jeffrey & Mischel, 1979; Murphy et al., 1985; Murphy, Gannett, Herr, & Chen, 1986; Williams, DeNisi, Meglino, & Cafferty, 1986). What is not apparent is whether raters are capable of doing a reasonably good job of evaluating performance (Banks & Murphy, 1985).

It is commonly acknowledged that humans have a limited capacity for processing information. At present, there is no way to determine whether these limits hamper the accurate evaluation of performance. It may be that the task of evaluating subordinates' performance is a relatively easy one that most raters are perfectly capable of doing well. As we will discuss in the section that follows, the fact that *ratings* do not discriminate good from poor performers does not indicate that *raters* cannot tell good work from poor work.

Performance Rating

In our model, we make a distinction between judgment and rating behavior. That is, the numbers that are recorded on PA forms do not necessarily reflect the rater's judgments. More concretely, the fact that one subordinate receives a higher rating than another on a dimension such as "timeliness" does not necessarily imply that the rater truly believes that the individuals differ in this respect or even that the higher-rated subordinate is necessarily the better performer. The rating merely indicates that the rater wishes to convey something to the audience who will read the rating form. Exactly what the rater chooses to communicate will depend on the rater's goals and on contextual factors.

The distinction between judgment and rating is not unique to this model; it is implied by a theory developed by Wherry in the 1950s (cf. Landy & Farr, 1983). Mohrman and Lawler (1983) distinguish between private and public evaluations and assume that they will not always correspond. Banks and Murphy (1985) distinguish between the rater's capacity to evaluate accurately ratee performance and his or her willingness to provide accurate ratings. What is unique to our model is the theoretical explanation for discrepancies between judgments and ratings.

Previous research has focused on leniency in rating, assuming that raters assign high ratings even when their private evaluation of ratees is not favorable (Landy & Farr, 1980, 1983; Murphy, Balzer, Kellam, & Armstrong, 1984). The assumption here is that raters hope to avoid the negative consequences (e.g., unpleasant confrontations) that are associated with harsh ratings (Bernardin & Buckley, 1981; Latham, 1986; Naiper & Latham, 1986). Other writers suggest that supervisors give high ratings because they do not know how to counsel workers who receive low ratings (Landy, 1985) or because they wish to avoid disapproval from others in the organization (Mohrman & Lawler, 1983).

The present model suggests that discrepancies between judgment and ratings cannot be explained solely in terms of a rater's attempts to avoid the consequences of low ratings. Rather, rating is a process of goal-directed communication. That is, the rater uses performance appraisal as a tool to achieve well-defined goals. Some of these goals may involve avoiding undesirable outcomes, but others involve positive end states. For example, if the rater believes that information from performance appraisal is used mainly as a basis for making promotion decisions, he or she may first decide who deserves a promotion and then fill out PA forms in a way that will maximize the likelihood that those promotions will occur (Cleveland et al., 1986).

Landy and Farr (1980) make explicit an assumption that appears to characterize most PA research—that ratings must contain some information about the ratee's performance. If performance rating is a goal-directed activity, however, there need not be any direct link between performance ratings and performance; in some settings, any correlation between true performance and rated performance might be spurious. In the example cited above, performance ratings will faithfully represent the rater's evaluations of each ratee's performance if and only if the rater decides who deserves a promotion solely on the basis of present performance. It would be entirely rational, however, for a supervisor largely to ignore present performance and to make promotion decisions on the basis of seniority, equity, past performance, or the perceived demands of the job that ratees might be promoted into. Under these conditions, ratings might bear little resemblance to the rater's private evaluations of each ratee's current job performance.

We assume that, under optimal conditions, raters are capable of forming accurate evaluations of important aspects of the performance of their subordinates (Borman, 1978). The question, then, is under what conditions the ratings that they record will also be accurate (i.e., will correspond with their judgment). Ratings are most likely to correspond with judgments if:

1. Organizational norms support distinctions between employees on the basis of their performance (Mohrman & Lawler, 1983).
2. Raters perceive a strong link between the ratings they give and specific outcomes (Landy & Farr, 1983; Thompson, 1967).
3. Raters believe that those outcomes should be based on present performance.
4. The valence of those outcomes is substantially larger than the valence of the negative outcomes that are associated with giving low ratings (Vroom, 1964).

The conditions listed above are most frequently encountered in research on the purpose of rating (Murphy et al., 1984). Here, ratings are collected for administrative purposes (e.g., salary, promotion) or for research or feedback purposes (i.e., they are not used to make decisions). It is likely that ratings collected for research purposes correspond closely with judgments; there are no adverse consequences for raters or ratees and probably no norms against giving truthful ratings. The same may be true for ratings collected in laboratory experiments (Latham, 1986; Wexley & Klimoski, 1984). There are several reasons to believe that the necessary conditions for strong links between judgments and ratings are not present in most other rating contexts.

First, ratings are typically used by organizations for a wide variety of purposes, ranging from salary administration to developmental feedback (Cleveland et al., 1989). It is unlikely that raters will believe that all of the decisions that might involve information about PA should be made on the basis of present performance. Even if they did believe so, different decisions emphasize different aspects of performance. For example, salary administration decisions reflect comparisons between individuals in terms of their overall performance levels, whereas training needs assessments involve comparisons of strengths and weaknesses within individuals. There is evidence that information from performance appraisals is often used for both within- and between-individual comparisons (Cleveland et al., 1989) and that when this is done, raters tend to focus on one set of comparisons (usually between individual) to the exclusion of the others (Cleveland et al., 1986). Thus, even when raters believe that decisions should be based on present performance, their ratings are likely to reflect only some aspects of their judgment (i.e., differences between individuals rather than individual strengths and weaknesses).

Second, the link between performance ratings and desired outcomes is often weak or uncertain. Factors other than present performance are, and should be, involved in making a variety of important decisions about ratees. Thus, the instrumentality link between ratings and desired outcomes may be weak (Mohrman & Lawler, 1983). In contrast, the link between low ratings and undesirable outcomes is likely to be strong; low ratings are almost certain to cause resentment and friction. This is the reason for our Condition 4 that ratings will correspond with judgments only if the valence of desired outcomes is substantially greater than the valence of the undesirable outcomes associated with giving low ratings to some subordinates.

Evaluation

The question of whether ratings are meaningful as a communication tool cannot be sensibly answered without considering the way in which these ratings will be used in organizations. The ratings that are recorded by supervisors will also be driven by the uses to which these ratings are applied. For example, when ratings are used to make salary or promotion decisions, raters are likely to emphasize differences between individuals and de-emphasize patterns of individual strengths and weaknesses (Cleveland et al., 1986; Cleveland et al., 1989). Consideration of the uses of PA information leads to alternate conceptions of the utility and accuracy of performance ratings.

Historically, performance ratings have been evaluated primarily in terms of their resistance to a variety of psychometric biases, or rater errors (Landy & Farr, 1980). The thrust of recent criterion research and development in the field of performance has centered around the importance of accuracy in performance ratings. We question whether this emphasis is always justified.

From the perspective of our model, it makes no sense to view rater errors, such as halo or leniency, as mistakes on the part of the rater (for a related argument, see Funder, 1987). For example, a high level of halo does not mean that the rater *cannot* discriminate among rating dimensions; it merely indicates that he or she *did not* discriminate. Saal, Downey, and Lahey (1980) note that many rater errors may in fact reflect desirable end states. For example, organizations do all they can to ensure that all subordinates perform at a high level, yet if everyone receives high ratings, psychologists suspect leniency rather than truly good performance. Our analysis suggests that many rater errors are consciously made and that failure to discriminate among persons or dimensions is often a highly adaptive behavior. Raters are not passive measurement instruments and should not be treated as such.

A number of serious questions may be raised about the practicality and adequacy of any particular method of operationalizing accuracy (Cronbach, 1955; Lord, 1985a; Sulsky & Balzer, 1988). A more general concern, however, is the extent to which accuracy is an appropriate criterion for PA ratings. Differences between actual and rated performance do not necessarily reflect measurement error; rather, they may simply reflect many forces in the organization that discourage accurate rating. Relatively context-free criteria, such as accuracy, may not make sense in the context-bound world of performance ratings. Consider why this is so.

A focus on accuracy is entirely appropriate when asking questions about the judgments that raters are able to make. Performance ratings are not simply judgments, however. They are a means of communicating a message to the organization or to the worker. At times, the most useful message may differ somewhat from the message that would be conveyed if perfectly accurate judgments were recorded and transmitted as performance appraisals. The most useful message may be a simpler one or one that takes into account demand characteristics present in the organization. In other words, it may include motivated distortion intended to improve the usefulness of the performance appraisal.

This distinction between performance judgments and performance ratings has important implications for the criteria used to evaluate them. As noted above, it is probably not reasonable to assume that discrepancies between performance ratings and employee work performance represent inabilities to make accurate judgments about that performance. Likewise, it can be seen that accuracy does not ensure the usefulness of performance ratings that are applied in a particular organizational setting.

The parallel between this example and the judgment-versus-rating distinction is straightforward. The study of errors in performance judgments (i.e., accuracy indices) assists in clarifying the judgment process, but the evaluation of ratings is more appropriately cast in terms of the mistakes (e.g., incorrect decisions) that they produce (Feldman, 1986).

Another implication of distinguishing between the evaluation of performance judgments and performance ratings concerns the difficulty in identifying individual raters who are particularly adept at their task. There are very few ways to tell a good rater from a poor rater, as long as each worker is evaluated by only one rater. In order to assess accuracy, multiple raters may be needed (Murphy, 1982b). In order to increase the usefulness of ratings, however, it may be more feasible and efficient to utilize an organizational intervention or perhaps simply to identify a high-performing rater and utilize the skills of that individual.

Even if a reliable distinction between good and poor raters can be made, this may not be the critical point, because the accuracy of raters in field settings is probably driven more strongly by situational variables than by individual difference variables. Moving a good rater to a different context, with strong situational demands, might very well produce a "poor" rater (as judged in terms of accuracy). Therefore, time might be better spent focusing on the context of performance ratings as a central theme, rather than concentrating strictly on individual raters as the primary source of variation in the effectiveness of an appraisal system.

SUMMARY

Previous psychological research on PA has focused on appraisal as a measurement process. The major concerns of this research have been whether performance ratings are accurate and valid measures and what technologies (e.g., scale formats) could be developed to increase accuracy and validity. This research has been characterized by models that do not facilitate the integration of science and practice in performance appraisal, because they do not identify the most important variables in appraisal and they fail to address concerns that are central to the practice of appraisal. Another approach to research and practice is needed.

The model we present in this chapter is intended to provide a guide to both research and practice. Ours is a social-psychological model rather than a psychometric model, and it treats performance appraisal as a communication process that occurs in a well-defined organizational context. Our key concerns are identifying what the rater is trying to convey to the organization; what features of the rater, the ratee, and the context affect that message; and how organizations should evaluate the information that is communicated to them by raters. Our model points to a variety of issues that are treated in depth in the chapters that follow.

2

█████████████████████████████████████

Environmental Influences

This chapter opens our discussion of the contextual factors that influence performance appraisal (PA) in organizations. One major theme of this book is that PA cannot be adequately understood outside of its organizational context—the same appraisal system, the same criteria for evaluating ratings, the same rater-training program, and so on are *not* the same if they exist in different contexts. We believe that the context is a major determinant of a rater's goal-oriented rating behavior, and that behaviors that seem to indicate rater error or an inaccurate rating when examined out of context, are often adaptive responses to the various contextual factors that surround performance appraisal. In this chapter, and in the two chapters that follow, we will discuss in depth the ways in which contextual factors affect PA processes and outcomes.

Context refers to a heterogeneous mix of factors, ranging from the social and legal system in which the organization exists to the climate and culture within the organization. One way to classify the various levels of context is to arrange them on a continuum from proximal to distal context factors. *Proximal* factors are those that impinge directly on the individual rater, whereas *distal* factors affect the rater indirectly (e.g., by determining norms for evaluating performance) (Cleveland & Hollman, 1991; Cleveland et al., 1986). A model for distinguishing between proximal and distal effects is illustrated in Figure 2.1.

Proximal context factors include the purpose of rating, the organization's policies regarding feedback, the need to document good versus poor ratings, and whatever else the rater is doing at the time he or she fills out performance appraisals. Distal context factors represent the internal and external environments of organizations. Distal context factors range from the climate of the organization to the sociopolitical system of the society (e.g., capitalism vs. socialism). This chapter is concerned with the more distal aspects of the context in which rating occurs and, in particular, with those factors that make up the external environment of an organization. We will examine the influence of these environmental factors as well as the mechanisms by which they might affect performance appraisals.

DEFINING THE ORGANIZATION'S ENVIRONMENT

There is no single definition of the external environment of an organization nor is there any clear consensus among organizational researchers regarding the most useful ways to define and study an organization's environment. Table 2.1 vividly illustrates the range of terms and concepts that have been used to describe organizational environments. This table is not comprehensive nor does it include the alternative definitions of several of these terms that have been used by different authors in the literature on organizational environments. Nevertheless, Table 2.1 does provide an indication of the complexity of the term *organizational environment*.

Katz and Kahn (1978) noted five aspects of the environment that organizations must monitor and respond to in order to be effective: (a) societal values, (b) the political/legal environment, (c) the economic/labor environment, (d) the information/technological environment, and (e) the physical/geographical environment. Each of these aspects of the environment is likely to affect PA in some way. Some have a more direct impact on

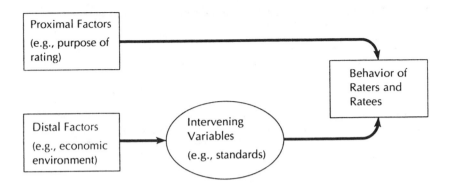

Figure 2.1. Effects of Proximal Versus Distal Context Factors

appraisal (e.g., legal environment), whereas others have an indirect, but nevertheless important, effect (e.g., societal values).

Each of the characteristics of the environment listed in Table 2.1 is multidimensional. Two of the most frequently cited facets of environments are turbulence and munificence (Katz & Kahn, 1978; March & Simon, 1958; Thompson, 1967). *Turbulence* refers to the extent to which the environment changes or remains stable. For example, Katz and Kahn (1978) note that the economic environment of Western nations was highly turbulent in the 1970s, with unpredictable swings between inflation and depression. Turbulent environments are thought to lead to uncertainty in organizations; this uncertainty could affect PA practices. *Munificence* refers to the degree of scarcity or abundance of critical resources in the environment. For example, when unemployment is high, the labor market is, from the organization's point of view, a munificent environment. Scarcity of critical resources is likely to lead to conflict within organizations (March & Simon, 1958). The implications of this conflict will depend largely on which environments are munificent and which are plagued by scarcity. For example, if the labor market is very tight, performance appraisals may be used quite differently than if the physical environment is characterized by scarcity.

Researchers have sometimes mentioned environmental variables as possible influences on performance appraisals; 12 of the environmental variables that have been discussed in the PA literature are (Carroll & Schneier, 1982; Landy & Farr, 1983):

TABLE 2.1 Terms Used to Describe Organizational Environments

Term	Definition
Distant (Secondary Environment)	Everything beyond environment's domain
Domain	Organization's goals and the functions undertaken to meet them
Industry	Set of organizations producing substitutable products
Market	Set of customers who use organization's products
Niche	Environmental configuration that favors survival
Organization Set	Organizations whose roles interlock with subject organization
Organizational Role	Goals or tasks of an organization
Organizational Saga	Collective understanding within an organization
Role	Exchange relation with the environment
Strategy Set	Plan for future relationship with environment
Subenvironment	Environment of one department
Task Environment	Parts of environment that are relevant to goal accomplishment
Territory	Subset of domain organization seeks to dominate
Value Environment	Subset of distant environment that sets norms

SOURCE: W. H. Starbuck, in M. Dunnette (Ed.), *Handbook of Industrial and Organizational Psychology* (Chicago: Rand McNally, 1976). Used by permission of M. Dunnette.

- Technological development
- Competition
- Unionization
- Economic conditions
- Workforce composition
- Market share
- Profitability
- Market predictability
- Local unemployment
- National unemployment
- Demands for diversification
- Local, state, and federal legislation

Landy and Farr (1983) note, however, that there is virtually no empirical research on the effects of these environmental variables on PA processes or outcomes. In this chapter we will draw on research from other areas of psychology and sociology to describe the potential effects of environmental variables on performance appraisal.

Objective and External Environments

Most discussions of environmental effects treat the environment as an objective variable that exists outside of the organization. It is typically assumed that there is some discernible boundary between the organization and its environment, and that the environment of an organization is discernible to an outside observer. Both of these assumptions are debatable. Research questioning these assumptions may have implications for the way environmental variables are linked to PA processes and outcomes.

Starbuck (1976) notes that the boundaries between an organization and its environment are often fuzzy. He uses a cloud or magnetic field as a metaphor for an organization and notes that when a person is either far enough inside or far enough outside of an organization, the organization appears to be a clear, distinct entity. If an individual is near the boundaries of an organization, however, the precise demarcation between the organization and its environment is not at all clear. A considerable amount of research literature has examined the roles of individuals who occupy positions near the boundaries of organizations (Adams, 1976). This literature suggests that occupants of boundary roles inhabit both the organization and the organization's environment. Although the literature is not completely clear on this point, we predict that the effects of environmental variables would be strongest for individuals near the boundary.

Yasai-Adekani (1986) notes that individuals and organizations do not react to objective aspects of the environment but rather to *perceived* aspects of the environment. In many cases perceptions of organization members will correspond closely with objective reality, but this is not always the case. For example, in the area of employment testing many personnel managers appear to believe that employment discrimination laws discourage the use of ability tests but allow the use of more subjective methods (e.g., the interview) without the same level of scrutiny (Cascio, 1987; Wigdor & Garner, 1982). In fact, the opposite is probably true. Nevertheless, personnel managers have acted on their perceptions of the legal environment, and during the 1960s and 1970s the use of ability tests appears to have declined (Hale, 1982).

If perceived environment is more important than the objective environment, one implication is that environmental effects might be highly variable within the same organization. For example, some managers might perceive the task environment as highly munificent, whereas others see scarcity. If all these managers were to rate the same subordinates, some differences in ratings would be expected solely as a function of the perceived environment. Thus, it may be that the organization is not the appropriate level of analysis for describing environmental effects. For some environmental variables, the effects on each department, or even on each rater in the organization, may need to be examined.

It is useful to examine the factors that lead some individuals to misperceive their environment. When these factors are present, wide individual differences in perceptions of the environment can be expected. These differences may also lead to significant variability in the extent to which the environment affects the rating behavior of various individuals. When these factors are absent, it may be predicted that all organizational members will develop similar perceptions of the environment, which may in turn lead to more homogeneous environmental effects.

Misperception of the environment is most likely when (a) environmental cues are ambiguous, (b) information about the environment is scarce, or (c) environmental cues are inconsistent. For example, if the economy is not clearly in a period of inflation, recession, or recovery, this may lead to wide individual differences in perceptions of the munificence of the economic environment. During periods of rapid technological advances, information about the technology that is likely to dominate one's market or niche is likely to be fragmentary, which could lead to considerable uncertainty in an individual's perceptions of the technological environment. It might be difficult to develop a consistent perception of the legal environment (especially in areas related to personnel administration), because of conflicting court decisions or because of conflicts between the executive and the judicial branches.

HOW THE ENVIRONMENT AFFECTS APPRAISAL

As discussed earlier, there is very little empirical research on the links between environmental variables and appraisal. Consequently, very little is known about the mechanisms by which environments affect appraisal processes and outcomes. By definition, these effects will be at least partially indirect (i.e., external environments represent distal cues), which means that some variable or set of variables will intervene between the environment and the behavior of individual raters and ratees. We can suggest several possible intervening variables, including:

1. Performance standards
2. Performance dimensions
3. Frequency of appraisal
4. Supervisor-subordinate relationship
5. Consequences of high versus low ratings
6. Legitimacy of appraisal

These six variables do not exhaust the list of possible mediating variables, but they do provide a basis for describing the different ways in which the environment might indirectly affect performance appraisal.

Environments are complex, and different aspects of the environment could have different effects on each of the intervening variables listed above. To help structure our discussion of environmental effects, we will restrict our attention to the effects of the munificence of the five aspects of the environment identified by Katz and Kahn (1978). Munificence can be defined in the following ways for each aspect of the environment:

1. Societal—the extent to which sociopolitical norms and values support the concept of performance appraisal, as typically practiced in organizations
2. Legal—the extent to which the legal system facilitates and allows typical performance appraisal practices
3. Economic—the extent to which general economic conditions are favorable for the organization
4. Technical—the extent to which an organization possesses or controls the technology and work methods needed to carry out the organization's functions
5. Physical—the extent to which necessary physical resources are available

Our predictions regarding the effects of munificence are summarized in Table 2.2. The rationale for these predictions is discussed below.

Performance Standards

We predict that the standards that define good and poor performance on the job will be strongly affected by four of the five aspects of the environment. For example, the question of whether one should expect all workers to perform well, or should set standards that allow some workers to succeed

TABLE 2.2   Effects of Environmental Munificence on Six Aspects of
Appraisal Systems

Aspects of Appraisal	Aspects of Environment				
	Societal	Legal	Economic	Technical	Physical
Standard	Strong	Moderate	Strong	Strong	Strong
Dimensions	Moderate	Moderate	Strong	Strong	Strong
Frequency	Weak	Moderate	Moderate	Weak	Moderate
Relationship	Moderate	Weak	Strong	Strong	Moderate
Consequences	Moderate	Strong	Strong	Weak	Moderate
Legitimacy	Strong	Strong	Moderate	Strong	Weak

and others to fail, is in part a philosophical one whose solution might depend on the values of society as a whole. A society that emphasizes competition and achievement might lead to different (probably higher) performance standards than one that emphasizes satisfaction with work.

The legal system probably also affects performance standards, although to a lesser degree. That is, the legal system may not have a main effect on standards (i.e., raising or lowering standards) but it is likely to affect the degree to which standards are made explicit, as well as the degree to which they are enforced. A legal system that is basically antagonistic to performance appraisal will probably lead to the formulation of explicit, concrete standards that are communicated directly to employees.

We would expect different (higher) performance standards during a business recession than during a period of economic growth or stability. We would also expect the technological position of a company to affect standards. A company that is behind-the-times technologically might try to compensate by setting high standards; a company that is technologically sophisticated might not see strong links between the performance standards enforced for individual workers and the output of the organization. Companies that employ assembly-line technologies might have different performance standards than companies that rely on semi-autonomous work teams to produce their product.

Finally, the effects of physical munificence are likely to be very similar in strength to those of economic munificence but perhaps in a different direction. When the physical resources needed for production are not available, it may be necessary to adjust performance standards downward (Peters, O'Connor, & Eulberg, 1985).

Performance Dimensions

The definition of what constitutes performance and the relative importance of different parts of the performance domain are likely to be affected by the environment. A comparison of U.S. versus Japanese management styles provides an example of societal influences. A U.S. manager is likely to emphasize individual task performance, whereas a Japanese manager is likely to emphasize ability to work with the group when evaluating the performance of the same subordinate (Pascale & Athos, 1981).

The legal system will probably also have a moderate influence. As the legal system becomes less munificent (i.e., less favorable to current appraisal practices), we predict that organizations will emphasize dimensions that involve clear, concrete, objective outcomes, and will de-emphasize interpersonally oriented performance dimensions.

The munificence of the economic environment will strongly affect the choice of performance dimensions. In an unfavorable economic environment, we expect that organizations will define performance in terms of short-term, bottom-line goals. Thus, a supervisor who is not good at producing products but who is good at developing subordinates might receive different evaluations, depending on the economic environment. The technical environment will also have a strong impact on the choice of performance dimensions. The importance of technically oriented dimensions will probably vary across industries (and companies) with varying levels of technical sophistication.

The munificence of the physical environment will strongly affect the extent to which performance is defined in terms of efficiency versus output. When resources are scarce, the worker who produces less but conserves materials and resources might receive a more favorable evaluation than a worker who produces a great deal but is wasteful. The reverse might be the case when resources are cheap and plentiful.

Frequency of Appraisal

Societal values will probably have a weak impact on the frequency with which an organization conducts appraisals. The practice of annual appraisals is a strong norm, however, and these values could affect an organization that tries to conduct appraisals less or more frequently than once a year. The legal system is likely to have a moderate, albeit indirect, effect on the frequency of appraisals. Many organizations make major administrative decisions (particularly salary decisions) on a roughly annual schedule. If the legal system encourages strong links between appraisals and administrative decisions, this might lead to a strong preference for annual or semi-annual appraisals that coincide with the organization's schedule for making administrative decisions.

Both the economic environment and the physical environment are likely to have a moderate effect on the frequency of appraisals. As the economic and physical environments become more unfavorable, there will be stronger incentives for frequent performance appraisals, coupled with programs to increase the output of poor performers. When the economic and physical environments are highly munificent, there will probably be less interest in performance appraisal.

We do not expect the technical environment to have a strong effect on the frequency of appraisals. Perhaps the one exception is the situation where the supervisor is not familiar with the technology of production. We might expect this supervisor to avoid doing performance appraisals, if at all possible, and to turn in appraisals that are not informative when they are demanded by the organization.

Supervisor-Subordinate Relationship

Societal values will have some impact on the nature of the relationship between supervisors and subordinates, particularly with regard to the extent to which this relationship is autocratic versus participative. Agervold (1975) notes that the decline of authoritarian methods of supervision in some Swedish industries is a direct result of a cultural value system that emphasizes workplace democracy. We do not think that the legal system will have a strong impact on supervisor-subordinate relationships, although an adverse legal climate might lead supervisors to try to avoid litigation by being more formal and retaining better documentation of the interaction with subordinates.

Both the economic and technical environments, and to a lesser extent the physical environment, are likely to affect supervisor-subordinate relationships significantly. Economic or physical environments that are unfavorable, or technical environments that are complex, are likely to increase the degree to which the supervisor is dependent on subordinates. When the economic or physical environment is unfavorable, there is likely to be pressure on the supervisor to produce; he or she must in turn depend on obtaining good performance from subordinates. As the technology becomes increasingly complex, the supervisor might also become increasingly irrelevant, especially if the supervisor cannot operate the computers, instruments, or machines used by subordinates.

Consequences of High Versus Low Ratings

As discussed in the previous chapter, one of the key determinants of whether a supervisor gives high or low ratings is the consequences that are attached to the ratings. Rating inflation is quite likely when ratings have a strong influence on salaries or promotions, and is least likely if ratings are not used to make administrative decisions (see Chapter 9). Four of the five aspects of the environment will have at least a moderate effect on the consequences of giving high versus low ratings; for two of the five aspects, this influence may be substantial.

Societal norms and values will have some influence on the consequences of high versus low ratings. The extent of this influence will be determined by the degree to which societal values support or discourage treating good and poor workers differently. For example, the question of whether individuals should be rewarded in proportion to their level of performance would probably be answered differently in the United States than in Japan. In socialist and communist states, the answer might be different from that in either the United States or Japan.

The legal system will strongly affect the degree to which performance appraisals are likely to be connected to administrative decisions. A legal system that is hostile to PA, as it is typically practiced, will also be hostile to the use of performance ratings as a primary basis for allocating organizational rewards. A legal system that strongly acknowledges management's rights to evaluate the performance of workers will also probably support linking rewards directly to performance ratings.

The lower the munificence of the economic environment (and, to a lesser extent, the physical environment), the greater the incentive to tie rewards to performance levels. We predict that organizations will be more likely to use performance appraisals to make administrative decisions—ranging from salary and promotions to layoffs—when the economic environment is unfavorable than when it is favorable. In part this is because organizations have less slack (i.e., less ability to survive given

42 UNDERSTANDING PERFORMANCE APPRAISAL

substandard performance) in an unfavorable economic environment than in a favorable one.

We do not predict that the munificence of the technological environment will affect the organization's decision of whether or not to link rewards to one's performance ratings. The technological environment might still have an effect on rating, however, especially if the supervisor is not capable of using the technology that workers employ. In this case, one might find range restriction. Our rationale here is that supervisors who do not understand or have never performed major portions of the job may be less willing (or able) to distinguish between good and poor performers.

Legitimacy of Appraisal

The question of legitimacy can be thought of in two ways. First, at the broadest level, it is likely that some people regard the evaluation of individual job performance as a perfectly legitimate managerial function, whereas others do not accept the idea of performance evaluation at all. Second, it is likely that some people will regard any particular performance appraisal system as acceptable, whereas others will not. The organization's environment might affect both aspects of the legitimacy question.

Societal values will be a strong determinant of perceptions of the legitimacy of performance appraisal per se, as well as perceptions of any particular appraisal system. In contrast, many European countries appear to place less emphasis on individual appraisal, and often place legal restrictions on assessment and appraisal systems that are not acceptable to employees (Pearn, 1993). If different countries were rank-ordered in terms of the degree to which the dominant culture viewed individual performance appraisal as a reasonable and acceptable activity, the United States would be at or near the top of the list. Countries in which the primary orientation was toward the performance of groups or classes of workers (e.g., Japan and some countries with socialist or communist systems) would probably be ranked lowest. The acceptability of any particular appraisal system would also depend on the degree to which the system was consonant with the society's values.

One function of the legal system, in this case, is to codify the societal values that are relevant to PA practice. For example, the U.S. legal system accepts the principle of performance appraisal but also demands certain safeguards be in place to protect workers from arbitrary and capricious supervisory judgments. The technological environment also has a strong effect on determining the legitimacy of performance appraisal, but the direction of this effect is not as easy to predict. If the technology is complex and the supervisor is not familiar with the technology, the idea of the supervisor evaluating subordinates' performance might not be acceptable. On the other hand, if the supervisor is familiar with or expert in the technology used by subordinates, there may be little resistance to using the supervisor as the primary or sole source of performance appraisals.

The economic environment might affect supervisors' and subordinates' assessments of the legitimacy of different PA methods. There is evidence that economic hardship contributes to conflict and suspicion in organizations (Whetten, 1987). Subordinates may most strongly resist supervisors' attempts to separate good from poor performers in situations where resources are tight and poor performance ratings may result in adverse outcomes.

Finally, we do not predict a strong effect for the munificence of the physical environment of the perceived legitimacy of performance appraisal. There is, however, one circumstance in which the effects of the physical environment could be strong. If there are strong situational constraints that prevent individuals from performing well, workers might not accept an appraisal system that tries to separate good from poor performers.

RESEARCH ON ENVIRONMENTAL EFFECTS

As noted earlier, empirical research that directly examines the role of environmental variables in performance is virtually nonexistent. Nevertheless, we can draw on research outside of the area of performance appraisal and from nonempirical papers in the PA literature to document some of the likely effects of environmental variables on performance appraisal processes and outcomes. As with the preceding section, our discussion is arranged around the five aspects of an organization's environment that are critical in determining the organization's health and survival.

Societal Environment

Research on the effects of societal norms and values on behavior in organizations has concentrated primarily on political issues, particularly the extent to which the sociopolitical system encourages democratic versus authoritarian systems of control, and capitalistic versus socialistic systems of ownership. Some studies have also examined the internal political environment of organizations (e.g., Longenecker, Sims, & Gioia, 1987); this research will be discussed more fully in Chapters 3 and 4.

Locke (1983) examined the practice of PA under capitalism, socialism, and a mixed economy. First, he concluded that, under capitalism, the market would help guarantee effective performance appraisals. His reasoning, similar to that often employed by classical economists, is that any personnel practice that survives for long periods in an organization must be an effective one; otherwise, organizations that used more effective methods would soon overtake the organization that was doing a poor job in evaluating its employees. (A similar line of reasoning is employed by sociobiologists, who argue that the long-term survival of any species-specific characteristic is an indication of its evolutionary value.) Second, he concluded that there was very little incentive for PA under socialism, noting that "socialism eliminates at the outset the foundation on which objective performance evaluation is based—namely the price system and its free market corollary, the profit system" (Locke, 1983, p. 317). Third, Locke concluded that in a mixed economy (a category that would include the United States, Europe, and much of the Third World), performance appraisal would be very difficult. (For an opposing point of view, see Lerner, 1983.)

We would be more willing to accept Locke's (1983) conclusions if there were more data available to support them. His arguments appear to rest on many of the assumptions of classical economics (e.g., that a completely free market can exist, and that decision makers possess the information necessary to make optimal decisions) that have been shown to be untenable (March & Simon, 1958). Relatively few studies have examined Locke's hypotheses to date. Thus, we regard the question of whether PA is easier under capitalism, socialism, or a mixed economy as unsettled.

Goldman (1983) examines performance appraisal from the Marxist perspective. Goldman does not address the question of whether it is possible to evaluate performance accurately, but rather asks whether performance *should* be evaluated, regardless of the technical capacity to do so. He argues that the practice of distinguishing among workers on any basis, such as their level of performance, is in the interest of management but is not in the interest of workers. According to Marxist thought, the primary basis for workers' power is their solidarity. Any procedure that singles out workers and separates them from their colleagues dilutes the workers' power and therefore increases the power of management to exploit workers. Implicit in this argument is the assumption that the gains associated with performance appraisal for individual workers who *are* good performers are smaller than the losses that workers as a group will have to endure if distinctions are made between good and poor workers.

Our discomfort with Goldman's (1983) conclusions closely mirrors our objections to those of Locke (1983). The argument would be more convincing if it were accompanied by more data. Unfortunately, empirical research has not, in general, supported key aspects of the Marxist position. For example, Form (1987) notes that Marxist theory assumes that capitalists will attempt to simplify jobs in order to increase efficiency, control, and profits. A careful review of the literature led Form (1987) to conclude that skill levels of jobs have not declined in modern history. The proportion of skilled to unskilled jobs in the economy has not changed substantially since the Industrial Revolution.

In his survey of the history of organizational theory, Perrow (1973) noted that the decline of scientific management was not because this method did not work but rather occurred because of social, political, and cultural changes that created dissatisfaction with the highly directive and paternalistic aspects of this approach.

Similarly, Agervold (1975) noted that the growth of movements for industrial democracy in Europe (particularly Scandinavia) was a reflection of a broader social and cultural norm that rejected authoritarian styles of leadership. If social norms are moving away from top-down (from authoritarian power structures toward more democratic structures), PA practices could change substantially. For example, under a more strongly democratic culture we might see more emphasis on self-appraisal, peer appraisal, and the use of appraisals for counseling and development, and less emphasis on using appraisal to rank-order workers.

Both historical and cross-cultural research is needed to assess the effects of the sociopolitical environment on performance appraisal. We have noted earlier that the sociopolitical environment of the United States is highly favorable to performance appraisal. A good deal could be learned about the ways in which such an environment affects PA by studying appraisal methods in other times or cultures. This topic is likely to become increasingly relevant with the growth of multinational organizations whose corporate appraisal policies are different from those typically encountered in the United States. Historically, our nation has been able to impose its sociopolitical values on workers in U.S. multinational corporations. With the rise in foreign-owned multinational corporations in this country, however, the situation is starting to reverse itself (i.e., values and practices from other cultures are being employed with U.S. workers). Cultural differences revolving around PA could become a significant problem for U.S. employees of foreign multinationals.

Legal Environment

Passage of the Civil Rights Act of 1964 dramatically changed the legal environment of performance appraisals. Prior to 1964, it was difficult for any employee to contest legally his or her performance evaluation, no matter how subjective, capricious, or inaccurate the appraisal. (One exception would be where a performance appraisal was used to carry out some unfair labor practice, such as giving all union organizers poor ratings.) The reason for this is that there was no legal requirement that private organizations accurately evaluate workers' performance. The same is true today, except in the case where a test or measure has adverse impact on some protected group (typically minorities or women). Adverse impact occurs when a test, measurement device, or procedure has markedly different outcomes for different groups. For example, if most men passed a strength test but most women failed, the test would have adverse impact on women if it was used to make decisions about hiring, firing, promotion, and the like. Any measure that has, or might have, adverse impact is potentially vulnerable to legal scrutiny. If adverse impact is demonstrated, the employer must establish the validity or business necessity of the PA system.

Legal issues connected with PA are reviewed by Barrett and Kernan (1987), Bernardin and Beatty (1984), Cascio (1987), Cascio and Bernardin (1981), and Latham (1986). Some general guidelines (Bernardin & Beatty, 1984; Feild & Holley, 1982) for complying with federal antidiscrimination laws in carrying out performance appraisals are:

- Performance appraisals should be based on specific dimensions whose relevance has been established through job analysis.
- Raters should receive training or instruction.
- Performance dimensions should be defined in terms of behaviors.

- Feedback should be given to the ratee, and there should be an appeal process for ratings that the individual feels are inaccurate.
- Raters should have adequate opportunities to observe the performance they will be asked to evaluate.
- Extreme ratings should be documented.
- If possible, there should be multiple raters.
- Appraisals should be frequent—at least annual.

All of these guidelines can be thought of as safeguards designed to protect employees from arbitrary or subjective evaluations that may more closely reflect the rater's biases than they reflect the ratee's performance.

There is clear evidence that the legal environment affects the way in which performance appraisals are done. Cleveland et al. (1989) surveyed more than 100 corporations to determine the degree to which performance appraisals were used for various purposes in organizations. In their confirmatory factor analysis of 20 potential uses, one of the four factors was labeled "Documentation" and referred to the uses of performance appraisals to meet federal, state, and local requirements, in particular to justify adverse personnel actions (e.g., firing a worker for poor performance).

The surveys showed that documentation represented one of the most frequent uses of performance appraisal. Although Cleveland and colleagues (1989) did not investigate the issue, we suspect that the use of PA to document personnel decisions is highest in organizations that are willing to fire poor performers and is lowest in situations where it is not possible to take action in the face of performance that is at least marginally acceptable (e.g., where a strong union prevails). Only the most foolish employer will now dismiss a worker for poor performance without first collecting clear and convincing documentation.

As we will discuss in Chapter 5, most PA systems rely on the direct supervisor as the sole judge of his or her subordinates' performance. Although the appraisal form might also require the signature of the supervisor's superior, the direct supervisor has the ultimate responsibility for assessing workers' performance. The legal system, although not hostile to this practice, nevertheless discourages it. The issue is not that the supervisor is less qualified than someone else to evaluate subordinates' performance but rather that it is impossible to rule out rater biases if only one person evaluates each worker's performance (see Chapter 10). No matter how explicit the rating form or how detailed the training program, there is no safeguard against conscious or unconscious distortion by any single rater. Although using multiple raters does not completely solve the problem of rater bias (e.g., if all raters are white males with similar backgrounds, they may share similar biases), it seems to be the only reasonable procedure if the problem of rater bias is serious. We do not know of any case that has been decided on the basis of whether the plaintiff used one rater or several but we would not be surprised to see this issue raised in lawsuits in the near future.

The current legal environment for performance appraisal clearly reflects the broader sociopolitical environment. At one time in our history, the right of the employer to use *any* personnel practice, except perhaps for those that placed employees at great physical risk, was basically unchallenged. This is no longer true. The current legal environment is one where the outcome of conflicts between the rights of the employer and the rights of employees cannot be easily predicted. However, even if the outcome of lawsuits challenging personnel practices is highly uncertain, it is likely that the legal environment will continue to have a strong influence on PA practice. Organizations are likely to take steps to prevent lawsuits from ever arising (even if an organization wins a lawsuit, the expense of defending the suit can be ruinous). We thus expect that the guidelines outlined above will continue strongly to affect performance appraisal.

Economic Environment

Organizational researchers have paid relatively little attention to the effects of the economic environment on behavior in organizations. It has long been known that the munificence of the environment affects the frequency and intensity of conflict within the organization (March & Simon, 1958). Low munificence is associated with heightened conflict. It is also known that economic conditions strongly affect strategic goals (Starbuck, 1976). The literature on economic environments has, however, had little to say about the influence of those environments on performance appraisal.

Although research on the growth and decline of organizations is not concerned solely with the economic environment, this literature is nevertheless the source for several hypotheses about the relationship between the state of the economy and the methods used to evaluate workers' performance. Early in their life cycles, organizations are often characterized by liberal goals and flexible structures. As organizations prosper and grow, however, they tend to become inflexible and autocratic (Whetten, 1987). As organizations decline, relationships within the organization become increasingly politicized (Pfeffer & Salancik, 1978). Decline leads to higher levels of conflict, secrecy, and scapegoating, and to lower levels of morale, satisfaction, and participation (Whetten, 1987). We might expect similar phenomena to occur during either highly prosperous (growth) or economically unfavorable (decline) times.

As organizations grow and prosper, we would expect that PA will become increasingly formalized. In part, this is a product of the size of the organization; as the organization gets larger, informal relations between workers at different levels become less likely. As organizations decline, documentation of poor performance is emphasized more, especially if the organization is forced to lay off a significant portion of its workforce. We might also expect less emphasis on feedback and development (as a result of the increasing emphasis on secrecy) and more interest in using PA as an instrument to increase production.

Negative economic trends probably have a greater impact on behavior in organizations than do positive ones. In particular, personnel practices that are adopted during hard times are likely to be retained when the economy rebounds. This is precisely the pattern with union-management relations in the early and mid-1980s. The recession in the early 1980s created conditions where unions were forced to make substantial concessions to management, often in the form of decreases in pay. When the recession ended, few organizations restored their earlier contracts; requests for pay cuts and other major concessions are still common in union-management negotiations.

Technical Environment

Changes in technology can have a substantial impact on PA processes and outcomes. In part, this is due to incidental changes in the organization of work that accompany new technology. For example, Woodward (1965) noted that as technology becomes increasingly complex, the span of control of first-line supervisors tends to increase. Thus the addition of new technology may increase the number of persons a supervisor is asked to evaluate. An increasing span of control also implies that the supervisor (a) has less time to observe each worker's performance, (b) must spend more time doing performance appraisals, and (c) has a larger comparison group available for evaluating each worker's performance. The first two factors may lead to lower levels of accuracy; the last factor may lead to increased levels of accuracy.

Another example of the indirect effects of technology on performance appraisal involves changes in supervisor-subordinate relations (Barley, 1986). Fry (1982) notes that when the technology becomes complex, the workers who use that technology may become more expert in their jobs than their supervisors. In the extreme case, the supervisor who cannot operate the current technology could become completely dependent on his or her subordinates. This change in relationship is likely to have several effects on performance appraisal.

First, as noted earlier, the frequency of appraisals may go down if the supervisor does not feel able to evaluate sensibly subordinates' performance. (In this case, we would also expect severe range restriction in whatever ratings were collected.) Second, workers may not accept appraisals from a supervisor who does not understand precisely what they do. One basis for the supervisor's power is usually his or her presumed expertise (French & Raven, 1959). The supervisor who does not understand the technology no longer has expert power. Third, in a related point, the supervisor may lose position power (French & Raven, 1959) as a result of the introduction of new technologies. Particularly in areas such as communications or computers, new technologies may change the nature of work in such a way that the supervisor becomes superfluous. A loss in position power will probably also lead to lower levels of acceptance of performance appraisals by subordinates.

Shamir and Salomon (1985) note that advances in telecommunications and microelectronics have made it progressively easier for a number of workers to work at home, rather than going to the workplace. It is possible that a supervisor will never see or even meet some of his or her subordinates. The performance of an individual who works at home can hardly be assessed in behavioral terms. In this case, PA might depend solely on a count of products, reports, or other results achieved. Furthermore, in evaluating the performance of a worker who is off-site, the supervisor (if there even is one) might be bypassed entirely, and performance counts may be recorded through the same medium (e.g., a personal computer) that the worker uses to submit the results of his or her work. We will examine the effects of telecommuting and other arrangements for working in dispersed sites more fully in Chapter 13.

Computerized monitoring of employees is increasingly common. Aiello (1993) notes that 20%-40% of all office workers might be subject to monitoring; as many as 70,000 U.S. companies may use some form of monitoring. Recent research on computerized monitoring (e.g., Aiello & Svec, 1993; Chalykoff & Kochan, 1989; Garson, 1988; Grant & Higgins, 1991; Office of Technology Assessment, 1987) suggests that its effects are far from simple. Depending on the task and the task environment, monitoring can enhance or hurt performance. A number of variables are likely to moderate the effects of monitoring, including participation, organizational climate, use of individual versus group monitoring, the level of secrecy inherent in the system, and the precise measures obtained through monitoring (Aiello, 1993).

Advances in technology have made it possible to automate some aspects of the PA process. Landy (1985) described the use of computers to measure the performance of claims processors at a health insurance office. The computers that these workers used not only recorded the results of their work but also monitored their performance. The computer recorded performance on a minute-by-minute basis, constantly comparing productivity to company production standards, and provided weekly reports on each worker's performance. Workers' pay was adjusted up or down, according to their performance levels. As might be expected, the workers reacted very negatively to this system and complained of fatigue, stress, and an assembly-line atmosphere at work.

The use of computers or other technological means to monitor workers' performance will inevitably lead to a debate over the employer's right to get full-time work for full-time pay, versus the workers' rights to protection against invasions of privacy. Regardless of one's position in this debate, this application of technology is not one we recommend. Although the use of automatic monitoring of performance may be legally permissible (this issue has not yet, to our knowledge, been ruled on in court), the practice is likely to be a public-relations disaster. Personnel policies that are regarded as invasive or unjustified are likely to lead both members of the organization and outsiders to develop a negative image of the organization, which may in turn affect the organization's ability to recruit, hire, and keep good employees (Cascio, 1987; Murphy & Reynolds, 1988b; Schwab, Rynes, & Aldag, 1987).

Even if the public-relations problem could be solved, we are not sure that there is anything one could or should do with minute-by-minute reports about each worker. First, suppose that it was found that an individual took frequent breaks. Wouldn't the evaluation of that individual still depend on what he or she accomplished between breaks? The minute-by-minute report might say more about an individual's style of work than his or her level of performance. Second, reports that cover a short period, such as a week, are probably not reliable indicators of an individual's overall performance. It is known in test theory that reliability increases with the number of opportunities to observe the subject's behavior (i.e., with the number of test items). This same principle also applies to performance appraisal. If reports are produced only for blocks of time that allow for reliable measurement (this might require several weeks or months, depending on the nature of the work), minute-by-minute reports will be so voluminous as to be useless.

There have been proposals for partially or fully automating performance appraisal by recording ratee behavior on checklists and then using algorithms that apply Kane's (1986, 1987) performance distribution model to derive performance indices from the behavioral data. This strategy is a variation of one that is often recommended in research on clinical versus statistical procedures for integrating multiple pieces of data (see Wiggins [1973] for a review). That is, human judges have the responsibility for collecting the data, and a statistical or mechanical procedure is used for integrating the data. We are somewhat skeptical about the practicality of this approach.

Although the use of some objective, automatic means to integrate data is appealing, the strategy is only as good as the data that are recorded. We doubt that checklists that include most or all of the important behaviors could be assembled for many jobs (e.g., personnel manager). Even if they were, it is not clear whether supervisors are capable of objectively recording the behaviors they have observed. Cognitive research suggests that supervisors' perceptions of subordinates' behaviors are far from objective records of what has happened (see DeNisi & Williams [1988] for a review). Rather, the behaviors that are checked are strongly influenced by subjective overall impressions about each ratee (Murphy, Martin, & Garcia, 1982).

A more modest proposal for partially automating performance appraisals would involve: (a) obtaining ratings on specific dimensions from raters; (b) assessing, via job analysis, the importance of each dimension; and (c) computing a composite measure of overall performance that weighted the dimensions in proportion to their importance. This would preserve the primary advantage of using an objective method to integrate information about performance (i.e., the absolute reliability of an objective function) without the need for a comprehensive checklist that contained all important work behaviors.

One final aspect of the technological environment is the increasing emphasis on workgroups. Many manufacturing technologies, for example, have moved away from a reliance on individual workers in the assembly line and now use teams of workers to perform complex tasks. Performance appraisal has traditionally been concerned with the performance of individuals. An increasing reliance on work teams may force organizations to develop methods of evaluating both individual and team performance. This topic is discussed in more detail in Chapter 13.

Physical Environment

Although the physical environment is rarely considered by PA researchers, there is a body of literature on situational constraints on job performance that examines the effects of munificence of the physical environment on performance and performance measurement. This literature has been reviewed by Peters and O'Connor (1980) and, more recently, by Peters and associates (1985). Of the 11 categories of situational constraints reviewed, 3 represent aspects of the physical environment that might constrain an individual's ability to perform well: (a) shortages of tools and equipment, (b) lack of materials and supplies, and (c) an unfavorable work environment (e.g., poor lighting).

Researchers have identified a number of consequences of situational constraints. First, there is evidence that situational constraints lead to lower levels of performance (Peters & O'Connor, 1980). This should not be surprising, because situational constraints are defined as variables that constrain one's ability to perform well. Second, it has been hypothesized that the presence of situational constraints will lead to decreased variability in performance, in part because of a ceiling effect. Empirical research, however, has not consistently supported this hypothesis (Peters et al., 1985; Peters, O'Connor, & Rudolph, 1980). As we will note below, the failure to find range restriction effects may say more about the extent to which situational constraints exist than about their effects. Third, situational constraints appear to lead to negative affective reactions and to lower motivation, although research results here are somewhat mixed (Peters et al., 1985; Phillips & Freedman, 1982).

In their review, Peters and colleagues (1985) note that serious situational constraints are rare. It may be that the small effect sizes found in situational constraint research reflect the fact that work environments are generally munificent and that the situational constraints that do exist are too minor to have much of an impact. This is another area in which cross-cultural and historical research methods may be worthwhile. Researchers may be underestimating the effects of situational constraints as a result of doing research in a time and place where these constraints are rare. We predict that there would be stronger effects in settings where the seriousness of situational constraints was variable rather than being uniformly low.

In circumstances where situational constraints cannot be removed, it is necessary to develop methods of measuring performance that take these constraints into account. It is hardly fair to compare the performance of someone who has all of the tools, equipment, and supplies necessary to complete the task to someone else who does not. Peters and associates (1985) review the results of several studies that have attempted to develop PA methods that take situational constraints into account. Unfortunately, the results of these studies have not been encouraging. It is unclear if any method will be developed that leads raters to adjust adequately for the presence or absence of situational constraints.

Some of the effects of the physical environment tend to mirror those of the economic environment. In both cases we expect that shortages and scarcity will lead to growing levels of conflict and to increasing politicization of the organization. Scarcity also leads to an emphasis on conservation and efficiency, which may lead to a change in the performance dimensions that are viewed as most important by an organization. The physical environment may have a more immediate and vivid impact, however. If the tools, resources, information, and so on that are necessary to do the job are not available, the consequences are felt immediately, whereas poor economic conditions may take a significant period to lead to changes on the shop floor.

EXTERNAL ENVIRONMENTS AND RATER GOALS

At the beginning of this chapter, we noted that context is a major determinant of the goals that the rater forms. Some raters may use performance appraisal to reward or secure promotions for particular employees.

Others will use appraisal as a tool for punishing least favored subordinates. Still others will use PA as a method of shifting their problem employees to some other supervisor—it is not unheard of to give high ratings to a particularly obnoxious employee to ensure that he or she is promoted out of your workgroup or department (Longenecker et al., 1987). Although the internal environment of an organization is likely to have a stronger impact on rater goals than will the external environment, there are some areas in which the effects of external environments will be substantial. This is particularly true of the societal, legal, and economic environments.

A societal value that will directly affect the rater's goals is the extent to which the society emphasizes individual advancement. In a culture where promotions are highly valued and/or rapid, raters are likely to use performance appraisal as an instrument for promoting employees whom they regard as deserving. In this same culture, raters might be very reluctant to give low ratings because such ratings could jeopardize the worker's future success in the organization. The legal system might also strongly shape goals. Our current legal environment is one in which most organizations will go to great lengths to avoid litigation. The rater who supervises a marginal performer may give high ratings to avoid any possible challenge. The other possibility is that the rater will carefully collect evidence to document the low ratings he or she wishes to give to the poor performer.

The state of the economy may also shape the rater's goals, and the direction of this effect might be the opposite from the effect of the economy on the *organization's* goals. When the economy is bad, organizations might become highly motivated to weed out poor performers. The rater might, however, be very unwilling to take steps that will eventually cost a subordinate his or her job if the prospects for getting another job are dim. When the economy is bad, raters might become more lenient, whereas organizations become more severe.

The technological environment will sometimes affect a rater's goals. As the technology becomes more complex, the supervisor will be more interested in retaining and motivating workers who are skilled in the technology. As a result, the rater may give higher ratings. The physical environment could also sometimes have an effect. If situational constraints are present, raters may be reluctant to distinguish among ratees and may use performance ratings as a device to encourage workers who are presently constrained from performing well.

SUMMARY

This chapter examined the influence of the external environment on performance appraisals in organizations. Although the research literature dealing with the relationships between organizations and environments is large, few definite conclusions can be drawn about how environments affect behavior in organizations or about what facets of the environment are or are not important. It is, however, possible to speculate about the ways in which environmental variables might affect PA processes and outcomes.

We identified several aspects of performance appraisal that are likely to be affected by environmental variables, including the standards used to evaluate performance, the definition of exactly what constitutes performance (i.e., the performance dimensions chosen), the frequency of appraisals, supervisor-subordinate relationships, the consequences of high or low ratings, and the perceived legitimacy of performance appraisal. All of these may be affected in varying ways by events and conditions in the sociopolitical, legal, economic, technical, and physical environment in which work is carried out.

It is very reasonable to assume that the external environment affects a number of practices in organizations, including performance appraisal. However, we still know very little about *how* environmental variables affect organizations, or *which* environmental variables are most or least important.

The challenge to researchers concerned with environmental effects is that the concept of environment is both broad and fuzzy. That is, everyone knows what it means, but nobody can provide a clear definition of precisely what the environment is or how it affects individuals, groups, or organizations. Better articulation of the links between environmental variables and performance appraisal processes and outcomes might be one small step in understanding the ways in which environmental variables affect organizations.

3

Organizational Influences

This chapter continues our discussion of the contextual factors that influence performance appraisal (PA) in organizations. In Chapter 2, the influence of factors in the environment external to the organization were discussed. In this chapter, we discuss the contextual factors internal to or within the organization that may influence the process and outcomes of performance appraisal. Before the literature on organizational context and appraisal is reviewed, we will describe what we mean by context, drawing from the social and personality psychology literature. In addition, we will identify the range of methods and approaches used to analyze and describe situations.

Although the meaning of a situation is important when discussing the environment external to an organization, we have placed this discussion within the current chapter for two reasons. First, we believe that the internal organizational context is a more salient set of variables that has greater impact on the rater and appraisal than distal, external environmental variables. Because they have more impact, a more extensive discussion of the terms *context* and *situation* is warranted in this chapter. Second, there is an extensive literature on the psychology of situations that is more appropriately applied to the organization as the general context.

This chapter also presents a range of context variables that are likely to influence performance appraisal. Further, we will identify relevant context factors that have not been extensively investigated in the context of PA and discuss how they might affect appraisal in organizations. Interactional psychology is then introduced as an approach to investigating the interaction between a pattern of organizational characteristics and a pattern of person (rater or ratee) characteristics as they affect the PA system.

WITHIN-ORGANIZATION CONTEXT

There is little research on organizational differences in appraisal process and outcomes (Davis & Dickinson, 1987; Landy & Farr, 1983). Most appraisal research has focused on the actual measurement and process of rating; few researchers have investigated the influence of the surrounding organizational context within which appraisals are conducted and utilized (for exceptions, see Davis & Dickinson, 1987; Eulberg, O'Connor, Peters, & Watson, 1984; Lawler, 1967). Before describing situational influences on behavior, it is important to understand what is meant by *situation* and *context.*

Brunswick (1952) and others (Magnusson, 1981) have urged psychologists to develop a better understanding of the dynamics underlying and defining situations. In order to understand more fully and predict the perceptions and behavior of individuals, psychologists should systematically investigate the relevant features of the context within which people behave. Brunswick and more recent theorists have urged psychologists to develop a "psychology of situations." There are a number of considerations in the process of defining situations.

Magnusson (1981) notes that the description and classification of situations raise many problems. He describes three major considerations: (a) units of analysis, (b) time and space measures, and (c) characteristics that can be used for description and classification of situations. We believe that research on PA can benefit from increased knowledge about the context of the appraisal. In order to conduct such research adequately, each of these issues warrants more discussion.

Units of Analysis

When managers refer to the context of appraisal, they can be referring to very different aspects of the appraisal situation, including the pattern of a ratee's past performance, the composition of workgroup performance, the nature of the job and/or department, the values of the organization, and so on. It is therefore critical to articulate clearly the unit of context under consideration.

The unit of context for situational analysis can range from microlevel (e.g., the type of task performed) to macrolevel (e.g., organizational climate) variables (Magnusson, 1981). Context variables can also be conceptualized as proximal, having a direct impact on an individual's behavior or perceptions, to distal variables, having a less direct influence on the perceptions or behavior of people (Cleveland & Hollmann, 1991; see Figure 2.1 in Chapter 2 of this book). According to Magnusson (1981), in research on situation variables there is a need to identify the appropriate unit of analysis along these dimensions (micro to macro) for each specific question or problem. Because there do not appear to be definite boundaries between one unit of analysis and another, however, the distinction among units of context may be somewhat arbitrary.

The concept of context or situation can also vary along two other dimensions: (a) from physical to perceived characteristics of the situation and (b) from molecular to molar units. For example, Magnusson (1981) described four uses of the term *situation* that vary along these two dimensions: the actual situation, the perceived situation, the situation type, and the life situation.

The *actual situation* refers to the physical and biological variables of a part of a total environment that are available to the individual for a certain amount of time. Further, attached to the biological and physical characteristics of context, there are sociocultural factors (e.g., norms, rules, roles, etc.) that contribute to the definition of the situation. Two subunits of the actual situation can be identified: situation stimuli and situation events. *Stimuli* refer to a sound or the presence of a supervisor on the shop floor, and function as signals in themselves. *Situation events* are specific parts of a total situation that can be classified in cause/effect terms. Studies of organization structure and design, and environmental psychology use the actual situation as the unit of analysis.

More important to our discussion of appraisal is the *perceived situation* as the unit of analysis, especially from the rater's perspective. The perceived situation is generally the actual situation as it is perceived, interpreted, and assigned meaning or as it is construed in the mind of the perceiver (Magnusson, 1981). This implies that the same actual situation leads to many different perceived situations, depending on the rater's interpretation. Magnusson (1976) identifies two units of analysis in perceived situations: within situation and overall or general situation. The former refers to the flow of stimuli and events as they are perceived and interpreted by the perceiver, whereas the latter refers to the factors that contribute to our interpretation of a total situation. As frames of reference, the overall situation factors may guide our selection and interpretation of specific stimuli and events, as well as our expectations and predictions regarding options and courses of action (Magnusson, 1981).

Both the situation type and the life situation reflect more molar units of analysis of the environment. The *situation type* refers to the general kind of actual or perceived situation without specification of time and space. Bem's (1981) and Cantor's (1981) work on situation prototypes employs concepts similar to the analysis of situation types. An example of a situation type might be "an appraisal assessment and feedback session," as opposed to a momentary situation such as "an appraisal of John's performance by his supervisor, Mary, on June 29 at 8:30, covering the performance period from January to June."

Life situation refers to those parts of the total world that an individual can experience and does perceive and interpret as having relevance to self and behavior. The life situation includes actual conditions under which a person finds himself or herself, including type of professional and work organization, family relations, geographic area, socioeconomic conditions, and so on, and the individual's own experiences and evaluations of the actual conditions.

Time and Space

A second consideration in the discussion of situation and relevant to the appraisal context involves time and space considerations. Situations change continuously; some circumstances, such as a 20-minute appraisal feedback session, have a clear beginning and end. Many events, however, are not so clearly defined. For example, "observing an employee's performance on the job" refers to an event without clear time or space boundaries.

The focus in appraisal research is usually on a momentary situation, which includes both a time dimension and a distal-proximal dimension. The physical information available on this situation includes (a) what is in the focus of attention; (b) what is considered, but peripheral and not attended to; and (c) what is not considered at all. The focus of attention and the peripheral considerations change continuously. The temporal or time dimension determines what is attended to and what is peripheral. That is, both are dependent at a specific moment on what happened before and to some extent on what will happen next in the process. Later in this chapter, we describe appraisal research that has demonstrated that a person's performance at a given time can influence the rater's perceptions of his or her past and subsequent performance (Murphy et al., 1985). This research is using past or subsequent ratee performance as part of the definition of rating context.

Situation Characteristics

No taxonomy of situation characteristics defined in terms of outcome variables is available. Further, there is no set of characteristics available that can be used to analyze all situations. The situation characteristics that might be used to analyze a situation may, in part, be determined by what features are most relevant to the specific context. Two general categories have emerged, however: actual situation properties and person-bound properties.

The *actual situation properties* include situation complexity (Schroeder, Driver, & Streufert, 1967), clarity, strength, promotion versus restriction, tasks, rules, roles, physical settings, and other persons (Magnusson, 1981). The most common among these is the analysis of situations in terms of their restrictive versus promotive effects on behavior. The nature of restrictions and promotions, the types of behaviors that are restricted versus promoted, and strengths of the reinforcements and punishments are assumed to be important for individuals in forming perceptions, interpretation, and methods of dealing within a situation.

Situations can also be described using *person-bound properties,* including goals, perceived control, expectancies, needs and motivation, and affective tones or emotions. Goals or intentions are a key situation variable.

They are important in guiding or directing an individual toward situations. Goals also influence what cues the individual attends to, what alternatives he or she has, and what strategies are applied. Long-term goals may be appropriate when the situation unit of analysis is the 10-year career pattern of an employee (factors important to the life pattern in a broad sense). Short-term goals may be bound to specific types of situations and may differ depending on different stages of development.

Both actual situation properties and person-bound properties are important to understanding the context of ratings. For example, organizations may inadvertently promote inaccurate performance ratings by rewarding raters on the rated performance levels of their subordinates, or the organization may restrict the accuracy of ratings by punishing the rater for being too harsh. Person-bound properties are also critical considerations in appraisal. For example, the goals of the raters must be considered in order to understand what the performance ratings are intended to convey. We believe that these person-bound properties, especially rater goals, are so important that we devote a more detailed discussion of them in Chapter 8.

Describing the Rating Context

Many of the studies that suggest typologies of situations identify specific aspects of an organization's context. These features may also affect rating processes and outcomes. The typologies listed in Table 3.1 can be grouped into two general categories: environmental and organizational.

In the class of environmental classification schemes, Moos (1973) discusses both the physical and social aspects of environments. He also conceptualizes three basic dimensions that characterize and discriminate among work environments. These include a relationship dimension (e.g., support, involvement, etc.), a personal development dimension (e.g., self-enhancement), and a system maintenance and system change dimension (e.g., control, order) (Moos, 1973). In Chapter 4, each of these three dimensions is discussed in more detail and reflects some of the purposes or uses of appraisals in organizations.

Krause (1970) categorizes social behaviors into seven groups that reflect different ways of personal interaction (e.g., joint working, sponsored teaching). The intended use of the classification was for research purposes. The categories can, however, be applied to assess the nature of interactions in the appraisal exchange. Ekehammar (1974) uses five dimensions to describe

TABLE 3.1 Characteristics Used in Classification of Context

Environmental

Moos (1973)
Ecological dimensions
Behavioral settings
Parameters of organizational structure
Personal and behavior parameters
  of environment
Climate, organizational, and
  psychological variables

Krause (1970)
Social situations:
  —joint working
  —trading
  —fighting
  —sponsored teaching
  —serving
  —self-disclosure
  —playing

Ekehammar (1974)
Physical and social characteristics
Need concepts
Single reaction elicited by situation
Individual's reaction pattern
  elicited by the situation
Individual perceptions of situation

Organizational

Forehand (1968)
Environmental variables
Personal variables
Outcome variables

Duncan & Weiss (1979)
Internal organizational environment:
  —personnel component
  —functional and staff units
  —organizational-level component

Argyle (1981)
Goal structure
Environmental setting
Roles
Skills and difficulties
Concepts
Repertoire of elements
Rules
Sequence of behaviors

Rotter (1955); Fredericksen (1972)
Taxonomy based on similarity of
  behavior evoked by situation

Fuller (1950)
Incentive value:
  —field incentives, field impedance
Complexity

Mischel (1977)
Strong, powerful situations:
  —lead everyone to perceive the
    situation in the same way
Weak situations:
  —not uniformly encoded

Etzioni (1975)
Coercive organizations
Utilitarian organizations
Normative organizations

Van Maanen & Schein (1979)
Functional
Hierarchical
Person's inclusion

a situation. Similar to other researchers (Endler, 1982; Endler & Magnusson, 1976), Ekehammar distinguishes between the subjective-psychological aspect and the objective aspects of the environment. The physical and social environment in which a person interacts is called *ecology*. Actual behavior occurs in a situation or a part of ecology that a person perceives and reacts to immediately (Endler & Magnusson, 1976).

Argyle (1981) uses another classification scheme to study the basic features of situations. His approach maintains that people continuously renegotiate their shared definition of a situation. Further, he states that individuals can alter the nature of the situation entirely. Both Frederiksen (1972) and Rotter (1955) suggest that understanding behavior would be enhanced if a taxonomy of situations was developed based on the similarity of the behaviors they elicited. Fuller (1950) describes three types of interactions that a person may display in order to reach a goal (directive, cybernetic, and effective interactions). Finally, Mischel (1977) classifies context into strong, powerful situations and weak situations. Strong situations differ from weak in a number of ways:

1. Strong situations induce uniform expectancies regarding appropriate behavior, whereas weak situations do not.
2. Strong situations provide adequate incentive for the performance of the behavior, whereas weak situations do not.
3. Strong situations require skills that everyone has, whereas weak situations fail to provide the learning conditions necessary for successful emergence of behavior.

The remaining authors listed in Table 3.1 attempt to describe situations by drawing from the organizational literature. In discussing the dimensions of organizational climate, Forehand (1968) states that three sets of variables are involved: (a) environmental variables external to the individual (e.g., size, structure, etc.); (b) personal variables, including abilities, aptitudes, and motives of organizational members; and (c) outcome variables, including employee satisfaction, motivation, and performance. He states that climate is the configuration of environmental variables as perceived by individuals.

Similar to Forehand (1968), Duncan and Weiss (1979) classify organizations as having internal and external components. The internal environment includes the personnel component (e.g., skills and education of employees), the functional and staff component (e.g., interdependence), and the organization-level component (e.g., goals, products, etc.). The external environment includes such components as customers, suppliers, and competitors.

Another model of the organization is to describe the environment in terms of organizationally defined roles. Van Maanen and Schein (1979) use three dimensions to define roles: functional (e.g., tasks performed by the organization, such as finance and marketing), hierarchical (e.g., centralized or decentralized), and the person's inclusion within the organization (e.g., newcomer or employee "on the edge"). Finally, Etzioni (1975) classifies organizations on the basis of how they exert control over their members. Specifically, an organization may exert control primarily through coercion (coercive organization), remuneration (utilitarian organization), or normative power (normative organization). Etzioni also identifies a fourth category, dual compliance structures, where two patterns of control occur with similar frequency.

METHODS OF SITUATION ANALYSIS

In addition to knowing what is meant by the rating context, it is also important to develop methods for assessing the features of the rating situation. There are a number of techniques already developed by situational researchers and personality psychologists that may be usefully applied to the organizational context. Among the first to classify situations empirically in terms of situation perception are Pervin (1968), who used a semantic differential technique, and Magnusson (1971), who used multidimensional scaling for analyzing similarity of information. Frederiksen (1972) suggested using cluster analysis and factor analysis as methods for categorizing situations.

Most studies that attempt to analyze situations do so in terms of how people perceive and interpret them. For example, Cantor (Cantor, 1981; Cantor & Mischel, 1979; Cantor, Mischel, & Schwartz, 1982) has investigated the lay perceiver's categorical knowledge about everyday situations. This knowledge is called a *prototype* and captures the meaning of the category. Using prototypes, Cantor's strategy for investigating perceptions of situations includes:

1. Establish taxonomies of commonly used situation categories and obtain agreement that taxonomies reflect hierarchies.
2. Ask subjects to generate prototypes for each category in each taxonomy, and then identify the characteristic subjects listed to describe the same category to obtain a consensual prototype for each situation category.
3. Assess the consensus to determine the depth and complexity of situation prototypes, the structure of situation taxonomies, and the content of the descriptions of everyday situations (Cantor, 1981).

Similar to Cantor's approach, Bem (1981) uses a template-matching technique. A *template* is a description of how one would expect a specific type of person to behave or what outcomes one would expect for a specific type of person in a given situation. Situations are similar to the extent that similar persons receive similar outcomes (Bem, 1981). Drawing from and extending the research by Block and Block (1981) on the Q-sort technique, Bem and Funder (1978) modified the Q-sort procedure to obtain information about a situation and perhaps identify sources of behavior inconsistencies across seemingly similar situations. They proposed that situations be characterized as sets of template-behavior pairs, with each template being a Q-sort description of an idealized type of person (Bem, 1981, p. 250). This person is expected to behave in a specified way in that particular situation or setting. The behavior of actual individuals in the setting is predicted by comparing one's own Q-sort with each template. It is predicted that individuals will display a behavior that is associated with the template of closest match. The actual method for constructing a template is described in Bem and Funder (1978) and Green (1980).

The previous techniques are examples of *idiographic* approaches in assessing situation similarities. In addition to using the Cantor and Bem methods, situations can be assessed through direct similarity ratings (Magnusson, 1971; Magnusson & Endler, 1977) in which subjects are asked to assess how similar various pairs of situations are, or by goal satisfaction similarities in which situations are grouped by how instrumental they are in satisfying goals (Lord, 1982). On the other hand, the *nomothetic* approach relies on consensus across individuals on situation similarity. There is evidence that the idiographic approaches are superior to the nomothetic approaches in predicting cross-situational consistency (Lord, 1982). Further, there are substantial individual differences in what people pay attention to as they move from one situation to the next (Magnusson, 1981).

MICROLEVEL CONTEXT VARIABLES
AND PERFORMANCE APPRAISAL

Major reviews and subsequent models of appraisal (Bernardin & Beatty, 1984; Carroll & Schneier, 1982; DeCotiis & Petit, 1978; Landy & Farr, 1980) have consistently acknowledged the importance of the situation or context within which appraisals are conducted. Although the organizational context is viewed as important by these authors, their books and reviews have given less attention to these variables than, for example, scale format or psychometric properties of formats. One reason for this may be that there has been little empirical research on situational factors and their impact on behavior in organizations, specifically on appraisals. A more plausible reason is that PA traditionally is viewed as a research and an applied topic within industrial or personnel psychology rather than as a topic within organizational psychology or organizational development.

As we noted in Chapter 1, appraisal scales have usually been treated as tests or instruments. Consequently, past research has emphasized instrument development and assessment in terms of accuracy, psychometric properties, and, to a lesser degree, utility of the instrument. In our model, we view appraisals in organizations as a social-communication-decision instrument. There is a need to develop and refine the measurement qualities of appraisals as scale instruments as well as acknowledge appraisals as a decision tool in organizations. Recognizing these needs, PA is clearly a topic that rests at the intersection of industrial and organizational psychology and would be best approached from both perspectives. The research literature reviewed here reflects a movement by researchers to apply knowledge about organizational behavior to the traditionally industrial topic of performance appraisal.

Researchers have investigated the influence of numerous contextual factors on appraisal outcomes (Cleveland et al., 1986; Davis & Dickinson, 1987; Dobbins, Cardy, & Platz, 1988). For example, Davis and Dickinson (1987) examined the influence of individual-level context variables and unit-level context factors on the utility of performance appraisals in organizations. They found that individual-level variables, such as role ambiguity, leader trust and support, and leader interaction and facilitation, accounted for systematic variance in performance ratings. On the other hand, ratings of the extent to which appraisals are used for salary and promotions was predictable from unit-level variables, such as participation in decision making, organizational communication, organizational goals and planning, and climate for innovation (i.e., encouragement of risk taking and creativity). Employee ratings of the administration, fairness, and accuracy of PA were predicted by a combination of individual and unit-level variables. We believe that more research like that conducted by Davis and Dickinson (1987) is needed. Further, we agree, in part, with these authors that it may be very fruitful to view the PA process as an organizational development intervention.

The literature on the psychology of situations is somewhat unclear as to what variables to include in a discussion of microlevel context variables. Cummings and Schwab (1973), however, suggested that three sets of factors comprise the performance environment: task design, leadership, and the reward systems. We believe that this taxonomy represents a useful starting point. Our review of the literature includes group, task, and leadership characteristics, and reward and punishment or threat considerations. We also believe that more recent research suggests other important situation considerations.

Focusing on the rater perspective and perceptions of context, recent research has examined the influence of past or previous performance and the performance level of the ratee on rating outcomes (Murphy et al., 1985; Murphy, Herr, Lockhart, & Maguire, 1986). In addition, rater and ratee acquaintance (interpersonal relations) and affect have been found to influence the effectiveness of appraisals. The work by Dobbins, Cardy, and Platz (1988) and others has highlighted the specific features of the appraisal systems as important in the quality of rating outcomes and in acceptance of the appraisal process. Finally, the goals and purpose of the appraisal (both organizational and rater goals) will be discussed as an important context factor.

In summary, the influence of microlevel context factors on appraisal quality, accuracy, and acceptance will focus on the following six sets of contextual factors: (a) group, leader, and task characteristics; (b) rewards, trust, threats, and punishment; (c) ratee past performance and level of performance; (d) appraisal system features; (e) rater acquaintance, commitment, and affect; and (f) goals and purpose of appraisal.

Group, Leader, and Task Characteristics

According to Hackman (1976), groups have a number of ways in which they can influence individuals. Groups can influence a person's skills and knowledge of individuals, the level of psychological arousal while working, and a person's effort and performance strategies. Further, norms or expectations develop within groups regarding acceptable levels of performance. These norms become stronger as the group increases in cohesiveness.

Not only do norms develop concerning productivity but also concerning the levels of acceptable performance ratings. For some groups, a norm develops that leads raters to believe that high or inflated ratings are the only acceptable ratings. It may be unacceptable for a rater to record ratings that depict average or below-average performance even when such ratings are accurate. Based on information from rater interviews, Cleveland and colleagues (1986) found that when there were high entrance or educational standards for admission into a group or job community, raters were reluctant to evaluate employees as average or below. The rater's rationale was that these individuals passed through numerous performance hurdles in order to gain access to the group, and all were therefore "superior."

The characteristics of a group, such as the performance variability of its members (Ilgen & Feldman, 1983; Liden & Mitchell, 1983) and the salience of specific group members (Brewer, 1979; Linville & Jones, 1980; Quattrone & Jones, 1980), also influence the accuracy and the leniency of ratings. Raters do not evaluate one person on a single occasion; rather, evaluation occurs for many people over an extended time or covering many tasks. There is therefore opportunity for other group members to influence specific ratings by providing raters with information for comparative rather than absolute judgments (Ilgen & Feldman, 1983).

Mitchell and Liden (1982) found that in a workgroup with one poor performer and two good ones, the evaluation of the poor performer was higher than it should have been and the evaluations of good performers were lower. This was especially true when the poor performer was portrayed as high in popularity and leadership skills. Also, the degree of task interdependence among group members was related to rating outcome and performance variability. Specifically, Liden and Mitchell (1983) found that good performers were rated higher and poor performers lower when group members were portrayed as working independently. On the other hand, when group members were interdependent, good performers were rated lower and poor performers were rated higher.

Liden and Mitchell (1983) suggest that in highly interdependent groups it may be difficult for the rater or supervisor to evaluate the contribution of the individual group members even when the performance of one member is poor in comparison to other members. Grey and Kipnis (1976) found that performance ratings of a compliant group member were higher when the others were inept and possessed a bad work attitude than when other group members were also compliant. This suggests that if an individual is, in some important way, different than the other members of a group, he or she may be evaluated differently than in a relatively homogeneous group. That is, the individual who is different may be more salient to the rater and may be characterized in a stereotypic way (Kanter, 1977).

Related to the heterogeneity of group members is the existence of in-group and out-group members of a workgroup (Graen, 1976) and leader perceptions and evaluation of these individuals. Supervisors do not treat all subordinates in the same way, nor should they. One theory of leadership, leader member exchange (LMX) theory, suggests that each supervisor-subordinate dyad may involve a somewhat different style of interaction (Dansereau, Cashman, & Graen, 1973). The theory suggests, however, that dyads can be classified into those involving members of the in-group and those involving members of the out-group. In-group members receive more information and trust from supervisors and perform more complex and interesting tasks. Mundane and routine tasks are relegated to members of the out-group (Dansereau, Graen, & Haga, 1975; see also Chapter 8 in this book).

According to Brewer (1979), factors such as intergroup competition, similarity, and status differentials of individuals affect in-group bias indirectly, by influencing the salience or distinctions between the in- and out-groups. Linville and Jones (1980) proposed and tested a model that assumes that people have more complex schema regarding in-group members than out-group members. As a result, appraisals of out-group members will tend to be more polarized. They found that when application credentials were positive, the out-group member was evaluated more positively than was the in-group member. When the credentials were weak, out-group members were evaluated more negatively than were in-group members. They also found support for the complexity-extremity hypothesis. That is, white subjects demonstrated greater schema complexity for whites than for blacks and greater complexity resulted in more moderate ratings. Brewer (1979) suggests that bias reflects increased favoritism toward in-group members rather than increased hostility toward the out-group.

Related to group features, task characteristics appear to influence both the consideration of what scale or evaluation approach to take and the accuracy of ratings. Lee (1985) suggests that matching the task with the appraisal format will increase appraisal effectiveness. Bernardin and Beatty (1984) also suggest that different types or purposes of decisions (i.e., promotion to the next level vs. individual feedback) may require different scale formats (i.e., trait vs. behavioral) in order to maximize appraisal utility.

Balzer (1986) found that the cognitive processes in ratings were influenced by the interaction of the centrality of the task to the rater and the rater's initial impression of the ratee. That is, when raters were told to observe a lecturer and learn the content of the lecture (low centrality), subjects with a positive initial impression recorded fewer behavioral incidents than subjects with a negative initial impression. When raters were told that the behavioral diary or the recording of behaviors was their sole task (high centrality), subjects with positive initial impressions recorded more incidents than those with a negative initial impression. This interaction affected raters' observation and coding of positive critical incidents and not negative incidents.

Rewards, Trust, Threats, and Punishments

Jones, Tait, and Butler (1983) found that actions that are perceived as rewarding by employees were characterized by public visibility, tangibility, implied esteem, and long-term implications. Actions perceived as punishment had similar qualities (although scaled in opposite directions), with visibility most closely related to perceived severity. Few empirical studies have investigated directly the influence of organizational rewards or punishments on appraisal ratings. Mohrman and Lawler (1983) and others have described how rater motivation contributes to accurate ratings. One factor that they say influences motivation is rewards. Longenecker et al. (1987) interviewed executives concerning the politics of appraisal and found that raters inflated appraisal outcomes in order to avoid negative or uncomfortable feedback sessions and to avoid negative consequences or actions for the ratees (e.g., a poor appraisal in the employees' permanent files). Further, Longenecker and colleagues (1987) found that the most frequently cited reason for rating inflation was to obtain rewards for the subordinate (e.g., maximize merit increases).

Bjerke, Cleveland, Morrison, and Wilson (1987) found similar results from interviews with navy officers (raters) and a small sample of industry personnel managers. In much of the military, there are few negative consequences for raters who give inaccurate, inflated ratings (i.e., raters are not penalized for inaccuracy); however, there are incentives for raters to inflate ratings, primarily to secure promotions for their junior officers. From managers interviewed, Bjerke and associates (1987) found that at times managers were punished for ratings that were seen as inaccurately favorable or unfavorable by their own superior.

Most of the research on the influence of rewards and punishments has involved field interviews or the manipulation of other variables (i.e., appraisal purpose) and explaining the outcomes by implied consequences of accurate ratings. More research is needed to address how organizational rewards and punishments influence appraisal processes and outcomes.

Related to the consequences of appraisals is the trust and/or threat perceived by the rater (and ratee) in the appraisal process (Bernardin, Orban, & Carlyle, 1981; Bernardin & Villanova, 1986; Kay, Meyer, & French, 1965; Longenecker & Gioia, 1988). Trust and threat appear to influence both the psychometric quality of rating outcomes (i.e., leniency) and the acceptance of the appraisal system. Organizational climates characterized by low trust, either between raters or across organizational levels, can lower the effectiveness of an appraisal system (Lawler, 1971).

Trust in the appraisal context reflects the extent to which raters believe that fair and accurate appraisals will be or have been made in the organization. Lawler (1971) notes that trust may be more important when appraisals are used for promotion or administrative decisions than when used as a basis for individual feedback (e.g., the interaction of two context variables such as trust and purpose of rating; see Chapter 4). Bernardin and associates (1981) found that trust in the appraisal process accounted for 32% of the variance in ratings. Regardless of appraisal purpose (i.e., promotion vs. feedback), raters with high trust provided ratings with less leniency, whereas raters low in trust provided more lenient ratings.

Perceptions of threat by subordinates are also related to attitudes toward the appraisal (Kay et al., 1965). A manager who attempts to assist employees by pointing out improvement needs is likely to be perceived by subordinates as threatening to their self-esteem, which can result in defensive behavior. Also, the more threats perceived by the subordinates, the less favorable their attitudes toward appraisal and the smaller the subsequent improvement in performance.

Longenecker and Gioia (1988) reported five sources of appraisal apprehension as identified by executives:

1. The quality of working relationship with one's supervisor (i.e., trust)
2. The extent to which the subordinate manager's job responsibilities, authority, and goals are ill defined

3. Whether or not the individual had been receiving specific feedback throughout the year
4. The appraisers' level of honesty or perceptions of a "hidden agenda"
5. The political nature of appraisals (discussed in Chapter 4 of this book)

In general, trust was highest when there was a good working relationship, well-defined roles, specific feedback, honesty, and a low tolerance for political manipulation.

Ratee Past Performance and Current Level of Performance

According to Magnusson (1981), one key consideration in situation analysis is time. Practitioners concerned with appraisal in organizations are also concerned with a time factor and have criticized laboratory research on appraisals for not taking into consideration the fact that the supervisor interacts with, observes, and assesses employees over a period of time. Evaluation does not occur after one performance episode. Rather, an employee performs a given task at a certain level for a period of time and this task or time period may be preceded or followed by performance at the same or at a different level of efficiency. A case could therefore be made that the employee's performance on a given task or on a given day is embedded in a context or pattern of employee performance over time. The rater observes the employee's performance over time; performance probably varies in level from one time to another.

Murphy and colleagues (Murphy et al., 1985; Murphy, Herr et al., 1986) investigated the effects of previous and subsequent performance on the evaluation of present performance. They (1985) conducted two studies to examine the influence of previous employee performance on ratings of current performance. In Study 1, subjects looked at videotapes of positive or negative performance followed by a video of an average performance by the same person. They found that exposing raters to positive or negative performance of a ratee had significant effects on subsequent ratings. Specifically, contrast effects were found, indicating that an employee who performed well initially was rated lower in current performance than if the same person had performed poorly in the first tape. In Study 2, Murphy and colleagues (1985) included a one-day delay condition. Results suggested that contrast effects did not occur when ratings were provided from memory.

Rather than strengthening the contrast, increased demands on memory appeared to lead to a decay in contrast effects.

In a study examining the effects of subsequent performance on evaluations of previous performance, Murphy, Herr, and associates (1986) asked subjects first to view an average performance videotape and then either a good or poor performance video. The researchers also had an immediate performance rating condition and a delay condition. They found an assimilation effect in the delay condition but not in the immediate rating condition. Subsequent performance (i.e., the second performance episode) influenced memory-based behavior ratings (e.g., the frequency with which a behavior occurred) but did not influence ratings on performance evaluation dimensions. Further, they found that under conditions posing minimal demands on memory, subsequent performance had a relatively weak effect. When demands on memory through delay were increased, however, subsequent performance exerted a stronger influence on ratings of previous performance. One implication of this finding is that supervisors may be biased in the direction of their current impression of the employee rather than correctly assessing past performance.

It has been suggested that the level of employee performance may contribute to the type of ratings that are given (DeNisi & Stevens, 1981). In particular, managers avoid evaluating low performers. Cummings and Schwab (1973) suggested that employees at different performance levels should be appraised differently. That is, different appraisal systems should be structured for low, average, and high performers. Distinguishing features of these systems would include type of information collected, frequency of performance reviews, and role of the employee in the appraisal process.

Appraisal System Features

The specific features of appraisal systems referred to here include type of scale, instructions and item content or anchors, purpose of rating, participation in the appraisal process, presence of a training program, frequency of evaluation, secrecy of appraisal process, and opportunity to develop action plans to correct performance weaknesses. Bernardin and Beatty (1984) suggest that if the purpose of rating is to predict future performance or potential, a trait scale may make more sense than a scale that asks for ratings of specific behaviors (based on the assumption that traits at one level predict performance in another job). Bernardin and Beatty

(1984) suggest, however, that behavioral definitions may help to decrease the subjectivity of trait ratings.

Wexley and Klimoski (1984) also suggest that the format of the scale (traits vs. behaviors) might be matched with the purpose of rating. Appraisals can reflect behavioral (process) or result (outcomes) measures. Result measures tell employees little about their relative strengths or weaknesses and why they did not meet an objective. Behaviorally oriented scales seem appropriate for development. Wexley and Klimoski (1984) suggest that the use of trait scales may heighten employee defensiveness in feedback sessions.

The scales used in the appraisal process can influence important appraisal outcomes in two other ways. First, Murphy and Constans (1987) found that the specific behavioral anchors in BARS scales can affect the cognitive processes of the rater. When the scales had anchors that were actually observed by the rater, but not representative of the ratee's overall performance, ratings were biased in the direction of the unrepresentative anchor. Murphy and Constans (1987, 1988) recommend that the representativeness of anchors be considered as well as whether the items reflect poor, average, or good performance.

Second, participation in scale development also has multiple, positive effects. Silverman and Wexley (1984) found that ratees who participated in the development of scales on which they were rated believed that:

1. The appraisal interview was more useful.
2. The supervisor was more supportive.
3. They were given more opportunity to participate.
4. Goals and objectives were set to a great extent.
5. They made a greater impact or contribution to the appraisal interview.

Those who participated in scale development were also more satisfied with the appraisal interview and more motivated to improve performance.

Dobbins, Cardy, and Platz (1988) examined the relationship between five appraisal characteristics (secrecy, opportunity to participate, opportunity to develop action plans, presence of a rater training program, and frequency of evaluation) and employee satisfaction with the appraisal process. They hypothesized that these five characteristics would be moderated by uncertainty, role ambiguity, and role conflict. In general, they found that ratees were more satisfied with the appraisal process when they were able to provide input into the process, assisted in the development of action plans, and were knowledgeable about dimensions and procedures of evaluation.

Dobbins, Cardy, and Platz (1988) also found that the three organizational characteristics moderated the relationship between appraisal characteristics and appraisal satisfaction. The relation between the development of action plans and satisfaction was moderated by role ambiguity and closeness of supervision. When there was high ambiguity and low closeness in supervision, this relationship was stronger. The relation between frequency of evaluation and satisfaction was moderated by role conflict and quality of leader-member exchange. More frequent evaluation was more important for ratees who experienced more conflict and when ratees had a low-quality relationship with their supervisor. Rater training was more positively related to satisfaction when the employee experienced high levels of role conflict or when employees could not be closely monitored by their supervisor. Finally, the relation between secrecy and satisfaction was most negative when employees were closely monitored or when employees experienced little role conflict. Dobbins, Cardy, and Platz (1988) suggest that high secrecy paired with role clarity or close supervision may send mixed messages to ratees.

Comparing managerial and employee satisfaction with a PA system, Mount (1983) determined that managers' attitudes reflected seven factors and employees' attitudes reflected five factors.

Managers' Attitudes	**Employees' Attitudes**
Content of appraisal forms	Content and ratings on appraisal forms
Ratings on appraisal forms	Company policy and appraisal procedures
Company policy regarding appraisal	Physical characteristics of appraisal forms
Appraisal procedures	Communication of the program
Physical characteristics of appraisal forms	General appraisal satisfaction
Communication of the program	
General appraisal satisfaction	

Managers appeared to have more complex, fine-grained perceptions of the appraisal system. Mount (1983) suggests that this may result from the different roles that managers and employees have. For example, managers perceive company policy and appraisal procedures as distinct, whereas employees tend to put them together.

Through factor analysis, Mount (1983) found that appraisal satisfaction for employees is due to a general satisfaction factor, including such items as overall experience with the appraisal system, quality of the appraisal discussion, how the forms aid discussion of performance, and how the forms help to formulate development plans (common variance 42.7%). On the other hand, the same factor accounted for only 4% of the variance in managerial ratings. Instead, the largest percentage of variance was accounted for by the type of ratings on the forms. That is, the extent to which performance ratings help communicate employee's performance seemed to predict a significant portion of the manager's satisfaction with appraisal.

Rater Acquaintance, Commitment, and Affect

Kingstrom and Mainstone (1985) investigated the influence of rater-ratee acquaintance on rating bias. They distinguished between task and personal acquaintance to examine how each relates to rating favorability (i.e., leniency and halo). No relationship was found between task and personal acquaintance and halo. Personal acquaintance and task acquaintance were related to leniency although the latter was less strongly related. Ratees who were assessed high in personal and task acquaintance received more favorable ratings. Using multiple regression, Kingstrom and Mainstone found that personal and task acquaintance accounted for variance in ratings not accounted for by actual sales productivity. Actual productivity, however, was related to supervisory perceptions of personal and task acquaintance. Therefore, more favorable ratings may be due, in part, to true performance differences, and personal and task acquaintance are correlates.

Freeberg (1969) found that appraisal ratings were more accurate when the raters possessed task-relevant acquaintance (e.g., relevant knowledge or contact) with the ratee than when raters possessed irrelevant acquaintance (e.g., socializing). Using interview data, Kallejian, Brown, and Weschler (1953) found a similar relationship between the supervisor's and the subordinate's interpersonal relationship and appraisal ratings.

Related to rater acquaintance with the ratee is the commitment of the rater to the ratee and the proximity between the rater and ratee. Bazerman, Beekum, and Schoorman (1982) assessed the influence of prior commitment of the rater to the ratee on performance evaluations. They predicted that raters who made an initial commitment (e.g., promotion) to the employee would be biased (i.e., more lenient) in their subsequent evaluations of that employee in order to justify the initial support of the employee. That is, a rater will evaluate a poorly performing person higher if the rater previously promoted this person than when another rater made the initial promotion decision, because they feel higher responsibility. Bazerman and colleagues (1982) found that high-responsibility raters gave higher performance evaluations, greater pay increases, more vacation days, and so on. These raters were also less likely to demote or lay off the employee.

Imada and Hakel (1977) did not find that rater proximity (i.e., whether the rater was the actual interviewer or an observer) influenced hiring judgment. They did find, however, that nonverbal cues, especially eye contact, smiling, attentive posture, gestures, and smaller interpersonal distance, were related to an interviewer's recommendation for hire. If the interviewee demonstrated the above behaviors, he or she was more likely to be recommended for hire. Imada and Hakel (1977) indicated that raters had very different affective responses to interviewees who demonstrated greater contact, smiling, and the like, suggesting that the interviewer may be more involved in an affective dimension of the interview then previously believed.

Tsui and Barry (1986) directly assessed the influence of interpersonal affect on rating errors. They found that the level of ratings given by raters with positive affect toward ratees was highest, followed by ratings from raters with neutral affect, and lowest for raters with negative affect. The average intercorrelation among ratings was highest for raters with negative affect and lowest for raters with neutral affect. This finding was similar across sources of ratings (e.g., supervisory, subordinate, and peer). Raters with neutral affect had the most range restriction.

Goals and Purpose of Appraisal

There is a good deal of research that indicates that appraisal goals and purpose influence the psychometric properties of ratings (e.g., halo, leniency, etc.), accuracy of ratings, and judgment processes. They also interact with other appraisal features (e.g., format, scale anchors, etc.) (Bernardin & Beatty, 1984; Cleveland et al., 1989; DeNisi et al., 1984; Landy & Farr, 1980). The stated purpose of performance appraisals (either organizational or individual purposes) could very well be the single most important contextual factor in understanding appraisal process and outcomes. Therefore, we devote a full chapter (Chapter 4) to a discussion of this issue. Further, the perceptions or interpretations of raters and the translation of these purposes into his or her own goals is discussed extensively in Chapter 8. In Chapter 14 we will discuss the design, implementation, and evaluation of goal-oriented performance appraisal systems.

MACROLEVEL CONTEXT VARIABLES
AND PERFORMANCE APPRAISAL

Macrolevel situational variables describe the more general, within-organizational context. In Chapter 2, macrolevel variables outside of the organization were described. In this section, we will discuss three macro-organizational variables and how they may influence the process and outcomes of appraisal. The set of variables includes (a) organizational life cycle and structure, (b) organizational goals, and (c) organizational culture, climate, and values.

We assume that macrolevel variables, both internal and external to the organization, are largely distal to the rater and the ratee. That is, they do not immediately impinge on the individual participants of appraisal. Further, employees may not be aware initially that these variables play a role in the judgments and decisions that they make. We believe that macro-organizational variables most often influence appraisal outcomes indirectly through more proximal, microlevel, situational variables (e.g., organization climate for cooperation may be reflected by tasks performed in teams, which in turn has direct implications for appraisal outcomes). We also recognize the possibility that macrolevel situational variables could have a direct impact on appraisal decisions. For example, if organizational goals or values are very strong, focused, or unidimensional (e.g., in the military, the main goal of appraisal is the development and promotion of future commanding officers), then a rater would probably be very aware of the influence such variables have on his or her own judgments and decisions.

Organizational Life Cycle and Structure

Whetten (1987) suggests that the structure and process within an organization are shaped to some degree by the stage a company is in, in its organizational life cycle. Borrowing from life-cycle models, Whetten and Cameron (1983) described four growth stages: (a) entrepreneurial—reflecting early innovation, niche formulation, and high creativity; (b) collectivity—including high cohesion and commitment; (c) formalization and control—emphasizing stability and institutionalization; and (d) elaboration and structure—reflecting domain expansion and decentralization. These stages cover the growth of an organization and may reflect groups of problems or issues that are specific to each stage.

Whetten (1987) suggests that we also examine possible stages in the decline of organizations. He notes that both growth and decline stages have four important applications in organizations. First, they serve as reasonable diagnostic tools. Awareness of the organization's current stage can convey information about problems and experiences that are likely to be encountered by organizational members. Second, it serves as a reminder that organizational goals, priorities, and criteria for effectiveness shift over the life span of the organization. Third, it is an important source of contextual information that must be factored into our analyses of organizational research results. For example, rapidly growing versus rapidly declining organizations may have different structural properties and internal processes. Fourth, an understanding of the clusters of problems that an organization is likely to encounter at different stages of development, as well as insights for effectively managing transitions between stages, represent important aids for organizational leaders and researchers (Whetten, 1987).

The life-cycle approach to organizational growth and decline suggests that appraisal systems in organizations are not static systems nor should they be assumed to be equally effective (if not altered in some important way) across different stages. The goals of organizations evolve and change; as a result, the purpose and format of the appraisal may be expected to change as well. The view that this book takes—that performance appraisals are a social and decision-making tool and, secondarily, a measurement instrument—is consistent with the notion that the context of appraisal is not static and the appraisal itself is a dynamic process. Typically, as a measurement tool, appraisals are assumed to measure stable characteristics of ratees, but they may also measure or be influenced by the constantly changing environment of which they are a part.

As Whetten (1987) suggests, the life stage of an organization may influence its actual structure. Further, the structure (i.e., the organization level that employees occupy) has been found to influence job attitudes and performance (Berger & Cummings, 1979). Specifically, Berger and Cummings (1979) found that there is a relatively stable pattern of relationships among organizational level and attitudes, such as job satisfaction and satisfaction with appraisal.

Schneier and Beatty (1978) found differences in performance expectations at different levels of the organizational hierarchy. Raters rated the same behavior lower than did subordinates. Davis and Dickinson (1987) found that appraisal utility decreased in organizational units where employees could take little action without permission from their supervisor. Berger and Cummings (1979) found little relationship between line versus staff positions in job attitudes. McCall and DeVries (1977), however, suggest that appraisals may be caught in a staff versus line conflict. That is, appraisals are designed by staff employees for personnel uses or for larger organizational concerns, yet they are completed by line managers. There is potential here for the appraisal not to meet the needs or goals of the line manager. In addition, there appears to be a small to moderate relation between span of control and job attitudes and performance. Finally, absenteeism increased with the size of the total organization (Berger & Cummings, 1979).

Although more research is needed to address the relationship between organizational structure and appraisal, there is sufficient evidence using other dependent measures to suggest that organizational structure probably does influence appraisal.

Organizational Goals

Organizations are systems that are activated and directed by goals (Katz & Kahn, 1978). These goals are not necessarily actively chosen or consciously established; they may emerge initially from the types of persons who established the organization (Schein, 1985). Cartwright and Zander (1968) draw a distinction between goals of an individual for a group and goals of a group or an organization. The first refers to individual attainment and the others to group or organizational attainment. Also, the first type of goal is held individually, whereas the last two are held collectively. Although there is research suggesting that organizational goals influence behavior and that conflict occurs when there are mixed goals (Zald, 1962), other researchers have criticized the concept of organizational goals. Etzioni (1975) suggests that goals be replaced with a systems model. That is, the criterion of effectiveness should reflect a balanced or optimum allocation of resources rather than when organizational goals are met or not met.

According to Mohr (1973), organizational goals have two aspects: intent and outcomes. The former could be viewed as the process that makes goal attainment possible, including appraisal and reward systems. It is reasonable to suggest that an appraisal system may be structured and administered differently depending on the goals of the organization. Davis and Dickinson (1987) found that appraisals were viewed more positively in units that possessed lateral and vertical communication. Further, employees in units having more complete and formal goals and planning practices viewed appraisals more positively. The second aspect, outcomes, refers to a criterion for organizational effectiveness (i.e., has the organization attained or accomplished goals?). The activation and guiding processes (i.e., goals) within an organization and the role of appraisal in this process need to be addressed more directly through research.

One contemporary theory of organizational effectiveness that might be usefully applied to evaluating performance appraisal is the constituency theory of effectiveness. A *constituency* is any group within or outside of the organization that has a stake in organizational performance (Connolly, Conlon, & Deutsch, 1980; Daft, 1986; Friedlander & Pickle, 1968). Each constituency may have different criteria for evaluating effectiveness, because each has a different interest in the organization. The various constituencies involved in PA include the rater, the personnel decision makers (e.g., persons involved in making salary or promotion decisions), and the courts, to name a few. It is likely that an organization finds it difficult to fulfill simultaneously the demands or goals of all groups.

Research on performance appraisal using the constituency approach as a general framework may yield some interesting theoretical insights, as well as practical recommendations. For example, if it is impossible to fulfill the expectations of all constituencies, the design of a PA system must include procedures for identifying the most important goals and constituencies for different parts of the appraisal system. We will develop this theme more fully in Chapter 14.

Organizational Culture, Climate, and Values

Schein (1985) distinguishes three levels of culture: basic assumptions, values, and artifacts (special jargon, rituals, dress, etc.). Martin and Siehl (1983) add a fourth level, management practices. These practices include training, allocation of rewards, and performance appraisal. Research suggests that culture offers an interpretation of an institution's history that members can use to decipher how well they will be expected to behave in the future. Culture can also generate commitment to corporate values or management philosophy, so that employees feel that they are working for something they believe in. Finally, culture serves as an organizational control mechanism that informally approves or prohibits some patterns of behavior (Martin & Siehl, 1983).

Culture is a more amorphous concept than organizational climate (Schneider, 1985). Culture refers to assumptions and values attributed to why certain behaviors and activities are rewarded and expected. Climate focuses on how the organization functions (i.e., *what* is rewarded, supported, and expected). Culture is transmitted through myths and stories, particularly when large groups of people share the interpretation of the myths (Schein, 1985; Schneider, 1985, 1987; Tagiuri & Litwin, 1968). For example, through interviews with naval commanding officers, Cleveland and colleagues (1986) found that the navy's values concerning the importance of warfare readiness influenced what raters thought about when completing evaluations of subordinate officers. That is, raters appeared to assess subordinates solely in terms of warfare readiness and the ability to be a good commanding officer rather than assessing their performance in specific assignments.

According to Schneider (1975, 1987), much of the climate research makes two assumptions: (a) people try to attain order in their environment and to create order through thought, and (b) people attempt to create order in their environment so they can effectively adapt their behavior to the work environment. Fredericksen, Jensen, and Beatrin (1972) found that the intercorrelations among dimensions of an in-basket varied as a function of the climate under which people worked. That is, the pattern of what was important and what covaried depended on the climate. Further, Fredericksen (1962, 1972) found that performance on the in-basket was higher when climates provided consistent cues to performance than in climates that reflected inconsistent information. Russell, Terborg, and Powers (1985) attempted to determine whether organizations that valued and emphasized training are more effective. A favorable training climate was found to have a positive relationship with organizational performance.

Schneider (1985) addressed the issue of the content or dimensions of the climate construct. He stated that the key question for determining the content of the perceptual climate is: Climate for what? Research that has defined climate globally has not found a strong relationship between climate and job performance (Pritchard & Karasick, 1973). On the other hand, specific domains of climate, including safety climate or a technical updating climate, are related to measures of performance (i.e., accident prevention, safety effectiveness, etc.) (Kozlowski & Hults, 1987; Zohar, 1980). To date, little research has been conducted on the influence of various climates on performance appraisals in organizations. We believe, however, that research on culture and climate will contribute to the understanding of performance appraisals.

APPRAISAL RESEARCH AND
AN INTERACTIONIST PERSPECTIVE

Interactional psychology may be usefully applied to appraisals in organizations; indeed, some appraisal research currently reflects the interactionist approach (e.g., Cleveland & Landy, 1983; Dobbins, Cardy, & Platz, 1988). One major advantage of the interactional approach is that the assumptions and questions posed can help in identifying future research needs in performance appraisal. We will describe the interactionist approach briefly and then relate it to the appraisal process specifically by identifying current research knowledge as well as research needs for the future.

Interactional psychology emphasizes continuous interactions between person and situation characteristics as the major determinants of behavior. That is, situations are as much a function of the person's behavior as the person's behavior is a function of the situation (Bowers, 1973). Interactionists recognize that situations vary in terms of cues, rewards, and opportunities, and that people vary in their cognitions, abilities, and motivations (Terborg, 1981).

Endler and Magnusson (1976) describe four propositions of interactional psychology:

1. Actual behavior is a function of a continuous, multidirectional process of interaction or feedback between the individual and the situation encountered.
2. The individual is an intentional, active agent in this interaction process; the person is both changed by situations and changes situations.
3. On the person side, cognitive, affective, and motivation factors and ability are essential determinants of behavior.
4. On the situation side, the psychological meaning of situation for the individual and the behavior potential of the situation for the individual are essential determinants of behavior (Terborg, 1981).

Thus, the situation is in some way a function of the observer. The observer's cognitive schema filter and organize the environment in a way that makes it impossible completely to separate the environment from the person (Bowers, 1973). Further, a great deal of a person's social environment is generated by his or her own behavior. For example, there is a fair amount of consistency in the kind of environments that people create for themselves (Bowers, 1973; Schneider, 1978, 1983a, 1985, 1987; Wachtel, 1973). Schneider (1983b, 1985) has applied the interactionist perspective to the notion of organizational effectiveness. He notes that organizations are defined by the kinds of people attracted, selected, and remaining in them. As a result of this cycle (attraction-selection-attrition), organizations can become too homogeneous, which may result in a decrease in capacity to adapt or change.

There are at least two major concerns in interactional psychology. The first is the attribution of cause either to internal or external factors. That is, causes of behavior could reside in the person, the situation, or both. The second issue involves the notion of coherence of behavior. It concerns whether behavior is inherently stable and predictable without necessarily being stable in absolute or relative terms. That is, interactional psychology asks whether the individual's pattern of stable and changing behavior across situations of various kinds is characteristic of that person. Interactionists say that coherence of behavior results from information processing. People are viewed as proactive perceivers who, through perceptions and cognitions, *actively* structure the external world. Further, the situation is not construed in research as the physical situation. The central notion is that active involvement (i.e., experience) in a situation through perception and other behaviors is the way that people come to understand situations. The interactionists' notion of active involvement has similar philosophical grounds as does the approach of action scientists (Argyris, 1980).

The application of interactional psychology to appraisals in organizations suggests that we need to understand fully the characteristics of individuals that affect rating processes and outcomes as well as the features of the situation that are instrumental in determining appraisal outcomes. Unfortunately, interactional psychology also informs us that it may be difficult to distinguish fully between the effects of the individual and the situation. The research on appraisals to date reflects an emphasis on the identification of person variables, including demographic variables (e.g., age, sex, etc.) and cognitive processes of raters. Currently, a good deal is known about how the rater observes, recalls, and makes judgments that lead to various appraisal outcomes. The largest portion of this book is therefore devoted to issues concerning the individual rater. Less is known about the context within which appraisals are conducted.

SUMMARY

Little is known about what context factors raters perceive or consider in determining what course of action to pursue through appraisal (e.g., type of ratings to give in a specific appraisal situation). In this chapter we have identified some contextual variables that may be relevant to understanding the appraisal process. For example, it is clear that the composition of the workgroup influences a rater's evaluation of an employee's individual performance. There are, however, a number of other organizational and contextual variables that are relevant to the appraisal process and effectiveness. These factors include organizational values, climate (cooperative, competitive, etc.), trust in the appraisal system, the centrality or status of the job or department in which the appraisal is conducted, entrance standards in the job community (Cleveland et al., 1986), and so on. There has been some research concerning these factors, but more research is needed to assess how each influences appraisal effectiveness. Each variable can be considered relevant to appraisals, although little is known about the influence of them on appraisal process and outcomes.

The literature on the psychology of situations and interactional psychology suggests that some context factors may be more important than others in their interaction with key person variables in the appraisal process. We believe that the purposes or uses of appraisal in an organization represent a critical contextual consideration and mediate the relationship among rater characteristics and appraisal effectiveness. Chapter 4 is therefore devoted exclusively to the discussion of the purpose of rating.

Related to the purpose of rating, a second key variable in appraisal is the rater's goals. Although rater goals might be classified as a person variable, we believe that it may be difficult to distinguish between the person and situation features of rater goals. That is, we can draw on the goal-setting literature that informs us how individuals set goals and how these goals guide subsequent judgments and behavior. However, we also must consider how the rater perceives and integrates information from the appraisal situation, what information the rater uses as cues, and how the rater integrates and interprets this contextual information to formulate his or her own goals in the rating process. Chapter 8 is devoted to a discussion of rater goals in performance appraisal.

4

Purposes of Performance Appraisals

In the previous two chapters, we discussed a variety of environmental and organizational context factors that may affect the outcomes and effectiveness of an organization's performance appraisal (PA) system. In this chapter, one context factor has been selected for more detailed attention—the purposes of performance appraisal. Discussion of these purposes is important for at least three reasons:

1. Performance appraisal is used for a wide variety of purposes within and across organizations.
2. The purpose of appraisal influences the ratings and the effectiveness of the system.
3. Purposes provide the key mechanism by which the context of rating interacts with the capabilities and cognitive and judgmental processes of the rater (Cleveland et al., 1989).

Understanding the effects of the purposes of PA on appraisal processes and outcomes will help advance the knowledge of contextual factors in appraisal.

A key concern of this chapter is that information from performance appraisals is used by raters, ratees, and organizations for many purposes. The goals pursued by the rater and ratee are not necessarily the same as those pursued by the organization (see Chapter 8). Therefore, the material presented in this chapter can be viewed as a transition from a discussion of external context factors and ratings to a discussion of the rater or decision maker's goals and his or her "survival" techniques in the organization.

First, we will survey the use of performance appraisal in organizations. Next, we will examine ways in which the purpose of rating influences the outcomes of PA. That is, we will identify and discuss what outcomes to expect as a function of the purpose of appraisal and how purpose influences various rater variables (e.g., judgment strategy). Third, because the purpose of an organizational appraisal often reflects the constituents it serves (the organization, the rater, the ratee), political and power issues are an integral part of the use of the PA system, and we will discuss these issues. Further, conflict may emerge among organizational and individual uses of performance appraisal; we will explore the potential conflict among incompatible purposes.

USES OF PERFORMANCE APPRAISALS

Historically, information from performance appraisals has been used as a basis for administrative decisions (Whisler & Harper, 1962). More recently, the purposes of appraisal have expanded considerably. In 1957, McGregor proposed that performance appraisal be used for feedback and developing employees (DeVries et al., 1986). Proponents of management by objectives (MBO) suggested using appraisals for organizational planning (Drucker, 1954; Odiorne, 1965). PA experts (Bernardin & Beatty, 1984; DeVries et al., 1986) predict that appraisal will continue to be used in the 1990s for human resource planning and replacement. Since the passage of the 1964 Civil Rights Act and the Age Discrimination in Employment Act, performance appraisal has also been used increasingly to safeguard organizations against discrimination lawsuits.

Performance appraisal is not only a U.S. phenomenon but is also widespread in Great Britain. Approximately 82% of organizations in Great Britain have some type of formal appraisal system, with a substantial increase in appraisals for nonmanagement employees during the past 10 years (DeVries et al., 1986). The most frequently cited uses of PA in Great Britain are to (a) improve current performance, (b) set objectives, and (c) identify training and development needs. Further, there is a recognition and trend toward the separation of performance review from potential review.

Performance Appraisal and Administrative Decisions. The most obvious purpose of a performance appraisal system is as a decision aid. Performance appraisals provide one basis for deciding who should be promoted, terminated, given a raise, and so forth. They are probably not the only basis for such decisions. Promotion decisions may depend as much on a prediction of future performance as on assessments of past performance. Salary decisions may depend as much on market forces as on assessments of job performance. Nevertheless, high-quality performance appraisal systems are an important consideration in making a wide range of personnel decisions in most organizations.

Figure 4.1 illustrates three very different ways in which performance appraisals might be related to administrative decisions. In what we call *lead* relationships, decisions are made on the basis of evaluations of performance. For example, a worker might receive a large salary increase because he or she is consistently rated as the best performer. Here, positive appraisals are the cause of subsequent administrative decisions. Much of the existing research on performance appraisal is based on the assumption that administrative decisions should be based (at least in part) on performance, and that high-quality measures of performance are therefore critical to making good decisions. Appraisals, however, do not always lead to administrative decisions, but rather may themselves be the result of such decisions.

In what we call *lag* relationships, performance appraisals are filled out to justify decisions that have already been made or to make it easier to implement a course of action already decided upon. For example, a supervisor who decides to fire a subordinate might have to provide one or more poor performance reviews to justify the decision. As we have noted elsewhere, rating inflation is the norm in American organizations, and the fact that most workers routinely receive positive appraisals (even when their performance is poor) makes it very difficult to fire a poor performer. Once you have decided to fire someone, it might be necessary to complete several performance appraisals that include low ratings, in order to "justify" a decision you made long ago.

Figure 4.1. Lead-Lag Relationships

Bjerke et al. (1987) present a vivid example of a lag relationship between performance appraisals and administration decisions in their analysis of the appraisal system used by naval officers. It appears that the rater first decides whether or not his or her subordinate deserves to be promoted and then fills out the performance appraisal form accordingly. As we note elsewhere, there is a complex set of implicit rules defining a "good" performance appraisal, but most senior officers seem to know how to write appraisals that will maximize the promotion opportunities of deserving candidates or that will end the careers of candidates they see as poor candidates for promotion.

Finally, the relationship between performance appraisals and decisions can include both lead and lag elements. For example, I might decide to fire a poor-performing employee, and therefore give low performance ratings. These low ratings, in turn, might flag that employee as a candidate for remedial training. In this case, my decision affects the appraisals, which in turn affect some other personnel decision. It is even possible that my decision to fire a poor performer may eventually turn him or her into a good performer (if the training works).

Performance Appraisal as a Feedback System. Some organizations develop essentially separate systems for performance feedback and for administrative decision making (Meyer et al., 1965; Department of the Air Force, 1988). Although this may seem a cumbersome procedure, it may be a very good idea. When the same appraisal system is used for feedback and for making administrative decisions (e.g., raises, promotions), both functions may suffer (Cleveland et al., 1989; Meyer et al., 1965). There is considerable evidence that performance feedback, if given appropriately, can lead to substantial improvements in future performance (Guzzo, Jette, & Katzell, 1985; Kopelman, 1986; Landy, Farr, & Jacobs, 1982), and it may be a grave mistake to let the administrative side of appraisal interfere with the use of appraisal as a feedback tool.

It is generally assumed that the type and frequency of feedback should be a central concern in designing a performance appraisal system (Cummings & Schwab, 1973). There have, however, been relatively few empirical tests of this assertion, or even of the more general idea that the purpose of an appraisal system should affect its design (Klein, Snell, & Wexley, 1987; but see Klein & Snell, 1993). As a result, relatively little is known about how the design of the appraisal system might affect the frequency or quality of feedback. Two topics that have received more research attention are subordinates' interest in receiving feedback and the effects of positive versus negative feedback.

There is clear evidence that individuals are motivated to seek feedback (Ashford, 1986; Ashford & Cummings, 1983). Feedback reduces uncertainty and provides information relevant to self-evaluations (e.g., levels of mastery). To the extent that feedback is seen as a valuable resource, individuals will be motivated to seek it. Feedback is not always welcome or accepted, however: Feedback acceptance depends on both the source and the favorability of the feedback. Feedback is most likely to be accepted if it comes from a source with high perceived credibility and if it is favorable (Ilgen, Fisher, & Taylor, 1979; Stone & Stone, 1985).

It is obvious that most people prefer positive to negative feedback. A more interesting question is what effects positive or negative feedback might have on future performance—and here, the evidence is mixed. For example, there is evidence that positive feedback may enhance self-efficacy (Bandura, 1986), but it is not clear whether this translates into higher performance. There is evidence that negative feedback can enhance subsequent performance (Podsakoff & Farh, 1989), but there is also evidence that it can lower subsequent performance (Liden & Mitchell, 1985). Feedback that is specific and behaviorally oriented is more likely to be useful than feedback that is general and vague (e.g., "when you lecture, you should use audiovisual aids to help make the point" is better feedback than "your lectures are confusing"), but even well-delivered feedback can lead to defensiveness and hostility if it is negative. On the other hand, feedback can be an extremely useful tool for development, especially when it includes both problem-oriented and solution-oriented information.

The Multiple Uses of Performance Appraisal. Tables 4.1 and 4.2 present the results of surveys conducted since 1970 of uses of performance appraisal in the United States. Administrative uses of performance information continued to be the most frequent application of performance appraisal in the 1970s and 1980s. In the 1970s, 50% to 85% of the organizations surveyed used appraisal for administrative decisions such as salary administration, promotion, and retention and dismissal. Cleveland and associates (1989) found that when asked to identify the most frequent use of information from performance appraisals, respondents (this study surveyed industrial/organizational psychologists) ranked salary administration and developmental feedback as the top two uses. As Table 4.2 indicates, the purposes for which appraisals are *infrequently* used include (a) criteria for validation studies, (b) determining organizational training needs, (c) reinforcing the authority structure, and (d) manpower planning.

In surveys from the 1970s, PA was used for validating selection procedures in only 12% to 23% of the organizations surveyed. More recent surveys suggest a greater emphasis on validation and, more generally, on the documentation and justification of personnel decisions. Cleveland and colleagues (1989) found that when 20 uses for PA were factor analyzed, a documentation factor clearly emerged as one of four major uses of information from performance appraisal. The specific items within the documentation factor included (a) criteria for validation research, (b) document personnel decisions, and (c) meet legal requirements.

The results of Cleveland and colleagues' (1989) analysis, which are summarized in Table 4.2, provide a useful classification of the purposes of performance appraisal. In addition to the documentation factor described above, this study suggests that organizational uses of PA can be grouped into three categories:

TABLE 4.1 Results of Surveys From the 1970s

Use	Lazer & Wikstrom (1977) (%)	Bureau of Nat'l Affairs (1974) (%)	Lacho, Stearns, & Villere (1979) (%)
Individual Performance Planning	73-82 (performance feedback)	57 (setting goals)	—
Salary Administration	63-70	85	80
Promotion	50-66	64	74
Training & Development	54-60	55	62—Development 44—Assessing training needs
Retention & Discharge	—	—	69—Dismissal 64—Demotion
Manpower Planning	23-34	37	—
Validation of Selection Techniques	12-13	23	23

SOURCE: D. L. DeVries, A. M. Morrison, S. L. Shullman, & M. L. Gerlach, *Performance Appraisal on the Line* (Greensboro, NC: Center for Creative Leadership, 1986), p. 22.

1. Between-person uses, including salary administration, promotion, retention/termination, recognition of individual performance, layoffs, and identification of poor performers
2. Within-person uses, including identification of individual training needs, performance feedback, determining transfers and assignments, and identifying individual strengths and weaknesses
3. Systems maintenance uses, including use of appraisal for workforce planning, determining organizational training needs, evaluating goal achievement, assisting in goal identification, evaluating personnel system, reinforcing authority structure, and identifying organization developmental needs

In general, both between-person (e.g., salary administration) and within-person decisions (e.g., feedback regarding strengths and weaknesses) were more frequently cited as purposes of appraisal systems. Systems maintenance (e.g., workforce planning) and documentation (e.g., documenting personnel decisions) were less frequently cited as important uses of appraisal information.

Jacobs and colleagues (1980) suggested that a critical decision in using information from performance appraisals is whether to focus on satisfying individual needs (e.g., employee development and feedback) or organizational

TABLE 4.2   Means, Standard Deviations, and Factor Loadings for Twenty Uses of Performance Appraisal

Factors/Uses	Mean	Standard Deviations
Between-Person Decisions		
Salary administration (.79)[a]	5.58[b]	1.16
Promotion (.68)	4.80	1.18
Retention/termination (.78)	4.75	1.40
Recognition of individual performance (.62)	5.02	1.52
Layoffs (.58)	3.51	1.68
Identify poor performance (.74)	4.96	1.54
Within-Person Decisions		
Identify individual training needs (.77)	3.42	1.40
Performance feedback (.77)	5.67	1.35
Determine transfers & assignments (.76)	3.66	1.53
Identify individual strengths & weaknesses (.75)	5.41	1.44
Systems Maintenance		
Manpower planning (.82)	2.72	1.58
Determine organizational training needs (1.0)	2.74	1.49
Evaluation of goal achievement (.74)	4.72	1.59
Assist in goal identification (.73)	4.90	1.62
Evaluate personnel systems (.82)	2.04	1.18
Reinforce authority structure (.16)	2.65	1.69
Identify organizational development needs (.98)	2.63	1.52
Documentation		
Criteria for validation research (.45)	2.30	1.35
Document personnel decisions (.91)	5.15	1.27
Meet legal requirements (.48)	4.58	1.80

SOURCE: Adapted from J. N. Cleveland, K. R. Murphy, & R. E. Williams, "Multiple Uses of Performance Appraisal: Prevalence and Correlates," *Journal of Applied Psychology, 74* (1989).
NOTES: a. Maximum likelihood estimates of loading are in parentheses.
b. Ratings were based on a 7-point rating scale measuring the impact of appraisal on a variety of organizational decisions and actions, where 1 = no impact, 4 = moderate impact, and 7 = primary determinant. Factors are boldfaced.

needs (e.g., administrative decisions such as promotion, salary increases, etc.). Others distinguish between administrative decisions and the identification of employee strengths and weaknesses (Wexley & Klimoski, 1984) or between-person decisions and within-person decisions (Cleveland et al., 1989). In addition, uses of performance appraisal have been categorized according to their impact on various organizational constituents (Balzer & Sulsky, 1990; Mohrman & Lawler, 1983). Thus, when discussing the uses of PA, it is important to distinguish among organizational goals, rater goals, ratee goals, and the performance appraisal researcher goals.

Further, Mohrman and Lawler (1983) discussed both private and public PA behaviors; the public-private distinction is similar to the rating-judgment distinction discussed in Chapter 1. Mohrman and Lawler indicate that rating behavior is an outcome of the rater's perception of the situation. There are two determinants of those perceptions: the appraisal system itself (format, frequency, etc.), and the context of performance. As noted earlier, the purpose of performance appraisal is one critical aspect of the rating context. It is thus reasonable to conclude that the purpose of appraisal will affect the rater's behavior.

With the proliferation of the organizational and individual uses of information from performance appraisals, researchers and practitioners have begun to observe that an appraisal system that is used for one purpose may not (under similar circumstances) yield the same outcome when the purpose is different. Also, information about performance collected under one set of conditions (purpose) may not be useful for other purposes. As we will discuss later in this chapter, the use of PA for a wide range of individual and organizational uses is not always effective or efficient. When several uses are incompatible or in conflict, attempts to use performance appraisal as an all-purpose tool may fail.

PURPOSES OF APPRAISAL AND
RATING OUTCOMES AND PROCESSES

In the previous section we discussed the many purposes or goals associated with performance in organizations (Jacobs et al., 1980; Landy & Farr, 1980; Murphy et al., 1984; Zedeck & Cascio, 1982). According to both the DeCotiis and Petit (1978) and Landy and Farr (1980) PA models, the intended use of information from performance appraisals is thought to have a significant impact on appraisal outcomes such as the properties of ratings (e.g., reliability, leniency, accuracy), and on the rating process. The research on the impact of purpose on rating can be divided into several areas, including: (a) impact on psychometric quality of ratings, (b) impact on the accuracy of judgments, (c) impact on rating and judgment processes, and (d) impact on the structure and administrative practices of performance appraisal. The first two areas are tied to outcomes; the latter two are tied to the rating process.

Rating Outcomes

Research that evaluates the effect of purpose on the measurement qualities of ratings (e.g., psychometric properties, accuracy) has covered a fairly wide range of topics. However, there is a substantial body of literature dealing with the effects of purpose of rating on one specific psychometric property of ratings—leniency.

Leniency. Starting in the 1950s, several studies documented the impact of purpose of rating on leniency, or the level of ratings. Field research, in particular, has consistently documented the impact of purpose. For example, Taylor and Wherry (1951), using ratings from army personnel, found that average ratings of officers were significantly higher for administrative purposes than when ratings were collected for research purposes. Using ratings of 400 job applicants, Heron (1956) obtained results similar to Taylor and Wherry's, with a negatively skewed distribution of ratings for administrative purposes. Sharon and Bartlett (1969) found that ratings used in making real administrative decisions were more lenient than ratings obtained for research purposes. Bernardin et al. (1981) found that probationary officers were rated significantly higher by police sergeants when ratings were used to make personnel decisions than when they were used to provide feedback. Other studies, however, have found no mean difference in ratings when comparing administrative and research purpose conditions (Berkshire & Highland, 1953; Borreson, 1967; Sharon, 1970) or comparing administrative and feedback purposes (McIntyre, Smith, & Hassett, 1984; Meier & Feldhusen, 1979).

It is important to note that field studies usually find greater leniency for ratings that are used for promotion or other administrative decisions than do laboratory studies that use students as subjects and use ratees that are not known to the student raters (Bernardin & Villanova, 1986; McIntyre et al., 1984; Murphy et al., 1984). Some of the inconsistency in findings regarding leniency may be an artifact of the different methods employed in research on the purpose of rating.

Purpose and Accuracy. During the past decade, PA researchers have used a number of accuracy measures to assess the effectiveness of ratings (see Chapter 10). Unlike much of the research on the psychometric properties of ratings, research on the accuracy of ratings has been largely conducted in laboratory settings using students as raters, rather than using real ratings collected in organizations. Results of these studies are mixed. Murphy et al. (1989) found that subjects were more accurate in evaluating teachers when performance evaluation was the primary purpose for observing teaching behavior than when the evaluation was the secondary goal (with the primary goal to "learn the lecture"). Accuracy in the evaluation condition did not hold up over time, however. When there was a delay between observation (of the lecture) and the actual rating task, subjects for whom performance appraisal was a secondary task showed higher levels of accuracy. It is important to note that in this study, the researchers varied the purpose of *observation*. In most other studies, the purpose of rating has been manipulated.

In a study of faculty ratings, Dobbins, Cardy, and Truxillo (1988) investigated both the accuracy and level of ratings collected for three purposes: (a) feedback, (b) scale validation or merit, and (c) promotion decisions. They found that male professors were rated more favorably than females only when the evaluations were made by men and used for administrative decisions. The accuracy measures indicated that men were rated higher than their true performance levels, whereas women were rated lower than their true performance levels.

Dobbins, Cardy, and Truxillo (1988) investigated the effects of two purposes: research versus merit pay and promotion, and individual differences in stereotypes of women (traditional vs. nontraditional) on the accuracy of appraisals. Here, female ratees were evaluated less accurately and less favorably by raters with traditional female stereotypes than by raters with nontraditional stereotypes of women. However, this difference in accuracy occurred only when ratings were used to make administrative decisions. Finally, McIntyre and colleagues (1984) assessed accuracy under three purpose conditions: hiring, feedback, and research. They found that ratings in the research condition were marginally more accurate than in the hiring condition.

Bernardin, Abbott, and Cooper (cited in McIntyre et al., 1984) suggested that the effect of purpose on ratings might be due to confounding the format of rating with the purpose of rating. When these researchers looked at purpose and held format constant, they found no influence of purpose on rating accuracy. Similarly, Murphy and associates (1984) found that purpose did not affect the accuracy of ratings collected using two different rating formats.

Summary. The purpose of rating appears to influence the psychometric quality of ratings. This especially holds in research conducted in the field using actual raters and ratees; this effect is less consistently found in laboratory research. The pattern of significant results in field research and the nonsignificant results in the laboratory is the reverse of what occurs in many other research areas. Because of the more highly controlled conditions and the demand characteristics that are present in laboratory studies, lab research will usually yield larger effect sizes than those found in field settings (Murphy, Herr et al., 1986). This is clearly not the case in research on the influence of rating purpose on rating outcomes.

Although more research is required to understand fully why purpose affects the outcomes of ratings, several hypotheses have been made. DeCotiis and Petit (1978) suggest that raters may inflate their ratings of subordinates so they (the raters) can receive a high rating or evaluation from their own supervisor. Ilgen and Feldman (1983) suggest that leniency is likely to occur when the appraisal has important consequences for the ratee (i.e., administrative decisions). Mohrman and Lawler (1983) suggest that leniency will occur when the rating has positive or negative outcomes for the rater as well. Waldman and Thornton (1988) and others indicate that when the rating is made public (and would probably have negative consequences for either rater or ratee), more lenient ratings are likely to occur.

Murphy and associates (1984) describe three ways in which appraisal purpose could affect ratings. First, purpose may directly affect ratings. Raters or decision makers may use one standard when rating for administrative decisions and another standard when rating for research purposes. Similar to Ilgen and Feldman (1983) and Mohrman and Lawler (1983), Murphy and colleagues (1984) suggest that raters will hesitate to give poor ratings because they are likely to lead to negative outcomes. Second, purpose may affect ratings indirectly, through basic cognitive processes including observation, encoding, and recall. This is also implied by Landy and Farr (1980) and DeNisi et al. (1984), the latter emphasizing information acquisition. Finally, Murphy and colleagues (1984) suggest that purpose may affect the way in which a rater integrates behavioral information when forming judgments about performance (see also Crowder, 1976). Decision strategies may differ in tasks that require high memory demands, and strategies are apt to change as the complexity of the task increases or when time pressures or distractions are present (Wright, 1974). Different purposes may pose different constraints or demands on the rater.

Rating Processes

There are two different ways in which purpose might affect the rating process. First, as noted above, purpose might affect the judgment process (we will expand on this notion below). Second, the purpose of rating might dictate a number of administrative features of rating, ranging from the frequency of ratings to the type of scales employed.

Purpose and the Judgment Process. Another area of research on the influence of purpose assesses its impact on the observation, attention, storage, memory, and retrieval processes involved in ratings (DeNisi & Williams, 1988; Henemen & Wexley, 1983; Waldman & Thornton, 1988; Williams et al., 1985; Zedeck & Cascio, 1982). DeNisi and colleagues have conducted a number of studies that indicate that the purpose of appraisal affects the way in which the rater acquires information. Williams and associates (1985) found that raters used information from appraisals differently when ratings were used to make decisions regarding pay (as opposed to promotion or remedial training). More lenient ratings were found for promotion than for the other two purposes. In a second experiment, Williams and colleagues (1985) found that raters searched for different types of information under the various purpose conditions.

Zedeck and Cascio (1982) investigated the effects of appraisal purpose on rating strategies and rating outcome. They used policy-capturing techniques to identify which performance dimensions contributed to students' ratings. Their analyses indicated that rater strategies varied with the purpose of rating. The researchers concluded that individual dimensions of performance were weighted, combined, and integrated differently depending on rating purpose. Specifically, raters differentially attended to positive and negative information reflected in the job dimensions as a function of perceived purpose. Zedeck and Cascio also found that accuracy of ratings varied by purpose, with accuracy highest for ratings of retention of a probationary employee, and decreasing for employee development and merit pay. Heneman, Wexley, and Moore (1987) noted that in this study the accuracy in ratings decreased when the magnitude of the decision increased.

Reilly and Balzer (1988) asked subjects to rate their teaching assistants and found that purpose influenced the psychometric quality of ratings and the recording of positive and negative behaviors. Ratings were more lenient in the administration condition than in the feedback condition. Further, in both the administrative and the administrative-plus-feedback condition, subjects rated positive behaviors as occurring more frequently than in the feedback-only condition. The authors suggest that this may be a way that subjects justify more lenient ratings.

Purpose and Characteristics of the Appraisal System. Few empirical studies have addressed the question of whether the purpose of rating determines the effectiveness of certain structural and administrative features of a PA system. At least four aspects of the rating process might be influenced by purpose.

The first issue is *who* should be evaluated. Cummings and Schwab (1973) suggest that employees at different overall levels of performance should be appraised differently. They suggest that separate appraisal systems should be structured for low, average, and high performers. It may also be that as one progresses higher in the organizational hierarchy, the purpose or use of performance appraisal changes. For middle managers, appraisal may be used as a control mechanism to identify and to distinguish among employee performance levels, and may possess a strong administrative component. On the other hand, for upper-level managers, PA may be used to assign executives to specific and challenging activities that develop targeted skills.

The second issue concerns the *source(s)* of the ratings. Although raters are most often the ratee's immediate supervisor, it may be more effective to use peers as raters when the purpose is to provide developmental feedback to the employee. Here, a clear separation could be made between the administrative and feedback purposes by obtaining ratings from different sources. Third, the purpose of rating might influence the *frequency* with which the appraisal is conducted. For administrative decisions, information may need to be updated yearly in order to correspond with budgetary cycles. On the other hand, if the purpose of rating is to provide developmental feedback, employees may want this information more often (and perhaps less formally) than on an annual basis. Furthermore, if an employee's performance is to improve, feedback may be necessary every 3 to 6 months, or even more often, depending on the task.

Finally, Bernardin and colleagues (Bernardin & Beatty, 1984; Bernardin & Villanova, 1986) note that the *purpose* of rating has usually been ignored when comparing rating scale formats. If the purpose of performance appraisal is to predict future performance or potential, traits or more general skill ratings may make more sense than somewhat specific behavioral ratings. On the other hand, behavior-based scales may be more meaningful, appropriate, and effective when used to provide developmental performance feedback to employees.

POWER, POLITICS, AND THE USE OF APPRAISAL

Few performance appraisal researchers or practitioners would deny that power and politics are important determinants of appraisal processes and outcomes. However, other than a few recent empirical articles (e.g., Longenecker et al., 1987; see also Ferris & Judge, 1991) and mention of the topics in books and chapters on performance appraisal (e.g., Bernardin & Beatty, 1984; Cardy & Dobbins, 1994; Carroll & Schneier, 1982; DeVries et al., 1986), power and politics (as associated with appraisal practices, generally, and with rating purpose, specifically) have received inadequate attention. In this section, we will attempt to specify the role of power and politics in performance appraisal, and explore the possibility that the influence of political considerations may depend on the purpose of appraisal.

Power and Appraisal

The notion that performance appraisal serves as a control system in organizations is not new (Lawler, 1976). In fact, a PA system, when operating as the organization designed and intended it, has inherent power. In such a system, raters evaluate employees accurately, identifying each employee's strengths and weaknesses and distinguishing among the good and poor employees, and ratings are followed by important organizational consequences. These consequences can be formal, including monetary rewards to good performers and dismissal or punishments to poor performers. Informal consequences might include a humiliating, demoralizing feedback session for a ratee or an uncomfortable awkward feedback session for the supervisor (Whisler, 1958). If raters were willing to provide accurate ratings and accurate feedback, the PA system would become a very powerful tool.

In addition to being linked with salient rewards or consequences, the performance appraisal system derives power from the organization when it serves to clarify lines of authority. In most appraisals, the organization assigns the responsibility for performance evaluation to managers. Further, these managers rate only the employees they manage (as opposed to peer evaluation or subordinate evaluation). That is, employees with more power in the organization provide ratings for employees occupying lower and less powerful positions (Pfeffer, 1981).

Power implies the ability to influence one's environment. Performance appraisal provides one means for the organization to influence its internal and external environments. When using an appraisal system for documenting the validity of selection and promotion practices used by the organization, the influence that the organization may have over its environment, especially the legal environment, is enhanced. If ratings provide thorough documentation of personnel decisions, employees may be less likely to perceive the system as unfair and less willing to bring a lawsuit against the company.

The organization's top management can influence employees by establishing the type, format, frequency, and purpose of its PA system. It can communicate to employees what it values in work activities and what it rewards, and it can set a climate for performance (Zand, 1981). A supervisor may attempt to exert power on the organization when ratings are used to make salary recommendations or promotion decisions. In addition, a supervisor may use the performance ratings of his or her subordinates as a means of competing for a valued project for the department or unit.

Performance appraisal has obvious implications when it is tied to the supervisor's attempts to influence his or her subordinates. In particular, when the purpose of appraisal is to make salary or promotion decisions, a supervisor possesses significant reward or coercive power to influence valued outcomes. When there is no apparent link between ratings and administrative outcomes (French & Raven, 1959), the supervisor will have less power over the subordinate. Finally, there are opportunities for upward influence from subordinate to supervisor in feedback sessions. Here, the employee is likely to have some opportunity to explain his or her performance and behavior. There also is an opportunity for the ratee to influence the supervisor by providing additional information that the rater may not have access to (Backburn, 1981; Mechanic, 1962; Porter, Allen, & Angle, 1981).

Although in theory the appraisal system provides a way to exercise power, in fact the many constituents of a performance system are likely to *obtain* power through their use of the appraisal system. Further, there may be power conflicts among constituents. The emergence of political behavior in the PA process is likely to occur. One consequence of such behavior may be that the appraisal system may not yield the information that was intended.

Politics and Appraisal

There are multiple constituents for any PA system; these include the organization, the rater, the ratee, and the researcher (Balzer & Sulsky, 1990; Mohrman & Lawler, 1983). Each of these constituents has its own set of needs and goals to achieve through performance appraisal. Although there may be overlap among these goals and constituencies, inconsistencies and conflict are not uncommon.

Longenecker and associates (1987) refer to politics of appraisal as the "deliberate attempts by individuals to enhance or protect their self-interests when conflicting courses of action are possible" (p. 184). Therefore, the authors state, political action is typically a source of bias or inaccuracy in employee appraisal. From interviews with 60 upper-level executives, Longenecker and colleagues (1987) found evidence of deliberate manipulation of formal ratings by executives. Much recent research on performance appraisal has been devoted to understanding and improving the accuracy of ratings—ways to perfect an instrument's measurement qualities. Longenecker and colleagues and others (Bernardin & Beatty, 1984) point out, however, that appraisal takes place in an environment that may not be completely rational, straightforward, or objective. In recent years, research on the political bases of appraisal and other human resource practices in organizations has progressed substantially (Ferris, Fedor, Chachere, & Pondy, 1989; Martocchio & Ferris, 1991). Recently, measures of the extent to which political factors affect appraisal have been developed and tested (Tziner, Latham, Prince, & Haccoun, 1994).

Managers often do not care about accuracy but rather about the extent to which they have discretion needed to balance effectiveness and survival.

If accurate performance appraisals can hurt the manager (e.g., by negatively influencing interpersonal relationships), it may be irrational to give accurate ratings. Managers therefore have their own motives and may manipulate ratings in order to accomplish their own goals or agendas. Longenecker and associates (1987) found that executives adjust or manipulate employee ratings in two directions—both higher and lower than the actual employee performance level. Inflated ratings occur frequently (most often on overall performance ratings rather than on specific performance items) and, not surprisingly, there are many reasons for inflation. Longenecker and associates and Cleveland et al. (1986) suggest that raters first determine the overall rating they want to give an employee and then go back and complete the specific items. Why? The most frequently cited reason from the Longenecker and colleagues' (1987) interviews was to maximize a subordinate's merit increases. Nearly all other reasons reflect the intense social nature of performance appraisal that, although not completely ignored, have apparently not been included in much current PA research.

Although executives hesitate to manipulate employee ratings downward, deflated ratings do occur. The reasons for deflating ratings cited by managers include (a) to shock the subordinate back into increasing his or her performance, (b) to teach rebellious subordinates a lesson regarding who is in charge, (c) to send a message to a subordinate that he or she should consider leaving the organization, and (d) to build a strongly documented record of poor performance that could expedite the termination process (Longenecker et al., 1987).

Both supervisors and subordinates engage in performance appraisal behaviors that can be described as political. As noted above, supervisors might be strongly tempted to manipulate appraisals in a variety of ways to affect the behavior of their subordinates or to affect their own standing in the organization. In the same vein, subordinates may engage in a wide range of impression management behaviors, all of which are designed to yield more favorable appraisals (Fodor, 1974; Kipnis, Schmidt, Price, & Stitt, 1980; Kipnis, Schmidt, & Wilkinson, 1980; Kipnis & Vanderveer, 1971; Villanova & Bernardin, 1989).

Longenecker (1994) points out that the label "political" carries negative connotations in organizations, and that raters who routinely manipulate the appraisals they give in an effort to achieve important goals deny that they are being in any way political. Rather, they are likely to view this manipulation as part of being a good manager, particularly if such manipulation increases the effectiveness of their unit. Managers routinely report, however, that *other* managers are political in their appraisal behavior. As research on attribution theory (Jones et al., 1972) would suggest, raters tend to view the same behavior in very different terms when it is done by someone else. When you manipulate ratings (e.g., to guarantee that your subordinates get above-average raises), you are likely to view it as an example of good management. When your peers manipulate ratings to achieve the same ends, you are likely to view that as "politics."

One interesting and potentially important finding in research on the politics of performance appraisal is that appraisals seem to become more political the higher one rises in an organization (Gioia & Longenecker, 1994; Longenecker et al., 1987). That is, the potential for manipulation of appraisals to meet the rater's particular agenda is strongest at the top of the organization, where job descriptions and performance expectations are most vague and subjective. As Gioia and Longenecker (1994) note, "performance is not necessarily the bottom line in the executive appraisal process" (p. 51). This could pose a significant problem, because the value of accurate and thorough performance appraisals is likely to increase as one moves up in the organization. Upper-level managers make decisions that can substantially affect the entire organization, and the costs of poor performance (or the benefits of good performance) at this level can be substantial. As we will note in Chapter 11, the costs and benefits of good versus poor performance are a key consideration in forecasting the economic implications of performance appraisal systems.

Although politics may always be a part of appraisal, the extent to which politics is operating in ratings may vary considerably, depending on political culture of the organization—in particular, whether the performance appraisal is taken seriously. There are a number of influences on the political culture of the organization (Longenecker et al., 1987), including the following:

- The economic health and growth potential of the organization
- The extent to which top management supports or does not practice political tactics when appraising its own subordinates
- The extent to which executives believe appraisal is necessary
- The extent to which executives believe they would be scrutinized by superiors on their appraisal of subordinates

- The extent to which organizations will train managers in performance appraisal
- The degree of open discussion of the appraisal process among executives and subordinates (i.e., trust)
- The extent to which executives believe that the appraisal becomes more political at higher levels of the organizational hierarchy

In general, when top management believes strongly in the necessity of performance appraisal, the influence of political factors on ratings is not likely to be substantial (Longenecker et al., 1987). When appraisal is not strongly and visibly supported by top management, political factors are more likely to emerge.

CONFLICTS AMONG ORGANIZATIONAL AND INDIVIDUAL USES OF APPRAISAL

Throughout this chapter we have identified a number of organizational uses for performance appraisal information. Further, we have discussed how appraisal purposes can influence the processes and outcomes of appraisals. Until now, we have discussed the impact of purpose as if only one purpose is operating at a time in a given organization. This is the implicit assumption of much of the laboratory research on the effects of purpose. However, appraisal experts recognize that information from any one performance appraisal system is likely to be used for multiple purposes. Cleveland and associates' (1989) survey specifically asked organizations to indicate the extent to which their PA system was used for various purposes. They found that more than 71% of the respondents indicated that information from appraisals was used "moderately to extensively" for both between-person decisions (i.e., pay, promotion, etc.) and within-person decisions (i.e., feedback). They noted that these two purposes are often in conflict.

Whether or not performance appraisal should be used simultaneously for personnel decisions, on the one hand, and for employee feedback, on the other hand, was questioned by Meyer et al. (1965). More recently, DeVries (1983) suggested that a performance appraisal system designed to improve employee performance may not be the most effective for salary administration. Further, DeVries and associates (1986) found that the uses of appraisal have expanded considerably within the past 25 years. The purposes that human resource managers have in mind and those that employees have may not always be the same. They warn that the several uses may conflict, giving way to less useful ratings and ultimately to dissatisfaction with the system.

It is important to understand what is meant by conflicting purposes in performance appraisal. Two types of conflict have been noted: (a) the conflicts between the multiple constituents of appraisal (i.e., the organization, the rater, the ratee, etc.) and (b) the conflicts that occur when appraisal is used to satisfy multiple organizational and individual purposes (e.g., using appraisal for both promotion decisions and employee feedback) (Cleveland et al., 1986; Cleveland et al., 1989; see also Chapter 14 of this volume).

Mohrman (1986) and others (Balzer & Sulsky, 1990) indicate that conflicts may arise among the constituents of an appraisal system. Specifically, raters may use appraisal to achieve different objectives or purposes than the ratee. Further, the ratee may think that appraisal is used for purposes quite different from those envisioned by the organization. Especially with a new PA system, there is a danger that the system will create a discrepancy between the espoused purposes and actual purposes of appraisal (Mohrman, 1986).

Closely related to the conflict that emerges among the various constituents is the conflict that may emerge for the rater when the appraisal he or she completes is used for multiple organizational and individual purposes. That is, given that the organization uses information from appraisals (e.g., to make promotion decisions, to terminate employees, to provide developmental feedback to employees), the rater must somehow weigh each of these purposes, incorporate his or her own agenda (Longenecker et al., 1987), and then decide what appraisal ratings to provide. There are a number of issues of concern here (assessments of compatibility among goals are considered in more detail in Chapter 14).

First, there is a need to understand what uses of PA are compatible and what uses are incompatible. For example, it is likely that a supervisor experiences little conflict when information from performance appraisals is used for providing feedback to employees regarding their strengths and weaknesses and to recommend employees for training programs. Both of these purposes reflect within-person decisions. These decisions require the rater to compare the strengths and weaknesses of different skills and behaviors for a given individual. On the other hand, raters may experience conflict when the organization uses the appraisal information for both developmental feedback and promotion decisions. The latter purpose reflects a between-person use (Cleveland et al., 1989), which requires the rater to make comparisons of good and poor performance among all of his or her subordinates.

Second, as suggested elsewhere (Cleveland et al., 1986), when operating in an organizational context that requests appraisal information as a basis for multiple and possibly conflicting uses, the rater may attempt to balance these purposes, frequently resulting in ratings that reflect political judgments rather than judgments about performance. There is also evidence that in some settings the rater will select one purpose or goal and then complete the appraisal with that purpose in mind (Bjerke et al., 1987).

A third issue involved when appraisal is used for multiple purposes is how the rater decides what to do (e.g., how to balance incompatible purposes) and, in particular, how limitations of the rater may affect this decision. Cognitive research suggests that the purpose of rating affects the way in which information about performance is acquired, categorized, stored, and retrieved (see DeNisi & Williams [1988] for a review). A particularly important finding in this research is that when the purpose of rating changes, raters might find it difficult to provide ratings that are useful for the new purpose. That is, when raters initially have one purpose in mind, this purpose interferes with the purpose in the subsequent task. The rater is less able to process information appropriately when completing ratings whose purpose differs from the purpose the rater had in mind when he or she observed the ratee's performance. These studies suggest that under multiple-purpose conditions, the organization may sometimes ask raters to perform an activity that is beyond their capabilities.

Finally, results from the laboratory and from interviews with raters in the field suggest that when a rater faces multiple and possibly conflicting purposes, the organization may be sacrificing not only accuracy but also the usefulness of the ratings (i.e., ratings are so inflated that they provide no meaningful information). It is conceivable that the rater selects one salient or consequential purpose and ignores the rest. The information provided by the rater may have some utility for that particular decision but may have little utility for other purposes. It is also conceivable that organizations are not obtaining useful information for any organization or individual purpose when the ratings are collected for multiple purposes. That is, if performance appraisal is attempted for a large number of incompatible purposes, there is a risk of putting the rater in an impossible situation, and the ratings he or she finally gives may be affected by so many confounds that the ratings are not useful for any of the system's purposes.

SUMMARY

Performance appraisals are used for many purposes in organizations. Different organizations might emphasize different purposes, and any given organization might pursue several different purposes with the same appraisal system. The variety of appraisal purposes often reflects the variety of goals different constituencies want to pursue when participating in performance appraisals. The goals of different constituencies are often in conflict; one result of these conflicts may be the use of power and politics in the appraisal process and outcomes. We suggest that organizations assess the compatibility of the various intended uses of performance appraisals. We strongly believe that appraisals cannot be used for all of the purposes they often appear to serve in organizations, and that attempts to use appraisals for a wide range of purposes may doom the system. PA systems will work best when the formal goals and organizational uses of performance appraisal are consistent with the goals of other appraisal constituents, including the rater and ratee.

5

Obtaining Information About Performance

The focus of this chapter is on understanding how supervisors evaluate the work of their subordinates and how those evaluations change as the work behaviors of subordinates change. As we discussed in Chapter 1, the supervisor's evaluation of a particular worker is not necessarily identical to his or her formal appraisal of that worker (i.e., the numbers that are recorded on a performance appraisal form). Supervisors are often motivated to give high ratings (or avoid low ones) even when they know that the worker is not performing well. Therefore, understanding the judgment process is not sufficient for understanding the ratings a supervisor will record. It does, however, provide a first step toward understanding the complex process of performance appraisal (PA) in organizations.

Figure 5.1 presents a simple model that will be used in the discussion about the performance judgment process. First, the supervisor must obtain information about the subordinate's performance. This information might include direct observation of work behaviors; reports from clients, customers, or other members of the organization; or inspection of the results of job performance (e.g., products, reports). Other sources of information include the supervisor's prior evaluation of the subordinate (Balzer, 1986; Murphy et al., 1985) as well as the subordinate's general reputation as a good or poor performer (March & March, 1978). The supervisor must then apply judgment strategy to combine, integrate, and make sense of this information. The term *strategy* should not be taken to indicate a conscious plan or well-formulated policy: Judgment strategies are often nothing more than simple heuristics and rules of thumb (Hogarth, 1980; Naylor, Pritchard, & Ilgen, 1980; Tversky & Kahneman, 1974), and judges are not completely consistent in using even the simplest of strategies (Dawes & Corrigan, 1974). The judgment strategy will, in turn, influence the type of information needed when evaluating others. Thus, the sales supervisor who believes that the sign of a good salesperson is a firm handshake will base performance appraisals on information different from one who takes into account such things as the salesperson's timeliness, accuracy of records, and sales volume. Finally, the product of the information and judgment strategy is an evaluative judgment—an assessment of whether the subordinate is a good, poor, or average worker.

This chapter is concerned with the first box in the model depicted in Figure 5.1—the acquisition of information about performance. We will deal with the question of how and under what circumstances supervisors obtain information about the performance of different subordinates. This chapter concentrates on "new" information about performance; Chapter 6 will discuss the impact of information that is already in the supervisor's head (e.g., reputation of individual as good or poor performer, prior impressions and previous evaluations of the individual). We will also discuss the types of information that might be available to persons other than the supervisor, such as peers or subordinates of the individual being evaluated. The use of multiple sources of evaluation provides an opportunity to consider information that is typically not available to the supervisor. As we will note in this and subsequent chapters, however, using a variety of sources for evaluating workers may lead to problems ranging from low levels of

Figure 5.1. The Performance Judgment Process

agreement among different sources to political difficulties that arise when the power hierarchy of an organization is violated (e.g., when a subordinate evaluates his or her supervisor).

WHAT SHOULD SUPERVISORS OBSERVE?

Before determining how supervisors obtain information about job performance, it is necessary to define what is meant by *job performance.* In other words, it is useful to define the thing that supervisors obtain information about before discussing how they obtain that information.

The fundamental question in determining the content of the job performance domain is whether performance should be defined in terms of behavior or in terms of the results of behavior (James, 1973; Smith, 1976). From the organization's point of view, there is a strong temptation to define performance in terms of results. After all, results are what count (at least in the short run). There are, however, several reasons for defining performance in terms of behavior rather than in terms of results. First, an exclusive emphasis on results is likely to lead to behaviors that are dysfunctional for the organization. Landy and Farr (1983) note that if performance is defined exclusively in terms of countable outcomes (i.e., results), incumbents will be strongly motivated to maximize those outcomes at the expense of other activities (e.g., maintenance, planning, conservation) that are vital to the organization. Second, results are more complexly determined than behaviors, in that results are a joint function of what the person does and the situation in which he or she does it. Defining performance solely in terms of results makes it difficult to determine what is being measured—the person or the situation in which he or she performs. Consider the case of sales clerks who work on different days or different shifts. Their sales volume may be a better measure of the number of customers in the store at different times than of their individual effectiveness in selling the product. A final point is that results-oriented criteria can lead supervisors and subordinates to ignore a wide range of behaviors (e.g., maintaining good interpersonal relations) that are critical to the survival and effectiveness of the organization but are not uniquely tied to any given product or result.

Our conclusion is that performance must ultimately be defined in terms of behaviors. The results of behaviors are, to be sure, extremely important in evaluating those behaviors. Nevertheless, we believe that the domain of performance is best defined as a domain of behaviors rather than as a set of outcomes.

The next question that must be answered is, What kinds of behaviors define performance on the job? In other words, what sorts of behavior does the supervisor need to know about in order to sensibly evaluate a subordinate's job performance? It seems reasonable to assume that the definition of job performance should not include *all* behaviors that occur on the job, but rather only some subset of relevant behaviors. One way to define *relevant* is in terms of those behaviors that are clearly linked to accomplishing the specific tasks that are included in a person's job. Carroll and Schneier (1982) take this perspective and define performance as the quality of task-oriented behavior. From this perspective, the growing body of research dealing with the determinants and the nature of task performance (cf. Fleishman & Quaintance, 1984; Salvendy & Seymour, 1973) provides the key to understanding job performance. If job performance is equated with task performance, research priorities in this field should be directed at developing better job descriptions and at aggregating measures of performance on several separate tasks into an overall measure of job performance.

There are several reasons to believe that job performance *cannot* be equated with task performance. First, most observations of work behavior confirm the common perception that workers spend relatively little time performing what would be regarded as tasks. For example, Bialek, Zapf, and McGuire (1977) reported that enlisted infantrymen spent less than half of their work time performing the technical tasks for which they had been trained; in many cases, only a small proportion of a soldier's time was in any way devoted to accomplishing the tasks specified in his or her job description. Campbell et al. (1970) noted similar patterns for managers. A substantial part of the manager's day is spent doing things that cannot be unambiguously linked to the accomplishment of specific tasks.

The fact that most people's work time is not devoted solely to tasks has serious implications for several aspects of criterion development. For example, many methods of job analysis are based explicitly on the assumption that most, if not all, of a worker's time is spent working on identifiable tasks. (This is true of the air force's task analysis system; see Christal, 1974.) Because much of the workday is spent doing something outside of the typical domain of tasks, indices of the percentage of time spent on different tasks present a warped view of the activities actually carried out by workers. Unless one is willing to ignore much of what a person does at work, it is difficult to equate job performance with task performance.

Second, many of the PA systems currently in use in the civilian and military sectors include specific measures or indices that are only tangentially related to task performance. Examples include measures of absenteeism and turnover, as well as supervisory ratings of broad traits such as dependability or motivation. Admittedly, the use of such measures does not prove that the job performance domain is broader than the task performance domain; it is possible that these measures, although widely used, are invalid. Nevertheless, the widespread use of measures that do not relate directly or solely to the accomplishment of tasks does suggest that the job performance domain is *perceived* to be broader than the domain of task performance.

A third argument for assuming that job performance cannot be defined solely in terms of task performance is that job performance must be defined over longer time periods and in relation to more organizational units than is true for task performance. This can be seen most clearly by considering the case of a machinist who successfully accomplishes his or her tasks by depleting all available reserves of material and by diverting resources from other work units. Although the individual successfully achieves the main task, the long-term implications of such task performance are clearly not favorable. In many jobs it would not be difficult to provide examples of individuals who successfully complete most tasks, but whose performance was judged to be poor.

An alternative approach to defining the set of relevant behaviors can be derived from Astin's (1964) definition of *conceptual criterion*. Astin noted that in developing criteria, the relevant goals of the sponsor or the measurer must be identified. In the context of work, the relevant goals of the organization would include short-term goals, such as the successful completion of specific tasks, as well as long-term goals, such as the maintenance of effective relations between workgroups, departments, and so on. According to Astin (1964), the conceptual criterion is nothing more than a verbal abstraction of the relevant goals or the outcomes desired; the set of possible criterion measures would include any observable index or state that is judged relevant to the conceptual criterion. If we substitute "performance construct" for "conceptual criterion" and "performance dimensions" for "criterion measures," it becomes possible to define the domain of performance and to indicate the set of behaviors that is included in that domain. *Performance domain* is defined as the set of behaviors that are relevant to the goals of the organization or the organizational unit in which a person works.

In order to specify the range of behaviors that define performance, one would have to know the relevant goals of the organization. Note here that the global set of goals that defines the overall effectiveness of the organization (e.g., maximize after-tax profits) are not as relevant as the set of goals that are defined for an incumbent in a specific position within the organization. The organization defines a set of goals to be met by an incumbent in each job, and the relevant goals may vary considerably from job to job or across different levels in the organization. This is particularly true when specific task goals are considered but will also be true for several nontask goals. For example, one goal that is likely to be broadly relevant but not tied to any specific task, is that incumbents must maintain effective interpersonal relations with their co-workers and with other organizational members with whom they interact. The type and extent of these interpersonal contacts will vary across departments and across levels of management. One might infer that the skills and behaviors that contribute to successful maintenance of interpersonal relations will vary from job to job. Nevertheless, within the great majority of jobs this general class of behaviors is likely to represent one aspect of effective performance.

Dimensions of Job Performance

The preceding section suggests that to evaluate subordinates' performance, supervisors must observe a wide range of behaviors that are relevant to the goals of the job. One way to impose structure on this task is to define the dimensions of job performance that can be used to classify behaviors into homogeneous clusters.

The traditional approach to defining the dimension of job performance is through a careful job analysis (McCormick, 1976, 1979). A variety of analytic methods have been used to define performance dimensions, ranging from the Job Element Method (Clark & Primoff, 1979) to critical incident methods (Flanagan, 1954; Latham, Fay, & Saari, 1979) to those that rely on structured questionnaires, such as the Position Analysis Questionnaire (Cornelius, Hakel, & Sackett, 1979; McCormick, Jeanneret, & Mecham, 1972).

Although formal job analysis provides an empirical basis for determining the dimensions of job performance, it does not provide a total solution (Murphy, 1989a). Research on the nature of job performance has consistently suggested that formal job analyses capture only some aspects of the job. In particular, several researchers suggest that "job performance" refers to two very distinct sets of behaviors—that is, those that are contained in a formal job description and those that are defined by the social context of work and organizations. For example, Ilgen and Hollenbeck (1991) differentiate between job elements (tasks formally prescribed for all job incumbents) and role elements. Role elements are not specified by the formal job description, but rather emerge through negotiation and interactions between the incumbent and others in the worksite. It is not necessary for every workgroup to continually redefine role elements. The traditions and the culture of the workplace and the organization may combine to create an informal job description that delineates the role elements associated with specific jobs or positions. These role elements represent real and important aspects of job performance, and although they are unlikely to be included in formal task lists or job analyses, they are crucial to effective performance.

Ilgen and Hollenbeck's (1991) model suggests that the ratio of job elements to role elements becomes smaller as jobs become more complex. One implication is that, for complex jobs, the exact requirements, duties, and expectations involved in a job are likely to be defined differently by different work teams. It may thus be necessary to study the individual position in its social context to obtain a complete picture of the job performance domain; formal job analyses are likely to overemphasize job elements and underemphasize role elements in defining the domain of job performance.

Borman and Motowidlo (1993) distinguish between task activities and "contextual performance" (see also Borman & Brush, 1993). Contextual performance does not directly support the technical core activities of a workgroup, but rather supports the organizational, social, and psychological environment in which the technical core must function. Central features of contextual performance include volunteering, persisting, helping, cooperating, following rules, staying with the organization, and endorsing organizational objectives. Contextual performance subsumes two concepts widely cited in organizational research, namely organizational citizenship behaviors (Smith, Organ, & Near, 1983) and prosocial organizational behaviors (Brief & Motowidlo, 1986). Similar concepts have been cited by Campbell (1990) in his model of soldier effectiveness. As one example of the potential importance of these aspects of performance, MacKenzie, Podsakoff, and Fetter (1991) found that insurance salespersons' evaluations were determined as much by organizational citizenship behaviors as by objective sales performance.

There is an emerging consensus that job performance involves a number of behaviors that are not directly relevant to accomplishing the tasks included in one's job description but that are nevertheless important to building and maintaining an effective workgroup. Furthermore, there is consensus that these behaviors become increasingly important as the job and the organizational context become more complex. Some researchers have suggested that behaviors of this sort should be included in assessments of performance in military jobs. For example, Edwards and Morrison (1992) note that in the future, officer assessment will need to measure citizenship, teamwork, customer-oriented behavior (as opposed to allegiance to the bureaucracy), and ability to adapt to a constantly changing external work environment.

Although important aspects of job performance are uniquely defined by the context in which one works (meaning that the same job will not have identical duties, requirements, etc., in all settings), it is important to recognize that there is considerable communality in the major dimensions of job performance across settings, jobs, organizations, and so forth. That is, although the specifics of jobs may vary with the context, it is nevertheless possible to capture important aspects of job performance with a relatively simple and common set of job dimensions. Jobs may vary in the importance of these dimensions and in the specific ways in which these dimensions are manifest, but it is nevertheless possible to describe performance in a wide variety of jobs in terms of a common set of major dimensions.

Campbell, McCloy, Oppler, and Sager (1992) proposed that performance in virtually all jobs could be described in terms of eight general dimensions, specifically: (a) job-specific task proficiency, (b) proficiency in tasks that are required in a wide range of jobs within the organization (e.g., in the navy, general navigation represents a non-job-specific task),

(c) written and oral communication, (d) demonstrating effort, (e) maintaining personal discipline, (f) facilitating peer and team performance, (g) supervision and leadership, and (h) management and administration. If this structure is indeed shown to apply to most or all jobs, it may be possible to derive a number of simple measures of job similarity and to develop appraisal methods that span a number of jobs while still giving each adequate coverage (Murphy, in press).

Other researchers have suggested alternate performance taxonomies that may provide useful bases for determining the content of appraisal systems. Morrison and Brantner (1992) studied the position of department head in surface vessels; their taxonomy included 11 roles grouped under three major factors: (a) leadership and management roles (e.g., personnel management), (b) working relationship roles (e.g., relationships with peers), and (c) technical-content roles (e.g., managing the maintenance and repair of equipment). Similarly, Mintzberg (1971) describes managerial work in terms of three groups of roles: (a) interpersonal roles (i.e., figurehead, external liaison, leader), (b) informational roles (i.e., as nerve center, disseminator, spokesperson), and (c) decisional roles (i.e., entrepreneur, disturbance handler, resource allocator, negotiator). Yukl (1982) developed a more extensive taxonomy that includes 23 aspects of managerial behavior (e.g., role clarification, goal setting, information dissemination).

Typical Versus Maximal Performance. In addition to thinking about the *content* of performance appraisals (i.e., which performance dimensions should be evaluated), it is useful to consider the *level* of performance that will be evaluated. There is a long-standing distinction in psychological testing between measures of typical performance and measures of maximal performance (Cronbach, 1990). In performance appraisal, it is important to distinguish between how well an individual *can* perform a job and how well he or she typically *does* perform a job. Research by DuBois, Sackett, Zedeck, and Fogli (1993) and Sackett, Zedeck, and Fogli (1988) confirms that maximal performance is not necessarily related to typical performance. That is, the individuals who are most capable of performing well are not necessarily those who are most likely to perform well.

The statement that typical performance is not the same as maximal performance would not come as a shock to any student of work motivation. Employees only perform to their maximal capacity when they are strongly motivated to do so *and* when their work situation allows them to perform at this level. Nevertheless, the recognition that a person's performance levels vary considerably carries a number of implications. First, some researchers (e.g., Kane, 1986) have used this truism to argue that we should not simply measure a person's average level of performance, but rather should also assess that person's consistency or inconsistency in performance. Second, research on the cognitive underpinnings of performance evaluation (this research is reviewed in Chapter 7) suggests that raters might pay undue attention to performance that is either unusually good or unusually bad. The main thing to keep in mind at this point is that evaluations of one's best performance, one's worst performance, or one's typical performance could all lead to different conclusions and actions.

Implicit Theories of Performance. Cognitive research suggests that the dimensions raters use to organize their observations of job performance are a product of implicit theories about the job (Borman, 1983, 1987). Although implicit theories often contain a great deal of accurate information (Lay & Jackson, 1969; Stricker, Jacobs, & Kogan, 1974), the dimensions used by raters are not necessarily the same as those that are derived through a formal job analysis.

In one of the few studies of supervisors' "folk theories" of job performance, Borman (1987) found that the dimensions that defined supervisors' conceptions of performance included the following:

- Initiative and hard work
- Maturity and responsibility
- Organization
- Technical proficiency
- Assertive leadership
- Supportive leadership

These dimensions are notable in two ways. First, several of them refer to global traits rather than to specific behaviors. The position that performance appraisal *should be* based on traits is accepted by only a few researchers (e.g., Kavanaugh, 1971). Borman's (1987) results suggest that, regardless of what should be done, performance appraisals *are* done in terms of global traits rather than specific behaviors. This position is also implicit in several of the recent cognitive models of performance appraisal (DeNisi et al., 1984; Feldman, 1981; Ilgen & Feldman, 1983; Nathan & Lord, 1983). Second, they range from those that are tightly focused on carrying out specific tasks (e.g., technical proficiency) to those that are more diffuse and more concerned with effective interpersonal relations (e.g., supportive leadership).

There is a clear need for more research on supervisors' theories of the job. At present we know very little about which dimensions of performance supervisors typically emphasize, about variation from supervisor to supervisor in the dimensions that are attended to, or about the circumstances that will lead to either widespread consensus regarding the dimensions of performance or widespread disagreement. Yet it seems likely that:

1. Supervisors hold implicit theories of the job that define, for them, the meaning of job performance.
2. The dimensions emphasized by supervisors will not always be the same as those that are derived through formal job analysis.
3. It is the implicit theory, not the job analysis, that guides the supervisor's observation, interpretation, and recollection of subordinates' job performance.

A better understanding of supervisors' theories of the job would help considerably in understanding judgments regarding job performance.

HOW IS INFORMATION OBTAINED?

Accurate observation is assumed to be the cornerstone of accuracy in evaluating performance (Ilgen, 1983; Spool, 1978). This assumption has received empirical support (Murphy, Garcia, Kerkar, Martin, & Balzer, 1982), but the mediating variables (i.e., judgment strategies) that link behavior observation with accurate evaluations of job performance are poorly understood (Lord, 1985a). It is useful in this context to consider *observation* as an umbrella term that covers the many methods that supervisors might use to obtain information about subordinates. These include direct observation of the subordinate's behavior, observation of the results of that behavior, or a variety of secondhand methods of obtaining relevant information, such as customers' reports, reports from co-workers, or reports from members of other organizational units.

Time Over Which Behavior Occurs

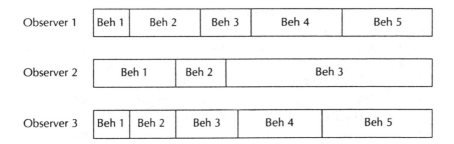

Figure 5.2. Consequences of Individual Differences in "Chunking" Ongoing Behavior

NOTE: Each rectangle represents a chunk, or discrete behavior perceived by the observer.

Direct Observation

It is an open question whether the direct observation of subordinates' behavior is feasible, even under the best of circumstances. Research on the perception of ongoing behavior suggests that individuals chunk behaviors into meaningful units, and the units employed by one supervisor may not be identical to those employed by another (Newtson, 1976; Sandlands & Calder, 1987). Consider the situation illustrated in Figure 5.2. Behavioral reports from these three observers are likely to vary in many ways. First, the observers may not report the same number of discrete behaviors. Some reports might refer to similar incidents (e.g., Behavior 1 for Observers 1 and 3), but others will report the same incident in fundamentally different terms (e.g., Behavior 1 + Behavior 2 for Observer 3 is the same as Behavior 1 for Observer 2).

In our judgment, individual differences in chunking of behaviors are not likely to pose a serious threat to the accurate observation of work behaviors. There are two reasons for believing this. First, work is a formally structured activity. Thus, discrete chunks are already built into much of what people do at work (e.g., specific tasks might define chunks). Extensive individual differences in the perception of behavior at work are not as likely as in other settings, where formal demands and preexisting structure are not so readily apparent. Second, several studies (e.g., Foster & Cone, 1980; Komaki,

Collins, & Thoene, 1980; Martinko & Gardner, 1985) have demonstrated that accurate behavioral observation in a work setting is possible. It may be very costly, however, to obtain an accurate behavioral record (a point we will return to later).

Although technically feasible, extensive direct observation of behavior is relatively rare. It is known that the accuracy of performance judgments increases as a function of the rater's opportunity to observe the ratee's behavior (Heneman & Wexley, 1983) and of the time actually spent observing behavior (Heneman et al., 1987), but apparently few organizations are willing to devote the resources necessary to ensure accurate observation. Indeed, several models of the appraisal process are based on the assumption that appraisals incorporate only limited samples of behavior. Although not phrased in these terms, the argument *against* relying on limited samples of behavior is essentially similar to that put forth by proponents of validity generalization (e.g., Schmidt & Hunter, 1981)—that small samples produce unreliable results. Some of the consequences of relying on insufficient samples of behavior in making performance-related decisions (i.e., promotion) include the following (March & March, 1978):

1. *False Record Effect:* Differences in career outcomes will be larger than true differences in ability or performance. This is because sampling error determines many promotions.
2. *Hero Effect:* The faster the rate of promotion, the less likely it is justified. A fast promotion rate implies very small samples of performance and thus extensive opportunities to capitalize on chance.
3. *Disappointment Effect:* Newly promoted employees are, on average, a disappointment. The best performers are promoted, but regression to the mean suggests that people who score best on a measure (especially an unreliable one) will not do so well on a subsequent measure of the same construct.

In addition to the problems associated with the limited reliability of small samples of behavior, insufficient sampling of behavior could be an issue if the validity of performance measures is challenged in a legal action (e.g., a suit charging violations of equal employment opportunity laws; see Barrett & Kernan, 1987; *Brito v. Zia,* 1973). Given the potential importance of accurately observing subordinates' behavior, it is useful to ask why direct observation of subordinates' behavior is not more frequently carried out.

Barriers to Direct Observation. The most obvious barriers to extensive observations of subordinates' behavior are the numerous demands on the supervisor's time. Simply put, supervisors typically have better things to do than to stand around watching their subordinates work. (Unfortunately, research on performance evaluation is often carried out in settings in which raters do not have anything to do but observe and evaluate ratees [Murphy et al., 1989]. Conflicting task demands or the lack of conflicting task demands almost certainly affects the accuracy of observation [Balzer, 1986].) This lack of time affects not only the frequency of observation but also the style of observation. That is, supervisors who can devote only limited periods to the direct observation of subordinates are unlikely to spend that time in passive observation. Rather, they are likely to have definite goals when observing subordinates' performance and are likely to use observation as a means of answering specific questions about subordinates (e.g., Is this worker having problems scheduling activities?).

It is well known that observational goals affect the way in which observers attend to, encode, store, and retrieve information (Murphy et al., 1989; Williams et al., 1985). Thus the behaviors that are observed and remembered by a busy supervisor may not be the same as those that would be noticed and recorded by someone whose sole task was behavioral observation.

Time pressures are not the only obstacle to accuracy in behavioral observation. First, the proximity of supervisors to subordinates varies greatly within and across organizations (Kaufman, 1960). Wherry's work on a psychometric model of performance rating suggests that evaluations are most accurate when supervisors and subordinates work in close proximity (Wherry & Bartlett, 1982); supervisors who do not work directly with employees may find it very difficult to observe subordinates' work behavior. Second, the information that is available to supervisors may interfere with their ability or inclination to observe subordinates' behavior. Supervisors often observe or are informed of the *results* of behavior, and knowledge of results may lead them to infer behaviors (Bernardin & Beatty, 1984) (see Murphy, Martin, & Garcia [1982] for a similar argument regarding inferring behaviors from global evaluations). If results are acceptable, the supervisor may give little thought to behaviors and may concentrate on observing subordinates whose results are not so impressive.

There is evidence that the *relevance* rather than the frequency of observation is the most important determinant of the accuracy of evaluations

(Freeberg, 1969; Kleiger & Mosel, 1953; Landy & Guion, 1970). Traditionally, it has been thought that increasing familiarity with the person and the job being observed would increase the accuracy of observations and judgments. This may not be so. Kingstrom and Mainstone (1985) note that frequency of observation is likely to be critical only when the subordinate is new to the job. Supervisors quickly develop impressions and global evaluations of each subordinate, and these are likely to affect all subsequent observations and assessments of work performance (Murphy et al., 1985). Thus the supervisor who is familiar with a particular subordinate's work may spend little time in the future observing that subordinate, and any behavior that is observed is likely to be interpreted according to the supervisor's general impressions.

Features of the job, organization, and environment can directly affect supervisors' opportunities, strategies, and inclinations toward observing the performance of their subordinates. Some jobs consist mainly of observable behaviors, whereas others consist of unobservable mental ability. Task environments can be highly stable or highly turbulent (Kane & Lawler, 1979; Thompson, 1967). Turbulent task environments (e.g., those in which technology, procedures, workgroup composition, etc., change frequently) are characterized by a high degree of uncertainty; more extensive observations may be needed to assess performance accurately in a turbulent environment than in a static one. Rambo, Chomiak, and Price (1983) suggest that performance in some jobs can be highly stable over time, but also note that stability of behavior and performance may depend as much on characteristics of the situation (e.g., design of the reward system) as of the person. Because the stability of performance directly affects the likelihood that limited samples of behavior will provide accurate assessments, the question of whether performance is stable is a highly relevant one (Murphy, 1989b).

Does Observation Affect Behavior? Supervisors must not only contend with barriers to direct observation but must also consider the possibility that the act of observing subordinates' behavior changes that very behavior. In fact, subordinates' belief that they are being observed may lead to changes in behavior. There are several explanations for this link. First, the presence of an observer can interfere with work activities (e.g., by distracting workers or by getting in the way) (Dornbusch & Scott, 1975). Second, it has long been known that workers resent and resist the routine observation of their activities (Kahn & Katz, 1953; Merton, 1957); this issue has received renewed attention since the introduction of computerized monitoring systems. They may adopt a variety of strategies to deal with this problem, ranging from strict enforcement of work norms, to filing a grievance, to removing the unwanted observer, and may not revert to their usual work habits until the observer is gone.

As we noted earlier, a distinction is made between a test of typical performance and a test of maximal performance (Cronbach, 1970). The former measures day-to-day performance; the latter measures performance under circumstances where the individual is motivated to perform at the highest level possible. This distinction is clearly relevant in comparing the behavior of subordinates who believe they are not being observed by their superiors to that of subordinates who believe they are being observed. It is likely that the maximal performance that is exhibited for the benefit of the observer (i.e., the supervisor) is different from more typical, day-to-day performance.

Several authors have noted that performance on standardized, closely observed work samples is not highly correlated with global ratings of performance (Campbell, Crooks, Mahoney, & Rock, 1973; Murphy, 1986; Schmidt, Hunter, & Outerbridge, 1986). This low correlation is usually taken as an indication of the dismal validity of ratings, but the present analysis suggests a different conclusion. Work samples are clearly tests of maximal performance (Murphy, 1986); measures based on work samples may not provide appropriate criteria for evaluating ratings. One piece of evidence in favor of this interpretation is the finding that objective measures of typical and maximal performance are not highly correlated (DuBois et al., 1993; Sackett et al., 1988). In a more general sense, it may be difficult, under conditions where observation itself affects behavior, to obtain via direct observation the information needed for valid assessments of an individual's performance level.

Observation Aids. Three strategies have been suggested to help increase the accuracy of behavior observation. The first revolves around training and experience. It is known that behavior observation skills training can be effective (Boice, 1983; Spool, 1978; Thornton & Zorich, 1980). In the 1950s, Wherry suggested that raters should be trained on what and how to observe (cited in Wherry & Bartlett, 1982); this suggestion is still a good one. There is also evidence that experience in activities that involve detailed observations of behavior (e.g., serving as an assessor in a managerial assessment center) leads to higher levels of accuracy in other observation tasks (Lorenzo, 1984).

A second strategy for increasing the accuracy of ratings is based on the use of Behaviorally Anchored Rating Scales (BARS). Although this point has not been emphasized in most applications of BARS, these scales were originally designed to aid raters in observing and categorizing the behavior of ratees (Bernardin & Smith, 1981; Smith & Kendall, 1963). The idea here is that by carefully defining scale dimensions and providing specific behavioral examples, BARS will provide raters with a standard frame of reference. The strategy of using BARS to improve observation might be especially helpful if it is combined with observation skill training. Here, BARS help tell the rater what to look for, and training will increase the rater's skills in observing and recording those behaviors.

Martinko and Gardner (1985) suggest the most comprehensive strategy for increasing observational accuracy. They describe the use of multiple methods, some of which are listed here, that can be applied in observation:

- Time sampling
- Behavior diaries
- Self-observation
- Use of multiple raters
- Use of large behavior samples

The authors suggest that it is technically feasible to obtain accurate behavioral records, but they also note a dilemma. A high level of accuracy in behavioral measurement at work may require the use of several methods, some of which are both cumbersome and expensive. It is not clear whether the results will always justify the cost.

Indirect Observation

Much of what supervisors know about subordinates' performance is probably the result of indirect rather than direct observation. As noted earlier, indirect observation encompasses many areas, such as viewing videotapes, reading descriptions of subordinates' behavior, receiving complaints or letters of praise, and hearing wholly unfounded rumors about the subordinate. Unfortunately, our understanding of these indirect methods of obtaining information about subordinates' performance is not commensurate with the scope or the importance of the problem. For example, communication specialists have long known that the same message has different meaning when conveyed via two different media (Shannon & Weaver, 1948). Thus, observing a subordinate insult a customer is a different thing from hearing about it. Hearing about it may mean different things, depending on the source (e.g., the customer vs. a rival worker) or the context.

Studies comparing the impact of direct versus indirect observation on performance appraisals and other evaluations in organizations are rare. Two studies from the interviewing literature help to illustrate issues that might arise in performance appraisal. Maier and Thurber (1968) showed that judgments are more accurate when based on audio or written records of interviews than on direct observation. There are several possible explanations for this effect. First, written and audio records contain less information than is obtained through direct observation, and much of the missing information is largely irrelevant (e.g., physical attractiveness, nonverbal interaction styles) (Banks & Murphy, 1985). Second, information that is presented in written or audio form may be encoded, stored, and retrieved differently than information that is obtained through direct observation (Murphy, Herr et al., 1986). This is particularly true for written stimuli; a different memory system (semantic vs. episodic) might be involved when reading a description of what a person does as opposed to observing him or her do it (Tulving & Thompson, 1973).

Imada and Hakel (1977) showed systematic differences between the perceptions of subjects who interacted with candidates in an interview and subjects who observed those interactions. Their results can be best understood in terms of the actor-observer distinction that has long been drawn in both social psychology and cultural anthropology. That is, persons who are actively involved in an event will observe different things than will be observed by uninvolved spectators. The supervisor's status as actor versus observer may be uncertain or unstable, particularly if he or she has input into the activities of the subordinate. Actor-observer status may even vary across subordinates, tasks, or time. Thus, the information obtained about different subordinates may vary as a function of the supervisor's perspective.

Although there has been little research on the effects of indirect observations on performance judgments, research from other fields provides a basis for speculating about the variables that are most likely to moderate the impact of indirect observations. Eight such variables are presented in

TABLE 5.1   Variables That Might Determine Impact of Indirect Observations of Performance

1. Source of the report	Colleague, customer, supervisor, etc.
2. Initiator of the report	Is report requested by supervisor?
3. Form of the report	Descriptive versus evaluative; detailed report versus summary
4. Medium	Letter, memo, conversation, etc.
5. Referent	Behavior versus results
6. Timing	Time elapsed since episode
7. Motive for the report	Why is information provided?
8. Consistency of report observations	With other reports and with supervisor's report

Table 5.1. The first consideration is the source of the message, which affects both its credibility and the weight that is attached to the message. Thus the observation that employee A did a particularly good job with a specific assignment will probably have a different impact, depending on whether it is received from a good friend and co-worker of the person being evaluated, a customer or client, or the CEO of the organization. The same comment from a customer might be received quite differently if it comes from a customer who frequently praises your employees' work, frequently criticizes your employees' work, or has never before commented on your employees' work.

The question of whether indirect observations are solicited by the supervisor, are volunteered by others, or are encountered by chance (e.g., accidentally overhearing a comment about one of your subordinates) is an important one. Information that is acquired incidentally is processed and stored differently from information that is consciously sought out (Balzer, 1986; Murphy et al., 1989). The supervisor who requests a report from some indirect source is probably pursuing a specific question and is likely to attend most closely to the information that is relevant to that question. Therefore the same report may be perceived differently when received on request than when it is encountered unexpectedly. The effect of unsolicited reports may be quite different when they are delivered directly to the supervisor than when they are encountered by chance. In the former case, the supervisor may interpret the report differently, depending on his or her interpretation of the sender's motives for delivering the report (see Point 7, Table 5.1).

The form of secondhand reports about a subordinate's performance can vary on many dimensions. One relevant dimension is whether the report is primarily descriptive or evaluative (Ilgen et al., 1979; Jacobs, Jacobs, Feldman, & Cavior, 1973). Descriptive reports consist primarily of recitations of what occurred, whereas evaluative reports consist primarily of an individual's subjective assessment of the quality or the effectiveness of what was done. Admittedly, the distinction between description and evaluation is not completely clear; most descriptions imply a positive or negative evaluation (Hoxworth, 1988). Nevertheless, a supervisor is likely to get different information from a descriptive report than from a report that takes the form of, "Bill did a good job on our project." The implication of both source and motive variables (see Points 1 and 7, Table 5.1) may be different for descriptive versus evaluative reports. That is, description from many sources might be credible and might affect the supervisor's judgments. The same supervisor may ignore some evaluative judgments and give great weight to others (e.g., those that come from credible sources).

Another related dimension for classifying the form of secondhand reports is the extent to which they provide detailed information as opposed to short summaries. Several methods of judgment research involve the use of short written vignettes in which subjects are asked to make judgments based on the information they read. The use of those methods in studying evaluation in organizations has been criticized (Gorman, Clover, & Doherty, 1978; Ilgen, 1983; Wendelken & Inn, 1981; cf. Dipboye, Stramler, & Fontenelle, 1984), at least in part because these vignettes contain too little information and are more neatly packaged than the observations that are typical of real decision makers. This criticism may apply when generalizing from judgment studies to direct observation but probably does *not* apply as strongly to indirect observation. In fact, it is likely that many of the reports received by raters are short ones that contain only a small amount of information. These reports probably contain little of the irrelevant information (e.g., physical attractiveness of the person being observed) that is present in direct observation (Banks & Murphy, 1985). The ratio of relevant to irrelevant information may be even higher for short summaries than for longer reports.

The medium by which a report is delivered could markedly affect the information conveyed. The same message presented verbally versus in written form will not convey the same information, especially if one medium allows for more interaction than the other (e.g., does the supervisor have a chance to ask questions?). The medium will probably also affect the form of the message (e.g., short vs. long; Point 3, Table 5.1), may be a function of who initiates the message (Point 2, Table 5.1), and may be affected by the timing of the message (e.g., a short verbal report is more likely than a long written one immediately after the event; Point 6, Table 5.1). Informal memos will probably contain different information than formal reports and are likely to be produced under different circumstances. A detailed, formal report is unlikely except when it is formally required or an unusual event (e.g., very good or very poor performance) occurs; a brief memo might be produced at the spur of the moment.

Earlier in this chapter, information was presented about the controversy over whether performance should be defined in terms of behavior or results. The same question arises when considering secondhand reports concerning performance. In general, short evaluative reports will probably refer to results; it is only the long formal reports that are likely to include extensive descriptions of behavior. Again, as noted earlier, results-oriented reports may require supervisors to infer behaviors. Because results are not perfectly correlated with behavior, these inferences will not always be accurate, even when the results report itself is entirely accurate.

The timing of reports about subordinates' performance will affect both the credibility and the use of those reports. Reports that occur shortly after the event may be more credible, particularly if a great deal of behavioral detail is required. Behavioral reports that are received shortly before a PA is to be completed might exert more influence than reports that were received long before the PA was due. The timing of reports may also vary as a function of the source of the report (e.g., the CEO might not rush to tell you about a particular subordinate's performance), the form of the report (e.g., short memos might come sooner and more often than long formal reports), and even the referent of the report (e.g., results may take a long time to determine).

The principal concern of attribution theory (Jones et al., 1972) is the way in which an individual explains the behavior of others. Depending on the supervisor's attributions, he or she may do anything from taking reports at face value to discounting them altogether. When receiving a report the first question a supervisor must ask is *why* the report was given; the interpretation of the report may vary depending on the answer to that question. For example, if the report is seen as an attempt to harm a rival or as an exercise to impress management, the report may receive little weight. There are multiple motives for most behaviors in organizations, and a report that is perceived as a means of furthering an ulterior motive will receive less weight than a similar report from a disinterested source.

The final issue noted in Table 5.1 is the consistency of the report with other reports and with the supervisor's own evaluation. Agreement among second-hand reports should increase credibility. If one report disagrees with all of the others, only that report will be affected. However, widespread and general disagreement among external sources may lower the credibility of *all* reports.

Inconsistency among a secondhand report and the supervisor's own observations and evaluations is a more complex matter. On the one hand, there is evidence of a pervasive confirmatory bias in human judgment. People tend to seek out information that confirms their initial impressions and discount information that does not (Darley & Fazio, 1980). Thus it is possible that supervisors will ignore or explain away inconsistent reports. On the other hand, some reports come from sources that have a great deal of power and/or credibility. It is possible that these reports will lead the supervisor to change his or her evaluation, at least in situations where the supervisor is not strongly committed (see Bazerman et al. [1982] for a discussion of what happens when a person is committed to an evaluation). However, the extent of this change (i.e., the impact of the report on the supervisor's judgment) may be complexly determined.

Research on attitude change and opinion revision (Freedom, Sears, & Carlsmith, 1981; Slovic & Lichtenstein, 1971) suggests that even when people do pay attention to information that is inconsistent with their prior observations or beliefs, they often do not give the information sufficient weight. To complicate matters further, the impact of reports that are inconsistent with the supervisor's prior observations might depend on the timing of those reports. There is evidence that inconsistent information is more easily remembered than information that is either neutral or consistent (the evidence is more equivocal for the latter than the former) with prior observations (Hastie, 1980; Murphy et al., 1985). Thus inconsistent information may have a greater impact on memory-based evaluations than on those that are formed immediately after the event or that are based on careful examination of records of the event.

The issues presented in Table 5.1 suggest (but certainly do not exhaust) a set of research questions that to date have been largely ignored. Supervisors cannot possibly obtain all of the information needed for accurate appraisals solely through direct observation. Time pressures and their physical separation from subordinates force supervisors to rely in part on secondhand reports when evaluating subordinates. There is a clear need for both descriptive research and process-oriented research. First, it is important to know more about what actually happens in organizations. What sort of information do supervisors receive through secondhand reports and how do they use this information? The eight points listed in Table 5.1 suggest several points of departure for process-oriented research. We look forward to progress in these areas.

The assumption throughout this chapter has been that supervisors use *some* information about a subordinate's behavior when evaluating his or her performance. This is not necessarily the case. A supervisor who has no information about a subordinate's behavior during a given period is unlikely to return a blank performance appraisal. It is well known that appraisals are heavily influenced by general impressions and that early evaluations exhibit a powerful influence on subsequent ones (Balzer, 1986; Kingstrom & Mainstone, 1985; Murphy et al., 1985). We are not sure that evaluations conducted in the absence of any relevant information would be much different from evaluations carried out by a well-informed supervisor. Unfortunately, if this is true, it might be hard to demonstrate that information that is obtained through direct or indirect observation makes much of a difference, at least after the supervisor has formed an initial evaluation.

We are not as pessimistic as the preceding paragraph might imply. Research on human judgment has focused on errors, inconsistencies, suboptimal strategies, and poor choices, in part because errors often more clearly illustrate underlying processes than do correct decisions (Funder, 1987). It is important not to lose sight of the fact that people generally do better in real-life judgment than in research studies designed to assess their errors. Thus the knowledge that initial evaluations can cloud later judgments or that appropriate weight is not always given to new information should not lead to the conclusion that supervisors are impervious to what is going on around them. Although there are many sources of error in performance evaluations, there is also some "true score" in a typical PA (Landy & Farr, 1983). We think that in most cases the subordinate's behavior *does* have an impact on the supervisor's evaluation. It is thus worthwhile to continue to pursue research on the ways in which supervisors obtain information about subordinates' performance.

WHO SHOULD OBTAIN INFORMATION?

The preceding section was built around the assumption that supervisors should be the people responsible for obtaining information about their subordinates' performance, and that information from other sources should be filtered through the supervisor. There is evidence that both raters *and* ratees strongly prefer using the immediate supervisor as the main (and perhaps sole) source of performance appraisals (Bernardin, 1979; Gosselin, Werner, & Halle, 1994).

Although the use of immediate supervisors as the primary source of performance appraisal information is certainly common practice in most organizations (Cleveland et al., 1989; Long, 1986), it is not clear that this is the optimal practice (Kane & Lawler, 1979). People other than the supervisor may be better qualified to evaluate. Even when the supervisor is the best evaluator, it is not necessarily advantageous for the supervisor to be the *only* evaluator. Peers, subordinates, customers, or colleagues of the supervisor might provide additional information or fresh perspectives on information that is available to the supervisor.

Kingstrom and Mainstone (1985) discuss the importance of *task acquaintance,* which they define as the amount and type of work contact the evaluator has with the person being evaluated. The quantity and quality of task acquaintance vary considerably as a function of level in the organization; peers and subordinates see different facets of an individual's task behavior than is seen by supervisors (Borman, 1974). This difference is even more pronounced for the behaviors that define interpersonal relations at work, which are critical in task performance (Murphy, 1989a). The frequency and style of interpersonal interactions will greatly reflect the power hierarchy of organizations. Thus one's boss, peers, subordinates, and so on, will all experience different social interactions with an individual and may evaluate interpersonal relations quite differently.

Table 5.2 lists five different potential sources of information about a person's work behavior and indicates whether or not each source is likely to have access to information about both behaviors and results of behaviors as they relate to task accomplishment and interpersonal relations at work. Some of the entries in Table 5.2 will probably vary across organizations. For example, subordinates have more opportunity to observe their supervisors' task behaviors in organizations where supervisors and subordinates

TABLE 5.2 Access to Information About Task and Interpersonal Behaviors and Results

	Source				
	Subordinates	Self	Peers	Next Level (Supervisor)	Higher Level (Upper Management)
Task					
Behaviors	Rare	Always	Frequent	Occasional	Rare
Results	Occasional	Frequent	Frequent	Frequent	Occasional
Interpersonal					
Behaviors	Frequent	Always	Frequent	Occasional	Rare
Results	Frequent	Frequent	Frequent	Occasional	Rare

work together than in organizations where they work apart. Nevertheless, the table provides a useful starting point for our discussion.

The frequency with which individuals at different levels in the organization encounter information about behaviors and results will vary, both as a function of the job itself (e.g., proximity between workers at different levels) and as a function of the roles of the observer and the person being observed. Individuals who are far removed from the target employee will only rarely have access to relevant information and will more frequently know about results than about behaviors. However, no one (not even the individual himself or herself) has frequent access to all of the relevant information. Thus a worker may know what he or she has done but may not be fully aware of the results of those behaviors. A manager who is several levels above the target employee may receive only occasional information about the results of tasks performed.

The research we review, which deals with the use of sources other than or in addition to the supervisor, is concerned with rating rather than with the behavioral reports that serve as data in forming evaluations of performance. As discussed in Chapter 1, rating, judgment, and the collection of information about performance are all separate activities. Nevertheless, research on ratings obtained from different sources does shed some light on those sources' access to relevant information. Unfortunately, this research raises some complex issues, because it deals with evaluation as well as with the collection of behavioral information. The recurring theme of much of this research is the impact of the power hierarchy of an organization on evaluations obtained from a variety of sources. Supervisory evaluations follow the natural flow of power and authority, in which the immediate supervisor is responsible for evaluations. Evaluations obtained from other sources will either bypass the natural lines of authority (evaluations from upper management), circumvent them (evaluations from peers, self), or reverse the usual authority structure of an organization (evaluations from subordinates).

Mahew (1983) surveyed societies and organizations ranging in time from the sixth century B.C. to the present, and in scope from the Achaemenid Empire of ancient Mesopotamia and Persia to the Columbus (Ohio) Police Department. He concluded that hierarchical differentiation with a unity of the flow of authority and power from the top down is essentially universal. That is, organizations are structured so that decisions, orders, and control flow from the top levels down, with very few instances of egalitarian or bottom-up rule. Dornbusch and Scott (1975) noted, "Evaluation is required if power is to be employed to control behavior" (p. 134).

One substantial barrier to the involvement of sources other than the supervisor (especially sources at or below the level of the person being evaluated) in performance appraisal is that it does not fit an apparently universal principle of hierarchical organization. Thus performance appraisals that incorporate input from peers or subordinates are rare and often not well received where they are applied. Nevertheless, Table 5.2 suggests there are potential benefits in involving multiple sources in PA, because no single source is likely to have access to all of the information needed for accentual appraisal.

We have chosen to classify alternative sources of information about individuals' performance in terms of their relative standing in the power hierarchy of the organization. This is not the only method that might be used; Carroll and Schneier (1982) classify alternative sources in terms of the roles they occupy. Thus the same individual might have access to different information about a person when interacting with him or her in different roles (e.g., assistant, mentor, friend). Although this role-based analysis has some merit, we find it more helpful to describe sources in terms of the one universal characteristic of all organizations—the power hierarchy.

One thing that must be kept in mind when examining research of rating sources is that different sources often give similar ratings. For example, in a meta-analysis of research on rating sources, Harris and Schaubroeck (1988) found an average correlation of .62 between peer and supervisory ratings (self-supervisor and self-peer correlations were .35 and .36, respectively). Although there are many reasons why different sources *might* give very different ratings, this does not always happen.

Subordinates as Sources

Involving subordinates in evaluation is a potentially serious violation of the status hierarchy (Dornbusch & Scott, 1975; Thompson, 1967). There is evidence that both subordinates and superiors are uncomfortable with subordinate evaluations of performance (Carroll & Schneier, 1982). Superiors' discomfort with subordinate ratings can probably be explained in terms of reversals of power; subordinates' discomfort may reflect concern that superiors will retaliate for low ratings.

Upward feedback has long been used in education, in the form of student ratings of teacher performance (Feldman, 1989), and is becoming increasingly popular in industry. Mount (1984a) reports some evidence for the reliability and validity of rating obtained from subordinates and notes that when supervisors, subordinates, and the target individual all provide ratings (the last source is a self-rating), supervisors and subordinates agree more closely with one another than either source agrees with self-ratings. It is not clear whether this latter result explains more about the validity of the ratings (and if so, which ratings are more valid) or the actor-observer differences.

Data in Table 5.2 suggest that subordinates only rarely have access to information about task performance, and when they do they are likely to know more about results than about behaviors. However, they do have frequent access to information about interpersonal behaviors and the results of these behaviors; direct subordinates will directly experience these behaviors and can testify firsthand about their results. Other subordinates (i.e., those who are at lower levels but do not work directly for the target individual) are also likely to be well informed about the interpersonal style of people higher in the organization, through both direct and indirect observation. It is axiomatic that power flows downward in organizations. It is equally axiomatic that gossip flows both sideways and down. We know of no empirical test but it is a common observation that workers frequently compare and discuss their bosses, especially if the boss has particularly bad or particularly good relations with his or her subordinates.

One of the keys to effective performance as a manager is the ability to get good work from one's subordinate (Mintzberg, 1980). That is, the manager who wishes to have a positive effect on his or her subordinates must communicate well with them and must earn their trust. There are, of course, some technical skills involved in managing. Interpersonal relations are an integral part of management, however, and the accurate evaluation of a supervisor or manager's performance may not be possible without information about interpersonal relations between the supervisor and the subordinate. Subordinates may be the optimal source for this information.

It is useful to consider the special characteristics of the one setting in which subordinate ratings are widely used—teacher evaluation. Student evaluations of teachers are conducted under special circumstances where the rater is anonymous and does not have to be concerned about the future consequences of giving high or low ratings. Teacher ratings are not always held in high regard as criteria, but the fact that they are widely used suggests that, in at least some situations, persons in a subordinate position will be willing and (some skeptics will dispute this) able to evaluate their superiors.

Workers' resistance to subordinate rating systems might not be so extreme if they could feel the same sense of anonymity and freedom from reprisal that is present in most teacher rating systems. Unfortunately, this would require a large number (N) of participants as well as a high level of trust. Subordinates who are qualified to rate a supervisor may often be too small in number to ensure anonymity. The supervisor whose average rating is low is in a better position to guess who gave low ratings when $N = 2$ than when $N = 15$. Trust may be an even more difficult problem (Bernardin & Beatty, 1984). In order to have a successful subordinate evaluation system, subordinates must believe that their ratings will not somehow become known to the supervisor being rated. Such a level of trust is probably not the norm.

Self as a Source

Although the use of self-ratings as the *sole* method of evaluating performance is rare (Bernardin & Klatt, 1985; Long, 1986), self-ratings are more likely than subordinate ratings to be included as a component of a PA system. As we will note later in this chapter, self-ratings are especially common in appraisal and feedback systems that seek to incorporate multiple sources of information. Table 5.2 suggests an obvious advantage to the use of the target individual as a source of information—being reasonably certain that this source will be well informed. The outstanding barrier to using self-ratings is the nagging suspicion that people tend to overrate their own performance.

There is evidence that self-ratings are typically more lenient (i.e., higher) than ratings obtained from supervisors (Meyer, 1980; Thornton, 1980). This by itself is not necessarily evidence of the invalidity of self-ratings, because it is possible that self-ratings are accurate and supervisory ratings are unduly harsh. Similarly, evidence that self-ratings are not highly correlated with supervisory ratings (Landy & Farr, 1983; Steel & Ovalle, 1984; Thornton, 1980) is difficult to evaluate, because supervisory ratings are not the optimal criteria for evaluating self-assessments. There are, however, two lines of evidence that would seem to point unambiguously to deficiencies in self-ratings.

First, self-ratings tend to move closer to supervisory ratings if extensive performance feedback is given (Steel & Ovalle, 1984). Although this finding may represent nothing more than criterion contamination (e.g., workers distort their self-assessments to correspond more closely with their supervisor's assessment), it may also indicate that feedback causes self-raters to adopt a frame of reference more similar to that of the supervisor. We would argue that this change would not occur if individuals were confident of the accuracy of their self-assessments. Thus the instability of self-assessments may be an indirect indication of their inaccuracy.

Second, there is at least one study showing clear evidence of distortion (i.e., leniency) in self-assessment. Farh and Werbel (1986) present evidence that self-ratings are less lenient if raters know that the ratings will be checked against some objective criterion. This may in part reflect a conservative bias among raters who do not trust the system (i.e., negative consequences are more likely if performance is overrated than if underrated), but the finding described above seems to point toward deliberate and conscious distortion in self-appraisal.

One interpretation of the inflation of self-ratings is in terms of a self-serving bias (Mitchell, Green, & Wood, 1981), which might occur in situations where the rater has a direct interest in receiving high ratings (e.g., where ratings are used to make promotion decisions). Attribution theory presents another explanation. At one time attribution researchers believed that people tend to explain the behavior of others in terms of internal causes (e.g., ability or effort) but tend to explain their own behavior in terms of external causes (e.g., luck or situational constraints). This phenomenon was referred to as the "fundamental attribution error" (Jones & Nisbett, 1971). Although no longer regarded as universal or fundamental, this tendency may still explain the leniency of self-ratings. Individuals tend to be aware of and make allowance for the external factors that cause them to perform poorly. Thus a person might explain away his or her own poor performance (i.e., give lenient ratings) much more readily than when evaluating the performance of others.

Self-ratings are usually higher than ratings obtained from others, but this is not always the case (Farh, Dobbins, & Cheng [1991] and Yu & Murphy [1993] present cross-cultural studies of modesty in self-rating). Yammarino and Atwater (1993) note that the consequences of self-other disagreements may depend on the direction of the difference. They distinguish between overestimators and underestimators. Overestimators, who rate themselves more favorably than they are rated by others, are common, but there are also those who underestimate others' evaluations. On the whole, the consequences of underestimating your performance are probably less severe than the problems encountered when you overestimate your performance or worth. Underestimators probably miss some opportunities, but overestimators encounter a much wider range of negative consequences (e.g., dissatisfaction with pay and promotions, distrust of supervisors, lack of acceptance of organizational rules and procedures, low commitment) as a result of distorted views of their own performance.

Although self-ratings may not be entirely trustworthy, there is still an argument for including the target individual as one source of information about the individual's behavior at work. The target individual clearly has access to information about his or her behavior and is probably well informed about the results of those behaviors. However, concerns regarding the leniency of self-ratings might also apply to self-generated descriptions of behavior. Research has clearly shown that the evaluation of the person being observed affects the behaviors that are attended to and recorded in diaries (cf. Balzer, 1986). Although this research has been conducted in settings where one individual evaluates another, this effect may also be present in self-evaluations. That is, self-generated descriptions of behavior might represent biased samples that contain too many positive and too few negative behaviors. This bias may exist even where there are no conscious efforts on the part of the target individual to bias or pad the record.

The considerations outlined above lead us to believe that self-generated descriptions of behavior are not useful as the *sole* source for obtaining information in performance appraisal (although they can be useful when combined with other information). Even when the ratee intends to provide an unbiased record, his or her observations and recollections regarding performance are quite likely to be biased. Although we know of no data linking bias in self-generated behavior records, it stands to reason that the extent of this bias is negatively correlated with performance levels. That is, we would expect the behavior reports of poor workers to be least credible, because they have the most to explain away. A final practical objection to self-generated behavior reports is that, regardless of their accuracy, supervisors will be inclined to disbelieve them. We foresee the potential of a vicious cycle in which supervisors interpret the behavioral records they read in an unfavorable fashion, which leads ratees to inflate their records of good behavior, which causes supervisors to further discount these behavioral records, and so on.

Peers as Sources

Research on peer rating suggests that peers can provide useful information about an individual's performance (Murphy & Cleveland, 1991). A variety of peer rating systems have been studied, and the available research supports the validity of peer ratings (Bernardin & Beatty, 1984; Harris & Schaubroeck, 1988; Kane & Lawler, 1980; Landy & Farr, 1983; Wexley & Klimoski, 1984).

There are three clear advantages of peer ratings. First, peers work more closely with the ratee and may have more opportunities to observe both task and interpersonal behaviors than do non-peers. Second, the presence of peers is less likely to affect the behavior being observed than the presence of supervisors or other external evaluators. When individuals know they are being observed by their supervisors, they are likely to censor their own behavior; peers may obtain a less biased sample of behavior. Third, and perhaps most important, peer ratings can be pooled, which can substantially increase reliability and partially remove idiosyncratic biases of any particular rater (Kenny & Berman, 1980; Murphy, 1982b).

Although peer ratings can be useful, many organizations are reluctant to incorporate input from peers in their performance appraisal systems. The resistance to peer ratings does not seem to be connected to concerns over their psychometric shortcomings. Rather, it appears that the resistance to peer ratings can be traced to two causes: (a) concerns over role reversals, and (b) concerns over distortion. The first issue, role reversals, has been noted earlier. Incorporation of peer ratings changes the power structure of an organization in such a way that people who are at the same level in the formal power hierarchy nevertheless have power over one another.

There are two considerations that lead many managers to conclude that peer ratings will be unduly lenient. First, it is widely believed that the friendship between peers will lead to inflated ratings (Landy & Farr, 1983). In fact, there is little evidence that friendship bias is an important factor, although bias might be a problem if the ratee is aware of individual raters' scores. A second problem, and a potentially more serious one, is range restriction. It is plausible that peers will be unwilling to differentiate good from poor performers in the workgroup for fear of "rocking the boat." Although this problem is no doubt present in some settings, there is not yet sufficient evidence to support or refute the proposition that peer ratings will generally exhibit range restriction. One final potential drawback to the use of peer ratings is that peers tend to be uncomfortable in the role of the rater. There is evidence, however, that peers are more comfortable in the role of rater when peer evaluations are used for developmental purposes than when they are used to make administrative decisions (Murphy & Cleveland, 1991).

The theoretical argument in *favor* of peer rating is suggested by Table 5.2. Because peers often work in close proximity, they have ample opportunity to observe each others' behavior. Wherry's theory of rating cites rater-ratee proximity as one key to accuracy in rating (Wherry & Bartlett, 1982). Thus peers' frequent opportunity to observe task behaviors, interpersonal behaviors, and results may make them a uniquely valuable source. Imada (1982), however, cautions that there is little data to support the assumption that peers' opportunity to observe behavior is related to the accuracy of their judgments. Considerations of the work roles of peers might even suggest that their observations will *not* be the best source of information about a particular individual's performance. We alluded earlier to actor-observer differences and to research showing that people involved in an event will report it differently from people who passively observe the same event (Imada & Hakel, 1977). Peers will often work directly with one another. Thus a co-worker who is at an individual's side all day has an excellent opportunity to observe that individual's behavior but is likely to record different observations than would be obtained from a disinterested passive observer. Note that we said that the behavior records would be different; the empirical evidence does not allow us to say which record would be more accurate or more useful. Peer ratings may vary as a function of the *rater's* performance level as well as the ratee's. Saavedra and Kwun (1993) present evidence that high-performing peers are more discriminating in their ratings than lower-performing workgroup members.

The behavior observed by peers is both quantitatively and qualitatively different from that observed by supervisors and subordinates because peers see more and different behaviors than do other sources. This is particularly true in the domain of interpersonal relations. An individual may be on his or her guard when interacting with superiors or subordinates but is more likely to behave naturally (whatever the person's natural style of interaction) among peers. Peers are also likely to encounter secondhand information about interpersonal behaviors. Colleagues tend to talk about colleagues, and interpersonal issues are likely to be a frequent topic of conversation.

Upper Management as Sources

It is common practice to involve the supervisor's supervisor (and perhaps higher-level superiors) in the performance appraisal process, at least to the extent that they "sign off" on the supervisor's evaluation (Long, 1986). As Table 5.2 suggests, higher-level supervisors and managers are likely to be informed about only a narrow range of behaviors; they may know the results of some tasks but are unlikely to know much about behaviors except in those rare circumstances that behavior is either so effective or so ineffective that it is brought specifically to their attention. However, higher-level supervisors may have a crucial yet indirect role in the behavior-observation process. That is, they are not well equipped to observe behavior, but they can have a significant impact in deciding what to observe.

At the beginning of this chapter, performance was defined as the total set of behaviors that are relevant to the goals of the position. One of the crucial functions of management is to set these goals. Another is to communicate those goals (House, 1971). Upper management can communicate these goals and the set of behaviors that define good performance directly, but this is rare. More frequently, goals and desired behaviors are communicated via the climate and culture of the organization (Koprowski, 1983;

Schneider, 1985). Effective managers and executives will communicate the goals of the organization, the company, and the work unit to organization members. Thus, one indirect indicator of effective upper management might be the extent to which supervisors understand the goals associated with the positions they oversee, and the extent to which they agree in their "theories of the job." If goals are made clear, one might expect that supervisors will look for similar behaviors when evaluating individuals in similar jobs. In an organization where goals are unclear or contradictory, every supervisor might look for different behaviors, and when two supervisors observe the same behavior they might evaluate it differently.

Disagreement Among Sources

Subordinates, peers, the target individual, and supervisors at all levels will have different perspectives when observing the behavior of an individual. This disagreement is neither general nor random: Some sources agree more frequently than others. For example, self-supervisor agreement can be low, but it is moderated by a number of factors, including knowledge of the appraisal system and of the standards imposed by the organization (knowledgeable individuals agree more with their supervisors; Williams & Levy, 1992). Furthermore, there is evidence that subordinates who are members of the supervisor's in-group show higher agreement about evaluations of *other* workgroup members than do out-group members (Lee, 1993). Nevertheless, it seems reasonable to believe that different sources will often disagree. We do not regard this disagreement as a problem to be resolved but rather as an indication of the benefit of multiple sources. If all sources agreed, there would be no reason to collect information from multiple sources (Campbell, 1982).

The potential for disagreement among sources need not be a serious problem. First, the disagreements that are noted in the research literature (e.g., Borman, 1974) are more likely to involve *evaluation* than description. That is, disagreements about whether a behavior was effective or ineffective are more likely than disagreements over what behaviors occurred. Second, and more important, the assumption that disagreements must be reconciled is not necessarily correct. As discussed in Chapter 1, performance appraisals are used for a wide variety of purposes (cf. Cleveland et al., 1989), and information from different sources may not be equally useful for every purpose. Thus information from peers and subordinates may be most useful in evaluating a person's interpersonal interactions, whereas input from upper management might be useful in deciding whether the individual is contributing to the goals of the organization.

Cleveland and colleagues (1989) note that two of the major purposes for performance appraisal are to make distinctions between individuals and to discriminate an individual's strengths from his or her weaknesses. The immediate supervisor is probably best qualified to evaluate overall performance levels; input from higher levels in the organization may be useful in determining which dimensions of performance should be emphasized and which behaviors are or are not valued. *All* sources may have insights regarding an individual's strengths and weaknesses but peers may represent the single best informed source.

Disagreement among sources may depend on the structure of the organization. For example, some organizations have very flat structures with minimal distinctions between levels in the hierarchy, whereas others have very sharply defined authority structures. In comparing the two types of organizations, two conclusions seem sensible: (a) use of sources at multiple levels will be easier in organizations with a very loose, informal structure than in an organization with a rigid power structure; and (b) disagreement among sources is more likely when there is a rigid, hierarchical structure than when the power structure is flat and loosely defined. These two conclusions lead to a third: (c) sharp disagreement between levels will be most often found in organizations whose structure is not amenable to the use of multiple sources. In other words, the higher the chance that multiple sources will be used, the lower the likelihood that they will seriously disagree.

360-Degree Feedback. In recent years, considerable attention has been devoted to the concept of 360-degree feedback, in which information from self-evaluations, supervisors, peers, and subordinates is used as a source of developmental feedback. Recent research on this method of feedback is presented in a special issue of *Human Resource Management* (1993, Vol. 32, No. 2 & 3). Although this type of feedback is usually considered distinct from the formal performance appraisal system, research on this feedback method has obvious implications for performance appraisal systems that incorporate multiple sources of information.

Tornow (1993) notes that disagreement among sources is both common and expected. After all, if peers, supervisors, subordinates, and so forth all had the same things to say about everyone, there would probably be little value in obtaining information from all sources. The implications of this disagreement may be different, however, when the information is used for feedback as opposed to evaluation. In a feedback session, this disagreement is evidence of the fact that different perspectives on your behavior yield different types of information. Thus, in this context, this disagreement represents an opportunity to obtain new and different information. In the context of formal performance appraisal, this disagreement represents a problem to be solved. Even if you average away the differences, the fact that sources disagree means that no single source is "right," and that the average of ratings from multiple sources might incorporate information that the organization decides is "wrong" (e.g., inflated self-ratings).

One surprise in research on 360-degree feedback is the apparent lack of concern with violations of the organizational hierarchy. As we noted earlier in this chapter, top-down evaluation is one of the defining features of hierarchical organization, and violations of this principle (e.g., the use of subordinate ratings) should represent a serious problem. Research on reactions to upward feedback suggests that reactions are not necessarily negative (Bernardin, Dahmus, & Redmon, 1993; Hautaluoma, Jobe, Visser, & Donkersgoed, 1993). However, this research also suggests that the administrative details of upward feedback can substantially affect acceptance of feedback from subordinates. Bernardin et al. (1993) showed that supervisors were generally favorable to upward feedback, but that they were much less supportive when input from subordinates was the *only* source of performance information and feedback. Hautaluoma et al. (1993) studied reactions to several methods of collecting and communicating feedback from subordinates to supervisors. Each of several variations on an upward feedback policy was seen as presenting both risks and benefits, but on the whole attitudes were reasonably positive toward such feedback. A feedback system in which subordinates presented upward feedback as a group (as opposed to one-on-one interactions with their supervisors) was seen as the least risky.

The pattern of results described above is probably true in performance appraisal systems in general. The use of multiple sources is probably less of a problem if information from nontraditional sources is balanced with the more familiar top-down evaluations and if input from nontraditional sources is presented in aggregated form (e.g., as group averages) rather than as individual observations. Even though the use of multiple sources violates the general principle of evaluation flowing downward, there are some aspects of this principle that receive support, even in research on subordinate appraisals. This research suggests that appraisals from sources other than the supervisor must be pooled and balanced with additional sources of information. In contrast, top-down appraisals obtained from a single supervisor are still the norm in the American workplace.

SUMMARY

Throughout this chapter we have noted that information from several sources might be necessary for accurate performance appraisals. Accuracy, however, is not always the ultimate criterion in organizations (see Chapters 1 and 11 in this volume), and even if it is, it may not be worthwhile for the supervisor to devote the time and attention needed to do accurate appraisals.

If performance appraisal is approached from the perspective of a cost-benefit analysis, the supervisor might be well advised *not* to bother with accurate performance appraisals. Mohrman and Lawler (1983) note that there are typically few rewards and many penalties for doing accurate appraisals. Workers are likely to regard a less-than-glowing PA as a punishment (even if it is richly deserved) and honest appraisals are likely to lead to ill will between supervisors and subordinates. This suggests to us that the organization that is truly interested in accurate performance appraisals must do two things.

First, the organization must create conditions that allow for adequate direct observation and a plan for collecting information from other sources that is sensibly related to the purpose(s) of the appraisal. Second, the organization must create conditions in which raters are motivated to seek out and use the information that is needed to form accurate appraisals. The extent to which an organization allows PA to be conducted in a haphazard fashion is a concrete indicator of the importance of accurate performance appraisals.

In creating conditions that allow for adequate observation, organizations might find it useful to ask who *can* do appraisals rather than asking who *should.* The almost universal reliance on the supervisor as the sole source of evaluations may make sense when considered from the perspective of the organizational power hierarchy, but it will not always make sense from the perspective of obtaining accurate evaluations. Thus the first question

that should be asked in evaluating the use of alternative sources in performance appraisal is who has the best opportunity to observe and obtain
information about each individual's performance. If the supervisor does not
have sufficient opportunities to observe, formal and regular channels should
be opened up for obtaining relevant information from other sources.

In creating conditions that motivate raters, more formidable problems
may be faced. First, raters must be buffered from the negative consequences
that are likely to occur if low ratings are given (e.g., deterioration of
interpersonal relationships). Second, some means of assessing the accuracy
of ratings must be established so that accurate raters can be rewarded. This
may be very difficult to do in most organizations because ratings are usually
collected from only one individual (the supervisor) and there is no readily
available standard for evaluating those ratings (Murphy & Balzer, 1989).
Chapters 10 and 11 will examine the problem of evaluating ratings in some
depth. It is sufficient to note here that there are no easy solutions to the
problem of evaluating the accuracy of ratings obtained in organizations.
Our present inability to discriminate inaccurate from accurate raters (and
to reward the latter) may be the most significant barrier to achieving
accuracy in observation, judgment, and rating.

6

Standards for Judging Performance

E*valuation* is a useful term because it makes it clear that judgments about performance (e.g., Is this individual a good, bad, or average worker?) involve *values* as well as objective information. That is, the same behavior may be judged to be very good, very bad, or neutral, depending on the values and standards of the judge. This chapter is concerned with the values and standards that are used in judging performance. In particular, we will discuss how the values that determine performance judgments (i.e., performance standards) are defined, developed, and used and whether different judges (e.g., peers, supervisors) are likely to have different values. As we noted in the preceding chapter, disagreements over the evaluation of what has occurred could result from either disagreements over facts (i.e., different perceptions of what actually happened) or disagreements over values (i.e., different opinions regarding what behaviors are acceptable, good, unacceptable, etc.). This chapter examines the latter perspective.

The term *value* is rarely encountered in research on performance appraisal (PA). (This topic is receiving increasing attention in related areas, however. The *Journal of Value-Based Management* was established to provide an outlet for this research.) There are two related terms that have very similar meanings in this context: *performance standard* and *performance norm*. The term *norm* has a relatively longer history and refers to a somewhat broader range of phenomena. For example, the normative regulation of behavior at work is a research topic that dates back to the Hawthorne studies (Roethlisberger & Dickson, 1939; Sonnenfeld, 1982) and was pursued actively by social psychologists in the 1950s (Dalton, cited in Whyte, 1955; Zaleznik, Christensen, & Roethlisberger, 1958). Hackman and colleagues have integrated research in several areas to present models of normative regulation that consider features of both workgroups and the work environment (Hackman, 1976; Hackman & Morris, 1975; Hackman & Oldham, 1980). Finally, Keller (1983) has explored normative regulation of a specific (and poorly understood) behavior—absenteeism.

Sherif and Sherif (1969) define a norm as "an evaluative scale (e.g., yardstick) designating an acceptable latitude and an objectionable latitude for behavior, activity, events, beliefs, or any other object of concern to members of a social unit" (p. 141). That is, norms represent beliefs about which behaviors are good or bad. Norms have typically been studied as properties of groups; in this context, norms refer to widely shared beliefs about acceptable and unacceptable behaviors (Sherif & Sherif, 1969). However, the concept applies equally well to an individual who is asked to evaluate others' performance (e.g., the supervisor). Understanding an individual's norms regarding good, poor, and average performance is thus one key to understanding evaluative judgments.

The term *performance standard* has essentially the same meaning as *performance norm* (as the latter term is used above). We prefer *standard* for two reasons. First, the term carries less excess meaning than *norm* and thus can be used more precisely to refer to an individual's beliefs about the effectiveness (or goodness, or acceptability) of specific behaviors at work. Second, the term *standard* allows us to establish links to several literatures in which terms such as *norms* would not necessarily be used. For example, cybernetic control theory incorporates the concept of "standard" in describing the feedback loops that control many complex systems (Miller, Galanter, & Pribram, 1960; Taylor, Fisher, & Ilgen, 1984). One such control mechanism is the TOTE (test-operate-test-exit) loop, illustrated in Figure 6.1. A

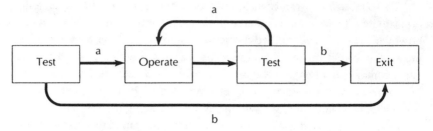

a — system does not match standard

b — system matches standard

Figure 6.1. A TOTE Loop

TOTE loop begins with information about the state of the system, tests that information against a standard, and either adjusts the system or exits the control loop. A thermostat is an example of a mechanism that is built around the TOTE loop.

Control theory has been applied to a variety of behavioral phenomena, including reactions to feedback and self-regulation of behavior (Carver & Scheier, 1981; Taylor et al., 1984). It is directly relevant to several phenomena in performance appraisal, particularly the problem of understanding how raters revise their evaluations of their subordinates (Murphy et al., 1985). Control theory suggests that this revision occurs only when the difference between previous and present performance is sufficiently large to trigger a reevaluation process.

Several models of judgment and evaluation include the assumption that evaluative judgments are made with reference to either implicit or explicit standards (DeCotiis & Petit, 1978; Higgins & Stangor, 1988; Ilgen, 1983; Sherif & Sherif, 1969). The process that is assumed to underlie evaluative judgment is illustrated in Figure 6.2. This figure suggests that evaluation involves (a) the judge's perception of what has occurred (behaviors), (b) the judge's standard(s) for evaluating that domain of behaviors, and (c) a comparison process. Depending on the nature of the standard(s), this comparison could range from a simple matching process, in which the judge scans a set of behaviors to determine whether one or more critical behaviors has occurred, to a complex integration process, in which the judge assigns values to all behaviors and combines those values to reach an evaluation.

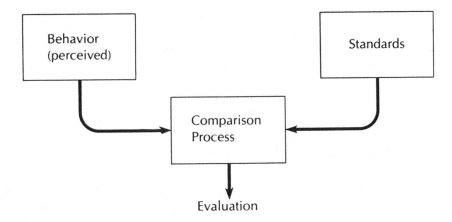

Figure 6.2. The Evaluation Process

The result of this process, the evaluation itself, is a classification of what has occurred (or what the judge perceives to have occurred) on a positive-negative or good-bad continuum.

Evaluations vary in their direction (good vs. bad) and their intensity (indifferent vs. extreme) but nevertheless are fundamentally the same regardless of what or who is being evaluated. That is, all evaluations fall along the same continuum, allowing for meaningful comparisons across persons, tasks, situations, and the like. The universal nature of this general evaluative dimension has been noted in several separate research literatures (Kim & Rosenberg, 1980; Osgood, 1962; Wegner & Vallecher, 1977). In the context of PA, the existence of a single and universal evaluative dimension implies that the consistent scaling of performance is at least theoretically possible. Even though the behavior of different workers may be qualitatively different (in the extreme case, there may be no overlap in actual behaviors), workers can still be meaningfully compared on a common good-bad dimension.

Figure 6.2 suggests two questions that must be answered in order to understand evaluative judgment. First, what do standards look like? In other words, what is the content of a performance standard? To answer this question adequately, we must first discuss types of standards and then discuss the process by which standards develop and change. Second, what is the nature of the comparison process? Are standards simply lined up side by side with behaviors to check for a match, with a negative evaluation resulting when they don't match, or is there a more complex process? Is the product (the evaluation) a function of the type of comparison process followed? These issues are explored in the two sections that follow.

STANDARDS

The specific types of standards that might be used in evaluating performance will vary depending on the job, the work environment, the judge (e.g., self, peer, supervisor), and so on. One useful way of categorizing and describing standards is to separate standards that are explicit and external to the judge from those that are implicit and internal. Thus, standards might range from production goals that are posted in the workplace (e.g., a furniture manufacturer might post the number of chairs a workgroup is expected to assemble each day) to a specific supervisor's definition of what constitutes good, average, and poor performance on a task. These two types of standards are not (or should not be) completely independent. Posted goals may help to define the supervisor's own implicit standards; these standards may be derived in part from the individual standards of the parties who decided on the posted standard. Nevertheless, it is useful to discuss these two types of standards separately. They may involve different behaviors or tasks, may lead to different comparison processes, and may result in very different evaluations of both behaviors and results.

External Standards

External standards for judging performance are those that are explicitly imposed by the organization. These may range from posted production goals to those that are passed on to new supervisors from more experienced members of the organization. These external standards are public rather than private and they exist independently of any particular decision maker.

External standards will often refer to results of performance. Thus a standard may exist that defines the minimum number of units that a worker or a workgroup is required to produce each day. External standards may also refer to behaviors, especially when these standards take the form of *rules*. Rules may exist that define sets of behaviors that are required at work (e.g., dress codes, standard practices) as well as sets of behaviors that are forbidden (e.g., substance abuse policies). In both cases, external standards may allow for simple and straightforward comparison processes. Thus, if a standard defines daily production quotas, evaluation may be a simple matter of comparing actual production to the quota. If standards define behaviors that are either required or forbidden, evaluation may be a simple matter of comparing the actual behaviors to the behaviors that are cited in the rules. It is important to note, however, that external standards do not guarantee that the comparison process that leads to an evaluation will be a simple one.

External standards are most likely to lead to simple comparison processes when the standards are concrete and specific and when the work environment is sufficiently stable to allow the consistent application of those standards. For example, standards may identify broad categories of acceptable behaviors (e.g., "appropriate attire will be worn at all times") or may specify the exact behaviors that are expected (e.g., "all employees will report to work by 8:30"). Standards that leave room for interpretation will necessarily also require more complex comparison processes. To apply a standard such as "appropriate attire will be worn at all times," the judge must first decide what constitutes appropriate attire. Depending on the latitude of the individual judge's definition of appropriate attire, the same behavior could be evaluated positively or negatively.

Even when standards are highly concrete and specific, the work environment may complicate their application. Environmental constraints may make it impossible to meet a specific standard. On the other hand, environmental opportunities may make it necessary or useful to adjust a previously defined standard. Standards may thus be set that determine sales quotas for a particular product. If the product suddenly becomes part of a consumer trend, demand may skyrocket and new standards will be needed to define good, poor, and adequate sales. The issue of adjusting standards to take into account environmental constraints and opportunities will be examined in the section of this chapter that deals with the comparison processes.

Standards need not refer to specific behaviors or results but could refer to *distributions* of behaviors and results (Kane & Lawler, 1979). That is, standards could define tolerances, in the sense that they refer to ideal outcomes, but also specify the extent to which deviations from the ideal are tolerated. Thus, a standard might define a specific level of output as "normal" and might also define a range of output levels that are treated as equivalent to normal. Performance that exceeds or falls below this range could possibly trigger rewards or sanctions.

Bobko and Colella (1994) note that standards are related to, but conceptually distinct from, goals. First, standards represent a tool for evaluation. That is, once an explicit definition of "acceptable performance" is defined, the performance of individuals or groups can be evaluated against this standard. Second, standards are not directly related to the individual's motivation to perform, whereas goals represent a key concept in several theories of motivation (Locke & Latham, 1990). Externally imposed standards might lead to or affect the nature of goals, particularly if the individual accepts the performance standard as reasonable. Goals and standards are clearly different, however, in the sense that goals are internalized whereas standards are externally imposed.

Bobko and Colella (1994) suggest that several characteristics of standards are likely to affect the degree to which they are accepted and incorporated into goals. In particular, standards that are clear, do not conflict with other standards, are tied to rewards, and that foster a sense of achievement are more likely to be accepted than those that do not show most or any of these characteristics. These standards might involve comparisons between persons (e.g., ranking within workgroup) or comparison to external goals (e.g., MBO; Ilgen & Schneider, 1991).

Participation in the process of setting standards probably increases their acceptability (similar findings have been reported in the goal-setting literature: Locke & Latham, 1990; Locke, Shaw, Saari, & Latham, 1981). Finally, it is important that standards be established in advance, communicated clearly, and explained to the individuals affected (Folger, Konovsky, & Cropanzano, 1992).

The lack of clear performance standards is one of the most frequent complaints in evaluating performance appraisal systems (Longenecker & Goff, 1992). This complaint even applies to MBO systems, which appear to incorporate specific, measurable goals. As we have noted earlier, the definition of "job performance" usually includes a wide range of behaviors, only some of which are likely to be captured in an MBO system.

Setting Standards. There are several processes that might be used in defining external performance standards. Specific standards are often defined in applications of human factors psychology and industrial engineering (Alluisi & Morgan, 1976; Campbell, 1983). Here, performance standards define optimal levels of functioning for the system for which standards are derived or defined. One industrial engineering concept that is broadly relevant to PA is that optimal standards are not necessarily the highest standards. The industrial engineering perspective suggests that one criterion for evaluating performance ratings may involve determining the degree to which the implicit and explicit standards that are used for evaluating performance are appropriate for a work situation in which they are applied.

Time-and-motion studies are often used to determine both work standards and the optimal procedures for achieving those standards. This method simultaneously defines standards for results (i.e., output levels) and behaviors (i.e., standard procedures to be followed). Although Taylor's system of scientific management (which relied heavily on time-and-motion studies) was regarded by many as a method that dehumanized work and exploited workers, it is useful to remember that Taylor's system was designed primarily to aid the worker. By carefully following the procedures that resulted from a time-and-motion study, workers could increase their output without increasing levels of exertion or effort. This increase in output would presumably lead to higher pay (especially where piece-rate systems are employed) and thus would maximize the benefit to both employers and employees.

The notion of standard operating procedures permeates the armed services, especially when applied to tasks that are carried out by enlisted personnel. Detailed manuals exist that describe standard methods for performing a wide variety of tasks (e.g., engine maintenance), and the evaluation of performance can depend on the extent to which standard procedures were followed, irrespective of the results actually obtained. Checklists comparing actual work methods to standard methods have been developed to provide "hands on" measures of job performance in the military (Green & Wigdor, 1988; Hakel, 1986; Wigdor & Green, 1991).

In the private sector, manuals that define standard procedures are common in a wide variety of repair occupations. Although deviations from standard procedures are not often used in assessing performance in the private sector, the question of whether standard procedures were followed is likely to be highly salient if a repair fails or if attempts to repair a problem only make things worse.

Standards are often set through negotiation, particularly when unions or other bargaining units are involved. Some of the issues that are likely to be negotiated as part of a union contract include the following (Saal & Knight, 1988):

- Determining disciplinary procedures
- Scheduling of work and overtime
- Determining work methods
- Determining production rates

Each of these defines a particular standard. Negotiations over disciplinary procedures determine what types and levels of behavior can be the focus for official sanctions, what time frames apply in applying discipline (e.g., maximum time that can elapse between the infraction and the response), and what procedures will be followed to determine whether discipline is required or allowed for specific incidents. Negotiations regarding schedules and overtime might determine both actual working hours and the degree of latitude in determining whether schedules are met (e.g., how late an employee has to be to be classified as late). Negotiations over work methods might determine the standard procedures that are followed.

In general, it is in management's interest to devise procedures that are labor efficient, whereas it is in the union's interest to devise procedures that are labor intensive. Here, the optimal set of work procedures may be those that achieve the best working compromise between these incompatible goals. Finally, production rates may be determined by negotiation and may be set in a way that maximizes benefits for both management and the union.

The processes of goal setting and Management by Objectives (MBO) involve creating explicit standards through negotiation, albeit not in the formal, adversarial mode that is typical of negotiations between management and unions. MBO often involves a process in which the employee proposes a set of standards or goals that will define performance on his or her job, the supervisor reviews the goals and suggests revisions (if needed), and the two parties negotiate to reach a set of mutually agreeable goals (Szilagyi & Wallace, 1983).

External Standards and Performance Judgments

Although research on external standards and performance judgments is lacking, it seems likely that external performance standards will deal with minimally acceptable levels of results and performance-related behaviors (Carroll & Schneier, 1982). For example, rules are likely to spell out in great detail the behaviors that are not acceptable, yet define the set of acceptable behaviors vaguely, if at all. Similarly, rules regarding production rates are more likely to specify the minimum acceptable level of production than they are to specify a maximum beyond which further production is not allowed. Manuals that describe standard procedures are perhaps an exception, in that they concentrate explicitly on what behaviors *are* required, but with this exception it seems reasonable to conclude that external standards will concentrate only on the breakpoint that separates acceptable from unacceptable performance.

The inference that can be drawn from this assumption is that external standards may often result in binary evaluation, in which workers are classified as either unacceptable or acceptable. This last category might better be labeled "not unacceptable." The point is, if external standards concentrate mainly on minimum performance levels, they may not be useful for the large number of workers who are not unacceptable. We will return to this point in our discussion of comparison processes.

Internal Standards

External standards may represent valuable information for determining performance evaluations, but they are generally not sufficient to account for judgments. As discussed earlier, the process of performance evaluation is one in which behavior is compared to some set of values. Some of these values are likely to be implicit and particular to the individual who is judging another's performance.

Figure 6.3 illustrates three factors that will influence the implicit, internal standards that are used to evaluate performance. First, the figure suggests that the effect of explicit external standards on individual judgments is indirect. That is, it is assumed that judgment occurs when behavior is compared to internal standards, which are in turn affected by the external standards defined by the organization. The influence of external standards on judgment may depend to a large extent on the degree to which the supervisor identifies with and internalizes the values of the organization (Mowday et al., 1981). Supervisors who are highly committed to the organization may form internal standards that conform to and build upon the external standards of the organization. Supervisors who are not committed or who do not view their superiors as credible sources for standards may form standards of their own that do not correspond at all to external standards that are defined by the organization.

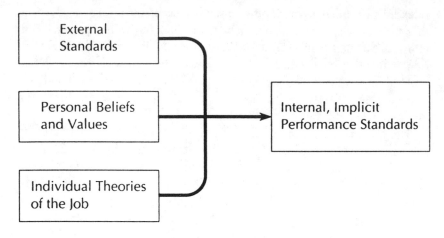

Figure 6.3. Factors That Influence Internal Standards

Personal values and beliefs are likely to influence implicit performance norms and standards. Most workers and supervisors have well-developed ideas of what constitutes a "fair day's work" (Dalton, cited in Whyte, 1955; Zaleznik et al., 1958). These ideas reflect the individuals' opinions about the amount of effort and production that should be exchanged for the pay and benefits associated with the job. General beliefs about human nature are likely to affect both the standards themselves and their application (Wexley & Youtz, 1985). For example, popular theories of management describe two sets of assumptions about human behavior that are likely to affect the choice of a leadership style (McGregor, 1960). Managers who subscribe to *Theory X* believe that workers are inherently lazy and that they must be motivated by external rewards and closely supervised in order to achieve acceptable levels of performance. Managers who subscribe to *Theory Y* believe that workers are intrinsically motivated and that they will respond most readily to challenges and opportunities for growth at work. A *Theory X* manager is likely to have a detailed, strict set of standards and is likely to give very low evaluations to behaviors that deviate from those standards. A *Theory Y* manager is likely to have standards that allow for greater latitude in behavior and that are less punitive with regard to behaviors that deviate from those standards.

Borman's (1987) research on "folk theories" of the job suggests a third influence on internal standards. Each judge may have a unique theory of what is and is not important on the job. Because norms and standards are generally developed only for important behaviors and results (Hackman, 1976; Sherif & Sherif, 1969), the judge's theory of the job may have a profound impact on implicit performance standards. Individual theories of the job will influence the levels of performance standards as well as their content. Thus, the level of performance in some specific area that is viewed as acceptable may depend on the judge's implicit theory of how the job is structured and how it is performed.

In discussing the cognitive requirements for accurate evaluations of performance, Feldman (1986) uses the concept of "performance model" to describe the standards that are used in evaluating performance on different tasks. This performance model defines reference points for evaluation; the nature of the task, in turn, defines the nature of the model. In Feldman's (1986) taxonomy, the methods appropriate for appraising tasks are classified as analytic, intuitive, and quasi-rational.

In analytic performance appraisal, standards are defined in terms of a small number of concrete behaviors or outcomes, and performance can be judged in terms of deviations from that concrete standard. In intuitive appraisal, standards are part of the raters' abstract task schema or their implicit theory of the task. Tasks in which several different procedures might lead to the same outcome or in which outcomes cannot be clearly ranked on a common evaluative scale are likely to be evaluated in an intuitive fashion. Feldman (1986) notes that the implicit theories that define the standards used in intuitive appraisal may vary considerably from judge to judge, and that measures of interrater agreement may say more about the extent to which judges share common task schema than about the extent to which they agree in their perceptions of ratees' behavior.

Quasi-rational PA represents a middle ground between analytic and intuitive methods of appraisal. Quasi-rational appraisal characterizes tasks in which performance cannot be fully described using a simple, objective model, but where objective standards partially define performance. Feldman (1986) suggests that most performance appraisals are examples of quasi-rational judgment tasks. One implication is that the standards that drive most performance appraisals are likely to include a mix of objective and highly subjective standards. Although the behavioral components of these standards may be defined objectively, it is likely that there will be no well-defined performance model for integrating that behavioral information in most PA applications.

One result of the quasi-rational nature of most performance appraisals is that there is room for honest disagreement. That is, all quasi-rational appraisal tasks incorporate at least some standards that represent the subjective values of individual raters. Chapter 5 stated that different sources (e.g., peers vs. supervisors) might observe different behaviors. Later in this chapter, we will take up the question of whether these sources are also likely to have different standards. One implication of potentially different standards is that a subordinate may view your performance as good, you might view it as average, your superior might view it as poor, and you all might be right. Because evaluation is ultimately a value judgment, differences in evaluation are not necessarily a sign of inaccuracy.

The preceding discussion suggests that the organization has a legitimate interest in trying to develop consistent standards among those who will evaluate other workers' performance. In part this can be accomplished if (a) supervisors identify closely with the organization and (b) the organization is able to articulate clear and consistent objective standards and work procedures. Another possible strategy for inducing common standards has been suggested in research on rater training. Frame-of-reference training is designed to provide all raters with a common set of standards regarding (a) which behaviors are most and least relevant for defining performance and (b) the effectiveness of each of these behaviors (Borman, 1979). Feldman's (1986) analysis suggests that frame-of-reference training will represent only a partial solution to the problem of developing common standards. The problem with frame-of-reference training is that it applies most readily to analytic tasks. Knowing the relevant behaviors and their respective values will not be enough to ensure consistency in a quasi-rational task, because a model to integrate those behaviors cannot be specified a priori. We will take up the question of either trying to change people's standards, norms, and goals or tailoring the appraisal system to existing norms and goals in Chapter 14.

Yet another approach to developing consistent standards can be derived from research conducted at McGill University in the 1950s (Webster, 1964). Researchers noted that interviewers made their decisions by comparing each applicant to their stereotype of an ideal applicant (i.e., their standard). Rather than trying to teach interviewers not to rely on stereotypes, the researchers suggested training interviewers to adopt a common, valid stereotype. In the parlance of social cognition, this suggestion boils down to providing a prototype that all interviewers can use to represent the category "good applicant." In performance appraisal, specific workers (or perhaps a hypothetical composite of several specific workers) might be held up as a common standard. The practicality of this strategy will depend on an organization's ability to locate individuals who clearly are good workers and whose behavior is well known to many raters, which may represent a tall order. Nevertheless, we think that this strategy has sufficient theoretical and empirical support to warrant further research.

Development of Standards

The process by which internal, implicit standards for evaluating performance are developed is poorly understood. For example, it is well known that some judges have unusually high standards and that others have unusually low standards (this disparity in standards may explain rater errors such as leniency/severity), but very little is known about *why* some judges are harsh and others are lenient (Vroom, 1969). Similarly, it is well known that standards can vary over time, but little is known about the circumstances under which they are likely to vary or to remain constant.

Standards refer to a wide range of phenomena; they may be tied to tasks, goals, behaviors, or results (Dornbusch & Scott, 1975; Lee, 1985). It is likely that different processes are responsible for the development of different types of standards. Objective methods such as time-and-motion studies or work sampling may provide information that affects analytic (vs. intuitive) standards (Carroll & Schneier, 1982), but many standards will refer to tasks in which objective definitions of "good" are effectively impossible. There is a need, then, to study the psychological processes by which these standards are formed.

There is little empirical work dealing directly with performance standards. There is, however, a substantial body of research dealing with a closely related topic—the development of norms—that can be used to identify processes that are likely to be involved in the development of performance standards. For example, we know that norms usually develop gradually (Hackman, 1976, 1992), although unusual events can trigger the quick development of a new norm (Sherif & Sherif, 1969). The same probably applies to performance standards. We also know that norms are highly resistant to change; research in both the lab and the field has shown that norms can be transmitted across generations, in the sense that a group norm may continue to influence behavior even after all of the group members who originally generated the norm have left the group (Jacobs & Campbell, 1961; Sherif & Sherif, 1969). If performance standards are somehow communicated from rater to rater, the same phenomenon may occur. That is, the organization's current standard for defining adequate performance may reflect the dead hand of history, in that it may be the result of standards that were set and articulated by supervisors who are no longer part of the organization.

Research on the development of norms suggests four mechanisms through which performance standards might be developed: (a) direct communication, (b) observation of reference groups, (c) direct experience, and (d) extension of values, attitudes, and beliefs from other domains.

Direct Communication. If taken literally, the implicit-explicit distinction would suggest that implicit standards cannot be communicated directly from one person to another. Although it may be impossible to communicate implicit standards in all of their details, the essence of these standards can probably be communicated quite clearly (Taylor et al., 1984). The popular literature on corporate culture suggests one medium for communicating performance standards—through corporate myths and stories. Thus, a widely told story about an especially effective (or ineffective) worker might serve to establish a prototype, and future workers may be evaluated in comparison to that prototype. Although the prototype may be widely shared, each judge will fill in whatever missing information is needed to flesh out the performance standard in a potentially unique manner. The same myth or story will not necessarily lead to the same standard for all judges.

Taylor and colleagues (1984) suggest that performance feedback can change the evaluation standards of the *recipient*. This is particularly likely when (a) the recipient has not formed a well-developed standard for evaluating that aspect of performance, (b) the feedback comes from a credible source, and (c) the feedback is repeated. Under these conditions, the performance feedback will define a standard for both self-evaluations and for evaluations of the performance of the recipient's performance.

Direct, explicit communication of performance standards (i.e., one person directly telling another what the standards are) is most likely when the recipient of this information is new to the organization. Experienced members of the organization may take on the formal or informal role of mentor and trainer; part of their job in socializing new members of the organization will be to communicate performance standards (Van Maanen, 1976). New employees are also the most likely to inquire directly about performance standards. Research on group norms suggests that allowances are typically made for newcomers' lack of knowledge of relevant norms (Sherif & Sherif, 1969). Thus, although it would be inappropriate for an established member of the group to inquire about important norms, this behavior would be tolerated and even encouraged for newcomers.

A variant on direct communication of standards is the situation in which organization members directly observe the *application* of those standards. Thus, if a rater publicly communicates his or her evaluation of a set of behaviors, this also communicates information about performance standards. If a highly credible judge publicly expresses approval or disapproval of certain behaviors (or allows his or her evaluations to become known), this may influence the performance standards of other judges. This is part of the rationale that is often cited when the organization (or some individual) decides to make an example of a particular employee. For instance, many organizations have programs for formally and publicly recognizing the "employee of the month" (or week or year). The main purpose of these programs is to motivate and reward employees, but they may serve the subsidiary purpose of establishing and clarifying performance standards. The supervisor who knows that the chosen employee is always an individual who shows initiative in dealing with customers is likely to incorporate "initiative in dealing with customers" as a dimension of his or her performance standard.

Informal communication among supervisors represents another channel for exchanging information about standards. Even if conversations among supervisors never directly address theories of the job or the values attached to different behaviors, results, or performance, they are likely to convey information about evaluation. This is conjecture, but we think it is likely that supervisors will occasionally talk about their best and worst employees. These conversations will certainly convey information about supervisors' standards and may help to establish some consensus regarding performance standards.

Finally, ratees are likely to seek information about performance standards (Ashford & Cummings, 1983). Therefore, one should not think of communication about standards as unidirectional (i.e., from supervisor to subordinate), but rather must also consider the subordinate's role in eliciting feedback about performance standards.

Reference Groups. Research on social norms suggests that these norms are often formed by incorporating some features of a particular reference group. In this context, a reference group is a group or person with which an individual identifies (Sherif & Sherif, 1969). Individuals adopt and internalize the norms of their reference groups, particularly when these groups are highly attractive. An individual typically belongs or aspires to belong to the reference group.

In the context of performance appraisal, the reference group is likely to represent individuals who are at the same or higher organizational level as the judge; the hierarchical nature of organizations implies that judges will not aspire to belong to groups at subordinate levels. Reference group research suggests that a judge will adopt standards that are similar to those he or she believes are held by the appropriate reference groups. For example, a supervisor may believe that managers higher in the organization have higher, more demanding standards. If that supervisor aspires to move up in the organization, reference group theory predicts that he or she will give harsh evaluations. This analysis suggests that some instances of inappropriate standards (e.g., leniency error in rating) may represent a combination of faulty diagnoses of the reference group's standards and ambition. The more ambitious the judge (i.e., the more he or she aspires to move up in the organization), the more critical the judge's accuracy in diagnosing the standards that are held by higher management.

The concept of comparison groups is related to that of reference groups, which suggests another mechanism by which performance standards may be formed. A comparison group is a group that is seen by the judge to be similar to the person being evaluated. This comparison group may be co-workers or contemporaries of the person being evaluated or may be made up of workers whom the supervisor has observed in the past. This comparison group may even be idealized, in the sense that it is made up of the judge's prototypes of different categories of workers. Regardless of its nature, the comparison group may define a performance standard, and the target individual's standing relative to that group may determine his or her evaluation. In particular, Haberstroh (1965) suggested that evaluations might be done by comparing an individual to the best performer in a comparison group. Thus, the difference between a target individual's performance and the performance of the best worker in the comparison group may define how far the target individual is from the top of the judge's evaluative scale.

Both reference and comparison groups have their greatest influence on the development of standards for evaluating performance on novel tasks (Lewin, Dembo, Festinger, & Sears, 1944). One reason for this is that judges are unlikely to establish firm standards for tasks they have never or rarely encountered and thus may have to rely on external sources for standards. Observation of comparison groups provides information about the range of performance that might be encountered in a novel task. There may even be reference groups in the organization for whom a particular task is *not* a novel one, and the judge may adopt that group's standards for evaluating the performance of his or her subordinates.

The choice of reference groups seems to depend more on characteristics of the judge (e.g., personality, motivational variables, etc.) than on characteristics of the situation (Oldham, Kulik, Stepina, & Ambrose, 1986). This suggests that the study of reference and comparison groups could provide an indirect method of studying a supervisor's "theory of the job" (Borman, 1987). For example, the composition of a comparison group chosen by a supervisor provides a concrete illustration of the jobs that are regarded by the supervisor as similar to that of the target individual.

Consider the case illustrated in Figure 6.4, in which two college deans are asked to nominate a comparison group for evaluating the performance of an associate professor of biology. Dean A chooses all associate professors from the natural sciences. Dean B chooses all biology faculty. Neither dean chooses faculty from the History Department. These choices would suggest that Dean A's theory of the job emphasizes rank and general area (e.g., natural science vs. humanities and social science) as relevant dimensions for defining the job. Dean B has a theory of the job in which the discipline or department (i.e., biology) is the most salient defining feature. Sociometric methods have long been used to describe structural characteristics of groups (Cartwright & Zander, 1968). These same methods might be useful for inquiring into the theory of the jobs that leads to the formation of these groups.

Studying comparison groups may provide valuable information about the supervisor's theory of the jobs he or she is evaluating. Studying the reference group whose norms and standards the supervisor adopts may provide information about the supervisor's theory of his or her *own* job. Does the supervisor identify with line or with staff? Does the supervisor identify with his or her own level or with higher levels of the organization? Answering questions like these may provide information about their supervisors'

Figure 6.4. Comparison Groups for Evaluating an Associate Professor of Biology

career aspirations as well as their visions of where their current jobs fit in the grand scheme of things.

Direct Experience. Supervisors' standards for evaluating performance may arise as a result of their own experience with the job or tasks they are evaluating (Ilgen, 1983). It is not uncommon for supervisors to rise through the ranks and to supervise workers in jobs they once held. This is probably more common for first-level supervisors than for middle- and upper-level managers, but, in general, it is likely that a supervisor will have some experience in the tasks he or she is asked to evaluate.

There are several reasons to believe that direct experience in carrying out the tasks one is asked to evaluate will lead to the development of somewhat inflated standards and expectations. First, supervisors are probably not chosen at random; individuals who are chosen to supervise are more likely to be superior performers than to be inferior or average performers. The supervisor who uses his or her own performance as the standard and who expects the same level of performance from all subordinates is likely to be disappointed.

Second, research on self-ratings (see Chapter 5) suggests that these ratings are inflated. One possibility is that to maintain positive self-images, individuals attend more carefully to their own positive behaviors, remember those behaviors more readily, and give those behaviors more weight when integrating them to form self-evaluations. (Research on the cognitive principles involved in evaluation is reviewed at length in DeNisi & Williams [1988] and in Ilgen & Feldman [1983].) Attribution research suggests that people will explain away the negative instances they *do* remember and will overestimate the frequency and importance of the positive ones (Jones & Nisbett, 1971). The net effect of this cognitive distortion is that supervisors are likely to view their own experience through rose-colored glasses and are likely to overestimate how well they actually *did* perform. When a subordinate shows exactly the same behaviors as were previously shown by the supervisor himself or herself, the supervisor is likely to perceive that behavior as worse than the standard set by the supervisor's past performance.

When the supervisor has no direct experience with the task itself, indirect or vicarious experience may still play a role in establishing standards. First, standards may be set on the basis of precedent (Dornbusch & Scott, 1975), which may be viewed as the accumulated experience of previous supervisors. As noted earlier, standards can be acquired from reference groups. It is possible that a supervisor chooses reference groups on the basis of their experience and thus indirectly inherits the results of their experience.

Vicarious experience may be obtained by forming a mental image of how the task is performed (Kosslyn, 1980). This image may be the product of the rater's theory of the job or performance schemata (Borman, 1987; Foti, 1988); his or her training (e.g., through viewing training films); his or her implicit theories of human behavior (Krystofiak, Cardy, & Newman, 1988); or job descriptions, procedure manuals, or observations of others performing the task. Once an image of how the task should be performed is created, that image may serve as a standard for evaluating the performance of others.

Experience in evaluation (as opposed to experience with the task) may itself lead to the development and crystallization of standards. Lorenzo (1984) noted that participation as an assessor in an assessment center increased managers' ability to record and evaluate behavioral information accurately and increased their effectiveness in communicating that information. One possibility is that having to judge others and to defend those judgments forces managers to develop specific, well-articulated standards.

Extending a bit on this line of reasoning suggests that highly experienced supervisors may have more detailed and more realistic standards than new supervisors. As we will discuss later (see Chapter 9), this tendency may be strongest in organizations that attempt to reward accurate appraisals. Supervisors who receive feedback about the accuracy of their appraisals will have a chance to test the adequacy of their standards. By receiving feedback from other parts of the organization about the performance of their subordinates, raters have a potentially unique chance to determine whether their standards are similar to the standards of others.

Values, Attitudes, and Beliefs. The values, attitudes, and beliefs of supervisors represent yet another source for performance standards. At the most basic level, different standards might be expected from a supervisor who subscribes strongly to the *Protestant Work Ethic (PWE)* than from one who does not. This value system emphasizes (among other things) hard work and dedication. A subordinate who achieves very good results through what appears to be a lackadaisical approach might be evaluated harshly by a strong proponent of the PWE.

Dickson and Buchholz (1977) describe five different sets of general beliefs about work that characterized the values of managers in the United States and Scotland. These belief systems are described in Table 6.1. Subsequent research by Buchholz (1978) and by Mora (1985) suggests that these beliefs generalize to other occupational groups (e.g., blue-collar workers) and cultures (i.e., Venezuela).

As noted above, belief in the PWE is likely to lead to performance standards that emphasize activity and effort. The *organizational* belief system, on the other hand, might lead to performance standards that emphasize the interpersonal dimensions of job performance (see Chapter 5). A worker who does not fit in well with the workgroup may be evaluated harshly by a supervisor who subscribes to the organizational belief system.

A *humanistic* belief system may lead the supervisor to develop performance standards that emphasize the tendency to seek challenge and growth through work. A worker who does his or her job but shows little or no intrinsic interest in the work itself or in the challenges posed by solving problems at work, might be evaluated harshly by a supervisor whose work beliefs are humanistic; this same worker might be favorably evaluated by a supervisor who accepts the PWE. The *Marxist* belief system might lead supervisors to emphasize the political dimensions of work. A worker who

TABLE 6.1   Five Work Belief Systems

Belief	Description
Protestant work ethic	Hard work is good in itself and bestows dignity on the person. Success is linked to one's own efforts.
Organizational	Work derives its meaning from the workgroup and organization. Work is a source of fulfillment through belongingness.
Humanistic	Work is meaningful if it is designed to fulfill higher-order needs.
Marxist	Workers are alienated from their activity and exploited by the ownership class. Workers should strive for more control.
Leisure	Work has no meaning itself, but provides money and resources for leisure. The less work, the better.

shows little interest in the class struggle might be evaluated more nega-tively than one who is actively involved in efforts to redistribute power to the workers. The *leisure* belief system might lead supervisors to give low ratings to workers who show too much interest in and enthusiasm for their jobs. (The Marxist and leisure belief systems are less common among U.S. managers than among other groups [e.g., other countries, labor, etc.] [see Mora, 1985].)

We noted earlier that most workers have a very specific idea of what represents a "fair day's work." The determination of what is fair probably depends on a combination of highly stable values and attitudes toward the organization. Equity theory (Adams, 1965) predicts that the determination of what is fair will depend in part on a person's perceptions of how he or she is treated by the organization. The organization distributes or controls a wide range of rewards (e.g., pay, promotion, opportunities to interact with co-workers), some of which are highly valued and some of which are not. An individual's own standard for what represents a fair exchange will depend on the perceived value of the rewards, his or her perception of the organization's policy for distributing those rewards, and the perceived value of the effort that he or she expends to achieve these rewards. A supervisor who places a high value on wages may develop an increasingly strict standard for evaluating performance as wages increase. A supervisor who believes that workers' efforts are not closely connected to the rewards they receive may develop more lenient and more flexible standards.

Values are often widely shared among organization members. In fact, it can be argued that the primary purpose of organizational socialization is to instill a common set of values in new members of the organization (Van Maanen, 1976). These shared values can directly affect PA, in that raters may use appraisals to attain valued outcomes (Bjerke et al., 1987). These shared values probably also affect appraisals indirectly, via their influence on performance standards. For example, in the navy, operational (i.e., warfare) skills and activities are most highly valued, and officers are evaluated according to those skills, even if the job is predominantly administrative (Bjerke et al., 1987). Not only are certain skills and performance areas emphasized over others (regardless of their relevance to the current job), it is also likely that the standards for evaluating performance in these areas are both stricter and less flexible. We noted earlier that norms are likely to be developed only for behaviors and tasks that are important. Values tell you what is and is not important.

Precision of Standards

Organizational researchers have noted that performance standards are often ambiguous and poorly defined (French & Caplan, 1973; Kahn & Quinn, 1970). Ambiguity of standards has been cited as a leading source of job stress (Kahn, Wolf, Quinn, Snoeck, & Rosenthal, 1964). The typical explanations for ambiguity in performance standards suggest that (a) supervisors have well-developed standards but do not communicate them effectively or (b) several persons evaluate an individual's work and they do not all share the same standard. Stress could result from not knowing what the standard is or not knowing which standard to apply.

Feldman's (1986) analysis suggests a third possibility. For tasks in which evaluation is wholly or partially intuitive, standards may be inherently unstable and imprecise. That is, there may be no fixed standard for evaluating performance on certain tasks. It is useful to make a distinction between shifting standards and shifting evaluations. The same behavior might be evaluated differently if exhibited by different persons, at different times, or in different environments without necessarily indicating shifting standards. It is possible that the standard stays constant but that the comparison process changes over ratees, tasks, environments, and so on. The subjective, intuitive nature of many performance standards suggests, however, that they may not always be fixed, stable quantities.

We know little about precisely how standards develop, and even less about why some standards might be invariant and others may shift. An analogy from psychometric theory helps in understanding the conditions under which standards might be highly stable and precise versus those in which standards are inherently unstable and imprecise. The classic theory of psychometrics suggests that observed scores can be broken down into true scores and random errors of measurement. More modern theories (e.g., generalizability theory, theories for imperfectly parallel tests; see Cronbach, Gleser, Nanda, & Rajaratnam, 1972; Lord & Novick, 1968) suggest a breakdown similar to this:

$$X = T + S + e$$

where:
X = observed score
T = true component
S = systematic error variance
e = random measurement error

In the context of standards,
X = standard that is actually applied
T = the part of the standard that is stable
S = systematic variation in the standard over time, occasions, ratees, and so on
e = random variation in the standard

The first and most obvious issue is the relative size of T, S, and e for standards of different types. Standards that are inherently stable will have small values for both S and e. Second, it is not clear whether e is always a relevant concept when applied to standards. Are the standards a person carries around in his or her head subject to some degree of random variation? If so, what is the explanation for that variation? If e exists at all in this context, is it a facet of the standard (e.g., some standards are unreliable), the person (e.g., some persons are unstable), or both? Does S exist in this context? If so, what are the facets over which one would expect systematic variation? Some possibilities have already been cited (ratees, occasions, tasks, environments). Are there others?

The precision of standards is an important topic for the simple reason that it places an upper bound on the precision of judgments, which in turn may affect the accuracy of performance ratings (although ratings do not always directly reflect judgments). In diagnosing inaccurate judgments, it is important to assess the potential role of (a) inaccurate perceptions of behavior, (b) unstable standards, and (c) improper comparison procedures. The first topic has been examined extensively but the other two topics have received little attention. We think there is a clear need for more research on the precision and stability of performance standards.

The final issue we wish to pursue in this section is the question of whether subordinates and supervisors are likely to have different standards. In general, the answer seems to be yes (Long, 1986). Supervisors and subordinates clearly disagree in their assessments of subordinate perform-ance (see Chapter 5). Although this may in part be due to different percep-tions of behavior, it is probably also due to differing standards.

Socialization processes can explain some of the differences in standards between supervisors and subordinates. It is well known that the norms and standards of new members of the organization differ from those of more established members (Schein & Ott, 1962; Van Maanen, 1975), and that socialization processes are designed to reduce these differences. The same phenomena no doubt occur at different *strata* in the organization. That is, new members of the upper strata (e.g., supervisors) are likely to take on the norms and standards of that stratum. Thus, if the general performance norms differ across strata, individual supervisors and subordinates are likely to adopt the standards of their own strata, leading to predictable differences in evaluation.

The socialization process presents only a partial explanation for differ-ences in the norms of supervisors and subordinates. This explanation is based on the assumption that, in general, the norms of these two strata will differ, but it provides little explanation for why they might differ. For example, why do supervisors and subordinates identify different dimen-sions of performance as important (Borman, 1974)? Why do supervisors have higher standards of performance than do subordinates (Beatty, Schneier, & Beatty, 1978; Schneier & Beatty, 1978)? The concept of egocentric bias may help to answer these questions.

We noted earlier that norms are developed only for behaviors that are considered important. Egocentric bias suggests that each group (i.e., super-visors, subordinates) will develop norms and standards for the behaviors that are relevant and important to *them* (Carroll & Schneier, 1982). For example, subordinates may develop elaborate standards for evaluating interpersonal and group-maintenance behaviors; these same behaviors may have little impact on supervisors' evaluation. Both behaviors and results probably differ in their relevance for supervisors and subordinates. The simplest explanation for supervisors' higher expectations and the tendency for self- and peer ratings to be lenient when compared to supervisory ratings is that supervisors consider high levels of output very important, even if little attention is paid to interpersonal relations. Subordinates, however, consider interpersonal relations to be very important, and care less about output levels.

Although some progress has been made in research on implicit theories of the job (e.g., Borman, 1987), little attention has been given to comparisons between the theories of supervisors and subordinates. Radical disagreements over the importance and centrality of different tasks, behaviors, and results are likely to lead to radical disagreements concerning standards. On the other hand, if supervisors and subordinates have similar implicit theories of the job (i.e., theories of the subordinate's job), more consistent evaluations, higher satisfaction with PA, feelings of equity, and so on can be expected. Our analysis suggests that some supervisor-subordinate conflicts stem from the fact that the two strata are likely to emphasize different criteria and develop different standards for evaluating job performance.

THE COMPARISON PROCESS

Research on cognition and judgment provides some useful insights into the processes that may be involved when comparing behavior to standards. Studies suggest that this process is complex rather than simple, depends on characteristics of the standards, and may not result in the same evaluation for a given behavior exhibited by different persons or in different situations.

One generalization that can be drawn from cognitive-perceptual research is that the complexity of the comparison process is a function of the complexity of the stimulus. With simple stimuli that can be characterized along a single dimension (e.g., comparing the loudness of two tones, the weight of two objects, etc.), comparison processes are simple, although the psychophysical functions describing these comparisons may look complex (Brown & Herrnstein, 1975). In evaluating performance, the stimuli are never simple. Even if evaluation is tied to a single concrete behavior, elaborate preprocessing of stimuli is needed to segregate the ongoing stream of behavior into discrete chunks (Newtson, 1976). To understand better the complex comparisons that are involved when evaluating job performance, some of the structural characteristics of standards must be described.

Characteristics of Standards

Sherif and Sherif's (1969) description of norms provides a starting point for a discussion of the structural characteristics of standards. They noted that norms could be categorized as ways of defining (a) the latitude of rejection—the set of behaviors that meet with disapproval, (b) the latitude of acceptance—the set of behaviors that are approved, and (c) the latitude of noncommitment—the set of behaviors that engage in neither approval nor disapproval. Much of their research from the 1940s to the 1960s dealt with features of the individual and the social situation that led to large or small latitudes of acceptance or rejection.

In PA, the latitude of acceptance spans the set of behaviors that are positively evaluated. Within this set, behaviors can be scaled from those that meet with mild approval to those that are highly valued. The latitude of rejection spans the set of ineffective behaviors (from slightly to very ineffective behaviors), whereas the latitude of noncommitment spans the set of behaviors that would not lead to any evaluation, positive or negative.

Jackson (1965) presented the return potential model (RPM), which is a structural model of norms closely related to Sherif and Sherif's (1969) formulation (Hackman [1976, 1992] describes several applications of this model). Several features of the model, which is depicted in Figure 6.5, are of interest. First, the latitudes of acceptance (Behaviors d and e), rejection (Behaviors a, b, g, h, i, and j), and noncommitment (Behaviors c and f) are clearly illustrated. The model allows one to compute (a) point of maximum return—the behavior that meets with the most approval (i.e., Behavior e); (b) potential return difference—the overall mean amount of approval, minus disapproval, over the whole range of behaviors; (c) intensity—the overall strength of the norm, defined as the amount of approval or disapproval assigned to the set of behaviors; and (d) crystallization—the degree of consensus regarding the amount of approval and disapproval assigned to specific behaviors.

Several phenomena in performance appraisal could be studied using the analytic procedures developed by Jackson (1965). For example, potential return difference is likely to be related to leniency and severity of judgment.

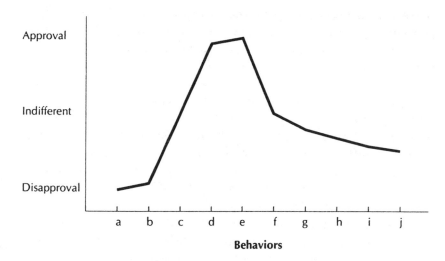

Figure 6.5. The Return Potential Model

A rater who assigns poor evaluations to most behaviors will tend to give harsh judgments. Second, intensity is likely to be related to central tendency or range restriction error. A rater who assigns little approval or disapproval to most behaviors is likely to evaluate most workers as "average." Finally, measures of crystallization might be used in investigating interrater agreement. Raters whose RPM graphs are very different might perceive behavior similarly but assign very different evaluations.

Research on cognitive categorization is also related to Sherif and Sherif's (1969) formulation for describing norms. (Lord and colleagues have, in several studies, examined categorization processes in perceptions of leadership. See, for example, Lord, Foti, & DeVader [1984]; see Lord & Maher [1991] for a general review of the role of cognitive theory.) There are stable individual differences in individuals' tendency to employ very broad versus very narrow categories for classifying specific behaviors, objects, or events (Garber & Miller, 1986). The category of "good worker" or "good performance" may be very broad for some raters and very narrow for others.

Category breadth is a concept that is closely related to latitudes of acceptance and rejection, especially in contexts such as PA, where categories are by their very nature evaluative. There is evidence that category breadth is domain-specific (Garber & Miller, 1986); it may also be level-specific. The same rater might thus have a broad category to represent good performance in some parts of the job and a narrow category to represent good performance in some others. The "good" category might be broader or narrower than the "poor" category.

Fox and Thornton (1987) present a model of evaluative judgment that incorporates another concept that is closely related to latitudes of acceptance, rejection, and noncommitment. They note that people have implicit theories about the *distribution* of behavior across both individuals and traits; these theories may even include assumptions about person-by-trait interactions. Implicit distribution theories may define boundary conditions for establishing norms and standards. That is, the latitudes of acceptance, rejection, and noncommitment are likely to be defined only over the range of behaviors that are seen as likely to occur. Thus, a supervisor whose theory leads him or her to expect only a narrow range of behaviors relevant to the trait "speaking style" is likely to have narrow latitudes of acceptance, rejection, and noncommitment. All other things being equal, the range of behaviors that are target for approval or disapproval will be directly related to the level of variability that categorizes a person's implicit distribution theory.

Higgins and Stangor (1988) draw a useful distinction between standards that are based on the distribution (or the mean of the distribution) of an attribute for members of a category and standards that are based on exemplars of different levels of that attribute (e.g., specific images of what constitutes good, average, and poor performance). At present, not enough information is known about performance standards to determine whether norm-based or exemplar-based standards predominate. These two types of standards may evoke slightly different comparison processes, however, especially if there are only a few exemplars. More research is needed to determine the implications of this distinction between types of standards for performance appraisal.

Assuming that standards are defined in terms of categories or *ranges* of acceptable and unacceptable behaviors, the comparison process is one in which the rater must sort the behavior he or she observes into the appropriate category. The process of categorization and category matching has been the subject of extensive research (see Gregson [1975], Rosch & Lloyd [1978], and Tversky [1977] for discussions of basic properties of categories and of similarity and category-matching judgments), little of which has dealt with contexts such as PA. In this case, the context might make a difference, because performance evaluation is characterized by the use of a set of *ordered* categories (e.g., good, average, poor) rather than a set of qualitatively different categories. Qualitatively different categories might be used in the *perception* of performance (see Chapter 7) but are unlikely to be used when the task is to map what has been seen onto a unidimensional evaluative scale.

The fact that the categories of evaluative judgment can be represented as points or regions on a single scale suggests that the matching process will have fewer degrees of freedom than in the typical social cognition experiment. First, behavior will be classified into one and only one category; the same incident will not be characterized as good, bad, *and* indifferent. Second, the number of categories is limited by their breadth. Because categories are aligned in order on a single scale, the use of broad categories necessarily implies the use of few categories. If a third of all behaviors fit into the "good" category and half of the behaviors fit into the "bad" category, there is not much room for a large number of intermediate categories.

Adjusting for the Environment. It is unlikely that standards are completely fixed. Rather, they are likely to include some provision for environmental variables that affect the likelihood of good or poor performance. Standards are probably least variable in stable environments (Thompson, 1967), but even when the environment is highly stable, situational variables can either depress or enhance performance. Standards might have to be adjusted to take this into account.

Peters and O'Connor (1980) called researchers' attention to the importance of considering situational constraints, such as the lack of the tools, supplies, equipment, or cooperation needed to perform a task, when evaluating performance or testing theories about the causes of job performance. Subsequent research has established the effects of situational constraints on both objective and subjective measures of performance (O'Connor et al., 1984; Peters et al., 1982; Steel & Mento, 1986). It is likely that the presence of situational constraints will cause a judge to shift his or her standard to a more realistic level. Thus, if workers usually produce 100 units but situational constraints make it impossible in a particular instance to produce more than 40, production of 39 units will not be judged as "poor." It is likely that the judge will adopt a sliding scale that takes into account unusual constraints or opportunities.

Very little is known about what happens when a supervisor adjusts his or her evaluative scale in reaction to the environment. For example, does the entire category shift downward or does the category move lower *and* become smaller? It is possible that the latitude of acceptance becomes narrower as the total range of behaviors shrinks, but at present there is little evidence one way or the other. Similarly, very little is known about which sorts of constraints lead to or fail to lead to shifts in standards. One might argue that workers are expected to overcome some situational constraints (e.g., lack of information) but not others (e.g., lack of materials). Some constraints probably lead to more adjustment than others but at present little is known about which ones or why.

Adjusting for Individuals. Norms do not apply equally to everyone (Jackson, 1965; Sherif & Sherif, 1969; Thibaut & Kelly, 1959); the same is probably true of standards. That is, there are probably systematic differences in the standards applied to different individuals, such that the same behavior is evaluated differently depending on who performs it.

The concept of in-groups and out-groups (Linville & Jones, 1980; Quattrone & Jones, 1980; see also Chapter 8 of this volume) is clearly relevant in discussing shifting standards for evaluating performance. Supervisors typically develop close working relations with some subordinates (in-group) and more distant, formal relationships with others (out-group). It is likely that the "good" category is broader for the in-group than for the out-group; the opposite is probably true for the "bad" category. The intensity of positive evaluation is probably greater for the in-group than for the out-group; the opposite is probably true for the intensity of negative evaluations. Research on the effects of affect and liking on performance appraisals is discussed in Chapter 7. One way to explain these effects is in terms of differential standards. An individual might apply standards for people he or she likes different from standards for people he or she dislikes.

Returning once again to Sherif and Sherif's (1969) formulation, it is generally the case that standards are linked to the status of the target individual. The size of the latitude of acceptance is positively related to status, whereas the size of the latitude of rejection is negatively correlated with status. In performance evaluation, the set of subordinates evaluated by a supervisor is likely to occupy equivalent places in the formal status hierarchy, but its informal status (e.g., in-group vs. out-group) will probably vary considerably. Employees often complain that their supervisors have different standards for evaluating different individuals; this claim may be well founded.

Current information regarding variation in the standards applied to different individuals does not encompass much beyond the rather obvious point that high-status, well-liked individuals are evaluated differently than low-status, disliked individuals. It does, however, suggest that much of the current cognitive and affective research dealing with this problem (see Chapter 7) takes an overly narrow focus. Status and liking effects on evaluations are probably due in part to differential perceptions of behavior (this is the line followed in most recent research), but the possibility of radically different standards cannot be ruled out.

Anchoring and Adjustment

The preceding discussion assumes implicitly that one starts with behavioral information, aligns that information with an evaluative scale, and makes a judgment. Here, *standard* refers to the evaluative scale. There is, however, another use of the term that treats *standard* as a starting point, the assumption being that behavioral information might move a person up (more favorable) or down (less favorable) from that standard point. Research on anchoring and adjustment processes in judgment is relevant to this use of the term *standard.*

Figure 6.6 illustrates the anchoring and adjustment phenomenon. If a standard provides a starting point, and the object or behavior to be judged deviates from that standard, research on anchoring and adjustment processes implies that the judgment will be closer to that standard than is warranted by the behavior (Lichtenstein, Slovic, Fischoff, Layman, & Combs, 1978; Poulton, 1968; Tversky & Kahneman, 1974; Wyer, 1976). If a standard represents what the judge usually expects, research on anchoring would suggest a chronic inability to evaluate deviant or unusual behavior accurately. When this behavior occurs, research on anchoring predicts an assimilation effect. If this is true, judges may habitually overestimate the stability of ratees' behavior. That is, they may evaluate unusual behaviors more conservatively (i.e., closer to the standard) than they should, and falsely conclude that performance rarely varies.

The possibility of assimilation effects is especially worrisome if past behavior defines the standard. Evaluation of the same person over several periods of time can be viewed as a Bayesian opinion-revision task in which previous behavior defines prior expectations, and new behavior may lead to a change in evaluations (Murphy et al., 1985). People are generally conservative in Bayesian tasks (cf. Edwards, 1968), in the sense that they typically do not change their opinions as much as they should, given the

Figure 6.6. Anchoring and Adjustment

new evidence. In the context of PA, this use of the term *standard* clearly implies that evaluations will not fluctuate as much as they should. It is possible that the persistence of first impressions can be explained in terms of anchoring or conservative opinion revision.

Although the uses of *standard* referred to in this section may help to explain some phenomena in judgment, it is not clear whether they apply to evaluative judgment. Referring back to Figure 6.6, one might ask how behavior can be placed on the same scale as the standard. If the scale is an evaluative one (as in Figure 6.6), it would seem that some sort of standard matching would be necessary before one could get to the situation illustrated in the figure. Nevertheless, it is useful to consider that there may be multiple levels of standards and that some of these may apply only after the standard and the behavior have been mapped onto a common scale.

SUMMARY

This chapter examined three issues that are rarely considered in psychological research on performance appraisal: (a) the nature of the external and internal standards that are used to determine whether a person's performance is good or bad, (b) the development and communication of these standards, and (c) the uniformity of precision of these standards as they are applied to different persons or situations or at different points in time. The research reviewed here suggests that the standards themselves and the ways in which raters use these standards to evaluate ratee behavior are affected by characteristics of the rater (i.e., his or her value system), the ratees (e.g., whether most subordinates are members of in-groups or out-groups), the organization (i.e., whether organizational norms encourage harsh or lenient evaluations), and the individual's progress in the organizational socialization process.

We believe that research on performance standards would provide important insights into a number of organizational phenomena. For example, disagreements between supervisors and subordinates over performance evaluations may not involve different views on *what* the individual did so much as they involve differences over whether it was good or bad. Similarly, conflicts between managers, or between a manager and his or her superior, may reflect, in part, differences in the standards that define good or poor performance.

There is a great temptation to make standards as explicit as possible. Most people want to know precisely what they need to do to be judged a good or poor worker. Although clarity of standards is certainly a good thing, attempts to make standards objective can only be taken so far. For example, a subordinate who is an insensitive loudmouth or a busybody is probably not very effective in his or her work and certainly will have a negative effect on the work of others. It is not clear what sort of objective standard could be written to cover that behavior. When standards are made completely clear and explicit, there is a strong temptation to work to those standards and to ignore anything that is not covered in an explicit standard. Some ambiguity in the distinction between a good worker and a poor one is probably inevitable. The standards actually used by raters to evaluate performance are almost certainly fuzzy, and attempts to make them completely explicit and uniform may be doomed to failure.

7

Processes in Evaluative Judgment

This chapter is concerned with the psychological processes that are likely to be involved in evaluating the performance of subordinates. We concentrate on cognitive processes, or on the way in which raters mentally process information about ratees, but will also discuss research on emotional or affective bases of evaluation. This chapter draws more heavily than others on experimental research conducted in laboratory settings. The relevance of this research for rating and evaluation in organizations has been widely debated; several of the issues in this debate will be discussed in the chapter.

It is useful to keep in mind that our focus here is on the evaluation that the rater arrives at, not necessarily on the rating he or she records. The model we presented in Chapter 1 suggests that this evaluation is partly context bound and partly context free. That is, the organizational context helps to define which behaviors or outcomes are valued and helps to define the meaning of performance. Concepts such as "good," "bad," "attractive," and so on exist independently of the organizational context, however, and judgments regarding performance will be heavily affected by these concepts. As we will discuss later, much of the research cited in this section is more relevant to the context-free aspects of judgment than to the context-bound aspects. This represents one of the potential barriers to generalizing from judgment research in the lab to actual judgments in organizations.

COGNITIVE PROCESSES

The first topic that must be examined in discussing cognitive processes in evaluative judgment is the meaning of cognitive. A quick survey of relevant research suggests that *cognitive* is a very broad term that includes almost any activity involving the mental manipulation or storage of information. Cognitive research might thus involve exploration of the basic processes in human memory (Craik & Lockhart, 1972; Tulving, 1974) or of person perception and social cognition (Wyer & Srull, 1986). Cognitive research also includes studies of the dynamics of halo error in rating (Cooper, 1981b), applications of personal construct theory (Borman, 1983), studies of attribution processes (Hogan, 1987; Kelley, 1971), research on the systematic distortion hypothesis (Shweder & D'Andrade, 1980), and examinations of the development and nature of tacit knowledge (Palermo, 1983; Wagner, 1986).

Given the wide range of things that might be included under the "cognitive" umbrella, it is a mistake to regard cognitive research in performance appraisal (PA) as a unitary field. Nevertheless, the majority of PA studies that would be labeled "cognitive" are concerned with the same basic issue—whether research in human information processing can be used to draw valid generalizations about the evaluation of job performance.

The rapid growth of research in cognitive processes in performance evaluation can be traced to several influential reviews that appeared between 1978 and 1982. Papers by Cooper (1981b), DeCotiis and Petit (1978), Feldman (1981), Landy and Farr (1980), and Wherry and Bartlett (1982) all called attention to the cognitive processes in appraisal and suggested ways of examining these processes and applying the results. Wherry and Bartlett (1982) described a model of rating developed by Wherry in the 1950s. Unfortunately, the paper describing the model was not published nor was the model widely known until it was described in Landy and Farr (1980).

More recently, two models of the judgment processes in appraisal have emerged, one presented by Feldman and colleagues (Feldman, 1981; Ilgen & Feldman, 1983) and another presented by DeNisi and colleagues (DeNisi et al., 1984; DeNisi & Williams, 1988). Much of the current cognitive research draws on these two models for hypotheses and interpretations of experimental findings.

Although the two models referred to above are in some ways different, they (as well as other cognitive approaches that have been applied to PA) can be described in terms of the five basic processes shown in Figure 7.1. First, raters must observe behavior, sorting relevant from irrelevant information (Banks & Murphy, 1985). Second, they must mentally represent, or encode, that information. This representation is not necessarily a totally faithful replication of what they have seen; it may lack many of the details that were observed and it may contain details that were not in fact present in the stimulus. This representation must then be stored in memory. It is likely that some information is lost in the transition from working memory, where immediate processing takes place, and long-term memory, where the memory traced is stored.

At some later time, raters must retrieve information from memory. Because performance appraisals are frequently conducted at annual or semi-annual intervals, demands on memory may be substantial and raters might find it difficult to retrieve all of the relevant information. Finally, raters must somehow integrate all of the information they have about each ratee. As discussed in Chapter 5, raters may have to integrate information from several different sources as well as from several different time periods. This last process, that of information integration, has received comparatively little systematic attention in cognitive models of performance appraisal, but has been a focus of considerable attention for judgment and decision researchers.

Lord and Maher (1991) show how the perspectives of cognitive science can be applied to understanding judgments in performance appraisal. Much of the cognitively oriented research in this area has drawn from the social-cognitive tradition of the 1960s and 1970s. In recent years, multidisciplinary research in cognitive science has taken a somewhat different direction, and it offers new perspectives on cognitive processes in appraisal.

The most fundamental difference between the social-cognitive approach that has dominated PA research and the cognitive science approach reviewed by Lord and Maher (1991) is the latters' emphasis on constructing

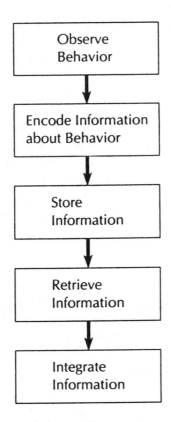

Figure 7.1. Basic Cognitive Model for Performance Evaluation

and testing models of fundamental processes involved in information processing. Cognitive science research suggests that the process of evaluative judgment probably proceeds simultaneously at several levels. Most generally, a distinction is drawn between connectivist models of cognition, which start from the neural level and attempt to explain cognitive processing in terms of neural networks, and symbolic models that take as their starting point the cognitive representation of concepts, events, and objects. Connectivist models emphasize "hard-wired" networks of neural associations, whereas symbolic models emphasize the representation and manipulation of knowledge. Cognitive science research suggests that *both* levels of analysis are useful for understanding tasks such as the evaluation of job performance, and that information processing involves multiple simultaneous processes.

Lord and Maher (1991) suggest a number of applications of a cognitive science perspective to problems in performance appraisal. For example, they show how apparently conflicting findings about the dynamics of halo error (in particular, the tendency of raters sometimes to overestimate and sometimes to underestimate levels of true halo: Murphy & Jako, 1989; Murphy, Jako, & Anhalt, 1993; Murphy & Reynolds, 1988a) might be explained in terms of the underlying cognitive architecture (i.e., connectivist vs. symbolic) involved in rating. To date, however, applications of this perspective to performance appraisal research and practice have been limited, and our presentation of research in this area will conform to the more traditional model outlined in Figure 7.1.

Information Acquisition

The process of information acquisition is active rather than passive. The rater does not simply bring in all of the available information from whatever he or she has an opportunity to observe. Rather, he or she selectively attends to some features of the ratees and their behavior and devotes little attention to others. Focusing for the moment on the perception of behaviors, cognitive research suggests that the attention devoted to any particular behavior is a function of three variables: (a) the behavior itself, (b) the context of observation, and (c) the purpose of observation. That is, some behaviors are likely to attract more attention, regardless of the context or purpose of observation.

Organizational norms and standards (see Chapter 6) define some behaviors as important, desirable, unacceptable, and so on. Behaviors that carry strong evaluative implications will probably receive attention, almost regardless of the local context (Murphy, 1982b; Wegner & Vallecher, 1977). Beyond this simple principle, cognitive research has had relatively little to say about the behaviors that are most and least likely to attract attention. Research in this area has concentrated most on the second two influences, the context of observation and the purpose of observation.

Research on context suggests two conclusions. First, the salience of most behaviors (i.e., the likelihood that they will be the focus of attention) varies across situations (McArthur, 1980; Taylor & Fiske, 1978). This is due in part to differences in the evaluative implications of specific behaviors in different situations. For example, a loud, verbally aggressive style of conversation may not attract any attention among a group of heavy-equipment salespeople but might be very noticeable in a receptionist; the behavior is appropriate in one situation but not in others.

Second, distinctive, novel features of the ratee or his or her behavior will be highly salient (Langer, Taylor, Fiske, & Chantowitz, 1976). Gender thus might be a very salient characteristic in an office where there is only one female but may not be at all salient if half of the employees are female (Cleveland, Festa, & Montgomery, 1988). Behaviors that are infrequent might become salient through their novelty; behaviors that are important but commonplace may attract less attention.

Research on the purpose of observation, sometimes referred to under the heading of *observational goals,* is highly relevant for understanding what behaviors will or will not be attended to by raters in organizations. In laboratory studies it is common for subjects to concentrate all of their attention on observing performance for the sole purpose of evaluating the performance of the individuals they have observed. In organizations this is rarely the case. Supervisors typically face multiple task demands and rarely have the luxury to devote all of their attention to behavior observation and evaluation (Balzer, 1986; Murphy et al., 1989). Thus, raters in organizations are likely to acquire information about ratees' performance while they are concentrating on tasks other than evaluation.

Murphy and associates (1989) demonstrated that the purpose of observation can have a direct impact on the accuracy of behavior ratings. In particular, they showed that raters who concentrate primarily on observing and evaluating ratees have a short-term advantage over raters for whom observation and evaluation are secondary tasks. This advantage disappears over the long term, however. It may be that raters who concentrate on observation take in more information, both relevant and irrelevant, than raters for whom evaluation is a secondary task. In most organizational settings raters may attend to relatively little information, but it is likely that what they do attend to will be relevant. A small amount of relevant information may lead to more accurate evaluations than a large amount of information that includes both irrelevant and relevant observations (Murphy & Balzer, 1986).

When raters *do* consciously seek out information about ratees, the purpose of observation will affect their information-acquisition activities. Raters will seek different information if they want information to find out about people, tasks, or characteristics of the group (Murphy, Garcia et al., 1982; Williams et al., 1985). For example, Cafferty et al. (1986) found that acquiring information in a person-blocked pattern (i.e., all information about Ratee #1 before moving on to Ratee #2), a task-blocked pattern (i.e., all information organized by task), or a mixed pattern had a direct effect on several measures of the accuracy of evaluations.

Most evaluations are concerned with assessing overall differences between persons—a purpose that might be most consistent with a person-blocked strategy (see Srull & Brand, 1983). This, however, is not always the case. Raters who are trying to assess the training needs of their work-group might focus on the overall strengths and weaknesses of the group; raters who are trying to decide which subordinate to recommend for which position might want to know about individual patterns of strength and weakness (Murphy, Garcia et al., 1982). The appropriate information search and acquisition strategy will depend on the demands of the task.

Before concluding this section, it is important to note that information-acquisition strategies have both conscious and unconscious aspects. That is, the rater might consciously develop a goal and might plan steps to achieve that goal (see Chapter 8). However, features of the stimulus and the context of observation may also unconsciously shape the rater's information-acquisition activities. Ilgen and Feldman (1983) note that many important information-processing activities are done in an automatic mode, where little if any conscious deliberation is carried out. Lord and Maher (1991) suggest that what appear to be mode-of-processing effects (i.e., effects of automatic vs. controlled processing) may in fact reflect differences in the level (e.g., neural networks vs. symbolic manipulation) at which various judgment tasks are carried out. Both the traditional social-cognitive and the cognitive science perspectives agree that information-acquisition activities can be affected without the rater's conscious knowledge.

One implication of this fact is that interventions to help direct the rater's attention to relevant and valid cues cannot concentrate solely on the conscious strategy the rater uses in searching for information but must also attempt to deal with differences in the natural salience, the novelty, and the distinctiveness of relevant and irrelevant behaviors. In order to efficiently redirect the rater's attention to the most relevant or valid behavioral indicators, changes may be needed in both search and acquisition strategies *and* the context in which behavior is observed (Cleveland & Hollmann, 1991).

Encoding and Mental Representation

At one time, a movie camera served as a reasonable analogy for the way in which perception and the mental representation of information was assumed to work. That is, the mental representation of information was thought to be relatively automatic and faithful. The more current thinking in cognitive psychology, and in particular in social cognition, is that the mental representation of what one has observed involves a complex process of categorization that may proceed automatically but often requires careful attention and mental effort. Furthermore, mental representations are not necessarily snapshots of what one has observed. Rather, some information may be lost when a stimulus is categorized.

In general, it is likely that one remembers the *category* rather than the *stimulus*. An example of this process is illustrated in Table 7.1. One mental category of people might represent persons who have the properties of (a) tall, (b) dark, and (c) handsome. An individual who is tall, dark, and average in appearance might be sufficiently similar to that category to be perceived as a member. If he or she is categorized in that manner, the information that will be later retrieved from memory is that the individual was tall, dark, and handsome (i.e., the person is now seen as having the properties of the category).

It is useful to distinguish among three related terms that are frequently encountered in research on encoding and categorization: category, prototype, and schema. A *category* is a group of related objects that takes the form of a "fuzzy set" (Rosch, 1977; Rosch, Mervis, Gray, Johnson, & Boyes-Braem, 1976). That is, categories do not have rigid boundaries but rather represent potentially unstable groups of objects that are held together by similarity or "family resemblance." A *prototype* is an exemplar of that category. It is an image that summarizes the typical and distinguishing features of a category. Thus, if the categories are "dependable economy car" and "American sports car," a Saturn and a Corvette might serve as prototypes of their respective categories. Finally, *schema* (or *schemata*) refers to higher-level memory structures that contain verbal or propositional information (Feldman, 1986; Ilgen & Feldman, 1983). Schema can be used to represent the self and/or well-known others in familiar situations (Ilgen & Feldman, 1983). One type of schema, referred to as a *script* (Abelson, 1976), pertains to a mentally stored representation of a familiar event (e.g., visiting a restaurant).

TABLE 7.1　Effects of Categorization on Memory

Properties of the Stimulus	Properties of the Category	What Is Remembered
Tall	Tall	Tall
Dark	Dark	Dark
Average Appearance	**Handsome**	**Handsome**

In the most general sense, categorization depends on the similarity between a target and each of the categories that are available to the rater (Rosch, 1978; Tversky & Gati, 1978). Thus, to understand the process of categorization one must address two separate issues: how similarity judgments are made and how categories become more or less available to the rater. Research on the similarity judgment process suggests that the process of assigning persons (or objects) to categories involves a comparison of the features of a person with the features of the prototype for each category. (Research in this area has not addressed *how* to compare stimuli and prototypes. The literature on similarity judgment—see Gregson, 1975— suggests that the similarity-matching process is not a simple one.)

Returning to our earlier example, a car will be classified as a "dependable economy car" if it shares many critical features with a Saturn. It will be classified as an "American sports car" if it shares many critical features with a Corvette. The features that are critical are those that best represent each category and that best distinguish between categories.

The concept of category accessibility is an essential one in this line of research. It is assumed that the set of all possible categories is extremely large and that individuals can work with only a subset of all the possible categories at any given point in time. The model of social cognition presented by Wyer and Srull (1986) suggests that *using* categories makes them more salient (see also Srull & Wyer, 1980). That is, if a person uses the category "American sports car" to classify the first car he or she sees, the likelihood that the person will use the same category for the next few cars is increased. Using a category also increases the accessibility of related categories. Thus, if the person does not categorize the second car he or she sees as an "American sports car," the likelihood that the person will use a related category is increased.

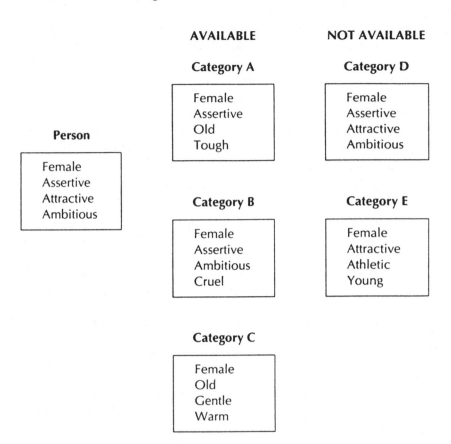

Figure 7.2. The Category Matching Process

NOTE: Properties of the person and the categories are listed in boxes.

The accessibility or availability of different categories may vary over time or situations. It follows that the same stimulus will not always be assigned to the same category. Figure 7.2 illustrates how this might occur. A person and five different categories are each described in terms of four properties. The match between the person and the category is a function of the number of properties the person and the category have in common. Of the five categories, the person fits Category D the best, but that category is not currently available. As a consequence, the person will be classified as a member of Category B. If, at some later time, the same person is encountered and Category D is then available, the categorization of the object will change.

There is evidence from several studies that processes like those illustrated in Figure 7.2 may in fact occur (Higgins & King, 1981; Higgins, King, & Mavin, 1982; Posner, 1978). Typical studies in this area involve presenting subjects with persons or objects that could conceivably be placed into several different categories, "priming" one of those categories (e.g., by having the subject use a specific category in a preexperimental task), and later testing the subject's memory for what he or she has seen. These studies have shown that construct availability at the time of encoding leads to both short-term and long-term effects on memory for what was observed (see also Jeffrey & Mischel, 1979; Cohen & Ebbeson, 1979).

Several models of the cognitive processes involved in evaluative judgment distinguish between automatic and controlled processes in encoding and (less frequently) in retrieval (Bargh, 1984; Ilgen & Feldman, 1983; Lord, 1985b; see also Lord & Maher, 1991; Motowidlo, 1986). There are three factors that distinguish automatic from controlled processes: (a) their development, (b) their demands, and (c) their consequences. First, automatic processes develop through what is referred to as *consistent mapping* or repetition of a stimulus-response sequence. Controlled processes are activated when there is no well-learned stimulus-response link. In the context of performance appraisal, automatic processing will occur for observations that are repetitive, frequent, or simple, whereas controlled processing will occur for novel or unusual observations. Second, automatic processing makes only minimal demands on processing capacity, making it possible to perform on several well-learned activities simultaneously (e.g., driving a car while carrying on a conversation). Controlled processes demand conscious attention and involve serial rather than parallel processing. That is, the controlled process of encoding occurs when raters consciously attend to observations and effectively screen out surrounding activities.

Finally, and most important, the consequences of automatic versus controlled processes in encoding can be substantial. Automatic processing involves a simple, unconscious matching of objects and categories and involves the loss of information about the object that is not shared by the category. Thus, in the example shown in Figure 7.2, automatic processing would involve the loss of information about one of the properties of the person (i.e., attractive); subjects would remember the object as possessing the properties female, assertive, ambitious, and confident (i.e., the properties of the category that most closely matches the object). Controlled processes involve an active search for information. The faithful representation of detailed information about the stimulus is probably more likely under controlled than under automatic processing.

The concepts of schema and prototypes have been applied to the area of leadership, as well as to PA (Lord, 1985b; Lord et al., 1984; Lord & Maher, 1991; Phillips & Lord, 1982). In fact, it is our opinion that the application of schematic theories has been more successful in the domain of leader perception and less successful in the domain of performance appraisal. The most obvious reason is that prototypes of leaders are more likely to exist and be similar across situations than will prototypes of good workers or successful performers. For example, Foti and Lord (1987) studied memory for leader behavior at a board meeting and were able to predict several important outcome variables using script and schema theory. One reason for this is that most people have at least a general idea of what behaviors are appropriate and expected from the leader of a meeting (i.e., scripts exist for this type of behavior). Thus it is possible to determine which of the behaviors actually observed are or are not consistent with a schema and to make fine-grained predictions.

In contrast, PA studies are often carried out in contexts where the subjects will have no clear idea of what represents good, average, or poor performance. In the language of schema theories, studies of performance appraisal are often carried out in situations where schema, scripts, and even performance categories are not well defined. As a result, it is difficult to use schematic theories to make specific predictions about appraisal outcomes. One of the few studies that was successful in applying this approach in studying appraisal led to very mixed results (Nathan & Lord, 1983).

Content of Categories. The outstanding weakness of schema and categorization theories as applied to PA has been a lack of attention to defining what performance-related categories look like. For example, is "good worker" a category? Is "average worker" another? Researchers in this area have argued both sides of this question but there has been little empirical work that addresses the content of job- or work-related categories (see, however, Blencoe, 1984; Ostroff & Ilgen, 1986). Cardy, Bernardin, Abbott, Senderak, and Taylor (1987) have presented evidence suggesting that raters do have prototypes of good and poor workers but their research has not examined the content question in any depth.

Although Borman (1987) was not directly concerned with the content of the categories that are used in encoding performance-related behaviors, his research on the personal constructs, or "folk theories," that raters use to describe job performance is highly relevant. He found that general dimensions such as maturity/responsibility, organization, technical proficiency, and assertive leadership were among the personal constructs most often used by raters in their descriptions of work. One possibility is that categories are characterized by different levels of particular dimensions or by different profiles of levels on several dimensions. That is, the dimensions identified by Borman (1987) might define the properties of each category, in that categories might be defined in terms of the presence or absence of each property. For example, one category might be people who are (a) high on maturity, (b) low on organization, (c) average on technical proficiency, and (d) very high on assertive leadership. Other categories might be defined in terms of relative and absolute strengths on different dimensions.

It is likely that the categories used in defining job performance change over time, especially when new raters are compared to experienced raters. In general, experience with the task and/or with evaluating performance on the task leads to an increase in the number and sophistication of the categories that are used in evaluation (Cardy et al., 1987; Kozlowski & Kirsch, 1986). In addition to the number and the detail of job-related categories, the content of these categories is likely to change with experience. One of the several aspects of organizational socialization may be to develop a category system that is comparable to the one used by other members of the organization. As new managers learn their jobs, they are also likely to learn categories that are useful for mentally representing the work of their subordinates.

One dimension that is likely to be highly central in defining categories is the general evaluative dimension (Murphy, 1982b; Murphy & Balzer, 1986). That is, categorization is very likely to involve placing each person along a good-bad, preferred-nonpreferred continuum. Cognitive models have generally assumed that evaluation was the end product of the cognitive process, but there is evidence that evaluation is primitive and universal and that evaluation may occur at the same time as or even precede other information-processing activities (Kim & Rosenberg, 1980; Osgood, 1962; Wegner & Vallecher, 1977; Zajonc, 1980).

Research by Hastie and Park (1986) suggests that evaluations are stored at the time that behavior is observed, and that subsequent memory may be for evaluations rather than for behaviors. (Hastie & Park's distinction between on-line vs. memory-based judgments is similar to the distinction Ilgen & Feldman [1983] draw between stimulus-based and memory-based judgments.) One implication of this is that overall evaluations of individuals may not be greatly affected by the encoding-storage-retrieval process, whereas perceptions of specific behaviors may be directly affected. Raters may be highly accurate in remembering their evaluations but may have a great deal of difficulty in remembering supportive detail. Indeed, there is evidence that raters may *infer* behavioral details from their evaluations, rather than (as is generally assumed) basing their evaluations on the total set of behaviors they have observed (Murphy, Martin, & Garcia, 1982).

One final point about categories deserves attention. It is widely assumed that categorization simplifies perception and encoding. Ilgen and Feldman (1983) assert that "categorization is necessary to cognitive economy; it reduces the amount of information that must be processed and stored" (p. 155). The assumption that categorization is more economical in terms of information-processing resources depends on the untested assumption that the number of categories is small relative to the number of stimuli that are encountered. In fact, the number of categories that might be used is potentially larger than the number of stimuli, because it is possible to construct categories that represent null sets. One such category of persons might be "female presidents of the United States" (hopefully, this category will not always be a null set).

It seems critical for proponents of the view that categorization is cognitively efficient and economical to demonstrate that this is in fact so. One way would be to show that stable categories exist only at a general level. For example, categorization will be economical if "good worker" and "bad worker" represent typical categories, but will not be economical if "good worker who sits at this desk and who is sometimes absent on Thursdays" represents a typical category.

Storage and Retrieval

Tulving (1983) noted that more than 100 years of experimental research on human memory have failed to produce any clear consensus on how memory works or on how many different types of memory exist. Memory researchers generally agree that it is useful to distinguish between short-term working memory and long-term memory, but several researchers have proposed different models for each type of memory. Thus, it is important to realize that the models we will describe here are not universally accepted, and that alternative theories can lead to different predictions about what behaviors will or will not be remembered at the time of appraisal.

There are two principal distinctions between working memory and long-term memory: duration and capacity. Working memory is assumed to have a limited capacity, both in terms of the number of items that can be held in memory and in terms of the length of time they can be held. It is assumed that some information enters working memory, where immediate information-processing activities occur, but is not transferred to long-term memory. Information that is not transferred to long-term memory within a very short period (often a few seconds) may be permanently lost.

Long-term memory is assumed to have effectively infinite capacity, both in terms of the number of items that can be stored and in terms of the length of time that they can be held. Although it is possible that the passage of time, as well as activities that intervene between storage and retrieval, may interfere with the ability to *retrieve* information from memory, it is assumed that information that is committed to long-term memory is not subsequently lost (Tulving, 1983).

One theory suggests that two separate memory systems exist: semantic and episodic memory (Tulving, 1983). More recent research suggests that transitional forms of memory that share features of both semantic and episodic memory may also exist. Semantic memory provides storage for verbal, factual, and propositional information, whereas episodic memory provides storage for actions, occurrences, and experiences (both direct and vicarious). Information about a subordinate's performance may be stored in *both* semantic and episodic memory, which may have implications for the way in which this information is used. Integration of information from two separate memory systems may not be as easy as integration of several pieces of information from the same memory system.

Wyer and Srull (1986) present an alternative model—one that has had a significant impact on cognitive research in PA. Some of the aspects of this model are illustrated in Figure 7.3. A storage bin is used as an analogy for human memory. It is assumed that there are several bins, each of which is designed to hold different types of information. Each bin has a label (or a prototype) that describes its contents. Information is stored in a bin in the

Figure 7.3. A Storage-Bin Model of Memory

order of receipt; the same information may be stored in several different bins. Information that is at the top of each bin is most accessible, and information is retrieved by first locating the appropriate bin and then by searching through the bin. Bins in this model are similar to categories. One implication of this model is that a memory search will not locate an individual piece of information unless the search includes the appropriate bin(s).

The model illustrated in Figure 7.3 suggests two major conclusions. First, some items (e.g., responds to feedback) can be found regardless of which bin is searched. Thus, categorization will not affect the *possibility* of retrieving this item, although it will be less accessible (i.e., the probability of locating the item will be lower) in a search of the poor-worker bin than in a search of the other two bins. Second, failure to search the correct bin(s) will result in a memory failure. Thus, if you search the average-worker or good-worker bins for the item "absent," you will report that you do not remember it; a search of the poor-worker bin is needed to locate that item.

Recognition, Recall, and Reprocessing. In describing retrieval procedures, it is useful to distinguish between *recall,* which represents a relatively unstructured effort to retrieve information from memory, and *recognition,* which represents an attempt to determine whether a stimulus that is present in working memory matches anything that is stored in long-term memory.

Recognition memory is typically better than recall (e.g., compare a multiple-choice test item to a short-answer item) but this is not always the case (Tulving, 1983). Murphy and Davidshofer (1988) suggest that some PA scales present the rater with a recall task, but other scales, particularly behavior-based scales, may present a recognition-like task. Rating scales that ask about the occurrence of specific behaviors (e.g., Behavior Observation Scales [Latham & Wexley, 1977]; see this book's Appendix for an example) appear to present a more structured retrieval task than do global trait scales. One implication is that questions about the occurrence of specific behaviors may be easier to answer than unstructured questions about what has occurred.

Memory research in the area of social cognition and person perception has been primarily concerned with the effects of categorization on memory. Several studies have shown that subjects recall traits that are consistent with the category used to represent persons mentally, even when those traits were not in fact present (Cantor & Mischel, 1977; Hastie & Kumar, 1979; Wyer & Srull, 1986). Other studies have established that manipulating category accessibility at the time of encoding will systematically affect long-term memory (Cohen & Ebbeson, 1979; Higgins & King, 1981; Higgins et al., 1982; Jeffrey & Mischel, 1979). At one point this research seemed to suggest that initial categorization determined the eventual contents of long-term memory. Recent studies of reprocessing suggest that this is not necessarily so.

DeNisi and Williams (1988) reviewed several studies of the effects of reprocessing on memory-related performance evaluation outcomes. Reprocessing occurs when information is obtained (and presumably encoded) for one purpose and subsequently used for another purpose. For example, Williams, DeNisi, Meglino, and Cafferty (1986) had subjects acquire information either for the purpose of making a designation decision (i.e., pick the best worker out of a group) or a deservedness decision (i.e., decide how well each worker performed), and then asked them, several days later, to rate all workers from memory. As expected, subjects in the deservedness condition were more accurate than those in the designation condition.

Williams and associates (1986) explain this finding by noting that subjects in the designation condition may have encoded workers' performance into two categories (such as "the best" and "not the best"). The subsequent PA task asked them to distinguish among all workers—something that was difficult to do for subjects who had initially categorized workers into two gross categories. It was not *impossible,* however, for subjects in the designation condition to distinguish among workers they had previously categorized into the same group, which suggests that information about individuals' performance was not completely lost in categorization.

It is possible that reprocessing may lead to recategorization. The evidence is not clear on this point, but close examination of Williams and colleagues' (1986) results suggests that the initial decision task did not cause raters to lose all of the information that was not relevant to the category (e.g., differences in performance among workers in the "not the best" category). Although most models incorporate the assumption that categorization entails the loss of category-irrelevant information (Ilgen & Feldman, 1983), research on reprocessing suggests that this is not always the case. DeNisi and Williams (1988) suggest that the initial categorization of each person may involve at least two separate codes: a behavior code and an evaluation code. Recategorization may involve changing the emphasis on the behavioral versus evaluative information as a result of the demands of different tasks.

Memory Aids. More than 40 years ago, Wherry proposed that raters use behavioral diaries as memory aids (see Wherry & Bartlett [1982] for a description of a model of rating developed by Wherry in the early 1950s); diaries are still advocated as a useful tool for appraisal (Balzer, 1986; Bernardin & Walter, 1977). The rationale here is that it is very difficult for raters to remember all of the relevant behaviors they observe, and that consulting a behavior diary before rating could lead to more accurate evaluations. Although empirical evaluations of the effects of keeping a diary are somewhat mixed, there are some aspects of memory research that suggest that diaries may indeed be useful.

In order to understand the role of diaries, it is important to assess the precise nature of the memory problems that are most frequently encountered in rating. The problem is not that the information that is needed is not in the system; anything that is stored in long-term memory could, in principle, be retrieved at some later date. Rather, the problem is typically one of retrieval. The entries in behavioral diaries probably serve as retrieval cues. One implication is that a diary entry such as, "Worker submitted a report that contained many typographical errors" will help to retrieve incidents of that behavior and will also help in retrieving incidents of conceptually similar behaviors (e.g., behaviors that are stored in the same memory bin). Diary-keeping not only aids the recall of behavioral information, it may also help the raters organize that information into coherent categories (DeNisi, Robbins, & Cafferty, 1989).

One unanticipated consequence of using behavior diaries may be a change in the method of categorization. Level-of-processing theories (e.g., Craik & Lockhart, 1972) suggest that consciously attending to and recording behaviors will shift categorization from an automatic to a controlled mode. This will imply more extensive searches for information and a greater likelihood of preserving specific details of what has been observed. It will also mean that raters may now process behavioral information in sequence rather than engaging in parallel processing. In the automatic mode raters can process many pieces of information simultaneously, but in the controlled mode they will process only one piece at a time and will not encode information about other stimuli that are present at the time. It was argued elsewhere (e.g., Murphy & Balzer, 1986) that preserving all of the behavioral details one observes does not necessarily lead to more accurate evaluations and may even detract from accuracy. Thus, the shift from automatic to controlled processing that may result from the use of behavioral diaries could be a mixed blessing.

Rater Training. Rater training might range from simple efforts to acquaint raters with the performance rating scales and the mechanics of the system to elaborate methods of developing skills in observation, rating, and delivering feedback; the variability in scope and the focus of rater training efforts reflect large differences in the purpose of training across organizations. Many training programs focus on developing skills relevant to observing and evaluating ratee behavior.

The purpose of many rater training programs is to increase the validity, fairness, and accuracy of ratings. Over the years the emphasis in training research and application seems to have shifted away from training designed to eliminate specific problems with rating data (e.g., training to reduce rater errors; Bernardin & Pence, 1980; Pulakos, 1984), and toward training methods that increase raters' ability to accurately observe, recall, and/or classify ratees' behavior. There is some consensus that one of the more successful training methods for that purpose is some variation of frame-of-reference (FOR) training (Bernardin & Buckley, 1981; Bernardin & Pence, 1980; McIntyre et al., 1984; Pulakos, 1984, 1986). FOR training is designed to provide raters with a common set of standards for evaluating their subordinates, and it typically involves training raters to match behavioral exemplars to performance dimensions and to map behavioral exemplars to a common evaluative rating scale. If successful, FOR training helps to "calibrate" raters so that particular scores on individual rating dimensions have at least roughly equivalent meanings for all raters.

Another promising method of rater training utilized cognitive modeling principles. Here, trainers encourage raters to "think aloud" or to make their judgment processes explicit, provide feedback about the way in which judgments are being made, and demonstrate judgment processes that are likely to be effective (Luthans & Kreitner, 1985; McIntyre, 1986). In this method of training, raters attempt to model their own judgment processes on those processes that are known to be effective.

FOR and cognitive modeling methods share a number of components that are likely to contribute to their effectiveness, in particular the use of practice and feedback (McIntyre et al., 1984; Pulakos, 1984, 1986). The apparently critical role of practice and feedback in rater training mirrors its role in general learning theory. There is evidence from a wide range of sources that practice and feedback enhance learning and retention (e.g., Bandura, 1986), and it is possible that the use of practice and feedback is more critical than the specific training method (e.g., FOR vs. cognitive modeling) that is used.

Integration

Both the DeNisi and the Feldman models imply that integration of different pieces of information to form an overall judgment occurs after encoding, storage, and retrieval (see also Cooper, 1981b), although both models allow for the fact that previous information may effect subsequent encoding. This possibility has been examined in a series of studies by Murphy et al. (1985) and by Murphy, Gannett et al. (1986). The main results of these studies are summarized in Table 7.2.

These studies showed that both previous and subsequent performance can affect evaluations of present performance. Also, the integration of

TABLE 7.2   Effects of Previous and Subsequent Performance on Evaluations
of Present Performance

Delay Between Observation and Rating	Previous Performance	Subsequent Performance
Short	Strong contrast effect	Weak assimilation effect
Long	Weak contrast effect	Strong assimilation effect

SOURCES: K. R. Murphy, W. K. Balzer, M. Lockhart, & E. Eisenman, "Effects of Previous Performance on Evaluations of Present Performance," *Journal of Applied Psychology, 70* (1985) pp. 72-84. Also: K. R. Murphy, B. A. Gannett, B. M. Herr, & J. A. Chen, "Effects of Subsequent Performance on Evaluations of Previous Performance," *Journal of Applied Psychology, 71* (1986) pp. 427-431.
NOTES: Contrast: Ratings are biased in the opposite direction from that of previous performance.
Assimilation: Ratings are biased in the same direction as that of subsequent performance.

information about present performance with information about previous and subsequent performance can lead to either assimilation or contrast effects. By itself, demonstration of assimilation and contrast effects in evaluation is neither new nor impressive but the overall *pattern* of results shown in Table 7.2 is highly informative.

First, previous performance sets up expectations for the future, and when present performance is different from previous performance, contrast effects occur. For example, if a worker usually does a very good job on a task, but this time does only an average job, this present performance will be perceived as poor rather than average. As memory demands increase, this contrast effect grows weaker. Second, when subsequent performance differs from present performance, assimilation effects occur. That is, if a worker is now performing at an above-average level it is likely that one will remember that his or her previous performance was also above average, even though it was in fact not that good. Assimilation effects grow *stronger* as demands on memory are increased.

A study by Steiner and Raine (1989) suggests some boundary conditions for the conclusions reached by Murphy and colleagues (1985, 1986). They noted that the likelihood of assimilation versus contrast effects in evaluations of performance depended in part on the average performance level of the ratee. In particular, an employee whose performance is typically average but whose present performance is discrepant with the norm must be performing either very well or very poorly during the appraisal period. An employee whose typical performance is either very good or very poor and whose present performance is discrepant from the norm may be an average performer during the appraisal period. Contrast effects are more likely when the performance being evaluated is average; assimilation effects are more likely when the performance being evaluated is extreme (Murphy et al., 1985).

The studies summarized in Table 7.2 suggest an ongoing integration process, in that previous and subsequent performance affect two distinct information-processing activities. First, the expectations that are generated by previous performance direct one's attention to instances of present performance that differ from those expectations. In terms of the Feldman model, present performance that is different from previous performance may be processed in a controlled mode, whereas performance that is consistent with expectations may be processed in an automatic mode. Increasing one's attention to behaviors that violate expectations will lead raters to overestimate the differences between present and past performance, which results in a contrast effect.

Second, when subsequent performance is different from previous performance, one's *memory* for previous performance is biased; here, assimilation rather than contrast effects occur. The effects of subsequent performance on ratings of present performance cannot be due to biases in attention and encoding (Murphy et al., 1986), because present performance is encoded before subsequent performance even occurs. The fact that attention and encoding are ruled out, together with the pattern of results shown in Table 7.2, suggest that subsequent performance affects the retrieval of information about present performance from long-term memory.

The results summarized in Table 7.2 have clear implications for performance evaluations in organizations. Because performance appraisals are typically conducted at infrequent intervals and are generally done from memory rather than using behavior diaries or other memory aids, results obtained when there is a relatively long delay between observations are most relevant. These results suggest that previous performance will have only a weak effect on evaluations, but that subsequent performance may lead to strong assimilation effects in rating performance that has occurred in the past.

In all, the results shown in Table 7.2 suggest that performance evaluations may lead to underestimates of the variability (over time) of a worker's job performance. If assimilation effects occur, raters will remember the past as being more similar to the present than is actually the case. Therefore, raters may have a very hard time accurately evaluating changes in their subordinates' performance.

Judgment Research. Although many cognitive models allow for the possibility of ongoing integration of information about performance (as described above), most models also assume that some summary integration is carried out at the time the performance is formally evaluated. Research on judgment and decision making has attempted to address processes that might be involved when judges are asked to integrate several pieces of information to arrive at a judgment.

Table 7.3 illustrates the type of task that is often used in studying judgment. Subjects are given multiple pieces of information about each person or object (in this case, about each bank) and are asked to make judgments on the basis of that information. Regression models, subjectively weighted models, and Bayesian opinion revision models have all been used in studying judgments of the type illustrated in Table 7.3 (Hammond, McClelland, & Mumpower, 1980; Slovic & Lichtenstein, 1971). Anderson and colleagues have applied more complex designs in studying algebraic models of human judgment (Anderson, 1971; Anderson & Alexander, 1971).

The approach illustrated in Table 7.3 uses an algebraic analogy to explain and explore information integration. That is, a judgment about a person or object is assumed to be the result of a weighting and averaging process. It is *not* assumed that people actually calculate the average of their evaluation of each property or cue when judging a person or object, but it is assumed that determining the weights assigned to properties will help to tell how much influence each property had on the final judgment. The term *policy capturing* is often used to refer to an approach in which a mathematical model of the judgment is used to infer the importance of each cue or property in judgment.

Although policy capturing has been used to study information integration in performance appraisal (Zedeck & Cascio, 1982), this approach is no longer as popular as it was in the 1960s and 1970s. The principal problem with policy capturing is that the mathematical models employed frequently lead to ambiguous or unclear results. This can be illustrated with a simple example. Returning to the type of study illustrated in Table 7.3, the policy-capturing approach would entail the following:

1. Ask each subject to judge a large number of different banks (typically 50 to 100), each described in terms of the four properties included in Table 7.3.

TABLE 7.3   Typical Task Used in Studying Information Integration in
Judgment

The properties of several banks are described below. Rate each bank on a scale from 1
(not very desirable) to 7 (very desirable) in terms of how desirable each bank might be
as a place to do business.

Rating

Bank #1   _____

Interest on savings—very high
Charges for checking—average
Accessibility—very easy to get to
Evening and weekend hours—very limited

Bank #2   _____

Interest on savings—very low
Charges for checking—very low
Accessibility—average
Evening and weekend hours—very often open

NOTE: This task was used by K. R. Murphy, "Assessing the Discriminant Validity of Regression Models
and Subjectively Weighted Models of Judgments," *Multivariate Behavioral Research, 17* (1982a) pp. 354-
370.

2. Transform the verbal information about each property into scaled values
   (e.g., Charges for Checking—average would have a scale value of 4 on a
   7-point scale).
3. Use the scores on the four cues as predictors and use the judgment about
   each bank as a criterion in a regression equation.

The regression weights in this equation are assumed to provide information
about the importance of each cue in judgment (Lane, Murphy, & Marques,
1982). Thus, if the regression equation computed to predict a subject's
judgments yielded regression weights of 1.0, 4.3, 0.20, and 0.33, respectively, for the four cues, you might conclude that (a) Charges for Checking
are very important in your evaluation of a bank and (b) you also pay some
attention to Interest on Savings but do not really care about Accessibility
or Evening and Weekend Hours.

The problem with the conclusions drawn above is that regression equations capture the *outcomes* of judgments, without necessarily capturing the
process. That is, the regression equation will accurately predict the actual
judgments, but that does not mean that the weights that define the equation
were actually applied. Many studies have compared subjective weights,

which are obtained by asking the subject how important each cue or property is in his or her judgment, with regression weights (see Hobson & Gibson, 1983; Murphy, 1979). There are two general findings in this literature. First, regression weights are often quite different from subjective weights. Second, subjective weights predict judgments just about as well as do regression weights. In fact, any weights are likely to work about as well as regression weights.

As long as cues are to some extent correlated, the choice of weights in a prediction equation has virtually no effect on the accuracy of predictions (Dawes & Corrigan, 1974; Wainer, 1976). It is therefore hard to argue that one particular set of weights captures the judgment process (i.e., the regression weights) when any other set of weights would do just as well in predicting judgments.

The relevance of judgment research for information integration in performance appraisal is doubtful. (For a different evaluation of policy capturing in PA research, see Hobson & Gibson, 1983.) This research is useful for describing situations in which the decision maker is given several pieces of information at the same time and is required to make judgments solely on the basis of that information. The process of graduate admissions is an example of this. Here, each member of the admissions committee reads a folder describing each applicant in terms of a number of common properties (e.g., grade-point average, etc.) and makes a judgment about each one.

Performance appraisal does not involve a single summary evaluation, but rather probably involves an ongoing process of evaluation and opinion revision. Some decision research is relevant to this sort of ongoing evaluation process (Slovic & Lichtenstein, 1971) but policy-capturing research probably is not. Our conclusion is that we still know relatively little about the information integration processes involved in appraisal, and that policy capturing and related approaches are unlikely to provide an accurate description of these processes.

Applications of the Cognitive Approach

One of the most frequently encountered questions in cognitive research in performance appraisal is whether this approach has led or is likely to lead to advances in the *practice* of PA. On the whole, this approach has not yet led to new advances in application, in part because researchers and practitioners have not cooperated fully (Banks & Murphy, 1985). Some of the areas where application has been tried have turned out to be blind alleys, whereas others have not yet been pursued on a sufficient scale to determine whether they will work.

In the areas where cognitive research *has* made a contribution, the contribution has often been negative. For example, behavioral anchors on rating scales have traditionally been regarded as useful guides for observing and evaluating ratee behavior (Bernardin & Smith, 1981). Murphy and Constans (1987) showed that behavioral anchors can be a source of bias rather than a source of validity in rating, and that anchors can misdirect attention and retrieval processes (but see Murphy & Pardaffy, 1989).

Other cognitive research (Ilgen & Feldman, 1983; Murphy, Martin, & Garcia, 1982) has served to further undercut the rationale that is typically put forth in arguing for behavior-based scales rather than for trait-based scales. This research suggests that the categories used in encoding and storage are more traitlike than behavioral, and the trait inferences cannot be avoided by simply phrasing scales in terms of behaviors. Rather, it is likely that people infer behavioral information from subjective trait judgments and that behavior-based scales are not as objective as they appear (Murphy, Martin, & Garcia, 1982).

At one time it appeared that cognitive complexity would provide one key to improving the appraisal process. It was argued that individuals differ in their cognitive complexity—or their ability to sort persons and behaviors into many rather than few categories—and that appraisal would be most effective when the dimensional complexity of the rating form matched the level of cognitive complexity of the rater (Schneier, 1977). For example, if all work behavior is mentally sorted into two categories (e.g., task accomplishment and interpersonal relations), it will be difficult to rate subordinates using a form that requires performance to be separated into 15 dimensions.

Studies by Bernardin, Cardy, and Carlyle (1982) and Lahey and Saal (1981) cast doubt on the cognitive complexity hypothesis. One major problem with this line of thinking is the construct validity of the measures that are typically used to assess cognitive complexity. In our opinion it is doubtful that there are stable individual differences in cognitive complexity (i.e., there may be no such thing as cognitive complexity). If there are, the construct is very difficult to measure.

Although the examples cited above suggest that, to date, applications of cognitive research have not advanced the practice of performance appraisal, there are reasons to be optimistic for the future. There are two areas where progress in cognitive research is likely to lead to progress in application.

The first area is in rating scale formats. Landy and Farr (1980) noted that the great majority of the studies of performance appraisal over the past 35 years have been concerned with determining whether one scale format was better than another. The contribution of this research has been so minimal (no one format is consistently better or worse than the others) that Landy and Farr (1980) called for an end to scale format research. Feldman (1986) and Murphy and Constans (1988), however, noted that previous research on scale formats has largely ignored cognitive issues. It is quite likely that different scales may involve different cognitive processes, which could have a definite impact on rating processes. Although no one scale is likely to be best in all situations, selecting the scale according to the cognitive demands imposed may lead to significant improvements in rating. For example, if the purpose of rating is to identify candidates for promotion, scale formats that concentrate on between-person differences (e.g., ranking rather than rating) may lead to more valid decisions than scales that concentrate on individual strengths and weaknesses.

A second area in which cognitive research has clear potential for improving practice is in the area of rater training. Feldman (1986) has suggested that training should provide raters with uniform and valid schema and prototypes. If all raters knew what good performance looked like and agreed in their definitions of good, average, and poor performance, it is likely that the quality of rating data would improve dramatically. Feldman's (1986) suggestions are similar to what is already done in frame-of-reference training (Bernardin & Beatty, 1984) and reflect ideas that were suggested in research on interviewing and on performance appraisals carried out in the 1950s (see Wherry & Bartlett [1982] and Webster [1982] for reviews). The advantage of the cognitive approach is that it provides methods of assessing the categories and prototypes that are currently being used (Lord, 1985b).

Assessment of the raters' current category systems represents one step in training needs assessment; if raters are already using valid schema and prototypes, training of this type may not be needed. However, in situations where prototypes vary over raters, or where the category of "good performance" is defined in ways that are inconsistent with organizational values and norms, this sort of training might be very useful.

Limitations of the Cognitive Approach

There are two very different criticisms of cognitive research in PA: (a) it is not good science, and (b) it does not lead to good practice. The scientific criticism of this approach centers on shortcomings of schema-based and categorization-based theories. It is important to note that *direct* evidence for categorization processes of the sort featured in the DeNisi and the Feldman models is hard to come by (Heneman et al., 1987; Ilgen & Feldman, 1983). Although research in this area has shown that categorization-induced errors *can* occur, there is little evidence that these errors are frequent or important (Funder, 1987). It is even more important to note that schematic theories themselves are open to attack. Alba and Hasher (1983) noted that schematic theories are not needed to account for many of the phenomena that are currently thought to result from categorization, and that some of the critical predictions of schema-based theories of memory have not been supported. Alba and Hasher's (1983) article asked the question, Is memory schematic? There is still no clear answer.

Social cognition research represents only one small section of the broader literature on human information processing (Lord & Maher, 1991). It is likely that cognitive research in performance appraisal will at some future point establish contact with that broader literature but this has not yet happened. The concepts that drive much of the current cognitive research described here are useful but they do not exhaust the possibilities. For example, an exchange of ideas with researchers in artificial intelligence (AI) would probably be fruitful for both groups. Much of the cognitively oriented research in AI is concerned with understanding the way in which experts make judgments and decisions. It is not known if raters in organizations could be considered experts in evaluation (Philbin, 1988), but even if they do not meet the standard definition of *expert,* many of the concepts from expert systems research may be useful for understanding performance appraisal.

Many other critics suggest that cognitively oriented research is too concerned with theory and not sufficiently concerned with application (Banks & Murphy, 1985; Ilgen & Favero, 1985; Latham, 1986; Wexley & Klimoski, 1984). Part of the problem is that the issues that are most often examined in cognitive research are not highly relevant to appraisal in organizations (Banks & Murphy, 1985).

There is even greater concern, however, over the issue of external generalizability. Cognitive research is almost always carried out in the laboratory, using college students as subjects. Although it is recognized that laboratory research can be used to make valid generalizations to the field (Locke, 1986), there is justifiable concern over the extent to which the typical lab study captures the essential features of appraisal in organizations. Bernardin and Villanova (1986) have described several critical features that are present in performance appraisals in organizations but are typically lacking in laboratory studies. These include: (a) the use of multiple ratees, (b) real consequences for the rater and the ratee, (c) time pressures, and (d) ratees who know the rater and who sign off on the rating form. The absence of these features may seriously restrict the generalizability of laboratory studies.

In our opinion, the debate over the external generalizability of lab studies of cognitive processes in appraisal has been somewhat misguided because of a failure to distinguish between performance *evaluation* (a private judgment) and performance *appraisal* (a public, written form that is submitted to the organization). Consequences for the rater and the ratee are the result of appraisals, not judgments. This suggests that Points b and d above may not be relevant when laboratory studies are used to make inferences about *judgments* in organizations. On the other hand, Point c is probably relevant to both judgments and appraisals.

For the most part, however, laboratory research is concerned with judgments rather than with decisions that have real consequences. It is incumbent on cognitive researchers to make this distinction and to indicate clearly what aspects of the overall appraisal process are or are not being examined in a particular study. It is incumbent on critics of cognitive research to recognize that laboratory studies do not have to mimic all of the features of performance appraisals in the field to provide useful information about the way in which raters transform their observations of ratee behavior to judgments about their effectiveness.

Research focusing on the cognitive processes involved in performance appraisal has made both theoretical and practical contributions (Ilgen, Barnes-Farrell, & McKellin, 1993). For example, it has advanced our understanding of such things as the role of attention, storage, and retrieval in complex judgment tasks. It has also suggested that early assumptions about the importance of behavioral-based as opposed to trait-based appraisal systems were unrealistic; it seems clear that incorporating behavioral information into appraisals does not solve the problem of subjectivity. However, it is hard to avoid the conclusion that, given the volume of research in this area, the overall contributions have been relatively minor.

AFFECT AND PERFORMANCE EVALUATION

Dipboye (1985) noted that recent research on the interview has addressed cognitive variables at length but has largely ignored several other important variables. In particular, both this literature and the PA literature have paid little attention to the issue of affect. Cognitive models portray evaluation as a "cold" process that does not explicitly involve emotion. It is more accurate to think of performance evaluation as an instance of "hot cognition" or of judgment that involves both cognitive and affective processes. Raters typically feel strongly about several of their subordinates and these feelings are likely to influence their evaluations (see Cardy & Dobbins [1994] for a review of research on the role of affect in appraisal).

Unfortunately, *affect* is a fairly broad term. PA research that has examined affect has generally concentrated on liking (Cardy & Dobbins, 1986; Dobbins & Russell, 1986). *Liking* can be thought of as directed affect—it represents an emotional reaction to a specific person. Not all affect, however, is directed toward a specific person. Rather, there are at least two categories of undirected affect: (a) mood—which represents transient undirected affect, and (b) temperament—which represents chronic undirected affect. It is likely that both mood and temperament influence evaluations. A rater who is in a good mood at the time of observation and/or evaluation may give more positive evaluations than one who is in a sour mood. Raters who have a very positive, upbeat disposition may evaluate performance differently than raters whose temperament is surly or mean.

It is likely that raters' reactions to demographic cues (e.g., race, gender), physical attractiveness, and nonverbal behaviors are more affective than cognitive (Demuse, 1987). That is, a rater may have a "gut reaction" to a person of a different race or to a very attractive (or unattractive) person; this reaction will color the rater's evaluation. Zajonc (1980) has argued that affective reactions may, in some instances, occur independently of cognitive reactions. Thus, if a rater "knows" that an attractive person does not necessarily make a better secretary than an unattractive one, this may not prevent the rater from reacting positively to the attractive person and negatively to the unattractive one. Affective biases may be very difficult to detect and remove.

Affect and Cognition

Affect can influence cognition in many ways (Robbins & DeNisi, 1994). First, one's affective reaction to a ratee could serve as one piece of information to be integrated with other pieces (e.g., observations of behavior, reports from customers). It is thus possible that affect directly influences evaluations (Isen, Shalker, Clark, & Karp, 1978). It is likely, however, that the influence of affect on evaluations is at least partially indirect. That is, affect may change the cognitive processes themselves, as well as serving as a cue to be cognitively processed.

Studies by Clark and Isen (1982) and Isen and Daubman (1984) have shown that mood can affect encoding and retrieval processes. There is some evidence for mood congruency effects (Bower, 1981; Teasdale & Fogarty, 1979), which occur when the similarity between one's mood at the time of encoding and one's mood at the time of retrieval is positively correlated with the likelihood of retrieving specific pieces of information. The reasoning here is that mood can serve as a retrieval cue. Although it has been shown that having the same cues available at both encoding and retrieval enhances memory (Tulving, 1983), it is still not clear whether mood congruency effects really occur, or if they do, whether they are strong enough to make any practical difference.

At one time the existence of mood congruency effects led to the suggestion that learning might be state-dependent, in that material learned under one mood (e.g., a positive mood) would be more easily remembered while the learner was in that same mood than when the mood at learning was different from the mood at the time of testing (Bower, 1981). This suggestion is no longer considered a viable one; if congruency effects exist at all, they are likely to be too weak to substantially affect learning.

Affect influences the categorization process in two ways. First, affect increases the salience of some categories (Tajfel, 1969). It is possible that some categories are conceptually associated with affective states (e.g., a category of "things you detest"); the association between affect and categories may even result from classical conditioning. If a category of stimuli is repeatedly paired with aversive (or desired) outcomes, that category may develop a strong affective connotation. Affect also influences category breadth (Sinclair, 1988). There is evidence that positive affect leads to an increase in the breadth of categories, in such a way that persons in a positive affective state will classify more persons or objects into a given category than will persons in a negative affective state.

Although the precise explanation is not yet clear, there is evidence that interrater agreement is higher among raters with similar affect than among raters with dissimilar affect (Tsui & Barry, 1986; Zajonc, 1980). This may be because affect itself is a piece of data that is integrated into the evaluation, but may also reflect the indirect influence of affect. That is, raters with similar affect may employ similar categorization strategies and may have similar retrieval cues available at the time of evaluation.

Research suggests that the effects of affect are not symmetric, in the sense that positive and negative affect do not necessarily lead to opposite outcomes (Isen, 1984). For example, positive affect is more strongly linked to halo than is negative affect (Williams & Keating, 1987). In one area, however—leniency—there is evidence of symmetric effects (Williams, Allinger, & Pulliam, 1988). Positive affect leads to lenient ratings, whereas negative affect leads to ratings that are unduly severe.

The current research on affective bases of performance evaluation and appraisal has barely scratched the surface of an important question. It seems reasonable that the influence of affect on evaluations can be as strong as or even stronger than the influence of cognitive variables. Managers like some of their subordinates, dislike others, and have no strong feelings about still others. Some managers have happy dispositions, whereas some focus on the negative sides of life. Managers are sometimes in good moods and sometimes in bad moods. All of these variables are likely to influence managers' judgments regarding the performance of their subordinates. Furthermore, affect effects the judgments of some raters but not others (Harris & Sackett, 1988). Current understanding of affective processes in performance evaluation and appraisal is not sufficiently advanced to allow us to predict the strength or direction of all of these effects, or to determine the circumstances under which affect will have a large or a small effect on evaluations. There is clearly need for more work in this area.

SUMMARY

Information processing has become a central concern in many areas of psychology. During the 1980s, performance appraisal research was swept up in the so-called cognitive revolution. Most current PA studies are carried out in the lab, using college students as subjects and using a variety of tasks that appear to mimic features of appraisals in organizations. This research has advanced our understanding of evaluative judgment, but it is not clear whether it has contributed to our understanding of appraisals in organizations.

Cognitive research has dealt with the acquisition, encoding, storage, and retrieval processes involved in judgment; less research has been devoted to the integration of information. One general conclusion that can be reached on the basis of this research is that the way in which information is initially categorized and encoded can have a substantial and perhaps decisive impact on the subsequent use of that information. This suggests that training raters to develop consistent and accurate categorization schemes (as in frame-of-reference training) are probably worthwhile.

Research on the influence of affect on appraisals suggests that affect is an important component of appraisal. The rater's mood, temperament, and like or dislike of individual ratees is almost certain to influence ratings.

The most significant challenge to cognitive and affective researchers is to develop applications for their findings. As we noted in this chapter, most of the applications of this research to date have been negative (i.e., demonstrations that existing techniques do not work). The field needs to move beyond this stage, which will require the active cooperation of researchers and practitioners. It may be several years before it is possible to determine whether research on cognition and affect will have an impact on performance appraisal in organizations.

8

Rater Goals

Performance appraisal (PA) research has traditionally treated appraisal as a measurement process in which the principal goals were to provide reliable and valid measures of ratee performance. As a result, many of the deficiencies of appraisal systems are blamed on inadequate measurement instruments (i.e., rating scales), inadequate training, inappropriate schema and cognitive structures, and so on.

As discussed in Chapter 1, it may be more useful to treat appraisal as a goal-directed *communication* process in which the rater attempts to use PA to advance his or her interests. Raters are not passive measurement instruments, and it is unwise to assume that they are always trying to provide accurate measures of each ratee's performance. This is not to say that the rater always, or even often, engages in cynical manipulation of appraisals. Rather, it is a simple recognition of the fact that raters are likely to consider the implications of the ratings they give and may sometimes conclude that they *should* give ratings that do not correspond with their true evaluations of the ratee (this topic is taken up in greater detail in Chapter 9).

In this chapter we discuss the nature and content of the goals that might direct the rater's behavior. Unfortunately, very little is known about the goals actually pursued by raters; most evidence at this point is anecdotal (Bjerke et al., 1987; Longenecker et al., 1987). A great deal is known about the general ways in which goals influence behavior, however, and we can draw several hypotheses about rater goals from this literature. After discussing the nature of rater goals we will examine the ways in which these goals develop, as well as the ways in which they are communicated to members of the organization. Next, we will discuss rater goals as a function of ratee performance levels. There is clear evidence that supervisors pursue different goals and use different strategies when working with good- versus poor-performing subordinates. Finally, we will discuss the relationship (or lack of relationship) between the goals of the rater and those of the organization.

NATURE OF GOALS

Studies of the political aspects of the appraisal process (e.g., Longenecker & Gioia, 1988; Longenecker et al., 1987; Patz, 1975) present several examples of goal-directed appraisal behavior in its most obvious and perhaps extreme form. The image that comes to mind when reading some of this literature is of managers sitting in their offices, scheming about ways to play with the appraisal system in order to achieve their particular ends. Although an analysis of the goal-directed aspects of performance appraisal must necessarily include this type of behavior, it should not be restricted to this somewhat simplistic case. Rather, *goal-directed behavior* refers to a much broader and more subtle range of phenomena.

The idea that behavior is best understood by examining the goals pursued by an individual has a long and distinguished history in psychology. The theories of McDougall (1908, 1932), Tolman (1932), and Allport (1937) dealt extensively with the concept of goal-directed behavior. The influential work of Miller et al. (1960) was largely concerned with the way in which behavior is structured by goals and plans. Similarly, Schank and Abelson (1977) stressed the importance of goals for understanding both scripts (i.e., stereotyped patterns of behavior in familiar situations) and plans (i.e., coherent patterns of goal-directed behavior in less familiar situations). European psychologists, particularly those interested in action theory, have devoted substantial attention to the role of goals in explaining human behavior (Frese & Sabini, 1985). Finally, Pervin (1983) articulated a theory of personality that explains the continuity and flow of human behavior largely in terms of the goals an individual pursues. He claimed that "much human behavior can only be understood in terms of its role in goal acquisition . . . the movement toward goals gives behavior its organized, patterned quality" (Pervin, 1983, p. 10).

Pervin's (1983, 1989) theory makes three points that are particularly relevant to our conception of performance appraisal as goal-directed behavior. First, he noted that an individual's behavior may be influenced by multiple and sometimes conflicting goals. Second, goals are complex and fuzzy rather than representing simple statements of the ends individuals consciously value and pursue. As a result, people are not always aware of the goals or of all aspects of the goals that they are pursuing. Rather, some goals or aspects of goals are assumed to be more accessible (i.e., more readily brought into consciousness) than others. Finally, Pervin (1983) noted that goals are acquired in a variety of ways, including both direct experience and vicarious learning, and that goals reflect both the values and the experiences of the individual.

Goals are central to action theory. For example, Sjoeberg (1981) distinguishes between behaviors that are not tied to a particular goal and actions that are goal directed. In Chapter 7 we noted that the processes by which individuals divide a stream of behavior into discrete chunks could have implications for ratings. Action theory suggests that the processes of perceiving behaviors versus actions may be quite different. In observing behaviors, the individual must impose structure, whereas actions have an inherent structure. One implication may be that actions (i.e., goal-oriented behaviors) may be perceived similarly by most observers, whereas behaviors may be perceived differently. The action-behavior distinction has some interesting parallels in job analysis, specifically in the distinction between behaviors and tasks. Tasks are defined in terms of specific operations and endpoints (e.g., install generator), whereas behaviors are defined in more generic terms (e.g., supervise others). As in task analysis, it may be useful to analyze rating behavior by first asking about the purpose of the behavior.

The literature on goal-directed action is not always clear in defining exactly what constitutes a goal. For example, social learning theory (e.g.,

Bandura & Walters, 1963; Rotter, 1982) generally treats goals as endpoints. That is, the goal object is regarded as the source of reinforcement for goal-oriented behaviors. Over time, however, the goal itself takes on reinforcement value that can persist even if the original goal object is withdrawn. In this literature it is first the goal object and later the process of goal achievement itself that provides the motivating force for behavior. Rotter (1982) ana-lyzed test faking in terms of differences in the goals envisioned by the examiner and by the respondent. Manipulation of ratings can be thought of as a sort of test faking and can be analyzed in analogous terms.

On the other hand, Rommetveit (1981) describes goals as means-end structures. That is, the goal not only implies the end to be pursued but also the methods that are used to pursue it. Finally, Stokols (1981) incorporates features of the environment in defining goals. Specifically, he notes that the environment can either facilitate or hinder the accomplishment of goals, and suggests that the motivating power of goals may depend on the degree to which they are seen as attainable.

We believe that there is a useful separation between environments, means, and ends when describing the types of goals that are likely to affect the behavior of raters. In part, this is because the choice of means and the evaluation of environments often involve consideration of subordinate goals or even goals that are not directly related to the end currently being sought by the rater. Thus, in this chapter we define rater goals in terms of the ends pursued rather than in terms of the environment in which they are pursued or the means used to pursue them.

Relating Goals to Behavior. The process by which goals actually influence behavior is not fully understood. In some cases the process is probably quite like that implied in discussions of the political nature of performance appraisal (i.e., sometimes people consciously consider their goals and the various strategies they might use to accomplish them). Goal-directed be-havior of this type mirrors the processes that have been extensively studied in research on rational decision making.

Theories of judgment and decision making have traditionally involved some sort of mental calculus, in which the individual evaluated and weighed several attributes of a stimulus or course of action and then acted to maximize the utility or desirability of the expected outcome (Edwards, 1980; Hammond et al., 1980; Keeney & Raiffa, 1976). Although theories of this sort have advanced our understanding of both judgment and decision making, there is growing discontent with these theories, especially with their ability to describe the processes decision makers go through. The idea that decision makers have the capability or even the inclination to assess accurately the probable costs and benefits or multiple alternatives and choose the one that has the highest expected utility simply does not fit current conceptions of cognition, perception, or choice. Image theory (Beach, 1990; Beach & Mitchell, 1987; Mitchell & Beach, 1990) has been proposed as an alternative approach that more closely mirrors the processes involved in decision making, especially in instances where decisions are either automatic or intuitive.

The theory suggests that the process of making decisions involves principles (i.e., beliefs, values, norms), goals (i.e., future states the decision maker hopes to attain), and plans (i.e., ways of attaining goals). Much of the formal theory is devoted to questions of when, and under what circumstances, people change plans and goals. The theory also examines the impact of the decision context on the way in which decisions are framed. This theory is directly relevant to performance, and it helps to clarify the often indirect ways in which rater goals might affect performance appraisal behavior. Image theory suggests that the process of fitting ratings to goals need not involve any cynical manipulation, but rather might involve a relatively simple (and often unconscious and automatic) assessment of the extent to which performance ratings are consistent with the goal the rater is pursuing, with gradual and unconscious modification of the performance evaluation if ratings and goals are inconsistent. Conscious manipulation of ratings (e.g., giving a high rating to someone you know is a very poor performer) may occur only when the gap between the rater's goals and the ratings he or she believes the ratee truly deserves is sufficiently large to trigger the search for alternative rating strategies.

Image theory suggests that patterns of rating behavior, which are initially directed at achieving a particular goal, may persist long after that goal has lost its relevance. For example, a new supervisor might initially choose to give lenient ratings in an effort to ingratiate himself or herself with subordinates. As long as there are no serious negative consequences to giving high ratings, this pattern might become habitual and might persist long after the rater has lost concern over the potential friction that might result from giving harsher ratings.

Multiple Goals

Behavior is often influenced by several goals, which may or may not be compatible (Argyle, 1981; Cleveland et al., 1989; Reither & Staudel, 1985). These goals may operate sequentially or simultaneously, and the same behavior might be a part of several distinct actions. As a result, the use of goals to unitize behavior (i.e., classify behavior in terms of discrete actions) may not be simple: Each rater behavior may reflect a complex set of goals. Furthermore, these goals may have different sources. Cleveland and associates (1989) note that the organization often imposes a number of goals on the rater (however, not all of these goals will be accepted by the rater). In addition, the rater might impose a number of his or her own goals. As we will note in Chapter 14, the goals of ratees, clients and customers, and society in general may affect performance appraisal. Some of the multiple goals involved in appraisal will be compatible, but others may come in conflict.

When multiple goals exist, how do we determine which one(s) are influencing behavior? This may depend in part on the structure of the set of goals. Some researchers suggest that this organization is hierarchical in nature (Beach, 1985; Maslow, 1970), but Broadbent (1985) suggests a heterarchic structure. A heterarchy implies a more fluid arrangement than a strict hierarchy. It allows for the possibility that one goal can sometimes be more important and sometimes less important than a particular alternative. Regardless of the structure (i.e., hierarchy vs. heterarchy), research on the organization of goals suggests that separate but compatible goals are grouped into relatively homogeneous categories. It may, therefore, be more useful to investigate the broad categories of goals pursued by raters than to catalog the specific goals that are pursued.

Awareness of Rater Goals

As noted earlier, individuals may not be aware of any or all of the goals they are pursuing (Argyle, 1981; Broadbent, 1985; Pervin, 1983, 1989). One implication is that simply asking raters what they are trying to accomplish may not be sufficient, even if raters try to answer the questions truthfully and completely. Rather, it may be necessary to infer goals from behavior.

A research strategy similar to that used in construct validation may be appropriate here. That is, PA researchers may need to start with a set of hypotheses about the goals that are most likely to influence rater behavior, then proceed to deductions about events, behaviors, and so on, that would occur if those goals were in fact being pursued, then determine whether those events, behaviors, and so on *had* occurred. If the answer is yes, this is evidence that the hypothesized goals are indeed being pursued (Murphy & Davidshofer, 1988). As in any construct validation study it may not be possible to *prove* that the hypotheses about rater goals are correct. As the body of evidence consistent with the hypotheses grows, however, the greater the likelihood that the hypotheses have captured at least some of the goals actually being pursued by the rater.

In Chapters 1 through 4 we discussed the influence of situational or contextual variables on rater behavior. Goals (both conscious and unconscious) may represent a very useful tool for analyzing and describing situations (Fuller, 1950; Magnusson, 1981; Pervin, 1981). That is, a description of the rating situation is more likely to convey useful information if it includes information about the goal or goals being pursued than if it does not. Furthermore, other characteristics of the situation may be used to make inferences about rater goals. For example, if the norms of the organization include a strong emphasis on maintaining good interpersonal relations in the workgroup, it is reasonable to infer that one goal that will affect the rater's behavior is that of avoiding negative interpersonal incidents. In this book we use rater goals as an integral part of describing the context of rating in organizations.

Typology of Rater Goals

The specific goals pursued by raters will depend on a wide range of factors, including the values and experiences of the rater, the climate and culture of the organization, the performance level of subordinates, and the like. Several years of good descriptive research might be necessary in order to describe the goals that are most frequently pursued by raters. One way to structure this research is to propose a set of general categories of goals that raters are most likely to pursue. We believe that many of the most frequently pursued goals can be identified with one of four general categories: (a) task-performance goals, (b) interpersonal goals, (c) strategic goals, and (d) internalized goals.

Task-performance goals involve using performance appraisal to increase or maintain ratees' performance levels. Specific performance goals will necessarily depend on whether the ratee being evaluated is in fact (or in the rater's opinion) performing well. If the individual is performing well, the rater's goal might be to maintain that performance level. If the rater is performing poorly, the rater's goal might be to increase motivation or to identify and correct weaknesses. Finally, task-performance goals may be future-oriented. Raters may use appraisals to guide the development of employees in such a way that they will prepare themselves for future assignments or jobs.

Interpersonal goals are those that involve using appraisal to maintain or improve interpersonal relations between the supervisor and subordinates. The interpersonal goal that has been discussed most frequently in the literature (e.g., Mohrman & Lawler, 1983; Naiper & Latham, 1986) involves maintaining a positive climate in the workgroup. Because low ratings can lead to resentment and perceptions of inequity, the maintenance of a positive workgroup climate often involves rating inflation. It is interesting to note that some studies (e.g., Naiper & Latham, 1986) have questioned the extent to which raters are concerned with interpersonal relations. If the rater does not care what others think of him or her, this goal may not influence the rater's behavior.

Many interpersonal goals may involve efforts to achieve or restore equity. If a supervisor believes that a specific subordinate deserved some reward that he or she did not receive (e.g., a promotion or raise), subsequent ratings may be distorted to achieve those outcomes. If workgroup members believe that rewards have not been distributed equitably, the supervisor might have a strong incentive to restore perceptions of equity. Yet another class of interpersonal goals are those that involve attempts to establish or maintain interpersonal influence. For example, a rater who demonstrates that he or she can have a substantial influence on administrative decisions (e.g., salary) may have a great deal of power and influence over subordinates.

Strategic goals involve using appraisal to increase the supervisor's and/or the workgroup's standing in the organization. There are several ways to accomplish this. First, uniformly high ratings might reflect positively on both the rater and the workgroup, especially if the rater is viewed as a credible source. Second, the standing of both the rater and the workgroup may be enhanced if workgroup members are given widely sought promotions and assignments; raters may distort their ratings to increase the likelihood of these valued outcomes. Third, both the rater and the workgroup might look better if the supervisor succeeds in transferring poor performers to someone else's workgroup. Again, performance ratings may influence this type of decision.

Internalized goals are the product of the rater's values and beliefs. For example, a rater who believes that he or she should be honest in completing performance appraisals may turn in very different appraisals than a rater who believes that he or she should obtain value rewards for subordinates. The rater's self-image may also affect rating behavior. A rater who believes he or she is or should be a participative leader will probably devote more time and attention to feedback that will a rater whose self-image is more authoritarian.

Communication Rules

Supervisors' and subordinates' role demands and constraints often make it difficult for them to pursue important goals openly. For example, a rater whose goal is to get rid of a poor-performing subordinate may not be able to turn in extremely low ratings; these ratings may lead to unfavorable reactions in the workgroup. Organizations (and units within organizations) frequently develop sets of unwritten rules that allow the supervisor to communicate the necessary information to the organization (i.e., that the ratee is a poor performer) without necessarily giving low ratings. Schall (1983) described these communication rules as "tacit understandings (generally unwritten and unspoken) about appropriate ways to interact (communicate) with others in given roles and situations; these are choices, not laws (although they constrain choice through normative, practical, and logical force), and they allow interactors to interpret behavior in similar ways" (p. 560).

Although not formally a part of the goal, communication rules are critical to the achievement of many goals, particularly goals involving subordinates who perform either very well or very poorly. For example, Bjerke and colleagues (1987) studied raters' approach to evaluating the performance of officers in the navy. Like many organizations, the navy is plagued by rating inflation; in some specialties, virtually everyone receives ratings at or near the top of the scale. However, raters were able to communicate their evaluations effectively in the narrative section of the appraisal. A poor-performing officer might receive high ratings, but the narrative section of his or her evaluation might be restricted to statements such as "is neat in appearance." A better performer might receive the same scores, but his or her narrative section might contain substantive comments about the most important aspects of the job.

In the example described above, raters developed a special language that allowed them to give high ratings and still discriminate between good and poor performers. We do not think this is unique to the navy, although there may be more uniformity in the armed services than in other large organizations. Very little is known about the communication rules that govern appraisal in organizations. However, appraisals are presumably more effective if there is widespread agreement about the appropriate communication rules, and presumably many of the deficiencies of appraisal systems involve incomplete or poorly understood communication rules. In particular, agreement regarding communication rules may make it easier to communicate the rationale behind ratings as well as the true meaning of the rating.

DEVELOPMENT OF GOALS

When they first start their jobs, it is unlikely that supervisors have well-articulated goals that direct their behavior in performance appraisal. Indeed, this group might be unique in that they function in a way that some appraisal researchers assume *all* raters function—their principal goal might be to do the best job they can in honestly and accurately evaluating subordinates' performance.

With more experience, raters are likely to develop a more complex, sophisticated set of goals that reflect the realities of their organization, department, or workgroup. In part, these goals will be shaped by their own experiences on the job. That is, they will learn what outcomes to expect as the result of giving good or poor ratings and will also learn which of these outcomes is of concern to the organization. However, this type of trial-and-error process is not the only one involved in acquiring goals and beliefs regarding PA. Organizations make formal and informal efforts to socialize their members, and one aspect of being socialized into the role of supervisor or manager is to learn the appropriate behaviors and strategies for evaluating subordinates.

Socialization Processes

Organizations are composed of a number of individuals who perform interlocking roles. Thus, it is important for newcomers quickly to learn the roles they are expected to carry out. Until newcomers learn their roles, co-workers whose jobs are in some way linked to theirs will find it more difficult to perform their jobs.

The socialization process refers to the transition from the status of a naive newcomer who knows little about the role, to that of a knowledgeable insider who understands the nuances of his or her role as well as the relationship between that role and the roles of others in the organization (Chao, 1988; Russo & Hartman, 1987). Much of this socialization occurs via the *role episode process,* in which other members of the role set (i.e., other persons with a vested interest in how well the newcomer performs his or her role) send information evaluating the focal person's role performance (Graen, 1976). Behaviors that are consistent with the role are met with approval, whereas behaviors inconsistent with the role are sanctioned.

The role socialization process can be intensive in the initial period in which an individual occupies a job. The critical experiences in organizational and job socialization typically occur during the first year (Buchanan, 1974). The model shown in Figure 8.1 (adapted from Feldman, 1976) illustrates the steps in the socialization process.

First, there is some anticipatory socialization that occurs before an individual enters the job. That is, individuals are likely to start with expectations about their role as well as the behaviors appropriate for that role. Socialization itself begins with the process of accommodation, which involves initiation to both the task and the group, role definition, and the development of congruence between one's standards and the prevailing standards of the role set. Next comes role management, which involves resolution of conflicts between the work role and other roles (e.g., family roles) as well as resolution of conflicting demands presented by the work role. The outcomes of role socialization range from job involvement and satisfaction to the development of influence in the organization.

The precise content of what is learned in role socialization will vary from job to job but there are some broad categories of learning that are likely to be present in most jobs (Fisher, 1986). First, and most obvious, the person must learn how to do the job. Thus, training activities (both formal and informal) are one component of socialization. Second, he or she must learn the values and norms of the immediate workgroup. Third, he or she must learn the values, culture, goals, and norms of the organization; these are not always the same as those of the workgroup. Finally, the individual must incorporate the new role into his or her identity or self-image. One implication

Figure 8.1. Steps in the Socialization Process

SOURCE: Adapted from D. C. Feldman, "A Contingency Theory of Socialization," *Administrative Science Quarterly, 21* (1976), pp. 443-452.

of this final category of learning is that a fully socialized individual will not only learn the role but will also internalize at least some aspects of the role.

It is clear that some aspects of role socialization are easier than others. For example, expectations about the content of work are easily changed through experience (Wanous, 1980). Values and general work orientation are much less easily changed. In part this is because values are more firmly entrenched and more central than specific expectations about the content of work. There is, however, another factor that influences the degree to which a person can be changed through socialization—the method of training.

Very few people object to participating in technical training that is designed to instruct them about how to do the job. Many people, however, would object strenuously to training programs that were designed to mold their values or their orientation toward work. It may therefore be difficult to impart values and norms; these may require somewhat indirect methods of socialization. Weiss (1978), for example, suggests that organizational values are learned through modeling the behavior (and apparent values) of others. The ease of modeling probably depends on the number of opportunities the focal person has to make relevant observations of others' behavior, as well as the power and status of the role sender (Fisher, 1986).

Organizational Culture and Rater Goals

Modeling the behaviors of specific role senders is only one way in which newcomers acquire the values of the workgroup and the organization. These values and expectations that define the climate and culture of the organization influence most of the interactions between the focal person and other members of the organization (Rousseau, 1988; Schneider & Reichers, 1983); therefore, these values will probably influence the development of specific goals for performance appraisal.

Martin and Siehl (1983) note that the culture of an organization offers "an interpretation of an institution's history that members can use to decipher how they will be expected to behave in the future" (p. 52). Thus, the culture defines the behaviors that are either accepted or sanctioned, and the process of transmitting that culture (e.g., through stories or rituals) may serve as a powerful socializing force. In the context of performance appraisal, the culture might determine what approach to appraisal and what behaviors are evaluated positively or negatively in the organization.

Although evidence about the content of organizational cultures is fragmentary and contradictory, it is reasonable to expect that beliefs, values, and norms regarding PA will often be a part of the organization's culture. In some organizations, appraisal is treated as important; in others, it is treated as a joke. Feedback is the norm in some organizations and the exception in others. Ratings are a critical determinant of decisions in some organizations and are ignored in others. It is possible that all of these aspects of appraisal are influenced by the culture of the organization and that newcomers must learn that culture before they can use the appraisal system effectively to achieve their goals.

Organizational cultures can be described in terms of both the content and intensity of the values and beliefs that are part of that culture (Rousseau 1988). The culture of an organization is most likely to affect the behavior of raters when (a) it includes beliefs, values, and so on that are directly relevant to appraisal; and (b) those values, beliefs, and so on are strongly held.

Returning to our earlier example of appraisal in the navy, there appears to be a strong norm in that organization that appraisals should be used to secure promotion for deserving subordinates (and for those who show promise of performing well in more responsible jobs). Most raters appear to accept this norm and fill out their appraisals with promotion in mind (Bjerke et al., 1987). These same conditions (i.e., strongly held beliefs about how appraisal should be done) may make it difficult to change the appraisal system in an organization without first changing its culture.

Contextual Factors Affecting Appraisal Goals

A number of previous reviews, models, and studies of appraisal (Bernardin & Beatty, 1984; Bjerke et al., 1987; Carroll & Schneier, 1982; Davis & Dickinson, 1987; DeCotiis & Petit, 1978; Dobbins et al., 1988; Landy & Farr, 1980; Murphy & Cleveland, 1991; Wexley & Klimoski, 1984) have acknowledged the importance of the situation or context within which appraisals are conducted. In most discussions of contextual or situational influences on performance appraisal, however, little attention has been paid to exactly how context influences the appraisal process. As suggested below, it is possible that goals serve as mediating variables in the relationship between context and appraisal behavior. That is, contextual factors may have a strong influence on the goals developed by raters, organizations, and ratees in the appraisal process, and thus indirectly influence the way in which appraisals are carried out, interpreted, and used. Before describing a model linking context, goals, and appraisal processes and outcomes, it is useful to describe in more detail what is meant by "context."

Proximal Factors. As we noted in Chapter 2, context variables that affect performance appraisal can be conceptualized as either proximal or distal (cf. Brunswick, 1952; Cleveland & Hollmann, 1991). Proximal variables directly impinge upon or influence the rater, the ratee, and so forth. Proximal variables thought to affect performance appraisal include group leader and task characteristics (Bernardin & Beatty, 1984; Bjerke et al., 1987; Brewer, 1979; Hackman, 1976; Lee, 1985; Liden & Mitchell, 1983; Linville & Jones, 1980); perceived rewards, trust, punishment, and threats (Bernardin et al., 1981; Bernardin & Villanova, 1986; Longenecker et al., 1987; Mohrman & Lawler, 1983); previous and subsequent levels of ratee performance (Cummings & Schwab, 1973; Murphy et al., 1985; Murphy,

Gannett et al., 1986); appraisal system features such as scale type, instructions and item content or anchors, presence of training program, frequency of evaluation, and so forth (Bernardin & Beatty, 1984; Dobbins et al., 1988; Mount, 1983; Murphy & Constans, 1987; Wexley & Klimoski, 1984); rater acquaintance, commitment, and affect (Bazerman et al., 1982; Freeberg, 1969; Kingstrom & Mainstone, 1985; Tsui & Barry, 1986); and finally, the purpose of rating (Bernardin & Beatty, 1984; Cleveland et al., 1989; DeNisi et al., 1984; Landy & Farr, 1980).

There is evidence that suggests that these proximal variables influence the outcomes of rating. For example, groups, which help define the context of ratings, can influence individuals in a number of ways (Hackman, 1976, 1992). Groups can influence the knowledge and skills of individuals, the level of psychological arousal while working, and the member's effort and performance strategies. Further, norms or expectations develop within groups regarding acceptable levels of performance (Sherif & Sherif, 1964). Not only do norms develop concerning productivity, but also concerning what are acceptable performance ratings. For some groups, a norm develops that leads raters to believe that high or inflated ratings are the only acceptable ratings. It may be unacceptable for a rater to record ratings that depict average or below average performance, even when such ratings are accurate. For example, based on information from rater interviews, Bjerke et al. (1987) found that when there were high entrance or educational standards for admission into a group or job, raters were reluctant to evaluate employees as average or below. The raters' rationale was that these individuals passed through numerous performance hurdles in order to gain access to the group, and therefore, were all "superior."

Characteristics of a group, such as the performance variability of its members (Ilgen & Feldman, 1983; Liden & Mitchell, 1983) and the salience of specific group members (Brewer, 1979; Linville & Jones, 1980; Quattrone & Jones, 1980), are also known to influence the accuracy and the leniency of ratings. Raters do not evaluate one person on a single occasion; rather, evaluation occurs for many people over an extended time or covering many tasks. Therefore, there is opportunity for other group members to influence specific ratings by providing raters with information for comparative rather than absolute judgment (Ilgen & Feldman, 1983).

Mohrman and Lawler (1983) and others (e.g., Padgett, 1989) have described how rater motivation contributes to accurate ratings. One factor that influences motivation is rewards. Longenecker et al. (1987) interviewed executives concerning the politics of appraisal and found that raters inflated appraisal outcomes in order to avoid negative or uncomfortable feedback sessions and to avoid negative consequences or actions for the ratees (i.e., a poor appraisal in the employees' permanent files, etc.). Further, Longenecker et al., (1987) found that the most frequently cited reason for rating inflation was to obtain rewards for the subordinate (e.g., maximize merit increases). Bjerke et al. (1987) found similar results from interviews with navy officers (raters) and from a small sample of industry personnel managers.

The level of trust and/or threat perceived by the rater (and ratee) in the appraisal process has been shown to affect ratings (Bernardin & Buckley, 1981; Bernardin & Villanova, 1986; Kay et al., 1965). Trust and threat appear to influence both the psychometric quality of rating outcomes (i.e., leniency) and the acceptance of the appraisal system. Organizational climates characterized by low trust, either between raters or across organizational levels, can lower the effectiveness of an appraisal system (Lawler, 1972). Personal acquaintance and task acquaintance are related to leniency, although the latter is less strongly related. Freeberg (1969) found that appraisal ratings were more accurate when the raters possessed task relevant acquaintance (e.g., relevant knowledge or contact) with the ratee than when raters possessed irrelevant acquaintance (e.g., socializing). Using interview data, Kallejian et al. (1953) found a similar relationship between the supervisor and the subordinate's interpersonal relationship and appraisal ratings.

Distal Factors. Distal context cues are those intra- and extra-organizational characteristics that may influence judgments, ratings, and assessment indirectly. Their effects are not only indirect, but frequently also implicit. That is, employees and raters may not be aware that these variables play a role in the judgments and decisions that they make. Distal context variables include organizational life cycle and structure; organizational goals; organizational climate, culture, and values; the status of the specific function or unit; and external/legal entrance standards to a functional unit or job type (e.g., lawyer, nurse, engineers, etc.). Examples of distal variables external to the organization include the state of the economy, the financial condition of the organization in comparison to competitors, and the legal climate.

There is evidence to support the effects of distal context factors. Cleveland et al. (1989) found that organizational complexity and organizational coordination were correlated with ways in which organizations used performance appraisals in making decisions. Organizations high in complexity and coordination were more likely to use appraisal for purposes such as feedback, identifying strengths and weaknesses in employees, and systems maintenance than other organizations. Cleveland et al. (1986) found support for the influence of an organization's value system upon ratings (see also Longenecker et al., 1987). Specifically, employees whose jobs or activities were perceived as more closely linked with the organization's mission or purpose were rated systematically higher than employees in jobs that were perceived as less central to the organization's mission. Finally, the impact of the economic environment (Starbuck, 1976), the technical environment (Barley, 1986), and the physical work environment (Peters et al., 1982) on appraisal has been documented.

GOALS AS A FUNCTION OF
SUBORDINATE PERFORMANCE

To some extent the rater's goals will be driven by the climate and culture that pervade the organization, as well as by the formal demands of the PA system. It is unlikely, however, that a given rater pursues the same set of goals when evaluating each of his or her subordinates. Rather, there are likely to be very different goals when evaluating a chronically poor performer than when evaluating someone whose work is usually excellent. In the case of poor performers, the rater's goals might be to improve the performance, to improve the chances that the worker will be transferred to some other work unit, or to justify a decision to discipline or dismiss the worker. The choice among goals such as these may depend in part on the extent to which the workgroup accepts the evaluation and supports the impending action. In the case of good performers, the rater's goals will probably center on maintaining current performance; giving ratings that lead to raises, bonuses, or awards might be one mechanism for accomplishing this goal.

Although goals will be somewhat tailored to the subordinate, it is important to note that some goals are probably relevant to *all* subordinates (e.g., the goal of maintaining a positive workgroup climate) and probably do not vary as a function of the subordinate's performance level. The goals that are most likely to vary as a function of the ratee's performance are those in the categories we have labeled "task performance" and "strategic" goals.

Before discussing the specific goals that are pursued for good versus poor performers, it is useful to discuss a related but somewhat more complex distinction among the individuals who report to a given supervisor. That is, the members of the workgroup can often be divided into two categories: those in the in-group and those in the out-group. Raters probably pursue different goals when evaluating members of these two groups.

In-Group Versus Out-Group

Supervisors do not treat all subordinates the same, nor should they. One theory of leadership, the leader-member exchange (LMX) theory (Dansereau et al., 1973), suggests that each supervisor-subordinate dyad may involve a somewhat different style of interaction. The theory also suggests, however, that dyads can be classified into those involving members of the in-group and members of the out-group. Naiper and Ferris (in press) propose a muitidimensional model of distance between supervisors and subordinates that produces a more complex description than this two-category scheme. However, the LMX theory provides a useful starting point for describing differences in the ways supervisors treat various groups of subordinates.

Members of the in-group are chosen on the basis of (a) competence and skill, (b) the degree to which they can be trusted by the supervisor, and (c) their motivation to assume responsibility at work (Liden & Graen, 1980). In-group members perform the tasks that are most critical and challenging, whereas out-group members perform more mundane tasks. Furthermore, members of the in-group receive more information as well as more confidence and concern from supervisors than do those in the out-group (Dansereau et al., 1975).

One way to characterize the difference between the in-group and the out-group is that in-group members are treated by supervisors as trusted assistants, whereas out-group members are treated as hired hands (Vecchio & Gobdel, 1984). That is, in-group members are treated as valued colleagues; out-group members are treated as if they are temporary employees who are not really the concern of the supervisor. Supervisors typically devote more attention, resources, and so on to in-group members, even though out-group members might have a greater need for assistance, information, and the like, to perform their jobs.

Research on the LMX model suggests that supervisors adopt very different leadership styles when dealing with members of the in- versus the out-group (Dansereau et al., 1975). In general, supervisors are more participative when dealing with in-group members and more directive or authoritarian when dealing with out-group members. In the context of performance appraisal, this suggests that supervisors will more readily incorporate information from in-group members in their evaluations and will usually devote more time and effort to feedback for in-group as opposed to out-group members.

Research on in- versus out-groups has dealt with several issues that are directly relevant to performance appraisal. First, and most fascinating, there is evidence that in-group status is related to subjective ratings of performance but *not* to objective indices of performance (Vecchio & Gobdel, 1984). This implies that the perceived competence of in-group members may be an effect rather than the cause of their assignment to the in-group. It is possible that supervisors who feel that they can trust certain subordinates will perceive their performance as better than it actually is.

A second relevant finding is that out-group members typically receive more extreme evaluations than do in-group members (Linville & Jones, 1980). These evaluations are usually negative, but the out-group member who actually does perform well may receive highly inflated ratings. One possible explanation for this effect is the fact that out-group members are expected to perform poorly. Performance that violates those expectations may attract more attention than performance that conforms to expectations (Hastie, 1980; Murphy et al., 1985).

Another finding in this research is that out-groups are seen as relatively homogeneous, whereas differences between in-group members are readily noticed by supervisors (Park & Rothbart, 1982). As a result, all out-group members may receive similar evaluations; stereotypes of the group as a whole may generalize to all group members. One implication of this finding is that performance evaluations may not provide feedback that is useful to out-group members; this feedback may reflect the group and may not be tailored to specific individuals in the group. Another implication is that there will often be range restriction in ratings of out-group members. Thus, raters who have small in-groups and large out-groups may be especially likely to provide ratings that do not discriminate among most subordinates.

The terms *in-group* and *out-group* are not synonymous with *good performer* and *poor performer.* Nevertheless, research on in- versus out-group status may be useful in forming hypotheses about the goals that raters are likely to have when rating subordinates who have performed well or poorly. In particular, this literature suggests that good and poor performers may differ not only in the ratings they receive but also in terms of how they are treated by supervisors in the appraisal process (e.g., the degree to which developmental feedback is given). In particular, there might be substantial differences in the goals being pursued by the rater when the ratee is a good, average, or poor performer.

Goals for Superior Performers

As will be discussed in the next chapter, rating inflation is the norm in most organizations rather than the exception. One implication is that raters might find it difficult to give ratings to truly good performers that adequately reflect their actual performance level. If nearly everyone receives ratings at or near the top of the scale, numerical ratings cannot be used to communicate to the ratee that he or she has really performed well. Thus, one goal that will often be relevant to the rater when evaluating a truly good performer will be to communicate to the ratee and the organization the fact that this individual's performance is in fact better than that of others who have received high ratings.

Raters may address this problem by developing a special vocabulary (Bjerke et al., 1987) or communication rules (Schall, 1983) that allow them to give ratings that are acceptable to all subordinates (in practice, this usually means giving inflated ratings to most ratees) and still communicate their evaluations of their subordinates. For example, a subordinate might receive a rating of 6 on a 7-point scale and may be described as "somewhat above average" in the narrative or comment section of the appraisal. A phrase such as "somewhat above average" might connote poor performance, however; phrases such as "excellent in all respects of the job" might be used to signal performance that is *actually* above average.

This process of developing special communication rules is especially likely to occur in organizations that have a strong and uniform culture. In such organizations, supervisors are probably well aware of what aspects of the job are treated as important and are probably also aware of the special meanings that are given to specific evaluative terms in that organization. This phenomenon is familiar to anyone who must read large numbers of letters of recommendation in which comments tend to be uniformly positive. Special terms are sometimes needed to convey that a particular individual really *is* a superior candidate.

A second goal that is highly relevant when evaluating good performers is to guide their development in such a way that they will be prepared for promotion or complex assignments. The supervisor might accomplish this, for example, by giving feedback on aspects of performance that are not relevant for the subordinate's current job but that are highly relevant for the next higher job in the organization. The popular literature contains many descriptions of *mentoring;* this approach to PA may correspond closely to one of the roles of a mentor.

One strategic goal that might be pursued is to bring higher management's attention to the accomplishments of superior performers. Exceptional performance by subordinates is likely to enhance a supervisor's standing; this is particularly true in organizations where the evaluation of the supervisor depends in part on the performance of the subordinates. We expect that the probability that this goal will affect rater behavior will be positively correlated with the subordinate's performance level. The better the subordinate's performance, the more the supervisor has to gain by bringing that performance to the attention of others in the organization.

Goals for Average Performers

It is reasonable to assume that in a large workgroup the true distribution of job performance is reasonably normal. One implication is that the number of truly good or truly poor performers will be small relative to the number of individuals whose performance can best be described as average. Although average performers are the most numerous, we believe that raters do not pay a great deal of attention to their goals for evaluating average performers. There are several reasons for this. First, good performers are probably in the in-group and will therefore naturally receive much of the rater's attention and concern. Second, poor performers require attention; their low level of performance can directly affect the overall output of the workgroup, particularly if the work performed requires a high level of interdependence. Third, average performance is probably not as salient (or interesting) as either outstandingly good or outstandingly poor performance. As a result, average performers may not receive the attention they deserve.

There are a few goals that might become relevant for average performers, depending on the characteristics of both the person and the situation. First, there might be some individuals who, because of their trustworthiness and responsibility, would be good candidates for the in-group. The rater's goal when evaluating these individuals might be to improve their performance and bring it up to the level of other in-group members. Second, the rater might have a strong incentive to help improve the performance of individuals who are members of specific groups. For example, the supervisor whose values encourage affirmative action efforts might devote considerable time and attention to the development of members of protected groups whose performance is at or below the workgroup's average. On the other hand, the supervisor who is prejudiced against members of specific groups might be inclined to give them harsh ratings; the underlying goal may be to remove these individuals from the workgroup.

Goals for Poor Performers

The literature dealing with supervisors' reactions to poor performance is extensive. Although relatively few studies deal directly with performance appraisal, several conclusions can be drawn about the appraisal goals that might be pursued when evaluating poor performers.

It is clear that managers prefer to avoid dealing with the problem of poor performance (Mitchell & O'Reilly, 1983). In the context of appraisal, raters might avoid the problem by giving relatively high ratings, accompanied by vague and noncommittal comments. In this case, feedback is likely to be perfunctory, and little effort will be expended to improve the subordinate's performance. In many cases, however, it may be impossible to ignore poor performance, either because it is extremely bad or because there are situational factors (e.g., co-workers' resentment) that force the rater to attend to the problem of poor performance.

The rater's reaction to a poor-performing subordinate probably depends on the attributions he or she makes when deciding about the cause of that performance (Mitchell & O'Reilly, 1983). Both supervisors and subordinates make sense of poor performance feedback by developing a causal model of why the person performed poorly (Bannister & Balkin, 1990). Depending on the attributions (e.g., situational constraints, low effort), very different actions might be taken.

Mitchell et al. (1981) described several different categories of attribution, including those that explain poor performance in terms of a lack of ability, a lack of values and standards, an unfavorable environment, or a variety of temporary barriers to performance (e.g., family crises). These specific categories of attributions can in turn be classified in terms of two dimensions that are frequently encountered in attributional research: (a) attributions to internal versus external causes and (b) attributions to stable versus temporary causes. The supervisor's response may be very different, depending on the type of attribution.

Attributions depend on a number of factors, including the behavior itself, and the values, standards, and inclinations of the supervisor (e.g., some supervisors make more internal attributions than others). Another factor that appears to influence the supervisor's attributions is the outcome of the behavior. The same behavior might be evaluated differently, and different causes might be cited for that behavior, depending on the seriousness of the outcomes of that behavior. For example, if two subordinates follow exactly the same unsafe work practices and one of them causes or experiences an accident, they will probably be evaluated differently, with harsher evaluations for the person involved in the accident.

Research on attributions suggests systematic differences in the supervisors' versus subordinates' explanations for poor performance. In general, supervisors make more internal attributions (e.g., the person did not perform well because of poor work values), whereas subordinates are biased in favor of external attributions (e.g., constraints in the situation made it impossible to perform well) (Gioia & Sims, 1985; Ilgen, Mitchell, & Frederickson, 1981). The tendency of supervisors to make internal attributions increases the likelihood that their responses will involve discipline or punishment for the poor-performing subordinate.

Arvey and Jones (1985) note that the topic of discipline or punishment in organizational settings has been largely ignored by behavioral scientists. Studies that have examined punishment suggest that performance appraisal is sometimes used as a vehicle for administering discipline. For example, Jones et al. (1983) studied the degree to which different supervisory behaviors were perceived by subordinates as punishing. Behaviors that were cited as being very punishing included (a) telling a superior about a person's mistakes, (b) documenting the negative things the person does, and (c) publicly praising everyone in the group but that person. These and other punishing behaviors may be used differently in in-groups and out-groups (Arvey & Jones, 1985); in general, the frequency and severity of punishment will be lower in the in-group.

If the attribution is external, the supervisor may avoid punishing the subordinate. Task performance goals for poor-performing subordinates (assuming that the attributions are external) will probably involve efforts to develop the subordinate, to maintain or increase motivation, and to move the subordinate to circumstances that are more favorable (e.g., a less difficult assignment or a different, more supportive workgroup). The rater who intends to develop a poor-performing subordinate will probably (a) give higher ratings than deserved, in an effort to avoid organizational sanctions and maintain motivation; (b) devote more attention to feedback; and (c) identify weaknesses in feedback sessions but not in the performance evaluation forms that are turned in to the organization.

When attributions are internal, strategic goals that involve getting rid of the poor-performing subordinate may strongly influence rating behavior. This will depend in part on how bad the performance really is. The worse the performance, the stronger the incentive to get rid of the subordinate. The strength of this goal may also depend on what specific aspects of performance are below standard. For example, supervisors might be more strongly inclined to get rid of subordinates whose poor performance reflects an inability to get along with co-workers than those whose performance reflects sincere effort but low ability. In general, performance deficiencies that may affect other co-workers may present a stronger incentive to get rid of the subordinate than will deficiencies that involve the individual only.

The exact rating strategy for accomplishing the goals described above will depend in part on the policies of the organization. For example, if the organization is very reluctant to fire poor performers, it may not be a good idea to give low ratings. If the subordinate consistently receives low ratings, it may be very difficult to persuade the organization to transfer him or her to another workgroup. The attractiveness of "dumping" a poor-performing subordinate on another workgroup will vary as a function of the nature and size of the organization. In a small organization, supervisors are more likely to know one another and to be friends. It may be very difficult, in this case, to transfer a poor-performing subordinate to someone else's workgroup without negatively affecting the relationship with that supervisor.

RATER GOALS AND ORGANIZATIONAL GOALS

It would be naive to expect that the goals pursued by the rater in performance appraisal are identical to those the organization wants him or her to pursue (Balzer & Sulsky, 1990). It is also unrealistic, however, to assume that the goals of the rater are completely inconsistent with those of the organization, even when the rater's behavior violates the organization's official policy. The personnel manual may state that accurate performance appraisals are expected, but if this will lead to such things as friction or decreased motivation the supervisor who skillfully inflates his or her ratings is acting in the organization's best interest (see Chapter 12). It is important to keep in mind that when organizational control systems such as PA make unrealistic demands or lead to unforeseen, undesirable consequences, managers who subvert the system may contribute more to the organization than do managers who are faithful to the system.

One reason that rater goals are not always consistent with organizational goals is that the goals of the organization are not always themselves internally consistent (see Chapter 14). Organizations pursue a wide range of goals in several different areas, ranging from the highly general (e.g., profitability) to the highly specific (e.g., improve market share for a specific product) goals. Furthermore, some goals are explicitly stated, whereas others are implicit and are communicated to organization members through the culture of the organization. Cleveland and colleagues (1989) noted that the explicit goals of PA (e.g., distinguish between good and poor performers, provide valid feedback) are sometimes mutually incompatible. When implicit goals, such as maintaining a positive workgroup climate, are added in, it may be impossible to satisfy all goals.

Assume for the moment that there are no inconsistencies in the goals of the organization. In this case, it might be possible for the rater's goals to match closely the goals of the organization. This match is most likely when the rater is socialized to the extent that he or she internalizes the goals of the organization. At least one organization we have consulted with uses "extent to which individual accepts the values of the organization" as a dimension for assessing its managers. If value congruence leads to goal congruence in performance, there may be some utility to including values in the assessment program. We should note, however, that empirical evidence for the validity or relevance of ratings of this dimension is lacking.

Our discussion of goal conflicts points to two pressing research needs. First, more research is needed in describing the range and the content of the goals pursued by raters. The typology we have offered here is a first step in that direction but it is based on speculation rather than on data. Second, more knowledge about how raters deal with goal conflicts is needed. We believe that conflicts between the goals of the organization and those of the rater as well as conflicts among the various goals pursued by the organization and the rater are the norm rather than the exception. We have reviewed some fairly limited data suggesting that raters choose one goal as primary and ignore the rest, but we do not know whether this always occurs, how raters make the choice, or whether those choices can be reversed. We regard the area of rater goals as a critical focus for future PA research.

SUMMARY

Performance appraisal researchers rarely take the rater's perspective in analyzing performance appraisal processes and outcomes. Thus, when ratings fail to correspond with other performance measures or with reasonable assumptions about ratees' performance levels, this lack of correspondence is taken as evidence of rater errors or problems in the appraisal system. This diagnosis makes sense if the rater is treated as a passive measurement instrument but makes much less sense when appraisal is treated as goal-directed behavior. Simply put, raters may distort their appraisals as a way to help achieve a variety of important goals.

It is useful to consider several classes of goals, including task performance goals, interpersonal goals, strategic goals, and internalized goals. Goals in each of these four categories may vary systematically as a function of the ratee's performance level.

Research on the development and application of rater goals represents several challenges. First, raters may not always be aware of the goals they are pursuing. Second, they may not be willing to admit that they are pursuing some goals (e.g., using performance appraisal to get rid of a poor performer). However, judgment research in several other areas (e.g., work motivation) has dealt successfully with similar constraints. Given the potential payoff of research on rater goals, the effort needed to mount a program of research is clearly worthwhile.

9

Rater Motivation

One of the most frequent complaints regarding ratings is that they are inflated (Ilgen & Feldman, 1983; Landy & Farr, 1983; Longenecker et al., 1987). It is not unusual for the great majority of all employees to receive extremely high ratings. For example, when ratings are done on a 7-point scale, 80% of all ratings are often 6 or 7. This is particularly true in the military (Bjerke et al., 1987) but is also true in both the public and private sectors. Rating inflation of this sort is typically treated as evidence of rampant rater errors or of a breakdown in the performance appraisal (PA) system (Saal et al., 1980). The typical treatment for rating inflation is some adjustment in the scale format or perhaps a new training program for raters.

There is an alternative explanation for rating inflation that would have very different implications for both research and practice. It may be that the tendency to give uniformly high ratings is an instance of adaptive behavior that is, from the rater's point of view, an eminently logical course of action. That is, it may make no sense for the rater to give low ratings, except in extreme circumstances. It may make perfect sense to give high ratings, *regardless of the true performance levels of one's subordinates.*

This chapter considers the implications—for the rater—of giving high or low performance ratings, and seeks to explain rating inflation in terms of the rater's rational pursuit of sensible goals rather than explaining this phenomenon in terms of errors and mistakes. There are several facets of the rating context that may motivate raters to inflate their ratings. In order to obtain accurate ratings, the organization may have to structure the rating environment to provide raters with rewards for accurate rating.

THE PSYCHOLOGY OF LENIENCY

As will be discussed in Chapter 10, research on performance appraisal is often characterized by the assumption that the rater is trying his or her best to evaluate performance accurately and just is not doing it very well. We believe that it is more reasonable to assume that raters are indeed capable of accurately evaluating performance, and that deficiencies in ratings are more likely to be a result of the rater's *willingness* to provide accurate ratings than of his or her *capacity* to rate accurately (Banks & Murphy, 1985; Padgett, 1989; Villanova & Bernardin, 1989). If the situation is examined from the rater's perspective, there are many sound reasons to provide inaccurate (typically, inflated) ratings. More important, there are surprisingly few good reasons for most raters to give accurate ratings. Leniency thus may not be an error but rather a behavior that allows the rater to obtain rewards and avoid punishments.

Figure 9.1 illustrates the model we use to try to understand the forces that motivate a rater to provide ratings that are either an accurate reflection of his or her evaluation of each subordinate (see Chapter 7) or that are distorted (i.e., inflated) and inaccurate. This motivational model is certainly not new (see DeCotiis & Petit, 1978; Mohrman & Lawler, 1983) but it does offer a different perspective than that which appears to dominate current PA research. The specific components of this model are discussed below.

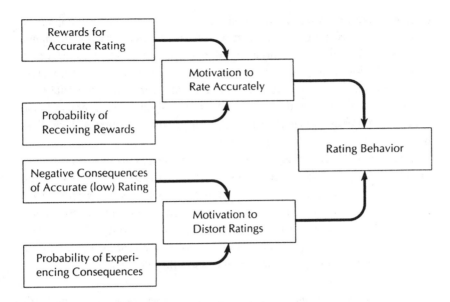

Figure 9.1. Model of Motivation to Provide Accurate Versus Distorted Ratings

Rewards for Accurate Rating

The first question that needs to be addressed is why raters *should* devote the time and energy (and possibly suffer the negative consequences) needed to evaluate performance accurately. From an expectancy theory perspective, it might be predicted that raters will be motivated to rate accurately when (a) valued rewards are available for accuracy in rating, and (b) the likelihood of achieving those rewards is connected to the accuracy of the ratings given (Mohrman & Lawler, 1983).

Availability of Valued Rewards. In most organizations valued rewards are not available, at least with regard to extrinsic rewards such as pay or promotions. That is, there are typically no rewards from the organization for doing accurate appraisals and few if any sanctions for inaccurate appraisals (Carroll & Schneier, 1982; Naiper & Latham, 1986). Indeed, organizations seem to send mixed messages to raters regarding the value of the whole enterprise. Official company statements frequently stress the value of good performance appraisals but organizations typically take no concrete steps to reward this supposedly valued outcome (Chapter 12 examines in more depth the implications of mixed messages in performance appraisal). We know of no organizations that include the rater's accuracy as an evaluator of ratee performance as a part of the *rater's* PA. A manager might infer that most organizations do not really care about the quality of PA data. If the organization is unwilling to reward good appraisers and sanction poor ones, we would argue that this inference is correct, regardless of the stated policy of the organization.

Even when the principal duties of a manager center around appraisal, as might be the case for an interviewer or a manager who is part of an assessment center staff, we know of no instances where raters are rewarded for accuracy or punished for inaccuracy. For most managers, performance appraisal represents an infrequent and unimportant activity. If the organization's willingness to provide rewards is taken as an indicator, we would conclude that most organizations feel exactly the same way.

Rewards Following Accurate Appraisal. Suppose an organization sets aside a portion of each year's salary increase budget to reward accurate appraisers. The rater might still doubt that rewards will follow if he or she turns in accurate appraisals. There are two issues here—a criterion problem and a problem involving trust in the system.

It is a common finding that both raters and ratees distrust the organization's PA system (Bernardin & Beatty, 1984; Bernardin, Cardy, & Carlyle, 1982). Ratees do not believe that providing accurate appraisals will be beneficial. Unfortunately, distrust of the PA system probably implies distrust for the reward system that is associated with the quality of one's performance appraisals. That is, raters who do not trust the system may not believe that promised rewards will follow desired behaviors.

When the problems in evaluating the accuracy of ratings are considered, a lack of trust might be well founded. As we will document more thoroughly in Chapter 10, it is very difficult to measure the accuracy of the ratings that are given by a single rater. For example, suppose an evaluator rates 80% of his or her employees as "excellent." How does the organization determine whether the rater is providing accurate or inflated ratings? The people who receive high ratings may very well be excellent workers. On the other hand, the evaluator might be unduly lenient.

A manager has every right to feel that he or she is placed in a dilemma by efforts to reward accurate ratings, especially if accuracy is defined in terms of someone's preconceived notions regarding the true distribution of performance. We will develop our arguments more fully in the next chapter. It is sufficient here to note that there is no simple solution to the criterion problem in most organizations. It may be impossible for the organization to sort accurate from inaccurate raters; thus, efforts to reward good raters may be doomed. Later in this chapter we will suggest some ways that organizations could approach the problem of rewarding good performance appraisals, but it is important to note that the problem of identifying good and poor raters is a formidable one, and raters may be right in distrusting the system.

Certain Versus Uncertain Outcomes. Accurate performance appraisal presumably leads to some rewards and some costs (e.g., negative reactions from subordinates who receive low ratings). Many of the costs or negative states associated with accurate appraisals are reasonably certain. That is, if a rater gives ratings that cost a subordinate a promotion, an unpleasant work situation is almost certain to ensue. Rewards, on the other hand, are quite uncertain. Unless the rater believes that the organization can identify accurate and inaccurate raters and is willing to provide rewards to those who evaluate performance accurately, the instrumentality of accurate ratings for achieving those rewards will always be less than perfect. Accurate PA may therefore be a behavior that carries certain costs and uncertain rewards. Unfortunately, this asymmetry in the certainty of costs and benefits could pose a serious barrier to achieving accurate appraisals.

Prospect theory (Kahneman & Tversky, 1979) provides a powerful tool for analyzing the effects of perceived costs and benefits on judgment and behavior. The theory suggests that (a) people undervalue gains and overvalue losses, and (b) certain gains and losses receive more extreme values than corresponding uncertain gains and losses. Thus, a loss of $10 is more negative than a gain of $10 is positive; a certain loss of $10 is worse than a 50% chance of losing $20. This theory suggests that if rewards and costs were of objectively equal value, raters would *not* choose to provide accurate appraisals. In order to balance costs that are certain to be incurred, the rater must believe that the probable rewards are considerably more valuable than the certain costs. Because rewards are typically meager, if they exist at all, this condition may be only rarely met in organizations.

Negative Consequences of Accurate Rating

It is important to keep in mind that the specific problem most often cited in ratings is inflation. That is, if ratings were accurate the ratings received by most or all individuals would typically be lower. There are several reasons why a rater might and should be reluctant to give lower ratings. We have grouped these reasons into four categories: (a) consequences for the ratee, (b) consequences for the rater, (c) avoidance of negative reactions, and (d) maintaining the organization's image.

Consequences for the Ratee. The most common reason cited for rating inflation is that high ratings are needed to guarantee promotions, salary increases, prestigious assignments, and other valued rewards (Lawler, 1976). Low ratings, on the other hand, will result in these rewards being withheld from subordinates. McCall and DeVries (1977) suggest that the availability of resources affects rating inflation in that inflation is most likely to occur when the supply of promotions, salary increases, and so on is either abundant or very restricted. When there are many resources available in the organization, the rater will be motivated to see that his or her subordinates receive their fair share. When resources are scarce, raters might be motivated to hoard them. In this context, this would mean trying to obtain valued resources (e.g., promotions) for one's subordinates.

The issue of consequences for the ratee has been examined most thoroughly in the voluminous literature on the effects of the purpose of rating. A number of studies have shown that ratings collected for administrative purposes (e.g., salary administration) are significantly higher than ratings of the same individuals collected for other purposes, such as feedback or research (Bernardin et al., 1981; Heron, 1956; Reilly & Balzer, 1988; Sharon & Bartlett, 1969; Taylor & Wherry, 1951; Williams et al., 1985; Zedeck & Cascio, 1982).

Some studies suggest that different psychological processes may be involved when ratings are collected for different purposes (Murphy et al., 1984; Reilly & Balzer, 1988). Other studies have failed to find a main effect for purpose (Berkshire & Highland, 1953; Borreson, 1967; Murphy et al., 1984), but the failure to find an effect may be due to low power or weak manipulations of the purpose variable (Reilly & Balzer, 1988). All in all, this literature suggests that raters who believe that ratings will have an impact on administrative decisions are more lenient than raters who think that ratings will not have any impact on salary, promotion, and the like.

It is useful to distinguish between the actual purpose(s) of rating and raters' *beliefs* about the purpose(s) of rating. Organizations use performance appraisals in a number of ways, and the actual uses of appraisal are not always communicated to raters (or raters might not fully believe these communications). Ostroff (1993) showed that even when the actual purpose of rating is held constant, raters differ somewhat in their beliefs about how ratings are used and why they are collected, and these differences affect their rating behavior.

The literature on the effects of the purpose of rating provides what we regard as strong evidence for the hypothesis that raters consciously distort their ratings when they think that ratings are tied to valued outcomes. Raters who provide ratings for feedback or research purposes seem to have no problem in distinguishing between good and bad performers. When ratings are not used for administrative decisions, inflation and range restriction are not serious problems. We believe that raters whose appraisals are used in making administrative decisions are just as capable of distinguishing good from poor performers but simply refuse to do so. Purpose of rating may not affect the *evaluation* of performance (Murphy et al., 1984) but it is likely to affect what is reported by the rater.

There is one interpretation of the difference between ratings for administrative decisions and ratings for research that does not depend on conscious distortion. It is possible that the purpose of rating affects the standards that are used to judge performance (Murphy et al., 1984; see also Chapter 7 of this volume). The same behavior might thus be evaluated favorably for one purpose (i.e., under one set of standards) and evaluated unfavorably for another. We do not know of any direct test of this hypothesis but it is an interesting one. Hypotheses about performance standards are quite difficult to test (Constans, 1987), but this hypothesis could explain a variety of phenomena, ranging from interrater disagreements (raters see the same behaviors but are applying different standards) to instability in ratings (the same rater applies different standards at different points in time).

Why should the rater care whether his or her subordinates receive valued rewards? We think there are two related reasons. First, raters are very concerned with establishing and maintaining high levels of motivation. Many raters believe that telling a poor worker that he or she is performing poorly will not be motivating and could discourage the poor performer (Longenecker et al., 1987). Negative ratings could represent a self-fulfilling prophecy, in that they discourage employees, who from then on perform at substandard levels.

Concerns over ratee motivation lead many raters to do two separate performance appraisals—a public appraisal that is turned in to the personnel department and a private, verbal appraisal that is shared with the worker during his or her appraisal interview (Longenecker et al., 1987; Mohrman & Lawler, 1983). The discrepancy between the written appraisal and the oral appraisal can itself be used as a motivational device. That is, the rater can inform the ratee that he or she knows about the ratee's poor performance but is still turning in good ratings. This may serve as an incentive or perhaps as a warning.

The second reason that raters should care whether ratees receive valued rewards is that raters and ratees have to work together. Raters often must maintain good interpersonal relations with subordinates to perform their jobs (McCall & DeVries, 1977), and even when good interpersonal relations are not required, raters are likely strongly to prefer a positive work atmosphere to a negative one. It is unlikely that relations will be good if the supervisor is seen as the reason why workers did not receive valued rewards (Smith, 1976).

From the rater's point of view the ability to maintain positive interpersonal relationships with his or her subordinates might be viewed as much more important than turning in accurate performance appraisals. Poor performance appraisals, especially if the organization's norm is to turn in high ratings for everyone, will probably lead to resentment, which may in turn make it impossible for the subordinate and the supervisor to work together effectively.

The idea that raters will give high ratings to avoid bad interpersonal relations with ratees seems quite reasonable. Naiper and Latham (1986), however, note that there is little empirical evidence of raters showing concern over the aversive interpersonal consequences that accompany low ratings. This finding must be interpreted cautiously, because there might be a strong social desirability factor present in research that examines raters' concerns over ratees' reactions to performance appraisals. A rater might be unwilling to admit that he or she is worried about the resentment that is likely to accompany low ratings that result in the loss of desirable outcomes such as raises or promotions. Nevertheless, their criticism must be taken seriously.

Consequences for the Rater. The second reason that raters may be motivated to give inflated ratings is that the ratings received by subordinates say something about the *rater's* job performance. One of the duties of a manager is to develop his or her subordinates and to get the best performance possible out of them. If a manager consistently rates his or her subordinates as poor performers, it will eventually appear as if the manager is not doing his or her job. This is particularly true in organizations where the manager's peers routinely turn in high ratings. Thus, the simplest explanation for rating inflation may be that high ratings make the rater look good and low ratings make the rater look bad.

There are some reasons to believe that accuracy in rating is in fact tied to the rater's true level of performance. Landy and Farr (1983) note that studies in the 1950s and 1960s indicated that better performers gave more accurate ratings. Because inaccuracy is not random but rather is manifest in the form of rating inflation, this line of research implies that the correlation between the rater's level of performance and the ratings he or she gives should be negative. That is, the better the rater, the higher the likelihood of low ratings. High ratings may be a signal that the rater wants to *look* good; low ratings may be a signal that the rater *is* good.

The rewards a manager receives are sometimes tied to the performance of his or her workgroup. Ilgen et al. (1981) showed that when supervisors' rewards are tied to the performance of subordinates, rating inflation occurs. One interpretation of this finding is that raters intentionally distort their ratings to maximize their own rewards. Evidence of intentional distortion is hard to come by, although anecdotal evidence has been collected (Longenecker et al., 1987). More information is needed about the contingencies raters perceive between the ratings they give and the rewards they receive. If raters believe that there is a strong link, this might motivate them to inflate their ratings.

Even if ratings are not tied to the rewards received by the rater, there is still a strong possibility that self-interest will lead to rating inflation. Longenecker and associates (1987) note that raters show little concern over whether their ratings are accurate but are greatly concerned about the consequences of the ratings they give for the future performance of their subordinates. That is, raters consider whether a high or low rating will be more effective in increasing the subordinate's future level of performance. They must also consider whether a high or a low rating will make it easier for them to perform *their* jobs in the future. It may be very reasonable to conclude that high ratings do more to facilitate future performance and low ratings only complicate the rater's life. It may make more sense, from the rater's point of view, to give the ratings that will do the most good for the workgroup's future effectiveness (i.e., high ratings) than to give accurate ratings that only interfere with the smooth functioning of the group.

Research on self-serving biases in attribution (Gioia & Sims, 1985; Miller & Ross, 1975; Mitchell et al., 1981) suggests another mechanism for explaining rating inflation. It is well known that individuals attribute their own successes to internal factors (e.g., ability, effort) and their own failures to external causes (e.g., situational constraints). Individuals attribute *others'* successes to external causes (e.g., luck, superior resources available to others), however, and others' failures to internal causes (e.g., they didn't work hard enough). In the case of performance appraisal, the supervisor may see himself or herself as an important external cause of subordinates' success. Therefore, if subordinates are evaluated as successful, the manager may attribute that success to his or her own ability as a manager, in effect taking credit for subordinates' performance. Note that this explanation probably operates at the unconscious level rather than involving conscious distortion. That is, it is unlikely that raters (a) know their subordinates are performing poorly, (b) consciously distort their ratings upward, and (c) take credit for the success of their employees.

Another possible explanation for unconscious distortion comes from research that shows that raters tend to view subordinates as more similar to themselves than they actually are (Rand & Wexley, 1975). Because most individuals attempt to retain positive self-images, it follows that the supervisor who sees similarities between subordinates and himself or herself will tend to rate subordinates favorably. Raters who commit the similar-to-me error (Rand & Wexley, 1975) will probably also inflate their ratings.

One final way in which self-interest can lead raters to inflate their ratings is through peer pressure. In an organization where the norm is to give high ratings, the rater who defies the norm might experience disapproval from his or her peers. There is a long history of research on the effects of peer pressure on the performance levels of workers (Sherif & Sherif [1969] review this research, much of which was carried out prior to 1960); the same phenomenon is probably present in management. Shop-floor workers put a great deal of pressure on "rate busters," whose level of performance makes them look bad. Managers probably react in exactly the same way when another rater makes them look bad. Pressures for conformity may be a significant factor in rating inflation.

Avoidance of Negative Reactions. Another reason why raters might tend to inflate their ratings is that they wish to avoid the negative reactions that accompany low ratings (Latham, 1986). This phenomenon is particularly relevant in understanding the performance feedback process. Negative feedback typically results in defensive reactions from ratees (Kay et al., 1965), which can create a very stressful situation for the rater. The simplest way to avoid unpleasant or defensive reactions in appraisal interviews is to give uniformly positive feedback (i.e., give inflated ratings). There is evidence that raters do indeed inflate their ratings when they believe they will be required to provide face-to-face feedback (Landy & Farr, 1983).

Both supervisors and subordinates dislike giving and receiving feedback (C. Fisher, 1974). In part, this may be due to the expectation on the part of both the rater and the ratee that subordinates will not be satisfied with the feedback they receive. Earlier, we noted that self-appraisals tend to be more favorable than appraisals from others (see Chapter 5), and suggested attributional mechanisms that would account for this effect (i.e., self-serving biases in attribution). As a result, the rater's own inflated rating might not be as favorable as the ratee's self-evaluation. There are some reasons to believe that poor performers evaluate their own performance less accurately than good performers (Mitchell et al., 1981). If this is true, it may also mean that truly poor performers are the most likely to be dissatisfied with the feedback they receive. Evidence from several studies suggests that the favorability of the PA is one of the major determinants of ratees' reactions to the rating process (Dipboye & dePontbriand, 1981; Landy, Barnes, & Murphy, 1978; Landy, Barnes-Farrell, & Cleveland, 1980).

There are several aspects of the rating process that, independent of the rating level, may influence subordinates' reactions to performance feedback. Performance feedback is most likely to be accepted by the ratee when:

1. Appraisals are frequent.
2. There is widespread agreement concerning job duties.
3. Feedback from any given source is consistent with feedback from other sources.
4. There is widespread agreement regarding what constitutes good and poor performance (Ilgen et al., 1979; Landy et al., 1978; Landy, Barnes-Farrell, & Cleveland, 1980).

It may be that when these conditions are met, negative feedback does not provoke a negative reaction. Greenberg (1986) notes that performance feedback is more likely to be accepted when the requirements of procedural justice are fulfilled (i.e., when procedures that appear reasonable and fair to *ratees* are followed). We suspect that the conditions specified above are typically *not* met in organizations. Therefore, a rater who gives low ratings might quite rightly be concerned over how feedback based on those ratings will be received.

Feedback acceptance may be important to the rater, even if feedback results in no behavior change. When the rater *does* give negative feedback, he or she runs the risk that it will be discounted or ignored by the ratee. In this case, the rater is likely to encounter all of the negative facets of giving low ratings and will not experience any benefits. Thus, the rater who believes that poor feedback will not be accepted may be likely to avoid giving poor feedback (i.e., to inflate ratings). One demonstration of the power of raters' desire to avoid negative reactions comes from research on the role of accountability in performance appraisal.

A fundamental assumption of several models and discussions of performance appraisal (e.g., Banks & Murphy, 1985; DeCotiis & Petit, 1978; Mohrman & Lawler, 1983; Murphy & Cleveland, 1991) is that ratings will be accurate only when raters are motivated to provide accurate ratings. One way to motivate raters may be to hold them accountable for their ratings. There are a number of studies showing that when decision makers are held accountable for the quality of their decisions, they are more careful, thorough, and accurate (Rozelle & Baxter, 1981; Tetlock & Boetteger, 1989; Tetlock & Kim, 1987). Details of exactly *how* raters are held accountable, however, may make a considerable difference. For example, one method of increasing accountability is to require raters to explain and justify their ratings to their subordinates (Tetlock, 1985a, 1985b). There is evidence, however, that ratings are more likely to be lenient when raters anticipate giving face-to-face feedback (Klimoski & Inks, 1990). This suggests that accountability might degrade the quality of ratings.

Maintaining the Organization's Image. Our final explanation for rating inflation is one that does not assume any conscious distortion of ratings but rather involves the inferential processes that are used to process information about job performance (see Chapters 5 through 7). We assume that many, if not most, raters have a reasonably positive image of the organization in which they work. That is, it is reasonable to assume that most managers think of their company as one that employs good people and that does a good job producing the goods and services the company provides. The mere fact that an individual is a member of the organization therefore conveys some information (probably favorable) about the person's performance. The fact that an individual has been able to get and keep a job in that organization may be used to infer that he or she must be a good worker (Ilgen & Feldman, 1983). The longer an individual stays with an organization and the higher he or she rises in the ranks, the more likely this effect.

The image of an organization is not necessarily uniform throughout the organization. Some parts of any organization are likely to be perceived as high-status areas that have high standards, whereas other parts of the organization are regarded as the dumping ground for substandard employees. If the image of each part of the organization influences evaluations, one might expect more rating inflation in high-status areas and more accurate appraisals in low-status areas. There is anecdotal evidence that this in fact occurs.

Bjerke and colleagues (1987) noted that high-status combat communities in the navy (e.g., nuclear submarine community) were more likely to suffer from rating inflation than were low-status support communities (e.g., supply and tanker fleets). In the high-status community, the mere fact that an individual is a member of the community is enough to justify ratings of "excellent" on many dimensions. We do not know of any research on this phenomenon in the private sector, but we would make two predictions. First, mean rating in each department of an organization should be correlated with that department's position in the status hierarchy. Second, the variance of the mean ratings calculated for each department in an organization should be positively correlated with the status differentiation within that organization. If some departments are very high in status and others are very low, we would expect that the average rating in the low-status area will be much lower than the average rating in the high-status area. In some high-technology firms there appears to be little differentiation in the status of different levels or functions in the organization. In those organizations, the mean rating is probably similar in all departments.

A person's reputation as a good or poor performer is one source of information that might be used in evaluating his or her performance (see Chapter 5). We suspect that the inferential process that is involved in evaluating an individual who has a reputation as a good or poor performer is similar to the inferential process involved when evaluating a person who works in an area where most workers are thought to be superior performers. In both cases, the reputation is a source of a prior hypothesis about the person's performance, and information about his or her behavior provides data that may be used to revise that hypothesis (Murphy et al., 1985). The effects of an individual's reputation are probably stronger than the effects of an organization's or a department's reputation, but in either case the ratings will probably be inflated when the reputation is a particularly good one.

A Framework for Research on Rating Inflation

We have suggested several reasons why raters might be motivated to inflate their ratings. It is important to realize, however, that not all raters inflate their ratings. Among those who turn in inflated ratings, there is substantial variability in the extent to which ratings are inflated. In predicting who will inflate ratings and to what degree, we find a combination of ideas from expectancy theory and techniques derived from decision research especially useful. In particular, we think that Edwards' (1980) Multiattribute Utility Technology (MAUT) (see Edwards & Newman [1982] for a review) provides a framework for organizing research on the psychological processes involved in rating inflation. Methods based on MAUT have been applied in measuring and evaluating the performance of individuals and groups (Jones, Buerkle, Hall, Rupp, & Roth, 1993; Pritchard, 1990; Pritchard, Jones, Roth, Stuebing, & Ekeberg, 1989).

MAUT represents a tool that can be used to structure evaluations of alternate courses of action that may affect several valued outcomes or attributes. In the context of rating inflation, MAUT might be used to describe and study the processes of choosing between providing inflated ratings or providing accurate ratings. This technique can easily be applied to a wider range of courses of action (e.g., the rater might choose among different levels of rating inflation), but it can be best illustrated by examining the decision of whether or not to inflate one's ratings.

In its simplest form, MAUT can be described in terms of the following five steps:

1. Identify the courses of action to be evaluated.
2. Determine the relevant attributes or value dimensions of the outcomes that may follow each action.
3. Determine the relative importance of each of the values.
4. Determine the probability that each course of action will result in valued outcomes.

5. Integrate importance measures from Step 3 with value measures from Step 4 (see Edwards & Newman [1982] for a more complete description).

The usual applications of MAUT are ones in which the values, importance weights, and so on are known and are integrated to recommend which of several courses of action should be followed. The same technology may be applied to predict which course of action the rater will follow, as we will illustrate below.

First, assume that the set of alternatives was limited to two—to inflate ratings or not to inflate ratings. The research reviewed above provides a starting point for the second step in the MAUT process, the specification of relevant valued outcomes. Table 9.1 summarizes outcomes that have been cited in this chapter that might be affected by the decision to inflate or not inflate ratings. Note that these outcome states are arranged hierarchically, indicating that some outcomes represent combinations or effects of achieving lower level outcomes. Note also that some of these outcomes are positively valued, whereas others have a negative value. Different courses of action have different probabilities of producing each outcome. Utility theory assumes that individuals choose the course of action that maximizes the likelihood of receiving positively valued outcomes and minimizes the probability of achieving negatively valued ones. (Expectancy theory makes the same assumption.)

To predict an individual's choice, we need to know (a) the perceived probability of each outcome for each course of action and (b) the value assigned to each outcome. The overall utility of each course of action is then determined by multiplying the probability estimates by the values, and summing over outcomes.

For example, assume that probability estimates and value judgments were obtained from two raters (the values are shown in Table 9.2). For the sake of simplicity, only the highest level of outcomes (Outcomes 1-4) are listed. The values are scaled so that the probability of outcomes sums to 1.00. Values are scaled so that numerical ratings are proportional to the relative value of outcomes (e.g., value ratings of 40 and 20 would indicate that the first outcome is twice as valuable as the second), and the absolute values for the four outcomes sum to 100.

The values shown in Table 9.2 were used to compute the utility of each course of action for each rater. The outcomes of these calculations are

TABLE 9.1   Valued Outcomes That Are Affected by Rating Inflation

Outcome	Value
1. Ratees receive valued rewards	+
a. Good interpersonal relations maintained	+
b. Ratee motivation is maintained	+
2. Raters look good	+
a. Rater's performance evaluated positively	+
b. Rater's job is easier to do	+
c. Rater enhances self-image	+
d. Rater experiences peer pressure	−
3. Negative reactions from ratees	−
a. Defensive reaction to feedback	−
b. Feedback is not accepted	−
4. Organization's image is maintained	+

shown in Figure 9.2. These figures indicate that for both raters, inflating ratings makes more sense than providing accurate ratings. That is, rating inflation is a course of action that maximizes rewards (positively valued outcomes) and minimizes punishments (negatively valued outcomes). The motivation to inflate ratings is stronger for Rater A than for Rater B, however; for Rater A, rating inflation appears more likely to lead to valued rewards than it does for Rater B. On the other hand, the costs of giving accurate ratings seem higher for Rater B than for Rater A; Rater B worries more about negative reactions, and even though he or she sees them as less likely than does Rater B, the possibility of negative reactions creates a strong motivation to *avoid* accuracy for Rater B.

In predicting which course of action the raters will actually take, it is necessary to compare the utilities of each possible course. In this case, both raters are likely to conclude that inflation will lead to valued outcomes and that accuracy in rating will lead to undesirable outcomes. Thus, both will probably give inflated ratings. Rater A, however, is more strongly motivated to inflate than is Rater B, because the *difference* between these two courses of action is larger for Rater A than for Rater B.

It is instructive to describe why the utilities for the two raters differed. In part, this difference reflects a difference in values. Rater A attaches considerable value to the rewards that might be obtained for accurate ratings. He or she also places a strong value on avoiding negative reactions from ratees (remember that this attribute is a negatively valued one). Rater

TABLE 9.2 Values and Probability Estimates for Two Raters

	Rater A		Rater B	
	p	v	p	v
Results of Inflating Ratings:				
1. Ratees will receive rewards	.70	50	.50	30
2. Raters look good	.10	15	.25	10
3. Ratees react negatively	.05	25	.05	40
4. Organization's image is maintained	.15	10	.20	20
Results of Giving Accurate Ratings:				
1. Ratees will receive rewards	.05	50	.10	30
2. Raters look good	.05	15	.20	10
3. Ratees react negatively	.75	25	.60	40
4. Organization's image is maintained	.15	10	.10	20

NOTES: p = probability that each outcome will occur
v = value of each outcome

B also shows concern over negative reactions and he or she values the ability to secure rewards for subordinates. These raters not only differ in their values, they also differ in their beliefs about the strength of the links between rating inflation and valued outcomes. Rater A believes that the principal outcome of accurate ratings will be negative reactions from ratees (Rater B also emphasizes this outcome). Rater B believes that rating inflation had a noticeable impact on evaluations of his or her own performance. If ratings are inflated, the probability of "looking good" is five times as great as will be achieved with accurate ratings. It might thus be inferred that Rater B is more concerned than Rater A with using ratings as a vehicle for impression management.

Our presentation has simplified many of the highly important technical issues that are dealt with by Edwards (1980) and has adjusted other concepts to fit the current problem of predicting and explaining rating inflation. Nevertheless, we think the MAUT framework provides a powerful tool for studying the problem. First, it directs attention to issues that have not been considered in depth in research on rating inflation, such as the attribute dimensions considered by individual raters, individual differences in values, and the origin and alteration of beliefs about the links between rating inflation and valued outcomes. Second, it provides a basis for describing the rater's approach to the rating task that we think may bring us much further than the approaches that have dominated the literature to date.

	Rater A	Rater B
Inflate Ratings	36.75	15.90
Give Accurate Ratings	−14.00	−17.00

Figure 9.2. Estimated Utility of Inflating Versus Giving Accurate Ratings for Two Raters

NOTE: To calculate the utility for Rater A of inflated ratings, the formula is:

$$\text{Utility} = (.70 \times 50) + (.10 \times 15) - (.05 \times 25) + (.15 \times 10) = 36.75.$$

Note that the utility of negative reactions is subtracted from the total of the other three outcomes, because this particular outcome has a negative value.

By eliciting the perceived probability of outcomes and the values of outcomes from raters, useful insights may be obtained about the rater's perception of the PA context. For example, it would be possible to develop a simple index of the degree to which the perceived probabilities of the set of relevant outcomes varies as a function of the course of action the rater follows (e.g., the squared distance between probabilities under accurate rating vs. rating inflation would provide one index). We expect that some raters see strong links between their choice of a rating strategy and valued outcomes, whereas others do not. The stronger the perceived link between rating behavior and valued outcomes (i.e., the greater the change in outcome probabilities with different rating strategies), the stronger the motivation to distort ratings, assuming that distorted ratings have higher utility than accurate ones. Examining the values that the rater emphasizes might provide information about the goals the rater is pursuing in rating (see Chapters 8 and 12 for a discussion of rater goals). For example, the rater who places a high value on avoiding negative outcomes will be motivated to act differently than a rater who values the rewards the organization provides to accurate raters.

Mohrman and Lawler (1983) advocated applying expectancy theory to the problem of understanding rater motives. The MAUT approach provides a technology that will achieve that goal and may allow us to approach the problem of rating inflation from an entirely different angle. Rating inflation is often a highly rational course of action from the point of view of the individual rater. The best hope for curing rating inflation may involve changing values and instrumentality beliefs rather than simply exhorting raters to avoid leniency.

STRATEGIES FOR REDUCING RATING INFLATION

The first issue an organization should consider is whether it really *wants* to reduce rating inflation. We have discussed many of the negative outcomes that might be associated with giving accurate ratings. The organization should not take steps to reduce rating inflation unless the benefits outweigh the costs. In many situations the benefits of accurate ratings might be minimal; assessment of the benefits of accuracy depends largely on the uses to which ratings are put (see Chapter 10). For example, if the organization uses ratings to determine promotions, the most relevant criterion will be the extent to which ratings sort incumbents into two categories: promotable and nonpromotable. Accuracy beyond this gross sorting may be irrelevant to the organization's actions (Feldman, 1986).

Assuming that the organization *does* want accurate ratings and is willing to pay the costs that may be associated with accuracy, three issues need to be addressed:

1. Valued rewards must be tied to rating behavior.
2. Negatively valued outcomes of accuracy must be reduced.
3. Raters must see clear links between their rating behavior and valued outcomes.

These issues are discussed below. The chapter ends with a brief discussion of units of analysis involved in attempts to reduce rating inflation.

Rewarding Accuracy

Few organizations incorporate the ability to evaluate subordinates accurately as a criterion for evaluating the supervisor's performance. If an organization really cares about accuracy, it should be willing to provide substantial rewards for accuracy in rating. That is, such things as salary increases, promotions, and assignment to choice positions should depend partly on the manager's ability to evaluate subordinates' performance accurately.

The key issue in any system that attempts to reward PA accuracy is the same criterion problem that has plagued PA research. At present there are few measures that can be applied in organizations that convincingly indicate accuracy in rating (see Chapter 10 for a detailed critique of existing measures). One practical approach we can recommend is to evaluate ratings in terms of the procedures followed by the rater. Does the rater have access to relevant information about the ratee's performance, and is there evidence that he or she has made efforts to obtain that information? Has the rater collected careful records of relevant observations? Has the rater been adequately trained, and has there been any meaningful follow-up to determine the transfer of training? The more closely the rater's strategy for evaluating performance corresponds to procedures that are likely to produce accurate ratings, the higher the likelihood that ratings will be accurate.

Another approach for evaluating raters is a variant of the approach one might take to assess the construct validity of ratings (see Chapter 10). The performance of individual workers should have implications for a variety of nonjudgmental indices of the group's performance and productivity. For example, one would suspect inaccuracy if all workers were rated high but the group's productivity was lower than that of comparable groups in the organization. If ratees receive high marks for dimensions such as "time management" there should be few instances of products or reports that are turned in late, there should be little use of overtime, and there should be few complaints about the timeliness of workers in performing their tasks.

The assessment of accuracy will be easiest when the organization can identify specific outcomes that should follow as the result of good or poor performance in specific aspects of subordinates' jobs. If the actual outcomes correspond closely to those that would be expected on the basis of the ratings, this is one piece of evidence that the ratings are accurate. If expected and actual outcomes differ, this might be evidence of inaccuracy. If rating inflation is indeed present, actual outcomes can be expected to be less favorable than those predicted on the basis of the ratings.

Research on scale development suggests that one of the principal benefits of developing behaviorally anchored scales is that it gets many raters involved in the design of the appraisal system, which leads to increased levels of acceptance and trust in the system (Landy & Farr, 1983). It is critical to develop high levels of trust, because providing accurate appraisals is a very risky behavior. An organization might use scale development as a tool to increase raters' awareness and acceptance of the PA system. The scales that are developed probably matter less than the possibility of changing raters' attitudes toward performance appraisal.

Reducing Negative Outcomes

Many of the negative outcomes of accurate performance appraisal are the result of the subordinates' perception that the rater is responsible for their receiving a poor evaluation, and that the rater is to blame if they fail to receive valued rewards (e.g., pay raises) from the organization. One strategy for reducing negative outcomes would involve diffusion of responsibility. That is, the ratee might not react as negatively if the rater was seen as only a part of the evaluation process rather than the sole judge of ratee's performance.

The use of multiple raters has been advocated for a variety of reasons, ranging from increased control over rater biases (Murphy, 1982b) to increased flexibility in developing criteria (Saal et al., 1980). This strategy may also have the benefit of reducing the perceived responsibility of the supervisor for the ratings received. If ratings are the product of multiple, independent evaluations, the immediate supervisor cannot be seen as the sole reason for a low rating. Having multiple raters may take the heat off of the immediate supervisor, and may leave the worker who is dissatisfied with his or her ratings no clear target at which to vent any anger.

Rater training might provide another method of diffusing the responsibility for low ratings. For example, frame-of-reference training (Bernardin & Beatty, 1984; Bernardin & Buckley, 1981; McIntyre et al., 1984), which involves exposing raters to vignettes of good, poor, and average performance and giving them feedback on the accuracy of their ratings of vignettes, could serve two purposes.

First, it could be used as a means of communicating information about the norms and standards the organization uses for evaluating performance (see Chapter 6). Second, and this is more germane to the problem of reducing negative outcomes, this type of training externalizes norms and standards. That is, the rater who has received extensive training in identifying good, average, and poor performance might be able to tie low ratings to the standards that are set by the organization. This will not resolve all of the ratee's complaints when ratings are low, but it will reduce the likelihood that ratees attribute their low ratings to the arbitrary standards of their supervisors.

A different strategy for reducing the negative consequences of accurate ratings is to reduce the links between the ratings a worker receives and the organizational rewards he or she receives. In the extreme case, ratings might be used solely for research or feedback, without linking them in any way to raises, promotions, and so forth. We would not advocate going this far. It might be possible, however, to reduce the link between any *particular* rating and organizational rewards. We are familiar with several academic departments that reward employees on the basis of their average performance over periods of several years, with the idea that one unusual year should not have a strong influence on one's salary. One benefit of this type of system is that it may reduce ratees' concerns over the ratings they receive in any one year; with this system, ratees may react less vehemently to a low rating.

A third strategy for reducing negative reactions to accurate appraisals comes from Meyer et al. (1965). They suggested that performance feedback and discussions related to salary increases should be done separately. This might be taken a step further by having separate PA systems for the purposes of feedback and administrative decision making (Cleveland et al., 1989). Rating inflation may not be a problem in salary administration; salary increases are often determined on the basis of factors other than performance (e.g., seniority, equity). Therefore, it may not be important whether the ratings turned in to the human resources department are accurate; the accuracy of the feedback given to employees may be more important than the accuracy of the numerical ratings that are turned in.

This strategy is especially appealing because it is already a de facto policy in many organizations. Raters often have one set of ratings that they turn in to the organization and another set that is used for giving feedback (Longenecker et al., 1987). It may be worthwhile institutionalizing this process, at least to the extent that developmental feedback is separated from evaluations of performance (there may, however, be legal problems with maintaining two sets of ratings, particularly if they are discrepant).

Several facets of the PA process, including the frequency of appraisals and the credibility of the source, affect subordinates' perceptions of the fairness and accuracy of appraisals. User acceptance may be a critical issue in reducing the negative reactions that accompany accurate appraisals. As Bernardin and Beatty (1984) note, when ratees do not accept or trust the appraisal system, it is unlikely that the system will function well.

The culture of an organization (Mitroff, 1983) may be an important determinant of the consequences of accurate rating. Some cultures support distinguishing between individuals in terms of their performance, whereas others do not. An organizational culture that stresses teamwork and group goals might discourage raters from distinguishing among their subordinates. Cultures that stress individual achievement might more readily support performance appraisals that recognize individual differences in performance. Cultures may also affect the power and authority structure of the organization, which will in turn have implications for the acceptability of accurate versus inflated ratings. Organizations with a clearly defined power structure and significant power differentials between levels of the organization may be more supportive of systems designed to produce accurate ratings than organizations with very flat and democratic power structures.

Linking Rating Behavior to Valued Outcomes

The preceding section outlined some methods of reducing the links between negatively valued outcomes and appraisal behavior. It is not enough to reduce the motivation to rate inaccurately, however. The organization must also provide good reasons to rate employees accurately. The issue of providing rewards for accurate appraisals was discussed previously. In this section, we concentrate on methods of building strong links between rating behavior and rewards and sanctions.

The best way to convince raters that they will be rewarded for accurate ratings is to give rewards, as publicly as possible, to raters who comply. If it is clear that people do receive better raises, promotions, and so on when they rate accurately than when they distort ratings, motivation to rate accurately will increase. We have made the point many times in this chapter that the organization's willingness to reward accurate appraisals is a good measure of the real importance of accuracy. Here, we are suggesting that one step toward achieving accuracy is to provide and publicize rewards for accurate raters.

An organization might use the concept of profit sharing to increase the links between rating behavior and valued outcomes. Ratings have a direct bearing on many of the decisions an organization makes, and the success of those decisions is sometimes measurable. This is particularly true for promotion decisions. The rater who correctly identifies high-potential employees should receive some reward, which could be tied to the success of the people who are promoted on the basis of his or her performance ratings.

For example, a rater who correctly identifies an employee who rises quickly through the ranks or who makes an important contribution to the organization's success might receive a bonus. On the other hand, the rater who gives high ratings to people who routinely fail after being promoted might receive a pay cut or some other sanction. Making the raters share in the subsequent success or failure of their subordinates might lead to more careful attention to performance appraisals and promotion recommendations.

Policies such as pay secrecy can work against achieving accurate performance appraisals. If the organization keeps both the method it uses to make salary decisions and the results of those decisions secret, it may be difficult for the rater to develop any well-informed opinion about the links between rating behavior and organizational rewards. Strongly perceived behavior-reward links are most likely when raters are well aware of the rewards or punishments that others have received for turning in accurate or inaccurate ratings. Organizations are most likely to create conditions that motivate raters to provide accurate ratings when they can establish and implement a clear policy linking the quality of rating data to rewards.

Cognitive Distortions and Rating Leniency. In this chapter we have made the case that motivated distortion is a key explanation for the pervasive evidence of leniency in performance ratings. That is, there are many good reasons to avoid giving low ratings (and few good reasons to give them). As a result, we see relatively few low ratings given in the field. High ratings are likely to lead to a variety of rewards for both the rater and the ratee. As a result, high ratings seem to be the norm. Nevertheless, we must be careful not to attribute leniency *solely* to motivated distortions in ratings. Hauenstein (1992) offered evidence that leniency biases were at least partly the result of raters' information-processing strategies. Raters who subsequently give high ratings seem to pay more attention to and more accurately remember positive aspects of their subordinates' performance.

The hypotheses that leniency is the result of after-the-fact distortions versus the result of information-processing biases at the time that performance is observed and evaluated may not be as distinct as they seem. Hauenstein (1992) notes that "it is reasonable to assume that the contextual factors that motivate raters to render lenient ratings can also bias the cognitive processes involved when raters form impressions of ratees" (p. 486). For example, if you know ahead of time that there is heavy pressure to record high ratings, even for poor performers, you may devote more attention to incidents of good performance and may over-emphasize the relatively rare incidents of good performance that even poor performers are likely to exhibit.

CHANGING THE RATER VERSUS
CHANGING THE CONTEXT

The final issue in this chapter involves the choice of a unit of analysis for interventions in the PA process. In the past, performance appraisal researchers have intervened by either changing features of the task (e.g., by changing the rating format) or by changing the rater (e.g., through rater training). We think that a better strategy is to change the rating context. That is, we do not believe that much can be achieved by changing the rater or the task if the context dictates that ratings will be inflated.

Performance appraisal researchers agree that approaches that focus on the rating scale have not been successful (Landy & Farr, 1983). There is also some disenchantment with rater training, because training often fails to change rating behavior in organizations (Bernardin & Beatty, 1984). This issue is sometimes discussed under the heading of *transfer of training,* but we think that the problem is more fundamental than one of simply transferring information learned in training to the work setting.

We suspect that the traditional diagnosis of the underlying problem in performance appraisal is incorrect. Raters do not fail to give accurate ratings because they are incapable of accuracy but rather because they are unwilling to rate accurately (Banks & Murphy, 1985). This problem will not be solved by increasing their capability; the environment must be modified in such a way that raters are motivated to provide accurate ratings.

Changing the rating environment is likely to be a formidable undertaking. Accurate rating is most likely in a context where the following conditions exist:

1. Good and poor performance are clearly defined.
2. The principle of distinguishing among workers in terms of their levels of performance is widely accepted.
3. There is a high degree of trust in the system.
4. Low ratings do not automatically result in the loss of valued rewards.
5. Valued rewards are clearly linked to accuracy in performance appraisal.

We know of organizations in which *none* of those conditions is met; we do not know of any in which *all* of them are met.

Changing the rating context may involve changing the value structure of the organization, the administrative procedures of the organization (e.g., pay secrecy vs. publicizing rewards), or the beliefs of individual raters about behavior-reward contingencies. At present very little is known about the strategies that might be effective for achieving any of these goals. We see a clear need for more and better research on contextual factors in performance appraisal, and we think that the ultimate solution to the problem of rating inflation will come through changing the context rather than changing the rater.

SUMMARY

Rating inflation is a way of life in most organizations. From the rater's point of view, there are often many good reasons to turn in inflated ratings and few good reasons to turn in ratings that reflect his or her honest appraisal of each subordinate. The consequences of giving low ratings to subordinates are often negative and immediate, whereas the rewards for turning in accurate ratings are often uncertain. It is therefore not surprising that most supervisors quickly learn to inflate their ratings.

Rating inflation has traditionally been treated as a rater error. This chapter suggested that inflation should be treated as an adaptive behavior. That is, accurate ratings can lead to a variety of negative outcomes. In the worst case, accuracy in evaluation could make it difficult for supervisors and subordinates to work together, and in the long run it could lower the actual performance of everyone in the workgroup. An organization that is successful in stamping out rating inflation may, in the long run, be worse off than a similar organization in which rating inflation is the universal norm.

Research in the areas of decision making and work motivation provides a variety of frameworks for analyzing and understanding rating inflation. This research also suggests that the best way to counteract rating inflation (assuming that one is indeed interested in accurate ratings) is to create conditions that reward accuracy in rating and punish inaccuracy. The fact that organizations rarely attempt to create those conditions suggests that accuracy in performance appraisal may not be an important organizational goal. Unless organizations are willing to reward accuracy in rating and sanction inaccuracy, it is unreasonable to expect that raters will turn in anything but inflated ratings.

10

Error and Accuracy Measures

It is important to know whether performance ratings provide an accurate reflection of the performance of the individuals being rated. The need for criteria against which ratings can be assessed is most obvious when evaluating an existing performance appraisal (PA) system or choosing among alternative systems. Presumably, some methods of PA are better than others. To make an informed choice it is necessary to know which system is best and how much better one system is than another.

This chapter opens our discussion of the methods that are or might be used to evaluate the quality of rating data. We concentrate here on what are typically referred to as *psychometric characteristics* of ratings. In the chapter that follows we will discuss alternative methods of evaluating ratings that examine the *uses* of rating data rather than the ratings themselves. There are advantages and disadvantages to both psychometric criteria and user-oriented (or decision-oriented) criteria. The chapter that follows will consider the issues involved in choosing between these two types of measures.

CRITERIA FOR CRITERIA

Measures of the psychometric qualities of rating data can be classified into three broad groups: (a) traditional psychometric criteria such as reliability, construct validity, and interrater agreement; (b) indices of rater errors that reflect response biases on the part of the rater; and (c) direct measures of the accuracy of ratings.

Rater error measures are the most common indices of the accuracy of ratings. Psychometric criteria are still employed, although their use appears to be declining. A variety of procedures for directly measuring accuracy rather than inferring it from the absence of rater errors or psychometric deficiencies have been employed in studies of rater training (McIntyre et al., 1984), cognitive processes involved in rating (Murphy & Balzer, 1986; Murphy, Garcia et al., 1982), and judgmental processes in the interview (Vance, Kuhnert, & Farr, 1978). To date, these accuracy measures have been confined to the laboratory, although it may be feasible (as we will note later in this chapter) to generalize these measures to the field.

Bernardin and Beatty (1984) list a number of specific measures that have been used in research to evaluate ratings; some of these criteria are the following:

Psychometric
- Reliability and internal consistency
- Interrater agreement
- Equivalence of alternate forms
- Convergent validity
- Discriminant validity
- Construct validity
- Criterion-related validity
- Utility

Rater Errors
- Leniency
- Central tendency and range restriction

- Halo error
- Correlational bias (distortion of correlations to fit implicit theories)
- Scale unit bias
- Distortion (inappropriate weighting of dimensions in forming judgments)

Rating Accuracy
- Elevation
- Differential elevation
- Stereotype accuracy
- Differential accuracy
- Halo accuracy
- Distance accuracy

Balzer and Sulsky's (1990) review indicates the extent to which different criteria are actually used to evaluate ratings. They surveyed the dependent measures used in published research on performance appraisal in 1976 and in 1986; the results of their survey are summarized in Table 10.1. First, rater error measures appear to be the most common criteria for evaluating ratings, although their use declined between 1976 and 1986; psychometric criteria (reliability and validity) showed a similar decline. Second, the direct measurement of rating accuracy is relatively rare. If recall/recognition measures are pooled together with accuracy measures, the percentage of studies employing accuracy measures as criteria is still relatively small (25% or less). Third, these results suggest that there is no clear consensus among PA researchers regarding the measures that are most appropriate for evaluating ratings. In part, this is because some measures are method bound (i.e., accuracy measures are confined to the laboratory), but it also indicates that none of the measures commonly employed to evaluate ratings are so obviously good that they dominate the others. To understand our apparent failure to develop widely accepted standards for evaluating rating data, it is necessary to examine in depth the measures currently used in evaluating ratings.

INDIRECT MEASURES OF ACCURACY

Both indices of the psychometric quality of rating data and measures of rating errors can be thought of as indirect measures of rating accuracy. In

TABLE 10.1 Dependent Measures in Performance Appraisal Studies

	1976 (%)	1986 (%)
Reliability/validity	31	10
Rater error	54	30
Rater accuracy	0	15
Recall/recognition	0	10
Other	16	70

SOURCE: From W. K. Balzer & L. M. Sulsky, "Performance Appraisal Effectiveness and Productivity," in K. R. Murphy & F. E. Saal (Eds.), *Psychology in Organizations: Integrating Science and Practice* (Hillsdale, NJ: Lawrence Erlbaum, 1990).
NOTES: Because multiple criteria were used in several studies, columns total to more than 100%.

fact, it seems more logical to regard these approaches as indices of *inaccuracy.* The argument for using these measures as indicators of accuracy is when raters cannot agree, or give unreliable ratings, or give ratings whose distributions make no sense, they must not be providing accurate measures of performance. For the most part, then, accuracy is inferred in the absence of psychometric deficiencies or apparent rater errors. As we will note later, this approach to indirectly inferring accuracy depends on some extremely restrictive assumptions about the true distribution of performance in organizations. These assumptions are so implausible that they may call into question the majority of the criteria that are presently used in evaluating rating data.

Psychometric Criteria

Establishing the reliability and validity of ratings has proved to be a very challenging task. The assessment of reliability has been hampered by disagreements over the most appropriate type of reliability for different purposes. Criterion-related validity studies are often difficult. Ratings themselves are often the best available measures of performance, and the criteria against which ratings are evaluated are often dubious. Construct validity has been difficult to establish because there is no consensus on the nature or the boundaries of the construct "job performance" (Murphy & Kroeker, 1988). Although traditional psychometric criteria are conceptually appealing, they have not been used as the principal criterion for evaluating rating data. It is useful to consider why.

Reliability. The most difficult issue in determining the reliability of performance ratings is to decide which definition of reliability to employ. The most common method for evaluating the reliability of psychological tests is to examine the internal consistency of the items (Murphy & Davidshofer, 1988), but this model does not apply to typical PA scales. Unlike test items, the dimensions included on PA scales are not chosen to represent a single dimension or construct. On the contrary, many of the uses of performance appraisal make it clear that each dimension on the scale provides what is thought to be unique information (Cleveland et al., 1989). Because most performance appraisals employ a single item (or a very small number of items) to measure each dimension, internal consistency reliability estimates will be misleading. In a typical performance appraisal a valid measure of performance would be expected to exhibit low internal consistency.

Validity generalization research (Hunter & Hunter, 1984; Schmidt & Hunter, 1977) has employed a test-retest model and has typically used a reliability coefficient of .60 to characterize the long-term stability of job performance measures (see Schmidt, Hunter, & Caplan, 1981). In essence, this research incorporates the assumption that 40% of the variance in job performance measures can be attributed to random errors of measurement. This assumption has been criticized as unrealistic (Hartigan & Wigdor, 1989; Schmitt & Schneider, 1983), and the correction for attenuation used in validity generalization research has been shown to be biased in the direction of supporting validity generalization (Paese & Switzer, 1988).

One conceptual problem that plagues the test-retest approach is that it confounds the effects of measurement error with those of true changes in job performance. This approach is reasonable only if it is believed that the *relative* levels of job performance of different individuals do not change over time. Accepting that assumption, however, it is difficult to justify the practice of annual or semiannual appraisals. If apparent changes in individuals' performance levels are due primarily to measurement error, frequent measurement of job performance will only add to inaccuracy.

Interrater agreement is sometimes used as a criterion for evaluating ratings (Saal et al., 1980). It is not at all clear whether this criterion provides information about the reliability of ratings, the validity of ratings, or both. For example, the research reviewed in Chapter 5 leads us to conclude that disagreements between raters (especially those at different levels in the organization) cannot be attributed solely to random measurement error; different raters observe different aspects of the same ratee's performance and will sometimes honestly disagree in their evaluations. Therefore, the correlation between ratings obtained from different sources provides only partial information about the reliability of ratings. Although the case for using interrater agreement as an index of validity is somewhat stronger, even here, there are problems. Raters who share common biases (e.g., two supervisors who do not approve of female subordinates) will agree in their ratings but this is hardly evidence that the ratings are accurate.

Generalizability theory represents the most comprehensive framework for defining reliability (Cronbach et al., 1972). The theory suggests that there is no single figure that represents *the* reliability of a measure. Rather, there are as many potential reliability coefficients as there are uses for the information that a test provides. Generalizability theory suggests that the problem of evaluating and interpreting reliability indices cannot be solved in a vacuum but rather must be based on the uses to which information obtained from performance measures are put. As a result, it is impossible to determine *the* correct model of reliability for PA research; different models are appropriate for different purposes. We will return to this point in the chapter that follows.

Validity. The validity of ratings is difficult to establish. Several researchers have attempted to establish criterion-related validity by comparing ratings to objective or results-oriented criteria (Heneman, 1986; Landy & Farr, 1976, 1983; Roach & Wherry, 1970). In general, the correlations between subjective and objective measures of job performance are small, indicating a low level of validity. However, it is not clear what is being validated. Objective measures are often unreliable and often provide only partial coverage to the domain of job performance (see Landy & Farr [1983] for a review). It is quite feasible that the correlations between subjective and objective measures would be significantly higher if objective indices were better measures of job performance.

As is often the case, criterion-related validity studies are used in this area to help establish the construct validity of ratings. Although the construct-oriented model for validating ratings has long been advocated (Astin, 1964; James, 1973; Smith, 1976), empirical research on the construct validity of ratings has been rare (Murphy, 1989a; Murphy & Kroeker, 1988). There have been several studies of the convergent and discriminant validity of ratings (Dickinson, 1987; Kavanaugh, MacKinney, & Wolins, 1971; Lawler, 1967), but convergent and discriminant validity are not synonymous with construct validity. That is, convergent and discriminant validity are desirable but they are neither necessary nor sufficient to establish construct validity.

Consider, for example, convergent validity. If one method provides a perfect measure of performance and another does not, the two will fail to converge. On the other hand, two measures that share common measurement biases will converge. Discriminant validity is more a function of the traits chosen than of the measurement procedures that are being evaluated. If different dimensions of performance are conceptually distinct, discriminant validity is likely. If performance dimensions overlap, discriminant validity is unlikely.

Unless the construct of performance is described in some detail (i.e., unless the construct is explicated), progress in construct validation research is difficult (Murphy & Davidshofer, 1988). To date there has been virtually no research that carefully describes the construct of job performance and then attempts to determine whether a particular index provides an adequate measure of that construct (Murphy & Kroeker, 1988). Therefore, the question of whether ratings are valid measures of job performance is still an open one. As noted below, however, there is a good deal of incorrect evidence of construct validity.

Construct Validity Evidence. Although there are few studies directly concerned with the construct validity of ratings, there are many studies that provide indirect evidence. First, there are studies indicating that raters agree and, in particular, that raters at different levels in the organization show considerable consistency in their ratings. Although ratings obtained from different sources often differ in *level* (e.g., self-ratings are usually higher than supervisory ratings [Meyer, 1980; Thornton, 1980]), there is substantial agreement among ratings from different sources with regard to the relative effectiveness and performance of different ratees. For example, in a meta-analysis of research on rating sources, Harris and Schaubroeck (1988) found an average correlation of .62 between peer and supervisory ratings (self-supervisor and self-peer correlations were .35 and .36, respectively). Mount (1984a) reports some evidence for the reliability and validity of rating obtained from subordinates, and notes that when supervisors, subordinates, and the target individual all provide ratings (the last source is a self-rating), supervisors and subordinates agree more closely with one another than either source agrees with self-ratings.

A second category of evidence comes from research on the utility of various personnel programs (this research is reviewed in Chapter 11).

Utility estimation often involves asking supervisors to determine the worth of highly successful versus highly unsuccessful performers to the organization. There is considerable evidence that these judgments are accurate (see Bobko, Karren, & Kerkar [1987] for a review and critique of this research), which suggests that supervisors can identify good and poor performers. If they were unable to tell who was doing well or poorly, it is hard to see how they would be able to evaluate accurately the value of the goods, services, and so on produced by good versus poor performers.

Another category of relevant research examines the correlations between ratings and other measures of performance. For example, Heneman (1986) showed that ratings are positively correlated with a variety of objective measures of job performance, although the correlations are often small. It is hard to tell whether the small correlations indicate any deficiencies in ratings as criteria, because the objective measures against which ratings are usually compared are themselves incomplete measures of job performance.

A fourth category of evidence comes from studies of the effects of performance feedback. There is clear evidence that appraisal feedback leads to increases in worker productivity, measured in terms of criteria such as production, error rate, backlogs, and so on (Guzzo & Bondy, 1983; Guzzo et al., 1985; Kopelman, 1986; Landy et al., 1982). The fact that performance feedback has a consistent and positive effect suggests that raters are reasonably accurate in the feedback they give.

A final category of evidence comes from the large number of validity studies that use supervisory ratings as criteria for validating selection tests. This literature shows that scores on most selection tests, particularly those that measure cognitive ability, are correlated with supervisory ratings (Hunter & Hunter, 1984). Furthermore, the validities for these tests for predicting subjective criteria (such as ratings) are as large as the validities for predicting objective measures of job performance (Nathan & Alexander, 1988; Schmitt, Gooding, Noe, & Kirsch, 1984). In theory, the abilities measured by these tests *should* be related to job performance. The fact that the validity coefficients obtained using supervisory ratings are consistently large (both in an absolute sense and in comparison with validities obtained using objective measures) suggests that ratings have some validity.

Caution must be observed in evaluating the evidence on the construct validity of ratings. This evidence shows that raters *can* provide reasonably valid judgments of the overall performance levels of their subordinates and can reliably identify their best and worst workers. As noted in several of the preceding chapters, this does not mean that raters *will* provide valid ratings.

Rater Error Measures

There are several well-known phenomena that suggest that performance ratings are flawed measures. First, it is not unusual to find that 80% to 90% of all employees are rated as "above average." (This phenomenon has been referred to by educators as the "Lake Wobegon Effect" because it is often found that all the children are "above average.") Second, differences in the ratings received by different employees often seem small, given the obvious differences in their performance. Third, ratings on conceptually distinct aspects of performance are often highly correlated. One explanation for these phenomena is that raters make systematic errors in their evaluations of performance.

Discussion of the three most common rater errors—leniency, range restriction, and halo error—can be traced back more than 60 years (Kingsbury, 1922, 1933). These concepts still strongly influence the ways in which rating data are analyzed (Balzer & Sulsky, 1990; Saal et al., 1980) and have provided the foundation for a large body of research. We find it useful to deal separately with two classes of so-called rater errors: distributional errors and correlational errors.

Distributional Errors. The rater errors of leniency/severity, range restriction, and central tendency are thought to be present when the distribution of ratings differs from the (assumed) distribution of job performance. For example, if the mean of all the ratings given by a particular rater differs substantially from the scale midpoint, the rater is thought to be either overly severe (low mean rating) or overly lenient (high mean rating). The assumption implicit in the above statement is that the true mean level of performance corresponds roughly to the scale midpoint. Similarly, if ratings cluster near the scale midpoint, central tendency errors are assumed. The assumption here is that the true distribution of performance is normal and that the true variability of performance is substantial. Finally, if the variability of ratings is small, range restriction is assumed.

The assumptions that characterize typical measures of leniency, range restriction, and central tendency have been criticized. First, the true distribution of performance is almost always unknown, and there is typically no empirical justification for the assumption that it is normal and centered around the scale midpoint. Statistical convenience appears to be the only justification for assuming this true distribution (Bernardin & Beatty, 1984). Second, organizations exert considerable effort to ensure that the distribution of performance is *not* normal. Saal and associates (1980) point out that a variety of activities, ranging from personnel selection to training, are designed to produce a skewed distribution of performance. Any rational personnel manager would be pleased if all of the employees in a company were exceptional workers.

Third, these assumptions imply that there is no variation, from workgroup to workgroup, in terms of their actual performance (Murphy & Balzer, 1989). Thus, if Rater A gives ratings whose mean is 5.0 (7-point scale) and Rater B gives ratings whose mean is 4.1, Rater A is likely to be labeled as the more lenient rater. It is entirely possible, however, that Rater A's subordinates *are* better performers than those of Rater B. There is a substantial literature on leadership that assumes that workgroups *will* differ in their performance, depending in part on the effectiveness of the leader (Landy, 1985). It seems illogical to assume that all groups perform at the same level, regardless of their resources, their leadership, their tasks, and so on.

The literature on rating errors contains a good deal of speculation about the causes of distributional errors. Saal and Knight (1988) list several possible explanations for leniency/severity effects, including (a) a desire to be liked, (b) unwillingness to give negative feedback, (c) fear that other raters inflate their ratings, and (d) abnormally high or low standards.

Similarly, central tendency and range restriction errors are often attributed to (a) an unwillingness to stick one's neck out, (b) inadequate opportunities to observe, and (c) an unwillingness to justify high or low ratings to the organization or the ratee. Although there is no lack of speculation, we know of little empirical work on the reasons behind apparent rater errors. The reasons cited above represent hypotheses that seem to be widely accepted, but to date they have not been adequately tested.

There are two reasons to be concerned about the use of distributional error measures to infer that ratings are accurate or inaccurate. First, as noted above, the true distribution of performance is almost never known. Indeed, if there were means available to determine the true distribution of performance, it is hard to see why ratings would be needed at all. It is doubtful that anyone would favor the use of subjective criteria *if valid objective criteria were available.* They typically are not, meaning that the assumptions that underlie distributional error measures are inherently untestable. We believe that they are also implausible. Second, ratings whose distributions *did* correspond to the (unknown) true distribution of performance are not necessarily more accurate than those whose distributions are obviously wrong.

Figure 10.1 illustrates how this could happen. Rater X's distribution very closely matches the true distribution, whereas Rater Z seems unduly severe (i.e., his or her ratings are systematically lower). Rater Z, however, is obviously more accurate in determining who is better or worse at their jobs. Although Rater X showed the "correct" distribution, that was one of the few things about the ratings that *was* correct. Although exhibiting obvious rater errors, Rater Z is clearly more accurate. That is, Rater Z ranked the 11 ratees in an order that corresponds almost exactly with their true performance levels (e.g., Ratee A, who was the best performer, received the highest ratings), whereas Rater Z was clearly off base (e.g., he or she rated Ratee H as better than Ratee A).

Correlational Errors. It has long been known that raters tend to give similar evaluations to separate aspects of a person's performance, even when those dimensions are clearly distinct (Newcomb, 1931; Thorndike, 1920). The result is an inflation of the intercorrelations among dimensions and is referred to as halo error. Cooper's (1981b) review suggests that halo is likely to be present in virtually every type of rating instrument.

Halo is typically described in terms of (a) the rater's tendency to let global evaluations color ratings on specific dimensions or (b) the rater's unwillingness to discriminate among separate aspects of a ratee's perform-ance (Saal et al., 1980). The first explanation more clearly corresponds with the name of the error; a positive evaluation could be thought of as a "halo" that colors the evaluation of specific dimensions. Building on this idea, Landy, Vance, Barnes-Farrell, and Steele (1980) suggested that halo could be statistically controlled by parceling out an overall rating from ratings of separate performance dimensions (see also Ritti, 1964). Harvey (1982), Hulin (1982), and Murphy (1982b) pointed out shortcomings of this method and suggested that it does more harm than good. Nevertheless, Landy, Vance, and colleagues' (1980) suggestion is conceptually appealing to those who adopt the first definition of halo.

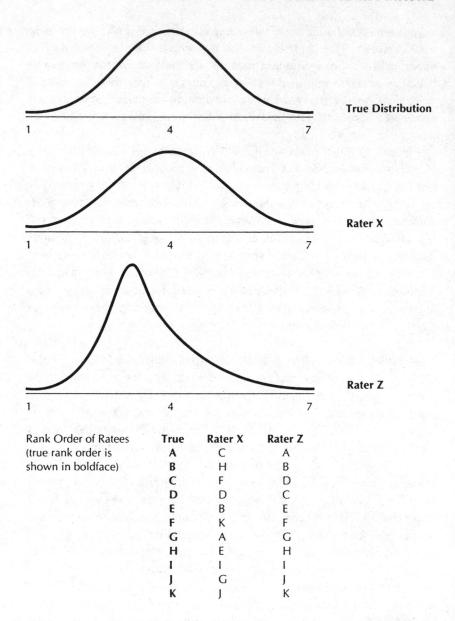

Figure 10.1. Why Distributional Errors Do Not Necessarily Indicate Accuracy

A second explanation is that halo is a function of the conceptual similarities among the dimensions being rated. The systematic distortion hypothesis suggests that raters tend to distort their ratings so that the correlations among dimensions correspond with the conceptual similarity among dimensions, regardless of the actual similarity of the behaviors being rated (Shweder, 1975; Shweder & D'Andrade, 1980). Although conceptual similarity has been used in several studies to predict halo levels (Cooper, 1981b; Murphy & Reynolds, 1988a), this approach has not always been successful. In carefully designed experiments, both Cooper (1981a) and Murphy and Jako (1989) failed to find substantial conceptual similarity effects. Thus, the current status of the systematic distortion hypothesis is unclear.

In addition to conceptual similarity, Cooper (1981b) reviews several possible causes of halo, including (a) failure to attend to hit rates, (b) confirmatory biases, and (c) discounting of inconsistent information. In addition to these cognitive distortions, halo is probably a function of the amount of information the rater has when making evaluations. Kozlowski, Kirsch, and Chao (1986) have shown that halo error is related to familiarity with the ratee and with job-related knowledge. Finally, Murphy and Anhalt (1992) present evidence that the level of halo present in performance ratings may depend more on the patterns of behavior actually observed than on characteristics of either the raters or the ratees (e.g., beliefs about the conceptual similarity of rating categories, familiarity).

Bingham (1939) was probably the first to distinguish between valid and invalid halo. Cooper (1981b) used the terms *true halo* and *illusory halo* to refer to these two explanations for the correlations among rating dimensions. One reason why ratings on separate dimensions may be correlated is that the behaviors being rated, although conceptually distinct, really *are* correlated. This is referred to as *true halo.* For example, if teachers were asked to evaluate the verbal ability and the quantitative ability of 10th-grade students, these ratings would undoubtedly be correlated. Although verbal and quantitative ability are distinct constructs, they are nevertheless correlated phenomena. It is assumed in this literature that *illusory halo,* or the part of the correlation that is due to cognitive distortion on the part of the rater, combines with true halo to produce the observed correlation among ratings. In essence, this formulation parallels the classic formulation of reliability theory, in which an observed score is partitioned into true score and error components.

Although it seems obvious that observed correlations reflect, in part, the true correlations among the behaviors being rated, it is difficult to demonstrate empirically the effects (if any) of true halo. Murphy and Reynolds (1988a) varied the true halo levels of sets of videotapes so that the behaviors to be rated would have average intercorrelations of .07 (low true halo), .43 (medium true halo), and .76 (high true halo). They found that the true halo levels of the stimuli being rated had an effect on the observed intercorrelations among rating dimensions, albeit a *very* small one, on observed levels of halo. In particular, observed halo was higher when the true correlations among dimensions was extremely high than when the true correlation was near zero, but the variance accounted for by true halo levels was hardly impressive, considering the extreme variation in true halo levels ($\omega^2 = .05$). Murphy and Reynolds' (1988a) results were replicated by Murphy and Jako (1989).

To understand why true halo is so weakly related to observed halo, it is useful to speculate about the conditions that would be necessary for true halo levels to have any real effect on rating behavior. The first and simplest condition is that raters must somehow be able to detect the level of true halo. This does not imply that they must be consciously aware of the intercorrelations among the dimensions they are rating, but they must also not be oblivious to that information.

Research suggests that subjects have difficulty estimating the correlation between variables, even when this information is reduced to a simple form, such as a scatterplot or a 2×2 contingency table (Peterson & Beach, 1967; Ward & Jenkins, 1965). Research on performance in multiple-cue judgment tasks suggests that judgment behavior is not affected by the true correlations among cues (Dudycha & Naylor, 1966; Lane et al., 1982; Slovic, 1966). Taken together, these studies suggest that subjects could not validly infer the level of true halo in complex behavior, even if detecting true halo was their primary task. We thus conclude that the idea that observed correlations among ratings represent a combination of true and illusory halo is not a useful one. One implication of this conclusion is that efforts to eliminate illusory halo without disturbing true halo (e.g., Landy, Vance et al., 1980) are likely to fail (Murphy et al., 1993).

Although true halo may have little or no effect on ratings, the concept is still useful for interpreting measures of halo error. As noted earlier, halo has usually been defined in terms of a tendency to give ratings whose correlations are *higher* than the true correlations. Recent research suggests that this definition is not adequate. Observed intercorrelations tend to be artificially high only when the true intercorrelations are low. Conversely, raters tend to *underestimate* true halo (i.e., give ratings whose intercorrelations are too low) when the true correlations among dimensions are high (Kozlowski & Kirsch, 1986; Murphy et al., 1984; Murphy & Jako, 1989; Murphy & Reynolds, 1988a).

This finding suggests that many of the traditional explanations for halo are probably incorrect. For example, if halo was the result of letting one's overall evaluation color evaluations of specific dimensions, observed correlations should be larger than true halo levels, regardless of whether true halo levels are high or low. Similarly, a failure to attend to hit rates, a confirmatory bias, or a tendency to discount disconfirmatory information (Cooper, 1981b) should lead to consistent overestimation of the true correlations among dimensions. The evidence reviewed above suggests that this does not occur.

One very simple explanation for halo error in ratings might be the demand characteristics of most rating tasks. The dimensions on a PA scale presumably all relate to overall performance, and thus will also be (at least conceptually) related to one another (Murphy, 1982b). On the other hand, the dimensions are unlikely to be seen as *completely* independent; if they are unrelated, how can they be put together to represent overall performance? We suspect that a rater who had no valid information on which to base his or her ratings would give ratings that showed moderate levels of intercorrelation, which would be interpreted as halo if true correlations are thought to be low.

Operational Definitions of Rater Errors. Saal and colleagues (1980) cataloged a variety of operations of each of the rater errors described above. The most frequently encountered definitions of the three types of rater errors are:

Leniency
- Shift of mean rating away from scale midpoint
- Skew of rating distribution
- Rater main effect in Rater × Ratee × Dimension ANOVA

Range Restriction/Central Tendency
- Standard deviation across ratees within dimensions

- Kurtosis of rating distribution
- Ratee main effect in Rater × Ratee × Dimension ANOVA

Halo

- Intercorrelations among dimension ratings
- Percentage of variance accounted for by first principal component
- Standard deviation of ratings across dimensions
- Rater × Ratee interaction in Rater × Dimension ANOVA (Saal et al., 1980)

Although the availability of multiple operational definitions of a construct is usually thought to be desirable (Murphy & Davidshofer, 1988), the existence of several operational definitions for common rating errors is problematic. There is clear evidence that different definitions of the same rater error are not equivalent (Saal et al., 1980). For example, Murphy and Balzer (1989) performed a meta-analysis of studies employing the two most common operational definitions of halo, leniency, and range restriction. The average correlation between alternate measures of the same rater error was .08. Balzer and Sulsky (1992) have noted that none of the available operational definitions of one widely studied rater error (i.e., halo) is fully acceptable.

If the conclusion is accepted that alternate definitions of rater error measures are not equivalent, it becomes important to develop methods of choosing among the alternatives. The merits of alternate definitions of halo have received the most attention. Pulakos, Schmitt, and Ostroff (1986) make a strong case for defining halo in terms of the averaged observed correlation coefficient, and make an even stronger case for abandoning the use of the standard deviation across dimensions as a halo index. As we will note later, their argument is weakened by its reliance on some debatable assumptions, but we do agree with their warning about the use of the standard deviation.

In choosing among alternate definitions of halo, leniency, and range restriction, two considerations are relevant. First, the operational definition should correspond with the conceptual definition of the construct. Second, the operational definition should not involve arbitrary cutoffs or decisions. The first requirement is met by some of the definitions shown above, but the second requirement is not really met by *any* of those definitions. For example, how high do the intercorrelations among dimensions have to be before they are judged to be too high? In Murphy and Reynolds (1988a), the observed average intercorrelation was .50 in the high true halo condition. This figure would probably be regarded by most individuals as a high correlation, but in this case it seriously underestimated the true halo level (average $r = .76$). How much variance does the first principal component have to account for to signal a high level of halo? How much skew and kurtosis are needed to indicate leniency and range restriction?

We do not know of any clearly defensible way of choosing one operational definition of leniency, range restriction, or halo. Rather than concentrating our efforts on this task, we suggest that researchers stop using rater error measures altogether. Our rationale is outlined below.

Are Rater Error Measures Useful as Criteria? Our answer is no, rater error measures are not useful criteria for evaluating performance ratings. We believe that ratings that show normal distributions, large standard deviations across ratees and dimensions, and low intercorrelations among dimensions, are not necessarily (or even likely to be) better measures than ratings that show all of the traditional rater errors.

We have two concerns regarding rater error measures. First, the unit of analysis for these measures is often defined incorrectly. For example, if halo is defined as a *rater* error, the individual rater should be the unit of analysis. However, halo is frequently defined at the organizational level (Murphy, 1982b). Although this may seem like quibbling, the example shown in Table 10.2 suggests that it can be an important problem.

Rater X gives a 7 to all ratees on all dimensions, whereas Rater Z gives a 1 to all ratees on all dimensions. The average intercorrelation among dimensions for each individual rater would be .00, because for each rater there is no variance in ratings. If data are pooled over raters, however, the average intercorrelation among dimensions is 1.00. This unit-of-analysis problem may not be as severe for other rater error measures but it is disconcerting to see apparently arbitrary choices when defining the unit of analysis for measuring rater errors.

Our most serious concern is over the assumptions that are implied by different rater error measures. Suppose the mean rating, the standard deviation across ratees within dimensions, and the average intercorrelation for three raters were calculated and the results were as shown in Table 10.3. It might be concluded that Rater Y is the most lenient, that Rater Y is most guilty of range restriction, and that both Raters X and Y have high levels of halo in their ratings. Unfortunately, these data do not support those

TABLE 10.2　Illustration of the Effects of Unit of Analysis on Halo Measures

Ratee	Dimension					
	A	B	C	D	E	
1	7	7	7	7	7	
2	7	7	7	7	7	Rater X
3	7	7	7	7	7	
4	7	7	7	7	7	
5	1	1	1	1	1	
6	1	1	1	1	1	Rater Z
7	1	1	1	1	1	
8	1	1	1	1	1	
9	1	1	1	1	1	

NOTE: Average: Rater X = .00; Rater Z = .00; Overall = 1.00

conclusions, because these interpretations depend on the assumption that the true performance levels of the workers supervised by Raters X, Y, and Z are equivalent in every respect. What if the workers assigned to Rater Z really are worse than average and really are worse than those assigned to Raters X and Y? It is not unreasonable to assume that workgroups vary in their true levels of performance. More important, we know of no justification for the implicit assumption that the true level of performance is constant across workgroups (see also Murphy & Balzer, 1981, 1989; Murphy et al., 1993).

　　Similar problems exist in interpreting measures of range restriction and halo. Is it reasonable to assume that the true variability in workers' performance is constant across groups? We believe it is more likely that true individual differences in performance are small in some groups and large in others. Is it reasonable to believe that the true correlations among performance dimensions are constant across groups? (Pulakos et al. [1986] make this assumption.) We believe it is more likely that the true correlations among the behaviors being rated vary from group to group and from time to time.

　　Researchers have long debated possible confounds between true halo and illusory halo. There is a similar confound between true leniency (sometimes everyone *did* perform well) and the rater error of leniency. The same principle applies to range restriction/central tendency. Some range restriction may reflect true differences (or the lack thereof) in performance, whereas other instances of range restriction may reflect real rater errors. It

TABLE 10.3 Hypothetical Results Illustrating Assumptions of Rater Error
Measures

	Rater X	Rater Y	Rater Z
Mean rating	4.0	5.2	3.7
Standard deviation across ratees	2.0	.09	1.9
Average observed intercorrelation	.50	.67	.09

NOTE: Ratings were obtained using a 7-point scale.

is time to face the fact that much of what has been labeled *rater error* in
the past may not be an error at all (Burnaska & Hollmann, 1974; Carroll &
Schneier, 1982; Murphy, 1982b; Murphy & Balzer, 1981, 1989).

Our overall conclusion is that rater error measures should be abandoned
(Murphy et al., 1993). They are based on arbitrary and often implausible
assumptions, and there are too many nonequivalent definitions of each one.
Fortunately, there are some alternatives to rater error measures. These
alternatives are reviewed in this chapter and in the chapter that follows.

DIRECT MEASURES OF RATING ACCURACY

The direct measurement of rating accuracy requires some standard
against which ratings can be evaluated. This standard is often referred to
as a *true score* and is thought to represent the rating that would be expected
from an unbiased, careful rater who completed the rating task under optimal
conditions. Questions have been raised about the adequacy of operational
definitions of such true scores (Heneman et al., 1987; Sulsky & Balzer,
1988) and about the meaning of accuracy in rating (Balzer & Sulsky, 1990;
Sulsky & Balzer, 1988). Nevertheless, accuracy measures have become
increasingly popular in recent years.

Two distinct types of accuracy measures have appeared in the literature:
behavior-based measures and judgmental measures. Behavior-based measures are considerably simpler and are often based on the rater's accuracy
in recognizing specific behavioral incidents (Cardy & Krzystofiak, 1988;
Lord, 1985a). For example, Murphy et al. (1989) studied the effects of
purpose of observation on behavior-recognition accuracy. They asked raters to indicate whether each of 36 behavioral incidents had or had not

occurred in the videotapes of performance they had observed. Because the true status of each behavior can be determined (here, 18 behaviors actually occurred and 18 did not), it was possible to measure observational accuracy in terms of true positives, true negatives, false positives, and false negatives. When responses are coded as true positives, true negatives, and so on, signal detection theory can be employed to derive measures of response bias and sensitivity (Lord, 1985a).

Although behavior-based measures are both simple and highly useful for testing several propositions from cognitive theories of evaluation, they are limited in their application. They rely on the rater's recognition of a short list of critical incidents. They do not incorporate any explicit evaluation of the behaviors nor do they guarantee comprehensive coverage of the performance domain. Further, the rater's task in studies involving behavior-based measures is not at all similar to the typical rater's task in real performance appraisals. It is hard to conceive of a PA system that consisted of a checklist of behaviors in which the rater's task was simply to indicate whether each behavior had occurred. On the whole, judgmental measures of accuracy seem more relevant and useful.

Measures of accuracy in judgment have been widely used, especially in cognitively oriented research on performance appraisal (Becker & Cardy, 1986; Borman, 1977, 1978, 1979; Cardy & Dobbins, 1986; McIntyre et al., 1984; Murphy & Balzer, 1986; Murphy et al., 1984; Murphy, Garcia et al., 1982; Pulakos, 1986). Sulsky and Balzer (1988) reviewed a variety of operational measures of accuracy, which can be broken down into three main types: (a) distance accuracy, (b) accuracy components, and (c) correlational measures of differential accuracy.

Operational Definitions. The simplest definition of accuracy is in terms of the distance (or squared distance) between ratings and true scores. This definition of accuracy has been employed in several studies (Bernardin & Pence, 1980; Heneman & Wexley, 1983; McIntyre et al., 1984), but there are serious drawbacks to this measure (Sulsky & Balzer, 1988). In a classic article, Cronbach (1955) showed that when N individuals are each rated on k traits, the distance between ratings and true scores (or any standard) is a function of several distinct types of accuracy, and that the interpretation of an overall distance accuracy measure is exceedingly difficult.

Cronbach (1955) recommended describing accuracy in terms of four separate components: (a) elevation, (b) differential elevation, (c) stereotype accuracy, and (d) differential accuracy (see Wiggins, 1973). *Elevation* refers to the accuracy of the average rating over all ratees and dimensions. *Differential elevation* refers to accuracy in discriminating among ratees, averaging over dimensions. *Stereotype accuracy* refers to accuracy in discriminating among performance dimensions, averaging over ratees (e.g., if dimensions include "Planning" and "Oral Communication," stereotype accuracy involves accuracy in determining whether a group of workers is better at Planning or at Oral Communication). Finally, *differential accuracy* refers to accuracy in detecting ratee differences in patterns of performance (i.e., accuracy in diagnosing individual strengths and weaknesses). If the rating data to be analyzed are structured in a ratee × dimension ($N \times k$) matrix, elevation can be thought of as the accuracy of the grand mean. Differential elevation refers to the accuracy of the row marginals, whereas stereotype accuracy refers to the accuracy of the column marginals. Differential accuracy refers to the accuracy of the row × column interaction.

Elevation reflects the difference between the observed and true grand means. Cronbach's (1955) remaining three accuracy measures reflect both accuracy in rank-ordering ratees, dimensions, or ratees within dimensions, and accuracy in evaluating the variability of performance (Balzer & Sulsky, 1990; Becker & Cardy, 1986; Wiggins, 1973). That is, they contain both correlational components and variance components. For example, a rater who accurately rank-orders employees but drastically underestimates the extent to which different ratees' performance actually differs might receive a poor score for differential elevation. Some researchers have questioned the practice of confounding accuracy in rank-ordering and accuracy in estimating the variance of performance (Balzer & Sulsky, 1990; Becker & Cardy, 1986; Sulsky & Balzer, 1988). As we will note in Chapter 11, the solution to this controversy depends entirely on the uses to which ratings will be put.

Borman (1977) has advocated concentrating on the correlational component of differential accuracy (see also Becker & Cardy, 1986; Wiggins, 1973). His index of rating accuracy is obtained by correlating ratings with true scores for each dimension and then taking the average of those correlations. This operational definition is somewhat different from Cronbach's (1955) definition of the correlational component of differential accuracy (Sulsky & Balzer, 1988) but the concepts behind the two definitions are quite close.

Researchers' preference for Borman's measure (as opposed to the four accuracy components described earlier) can be explained in terms of simplicity and a belief that this measure represents the most important component of accuracy (Borman, 1977; Wiggins, 1973). It is hard to dispute the claim that one measure is simpler than four, but we disagree with the claim that Borman's index is a measure of the most important aspect of accuracy.

Murphy, Garcia, and colleagues (1982) argued that differential elevation is much more important than differential accuracy. If administrative decisions, such as promotions or salary increases, are based on performance ratings, it is differential elevation, not differential accuracy, that determines the accuracy of those decisions. Differential accuracy is important only in situations where different decisions might be made, depending on the pattern of performance. For example, if Ratee A is high on "Planning" and low on "Oral Communication" and Ratee B shows the opposite pattern, accuracy in detecting this difference is important only if Ratee A is to be treated differently from Ratee B. That is, differential treatment based on patterns of performance is justified only if an Attitude × Treatment Interaction (ATI) exists (Cronbach & Gleser, 1965; Cronbach & Snow, 1977).

In the rating context, an ATI would exist if someone with ratings of 4 and 6 on the dimensions "Time Management" and "Planning" and someone with ratings of 6 and 4 on those same dimensions should be treated differently. ATIs are rarely found in educational settings (Cronbach & Snow, 1977), and we suspect they are even rarer in industry. If a researcher must concentrate on a single accuracy measure, we would advocate differential elevation rather than differential accuracy.

Our recommendation that attention be directed at accuracy in distinguishing among ratees, as opposed to accuracy in distinguishing among ratees within dimensions, has interesting implications for research on halo error. As we noted earlier, it is doubtful that halo error (as it is typically measured) really is an error. Even if halo *was* an error, the preceding paragraph suggests that it may not be a bad or costly one. In fact, it may be better to make halo errors than to avoid them, in that halo errors make it easier to distinguish among ratees.

To understand why this is so, it is useful to note that the variance of a linear combination of p variables is a function of the variance of each variable and the sum of the covariances among the variables. High halo will lead to large correlations among variables, which means large covariances. All things being equal, the rater who commits halo errors will give ratings that more clearly discriminate between ratees than will the rater who avoids halo error. Although halo error restricts one's ability to differentiate among ratees whose overall levels of performance are equivalent but whose patterns of performance differ, the loss may be trivial when compared to the gain in differential elevation. Murphy and Balzer (1986) have empirically demonstrated how halo error contributes to accuracy in rating.

The proliferation of accuracy measures has been noted in several reviews (Balzer & Sulsky, 1990; Becker & Cardy, 1986; Heneman et al., 1987; Sulsky & Balzer, 1988). Research suggests that the different accuracy measures are not highly correlated (Sulsky & Balzer, 1988). For example, Murphy and Balzer (1981) noted that the average correlation among Cronbach's (1955) four measures is essentially zero. This is not as serious a problem as with rater error measures, because the different accuracy indices are designed to measure distinct facets of accuracy. Nevertheless, it is disconcerting to note that one's results may depend more on the choice of accuracy measures than on the phenomenon being studied (Becker & Cardy, 1986).

At present there is no clear consensus among researchers regarding the best or most appropriate accuracy measures. Our recommendation is that multiple measures should be used if at all possible. In most cases, the researcher who has the data needed to compute one type of accuracy will have the data needed to compute several types. Situations in which the use of a single accuracy measure would be optimal are likely to be few and far between.

True Score Estimation. The validity of any accuracy measure depends primarily on the quality of the standards, or true scores, that are used to judge the ratings. In evaluating the procedures that have been or might be used to generate estimates of true scores, it is necessary to understand what is meant by *true score.* In the classical theory of reliability, this term has taken two distinct meanings. Some researchers define true scores in terms of objective reality (Platonic true scores). Thus, if a person's true score is 7 on a 7-point scale, he or she really is an excellent performer. Others define true scores as the expected values of observations obtained from a particular population (Cronbach et al., 1972; Lord & Novick, 1968). Here, the population could be a population of raters, occasions, and so on.

The Platonic true score concept has not proved useful in psychometrics (Lord & Novick, 1968) and is probably even less useful in the context of performance appraisal. Performance evaluation is, in the final analysis, a value judgment. It seems illogical to argue that a particular person *really* is a 7.0 and not a 6.9 or a 6.8; the exact evaluation of the individual's performance depends in part on the values of the rater. We prefer to define true score in terms of the expected value one would obtain from a specific population. The question that must then be answered is which population.

The most widely used procedure for computing true score estimates was developed by Borman (1977) (see also Murphy, Garcia et al., 1982). This procedure involves the use of multiple expert raters who evaluate performance under optimal conditions. For example, in Murphy, Garcia, and colleagues (1982), 13 graduate students served as expert raters of videotaped lectures. Videotapes were designed to exemplify specific levels of performance on each of several dimensions; these levels are sometimes referred to as *intended true scores*. Raters were given copies of the lecture scripts and had multiple opportunities to view the tapes before rating them. Estimated true scores were computed for each tape and dimension by averaging over these 13 raters. These true scores showed evidence of convergent and discriminant validity, as well as high correlations with intended true scores (see also Borman, 1978).

This procedure implicitly defines the population of raters in terms of their expertise with the task, as well as the conditions under which performance is observed. It would be possible to develop true scores from other populations with less expertise or who had fewer opportunities to observe performance, but it is unlikely that any other population would be regarded as superior to the population of raters used in Borman's (1977) procedure. Although there has been some criticism of this approach to developing true scores (Heneman et al., 1987; Sulsky & Balzer, 1988), we think this approach is the best available. The problem with this approach is that it limits the study of rating accuracy to the laboratory (Latham, 1986). This approach requires that the same behavior that is viewed by raters must also be viewed by experts, which is practical only when the performance to be evaluated consists of short videotaped vignettes.

There is an alternative method of defining true scores that might allow for the study of accuracy in the field; to our knowledge, this method has not yet been applied. If m raters each evaluated N ratees on k dimensions, it would be possible to define true scores for each ratee and dimension by taking the mean across all m raters. Taking the mean provides a reasonable estimate of the expected value for this population of raters. That is, the true score could be defined as the expected value of the rating obtained from the population of raters who are actually engaged in performance appraisal.

This definition of true score has several interesting implications. First, this definition identifies accuracy closely with interrater agreement. If all raters agree in their evaluations, ratings must, by this definition, be accurate, because any rater will be close to the mean of all raters. Second, the components of accuracy are defined in terms of how far a particular rater deviates from the mean of all raters. Thus the mean square for raters provides an overall index of the amount of elevation present in the ratings; each rater's elevation is measured by his or her deviation from the grand mean. Similar interpretations can be drawn for other accuracy measures. For example, the mean square for ratees provides one index of differential elevation; the mean square for dimensions provides one index of stereotype accuracy. (Dickinson [1987] provides a similar method of analysis that incorporates externally defined true scores in a Rater × Ratee × Dimension design.)

There are two potential objections to the method outlined above. First, does the mean over a group of raters really define a person's true level of performance? We would argue that it does, as long as the precise meaning of *true* is kept in mind. That is, the average over a set of raters is a reasonable approximation of what a person would receive if his or her performance was evaluated by every possible rater in the organization. Proponents of the Platonic true score concept might argue that the mean over all possible raters did not define the "real" performance level, but this position is a hard one to support. Even if it is accepted it may not be relevant, because we are interested in defining the "real" *evaluation* of performance, not merely its "real" level.

Second, and more important, this approach may not be practical. It might be very difficult to assemble more than a few individuals who are qualified, in terms of their job knowledge and their opportunities to observe performance, to evaluate an individual's performance. The use of the observed mean as an estimate of the expected value is justified primarily by application of the law of large numbers. If the number of qualified raters is two, we cannot place much faith in the mean as a true score estimate.

Vance, Winne, and Wright (1983) suggest a practical alternative to the fully crossed Rater × Ratee × Dimension design described above. They note that ratees are often nested within raters (i.e., are evaluated by a single supervisor) at any single point in time, but are sometimes partially crossed with raters (i.e., are evaluated by multiple raters) over longer periods of time. It is possible in this partially nested design to estimate both rater and ratee effects. More important, this design provides for multiple raters per dimension, which makes it possible to estimate expected-value true scores.

Finally, Englehard (1994) has developed a model for investigating rater errors and rating accuracy that incorporates the principles of item response theory. This method requires the sort of multirater design that is not always encountered in performance appraisal settings, but in the contexts where it is applicable it has the considerable advantage of bypassing the direct estimation of true scores and providing well-calibrated measures of several rating tendencies.

Rater Errors and Rating Accuracy. For those researchers who are already skeptical about the use of rater error measures as criteria for evaluating ratings, research on the relationship between rater errors and rating accuracy will drive the last nail into the coffin of rater error measures. The general trend in this literature is clear—rater error measures are largely unrelated to direct measures of the accuracy of ratings (Becker & Cardy, 1986; Bernardin & Pence, 1980; Borman, 1977; Murphy & Balzer, 1981, 1989).

As discussed earlier, rater error measures are used to infer accuracy indirectly. The presence of rater errors is generally taken to indicate inaccurate ratings, and the absence of rater errors is seen as an indication of accuracy. Until the development of direct measures of rating accuracy (Borman, 1977), the validity of this inference was impossible to evaluate. Several recent studies have measured the correlation between different measures of rater errors and rating accuracy. The results of Murphy and Balzer's (1989) meta-analysis, shown in Table 10.4, illustrate the relationships between error and accuracy measures.

Murphy and Balzer (1989) computed accuracy component scores and the two most common measures of each of three rater errors (halo, leniency, and range restriction) for each of 854 raters, drawn from eight separate studies. They calculated the correlations between error and accuracy measures in each study and then averaged the eight correlation matrices, weighting for sample size. The mean of the correlations shown in Table 10.4 is small and negative ($r = -.09$). Furthermore, the only substantial correlations between error and accuracy scores are negative. If the absence of error indicated accuracy, these correlations should be positive. (Accuracy scores are deviation measures where small deviations indicate high levels of accuracy.)

TABLE 10.4 Correlations Between Rater Error and Rating Accuracy
Measures

	Elevation	Differential Elevation	Stereotype Accuracy	Differential Accuracy
Halo				
Median correlation	−.11	−.14	−.16	−.31
Variance within ratees	−.01	.02	−.34	−.60
Leniency				
Difference between				
mean and scale midpoint	−.26	−.04	−.03	.00
Skew of ratings	.17	.15	.00	.00
Range Restriction				
Standard deviation across				
ratees	.11	−.25	−.18	−.22
Kurtosis of ratings	.06	−.14	−.06	−.09

SOURCE: From K. R. Murphy & W. K. Balzer, "Rater Errors and Rating Accuracy," *Journal of Applied Psychology, 74* (1989). Copyright 1989 by the American Psychological Association. Reprinted by permission of the publisher.

Thus, if there is any relationship between rater errors and rating accuracy, it is a paradoxical one in which rater errors contribute to rating accuracy.

The unusual relationship between errors and accuracy has been noted most often in research on halo error (Becker & Cardy, 1986; Cooper, 1981b; Murphy & Balzer, 1986) and has been labeled the *halo-accuracy paradox.* The data in Table 10.4 suggest that the strongest relationships between errors and accuracy do indeed involve halo and accuracy measures and are in the opposite direction that would be predicted if rater errors were valid indicators of accuracy. Fisicaro (1988) suggested that this paradox is due in part to the definitions of halo and accuracy commonly used in the literature, and showed that it disappears when different definitions are employed (see also Becker & Cardy, 1986).

We think that a better resolution of the halo-accuracy paradox is to admit that there is no paradox at all. The halo-accuracy relationship is paradoxical only if one assumes that the typical operational definitions of halo error are valid representations of the construct. We think there are sufficient problems with current operational definitions of *all* of the frequently cited rater errors to question their validity, and that there is no need for an elaborate theory to explain apparent paradoxes in measures of such dubious validity.

There is evidence of a systematic relationship between halo and the criterion-related validity of tests, which once again calls into question the traditional interpretation of halo measures. Nathan and Tippins (1990) showed that validity coefficients were *positively* related to measures of halo. That is, the more halo that seemed to be present in performance measures, the *higher* the validity of selection tests. This effect is probably due to the relationship between halo and reliability noted earlier; higher halo increases the reliability of overall ratings. In any case, the usual assumption that halo error would lower validity is not at all consistent with the data.

One final indication of the dubious relationship between rater errors and rating accuracy comes from the rater training literature. A favorite method of training has been to inform raters of the existence and nature of rater errors and exhort them to avoid those errors. This method does indeed reduce rater errors, but it also reduces the accuracy of ratings (Bernardin & Beatty, 1984; Bernardin & Pence, 1980; Borman, 1979; Landy & Farr, 1983). It appears that rater error training leads raters to substitute an invalid rating bias (avoid rater errors) for whatever strategy they were using before training. Avoiding errors simply does not address the question of accuracy.

Psychometric Criteria and Accuracy. We know of little empirical research on the relationship between the reliability, construct validity, and accuracy of ratings, although in theory these concepts should be related. In particular, reliability probably places an upper limit on accuracy: Ratings that are plagued by random measurement error are unlikely to be accurate. Construct validity probably also places some limits on accuracy, although the relationship is not so direct. For example, ratings might not provide valid information about separate dimensions of performance but might still provide a valid indication of ratees' overall level of performance. Here, a lack of construct validity would limit the stereotype accuracy and the differential accuracy of ratings but would not necessarily limit their differential elevation.

Sulsky and Balzer (1988) make the point that reliability and validity might be necessary but would not be sufficient to ensure accuracy. One reason for this is that many accuracy measures reflect both rank-ordering accuracy and accuracy in estimating the variability of performance. Sulsky and Balzer (1988) maintain that the first type of accuracy is a function of reliability and validity, but that the second is not. One solution is to separate the correlational components of accuracy from the variance components (Becker & Cardy, 1986). This approach is especially appealing if ratings are to be used solely to rank-order ratees (e.g., to determine priority for promotion) but will not always be appropriate. Pay-for-performance plans attempt to reward individuals in relation to their contribution to the organization. In this case, the best worker should receive a higher bonus if he or she is vastly superior to all other employees than if he or she is marginally better than other workers.

There is a need for more research on the reliability and construct validity of ratings. We believe that reliability and validity indices *will* be related to rating accuracy. Furthermore, the strength and pattern of this relationship will help in the future in choosing among the bewildering array of accuracy measures that are currently in use (Balzer & Sulsky, 1990). Murphy (1991) noted that different performance appraisal researchers advocate substantially different measures of rating accuracy as *the* best measure. It is probably more realistic to conclude that no single measure is always best, even for research purposes, and that when choosing criteria for evaluating ongoing performance appraisal systems, the choice is even more complex. As we have noted elsewhere, the use of accuracy (no matter how it is assessed) as a primary criterion for evaluating appraisals is not always appropriate.

RESEARCH DESIGN ISSUES

In most applications of performance appraisal, each individual is evaluated on several dimensions by a single rater (i.e., the supervisor). If the Analysis of Variance (ANOVA) were used to analyze these data, the design would be a nested one (Ratee × Dimension, nested within Raters). This design makes it empirically impossible to separate rater effects from ratee effects (Vance et al., 1983). For example, if a rater gives ratings of "excellent" to all ratees, it is impossible to tell if the rater is lenient or if the ratees really are excellent.

A fully crossed Rater × Ratee × Dimension design is needed to understand rating data. This design is impractical for most organizations because it is unlikely that all raters are qualified to rate all ratees, but a smaller-scale version of this design might be achieved by having each rater evaluate all ratees whom he or she has observed and then constructing separate Rater

× Ratee × Dimension matrices for all possible groupings of raters and ratees. This would provide multiple (but nonindependent) replications of the basic Rater × Ratee × Dimension design, and if a sufficient number of raters was available for each ratee it would be possible to separate rater biases from ratee differences. Another possibility for analyzing data from such a study is to perform a Rater × Ratee × Dimension × Group analysis, where each group consists of ratees who are evaluated by the same raters (Saal et al., 1980).

Saal and colleagues (1980) recommend the use of a Rater × Ratee MANOVA (Multivariate Analysis of Variance) in analyzing data from a Rater × Ratee × Dimension design. They suggest four criteria that should be used in evaluating the ratings:

1. The overall mean rating should be near the scale midpoint.
2. The ratee effect should be large; there should be clear differences in the mean ratings assigned to different ratees.
3. The rater effect should be small; there should *not* be sizable differences in the mean ratings from different raters.
4. The number of latent roots (i.e., eigenvalues of the correlation matrix that are sufficiently large to indicate the presence of a substantive factor) should be large.

Saal and associates (1980) suggested that the number of latent roots indicates the extent to which ratees are rank-ordered differently on different dimensions (i.e., the amount of halo in rating).

There are two difficulties with the approach outlined above. First, some criteria seem arbitrary. For example, the number of latent roots might indicate whether dimensions have been chosen that are similar to or different from one another and may not provide useful information about the quality of the rating data. Second, these recommendations imply that the organization should serve as the unit of analysis. There is some merit to this position. This unit of analysis allows one to determine whether or not the PA system as a whole is working in the way one would expect from a valid and accurate system. This approach, however, does not provide information to or about individual raters. Perhaps the best approach is to use *both* the rater and the organization as units of analysis. A Rater × Ratee MANOVA could provide information about the PA system as a whole, whereas an analysis for each individual rater could provide valuable diagnostic information. In the event that the system as a whole is deficient, an analysis of each rater's data could help determine whether the problem is systemic or whether it is concentrated in some group of raters. This rater-level analysis could serve as a type of individual needs analysis when deciding who to assign to rater training programs.

In addition to untangling rater and ratee effects, it is often important to untangle ratee effects from the effects of the group in which the rater works. Research clearly shows that the performance of other workgroup members affects evaluations of the performance of each member of the group (Grey & Kipnis, 1976; Liden & Mitchell, 1983; Mitchell & Liden, 1982). Yammarino, Dubinsky, and Hartley (1987) suggest analytic methods for separating individual effects from group effects in rating. Their methods are conceptually similar to those that might be employed in a Rater × Ratee ANOVA, in which ratees are nested within groups. They propose interpreting within-group and between-group differences as indices of specific rater errors. As with most other rater error measures, this method depends heavily on implicit assumptions about the true distribution of performance (e.g., that individuals differ more than groups differ) that are debatable and that have not been demonstrated empirically.

The final research design issue that needs serious consideration involves the choice of dimensions for the appraisal instrument. As we have noted elsewhere, indices of convergent and discriminant validity are difficult to interpret unless the proper relationship among dimensions is known. We would be more impressed with modest evidence of discriminant validity for dimensions that are conceptually similar than for dimensions that were obviously unrelated. Likewise, we would be more impressed with evidence of convergent validity for unrelated dimensions than for conceptually similar ones. When dimensions are redundant, convergent validity depends solely on the differences in the average level of performance of employees.

The choice of dimensions for a PA scale has generally been dictated by a careful job analysis (Bernardin & Beatty, 1984). We think that job analysis is important but that it is not enough. More attention is needed about the explication of the construct of job performance (Murphy & Kroeker, 1988) and the important parts of the performance domain that may not show up in a job analysis. For example, maintaining at least adequate interpersonal relations with co-workers is frequently critical, but it is unlikely to appear on any task analysis. Research on the criteria that should be used to evaluate performance appraisals will continue to flounder unless more progress is made in the area of the construct validity of job performance ratings.

SUMMARY

It is surprisingly difficult to determine whether or not performance ratings provide valid and accurate indications of individuals' performance. Several methods and measures have been proposed over the years, including a variety of indices drawn from psychometric theory, a number of so-called rater error measures, and, more recently, direct measures of rating accuracy.

Over the past 30 years rater error indices have been the most common measures of the quality of rating data. The popularity of these measures seems to be declining, in part because of research questioning the relationship between rater errors and rating accuracy. Direct accuracy measures have become more common but are limited almost exclusively to laboratory experiments. As noted in this chapter, it might be possible to measure rating accuracy in the field, although this will require substantial changes in the way in which ratings are done in most organizations. In particular, it will require the routine use of multiple raters.

Psychometric criteria continue to be important and should probably be used in more studies. Research on the psychometric characteristics of ratings is both scarce and fragmented. Nevertheless, a substantial body of indirect evidence for the construct validity of ratings exists. This research suggests that supervisors are indeed capable of telling who is performing well or poorly. This, however, does not necessarily mean that their ratings will reflect the judgments they have made. Raters' tendency to distort their evaluations when filling out performance appraisal forms may continue to be the most difficult issue in evaluating the validity and accuracy of ratings.

11

Criteria That Reflect
the Uses of Ratings

Chapter 10 examined the criteria that are most often used to evaluate ratings: rater error and rating accuracy measures. Both of these classes of measures attempt to address the question: Are ratings any good? Neither of these measures does a completely adequate job. We think the problem is not with the specific measures themselves but rather with the underlying question. Rather than asking, Are ratings any good?, it is more accurate to ask, What are they good for?

As discussed in several earlier chapters, it is the organizational context that defines the form and function of a performance appraisal (PA) system. Methods of evaluating rating data that are context free (e.g., rating accuracy scores) are not likely to provide an adequate basis for evaluating ratings. It is possible to envision situations in which ratings were highly reliable and

299

valid, and showed no leniency, halo, or central tendency, but still were absolutely useless to the organization. On the other hand, ratings that do poorly on all of the criteria outlined in Chapter 10 could still make a substantial contribution to the organization's ability to function and survive.

Balzer and Sulsky (1990) noted the growing proliferation of measures that are used to evaluate rating data and noted further that there are no clear guidelines for choosing among measures. This chapter will provide guidelines for evaluating rating data that incorporate contextual factors as well as psychometric ones.

We open this chapter with a review of research on the utility of accurate performance ratings. We will note that utility and usefulness are not necessarily the same thing, and that utility formulations may lead us to a narrow focus on only a few aspects of the organizational context. Next we will review literature that considers the match between the uses of rating data and the selection of criteria for evaluating these data. Consideration of this link could help move us from context-free to context-determined criteria, by shifting our attention from a global evaluation of ratings to the question of whether they efficiently accomplish a specific purpose in an organization. Finally, we will consider the problem of integrating information from several distinct criterion measures to form an overall evaluation of a PA system.

UTILITY

Very few people are interested in tests or other psychological measures solely as exercises in measurement. Rather, measurement is a critical social concern because test scores are used to make important decisions. The same principle applies to performance appraisals. No rational manager is or should be interested in measurement for measurement's sake. Performance appraisal is an important activity because it affects a wide range of organizational and individual decisions. Utility theory represents a decision-oriented method of evaluating appraisal systems or procedures that can be applied to assessing the value of accurate ratings, well-structured feedback, and so on, to the organization. There is substantial literature applying utility theory to employment testing (Boudreau, 1991; Boudreau & Berger, 1985; Cascio, 1982; Cascio & Ramos, 1986; Cascio & Silbey, 1979; Hunter & Hunter, 1984; Wyer, 1988). Landy et al. (1982) applied this same approach to the evaluation of performance appraisal systems (see also Landy & Farr, 1983).

The basic equation for assessing utility can be traced to the early works of Brogden (1949), and Cronbach and Gleser (1965), which were concerned primarily with personnel selection. The increase in utility associated with using a valid test in personnel selection is given by:

$$\text{Gain in utility} = N_s r_{xy}(\phi/p)SD_y - C \qquad (11.1)$$

where:

N_s = number of persons selected

r_{xy} = correlation between test scores and performance

p = selection ratio (number of positions/number of applicants)

ϕ = ordinate of the normal curve that corresponds to p

SD_y = standard deviation of performance

C = cost, per person, of testing

Equation 11.1 is nothing more than a simple regression equation. The term ϕ/p corresponds to the average standard score (z score) of those who are selected. Because candidates with the highest test scores are hired and candidates with the lowest scores are typically rejected, it follows that ϕ/p will generally be positive and will increase as the ratio of applicants to positions increases. (For example, if the selection ratio [SR] is .15, $\phi/p =$ 1.55; if SR = .10, $\phi/p = 1.76$.) Thus, ϕ/p represents the increase in the average test score if the highest-scoring candidates are hired rather than hiring people at random (Murphy, 1986).

When this z score is multiplied by r_{xy}, the result is the expected increase in Y (performance), measured in standard score units. Thus, if SR = .15 and $r_{xy} = .50$, using the test to select applicants will result in an average increase in performance of .775 standard deviation units, per person hired. Multiplying this figure by the number selected (N_s) gives the total increase, in standard deviation units. Multiplying this figure, in turn, by the standard deviation gives the increase in utility in whatever units are used to measure the standard deviation (usually, the dollar value of performance).

Finally, the costs of testing should be subtracted from the total utility estimate to obtain a comprehensive estimate of net gain. In many testing applications, however, these costs are so low that they can effectively be ignored (Murphy, 1986). Elaborate procedures, such as those used at some assessment centers, may involve more substantial costs.

Utility is typically expressed in dollar terms. This is accomplished by measuring the standard deviation of performance in terms of dollars, which can be done either through cost-accounting methods (Cronbach & Gleser, 1965) or by using supervisory judgments (Schmidt, Hunter, McKenzie, & Muldrow, 1979). For example, if the value of the goods and services produced by a highly superior worker (i.e., someone in the 85th percentile) is $60,000, and the value of the goods and services produced by an average worker (i.e., someone in the 50th percentile) is $40,000, this difference provides a concrete measure of SD_y. The 85th percentile is approximately one SD above the 50th percentile in a normal distribution, so the standard deviation of performance, measured in dollar terms, is approximately $20,000. Dollars, however, are not the only metric that might be used. For example, if the standard deviation of performance were measured in terms of the number of units produced per year, Equation 11.1 would give you a way of predicting the increase in production associated with the use of a valid test to select employees.

There is a substantial body of literature on the validity of utility estimates obtained by applying Equation 11.1 (see Bobko et al. [1987] and Boudreau [1991] for discussions of the boundary conditions of utility equations and SD_y estimation). Caution must be observed in evaluating the results of analyses of selection utility. Nevertheless, utility analyses suggest that the productivity gain associated with valid selection could be substantial. For example, Hunter and Hunter (1984) estimate that the use of valid selection tests for entry-level federal jobs would result in savings of $15 billion per year.

Applications to Performance Appraisal. Landy and colleagues (1982) noted that if a poorly designed PA system were replaced with one that provided workers with valid feedback about performance, there should be an increase in productivity. Equation 11.1 can be adapted to estimate the size of this increase. The annual gain to an organization associated with the installation of a valid performance appraisal and feedback system is given by

$$\text{Gain in utility} = [N_{Tp} (r_1 - r_2) SD_y (\phi/p)] - [N_{Tp} (C_1 - C_2)] \quad (11.2)$$

where:

r_1 and r_2 = validity of the new and the old appraisal systems, respectively

C_1 and C_2 = costs, per person, of the new and the old appraisal systems, respectively

N_T = total number of persons involved

p = proportion who receive new appraisal

Equation 11.2 is simply a more general case of Equation 11.1. The validity of a PA system (r_1) can be thought of in terms of analysis of variance (ANOVA) as the square root of η^2, where η^2 refers to the percentage of the total variance in responses accounted for by differences between those who use the new PA system and those who do not.

Equation 11.1 is based on the assumption that the current selection system has no validity whatsoever (i.e., selection is done at random), which implies that r_2 is zero. If selection is done at random, the costs of the old system (C_2) will also be zero. The only other difference between the two equations is that N_s is replaced by N_{Tp}. In most settings, all incumbents will receive the new appraisal system, which means that $p = 1.00$ and $N_T = N_S$.

Landy et al. (1982) suggest that utility analyses can be more easily understood if the effect of the appraisal system is expressed in terms of the difference in the mean levels of performance as the result of a new appraisal system (d_t), rather than expressing this same difference in correlational terms ($r_1 \times \phi/p$). The term d_t is approximately twice the size of $r_1 - r_2$. Because p generally equals 1.00 (i.e., all employees typically participate in a new appraisal program), the term ϕ/p usually drops out of the equation. If the validity of the old appraisal system equals zero (or if there was no previous system), and the new system is used with all employees, Equation 11.2 reduces to:

$$\text{Gain in utility} = N_T[(2\ r_1\ SD_y) - C_1] \qquad (11.3)$$

Landy and associates (1982) illustrate the application of Equation 11.3 in a hypothetical organization with 500 managers, where the validity of a new system is .30, $SD_y = \$20,000$, and $C_1 = \$700$. Equation 11.3 yields an estimated gain of $5.3 million per year.

Research on utility estimation has generally treated job performance as a unitary dimension. There is typically one r_{xy} value in a utility formula that represents the correlation between the X variable (e.g., a test or a new performance appraisal system) and overall job performance. This approach appears to embrace a concept that has been largely abandoned by PA researchers—the concept of the "ultimate criterion" (Thorndike, 1949). Job performance is more likely to be multidimensional, and the concept of overall job performance may have no meaning (Murphy & Kroeker, 1988). As we will note below, the failure to consider the multidimensional nature of performance may represent a serious problem in current approaches to utility estimation.

Credibility of Utility Estimates. Suppose an individual had just carried out the utility analysis described above. Based on those figures, should the individual conclude that there is now an extra \$5.3 million to spend? We think the answer is no. First, there are some technical objections to the procedures typically used to estimate SD_y (Bobko et al., 1987). Although the literature generally supports the validity of those estimates, there is also evidence of bias in the judgments that go into estimating SD_y. In particular, SD_y judgments may be based in part on the salary level of the job (Bobko et al., 1987). Thus, if workers in two separate plants do exactly the same thing but receive different salaries (e.g., if one plant is unionized and the other is not), higher SD_y estimates could be expected where the salary levels are higher.

Second, the equations do not account for the possibility that some employees may use the new program and others may not (Murphy, 1986). In personnel selection, some applicants who receive job offers may turn them down. In performance appraisal, some raters might be more willing to provide valid feedback than others. Murphy (1986) showed that utility equations, such as Equations 11.1, 11.2, and 11.3, typically overestimate the actual gain that can be expected as the result of a new test or appraisal system.

Third, and most important, it is uncertain that the outcomes of implementing a new PA system can adequately be summarized in terms of either a single validity coefficient (r_1) or in terms of a single outcome variable (dollar value of the increase in performance). There are multiple outcomes associated with any new system, some of which will be positive and others of which will be negative. The following list shows a number of outcomes that might reasonably be expected if a managerial PA system was instituted in a company that previously had no system.

Positive Outcomes
- More awareness of performance level

- More awareness of strengths and weaknesses
- Better development plans
- More effort to address current weaknesses

Negative Outcomes
- Interpersonal strain between managers and their superiors
- Perceptions of inequity (if rewards are not commensurate with ratings)
- Discouragement (average and poor performers see fewer opportunities for promotions and other rewards)
- Less willingness to help peers

Presumably, the value of these outcomes would vary (both in terms of sign and the magnitude) and the "validity" of the appraisal system for producing each outcome would also vary. For example, effort by managers to address current weaknesses may be more valuable to the organization than awareness of one's performance level. The tendency of an appraisal system to reduce a manager's willingness to help peers (under the new system, peers may be seen as competitors for promotions, salary increases, etc.) might be seen as more harmful than increasing interpersonal strain between managers and their supervisors.

Differences in the values of outcomes would not be a problem if the likelihood of each outcome were the same. Unfortunately, it is likely that there will be a different validity coefficient (r_{xy}) for each outcome variable. For example, valid feedback will, by definition, almost certainly lead to higher awareness of strengths and weaknesses. However, this does not necessarily mean that the quality of developmental plans will also increase. In utility theory terms, performance appraisal and feedback may have more validity when the outcome variable is awareness of strengths and weaknesses than when the outcome variable is the quality of developmental plans.

More realistic estimates of utility will require the identification of multiple outcome variables, estimation of the dollar value of each, and estimates of the validity of the proposed appraisal system in relation to each important outcome variable. Multiattribute Utility Technology (MAUT) (Edwards & Newman, 1982) provides some methods for identifying important outcome variables and estimating their relative value.

For example, applying MAUT methods might lead to the identification of the three outcome variables listed in Table 11.1. In this case, a new PA

TABLE 11.1   Utility Estimation With Multiple Outcome Variables

	Outcome Variable		
	Awareness of Strengths and Weaknesses	Better Development Plans	Perceptions of Inequity
N_T	500	500	500
Validity (r_1)	.60	.15	$-.20^a$
SD_y	$3,000	$17,000	$10,000
Cost per person (C_1)	$600	—^{b}	—^{b}
Gain or loss in utility	$1.2 million	$225,000	-$2 million

NOTES: a. Negative validity coefficient indicates that people with higher perceptions of inequity perform worse than those who perceive little inequity.
b. The cost of the system does not increase if there are multiple outcome variables, and should be subtracted from only one of the utility estimates.

system might be likely to lead to better awareness of strengths and weaknesses ($r = .60$). Workers who are highly aware of their strengths and weaknesses might produce goods and services that are worth $3,000 more than workers whose awareness of strengths and weaknesses is only average. If there are 500 participants, Equation 11.3 suggests that the utility for this outcome variable has a value of $1.2 million. The new system has considerably less validity for increasing the quality of developmental plans ($r = .15$), but the difference in performance of someone with highly superior versus average developmental plans is substantial ($17,000). The net utility for this outcome is $225,000.

Finally, the new system has some potential for leading to perceptions of inequity. Because this outcome is negative, the validity coefficient for this outcome should also be negative ($r = -.20$). Workers who perceive a high level of inequity will not perform as well as workers who are at the mean in their perceptions of inequity; the difference in their levels of productivity leads to a SD_y estimate of $10,000 for this outcome variable. Equation 11.3 suggests that the utility for this outcome will be a *negative* $2 million. In other words, considering the effects of the new performance appraisal system on perceptions of inequity; it may be concluded that one is worse off with the new system than without it.

In this example, the utility estimates for three outcome variables were $1.2 million, $225,000, and -$2 million, respectively. It is not clear how to go about combining these estimates to arrive at an overall utility estimate. Simply adding them together gives an estimate of -$575,000, which implies that the system will do more harm than good. Unfortunately, simply adding the separate estimates for each outcome variable might not result in an accurate estimate, because outcome variables are not likely to be independent. For example, the extent to which an appraisal system leads to better developmental plans is almost certainly correlated with the extent to which the system makes workers aware of strengths and weaknesses. Thus, some of the gain associated with better development plans is redundant with gains associated with better awareness of strengths and weaknesses, as is illustrated in Figure 11.1. The net gain for these two outcomes is almost certain to be less than the sum of the separate utility estimates. More research is needed on methods of combining separate estimates.

The most critical problem in multiattribute utility estimation is determining all of the important outcomes of implementing a performance appraisal system. It is possible that outcomes that are of concern to the organization *not* listed in Table 11.1 might also result from the introduction of a PA system, and failure to include those outcome variables could lead to substantial distortions in utility estimates.

In our opinion, accurate estimation of utility is not possible unless most of the important outcome variables can be identified. The most reasonable way to identify important versus unimportant outcomes might be to examine SD_y estimates. If SD_y is small, that outcome variable cannot have much impact on productivity: Workers who are at the top of the distribution of that variable will not perform much better than workers who are near the middle.

Usefulness of Utility Estimates. Assuming that accurate estimates of the utility of different performance appraisals were available, it might be argued that utility estimates that are ignored or discounted by organizations are not useful. Although there is a growing body of research on utility estimation itself, the question of whether utility estimates are in fact used by organizations has not received much attention.

Organizations rarely ask for utility estimates expressed in dollar terms. There are reasons to believe that utility estimates are more impressive to researchers than to managers in organizations. For example, although expressed in dollar terms, these estimates typically do not account for a variety of factors that would be routinely considered by accountants and financial managers, such as the tax rate or the interest that could be earned on money that is devoted to the personnel program under consideration (cf. Cronshaw & Alexander, 1985). Thus, the projected gain obtained from a

Figure 11.1. Overlap in Gain Associated With Awareness of Strengths and Weaknesses and Better Developmental Plans

utility equation is, at best, likely to be viewed by managers as a rough approximation (and probably an overestimate).

In the area of performance appraisal, utility estimates clearly have had little impact on organizational decisions. There are two lines of evidence to support this contention. First, although the estimated utility of valid performance appraisal is probably substantial (Landy et al., 1982), many organizations *act* as if performance appraisal is not very important. As noted in Chapter 9, organizations rarely reward supervisors for doing good performance appraisals or punish supervisors for doing bad ones. Longenecker et al. (1987) interviewed 60 executives to assess their perceptions of PA. A quote from one of these people very neatly summarizes the attitude of many managers and supervisors toward performance appraisal: "At some places, the PA process is a joke—just a bureaucratic thing that the manager does to keep the IR (industrial relations) people off his back." If organizations really believed that valid performance appraisal could lead to savings in the millions, they would hardly treat performance appraisal in such a cavalier fashion and would not tolerate executives who regarded appraisal as a joke.

Executive Appraisal: A Field Test of the Uselessness of Utility Estimates. Longenecker and Gioia (1988, 1992) note that although formal performance appraisal is nearly universal for lower-level employees, it is rarely carried out for executives. In their 1992 paper they discuss some of the myths that may impede the implementation of performance appraisal systems for executives and suggest ways of implementing appraisal systems at the top level of an organization.

Longenecker and Gioia (1992) refer to the scarcity of executive appraisals as a paradox, and suggest that high-quality appraisals are especially important at the top. This perspective is strongly reinforced when utility theory is applied to appraisal. Indeed, utility theory suggests that the potential gains from a good appraisal system (or the potential losses from a bad one) are greatest for high-level executives. The difference between the achievements of an average top executive and those of an excellent or poor executive should be correspondingly large. (SD_y estimates are usually proportional to the salary level of the job. An executive whose salary is $200,000 will probably receive an SD_y estimate that is roughly four times as large as a manager whose salary is $50,000.) The fact that appraisal becomes *less* likely rather than more likely as one moves up in the organization suggests that top-level executives either are not aware of or do not accept existing estimates of the utility of performance appraisal.

In a provocative paper entitled "The Futility of Utility Analysis," Latham and Whyte (1994) present evidence that information from utility analyses can actually *lower* managers' support for a valid selection procedure. They suggest that utility estimates may lack credibility (in part because they often incorporate a number of questionable simplifying assumptions), and more important, may fit poorly with managers' decision-making styles. There is clear evidence that managers value "soft" information (e.g., speculation, personal impressions) at least as much as they value "hard" quantitative analysis in evaluating programs (Mintzberg, 1977, 1989); the apparent objectivity and the aura of science that surround utility estimation may not be as much of an advantage as we would like to think it is.

What Can Be Done to Enhance Usefulness of Utility Estimates? It is likely that estimates of utility are more useful in making choices among alternatives than in projecting the real savings that will result from a valid PA system (Murphy, 1986). If two different PA systems with estimated utilities of $2 million and $5 million per year are being considered, we would be more confident in our choice of systems (choosing the latter) than in the prediction that there will be $3 million more available next year as the result of adopting the better performance appraisal system. It is interesting to note that the use of a dollar metric has no effect whatsoever when choosing among programs. The same choice will be made if SD_y is measured in dollars, time saved, increased output, or any other metric. Thus, the sizable literature on SD_y estimation (see Bobko et al., 1987) may be dealing with a question that is entirely academic.

At present, utility estimates appear to be useful but rarely used. Latham (1986) notes that researchers' emphasis on estimating financial gain is not shared by many managers: Managers rarely ask social scientists for utility estimates. It may be that the present emphasis on the financial impact of personnel programs *decreases* the credibility of results. Estimates of financial gain that do not consider the rudiments of accounting are not likely to impress a sophisticated business manager. They are more likely to reinforce the stereotype that social science researchers do not understand the realities of management and business. We believe that future research should emphasize estimating the *comparative* utility of alternative appraisal systems rather than trying to estimate the dollar savings expected as the result of a particular system.

SOME NEGLECTED CRITERIA

The dominance of psychometrically oriented criteria (e.g., reliability, halo) and, more recently, accuracy-oriented criteria (e.g., rating accuracy, behavior recognition accuracy) has directed the attention of researchers and practitioners away from a number of "soft" criteria that might be highly critical in evaluating whether a performance appraisal system has met its major goals. In particular, little recent attention has been given to three classes of criteria that might be extremely important in determining the success of an appraisal system: (a) reaction criteria, (b) practicality criteria, and (c) criteria that reflect the contributions of the appraisal system to the *process* of making decisions.

Reaction Criteria

Kirkpatrick (1967) suggested that one type of criterion that could be used to evaluate the effectiveness of a training program would deal with reactions to the program. This criterion is also highly relevant when evaluating a performance appraisal system. Regardless of the technical sophistication of an appraisal system, the system will not work if the raters and ratees do not accept or believe in the system.

We noted earlier that some managers regard performance appraisal as a joke (see Longenecker et al., 1987). We would regard this type of reaction as a potentially fatal flaw in a PA system and would predict that a system that is regarded as pointless pencil-pushing by the raters will not be effective in meeting important goals. On the other hand, a system that is well accepted by raters and ratees *may* work well, although there is no guarantee of this. Reactions to a performance appraisal system probably place a ceiling on the possible effectiveness of the system, in that acceptance of the system by raters and ratees may be necessary but not sufficient for the system to be effective.

Acceptance by the raters and ratees is a function of both the process and the outcomes of performance appraisal. In order to convince raters and ratees that the appraisal system is a reasonable one, the system must refer to relevant and important dimensions of work behavior, and raters must be in a position to provide well-informed judgments about the aspects of performance measured. In addition, there must be clear and visible support for performance appraisal in the organization. If appraisal systems deal with irrelevant aspects of performance or require raters to make judgments they plainly are not qualified to make, or if appraisal is treated as an unimportant activity by most organization members, reactions to the PA system are likely to be negative.

A second important component of reactions to performance appraisal is the acceptability of the *outcomes* of using the appraisal system. Some outcomes are politically more acceptable than others, and an appraisal system that leads to unacceptable outcomes will not be useful or successful in an organization. For example, if performance appraisals are used for salary administration, and high-rated employees in one job grade receive higher pay than low-rated employees in a higher pay grade, this outcome might be unacceptable and, as a result, the appraisal system may fail.

Most of the research on reaction criteria has concentrated on factors that affect perceptions of the fairness and accuracy of appraisal systems (Bernardin & Beatty, 1984; Dipboye & dePontbriand, 1981; Dorfman, Stephan, & Loveland, 1986; Landy et al., 1978; Landy, Barnes-Farrell, & Cleveland, 1980; Lawler, 1967; Mount, 1984b; Waldman, Bass, & Einstein, 1987). In general, this research suggests that performance appraisals are most likely to be perceived as accurate and fair when the following criteria are met:

1. Appraisals are conducted frequently.
2. There is a formal system of appraisal.
3. Supervisors have a high degree of job knowledge.
4. Ratees have an opportunity to appeal or to express their concerns over ratings.
5. The performance dimensions are seen to be highly relevant.
6. Action plans are formed for dealing with present weaknesses.

Although this literature does not deal at any length with the facets of organizational climate and culture that lead to perceptions of fairness and accuracy, it seems reasonable to expect that performance appraisals will be received better if the climate is cooperative rather than competitive, if supervisor-subordinate relations are close, and if trust is a valued norm within the organization.

Meyer (1991) notes that the top-down nature of most performance appraisal systems represents a significant barrier to their acceptance. In most organizations, appraisal systems are developed without substantial input (if any) from those who will be evaluated. Furthermore, most organizations require supervisors to evaluate their subordinates with little meaningful input from the subordinate. There is, however, considerable evidence that subordinates' participation in performance appraisal is directly related to their satisfaction with and acceptance of the appraisal system (Cawley & Levy, 1993). The strength of the participation-satisfaction relationship varies somewhat as a function of the type of organization and the employee's level in the organization, but it is nevertheless clear that giving subordinates a chance to participate increases satisfaction (Dipboye & dePontbriand, 1981; Dobbins, Cardy, & Platz-Vieno, 1990). A recent meta-analysis (Cawley & Levy, 1993) suggests that the relationship between participation and satisfaction with performance appraisal is relatively strong (mean $r = .53$), but that it is stronger for nonprofessional than for professional samples. As we note below, participation might be important because it enhances feelings of fairness in appraisal.

The literature on perceptions of justice in organizations may provide a rich theoretical framework for further research on factors that affect perceptions of fairness and accuracy (Greenberg, 1986; Thibaut & Walker, 1975). As noted in several earlier chapters, this literature suggests that there are two dimensions to the perceived justice of any act or policy: procedural justice and distributive justice (Folger & Greenberg, 1985; Greenberg &

Folger, 1983). These two types of justice correspond nicely with the distinction made above between reactions to the process of appraisal and reactions to the outcomes of appraisal. The research on perceptions of justice suggests that both of these facets must be present in many instances in order to guarantee that the act or policy will be perceived as fair. Thus, an appraisal system that follows sensible procedures but leads to unacceptable outcomes might fail. A system that leads to completely acceptable outcomes but follows procedures that are not accepted by raters or ratees may also fail.

Organizational justice researchers have devoted increasing attention to performance appraisal and suggest that a variety of mechanisms for increasing the apparent fairness of the appraisal process (e.g., participation, giving opportunities to voice grievances) can increase satisfaction with appraisal, even when ratings are not high (Folger et al., 1992; Greenberg, 1986; see also Lind, Kanfer, & Earley, 1990). Folger et al. (1992) suggest that there are three features of due process that are important in determining perceptions of the procedural fairness of appraisal systems. First, performance standards (see Chapter 6) must be adequately publicized and explained. Second, the individuals evaluated must have an opportunity to present their own point of view on their appraisals and to challenge assessments that they regard as unfair. Finally, appraisal judgments must be seen as based on evidence (i.e., reflecting real performance) rather than being based on such things as personal biases or favoritism. There is evidence (e.g., Greenberg, 1986, 1987) that appraisal systems that possess some or all of these characteristics are indeed seen as more fair than systems that do not.

Another reaction criterion that has received some attention in the research literature is the perceived utility of performance appraisals. Davis and Dickinson (1987) studied features of the organizational context, such as job standardization, leader trust and support, and climate for innovation, that determined the extent to which PA was perceived as useful for making both salary administration and promotion decisions. They found that the perceived utility of performance appraisal for these two purposes was related to (a) the extent to which the organization encouraged participation in decision making and had open lateral and vertical communications (interestingly, these two factors were *negatively* related to the perceived utility of performance appraisal); (b) the extent to which the climate encouraged innovation; and (c) the extent to which planning for goals was formal and structured.

Although we encourage more research on perceptions of fairness, utility, and accuracy, it is important not to lose sight of the fact that these perceptions represent only a few dimensions of a complex set of reactions to performance appraisal. That is, a system may be seen as basically fair and may lead to acceptable outcomes, but still might not be well received. As discussed in Chapter 2, both individuals and cultures vary in the extent to which they are likely to view the whole process of appraisal as acceptable or unacceptable. An individual who is basically uncomfortable with rigid authority structures might react negatively to *any* appraisal system. An organization in which the climate is highly democratic and participative might react negatively to the typical top-down appraisal system.

One reason that performance appraisal so often receives reactions ranging from indifference to disgust is that organizations, regardless of their stated policies, treat PA as a joke. As discussed in Chapter 9, organizations rarely reward good raters or punish bad ones. Performance appraisal often occupies only a minimum of the busy supervisor's time, and organizations rarely take concrete steps to encourage more thorough or deliberative appraisals. Organizations do not bother to provide appraisals to top management, who represent their most influential employees. None of these practices is likely to lead to the perception that accurate performance appraisal is important or that the judgments of the raters will have any real impact on the actions of the organizations.

The first question that should be faced by organizations that consider reaction criteria in their evaluations of appraisal systems is whether there is any good reason for a positive reaction. If the appraisal system is seen by most raters and ratees as a waste of time, it is hard to see how the appraisal system will aid in accomplishing any worthwhile goals. Reaction criteria are almost always relevant, and an unfavorable reaction may doom the most carefully constructed appraisal system. One of the most difficult challenges that may lie ahead of PA researchers will be to convince organizations to (a) take reaction criteria seriously and (b) create conditions in their organization that will lead to favorable reactions to the performance appraisal system.

Practicality Criteria

With a few exceptions (e.g., Cascio, 1987) the issue of practicality is rarely discussed in evaluating appraisal systems. Practicality concerns, however, are likely to influence strongly an organization's decisions regarding a new appraisal system, particularly one that is unusually complicated or involved. An appraisal system that calls for multiple raters, at different levels in the organization, all using detailed behavior diaries and behavior-based rating scales, might represent the technical state of the art, but it is likely to be rejected on the simple ground that it is impractical.

Practicality concerns are considered, to some degree, in utility estimates. As discussed earlier, one of the formulas widely used in utility estimation can be expressed as:

$$\text{Gain in utility} = N_T[2(r_1 - r_2) \times \text{SD}_y - (C_1 + C_2)] \qquad (11.4)$$

Practicality concerns are represented by the cost terms (C_1 and C_2). One implication of Equation 11.4 is that when two alternative appraisal systems are being considered, differences in the costs of the alternatives must be offset by differences in validity to justify the choice of the more costly system. (One possibility is to compare the costs and benefits of a single appraisal system, with the alternative course of action being no performance appraisal. In this case, Equation 11.4 reduces to Equation 11.3.)

For example, suppose one system uses multiple raters and new, complex scales that cost $1,500 per person to implement, and another system employs supervisors as raters and uses existing scales that cost $200 per person. Practicality considerations suggest that the complex system should not be adopted unless it leads to some benefit that offsets the additional cost.

The differences in validity, multiplied by SD_y, provide a measure of the differences in the value of the benefits of the two systems. In the example cited above, if SD_y is equal to $10,000, the validity of the complex system (i.e., the correlation between using the system and attaining valued goals) must be .065 larger than the validity of the simpler system (i.e., if $r_2 = .45$, r_1 must be .515) to justify the choice of the more complex system. Otherwise, choice of the more valid but more expensive system will lead to a net loss in utility.

Utility equations are useful for capturing some aspects of practicality but they may ignore or underestimate some important variables that distinguish highly practical from highly impractical systems. For example, some appraisal systems require substantial commitments of time on the part of both the raters and the ratees. To our knowledge, the raters' and ratees' investment of time is not typically fully factored into the costs that are considered in utility equations. The tendency of some systems to lead to unacceptable outcomes can also be considered a facet of practicality. A system that is politically unacceptable to the organization is not practical and will not succeed.

Ease of installation is yet another facet of practicality that is not always factored into utility equations. Some systems require long training periods. Other systems have complex reporting requirements that require many workers at all levels to readjust their schedules and routines. In general, an appraisal system that can be installed in an organization with a minimum of disruption of the organization's routine will be preferable to a more disruptive one, unless the disruptive alternative is substantially more valid than the simpler one.

Decision Process Criteria

One final criterion that is frequently overlooked is the extent to which PA contributes to the decision-making process in organizations. Utility equations estimate the effect of alternative systems on the *correctness* (or the dollar value) of decisions. There are two additional ways that performance appraisal might affect the decision-making process. First, several characteristics of the appraisal system will affect the degree to which decisions are accepted by the members of the organizations. Second, the characteristics of a PA system will have a considerable impact on the ease with which specific decisions are made.

In our brief discussion of procedural and distributive justice, we noted that the perceived fairness and accuracy of an appraisal system can be an important determinant of its success. The fairness of decisions (e.g., raises, promotions) made on the basis of performance appraisals must also be carefully considered. An appraisal system that does a poor job of measurement but that leads to decisions that are accepted as fair by organization members may be preferable to one that provides accurate measures that lead to decisions that are not accepted by raters or ratees.

Throughout this book we have argued that performance appraisal should be viewed as a decision aid rather than as a measurement tool. One way that performance appraisal can contribute to the organization is to streamline and rationalize the process of making administrative decisions. The extent to which a PA system contributes to the ease of decision making is a direct function of the match between the measurement properties of the system and the goals of the different constituent groups.

For example, a manager might use performance appraisal as a tool for deciding which 3 of his or her 10 subordinates should be promoted. The only measurement characteristic that is relevant to that goal is that the appraisal system should allow the rater to separate quickly and easily the total group into two subgroups: the promotable group ($N = 3$) and the nonpromotable group ($N = 7$). An appraisal system that does not allow the rater to separate these two groups, or one that requires substantial effort or calculation on the part of raters to decide who should and should not be promoted, may not make a worthwhile contribution to the process of making administrative decisions (Feldman, 1986).

The contribution of a PA system to the decision-making process may be more a matter of perceptions than reality. If organizational members *believe* that a performance appraisal system makes decisions easier and better, the system will have some benefits regardless of its actual contribution to the ease and the quality of decisions. As we noted earlier, the procedural justice literature may provide a framework for research on the contributions of a performance appraisal system to perceptions of equity. Survey research might provide some clues to the facets of PA systems that contribute to the perception that appraisals simplify the decision-making process.

INTEGRATING MULTIPLE CRITERIA

Because most performance appraisal systems are driven by multiple goals, multiple criteria will generally be needed to evaluate an appraisal system fully. One problem the researcher or practitioner must face is to integrate the evaluations reached on the basis of each individual criterion into an overall evaluation of the PA system. Research on multiattribute evaluation (Edwards, 1980; Edwards & Newman, 1982) and on decisions with multiple objectives (Keeney & Raiffa, 1976; Raiffa, 1968) provides some useful guidelines for this sort of integration.

Consider the case illustrated in Table 11.2. Here, a performance appraisal system whose primary goals are to help make promotion decisions, to document personnel actions and decisions, and to motivate employees is being evaluated in terms of three criteria that can be derived from those goals: (a) the rank-order correlation between ratings and some externally validated measure of promotability, (b) the amount and specificity of the information recorded about each ratee, and (c) the change in levels of motivation. Because these criteria are qualitatively different, they will need to be put on a common scale before they can be sensibly integrated. One simple approach, which is illustrated in Table 11.2, might be to express each criterion in terms of where the obtained value would be located on a percentile scale ranging from the worst possible value for that criterion (i.e., 1st percentile) to the best possible value for that criterion (i.e., 99th percentile).

For example, the worst possible value for the rank-order correlation between ratings and some externally derived measure of promotability is r = .00 (assuming that a system with negative validity would never be seriously considered). The best possible value is $r = 1.00$. One interpretation of the correlation coefficient is in terms of the distance between the best possible decision and decisions made at random. Therefore, the correlation of .50 can be expressed as a score of 50 on a 100-point scale. The score of 85 for the third criterion, changes in levels of motivation, indicates that the observed change is nearly as large as the increase in motivation that would result if the best possible system were instituted.

Although the percentile-based approach illustrated in Table 11.2 solves some problems, it does not provide a basis for integrating the values of different criteria. The reason for this is that criteria vary in their importance as well as in the relative value that might be assigned to the same percentage score on different criteria. For example, a validity coefficient of .10 might be an indicator that a PA system is not very useful for making promotion decisions, whereas an increase in motivation that has a percentile value of .10 might be considered worthwhile.

To further complicate things, the difference between the value of a given score on one criterion and the value of the same score on another criterion might not be constant. For example, a value of .20 on the motivational criterion might be twice as good as a value of .20 on the validity for promotion criterion. A value of .60 on the motivational criterion might be five times as valuable as a value of .60 on validity for promotion, because motivational changes affect all workers but promotions affect only a small number of workers. In order to integrate multiple criteria, more is needed than a common scale of measurement (e.g., the percentile scale). In particular, a common scale is needed for the *value* of the outcomes associated with each criterion.

Decision theory (Keeney & Raiffa 1976; Raiffa, 1968) provides a method for scaling qualitatively different outcomes on a common value

TABLE 11.2 Evaluating a Performance Appraisal System Using Multiple Criteria

Criteria	Evaluation	Percentile[a]
Rank-order correlation between ratings and some externally validated measure of promotability	r = .50	50th
Amount and specificity of information recorded about each ratee	Little information but highly specific	70th
Change in levels of motivation to perform well	Motivation to perform increases by 25%	85th

NOTE: a. Percentile: Location of the appraisal system on a scale where 0 = worst possible value of this criterion measure and 100 = best possible value of this criterion measure.

scale. This method allows one to predict value trade-offs and to aggregate value indices for different attributes or outcomes. The method involves the use of *indifference curves,* which can be constructed by asking an individual or a group of decision makers for their preferences among outcomes (see Figure 11.2). For example, a group of managers might be asked a series of questions in the following form:

Which outcome would you prefer or value more?

1. A promotion validity of .20 (20th percentile) or
2. An increase in motivation at the 25th percentile

For some questions, the preponderant majority will prefer one of the two alternatives (e.g., here, 85% of the managers may prefer Item 2). For other questions, however, approximately 50% of the managers will prefer Item 1 and approximately 50% will prefer Item 2. According to decision theory, if the group is indifferent about receiving 1 versus 2, these two outcomes must have equivalent value (see Raiffa [1968] for a highly accessible introduction to this technique and its applications in multiattribute evaluation).

The indifference curve represents a plot of those alternatives that have equal value to the respondents. For example, Figure 11.2 implies that a validity for promotion of .20 and an increase in motivation at the 20th percentile are equally valuable. Similarly, a validity of .40 and an increase in motivation at the 80th percentile are seen as equally valuable. All points

Figure 11.2. Indifference Curve Comparing Promotion Versus Motivational Criteria

NOTE: Area above the curve: Promotion outcome preferred to motivational
Area below the curve: Motivational outcome preferred to promotion
Curve itself: Value of promotion and motivational outcomes is equal

above the curve (e.g., validity of .60 and increase in motivation at the 25th percentile) represent trade-offs where the promotion outcome has more value than the motivational outcome. All points below the curve represent choices where the motivational outcome is more valuable than the validity for promotion outcome.

The indifference curve allows one to rescale different outcomes on a common value scale. For example, Table 11.2 includes values of 50 and 85 for the promotion and motivational criteria, respectively. The indifference curve suggests that a validity coefficient of .5 is equal in value to an increase in motivation that is approximately at the 88th percentile. When the two outcomes are expressed on a common scale, it becomes clear that the evaluation of this appraisal system in terms of its effect on promotion validity is very similar to the evaluation of the system in terms of its impact on work motivation levels (scores of 88 and 85, respectively), and that the system does a very good job of meeting both goals. If the remaining criterion dimension (amount and specificity of information) were also scaled on this value dimension (this would require another indifference curve), it would be possible to measure the effectiveness of the appraisal system with multiple criteria that all shared a common value scale.

In principle, any one dimension can be chosen to provide a common value metric. In practice, it is best to choose a dimension that is both important and highly concrete. For example, organization members might find it easier to evaluate an appraisal system that is scaled in terms of its motivational impact than one that is scaled in terms of the specificity and amount of behavioral information provided. Once all criterion dimensions are measured on a common value scale, the only remaining issue is to combine the dimensional assessments into an overall assessment. This can be done by forming a weighted linear combination of scores on the separate dimensions, where the weights are proportional to the relative importance of each criterion.

The method of forming indifference curves to express value trade-offs is not only useful for multiattribute evaluation, it is also useful for comparing different appraisal systems that address totally different goals. For example, suppose that one system did a good job of improving motivation and a moderately poor job of assisting in making salary decisions. Suppose that another system did a good job of identifying promotable workers and did a fair job at providing a detailed record of each individual's performance. The use of indifference curves will allow one to compare these two systems sensibly and to choose the one that best meets the most important set of goals. To our knowledge, indifference curves and related methods from decision theory have not yet been applied to the evaluation of PA systems. We think these methods have great potential and expect that they will be more widely used in the future.

Daniels and Keller (1992) present alternatives to indifference-curve methods that are simpler and may produce more reliable results. In general, we see the indifference curve as a valuable heuristic rather than as a general solution to the problem of scaling outcomes. That is, the general idea that trade-offs can (and must) be established between complex sets of decision outcomes is an essential component of applying a variety of decision models and theories to the problems faced daily by supervisors when conducting appraisals. Although the tasks and models described in the formal decision literature may seem abstract and difficult, it is important to keep in mind that people do this sort of thing every day. As our earlier chapters have suggested, raters must consider a wide range of possible implications of giving high or low ratings to each subordinate (we will develop this theme further in Chapter 12) and must somehow balance outcomes that vary greatly in their seriousness and nature (e.g., increased motivation vs. complaints from co-workers if you give a high rating to a particular subordinate). Decision research provides a powerful set of tools for examining these trade-offs.

SUMMARY

The most common criteria for evaluating PA systems (e.g., rater error and accuracy measures) do not take into account the actual use(s) of ratings in organizations. This chapter reviewed several methods of evaluating PA systems that reflect the degree to which PA helps the organization achieve or advance important goals. For example, utility formulations allow one to estimate the impact of good versus poor appraisal systems on the productivity of the workforce. It is much more important to know whether or not PA contributes to productivity than to know merely whether or not appraisals are accurate.

Several challenges await researchers and practitioners who attempt to develop criteria that reflect the impact of appraisal systems on the organization. The most obvious challenge is to identify the goals (both implicit and explicit) that PA systems are designed to serve. It is likely that different groups (e.g., raters, ratees, upper management) have very different goals in mind when participating in appraisal. Indeed, it is likely that each individual will pursue multiple goals in appraisal. The identification of relevant goals and the reconciliation of inconsistent goals may be the most important step in evaluating PA systems.

There are numerous criteria, including measures of reactions to performance appraisal systems, measures that reflect the practicality of PA systems, and measures of the contribution of appraisal to decision-making processes in organizations, that are usually dismissed as "soft" criteria that are of secondary importance. These criteria are often critically important, and the acceptability, practicality, and apparent contribution of PA systems to fair and accurate decisions may be the most important criteria. PA systems that are highly accurate but that appear to produce unfair outcomes or that are cumbersome and expensive to install and use may be doomed from the start.

One final problem considered in this chapter is the integration of different criteria in evaluating PA systems. Every PA system serves multiple goals and is more relevant to some goals than to others. This chapter suggested some ways of adapting the methods of decision research to the problem of integrating information about the impact of PA on the various goals that appraisal systems serve.

12

Does Performance Appraisal
Help or Hurt the Organization?

From the organization's perspective, performance appraisal (PA) systems are a mixed blessing. On the one hand, they are a constant target of criticism and complaints. As we noted in Chapter 1, dissatisfaction with performance appraisal is the norm in most organizations, and there appears to be little human resource managers can do to improve the image of performance appraisal. Even if a successful system is developed, it is likely that enthusiasm for the system will soon wane, and in a few years the new system will look as bad as all of the ones that have come before it (this is the common fate of many innovations in organizations). On the other hand, it is hard to imagine doing without performance appraisal altogether. Appraisal serves a number of important functions in an organization (both implicit and explicit), and if the formal performance appraisal system were abandoned, it is likely that something like it would eventually emerge in the informal workings of the organization.

This chapter considers the question of whether the benefits of PA to an organization are likely to outweigh the costs. Our focus here is on the organization's perspective, and it is likely that the costs and benefits of performance appraisal to raters, ratees, or other participants in the appraisal process will be quite different from those experienced by the organization. Nevertheless, we think it is worth asking whether organizations are better off with or without performance appraisal systems.

In evaluating the costs and benefits of performance appraisal to an organization, it is possible to enumerate a number of ways appraisal might either help or hurt the organization. As will be seen, however, some of the apparent benefits of appraisal may not be as valuable as they first seem. Similarly, many of the apparent costs of performance appraisal may not be as weighty as they initially seem. In a section that examines the relationship between "bad" appraisal and good management, we will consider the question of whether many of the shortcomings of performance appraisal systems should be considered as costs or benefits. After presenting potential costs and benefits, we will describe a specific application of performance appraisal (in pay-for-performance systems) that exemplifies the ambiguous nature of appraisal. Virtually any method of conducting and/or using performance appraisal presents a mix of costs and benefits, and balancing the costs against benefits may be a very complex task.

In asking whether the benefits of PA are likely to outweigh the costs, we will not consider some of the very real constraints on deciding whether or not to do performance appraisal. In particular, an organization may be bound by a contract or by legal guidelines to conduct appraisals (and to conduct them in certain ways). Thus, even if there is unanimous agreement that performance appraisals serve no useful function in the organization, the system may survive, propped up by a set of legal or contractual requirements. Similarly, we will not consider the potentially substantial costs of developing, implementing, or maintaining the appraisal system. For the purposes of this chapter, we want to think about the issues an organization would face in deciding whether or not to conduct appraisals if such costs and external constraints did not exist. We acknowledge that this hypothetical case is an unrealistic one, but nevertheless it helps to provide a framework for thinking about the range of costs and benefits of performance appraisal to organizations.

HOW APPRAISAL CAN HELP THE ORGANIZATION

We believe that performance appraisals can help organizations in several ways. First, they can enhance the quality of organizational decisions, ranging from reward allocation to promotions, layoffs, and transfers. Second, they can enhance the quality of individual decisions, ranging from career choices to decisions about where to direct one's time and effort. Presumably, if the members of an organization make good decisions about how to direct their time and effort in their current jobs and in their future development, organizations will benefit. Third, they provide a set of tools for organizational diagnosis and development. Knowing how people perform in various parts of an organization is vital for assessing the effectiveness of current or planned ways of functioning. Finally, performance appraisals can affect employees' views of and attachment to their organization. An organization that does a good job with performance appraisal may help to build and cement employee commitment and satisfaction. Of course, none of these benefits automatically flows from the mere presence of a performance appraisal system. Nevertheless, an organization that does a good job at performance appraisal might benefit in a number of ways.

Increasing the Quality of Organizational Decisions

It is common to base decisions about pay, job assignments, training opportunities, and so on, on a number of factors, including individual job performance (Gerhart & Milkovich, 1992; Lawler & Jenkins, 1992; Schuler, 1987). A good PA system has the potential to support a wide range of personnel decisions. As we noted in Chapter 4, PA also provides a basis for evaluating the quality of personnel decisions. For example, performance ratings often provide criterion measures for validating personnel selection systems or for assessing the impact of training programs.

Although performance appraisal has the potential to make an important contribution to the quality of organizational decisions, there are several factors that might limit that contribution. First, as we have noted in several previous chapters, performance appraisal systems serve several functions other than (and sometimes in direct opposition to) accurately measuring job performance. If the organization's decision requires an accurate assessment of performance, the failure of most performance appraisal systems to deliver such measures will represent a major limitation. More fundamentally, questions are often raised about whether such decisions should be based (partially or in full) on job performance.

Consider the decision to base pay on performance. On the surface, this might seem entirely reasonable, but a strictly performance-based system ignores several factors that are believed to be relevant to compensation (e.g., job demands, skill levels of employees, situational constraints, performance of the organization, market factors. See Gerhart & Milkovich, 1992; Lawler & Jenkins, 1992). Systems that link pay to performance also appear to heighten concerns over the fairness and accuracy of performance appraisals (Milkovich & Wigdor, 1991), and links between performance and pay may pressure raters to distort performance ratings upward (Cleveland & Murphy, 1992; Murphy & Cleveland, 1991).

Basing promotion decisions on job performance brings to mind the well-known "Peter Principle," which states that people will be promoted to their own level of incompetence. For example, promoting the best engineer into management may cost the organization its best engineer and give it a poor manager. If the demands, duties, and so on, of the two jobs differ substantially, promoting the best performer in Job A into Job B may not be the most effective policy.

Finally, the assumption that selection, promotion, or pay on the basis of performance is the "right" thing to do is not universally accepted. Reviews of European (Shimmin, 1989) and Scandinavian (Ekvall, 1980) research on selection and assessment suggest that assumptions about whether people should be treated differently on the basis of their job performance vary considerably, and that the very notion of linking rewards to performance is not universally accepted.

Although all of the limiting factors described above are important, we should not lose sight of the potential value of linking valid and accurate information about job performance to personnel decisions. The major purpose of the personnel and human resource department or function in an organization is to maximize the contributions of employees to the goals of the organization, and assessments of their job performance can play a key role in carrying out that function.

Increasing the Quality of Individual Decisions

Individual employees must make a number of decisions about their present and future roles in an organization. For the present, they must decide how to allocate their time, talents, and effort in performing their jobs. They must also decide how (or if) to develop future strengths and what sorts of career goals they should pursue. Performance appraisal systems that provide accurate, timely, and detailed feedback can contribute substantially to the quality of these decisions.

The role of performance feedback in organizations has been studied extensively (Ashford & Cummings, 1983; Davis & Mount, 1984; Fisher & Taylor, 1979; Fletcher, 1978; Greller, 1975, 1978; Guzzo et al., 1985; Landy et al., 1982; Meyer et al., 1965). One of the major themes of this research is that several conflicts are built into the appraisal and feedback process. For example, ratees desperately want feedback, but they also want to hear only positive feedback and tend to dismiss negative feedback (see Chapter 9 for a review of feedback credibility). Feedback involves seeking out information that may not be readily available to the ratee (Ashford, 1986), but during the appraisal interview, ratees like to talk about as much as they listen (Fletcher, 1978; Greller, 1975, 1978). Performance appraisal puts the rater in the uncomfortable position of both counselor and judge, who must both evaluate performance (and sometimes pass on bad news) and give advice about future development (Meyer et al., 1965). Yet, despite all of the problems and conflicts encountered in giving and receiving feedback, there is clear consensus that high-quality feedback can be extremely beneficial to both individuals and the organizations that employ them (Landy et al. [1982] illustrate methods for evaluating the economic benefits of performance appraisal; see also Chapter 11 of this volume).

There is an extensive body of research showing that accurate performance feedback is an important component of the success of training (Goldstein, 1986), that it provides critical input for forming realistic self-assessments in the work setting (Ashford, 1989), and that it is a key to maintaining high levels of work motivation (Locke & Latham, 1990). Performance feedback is also thought to be a key to self-development, both in the sense that it helps to identify areas of strength and weakness and in the sense that it motivates future development (Bandura, 1982, 1986).

The greatest potential limitation to the value of performance feedback is the strong likelihood that feedback will be biased, incomplete, and inaccurate. First, as noted in Chapter 5, the person most likely to give performance feedback (i.e., the supervisor) may not know how well workers have performed or what constraints exist that limit their performance. If employees are working in a context where the tools, information, or resources necessary to do the job are not available, it probably does not help to be told that they are not performing up to a standard. Second, as we will note later in this chapter, performance feedback tends to focus on the individual and ignore the system variables that affect performance. If employees produce little because the production line is moving very slowly, feedback about their low level of output is probably not helpful. Third, as we noted in Chapter 9, there are strong pressures to give high ratings and favorable feedback, even in contexts where the individual is not performing well.

If performance feedback is biased, inaccurate, or simply incomplete, the actual benefits achieved as a result of receiving feedback may be limited. It is even possible to envision cases where low-quality feedback could be harmful. For example, subordinates may develop unrealistic ideas about their capabilities and performance level, and may be dissatisfied if their rewards do not match the inflated self-assessments that are formed on the basis of inaccurate feedback. Nevertheless, performance feedback carries such a wide array of potential benefits that even a limited amount of usable feedback may be worthwhile.

Enhancing Attachments Between the Organization and Its Members

The type, frequency, and quality of performance feedback received affect ratees' evaluations of their PA system (Dipboye & dePontbriand, 1981; Landy et al., 1978; Landy, Barnes-Farrell, & Cleveland, 1980). More generally, the performance feedback ratees receive can affect their view of and understanding of the organization. Several researchers have examined the factors that lead to perceptions of fairness or unfairness in the appraisal process and the effects of these factors on more general views of the organization (Folger et al., 1992; Greenberg, 1986, 1987). There is clear evidence that the quality of PA and feedback has a role in perceptions of the fairness, legitimacy, and rationality of a wide range of organizational practices. When performance feedback is sketchy, inaccurate, or not given at all, concerns about the appraisal process may spill over into perceptions of other human resource systems, and the procedures for making pay, promotion, and other reward-related decisions may appear suspect. When performance feedback is prompt, fair, and complete, it is more likely that incumbents will view other human resource systems in a favorable light.

Employees who believe that an organization's decisions are irrational, capricious, or unfair are unlikely to develop strong commitment to that organization. Low commitment, in turn, has been linked to withdrawal behaviors (e.g., turnover, absenteeism), satisfaction, and job performance (Hom, Caranikas-Walker, Prussia, & Griffeth, 1992; Mobley, 1982; Mowday, Porter, & Steers, 1981). A belief that the decision processes are chaotic or unfair may in turn heighten concerns over the fairness of decision outcomes. A distinction is often made between the fairness of procedures themselves and the fairness of the outcomes of these procedures (i.e., procedural vs. distributive justice. See Folger & Greenberg, 1985; Greenberg & Folger, 1983). Research on the relationship between these two aspects of justice in organizations suggests that when the procedures seem fair and reasonable, it is easier to accept negative outcomes. For example, if performance appraisal feedback is seen as thorough, accurate, and fair, people who receive small raises or who are passed over for promotion may be more willing to accept that outcome. On the other hand, if performance appraisal and feedback systems are seen as incomplete, inaccurate, and unfair, people who fail to receive valued rewards are likely to react very negatively.

In this section, we have consistently used phrases like *performance appraisal and feedback* rather than talking about feedback itself. Our reason for doing this is that the performance feedback is probably the single most important piece of information ratees have about the performance appraisal system. Ratees may or may not be aware of the rater training or scale development processes, and they may not be well informed about the various ways organizations use appraisals. Their major contact with the appraisal process is likely to be their individual appraisal and feedback interview. As a result, when feedback is of low quality, ratees are likely to infer that the entire appraisal system is also of low quality, and that the decisions that are made on the basis of such a system are suspect.

Performance feedback sessions provide an opportunity to build and enhance positive impressions of the organization and its decision-making processes. As we have noted in previous sections, however, this opportunity is double-edged. That is, when feedback is incomplete, inaccurate, or difficult to use (e.g., feedback that refers to broad and general traits is not very useful), employees' experiences with the performance appraisal and feedback system may be a significant source of dissatisfaction and disillusionment.

Providing a Foundation for
Organizational Diagnosis and Change

Finally, PA provides useful information for diagnosing the organization's level of functioning and for suggesting avenues for change. There is a substantial body of research and practice aimed at introducing planned changes into the way organizations function, and there is a growing consensus that the key to successful organizational development (OD) is to change the on-the-job behaviors of individual members of the organization (Porras & Robertson, 1992). Valid and accurate information about individual and group performance provides a diagnostic tool for focusing planned change efforts.

Performance appraisal itself can be thought of as a type of OD activity, particularly when new appraisal systems are introduced. In Chapter 5 we discussed 360-degree appraisal feedback and appraisal systems (research on 360-degree systems is reviewed in a special issue of *Human Resource Management,* 1993, Vol. 32, No. 2 & 3). The use of appraisal and feedback systems that incorporate input from superiors, peers, and subordinates might change the organization and its function in a number of ways. Traditionally, power, influence, and evaluations in organizations flow from the top of the organization down (Mahew, 1983; Thompson, 1967). In fact, the ability to evaluate another's performance is one of the key indicators of power and authority in an organization (Dornbusch & Scott, 1975). An organization that introduces 360-degree appraisal and feedback disrupts the network of power and authority in ways that might substantially affect future interactions among peers, supervisors, and subordinates. One implication of a 360-degree appraisal and feedback system is that distinctions between levels of authority in an organization are likely to break down, at least to some extent. In Chapter 13 we will note that ongoing changes in the structure of work organizations may also lead to more permeable barriers between levels of authority and to less emphasis on hierarchical differentiation in organizations. Changing the performance appraisal system could be one avenue for breaking down those barriers.

Even though there seems to be widespread support for changing appraisal systems in ways that lower barriers between supervisors and subordinates, there are subtle signs of resistance to this trend. For example, supervisors often express positive attitudes toward subordinate appraisals, but they are most favorable when they receive appraisals from subordinates and supervisors, and least supportive when they receive appraisals from subordinates only (Bernardin et al., 1993). One way to interpret these results is to note that total reversals of the power hierarchy seem very uncomfortable to supervisors, whereas appraisal systems that balance upward feedback with the traditional downward feedback are less threatening.

Unlike many human resource interventions (e.g., personnel selection, training, job redesign), OD efforts are not generally aimed at improving individual job performance. Organizational development interventions often involve changing the environment, structure, physical layout, culture, and/or communication pattern of an organization or organizational unit (Porras & Robertson, 1992). Information about job performance, however, can be used both to identify areas where change is needed and to evaluate the effects of change. As Porras and Robertson (1992) note, although changes are often conceptualized and implemented at the broad system level, the whole point of OD is to change the behavior of individuals in ways that will contribute to the efficiency and health of the organization. Performance appraisals have the potential to inform and direct OD efforts.

In the preceding sections, we have cautioned that the extent to which organizations realize the potential advantages of appraisal may depend on the quality, accuracy, and completeness of the appraisals, and that problems in the appraisal system can limit the benefits actually achieved by organizations. The same caution applies here: A bad performance appraisal system could give misleading information about where OD efforts are needed or about their success. In this particular context, however, a bad appraisal system might itself be an impetus for organizational development. It is useful to keep in mind that performance information is only one of many sources of diagnostic data that might be considered in designing and evaluating OD efforts, and the typical shortcomings of performance appraisal systems may themselves provide useful information for designing and implementing OD efforts. For example, if the "problem" with appraisal is rampant rating inflation, one possible OD strategy is to modify the culture that supports and validates such rating behavior.

HOW APPRAISAL CAN HURT THE ORGANIZATION

In the sections above, we outlined several advantages of performance appraisal. If performance appraisals are done well, organizations stand to benefit in a number of ways. However, there are also a number of ways performance appraisal could hurt an organization, even if it is done relatively well. Furthermore, some of the potential drawbacks of performance appraisal could be magnified if, as is so often the case, performance appraisal systems fail to provide useful measures of job performance.

There are several ways a performance appraisal system could hurt the organization. First, the system can interfere with teamwork and with understanding performance successes and failures, by overemphasizing the individual and underemphasizing the system and the team. Second, appraisal systems often send mixed messages about what aspects of job performance are most and least important and about the importance of performing well. Third, as we have noted earlier, performance appraisal is itself often a source of discontent for both raters and ratees.

Appraisals Overemphasize the Individual and Underemphasize the Team or System

Deming (1986) and others (e.g., Joiner, 1994) have argued that individual appraisal is dysfunctional because it interferes with teamwork, fosters mediocrity, focuses on short-term outcomes, and overemphasizes individual differences in performance. Deming, in particular, criticizes appraisals as overly subjective and incorrectly focused (i.e., they focus on the product rather than the process). Furthermore, his approach to quality management (often referred to under the heading of total quality management, or TQM) suggests that almost all of the meaningful variation in performance is due to system characteristics rather than to person characteristics (Gabor, 1990; Nagy, 1993). On this basis, Deming suggested that individual performance appraisal should not be done; in his view, the pain outweighs the gain. Studies by Carson, Cardy, and Dobbins (1991, 1992) have examined Deming's criticisms. These studies support some of the points made by Deming and his followers (e.g., raters find it difficult to separate performance variability due to persons vs. systems), but they do not fully support the suggestion that appraisals should be abandoned.

In our view, the importance of the critiques raised by Deming and other proponents of TQM depends substantially on the nature of the job, the organization, and the product. In some settings (e.g., traditional assembly lines) there is probably little individual variability in performance, at least compared to the performance variability caused by the production system.

Attempting to apply individually oriented performance appraisal strategies in those contexts will probably lead to many of the negative consequences predicted by TQM advocates. On the other hand, job performance in service industries may depend heavily on the characteristics and actions of individuals, and there may be relatively little "system" variability. In these contexts (which represent an increasingly important part of the American economy—see Chapter 13) it may be both possible and important to assess the performance of individuals and to use those appraisals to guide a wide array of administrative and developmental activities (e.g., raises, promotions, training).

The potential problems with human resource systems that emphasize systems rather than individuals can be illustrated by examining the experiences of organizations that employ just-in-time (JIT) systems of manufacturing. JIT requires teamwork, as well as integration between teams, commitment, flexibility, high skill levels, and concern for quality (Amaya, 1990). Although the rhetoric surrounding JIT and related management techniques is often humanistic and benign (e.g., concern for empowering employees, lifetime security, reciprocal loyalty between employers and employees), the reality of JIT as implemented in Western organizations can be quite different (Delbridge & Turnbull, 1992). JIT management systems incorporate many elements of classic Scientific Management, including standardization of production techniques, short work cycles, and a fast pace of work. These systems employ blame, peer pressure, and relentless stress on employees and managers to achieve production goals. Sewell and Wilkinson (1992) note that organizations employing JIT and related production management systems often engage in extensive surveillance and monitoring of their employees (Austrin [1991] and Fuller & Smith [1991] present examples of employee surveillance in other industries), and that these systems can be highly coercive in their treatment of individual workers who deviate from system norms. On the whole, research in this area suggests that it is unwise to ignore either the person or the system when evaluating and understanding performance (for an extensive discussion of person- vs. system-oriented appraisal systems, see Cardy & Dobbins, 1994).

Although many proponents of TQM insist that individually oriented performance appraisal is incompatible with their approach to production and quality control, there is evidence that performance appraisal can be integrated with TQM (Nagy, 1993). For example, a carefully developed performance appraisal system can help raters separate person from system variability. Though there is evidence that supervisors and subordinates differ in their tendency to attribute poor performance to the system (Carson et al., 1991; consistent with a large body of research on attribution, individuals who receive low ratings tend to make external attributions. See Mitchell et al. [1981] for a review of research on attributions involved in evaluating poor performers), appraisal research suggests that raters can make useful and valid assessments of performance, given the motivation and the tools (Milkovich & Wigdor, 1991). Some researchers (e.g., Kane & Kane, 1992a, 1992b) have suggested specific methods of appraisal that might be most closely aligned with the goals of TQM, but to date there has been little research testing the viability of specific appraisal-TQM links.

Deming's (1986) critique of performance appraisal raises important questions about the potential drawbacks of individually oriented performance appraisal. As other researchers (e.g., Peters & O'Connor, 1980; Peters et al., 1985) note, PA systems often fail to consider the role of situational variables in determining performance. Focusing on the individual and ignoring the situation (and the overall production system) will develop a distorted picture of why people perform well or poorly, and what can be done about it. For example, if an employee is performing poorly, the individually oriented perspective might suggest that his or her supervisor should intervene to increase his or her motivation to perform (e.g., by manipulating rewards or punishments). If the real reason for poor performance is that the situation constrains performance, or that the system makes it difficult to perform well, such individually oriented strategies have little chance of success. On the other hand, Deming's critique can be taken too far. There is clear and compelling evidence of consistent individual differences in job performance (Judiesch, Schmidt, & Mount, 1992; Schmidt & Hunter, 1983), and it is reckless to ignore such differences. Although performance appraisal systems can overemphasize individual contributions to job performance, organizations that attempt to function without individual performance appraisal may be forced to ignore an important source of variability in job performance (Gerhart & Milkovich, 1992).

Performance Appraisal Systems
Send Mixed Messages

Earlier in this chapter, we commented on the gulf between appraisal systems as they are described in most employee handbooks and as they actually function in organizations. Our experience working with the performance appraisal systems employed in the armed services provides compelling examples of this gap.

Bjerke et al. (1987) described the performance appraisal system used by the U.S. Navy for evaluating officers' job performance. The appraisal form includes numerical ratings, rankings, and narrative summaries of performance. In theory, this system is used for a wide range of individual and organizational decisions, ranging from job assignment to career advisement. In fact, a culture has developed in this organization that targets the appraisal system at one particular function—that is, determining whether an officer should be promoted. Because of the "up or out" career system (i.e., officers who are passed over for promotion a certain number of times must resign from the service), this promotion decision is also a decision about whether this individual should remain in the organization. Raters have developed an elaborate set of implicit rules for communicating who should or should not be promoted (see Chapter 8), and there seems to be a clear understanding of the "real" purpose of appraisal.

This example refers to the mixed messages an organization sometimes sends about the purpose of performance appraisal. Organizations also send mixed messages about which aspects of job performance are or are not important. The most obvious example is the gap between rhetoric and reality concerning the importance of performance appraisal itself. Organizations routinely claim that performance appraisal is an important part of the supervisor's job, but as we noted in Chapter 9, they rarely reward managers who do a good job evaluating their subordinates or punish raters who do a consistently poor job in evaluating their subordinates (Cleveland & Murphy, 1992). Similarly, the dimensions rated on performance appraisal forms should reflect the most critical aspects of job performance. In fact, the dimensions rated may capture only a few important aspects of any particular job or may be so broad and vague that they do not refer in any clear way to the job itself. This is particularly likely in an organization that attempts to use a single appraisal form to cover many or all jobs.

A final mixed message often sent by organizations concerns the importance of performance appraisal for the ratee. Again, the "party line" in most organizations is that job performance and performance appraisal are critical determinants of administrative decisions and of the success of the organization. In fact, the links between performance appraisals and organizational decisions are often obscure and inconsistent. As we noted in Chapter 9, there is an extensive body of research on the effects of the purpose of rating on rating behavior and rating outcomes. One of the themes of this line of research is that ratees often have no clear idea what is actually done with ratings, in part because organizations often have no clear or consistent policy describing how they actually use performance appraisal to make important decisions.

Earlier in this chapter, we discussed the role of performance appraisal in conveying and reinforcing the belief that the organization is rational, thorough, and fair in its decisions and policies. Mixed messages in performance appraisal do little to reinforce the impression that the organization knows what it is doing. On the other hand, it is not clear that an organization can or should be absolutely clear or consistent in its administration and use of performance appraisal. The most "rational" organizational form is the classic bureaucracy, where there are detailed rules and procedures that govern every decision and action. In our view, mixed messages are a price that is paid for the flexibility and adaptability of a nonbureaucratic organization. Although it might be better to be consistent in the way PA is talked about and thought about in organizations, such consistency may be possible only under an absolutely stifling set of rules, guidelines, and procedures. As Milkovich and Wigdor (1991) note, attempts to make performance evaluations completely objective have met with little success. Attempts to make the entire performance appraisal system completely rational, consistent, and predictable would probably fare no better.

Appraisal can be a cause of dissatisfaction and dissent. There are a number of reasons why performance appraisal is such a frequent target of complaints and ridicule and such a frequent source of dissatisfaction in organizations. First, appraisal systems often force raters to make distinctions that are simply not realistic or functional. Joiner (1994) describes ranking, rating, and forced distributions as "the three great demoralizers," because each tends to force distinctions that may or may not be there. Similarly, Ilgen et al. (1993) note that if a task requires teamwork and cooperation, rating systems that point out differences between performers may interfere with the team's ability to function as a unit.

Second, performance appraisals routinely disappoint ratees, in part because of actor-observer differences in evaluation. As we noted in Chapters 5 and 6, self-assessments are usually more favorable than others' assessments of job performance. Because of predictable differences in the way we perceive, interpret, and remember our own performance versus that of others, it is normal to expect that many ratees will feel that their performance has been unfairly evaluated, even when performance ratings are in fact completely accurate. It may not be possible to develop an appraisal system that produces ratings that are viewed as fair by all, or even most ratees.

Third, as Meyer et al. (1965) noted, performance appraisal systems put raters in the uncomfortable role of both judge and counselor. That is, raters must both evaluate their subordinates and provide them with support, feedback, and direction for future improvement. Raters are often uncomfortable in these roles, especially in giving feedback (Landy & Farr, 1983; Latham, 1986); being forced to carry out both roles at the same time can be especially stressful.

Fourth, performance appraisals often appear to violate the requirements of procedural justice. Evaluations of performance are necessarily subjective (Milkovich & Wigdor, 1991), and subjective evaluation systems can present the appearance of bias and unfairness, even when they are in fact fair and thorough. As we noted above, many employees are likely to believe that they performed better than their appraisals indicate. Furthermore, they are likely to attribute these "unfairly" low appraisals to systematic errors and biases on the part of the rater, especially in cases where there is no clear and concrete definition of good or poor performance (Mitchell et al., 1981). As a result, performance appraisal systems can become lightning rods for generalized concerns over fairness and equity.

Finally, the generally poor reputation of performance appraisal can itself be a source of dissatisfaction. Imagine being a busy entry-level manager who must devote time and effort to a human resource system that is widely regarded as a joke and an imposition. Even if you initially think the appraisal system looks reasonable, the very fact that it is the constant target of ridicule may make you lose interest and faith in the system. Managers may be socialized to the idea that performance appraisal is a waste of time they should complain about, and this socialization will eventually make them dissatisfied and disillusioned with the appraisal system.

IS "BAD" APPRAISAL GOOD MANAGEMENT?

As we noted at the beginning of this chapter, the fact that managers turn in inaccurate appraisals is often regarded as a problem. The goal of many performance appraisal interventions is to increase raters' ability (Landy & Farr, 1980) or willingness (Banks & Murphy, 1985) to provide complete and accurate appraisals. It is not at all clear, however, that replacing distorted, inaccurate, or incomplete appraisals with accurate ones would be beneficial. First, rating distortion is often a highly adaptive strategy, and forcing raters to be accurate may expose them to a number of negative consequences (Cleveland & Murphy, 1992; see also Chapter 9 of this book). Second, there are many instances in which distortion of ratings is a consciously chosen management strategy (Ilgen, 1993; Longenecker, 1994). "Bad" appraisal might be nothing more than good management.

At the most general level, a manager's job is to get the most possible out of the resources and personnel assigned to him or her. Managers are asked to motivate, direct, and develop their subordinates, and to provide them with what is needed—resources, assistance—to perform their jobs. As we have noted in several earlier chapters, raters must consider a number of issues in completing performance appraisals, and the accuracy of the appraisal may be a minor issue compared with the appraisal's effect on present and future performance. Simply put, managers often have more important things to do than to rate accurately.

A manager who "plays by the rules" at all times is probably not a good manager. Officially, performance appraisal is usually treated as a measurement system designed to assess each subordinate's performance (this is also the perspective that dominated research on performance appraisal until the 1990s), but it seems clear that performance appraisal is something much more complex. Appraisal serves as a communications tool (e.g., a way of communicating performance standards and expectations), a motivational tool (e.g., as a way to gain access to rewards), a diagnostic tool (e.g., for targeting OD efforts), and so on. There is evidence (e.g., Longenecker, 1994) that effective managers understand that PA is a tool for managing rather than a tool for measuring their subordinates, and that they know how to use this tool to motivate, direct, and develop their subordinates and to maximize access to important resources in the organization.

If this line of reasoning is correct, measures of rating accuracy might be useful for evaluating performance appraisals, but their interpretation might be very different from the current interpretation of such measures. A manager who consistently turns in accurate performance appraisals might be an ineffective manager, especially if his or her peers successfully manipulate the system to motivate subordinates or gain access to required resources. This does not mean that inaccuracy in rating is a good thing, but targeted inaccuracy might be a very good thing. Raters who never distort or manipulate performance ratings may be passing up on the use of an important managerial tool.

PAY-FOR-PERFORMANCE SYSTEMS

In this section, we will examine in detail the operation of pay-for-performance systems. These systems help to move performance appraisal from the periphery of personnel decision making to the center by forming immediate links between performance ratings and valued outcomes (i.e., pay). As such, pay-for-performance systems illustrate both the potential contributions and the potential drawbacks of performance appraisal, and they also illustrate a number of boundary conditions that determine whether the benefits of performance appraisal are likely to outweigh the costs. By considering how performance appraisal fits within a broader personnel system (here, the compensation system) we can move from discussing performance appraisal in the abstract to considering how performance appraisal might affect important decisions made by the organization.

The How and Why of Pay for Performance

The best way to understand pay-for-performance systems and the role of performance appraisal in the success or failure of such systems may be to consider the three reasons most often cited for implementing pay-for-performance systems: (a) they can provide an incentive to motivate future performance, (b) they help communicate performance standards and expectations, and (c) pay for performance is the "right thing to do."

Incentive Effects. There are many ways that pay might be linked to performance, and choice of a specific method of establishing such a link could substantially affect the incentive value of paying for performance. The most direct pay-performance links are found in piecework systems, where an employee is paid a specific amount for each unit produced (Milkovich & Wigdor, 1991). This system is especially attractive to highly productive employees (Gerhart & Milkovich, 1992), but can be a source of tension (because it sets up implicit competition among employees) and can lead to a focus on short-term productivity, to the exclusion of behaviors such as maintenance and teamwork.

Merit pay systems establish a less direct link between individual performance and pay. In systems employing merit pay, some proportion of pay is put at risk (i.e., some part of the pay pool is distributed on the basis of performance), and the remainder is retained as base pay; merit increases may or may not be added into the following year's base pay. Because large portions of total pay are not contingent on performance (i.e., base pay), these systems necessarily establish weaker links between pay and performance than might be found in piece rate systems. Indeed, several studies show that pay-performance links in merit pay systems are generally weak (for reviews see Heneman, 1990; Milkovich & Wigdor, 1991). Gerhart and Milkovich (1992) note that some important pay-performance links may, however, be indirect. In particular, when performance appraisals are used to make both pay and promotion decisions, the eventual impact of performance appraisals on pay could be substantial (because promotions usually imply salary increases) even if the amount of merit pay itself is relatively small.

Finally, gainsharing systems link pay to overall profitability or to some sort of group outcome. Though there is evidence that gainsharing increases subsequent output (Milkovich & Wigdor, 1991), this particular form of pay for performance establishes the weakest links between an individual's on the job behavior and the rewards he or she receives. Extremely good performance does not guarantee an increase in pay, and extremely poor performance does not prevent one. In theory, the incentive effects of paying for performance should be strongest under piecework systems and weakest under gainsharing systems.

Empirical research on the motivational consequences of linking pay to performance suggests that procedural factors do make a difference. If the performance appraisal system is seen as fair and reasonable, this increases the likelihood that the pay increases that are linked to appraisal will also be seen as fair. It is clear, however, that the outcomes of pay for performance are more important than the process (Miceli, Jung, Near, & Greenberg, 1991). That is, the key question in pay-for-performance systems seems to be whether "deserving" employees receive rewards. A process that seems fair and reasonable on the surface but that fails to reward good performers will not provide an effective incentive.

Milkovich and Wigdor's (1991) review suggests that the single most important factor governing the success of a pay-for-performance system is the total amount of money available for performance-linked increases. On the whole, systems that reward everyone handsomely seem to be viewed more favorably than those that attempt to target increases to the highest performers. Despite the widespread support for the principle of pay for performance, in the end, good pay is probably more important than fairly administered pay. The best incentive may be the guarantee that rewards are available, not that the few available rewards will be distributed fairly.

Communicating Performance Expectations. One role of PA is to define and communicate performance standards. Attaching dollars to appraisal outcomes might enhance the effectiveness of such communication, but the typical pay-for-performance system is structured in such a way that the wrong message might be communicated.

Gerhart and Milkovich (1992) note that the difference in total salary received by good and poor performers is often quite small. In part this is because merit pay pools (or other mechanisms for linking pay to performance) often contain only a small fraction of the total compensation budget. Even where there is a good deal of money available in a pay-for-performance system, managers are often unwilling to discriminate good from poor performers (assigning high ratings to everyone), which makes it difficult to reward good performance or to fail to reward poor performance. When almost everyone receives a similar performance-based pay increase, the message being communicated to ratees may be that the organization does not really care about performance. If the merit pay received by the brightest star in the department is essentially the same as that received by the most marginal performers, it is difficult to avoid the conclusion that the organization values other things (e.g., avoiding complaints and lawsuits) more than it values job performance.

Gerhart and Milkovich (1992) suggest that the organization's ability to convey performance expectations with a pay-for-performance system depends on two basic factors: (a) the organization's willingness to put pay at risk, and (b) the raters' willingness to discriminate good from poor performance. When raters are willing and able to discriminate good from poor performance and there are clear consequences to those who perform well or poorly, it is likely that ratees will pay considerable attention to the performance appraisals and feedback they receive and will attempt to incorporate feedback into their future work behavior. If the performance-based part of salary is small, or if raters fail to discriminate good from bad performance, attempts to link pay to performance may convey precisely the wrong message—that is, that the organization does not value job performance.[1]

Doing the Right Thing. The belief that people should be rewarded for their individual efforts is basic to many Western cultures (managers and employees in some Eastern cultures sometimes emphasize the contributions and welfare of the group more highly than those of the individual: Farh et al., 1991; Ralston, Gustafson, Chueng, & Terpstra, 1992. See, however, Yu & Murphy, 1993). As a result, pay for performance may seem like a compelling idea, independent of its incentive effects or its value as a communication tool.

The position that pay for performance is something that should be valued in and of itself is likely to lead to an emphasis on procedural rather than distributive criteria for evaluating the system. If performance can be accurately measured and rewards tied to actual performance levels, the criterion of "doing the right thing" will be satisfied. Unfortunately, there may be many obstacles to establishing a fair and consistent system for linking pay to performance. First, the amount of money made available for performance-related pay directly limits one's ability to reward the deserving. Second, the common policy of putting only a small portion of each employee's pay at risk limits one's ability to withhold rewards from those who do not deserve them. Finally, it may be very difficult to convince raters to go along. As we have noted in this chapter, raters often have much more important things to do in performance appraisal than provide accurate measures of ratee performance, and the difficulty of obtaining fair, accurate, and complete measures of performance may make it impossible to "do the right thing."

How Does Pay for Performance Affect Performance Appraisal?

There is evidence that pay-for-performance systems can have beneficial effects for the organization (Milkovich & Wigdor, 1991). The effects of linking pay to performance on performance appraisal itself are less well understood, although the research reviewed in Chapters 8 and 9 provides a basis for making concrete predictions. In general, linking pay to performance heightens the consequences of giving and receiving high or low performance ratings, which in turn is likely to have several effects on performance appraisal.

Consider first the implications for the rater. As we noted in Chapters 8 and 9, there is often significant pressure on raters to give high ratings and positive feedback. The costs of giving low ratings can be high and the benefits both small and uncertain. As PA is more and more closely linked to important rewards, we expect that the pressure to give high ratings will become even more severe. First, as the consequences of performance appraisal become more concrete and substantial, reactions to low ratings are likely to become more extreme. Second, the benefits of giving high ratings increase (e.g., high ratings will now lead directly to higher pay). At the same time, however, the costs of giving high ratings or the benefits of giving low ones might not be substantially affected by tying pay to performance. As a result there will be increased pressure to give high ratings and avoid low ones. Systematic rating inflation will, of course, defeat the purpose of pay-for-performance systems. If everyone is rated high, it may be very difficult to identify and reward the truly good performers.

From the ratee's perspective, linking pay to performance ratings is likely to have a mix of positive and negative consequences. On the positive side, policies that increase the importance and (literally) value of performance appraisals will probably also enhance the importance and value of performance feedback. In a pay-for-performance system, performance feedback represents advice for increasing future pay (by increasing performance, or at least more favorable evaluations of performance), which should enhance the impact and credibility of the performance feedback.

On the negative side, anything that increases the importance and consequences of performance appraisal will also probably increase ratees' concerns over the fairness, accuracy, and completeness of their appraisals. Recall that one recurring problem in appraisal is that many ratees will be disappointed (i.e., their self-appraisals will be more positive than appraisals they receive from others). When the consequences of appraisal are minimal, this disappointment may also be minimal. As appraisal becomes more important, concerns about the fairness and accuracy of performance appraisals may also become more important.

Pay for Performance and the Benefits of Appraisal. In the first section of this chapter, we cited four ways performance appraisal can benefit an organization: (a) it can enhance the quality of organizational decisions, (b) it can enhance the quality of individual decisions, (c) it can enhance the relationship between the individual and the organization, and (d) it can provide a foundation for organizational development and change efforts. Embedding performance appraisal in a pay-for-performance system can affect the likelihood that each of these benefits will be realized by the organization.

Pay-for-performance systems are likely to have mixed effects on the quality of organizational decisions. On the one hand, there is evidence that linking performance appraisals to valued rewards does indeed inflate ratings and diminish between-ratee distinctions (this evidence is reviewed in Chapter 9). This will make it difficult to use appraisals for a wide range of purposes (e.g., promotions, layoffs), and it may even affect the usefulness of performance ratings as criteria in validity studies (because it will lead to range restriction). On the other hand, the most important single administrative use of performance appraisals is probably in salary administration, and a good pay-for-performance system establishes a systematic policy for translating ratings into salary adjustments.

Using performance appraisals to make decisions about pay may indirectly limit their usefulness for making individual decisions. When a salient and concrete outcome such as pay or promotion depends on performance appraisals, raters are likely to focus on that outcome and on information relevant to that outcome and pay less attention to other aspects of performance, such as individual strengths and weaknesses (Bjerke et al., 1987). In the worst case (which may also be the most common one), raters may make pay decisions first (i.e., they first decide who deserves a raise, or whose performance will be most affected by a raise) and then rate accordingly. The ratings employees receive may say relatively little about their actual performance and may provide little help in making decisions about one's own career, development, or future performance.

Paying for performance has the potential to enhance employees' commitment to and favorable impression of the organization. An organization that attempts consistently to link rewards to performance is likely to be seen by its employees as, for example, caring, fair, or rational. On the other hand, a poorly run pay-for-performance scheme might do more harm than good. Organizations that show little obvious regard for the real contributions of their employees when designing compensation packages are unlikely to inspire loyalty, commitment, or trust. For example, we know of many organizations that claim to consider performance when setting merit pay, but in fact assign the best and worst performers virtually the same merit increase every year. On the whole, these organizations would be better off without the pretense.

Finally, pay-for-performance systems might present both opportunities and challenges when using performance appraisal to help guide organizational development efforts. On the one hand, these systems may bring into the open conflicts that hamper the effective functioning of the organization. Linking pay to performance increases the likelihood that existing concerns about both pay and performance appraisal will come to the surface. On the other hand, linking pay to performance appraisals may diminish the diagnostic value of the ratings themselves. As we noted earlier, when pay is linked to the performance ratings workers receive, they are likely to learn a great deal about who (in the raters' eyes) should receive pay raises and perhaps less about who is or is not performing well.

Pay for Performance and the Costs of Appraisal. Earlier, we cited three ways performance appraisal could harm an organization: (a) it can overemphasize the individual and underemphasize the contributions of teams and systems; (b) it can send mixed messages to raters, ratees, and users of appraisal; and (c) it can itself be a source of dissatisfaction and dissent. Once again, embedding performance appraisal in a pay-for-performance system can affect the likelihood that each of these costs will be experienced by the organization.

Deming (1986) and others suggest that individual performance appraisal causes us to misattribute performance successes and failures to individuals. Linking pay to performance (especially in individually oriented piecework or merit pay systems) probably increases the extent to which we pay attention to the individual and ignore the team or the system (Deming, 1986). This may, in turn, interfere with teamwork and present a distorted picture of the reasons for good and poor performance (as well as the types of interventions most likely to improve performance). Although it is important to consider the contributions of individuals (Gerhart & Milkovich, 1992), there are clear costs associated with focusing on the individual and ignoring the system. Individually oriented pay-for-performance systems may need to be supplemented with systems that are sensitive to the external factors that limit or enhance job performance.

A pay-for-performance system can either solve the problem of mixed messages in performance appraisal or make it considerably worse. The mixed message problem is solved when raters adopt the common goal of providing good measures of performance, and the organization meaningfully links pay with the resulting performance measures. The mixed message problem is exacerbated when the appraisal system does not, in fact, measure performance and/or when the organization is unwilling to strongly link pay and performance. In either case, there will be a significant gap between the rhetoric ("this organization pays for performance") and the reality.

Finally, a pay-for-performance system can act as a magnifying glass, enhancing all of the advantages of appraisal and making all of the problems more serious. Even when the consequences are relatively small, perform- ance appraisal systems can evoke a range of negative reactions ranging from distrust to disgust. As the consequences of appraisal become more important and concrete, the reactions to appraisal are likely to become more extreme. An appraisal system that once was regarded as a mere nuisance can become an ongoing disaster if the stakes are raised. On the other hand, a generally good performance appraisal might look even better if valued rewards are consistently attached to high performance ratings. Thus, our final comment on the effect of embedding performance appraisal in a pay-for-performance system is that linking pay to performance is likely to enhance both the pain and the gain. Pay for performance is neither the salvation nor the destruction of performance appraisal, but it does raise the stakes, and it certainly makes the raters' and ratees' lives more interesting.

SUMMARY

This chapter considered the question of whether organizations might be better off with or without performance appraisal systems. This question probably cannot be answered in the abstract: Performance appraisal carries a number of potential costs and benefits, and the extent to which the benefits are achieved or the costs are experienced probably depends on a number of features of both the appraisal system and its organizational context.

There are four main benefits to performance appraisal. It can contribute to the quality of organizational decisions, ranging from salary administra- tion to selection system validation. It can contribute to the quality of individual decisions, ranging from decisions about how time and effort should be directed on the job to how careers should be structured. When performance appraisal is done well, it probably enhances attachments between the individual and the organization, which in turn is likely to affect satisfaction, motivation, withdrawal, and so on. Finally, PA provides information that can be used to direct and focus organizational development efforts.

There are also several costs to performance appraisal. First, individually oriented appraisal systems may overemphasize the individual and under-emphasize the production system or the team. If the major sources of variability in performance have little to do with the individual, performance appraisal systems may be seriously misleading about the causes of and possible solutions for poor performance. Performance appraisal systems also send mixed messages about what aspects of performance are most or least important, about the extent to which the organization values good performance, and even about the value of performance appraisal itself. Finally, performance appraisal is a headache for everyone involved and can be a major source of dissatisfaction and dissent in an organization.

One reason it is difficult to evaluate performance appraisal sensibly is that some of the benefits turn out to be less helpful than one would think, and some of the shortcomings turn out to be less of a problem than they first appear. This is most obvious when considering the possibility that such things as distortion or inaccuracy in performance appraisal is nothing more than good management. Managers who shamelessly manipulate the per-formance appraisal system to achieve their primary goals (i.e., get the most possible out of the human and physical resources at their disposal) do more for their organizations than managers who follow all of the rules and who turn in accurate performance appraisals, regardless of the consequences.

Embedding performance appraisal in a pay-for-performance system affects both the potential benefits and the potential costs of performance appraisal. At the most general level, paying for performance raises the stakes in performance appraisal, and probably enhances both the benefits and the costs of performance appraisal. Even in a specific context (such as pay for performance), the task of balancing the costs and benefits of performance is likely to be a complex one.

NOTE

1. It can be argued that an organization that is not willing to link pay to performance does not, in fact, value performance highly. The alternative explanation for the frequent failure to link pay to performance ratings is the belief (perhaps well founded) that the performance appraisal system is not adequate for the task.

13

Performance Appraisal
and the Changing Context
of Work and Organizations

M any of the personnel and human resource systems used today, including performance appraisal (PA), were developed during a time when the typical organizations were large and hierarchically organized, when markets and organizational environments were relatively stable, when the workforce was homogeneous and relatively well qualified, and when long-term employment was the norm. The context and organization of work are changing in such a way that none of these conditions is likely to exist in the future. Organizations are becoming more decentralized and flatter (i.e., they have fewer levels). The social, political, and technical environments in which organizations exist are increasingly turbulent, and markets are becoming more volatile. The workforce is no longer homogeneous and is not necessarily well prepared for the complex jobs of today's organizations. Workers are increasingly likely to change jobs, organizations, and even occupations. All of these changes have implications for the way performance appraisal should be done and used in evolving organizations.

This chapter examines how changes in four aspects of work and organizations—changes in organizational structure and function, the use of teams as a basis for work organization, changes in the workforce, and changes in the schedule and place of work—are likely to affect performance appraisal. The final section of this chapter proposes directions in which performance appraisal systems should evolve to remain compatible with the rapidly changing context of work in the global economy of the next century.

CHANGES IN THE STRUCTURE
AND FUNCTION OF ORGANIZATIONS

Change is the buzzword in virtually every business magazine and management journal. After several decades of unchallenged superiority in the global market (starting with the end of World War II), North American manufacturers are finding it increasingly difficult to keep up with foreign competition. The structure and function of American organizations are changing in ways that few organizational theorists of the 1950s to 1970s could have foreseen. As wrenching as these changes in the workplace may seem, however, it is important to keep in mind that they are part of a very normal process of evolution in work organizations that has been going on since ancient times. Burrell (1992) and Wardell (1992) note that the history of work organizations is a history of change, and that the nature of organizations has gone through a number of change cycles over the centuries.

Changes in the Structure of Organizations

In the postwar era the typical organization has been characterized by a high degree of specialization within departments or organizational units, many levels of authority or management, a concentration of authority and decision-making power (often at corporate headquarters), a large number of managers relative to the total workforce, and the ability to turn out high volumes of the same set of products. In the past 10-15 years there has been a clear shift in the way organizations are structured, with more emphasis on decentralization, a preference for smaller workplaces and fewer levels of management and supervision, dispersal of plants and units, and a greater use of subcontracting arrangements (Whitaker, 1992). Even in traditional manufacturing organizations, there is a greater emphasis on decentralization, more use of temporary employees and contractors, and a redefinition of human resource functions (Kirkpatrick, Davies, & Oliver, 1992; Whipp, 1992). As a result of mergers, buyouts, and the collapse of competition, many organizations have become larger and more complex. Even within these diversified giants, however, there is substantial emphasis on decentralization and flexibility.

Nirenberg (1993) suggests that in the future, organizations will gravitate toward structures that incorporate greater degrees of accountability, democracy, and community. In particular, he suggests that organizations are most likely to succeed and endure if they assume a structure he terms a "solacracy," in which there are multiple centers of power, responsibility, and accountability, based on task relevance. One aspect of this structure is the idea that "everyone is a manager." In this structure, work roles are negotiated, and they change as, for example, the product or the conditions of work change.

It is difficult to evaluate Nirenberg's (1993) predictions about the future structure of organizations. One way to structure such an evaluation is to think about why organizations adopt different structures. Organizational forms and structures reflect broad, macro-level influences (e.g., financial and social systems, markets; Whitley, 1992), but they also reflect a variety of internal influences, including bottom-up pressure from the workforce on organizational decision making (Wardell, 1992). Nirenberg's predictions appear to be based on this bottom-up pressure for a more meaningful experience in the workplace. The traditional top-down structures that developed with the early industrial age were generally consistent with a broader societal consensus about the role of class and authority in determining behavior. As our society has moved toward a more open, egalitarian form (a movement that in this country can be traced as far back as the Civil War), it is likely that organizational structures that concentrate authority and that treat workers as cogs in an industrial machine will become increasingly rare.

Changes in organizational structure are likely to affect the performance appraisal process in a number of ways. First, with a stronger orientation

toward responsibility and flexibility, jobs are likely to become more complex and more open to negotiation and change (Ilgen & Hollenbeck, 1991).
In a traditional manufacturing organization, it was common to develop
reasonably precise job descriptions and to treat the job as a static entity that
changed little over time or across manufacturing sites. Jobs are becoming
more fluid, in the sense that two individuals with the same job title are
increasingly unlikely to do exactly the same things, but rather are likely to
adapt their work to the requirements of the moment. One implication is that
supervisors and subordinates are more likely to disagree about the fundamental nature of the job and will not have the same set of resources (e.g.,
detailed job descriptions) to resolve their disagreements. The second notable change will be a decrease in the number of managers and supervisors,
relative to the nonsupervisory workforce. In the future, supervisors and
managers will be forced to do a more complex job in evaluating their
subordinates, and they will be forced to do it for a larger number of
subordinates (also, as we noted in Chapter 5, they may also be asked to
provide performance feedback to their superiors). We will elaborate on the
potential effects of changes in organizational structure on performance
appraisal later in this chapter.

Changing Function of Organizations

Organizations are not only changing *how* they do business, they are also
changing *what* they do. The North American (and to a lesser extent European) economy is in the midst of a massive shift from heavy manufacturing
to high technology and service industries as the dominant type of work
organization. Changes in what American organizations do are likely to have
substantial effects on the types of human resource systems that are most
likely to develop and survive (Lloyd & Rawlinson, 1992).

High technology firms now represent 13.1% of the total civilian workforce (Belous, 1987). These firms encounter more turbulent environments
(both internal and external) than traditional manufacturing, in part because
of the rapid pace of technological development. Unlike a traditional manufacturing organization, a high technology firm typically cannot produce the
same product or follow the same development strategy for long periods of
time and expect to survive. One implication of this turbulence is that the
political environment of a high technology firm is likely to be quite
different from that of a more traditional manufacturing firm (Martocchio

& Ferris, 1991). Organizational politics are likely to be more complex and more fluid; because the orientation of the organization and its product line change more rapidly than in a traditional heavy manufacturing organization, it is likely to take more political skill to thrive in a high technology firm than in firms that occupy a more predictable and stable environment.

In high technology firms, jobs, roles, and relationships among functional units are likely to change at a fairly rapid pace. One implication is that performance appraisal in such a firm may be more subjective and more difficult to do well than in a firm where the job and its contribution to the organization's mission are relatively fixed. As noted in the previous section, the existence of fluid job requirements, role relationships, and so on, is likely to be a source of tension in PA, because it may be more difficult for supervisors and subordinates to come to any agreement about the basic nature of the job, much less how well the subordinate performs it.

The second major change in what organizations do is the move toward a service economy. The fastest growing sectors of the American economy include fields such as health care, financial services, tourism, and information technology; some of our most successful exports come from the entertainment industry. In service industries, the "product" is the satisfaction of the customer's needs, and the evaluation of job performance is potentially complex because "performance" depends as much on how the customer/client evaluates the service as on what the individual being evaluated actually did. It is useful to note that this particular issue is not unique to service industries; even heavy manufacturing organizations have become more customer-oriented in their philosophies. The problem of how performance is defined and evaluated, however (i.e., is performance something the individual does or is it the customer/client's reaction to it?), is likely to be more complex in service industries than in traditional manufacturing industries.

By their nature, service industries require much more direct contact between employees and customers/clients than is the case in manufacturing. That is, many service employees occupy "boundary spanning" roles in which they must deal with both the internal and the external environment of the organization. Research on the nature of service work and the personality characteristics that contribute most to success in this role (e.g., Hogan, Hogan, & Busch, 1984) suggests that these roles are stressful and demanding and that they require interpersonal skills different from those needed to work in manufacturing environments. As has been noted earlier with respect to changes in organizational structure and technology, the most obvious effect of this emphasis on interpersonal skills is to make performance appraisal more difficult and subjective. These skills are less concrete and more subject to interpretation than some of those involved in production, and there will probably be more room for disagreement in appraisals in service industries than in industries where jobs are more structured and where most workers have no contact with the external environment of the organization.

In a service industry, customers and clients are likely to have a much more direct role in performance appraisal than in manufacturing or other traditional industries. It is common for hotels, restaurants, airlines, and even health care facilities to solicit comments from their customers and clients, and this input is taken seriously. In manufacturing, customer input is likely to focus on the product and have less bearing on the evaluation of individual employees. In service industries, the distinction between product and process is not so profound, and it is often possible to obtain extensive feedback about each individual who has direct contact with the customer or client.

Another way to think about the changing function of organizations is to consider changes in business strategies. In traditional manufacturing organizations, the usual business strategy was to focus on efficiency, formalization, and maintenance of existing profits. In more turbulent business environments, strategies such as entrepreneurship (emphasizing new, high-risk, high-return ventures), dynamic growth (emphasizing a balance between current ventures and the development of new, moderate-risk ventures), or divestiture (emphasis on cutting losses, reducing expenditures) are increasingly common. The choice of a business strategy is a product of both the organization's particular mission and goals and the broad social context (e.g., the national economy, the political system) in which a firm operates (Lodge & Vogel, 1987). Strategies, in turn, help to determine the human resource policies of the firm (Whipp, 1992).

Schuler (1987) notes that different business strategies will lead to different methods for planning, staffing, training, compensation, and performance appraisal. Focusing on performance appraisal, he suggests that the degree to which appraisal focuses on behavior versus results, the long versus the short term, participation versus top-down evaluation, and future-oriented versus past-oriented applications (e.g., development vs. rewards) will all depend on the business strategy pursued by the firm. Furthermore, the match between the business strategy and a variety of human resource systems may be a key determinant of their success. For example, in an organization that adopts a highly entrepreneurial strategy, appraisal systems that are highly formalized, standardized, and that involve minimal participation on the part of employees will probably fail. This business strategy requires high levels of involvement and flexibility, and appraisal systems should be designed to reflect these job requirements (e.g., PA should directly involve the employee by using self-ratings and frequent feedback sessions).

How Do These Changes Affect Performance Appraisal?

There are three broad themes running through research on the implications of changes in the form and function of organizations for performance appraisal: (a) decentralization, (b) changing ratios of managerial to non-managerial employees, and (c) changing definitions of jobs and their role in the organization. The trend toward decentralization presents both opportunities and barriers for innovation in human resource management. In a decentralized organization, for instance, it is possible to tailor a variety of human resource policies and tools, including performance appraisal, to the demands and nature of the work. For example, rather than using the same PA form throughout the organization, appraisal forms reflecting important aspects of work in each functional unit might be developed. This advantage comes with a price, however. It might be necessary for the human resources department of each unit of a decentralized organization to reinvent the wheel continually, in the sense that each must develop its own appraisal and reward systems. Nevertheless, the ability to tailor appraisal systems to the actual needs of the organization rather than to the dictates of corporate headquarters represents an important advantage in developing successful personnel systems.

The greatest potential problem that may be associated with decentralization is a shift from a long-term developmental orientation toward employees to an orientation that treats employees as a troublesome commodity (particularly in organizations whose present business strategy focuses on divestiture and liquidation) or as a source of potential variance and error in the production process (Kirkpatrick et al., 1992). As organizations break down into a number of relatively small, semi-autonomous units, it may become increasingly difficult to maintain a focus on long-term development, particularly for a career in another unit of the parent corporation. The key to maintaining a focus on long-term development in such an organization may be to encourage movement within the organization and to orient the career systems toward lateral transfers (involving new skills or duties) rather than movements up the chain of command.

As organizations become flatter (i.e., fewer levels of authority, larger numbers at each level), several facets of the appraisal process are likely to change. Judge and Ferris (1993) suggest that as supervisors have fewer opportunities to observe (e.g., because more of the work is done autonomously) and as they have larger spans of control, ratings are likely to get lower. Their data provided support for the former suggestion, but not the latter. That is, supervisors who have fewer opportunities to observe their subordinates do tend to give lower ratings; the effects of span of control are less clear.

Increasing the span of control also affects peers' ability to observe and evaluate each others' performance. On the one hand, appraisal systems that include peer ratings allow raters to obtain more data about each individual as the number of peers increases. On the other hand, the overall quality of the data provided by peers might be lower when there are many than when there are few co-workers (e.g., large groups may provide fewer opportunities for direct observation of any particular member).

A more pressing problem may be the implications of flattening organizations for their career systems. Until recently, the term *career* tended to imply a series of promotions to successively more responsible positions, each at a higher level of authority than the last. An organization that has few levels cannot operate such a career system, and the implications for performance appraisal may be substantial.

Traditionally, one function of performance appraisal has been to identify promising candidates for promotion. Appraisal systems geared toward promotion tend to focus on differences between employees and have paid less attention to within-person differences in performance (i.e., individual strengths and weaknesses; see Chapter 2). In a relatively flat organization, career moves are likely to be horizontal rather than vertical (i.e., transfer to another functional area rather than promotion to another level), and between-person comparisons might not be as useful for such purposes. Appraisal systems in flat organizations might need to pay more attention to individual strengths and weaknesses and to the fit of each individual with other functional areas or work teams (Prieto, 1993) and less attention to overall rankings of workers from best to worst.

INDIVIDUALS VERSUS TEAMS AS WORK UNITS

There has been a substantial upsurge in interest in teams (Bettenhausen, 1991; Hackman, 1990; Osburn, Moran, Musslewhite, Zenger, & Perrin, 1990; Rosen, 1989; Tjosvold, 1992) and team performance (Fleishman & Zaccaro, 1992). In part, this attention to teams is part of a broader movement toward some form of Total Quality Management (see Chapter 12); in part, it represents nothing more than a bandwagon effect (i.e., if all of your competitors use teams as a basis for work, you will probably also consider teams); and in part, it is based on the belief that teams are simply better for a wide range of tasks than individually based methods of work.

Although teams are often beneficial, it is not always clear that teams perform better than individuals working alone. A critical review of research on decision-making groups (Davis, 1992) makes it clear that many of the intuitions that guide our thinking about the advantages and disadvantages of teams are simply inconsistent with the large body of relevant research. For example, the assumptions that teams make better decisions than individuals (but that they are also more prone to take risks), that brainstorming produces better solution sets than other methods, that there is an optimal size for decision-making groups, and that fairly small procedural factors (e.g., the use of straw votes) substantially affect group decisions seem to be at best weakly supported and often inconsistent with the literature. Nevertheless, there do seem to be areas in which teams seem to function better than individuals working alone (e.g., in complex assembly tasks), and the apparent success of team-based organizations makes it likely that teams will be an important component of work organization for some time to come.

Team Performance

Team performance is often something different from the average of each member's performance, in part because many team tasks are interdependent. In addition, many of the tasks carried out by a team involve or require coordination with other groups or teams. Especially in a team-based organization, effectiveness of relationships with other groups could substantially determine effectiveness of the team (Ancona & Caldwell, 1988).

Saavedra, Earley, and Van Dyne (1993) suggest that interdependence is itself complexly determined. First, the task may require the exchange of information and/or resources (Thompson, 1967). Second, goals may exist at the individual or the group level; group goals imply some level of mutual dependence. Third, performance feedback may be done at the individual or the group level. Saavedra et al. (1993) suggest that the overall level and type of interdependence in a group are a function of all three, and furthermore that group performance will be highest when all three are congruent. For example, Saavedra et al. (1993) suggest that when the task requires sharing information and the goal pursued is a group goal rather than a series of individual goals, the team is more likely to be effective if performance is assessed for the team as a whole than for each team member individually.

The term *team* can take on a wide array of meanings, depending largely on the degree to which the work of team members is independent versus interdependent. Crown (1992) notes that in some teams each person works on his or her own tasks, with minimal input from or influence on other team members. In highly interdependent teams each person's task performance serves as input for another's task, and poor performance of one team member may translate into poor performance for the team as a whole. The degree of interdependence may dictate the best strategy for measuring team performance. Crown (1992) suggests that methods of measuring team performance be placed on a summative-nonsummative continuum. In summative measurement, the group's performance is the sum of each individual member's performance. In nonsummative measurement, the group product is different from the sum of the individual products (B. Fisher, 1974). Summative measurement is appropriate when interdependence is low. Nonsummative measurement is likely to be required when teams are highly interdependent.

A wide variety of methods of defining and assessing team performance have been developed. Jones et al. (1993) demonstrated how utility theory (see Chapters 8 and 9) could be applied in measuring team performance (for detailed descriptions of these methods, see Pritchard, 1990; Pritchard et al., 1989). Other methods have incorporated more traditional evaluation tools, including self- and peer appraisals (Norman & Zawacki, 1991). Recent models of team performance have examined ways in which the

organizational contexts in which teamwork occurs can affect the performance of the team (Salas, Dickinson, Converse, & Tannenbaum, in press;
Tannenbaum, Beard, & Salas, 1992); tools for incorporating information
about the team's context into assessments of its performance are not yet
available, but this is clearly a promising direction for future development.

In defining and measuring team performance, a useful distinction is
often drawn between team activities that are process oriented and those that
are task or product oriented. Process-oriented aspects of team performance
are often referred to as "teamwork," and they include a wide range of
activities geared toward maintaining and improving the way a team functions. Examples include a willingness to pitch in, support, and encourage
others; to volunteer to work on problems; and to avoid adversarial "me-
against-you" situations (Wellins, Byham, & Wilson, 1991).

A number of researchers (Brannick, Roach, & Salas, 1991; Morgan,
Glickman, Woodward, Blaines, & Salas, 1986; Prince, Salas, & Franz, 1990)
have identified the critical teamwork behaviors related to team success or
failure. These behaviors are organized under seven behavioral dimensions:
backup behavior, communication, coordination, feedback, monitoring, team
leadership, and team orientation. *Backup behavior* involves assisting the
performance of other team members. This implies that members have an
understanding of other members' tasks. It also implies that members are
willing and able to provide and seek assistance. *Communication* involves
the exchange of information between two or more team members in the
prescribed manner and by using proper terminology. Often the purpose of
the communication is to clarify or acknowledge the receipt of information.
Coordination refers to team members' executing their activities in a timely
and integrated manner. It implies that the performance of some team
members influences the performance of other team members. This may
involve an exchange of information that subsequently influences another
member's performance. *Feedback* involves the giving, seeking, and receiving of information among members. Giving feedback refers to providing
information regarding other members' performance. Seeking feedback
refers to seeking input or guidance regarding performance. Receiving
feedback refers to accepting positive and negative information regarding
performance. *Monitoring* refers to observing the activities and performance
of other team members. It implies that team members are individually
competent and that they may subsequently provide feedback and backup
behavior. *Team leadership* involves providing direction, structure, and

support for other team members. It does not necessarily refer to a single individual with formal authority over others, but rather can be demonstrated by several team members. *Team orientation* refers to the attitudes that team members have toward one another and the team task. It reflects acceptance of team norms, level of group cohesiveness, and importance of team membership.

Teamwork is clearly necessary for the continuing function of a team, but it is not always included in performance measurement systems. After all, it is not any particular person's job to back up others, to go beyond the requirements of the job description, to coordinate others' activities, and so on, and if the performance measurement system is focused solely on task performance there may be disincentives to engaging in teamwork. One useful function of a performance appraisal system that explicitly includes evaluations of teamwork is that it drives home the importance of this critical category of behavior.

There is evidence that judges can provide valid ratings of teamwork (i.e., showing both convergent and discriminant validity), but that these ratings show little convergence across tasks or scenarios. That is, teams that are rated high on particular dimensions in one task or scenario may be rated low on another (Brannick, Prince, Salas, & Prince, 1993). Also, knowledge of performance outcomes affects observers' reports of team processes and behaviors (Martell & Guzzo, 1991; Martell & Willis, 1993).[1] If a rater knows that the team was highly successful, he or she is likely to rate team process variables favorably, even if the team succeeded through dumb luck rather than through careful teamwork. The implication is that it may be difficult to separate evaluations of how a team does things (teamwork) and how well a team does them (the outcomes of team performance).

Prieto (1993) notes that the use of teams does not necessarily mean that individually oriented appraisal should be abandoned. He suggests that rather than evaluating individual job performance, we should evaluate an individual's contribution to the work effectiveness of his or her unit. This suggestion is particularly important for team-based organizations. One individual who spends most of his or her time doing teamwork, as opposed to the team task, may still deserve high performance ratings.

How Do These Changes Affect Performance Appraisal?

The move toward team-based systems for organizing work may have profound implications for performance appraisal. In particular, the use of teams rather than individuals as a basis for organizing work changes: (a) who is appraised, (b) the way appraisals are used, and (c) the definition of performance.

Despite Prieto's (1993) suggestion that individual performance measurement can be compatible with team-based work system, many organizations that use teams are likely to evaluate the team's performance rather than evaluating the performance of each team member. As we noted in Chapter 12, some proponents of team-based production systems (e.g., Deming, 1986) have gone so far as to claim that individual PA undermines the team's ability to function as a unit.

Appraisals of the team rather than the individual team member are likely to raise questions of equity and fairness (for reviews of research on perceptions of fairness in appraisal, see Folger et al. [1992] and Greenberg [1986]). No matter how strong the team orientation, some team members are likely to believe that they performed better than others, and appraisal systems that ignore potential differences in team member performance may be viewed as unfair by substantial numbers of employees. As we noted in Chapter 5, many workers seem to overestimate their own level of performance, and it is possible that the great majority of team members will believe that their own performance is better than the overall performance of the team. Giving the same evaluation to all members of a team may lead to massive perceptions of inequity.

A second problem associated with team versus individual performance measurement is the role of such measures in the organization's career system. We noted earlier that the opportunities for promotion in relatively flat organizations may be relatively infrequent, but there still is a need to make decisions about who moves into what roles in the organization. Team-based evaluations may mean that performance appraisals will have less of role in the career system than has been typical for individually based appraisal systems. Organizations are unlikely to promote or transfer an entire team; if the team is the unit of analysis for job performance measurement, it is unlikely that appraisals will be useful for a wide array of career-oriented applications. Organizations that use teams as a basis for production may choose to supplement their performance appraisal system with other evaluation methods when making career decisions. For example, team members may be asked to nominate candidates for promotion or transfer.

In Chapter 4 we noted that the uses of individually oriented performance appraisals could be grouped into four categories: (a) for assessing differences between individuals (e.g., ranking workers for salary adjustment), (b) for assessing differences within individuals (e.g., assessing individual strengths and weaknesses), (c) for systems maintenance (e.g., evaluating individual or group training needs), or (d) for documentation of performance levels (e.g., meeting legal requirements). Team-based appraisals are most likely to be useful for systems maintenance purposes but may provide little information for between- or within-individual comparisons or for documentation purposes. Although it violates the philosophy of team-based organizations, we believe that organizations that are built around teams will nevertheless find it necessary to regularly evaluate the performance of their individual employees. In fact, organizations may find it useful to maintain several parallel systems (e.g., individually oriented, team-oriented, team nomination systems) that are used for different purposes.

A team-based organization is likely to develop a different definition of "individual job performance" than an organization that makes little use of teams. In particular, teamwork is likely to constitute an important part of the core definition of job performance. Similar behaviors have received attention in research on individually based appraisal systems, often under the headings of organizational citizenship behavior or contextual performance (Borman & Motowidlo, 1993; Brief & Motowidlo, 1986; Organ, 1988; Smith et al., 1983, chap. 1). In an individually based system these behaviors are seen as going beyond the requirements of the job; they are often, by definition, behaviors that are not strictly required by the job or role description (although they are necessary for the survival of the workgroup and the organization). In team-based organizations, these same behaviors are likely to be part of the formal or informal description of what the job entails, and individuals who perform their tasks well but who do not engage in these behaviors are not likely to be seen as adequate performers. In a team-based organization the basic definition of job performance is likely to include a wide range of behaviors that are seen as exceptional and noteworthy in traditional organizations.

NONTRADITIONAL PLACES AND SCHEDULES FOR WORK

Traditionally, most employees in the same functional unit of an organization have worked in the same location and have followed similar schedules. Many organizations are moving toward systems in which employees are dispersed, both in terms of where they work and in terms of when they work.

Telecommuting

Toffler (1980) suggests that the structure of work in the developed world is undergoing a change comparable in scope and importance to the Industrial Revolution. He suggests that the future locus of work will be the "Electronic Cottage," where workers are linked to their organizations through, for example, telecommunications and/or computer systems. This electronic cottage seems to be taking two distinct forms, one in which the individual works from his or her home and is linked to the organization by phone, fax, and/or computer (i.e., telecommuting), and a second in which individuals work at dispersed sites that are close to their homes and once again are linked to the organization via some electronic medium.

Telecommuting is growing at a rapid pace (Gordon & Kelly, 1986; Mahfood, 1992; Ramsover, 1983). More than 3.6 million American workers work at home at least one day per week, and 20%-25% of the workforce participates in some formal or informal telecommuting (Telecommuting, 1992). Continuing developments in computer and telecommunication technology (e.g., increasing sophistication, portability, user-friendliness, and affordability of computers and telecommunication devices) are likely to make it easier for an increasing number of workers to telecommute.

Perhaps the ultimate extension of telecommuting is the mobile office. It is no longer difficult to equip a car with all of the equipment needed to work effectively on the run. With a portable computer, portable fax machine/printer, and a cellular phone it is possible to work quite effectively while driving down the highway. In fact, there are growing concerns that such mobile offices constitute a major traffic hazard. It is hard to pay attention to the computer, the fax, the phone, and to driving at the same time, and some mobile office users cope with this by paying little attention to their driving.

A variation on the theme of working from one's home or car is to work at dispersed sites. A growing number of organizations, especially those located in large metropolitan areas, offer the option of doing some or even most work at dispersed sites. Each of several sites is linked to the central organization via computer and telecommunication devices, and it is often just as easy to communicate with other employees working at a variety of sites as it would be if they all worked in the same location. For example, a major defense contractor has a system of dispersed sites where employees check in, are assigned to a cubicle, connect their computer to the organization's electronic communications system, and do their work from that site. Phone calls, faxes, and electronic mail are automatically routed to whatever site and cubicle the worker uses that day, and as far as most members of the organization are concerned, there is no practical difference between having that individual work at a dispersed site and working in his or her regular office. Employees may come to their regular offices 1 or 2 days a week, mainly to pick up mail and attend meetings, but the regular workplace may be one of the dispersed sites rather than the "office."

One point of using dispersed sites is to minimize the time spent and the energy consumed in commuting to the regular work site. In major metropolitan areas, commutes are often measured in hours rather than minutes, and the option of working at a site close to home (at least some days each week) is likely to be appealing to anyone who has spent much time commuting. These flexible work arrangements also make it easier to balance the demands of work and family and might be especially appealing to dual-career families.

Although telecommuting and the use of dispersed sites seem to be linked to higher productivity, and certainly to lower energy use, there are also some downsides. In particular, there is less direct communication or social contact between supervisors and subordinates or between peers (Ramsover, 1983). The manager's role becomes more complicated, and more of a premium is placed on skills such as planning, delegating, and providing feedback (Gordon & Kelly, 1986). Appraisals of telecommuters or off-site workers are likely to become more results-driven (Gordon & Kelly, 1986; Ramsover, 1983), in part because the supervisor has limited opportunities to observe anything other than the results achieved by a particular worker. When employees work at dispersed sites, the supervisor's role in appraisal may become more similar to that of clients and customers, in the sense that he or she sees the final product but not necessarily the work process that produced that product.

Flexible and Compressed Work Schedules

Even when workers all share the same worksite, they might not share the same hours. First, many organizations, especially those involved in production or health care, must operate multiple shifts. There is a very substantial body of research on shift work, much of which is concerned with the potential stresses involved in alternative shift structures (Harrington, 1978; Office of Technology Assessment, 1991; Waterhouse, Folkard, & Minors, 1992). Our particular concern here is with swing-shift workers, whose work schedules change on a regular basis (e.g., night shift for 2 weeks, followed by morning shift for 2 weeks, followed by afternoon shift for 2 weeks) and with workers whose schedules require them to work for long blocks of time, with long blocks of time off in between work schedules (e.g., some firefighters work a schedule with 3 days on the job followed by 4 days off). When shifts or working days change regularly, it is possible that a worker's schedule will not coincide fully with that of co-workers and/or supervisors, which may limit their opportunities to observe work performance.

Flexible work schedules have long been popular (Schuler, 1987) and appear increasingly common. The most basic flextime arrangement is one in which employees are required to put in a certain number of hours each day and are all required to be present during some core time (e.g., 10 a.m. to 2 p.m.), but are given the option each day of starting their work day early (e.g., an 8-hour workday might run from 6 a.m. to 2 p.m.) or ending it late (e.g., the workday might go from 10 a.m. to 6 p.m.). Flextime gives workers some degree of control over their schedules and can be especially helpful in dealing with the time pressures of a dual-career household.

As with swing shifts, one potential problem encountered in a flextime system is that an individual's supervisors and/or co-workers may see only part of each day's work (possibly only the work accomplished during core time). As we will note below, limits on the supervisor's opportunities to observe employee work behavior might affect both the quality and the emphasis of performance appraisals. One way to deal with the limits imposed by the use of work schedules that are not fully coordinated with that of a supervisor is to employ multiple sources in appraisal, but even here, the fact that a worker's schedule can be different from that of his or her peers may mean that each rater (both supervisors and peers) may have only a limited opportunity to observe behavior.

Finally, compressed work schedules allow workers to complete their 40 hours in 3 or 4 days per week rather than the traditional 5. Schuler (1987) described a scheduling system in which employees who worked two 12-hour shifts on the weekend could be considered full-time employees (with overtime, 24 weekend hours would be treated the same as 36 hours during the normal working week). Compressed work schedules present the same potential problem as the other scheduling systems described here: that is, limited opportunities for supervisors and co-workers to observe performance, particularly if their compressed schedule does not correspond with the ratee's.

How Do These Changes Affect Performance Appraisal?

A recurring theme of this section is that nontraditional places and/or schedules of work limit the supervisor's and co-workers' opportunities to observe worker performance. This is likely to have two effects, one obvious and one not so obvious.

The obvious problem encountered when a supervisor has limited opportunities to observe work performance is that the quality of the performance evaluations and the performance feedback may suffer. If supervisors do not know half of what workers do, they are unlikely to be a valuable source of information about the quality of performance or the steps that workers should take to increase work quality.

The less obvious effect of limiting the rater's ability to observe work performance is that it might shift the basis of evaluation from behavior to results. Although many management texts advocate results-oriented evaluations, we have argued that performance appraisals are most useful when they focus on what a person does rather than on the results of that behavior (see Chapter 1). When a supervisor has limited opportunities to observe worker behavior, it is no longer possible to base appraisals on behavior (the sample of behavior he or she sees might not be representative), and it is natural to start paying attention to results (or to second- and thirdhand reports) rather than to direct observations of work behaviors.

Finally, changes in the place or time of work change the context in a way that might directly affect work performance. That is, working at a distant site or on a different schedule than one's co-workers or supervisors might itself change one's job performance. Some jobs allow more independence than others, and some people function better working independently than others. If the job requires face-to-face contact, or if the employee works best in a group setting, the use of distant sites or uncoordinated work schedules might be a direct cause of poor job performance. One result is that comparisons of performance ratings obtained under traditional work arrangements (i.e., same site, same schedule) versus under nontraditional site or schedule arrangements might be difficult to interpret. If ratings are lower in one context than in the other, this might be a reflection of differences in how appraisals are done (e.g., opportunities to observe, focus on results vs. behavior), or it might be a reflection of real differences in performance across the two ways of arranging work sites and schedules.

THE CHANGING WORKFORCE

The workforce is changing both in terms of its demographic characteristics (e.g., age, gender, race) and in terms of its connection with the organization (e.g., permanent, full-time employment vs. temporary and/or part-time employment). Both of these changes are likely to affect the ways in which appraisals are carried out and used in organizations of the future.

Demographic Changes

The composition of the American workforce is changing in a number of ways. A large proportion of the new entrants into the workforce are women, minorities, and immigrants (Johnston & Packer, 1987). In sheer numbers, the most dramatic changes in the workforce, as compared to a generation ago, are in the number of women with children who are employed on a full-time or part-time basis (Blau & Ferber, 1985). Women now make up more than 40% of the American workforce (Johnston & Packer, 1987) and this proportion is likely to grow. There has been particularly rapid growth in the proportions of black, Asian, and Hispanic women in the workplace (Thomas, 1991). The explosive growth in the number of non-white women in the workplace is part of a broader demographic trend, the rapid growth of the black, Hispanic, and Asian workforce (Exter, 1992)

The American workforce is also aging, reflecting another general demographic trend. This change is especially striking given the recent growth in early retirement. Although a smaller proportion of workers age 65 and older are employed today than a generation ago, the average age of the workforce has nevertheless risen and shows every sign of continuing to rise.

Another broad demographic change is that the entry-level workforce is getting smaller. During the baby boom years of the 1960s and 1970s there was a glut of entry-level workers, but this is no longer the case. The situation is even more serious when you consider the number of *qualified* entry-level workers. Jobs have become increasingly complex, and even lower-level production jobs sometimes require the use of sophisticated technologies and analytic tools (e.g., statistical analyses are a common part of many quality improvement programs). The qualifications of the entry-level workforce have not, in general, kept up with the demands of increasingly complex jobs. Many organizations find it necessary to supply the most basic remedial training, often stressing literacy and basic mathematics. For example, Smither (1994) describes basic education training programs at Big Three auto manufacturers (i.e., General Motors, Ford, Chrysler). Tens of thousands of workers have learned to read and do simple calculations through such programs.

A final change in the demographic characteristics of the workforce is the increase in multinational ventures. Cultural differences in beliefs about how performance appraisals should be conducted and used can be substantial. For example, self-ratings are usually higher than ratings of performance obtained from others (see Chapter 5), but in some cultures, self-assessments can be less favorable than supervisory ratings (see Farh et al. [1991] and Yu & Murphy [1993] for contrasting views on modesty biases in self-ratings collected in China). In North America, organizations are assumed to have the right to use a wide range of assessment methods, but in many European countries, assessment methods that are not acceptable to employees are banned by law (Pearn [1993] and Prieto [1993] provide European perspectives on assessment and selection). The same performance appraisal system may work in very different ways in different nations or cultures.

Part-Time and Temporary Workers

Earlier, we noted that organizations are making increasing use of temporary and/or part-time workforces. Even when employees are classified as full-time workers they are less likely than in the past to stay in the same job or the same organization for long periods of time. Many employment counselors advise current entry-level workers to prepare for multiple changes of employer and even multiple changes in occupation. The permanent employee who occupies the same job or a series of related jobs in a single organization over the majority of his or her career is quickly becoming a thing of the past.

From the organization's perspective there are many financial advantages to using part-time or temporary employees. These workers typically receive lower pay, and more important, are likely to receive substantially fewer benefits (e.g., insurance, pension, vacation and sick time) than their full-time permanent counterparts. On the downside, these employees may be less loyal and committed to the organization and may be less willing to engage in teamwork, organizational citizenship, or other critical behaviors not strictly required by their current contracts. An organization that views its employees as interchangeable commodities cannot reasonably expect commitment or the willingness to engage in extra-role behaviors that are often critical to the success of a work unit.

Both the career systems and the reward systems used with part-time and temporary employees are likely to be different from the systems used for long-term, full-time employees. In particular, human resource systems for part-time and temporary workers are less likely to focus on development or career progress than will be the case for more permanent employees. If the duration of employment is relatively short, there may be little point to evaluating job performance. By the time appraisals are completed, the worker may have moved on or may be ready to move on. Even if there is some appreciable time left in an employee's contract, the knowledge that his or her relationship with the organization is strictly temporary may diminish the value of appraisals and performance feedback.

How Do These Changes Affect Performance Appraisal?

Changes in the demographic characteristics of the workforce are likely to have substantial effects on performance appraisals. At present, there is some evidence for age, gender, and race effects on performance ratings, but these effects have generally been small (Kraiger & Ford, 1985; Landy & Farr, 1980; Waldman & Avolio, 1986, 1991). As the workforce becomes more diverse, it is possible that these effects could either go away entirely or that they might become substantially larger.

Reviews such as that by Kraiger and Ford (1985) suggest that increasing diversity may lead to smaller race, and perhaps sex and age, effects in appraisal. Kraiger and Ford found that as the percentage of minorities in the workforce increased, the effects of race on ratings decreased. The most plausible explanation for this effect is simple salience. When there are only a few members of minority groups they tend to receive more attention and they tend to seem more different. As the workforce becomes more diverse, a person's race or gender may become less salient, and workers are more likely to be evaluated on the basis of their performance than on the basis of their status as "different." Similar findings have been reported in research on sex bias in performance ratings (Kanter, 1977).

A more worrisome possibility is that race, sex, and age effects in performance appraisal will become stronger as the workforce becomes more diverse. When only a small proportion of the workforce is different from the traditional white male mainstream they pose little threat to the status quo. As the proportion of workers who do not fit this traditional mold grows, workplace diversity is likely to be seen as a threat to the traditional order, and evaluations of individuals who do not fit the traditional stereotype for a particular job may be biased downward.

Research on the experiences of women and minorities attempting to enter top levels of management provides vivid evidence of the problems that can be encountered by workers who do not fit the prevailing stereotype. The top executive ranks of American businesses remain incredibly homogeneous, and relatively few women or minority group members have been able to crack the "glass ceiling." Smither (1994) notes that "top positions in the United States are almost routinely filled by White Protestant males who attended prestigious schools. Top managers dress alike, have similar cars and homes, belong to the same social organizations, and are almost universally clean shaven. Even the decor of executive offices is strictly regimented" (p. 358). In this highly homogeneous context, anyone who is different is likely to stick out, and it is likely that the smallest mistake made by a woman or minority group member in this setting will be substantially magnified in performance evaluations.

On the whole, the effects of increasing diversity on PA may depend very much on the current context. Where there is a strong stereotype of the "right" kind of worker for a job, individuals who deviate from that stereotype may be harshly evaluated (Cleveland & Landy, 1983; Heilman, 1983). On the other hand, performance appraisals in jobs that are now held by a reasonably diverse group of workers will probably not be greatly affected by the increasing diversity of the workforce.

The growth of the part-time and temporary workforce is likely to affect both the appraisal process and the ways performance appraisals are used. With the exception of some permanent part-time workers (whose status is similar to that of their full-time counterparts), most workers in this category are likely to have weaker ties to the organization than the traditional full-time permanent employee. They are less likely to be invested in the organization's career development system and are less likely to experience substantial links among their performance ratings and their pay or their status with the organization. Supervisors of temporary or part-time workers may also be less invested in the process, especially when the expected period of employment is relatively brief. As we have noted in several earlier chapters, raters tend to see motivation, development, and feedback as the most important purposes of appraisal. When the duration of employment is relatively short, there may be little opportunity to motivate employees and little point in attempting to develop new skills or to strengthen areas of performance that are currently weak. Even if development efforts succeed, the organization may have little time to utilize or profit from newly developed skills and competencies. A manager who supervises large numbers of temporary employees may be smart to spend as little time as possible on evaluating their performance.

Part-time employees may experience a different set of problems from those experienced by temporary employees. In general, part-time employees may be seen by their managers as less committed to the organization than their full-time counterparts, particularly when they themselves choose to work part-time. Part-time employees may also be assigned to different types of work than their full-time counterparts and will more often find themselves in support roles or working on lower-priority projects. All other things being equal, it is reasonable to believe that workers whose commitment to the organization is seen (perhaps unfairly) as questionable and who are assigned to less important tasks will tend to receive lower performance ratings.

Performance appraisals might serve a somewhat different function for part-time workers than for their full-time counterparts. In particular, part-time workers may have few opportunities for either career progression or for structured development programs. An organization that invests strongly in its full-time, long-term employees often offers a wide range of training and development opportunities, including everything from classroom instruction to off-site seminars. Part-time employees are less likely to have access to these expensive resources and may find it more difficult to develop new skills or competencies. Finally, part-time workers may have fewer opportunities for salary advancement than their full-time counterparts. On the whole, the performance appraisals received by part-time workers may have less influence on administrative decisions (e.g., pay, promotion, training) than would be the case if they were full-time, long-term employees.

PERFORMANCE APPRAISAL IN THE 21st CENTURY

The question we wish to explore in this section is where all of the changes described in this chapter are likely to take us and how performance appraisal systems are likely to change in reaction to these substantial changes in the context of work and organizations. In our view, there are three broad trends that are likely to drive the way PA systems of the future will operate. First, organizations are becoming less structured. Elaborate, detailed, multilevel organizational charts are giving way to relatively flat organizations with less rigid boundaries between functional areas and less micro-management from corporate headquarters. These changes in the structure of organizations are likely to have profound changes on career systems and even on peoples' understanding of what constitutes a career.

Second, we are moving from work systems in which each individual has a fixed set of responsibilities and tasks to systems in which groups or teams are given responsibility for entire processes and are given the autonomy to determine how tasks, responsibilities, and so on, will be divided among group members. This change in the basic unit of organization of work (i.e., movement from the individual job to the team as a basic unit) is likely to change our conception of what a job is and what job performance is. It is also likely further to erode the traditional distinction between management and labor. In traditional manufacturing firms, nonsupervisory workers had clearly delineated jobs, schedules, and pay rates, and it was only the managers whose jobs were fluid (there is still considerable disagreement about exactly what a manager does), whose schedules were driven by the demands of the project rather than by the clock, and whose pay was relatively independent of the amount of time spent in the office. We are moving toward organizational forms and methods of work organization where everyone is a manager, at least in the sense of having some level of flexibility and responsibility in his or her work.

Finally, the workplace and its inhabitants are changing. Fifty years ago, the workforce was highly homogeneous (i.e., white, male), and the great majority of employees worked at the same place and at the same time. This is no longer the case. Face-to-face interactions are becoming rarer in the world of work, and when they do take place, they are no longer necessarily between people whose backgrounds, status in the organization (e.g., temporary vs. full time, long term), and demographic characteristics are similar.

In thinking about how performance appraisal systems are likely to adapt to these changes, it is useful to deal separately with how appraisals are conducted versus how they are used.

How Will Appraisals Be Conducted?

The most common method of PA today involves obtaining judgments about performance from one's immediate supervisor. In a well-designed system the performance dimensions are based on a careful analysis of the job, and the rater is trained in both performance rating and in giving useful performance feedback. This system is unlikely to survive the ongoing changes in the context of work and organizations. In the future we expect that performance appraisals will routinely incorporate information from multiple sources, and that peer input will be the most important source of performance appraisal information. Rather than basing appraisals on a fixed set of dimensions obtained from a job analysis, appraisals in the future are likely to have as their basis evaluations of a core set of performance dimensions common to the functional unit, together with an individual's contribution to and fit with his or her work team. This implies an increasing emphasis on interpersonal factors and citizenship behaviors and a higher level of subjectivity in the whole process. On the whole, however, the use of multiple sources of appraisal information may outweigh the increasing subjectivity of the appraisal dimensions, and it is not clear that assessments of fit obtained from multiple sources will turn out to be any more subjective than job-analysis-based performance appraisals obtained from one's immediate supervisors (Milkovich & Wigdor [1991] note that attempts to remove subjectivity completely from the performance appraisal process have never succeeded).

A second probable change in how appraisals are conducted involves timing. Annual performance appraisals have attained a near-ritual status in American organizations, but this may change in the foreseeable future. In the future, appraisal cycles may become more tightly linked with task cycles than with annual pay cycles. That is, if a work team has a project that takes 9 months to complete, it may make more sense to do performance appraisals at the 9-month mark than to wait for the annual appraisal day. The annual cycle for performance appraisal seems to be an artifact of the linkage between appraisals and pay (Milkovich & Wigdor, 1991); many organizations complete their performance appraisals shortly before starting the process used to make salary adjustments. Although we expect to see a continuing link between performance appraisals and reward systems, it is entirely possible that the flexible, decentralized organizations of the future will break away from the current lock-step system in which virtually everyone's pay raise is determined at the same time each year.

Obtaining appraisals from multiple sources may have a substantial impact on the feedback process. Supervisors have often been reluctant to give feedback (positive or negative), in part because it put them on the line. In the future, the supervisor (if any such position exists) might become the conduit for feedback rather than both the source and the messenger. This might make it easier to give candid feedback and especially to discuss performance shortcomings with the ratee. If the feedback is aggregated from multiple sources, this helps to diffuse responsibility for bad news, while at the same time increasing the credibility of the message.

How Will Appraisals Be Used?

In Chapter 4 we noted that the two most important uses of performance appraisals (at least from the organization's perspective) were to distinguish between individuals (in terms of their overall level of performance) and to distinguish within individuals (to distinguish individual strengths and weaknesses). An organization interested in using appraisal to make decisions about salary, promotion, layoffs, and so forth, is likely to concentrate on differences between individuals, whereas an organization interested in using appraisal to guide training and development activities is likely to concentrate on differences within individuals. Cleveland et al.'s (1989) survey suggested that the most important uses of appraisal were for distinguishing between individuals, but this might be changing. In particular, as organizations become flatter (i.e., fewer levels of management or authority), their career systems are likely to emphasize lateral career moves (i.e., transfer to another team, department, field) rather than traditional horizontal ones (i.e., promotions). As the emphasis in career systems moves from identifying the best people to identifying the best fit for each person, the relative value of between- and within-individual comparisons is likely to change.

Although we expect that institutional uses of appraisal (e.g., for salary, promotion, transfer, etc.) will stay with us for some time to come, it is reasonable to predict that the emphasis will shift from institutional to individual uses of appraisal in the future. That is, the ultimate value of appraisal in organizations of the future may not be in helping the organization make decisions about an individual, but rather in helping the individual make decisions about his or her own current performance and future development.

This shift to an individual orientation is likely to be most pronounced in a team-based organization. In that context, the ultimate purpose of appraisal may be to provide information to employees about the degree to which they are seen as contributing to and fitting with their team. An individual who appears to be competent but who is perceived as not contributing or not fitting into the team might pursue one of two options: (a) change his or her behavior, or (b) change the team. Here, the organization might act as a sort of employment/placement office, with the task of finding the team that is best for each of its employees, particularly those who appear to be competent but who clash with their present teams.

If appraisal is heading in the direction outlined above (i.e., providing a measure of fit between an employee and his or her work team), the increasing diversity of the workforce may lead to predictable biases in appraisal. As we noted earlier, the effect of race, age, and sex on appraisal seems strongest when there are only a few individuals who differ from the workplace norm (usually, this means white male, but not in all cases. A male nurse might encounter problems similar to those faced by a female engineer). As work teams move from being completely homogeneous to having a few members who are "different," evaluations of fit to the team may be downwardly biased for the new team members. After all, one dimension of lack of fit is being different from everyone else. Eventually, as the workforce becomes sufficiently diverse, variables such as race, sex, or age may no longer cause a particular person to "stick out," and it may be possible to get fair and unbiased ratings of fit to the team, regardless of race, sex, or age. During the transition from a homogeneous to a diverse workforce, however, organizations should be particularly mindful of the potential bias in ratings of fit given to women, members of minority groups, or members of any easily identifiable group that is not traditionally associated with that particular job (Heilman, 1983).

SUMMARY

One of the major themes of this book has been the importance of contextual influences on performance appraisal. The context of work and organizations is changing rapidly, and it is likely that PA will change as a result. This chapter examined four aspects of the workplace and organization that are undergoing changes that are likely to have an impact on how performance appraisals are done and used. First, we noted that organizations are moving from complex, highly differentiated organizational structures, with large numbers of management, toward flatter, less rigidly structured, and less centralized structures. One of the reasons for this change in organizational structure is a massive change in organizational function. We are moving from an economy based on heavy manufacturing toward one based on high technology and services.

Changes in the structure and function of organizations are likely to lead to substantial changes in performance appraisal, especially in how appraisals are used. There is evidence that the orientation of appraisal in many organizations is shifting from future oriented (i.e., using appraisal to guide development, to decide about promotions) to past oriented (i.e., using appraisal to reward high performers), and this may be a reflection of the effect of changing structures on career systems. In traditional manufacturing organizations, one key use of appraisal is to help determine promotions. In a relatively flat organization, there are few positions to promote most people into, no matter how good their performance, and promotions are not likely to be an important purpose of or influence upon performance appraisals.

The second major change is the increasing use of teams (as opposed to individual workers) as the basic unit for organizing work. The adoption of a team-based approach might affect virtually all aspects of PA, most notably, who is appraised and on what basis. The decision to conduct appraisals of the team, its individual members, or some combination of the two is a critical one. If individuals are evaluated, this might negatively affect the team's ability to function as a unit. If the team is evaluated but not the individual members, the organization may lose important information about differences in performance.

In individually oriented production systems, behaviors such as helping others with their work, coordinating with others, or sharing information are sometimes referred to as "extra-role" behaviors in the sense that they are not a part of the actual job description. In a team-based system, these aspects of teamwork become part of the core definition of what the job entails and what is meant by job performance. The implication of this changing definition of job performance is that performance appraisals are likely to become subjective and possibly more contentious. The individual who refuses to engage in "teamwork" but who does his or her assigned tasks well might receive a poor evaluation in a team-based organization.

The past several years have seen substantial changes in where and when people work. Options such as telecommuting (i.e., working from home or car) or the use of dispersed worksites are becoming more popular. Several variations to the standard 40-hour workweek schedule have become popular, particularly the use of flextime and compressed work schedules. Changes in the place and time of work have somewhat similar effects, at least as they affect performance appraisal. All of these changes limit a worker's interactions with peers and supervisors, and therefore limit their opportunities to directly observe the worker's performance. This is likely to lead to a shift from an emphasis on behavior (which the raters may not have the opportunity to observe) to one on results. Whether this is good or bad is a topic of considerable debate in management circles, but it is a predictable effect of adopting a schedule for working that puts workers in limited contact with their supervisors.

Finally, the workforce is changing. The majority of the entry-level workforce are women, members of minority groups, and/or immigrants. Furthermore, this entry-level workforce is shrinking, and the workforce in general is getting older. The workforce also holds increasing numbers of part-time and/or temporary workers. These changes might affect appraisal in a number of ways. First, the increasing diversity of the workforce is likely to have an impact on the incidence of sex, age, or racial biases in performance appraisal, but the direction of these effects is not necessarily easy to predict. There are cogent arguments that increasing diversity will lead to an *increase* in bias in appraisal. There are equally cogent arguments that it will lead to a *decrease* in bias in appraisals.

The effects of growing numbers of part-time and temporary workers on appraisal are a bit easier to predict. These workers may get little benefit from appraisals, and supervisors who decide to devote little time and energy to appraising the performance of these workers might be making the correct decision. In any case, we can predict that whatever part-time and temporary employees get out of appraisal, it will not have a strong future-orientation. That is, part-time or temporary workers may get little help in developing their areas of weakness or even in maintaining their present skills.

The final section of this chapter made four predictions about the future state of performance appraisal. First, we believe that organizations are moving away from the traditional model—where the direct supervisor was the only rater—to multiple-rater systems. Second, we believe that the content of appraisals will shift from a focus on individual task accomplishment toward one that emphasizes an individual's contribution to the work and an individual's fit to the work team. Third, we suggest that the current practice of annual performance appraisal may give way to a cycle of appraisal that is tied directly to task accomplishment. That is, it might make more sense to appraise ratee performance at the end of each major project rather than obtaining an annual evaluation at a date that is set independently of actual work (e.g., many organizations do appraisals on the anniversary of a person's hiring). Finally, we believe that there will be a shift in emphasis from institutional uses of appraisal (i.e., using appraisal results to make decisions about individual uses of appraisal) to individual uses (e.g., using appraisal results in deciding whether to stay in a group). In the future, we expect that performance appraisals will provide team members an opportunity to give formal feedback to their peers, and that this feedback will largely be based on shared perceptions of a worker's fit to the team.

NOTE

1. The same sort of hindsight bias (Fischoff, 1975) is probably present in individual performance appraisals as well.

14

Designing, Implementing, and
Evaluating a Goal-Oriented
Appraisal System

The traditional strategy for designing, implementing, and evaluating a performance appraisal (PA) system is to start with a general definition of a "good" appraisal system and apply the tools provided by psychologists and human resource management specialists (e.g., rating scales, training programs) to approximate that goal. In this tradition, a "good" appraisal system is usually defined as one that provides accurate, complete, and fair evaluations of each person's performance and that provides information useful to both the organization (e.g., information that can be used to help make promotion decisions) and to the individual (e.g., frank and detailed performance feedback). In this chapter we will suggest a different strategy for developing and evaluating PA systems that takes as its starting point the goals pursued by the various players in the appraisal process.

WHY DEVELOP GOAL-ORIENTED
APPRAISAL SYSTEMS?

Much of the available research on performance appraisal has been designed to address the core question of why appraisals are so bad. As we have noted in several earlier chapters, performance appraisal is a constant source of disagreement and grief in organizations, and researchers in several disciplines have struggled with ways of improving the quality, acceptability, and/or usefulness of performance appraisals.

The type of solution attempted depends largely on one's diagnosis of the problem. From the 1950s to early 1980s most suggestions for improving PA were based on the assumption that the shortcomings of appraisal were primarily due to the rater's inability to evaluate his or her subordinates accurately or to communicate his or her evaluations accurately to the organization (Murphy & Cleveland, 1991). To deal with this problem, a wide range of appraisal tools and technologies (e.g., better scales, rater training, behavior diaries) were developed.

More recent research on appraisal reflects the assumption that the shortcomings of appraisal systems are due primarily to the fact that raters are *unwilling* to provide accurate appraisals of subordinates' performance (Banks & Murphy, 1985; Padgett, 1989; Villanova & Bernardin, 1989). That is, raters often seem to know who is performing well or poorly but may decide not to report this information on a rating form. This has been recognized in research on political behavior in ratings (Longenecker et al., 1987) and on rater motivation (Mohrman & Lawler, 1983; Padgett, 1989) but has not been sufficiently incorporated into the models that are typically used to portray and analyze the appraisal process. More important, it has not been explicitly incorporated into the design and evaluation of performance appraisal systems.

Raters' tendency to distort ratings or turn in appraisals that do not reflect their actual evaluation of their subordinates' performance is typically treated as some sort of error or as an aberration. The research we have reviewed in this book (see especially Chapters 3, 4, 8, and 9) suggests that the apparent shortcomings, errors, and aberrations in the rating process can be much more easily understood if one treats raters, ratees, and so forth as active participants in the appraisal process, each of whom is pursuing a complex set of goals that substantially affect their behavior. If you accept the suggestion (which will be elaborated further in this chapter) that the shortcomings of performance appraisals in organizations can best be understood by analyzing the goals pursued by the various players in the appraisal process, it follows that there are two general strategies for improving performance appraisals: (a) change participants' goals to fit the needs of the system, or (b) change the system to fit participants' goals.

Change the Goals. If the "problem" is that raters (or other participants in the appraisal process) are pursuing goals that interfere with the quality, usefulness, and so on, of ratings, one solution is to try to change the goals pursued by raters. Here, the strategy might involve a program of structured socialization and/or training that would focus on developing a consensus about the way appraisals should be done and used in organizations. To some extent, this is a goal of "frame-of-reference" training (Bernardin & Beatty, 1984; McIntyre et al., 1984). That method is designed to ensure that raters adopt a common perspective about what constitutes good performance and about which behaviors relate to which aspects of performance. The same idea might be broadened to developing a consensus about how PA "should" be used. That is, it might make sense to try to develop a common set of norms about what behaviors are appropriate or inappropriate in performance appraisal and about whether and to what extent raters should provide accurate appraisals of their subordinates' performance (Murphy [1993] suggested a similar process of norm development to deal with workplace dishonesty). For example, if the "problem" is that raters distort appraisals to gain valued rewards for employees (e.g., promotions, raises), one potential solution is to try to reach a shared set of norms about whether and when this type of behavior is appropriate and acceptable.

Research on organizational socialization (e.g., Van Maanen, 1975) suggests that it might be possible to shape norms about how appraisals should be used, particularly if you intervene early in an individual's tenure with an organization. The most difficult challenge in this area may be developing a realistic and enforceable set of norms. Virtually every training program and organizational handbook we have ever seen includes some sort of description of how the appraisal system is supposed to work, but there is often a significant gap between what the handbook says and what people actually do. In Chapter 12 we noted that much of the distortion and "politics" that are criticized in research on performance appraisal may be nothing more than good management. A supervisor who goes "by the book" with no regard for the consequences is not necessarily a good manager. Rather, a manager who never turns in an accurate appraisal but who uses the appraisal system effectively to guide, motivate, and reward his or her subordinates may be doing a much better job than is a manager who turns in exactly the sort of appraisals requested in the personnel handbook.

Even if it is possible to develop a workable set of norms and to socialize new managers to follow these norms in evaluating their subordinates, the strategy of changing the goals to fit the needs of the system may be a very difficult one to carry out. First, there are probably some managers whose strategies and norms for doing PA are fairly well established and whose behavior might be quite difficult to change. Second, the goals, norms, and so forth that present barriers to the effective use of appraisal are not likely to have grown up in a vacuum. Rather, the goals pursued by raters, ratees, and others are shaped by a number of personal and situational factors (Cleveland & Murphy, 1992), and if these factors remain in the work environment it is likely that a new consensus that is developed about how performance appraisals should be done will not survive for long. For example, when resources and rewards are scarce, raters might consciously decide to use performance appraisal to guard the resources their subordinates currently have and to maximize access to new resources and rewards. If the norms are changed to encourage a more honest and objective approach to appraisal, but rewards and resources remain scarce (and competition for them remains intense), it is likely that raters will soon revert to their old strategy of distorting appraisal to gain access to rewards.

Change the System. An alternative to changing the people to fit the system is to change the system to fit the people. This strategy involves assessing the goals pursued by participants in appraisal, then tailoring the system to best fit those goals. This perspective is based on two assumptions. First, the idea that the system should be fitted to existing goals is based on the assumption that it may not be possible to pursue the opposite strategy (i.e., change goals to fit the system). As we will note below, the very complexity of the set of relevant goals may make it impossible to develop a working consensus about how appraisals should be done, and to socialize all of the parties involved in appraisal to accept that consensus. Second, we assume that the goals pursued by various participants in the appraisal process evolve in reaction to real and important environmental pressures and demands. That is, many of the apparently dysfunctional behaviors criticized in PA research (e.g., leniency in rating) are in fact likely to represent adaptive responses that are entirely appropriate to the situations faced by raters, ratees, and the various users of performance appraisal. Even if we can temporarily change the goals pursued by raters, ratees, and others, it may not be a good idea to make those changes. Rather, it might be best to actively assess the goals pursued by those involved in performance appraisal and to develop appraisal systems that are as consistent as possible with the important and legitimate goals pursued by each of the major constituencies involved in appraisal.

DESIGN AND IMPLEMENTATION
OF GOAL-ORIENTED SYSTEMS

The development and implementation of a goal-oriented appraisal system starts with an assessment of the goals pursued by raters, ratees, the organization, and other interested parties. Conflicts among these goals must be assessed and priorities among conflicting goals must be set. Once a set of consistent and important goals can be identified, it is then possible to assess the compatibility of several possible appraisal system features with those goals. The endpoint of this process is the design and implementation of an appraisal system that includes the features that are most consistent with the key goals pursued by each of the constituencies involved in appraisal.

Defining and Assessing Goals

Balzer and Sulsky (1990) suggest a general framework for eliciting goals and selecting criteria that are relevant to those goals; this framework is quite similar to procedures used in decision research (Edwards & Newman, 1982). First, the set of individuals who have a stake in the performance appraisal system of an organization must be identified. Balzer and Sulsky (1990) assume that there will be groups of individuals who share common goals; they refer to these groups as stakeholders. There are three groups who have an obvious stake in the outcomes of appraisal and whose goals are clearly relevant in developing and evaluating a performance appraisal

system: (a) raters, (b) the organizational users of information from performance appraisals (e.g., management, human resource departments), and (c)
ratees. In addition to these three sets of stakeholders, clients/customers
often have a legitimate interest in appraisal, particularly when the job in
question represents a boundary role that involves substantial contact with
the client and/or customer. Finally, one can argue that society in general has
a legitimate interest in the process and outcomes of appraisal. For example,
if appraisals are conducted in such a way that there is systematic bias
against disadvantaged groups, there might be a valid societal stake in
reducing or eliminating this bias.

In this section we review research on the goals that raters, organizational
users of appraisal, ratees, and other key stakeholders are likely to pursue in
appraisal. Following this discussion of goals, we briefly discuss procedures
for assessing the goals actually pursued in a particular setting.

Rater Goals. In Chapter 8 we discussed in some detail the types of goals
often pursued by raters. It is useful to summarize the key points made there
about rater goals in performance appraisal; these points are summarized in
Table 14.1.

In thinking about the goals listed in Table 14.1 you might notice that
there are four separate types of goals, each of which leads to the same
behavior, that is, rating inflation. Our point in constructing this table was
to remind the reader that simply looking at what the rater does (i.e., giving
high ratings) might not provide a sufficient basis for understanding his or
her behavior. The same rating behavior might occur for a number of
reasons, and the appropriate response to that behavior might depend on the
reason the rater has for giving high or low ratings.

It seems likely that raters consider at least four questions (corresponding
to these four goal types shown in Table 14.1) when completing a performance appraisal form: (a) How will a high or low rating affect the subordinate's future performance? (b) How will that rating affect my future
relationship with that subordinate? (c) How will that rating affect my own
standing in the organization? (d) What rating does the subordinate deserve?
The relevance and importance of each of these questions may vary across
raters, ratees, or both. For example, a highly "political" manager might
always think about how ratings will affect his or her standing. Other raters
with a less political focus might give little thought to this dimension of
performance rating. Questions about how ratings might affect future per-

TABLE 14.1 Goals Pursued by Raters

Goal Type	Characteristics
Task performance goals	Using appraisal to increase subordinates' performance (e.g., giving high ratings to motivate employees)
Interpersonal goals	Using appraisal to build and maintain good working relationships (e.g., giving positive feedback to avoid the discomfort and dissatisfaction caused by criticism of performance)
Strategic goals	Using appraisal to enhance one's own status in organization (e.g., giving high ratings in an attempt to convey positive image of one's own effectiveness as a manager)
Internalized goals	Using appraisal to implement personal values (e.g., giving high ratings to "deserving" subordinates)

formance and future rater-ratee relationships probably take on a different meaning for poor performers than for good performers. Some rater-ratee combinations might make particular goals highly relevant and make others less pressing. Nevertheless, this set of goals is likely to have some bearing on the appraisals completed by each rater in the organization, and knowing which goals are most or least important may help in understanding why particular raters assign high or low ratings.

Organizational Goals. In Chapter 3 we discussed the taxonomy of organizational uses of performance appraisal developed by Cleveland et al. (1989); the four general categories of uses are shown in Table 14.2. The most widely cited uses of (or goals for) appraisal fall under the first two categories, that is, using appraisal to provide information useful for distinguishing between individuals and for distinguishing individual strengths and weaknesses. Both types of distinctions provide valuable information for both organizational and individual decision making. Differences in overall levels of performance form one basis for making administrative decisions (e.g., salary administration, career advancement), whereas within-individual differences in performance are an important consideration in choosing areas and strategies for future development. Performance appraisals might also be used as a source of information for developing and maintaining other personnel systems or for documenting and validating personnel decisions and decision-making systems.

TABLE 14.2   Organizational Uses of Performance Appraisal

Category	Examples
Between-person distinctions	Using appraisal for salary administration, individual recognition, identifying targets for layoffs
Within-person distinctions	Using appraisal to identify training needs, make placement and transfer decisions, provide performance feedback
Systems maintenance	Using appraisal to evaluate personnel systems, identify organizational development needs
Documentation	Using appraisal to justify personnel actions, to validate selection and assessment systems

Both individuals and organizations are likely to pursue a number of goals with their performance appraisal systems. Performance appraisal researchers (Bretz & Milkovich, 1989; Cleveland et al., 1989; DeCotiis & Petit, 1978; Jacobs et al., 1980; Mohrman & Lawler, 1983; Tiffin & McCormick, 1958; Wexley & Klimoski, 1984) and practitioners (Burchett & DeMeuse, 1985; Cocheu, 1986; Friedman, 1986; Haynes, 1986; Martin, 1986; Massey, 1975; Olson & Bennett, 1975) have promoted the idea that there are many uses for PA. Recently, however, there has been an increasing awareness that although appraisal can be used effectively for many purposes, a single performance appraisal system may not address all of these purposes equally well (Cleveland et al., 1989; DeVries et al., 1986). In a later section of this chapter we will examine the possibility of conflict among the multiple goals of performance appraisal.

Ratee Goals. Relatively little attention has been paid to the goals that are likely to be pursued by ratees in performance appraisal (Fisher, 1989). We believe, however, that a brief discussion of ratee goals is important for at least two reasons. First, ratee goals may indirectly affect performance ratings. Both the expectations that ratees bring to the performance discussion and the rater's perceptions of the ratee's reaction to performance appraisal may influence the actual ratings (Padgett, 1989). This is especially true when we view performance appraisal as an ongoing process, rather than a one-time review. Second, self-appraisals represent an increasingly common component of performance review systems (Ashford, 1989; Campbell & Lee, 1988; DeGregorio & Fisher, 1988). Therefore, as with supervisory raters, it is essential to determine the goals and information that

TABLE 14.3   Ratee Goals in Performance Appraisal

Goal Type	Characteristics
Obtain information	Use appraisal to obtain information about absolute and relative performance levels, performance standards
Convey information	Use appraisal sessions to convey information about factors that limit performance, about willingness to develop or improve
Influence evaluations	Use appraisal sessions to manage impressions, to suggest high levels of performance

the ratee wants to convey to performance appraisal users. Table 14.3 lists a number of goals ratees are likely to pursue in performance appraisal.

First, ratees may actively seek feedback (Ashford & Cummings, 1983), particularly regarding their relative standing in the workgroup (Fisher, 1989). Performance feedback not only informs the employee about his or her own behavior, it also provides an opportunity to acquire information on performance standards and organizational expectations of good or successful performance. Ratees may use the appraisal and feedback process to seek information about the norms and standards of the organization.

Employees also have the goal of conveying information to the rater, which can directly influence the present and future outcomes of appraisal. For example, ratees may want to convey information about situational constraints on their performance (Peters et al., 1985), particularly when their performance is below standard. Although they may not think of it in these terms, ratees are likely to be concerned about the attributions that a rater makes about the reasons or causes of their performance. Research on actor-observer biases in attribution suggest that ratees *should* be concerned over the possibility that raters will not sufficiently weigh situational constraints. This research has shown that raters will consistently attribute performance to internal factors, and that this tendency becomes stronger over time (Burger, 1986). On the other hand, ratees often make different attributions, claiming credit (e.g., citing internal factors such as ability) for success and indicating external or situational causes for failure or negative outcomes (Jones & Nisbett, 1971). When performance is poor, ratees are likely to make efforts to bring external constraints to the attention of the rater.

Ratees may also want to convey a willingness to improve or modify their work behavior. This information can affect evaluations of present performance (ratees who appear to be trying are likely to be evaluated more favorably), but it also can be used to influence future impressions of ratee performance. According to self-enhancement theories, people strive to see themselves favorably and as competent (Bandura, 1982; Brown, 1986). A corollary of self-enhancement theory is that individuals strive to make a good impression on others (Schlenker, 1980). Several empirical studies have investigated the influence of employee impression management on supervisory performance appraisal ratings (Kipnis & Vanderveer, 1971; Wayne & Ferris, 1990; Wayne & Kacmar, 1991). Both Kipnis and Vanderveer (1971) and Wayne and Rubinstein (1987) found that some impression management activities (e.g., ingratiation) by ratees seems to lead to higher performance ratings (see, however, Fodor, 1974).

Customer/Client and Societal Goals. The customers and clients who deal with an organization have a valid interest in the way performance appraisals are conducted and used. In particular, they are likely to be interested in the impact of human resource systems (including performance appraisal) on the quality and consistency of the product and/or service the organization provides. Thus, customers and clients are likely to be more interested in the outcomes of appraisal than in the appraisal process. In contrast, there is a legitimate societal interest in both the process and outcomes of appraisal. Societal concern about the appraisal process itself is one aspect of a widely shared belief that workers have a basic right to be treated with some level of dignity; fair and unbiased assessments of performance and assessment represent one component of this type of treatment (as Schuler, Farr, & Smith [1993] point out, the belief that workers have a basic right to be treated with dignity is almost universally accepted in Europe but is still debated in the United States).

The interests of customers/clients and society in general in the process and outcomes of appraisal need to be taken into account when developing an appraisal system that is most compatible with important goals of key stakeholders. Both customers/clients and society in general have a legitimate interest in how performance appraisals are done and used in organizations, and appraisal systems that pay no attention to these goals are unlikely to survive. If nothing else, such systems may be more tempting targets for lawsuits than are systems that attempt to address the societal interests.

Assessing Goals. We have suggested types of goals that might be pursued by raters, ratees, organizational users of appraisal, and other key stakeholders. To build an appraisal system that is maximally consistent with the key goals pursued by each set of stakeholders, it is necessary to move from a general idea of what types of goals they *might be* pursuing to an assessment of the goals they *actually are* pursuing. This process of goal assessment is likely to include a variety of direct and indirect methods. This can best be illustrated by thinking about ways one might assess rater goals.

As we noted in Chapter 8, raters are not always aware of their goals, and even when they are aware of them, they may not be willing to describe them. This does not mean self-reports are worthless for investigating rater goals, but rather that these methods will probably not be sufficient. Fortunately, we can draw on research in motivation and decision making to make some inferences about the content of rater goals.

Instrumentality theory (Porter & Lawler, 1968; Schwab, Olian-Gottlieb, & Heneman, 1979; Vroom, 1964) represents one of the most widely applied theories of work motivation. In its most basic form the theory says that the motivation to work is a function of the value attached to the various outcomes of good performance and the individual's belief that specific levels of effort or specific behaviors will lead to those outcomes. This theory provides a useful framework for determining what goals are likely to operate in different organizational settings. For example, in determining the probable content of rater goals it is useful first to list the outcomes that might reasonably be associated with giving good, average, or poor ratings. Some of these outcomes will be valued by raters, and these are likely to represent goal objects. Other outcomes might be valued by the organization but not by the rater (e.g., determining which member of the workgroup performed best this year); raters will not necessarily direct their behavior toward achieving those goals.

Raters may find it difficult to describe accurately the relative values of outcomes (assuming they are willing to try). Decision research provides methods that may prove useful for measuring rater values. For example, the first step in the assessment of multiattribute utility is often to ask questions about the values associated with different decision outcomes (Edwards, 1980; Edwards & Newman, 1982). This sometimes involves asking the decision maker to respond directly to a structured set of questions but may also involve more indirect methods in which values (i.e., utilities) are inferred from the choices an individual makes (Raiffa, 1968). For example, raters might be presented with scenarios describing a variety of appraisal outcomes and asked to indicate their preferences among sets of outcomes. Raters who consistently choose one set of outcomes over another (e.g., high-quality feedback regarding strengths and weaknesses vs. identifying best and worst performers) probably value that outcome more.

A similar inferential process might be applied to assessing ratee and organizational goals. That is, assessment of key goals will probably combine some fairly direct self-report methods with indirect inferential methods that assess the perceived gains and losses associated with pursuing various strategies in performance appraisal. We expect that the technology for assessing and inferring key goals will continue to develop, but at this point the assessment of goals remains an imprecise art. Nevertheless, simply asking the question of what each set of important players in performance appraisal is trying to accomplish is likely to provide a wealth of insights into how PA operates in an organization and how the system can be refined to be consistent with the goals of key stakeholders.

Goal Conflict

Conflict among the multiple goals pursued by each of the stakeholders in performance appraisal is probably common, for two reasons: (a) incompatibility between goals of different stakeholders—for example, organizations attempt to obtain information about performance, but raters may decide to use appraisal as a motivational tool, not a measurement tool; and (b) incompatibility between multiple goals pursued by the same stakeholder—for example, organizations usually attempt to assess both between- and within-ratee differences, but doing one typically interferes with the other (see Chapter 3).

Mohrman (1986) and others (Austin, Villanova, Kane, & Bernardin, 1991; Balzer & Sulsky, 1990) have suggested that conflicts among the stakeholders of an appraisal system are the norm. In particular, raters may use appraisal to achieve different objectives or purposes than the ratee. Further, the ratee may think that appraisal is used for purposes quite different from those envisioned by the organization. Especially with a new performance appraisal system, there is a danger that the system will create a discrepancy between the espoused purposes and actual purposes of appraisal (Mohrman, 1986). Mohrman (1986) found that although managers and subordinates sometimes agreed on the extent to which different purposes should be achieved through the performance appraisal system, subordinates rarely perceived that the actual goal of appraisal was achieved to the extent that managers did. Further, subordinates and managers differed in terms of the extent to which they believed that some purposes should be stressed. For example, Mohrman (1986) found that subordinates wanted an explanation of pay during appraisal, but managers did not think it was necessary. Neither constituent viewed pay as being discussed to any great extent; subordinates often felt that this need remained unmet after leaving the appraisal session (Mohrman, 1986).

Conflicts among goals held by the same stakeholder have been documented extensively in the research literature, especially in research on the multiple organizational uses of appraisal. For example, Cleveland et al.'s (1989) survey specifically asked organizations to indicate the extent to which their performance appraisal system was used for various purposes. They found that more than 71% of the respondents indicated that information from appraisals was used "moderately to extensively" for both between-person decisions (i.e., pay, promotion, etc.) and within-person decisions (i.e., feedback). Thirty years ago, Meyer et al. (1965) questioned whether performance appraisal should be used simultaneously for personnel decisions and for employee feedback. More recently, DeVries (1983) made a similar suggestion, noting that a performance appraisal system designed to improve employee performance may not be the most effective for salary administration.

Dealing With Conflict. Conflict among the goals of an appraisal system can be a significant source of dissatisfaction with performance appraisal and may substantially limit the effectiveness of any appraisal system. Results from the laboratory and from interviews with raters in the field suggest that when a rater faces multiple and possibly conflicting purposes, the organization may be sacrificing not only accuracy but also the usefulness of ratings (i.e., ratings may become so inflated that they provide no meaningful information). There is both research evidence (Cleveland et al., 1989; Meyer et al., 1965; Sharon & Bartlett, 1969; Williams et al., 1985) and anecdotal evidence from raters (Cleveland et al., 1986) that organizations convey mixed and conflicting messages to raters when an appraisal is used to achieve both individual (e.g., employee feedback) and administrative goals (e.g., personnel decisions) (DeCotiis & Petit, 1978; also, see Chapter 12). It is conceivable that the rater selects one salient or consequential purpose and ignores the rest when dealing with mixed messages from the organization. A more dismal possibility is that the attempt to use PA for a large number of distinct purposes puts the rater in an impossible situation, and the ratings he or she finally gives may be affected by so many confounds that they are not useful for *any* of the system's purposes.

Given the potential problems caused by conflicting goals, the question of what to do when conflicts arise is an important one. The first step in dealing with goal conflict involves determining which goals are or are not compatible. There are three ways in which performance appraisal goals might come into conflict. First, accomplishing one goal might directly block accomplishing another. For example, a rater who gives high ratings to avoid interpersonal conflicts might find it difficult to reward truly good performance. Second, acquiring information required for one goal might interfere with accomplishing other goals. For example, requiring detailed behavioral documentation (which satisfied one major organizational requirement for appraisal, i.e., that it provide documentation and justification for personnel decisions) removes the supervisor's flexibility to use the appraisal system as a motivational tool. Finally, pursuing one goal may direct attention away from another. For example, if ratings are collected for developmental purposes, raters may pay more attention to differences within individuals than to differences between individuals. If ratings are later used to make administrative decisions (e.g., salary administration), this initial focus on within-person differences may limit their usefulness for distinguishing between individuals.

The set of goals pursued by raters, the organization, ratees, and so on, is likely to contain a core of mutually compatible goals together with a set of goals that are fundamentally in conflict. If conflicts cannot be resolved, the next best step is to establish priorities among goals and to focus the appraisal system on goals that are both important and compatible.

It is reasonable to assume that different stakeholders will have different beliefs about which goals are most and least important. It is also reasonable to assume that priority-setting will be a difficult task, and that direct judgments about the relative importance of goals may not be sufficient to establish those priorities. This implies that the best way to determine the relative importance of the goals pursued by various stakeholders may involve a broad consideration—taking into account the viewpoints of multiple constituencies—of the consequences of meeting or failing to meet key goals. To illustrate this idea, consider the set of goals listed in Table 14.4.

Imagine an organization in which the primary goals pursued by raters are to motivate subordinates and reinforce perceptions of fairness. The

TABLE 14.4   An Illustration of Multiple Goals Involved in Appraisal

Rater Goals
  Motivate subordinates
  Reinforce perceptions of fairness

Organizational
  Distinguish between individuals
  Distinguish strengths and weaknesses[a]
  Document performance levels

Ratee
  Obtain feedback about overall performance
  Convey information about reasons for good and poor performance

Customer/Clients
  Enhance smooth function of organization

Societal
  Guarantee fairness and equity in assessment

NOTE: a. Note that this goal is incompatible with the organizational goal of distinguishing between individuals and with the ratee goal of obtaining information about overall performance.

organization uses appraisal to distinguish between individuals, distinguish strengths and weaknesses (note that these two goals are in conflict), and document performance levels. Ratees are most concerned with obtaining feedback about their overall performance level and conveying information about reasons for good and poor performance. Customers and clients are interested in human resource systems that enhance the efficiency of the organization but may have little interest in the process of assessment. Society in general has an interest in the fairness and equity of assessment.

Before assessing priorities, it is useful to evaluate possible goal conflicts; if all goals are mutually compatible, it might not be necessary to consider priorities. In this example, there is an obvious conflict between the two organizational goals of distinguishing between individuals and distinguishing strengths from weaknesses. There is a less obvious (but still important) conflict between the organizational goal of assessing strengths and weaknesses and the ratee goal of obtaining feedback about overall performance. In deciding which goals should be met by an appraisal system, consider the consequences of either not obtaining detailed information about strengths and weaknesses or not obtaining information and feedback about overall performance levels. An organization that fails to obtain high-quality information about strengths and weaknesses may be hampered in developing employees. Information about strengths and weaknesses can help target training and development activities and can provide a useful starting point for validating these activities. On the other hand, the failure to obtain high-quality information about overall performance levels may hamper the organization's ability to make administrative decisions (e.g., pay for performance), and it may also frustrate ratees' desire to know how they are doing. In deciding which set of goals is more important, it is necessary to factor in the ability of each stakeholder actually to accomplish the desired ends using appraisal. For example, if the organization does not have (or does not intend to develop) an intensive program of training and development, the fact that the appraisal system provides little information about strengths and weaknesses may be of little consequence. On the other hand, resources and promotion opportunities may be so restricted that the organization is unable to act on whatever information it obtains about overall performance levels. In this case, there may be little point in focusing on overall performance.

Suppose, in this example, it was decided that information about overall performance was more important than information about strengths and weaknesses. In that case, all of the goals except for obtaining information about strengths and weaknesses would form a reasonably compatible set, and if we dropped that one goal it would then be possible to move to the next step of matching appraisal system features with key stakeholder goals.

Appraisal System Features in Relation to Key Goals

Several critical decisions must be made in designing a performance appraisal system. First, you must decide who evaluates performance. Appraisals might be obtained from supervisor, peers, self-ratings, or some combination of these sources. Next, you must decide the basis upon which individuals are evaluated. For example, evaluations might be done on the basis of direct observations of job performance or they might be based on information about the results of job performance (e.g., evaluations of salespersons are often based primarily on results, in part because it is almost impossible to observe their performance directly).

You must decide about the level of analysis in defining and evaluating performance, particularly whether appraisals should be framed in terms of specific behaviors or broad and general traits. You must also decide whether employees will be evaluated in comparison to other employees (e.g., as in a ranking system) or in comparison to specific performance standards. You must also decide how appraisals will be used (e.g., for making administrative decisions vs. for development), and about what is communicated to ratees (e.g., performance level, relative performance, strengths and weaknesses).

The process of matching appraisal system features to the key goals of major stakeholders begins with an assessment of the extent to which each of these goals is either consistent with, inconsistent with, or irrelevant to major components or features of an appraisal system. Table 14.5 lists examples of judgments about the consistency or inconsistency among eight goals and 15 appraisal system features. The eight goals are taken from Table 14.4 (remember that the goal of distinguishing strengths and weaknesses was judged to be low in priority and incompatible with other goals, and was dropped). The 15 appraisal system features include using supervisors, peers, or self-ratings to evaluate performance; basing evaluations on direct observation, results, or feedback from clients and customers; evaluating performance in terms of behaviors, traits, or accomplishments; comparing performance levels to others, performance standards, or past performance; using appraisal for salary administration, feedback, or for no apparent purpose; and communicating information about absolute performance, performance relative to others, or individual strengths and weaknesses. For each goal we estimated the degree to which features of an appraisal system were either consistent (C), inconsistent (I), or neither consistent nor inconsistent (N) with accomplishing that goal. For example, if a key goal of an appraisal system is to provide detailed feedback for improving performance, appraisal scales that called for global trait ratings or for comparisons between employees in terms of their overall performance would be inconsistent, whereas appraisal scales that called for detailed behavioral assessments might be more consistent.

These consistency judgments are admittedly subjective, and they do not exhaust the possible set of goals or appraisal system features. They do, however, provide some guidance for evaluating the extent to which various appraisal systems are likely to match the key goals pursued by stakeholders. For example, the information in Table 14.5 suggests several conclusions about the design for an appraisal system. First, supervisors should have the responsibility for evaluating performance, but it might be reasonable to incorporate peer ratings. Use of supervisory or peer ratings is consistent with a wide range of goals, but the use of self-ratings is, in this example, inconsistent with a number of important goals, including distinguishing

TABLE 14.5   Appraisal System Features in Relationship to Key Goals

Goals	Who Evaluates Performance		
	Supervisor	Peers	Self
Organizational			
Distinguish between	C	C	I
Document	C	N	I
Rater			
Motivate	C	N	I
Perceived fairness	C	C	C
Ratee			
Obtain feedback	C	C	I
Convey information	N	I	C
Customer/Clients			
Smooth function	C	C	C
Societal			
Fairness	C	C	C

Goals	Basis for Evaluating Performance		
	Observation	Results	Feedback
Organizational			
Distinguish between	C	C	I
Document	C	C	N
Rater			
Motivate	C	C	C
Perceived fairness	C	N	C
Ratee			
Obtain feedback	C	N	C
Convey information	C	I	C
Customer/Clients			
Smooth function	C	C	N
Societal			
Fairness	C	C	C

Goals	Performance Evaluated in What Terms		
	Behaviors	Traits	Accomplishments
Organizational			
Distinguish between	C	C	N
Document	C	I	I
Rater			
Motivate	C	I	I
Perceived fairness	C	I	N
Ratee			
Obtain feedback	C	I	I
Convey information	C	I	I
Customer/Clients			
Smooth function	N	N	C
Societal			
Fairness	C	I	N

TABLE 14.5 *Continued*

Goals	Performance Compared To		
	Others	*Standards*	*Past*
Organizational			
Distinguish between	C	N	I
Document	I	C	I
Rater			
Motivate	C	C	C
Perceived fairness	N	C	N
Ratee			
Obtain feedback	I	C	C
Convey information	I	C	N
Customer/Clients			
Smooth function	C	C	N
Societal			
Fairness	C	C	N

Goals	Consequences of Appraisal		
	Salary	*Feedback*	*None*
Organizational			
Distinguish between	C	I	C
Document	N	C	I
Rater			
Motivate	C	C	I
Perceived fairness	N	C	I
Ratee			
Obtain feedback	I	C	C
Convey information	N	C	N
Customer/Clients			
Smooth function	C	N	I
Societal			
Fairness	C	C	I

Goals	What Is Communicated		
	Absolute Level	*Relative Performance*	*Strengths*
Organizational			
Distinguish between	N	C	I
Document	C	I	N
Rater			
Motivate	N	C	I
Perceived fairness	C	I	N
Ratee			
Obtain feedback	C	I	C
Convey information	C	I	C
Customer/Clients			
Smooth function	C	N	N
Societal			
Fairness	N	C	C

NOTE: C = Consistent, I = Inconsistent, N = Neither consistent nor inconsistent between, motivating, and providing feedback to employees. Second, ratings should be based on observations of behavior on the job, but it might be reasonable to incorporate feedback from clients or customers. Again, these practices are consistent with a number of important goals, whereas results-based evaluation is inconsistent with a number of important goals.

Table 14.5 suggests that rating scales should be behavior-based and that performance should be evaluated in terms of defined standards (rather than comparisons with others or with past performance). The decision to use ratings for salary versus feedback is a complex one; both uses are inconsistent with at least one important goal. The decision to use appraisals for salary or for feedback will probably depend on the relative importance of distinguishing between individuals versus providing useful feedback to ratees. Finally, Table 14.5 suggests that feedback should be phrased in terms of absolute levels of performance. Providing feedback about relative performance or about strengths and weaknesses would be inconsistent with a wide range of goals.

EVALUATING PERFORMANCE APPRAISAL SYSTEMS

Traditionally, performance appraisal systems have been evaluated in terms of context-free criteria such as rater error or rating accuracy measures (see Chapter 10). That is, criteria such as reliability, validity, accuracy, and freedom from rater errors are usually assumed to be important for assessing any performance appraisal system. Because there are a wide variety of criterion measures, all of which are supposedly relevant, PA researchers and practitioners seem to face a dilemma in choosing criteria, in that the choice of any specific set of measures can be criticized as arbitrary (Balzer & Sulsky, 1990). Rather than relying on the same context-free criteria for evaluating performance appraisal systems, we suggest that the choice of criteria be determined by the goals of the system. The goals of the system are, in turn, determined by the organizational context, and in particular by the implicit and explicit purpose(s) of performance appraisal in that organization.

The preceding section suggested that the first steps in designing and implementing a performance appraisal system involve assessing key goals and deriving a core set of goals that are mutually compatible and important to the major stakeholders in appraisal. These goals not only form the basis for designing an appraisal system, they also form the basis for evaluating that system. In this evaluative framework, a good performance appraisal system is one that helps the key stakeholders achieve their goals. A poor appraisal system is one that interferes with goal attainment.

This framework for evaluation implies that the "criteria for criteria" cannot be determined without assessing the *real* purpose and function of appraisal in an organization (which might be quite different from the function described in the personnel handbook), and that the criteria appropriate for evaluating an appraisal system are unlikely to be the same from organization to organization or even from time to time in the same organization. For example, there may be no real point in assessing the presence or absence of halo error in ratings even if appropriate measures of this rater error can be developed (for critiques of halo measures, see Murphy & Anhalt, 1992; Murphy et al., 1993). If distinguishing individuals' strengths and weaknesses is *not* an important goal of an appraisal, the fact that ratings show levels of halo that make these distinctions troublesome is of little consequence.

In evaluating the contribution of a performance appraisal system to attaining key goals, three classes of evidence are likely to be relevant. First, it is useful to assess the logical consistency between appraisal system features and key goals. This is exactly the process sketched out in the preceding section, and it provides the first type of data for assessing the links between a performance appraisal system and key stakeholder goals. It may not always be possible to design a system that is consistent with all of the relevant goals (the likelihood of achieving consistency with all key goals probably decreases as more goals are added), and even if such a system is possible in theory, it may not be possible in practice. For example, the appraisal system that seems optimal in the example presented in Table 14.5 will include performance ratings that are based on direct observations of ratee behavior. If supervisors have limited contact with their subordinates (which might occur if they work at different sites; see Chapter 13), it may not be possible to build this desirable feature into an appraisal system. Thus, the first step in evaluating an appraisal system might be a simple comparison between the actual system and the type of system that would best meet the goals of stakeholders. If the appraisal system actually in use differs substantially from the type of system that is most consistent with key goals, this may limit the possible effectiveness of the existing appraisal system.

Second, reaction criteria might be very useful. In Chapter 11 we noted that assessing raters', ratees', and organizational users' reactions to performance appraisal systems could provide useful information. Here, we take this suggestion one step further. It might be very useful to obtain stakeholders' assessments of the consistency between the appraisal system and the goals they view as most important in appraisal. That is, if raters, ratees, and others *believe* that an appraisal system is useful for a particular purpose (e.g., for motivating subordinates), this belief may be an important component of the appraisal system's success. On the other hand, an appraisal system feature might be logically consistent with a particular goal or set of goals, but if the key participants in the appraisal process do not see or accept the link, the system may fail.

Third, it is often possible and desirable empirically to evaluate the impact of an appraisal system on specific goals. That is, if an important goal of performance appraisal is to motivate employees, it makes sense to assess levels of employee motivation. Similarly, if an appraisal system is designed to enhance the quality of feedback received by subordinates, it is important to determine whether the feedback in fact improves. In evaluating the impact of a performance appraisal system on the attainment of key goals, it is important to consider both the strengths and limitations of alternative research designs and the process of translating general goal statements into actual criterion measures.

Research Design. The task of evaluating an intervention such as a new performance appraisal system is surprisingly complex, and it may require a carefully crafted research design. This is most clearly illustrated by considering the strengths and weaknesses of the simple design illustrated in Figure 14.1.

Here, the principal goal of the appraisal system is to motivate subordinates. Accordingly, a measure of employee motivation is obtained before implementing the appraisal system (pretest), the system is implemented, and motivation is measured again after the system has been in place for a while (posttest). If motivation is higher after the system has been installed than it was prior to the system, this might be an indication that the performance appraisal system worked.

Unfortunately, there are a number of equally plausible explanations for the change in motivation that have little or nothing to do with the appraisal system. Campbell and Stanley (1966) label these "threats to validity" (for the latest enumeration of these threats, see Cook, Campbell, & Peracchio, 1990). First, the increase in motivation could be due to some event or

A Simple, But Potentially Weak Design

Measure Motivation---Implement Appraisal System------Measure Motivation
(pre-test)   (post-test)

A More Complex, But More Powerful Design Group

---

1. Measure Motivation----Implement Appraisal System---Measure Motivation
2. Measure Motivation--Measure Motivation
3.   Implement Appraisal System----Measure Motivation
4.   Measure Motivation

Figure 14.1. Two Research Designs for Investigating the Effects of a New Appraisal System

combination of events in the external environment that are independent of the PA system. For example, it is possible that the economic position of the company improved about the time the appraisal system was put into place, making more promotion opportunities and raises more readily available. The increased motivation may be the result of increased rewards that are now available and may have nothing to do with the appraisal system.

Another possibility is simple regression to the mean. Perhaps the first measurement was taken at a point when ratee motivation was unusually low. In that case, there is nowhere to go but up, and an increase in motivation should come as no great surprise. The increase in measured motivation cannot necessarily be taken as an indication of the appraisal system's success.

Finally, it is possible that the measurement itself affects motivation. That is, the first measurement of employee motivation may alert both raters and ratees that the organization is interested in the degree to which employees are motivated to do their jobs and in the effects of the appraisal system on this motivation. The fact that the organization is showing this interest can alter the behavior of raters and ratees in such a way that subsequent measures will suggest higher motivation, regardless of how a new performance appraisal system is designed.

A more complicated, but potentially stronger, design is also illustrated in Figure 14.1. Here, there are four groups. The first received the pretest, then the new appraisal system, then the posttest. The second receives the pretest and the posttest but does not receive the new system. The third receives the new appraisal system and the posttest but no pretest. The fourth group receives the posttest only.

If the appraisal system is really responsible for the increase in motivation, high posttest scores should be seen for the first and third groups (who receive the new system) and lower scores in the second and fourth groups (who do not). A comparison of scores in the first and third groups tells you something about the effects of having a pretest measure. If the pretest itself causes some or all of the increase in motivation, posttest scores should be higher in the first group than in the third. Similarly, if it is the pretest rather than the treatment that explains the apparent increase in motivation, posttest scores should be just as high in the second group (who did not receive the new appraisal system, but who received the pretest) as in the first (who received the appraisal system). Finally, if there is some event in the external environment that explains the high level of motivation at posttest time, the fourth group (who received the posttest only) should have posttest scores as high as those in any of the other groups.

Cook et al. (1990) elaborate many variations on research designs that might be applied to evaluate the success of a performance appraisal system. One principle (that might be apparent from Figure 14.1) is that a truly informative design can be very difficult to implement, and that the evaluation of a performance appraisal system is likely to be a much more complex endeavor than has been attempted in most of the existing research on appraisal system effectiveness.

Measuring Goal Attainment. One of the problems in evaluating a goal-oriented appraisal system is that broad statements about desirable outcomes of appraisal must be translated into concrete measures. Table 14.6 illustrates the process of linking the choice of criteria to the goals of the appraisal system. In constructing this table, we translated the four uses of performance appraisal reviewed by Cleveland et al. (1989) into specific operational measures. The first step was to define the goal in terms of the measurement principles that apply. For example, a system that is used solely to make promotion decisions implies an ordinal system of measurement in which the major criterion for evaluating the system is its validity in rank-ordering candidates. A system that is designed to give feedback about strengths and weaknesses must allow one to scale different performance dimensions on a comparable scale that allows for meaningful comparisons among performance levels in qualitatively different areas. A system that is used to identify

TABLE 14.6 Using the Goals of the Appraisal System to Develop Operational Criteria

Purpose of Appraisal	Major Goal of System	Criteria Most Appropriate for Evaluating the System
Promotion	Rank ratees	Rank-order correlation between ratings and true overall performance level
Feedback on strengths and weaknesses	Scale performance in different areas using a common metric (e.g., ability to measure all dimensions on a common evaluative scale)	Stereotype accuracy, comparability of scores on different dimensions
Determine organizational development needs	Scale average performance level on each dimension on a common metric	Stereotype accuracy of the mean rating on each dimension, comparability across dimensions
Document personnel actions	Provide detailed, objective record of past performance	Amount and apparent objectivity of supporting information

organizational development needs must provide a valid measure of overall strengths and weaknesses in an organization. A system that is used to document personnel decisions or actions must provide a detailed and relatively objective record of an individual's past performance. The best criterion for evaluating such a system may be the amount of specific information about performance that can be recorded, rather than the accuracy of performance evaluations.

These measurement principles, in turn, provide guidance for developing operational criterion measures. For example, if the major goal of an appraisal system is to rank employees correctly from best to worst, the appropriate criterion measure involves a comparison between a ranking based on performance appraisals to a ranking based on a composite of other measures of performance (Chapter 1 discusses alternatives to performance ratings).

Once again, we cannot offer a cookbook for developing operational criteria for all possible performance appraisal systems. We can, however, suggest a process. In our view, the process of developing operational criteria involves determining what should be measured, but even more fundamentally, at what level it should be measured. Consider the case in which a performance appraisal system is used to make promotion decisions. Reliability, validity, and accuracy are not completely relevant in deciding whether the performance appraisal system is fulfilling its function (Sulsky & Balzer, 1988). As Feldman (1986) notes:

> the practical level of accuracy needed is only great enough to support decisions in the same way that the ideal system would if it were available. That is, if it is necessary to divide employees into promotable and non-promotable groups . . . a less than perfect appraisal system may be able to generate this dichotomy with the same level of accuracy as a schematically perfect one. (p. 77)

In other words, a system that did nothing more than allow the making of correct promotion decisions would be a good system, even if the indices used to measure performance were inaccurate or measured the wrong set of constructs. In a similar vein, Schmitt and Schneider (1983) note that if an appraisal system is used primarily to rank-order workers, accuracy in multidimensional evaluations is not really a relevant criterion. Rather, the system must be evaluated in terms of its ability to rank-order workers validly.

SUMMARY

This chapter began with the suggestion that many of the shortcomings of current PA systems can be traced to incompatibility between the system and the goals being pursued by raters, ratees, organizational users of appraisal, customers/clients, and society in general. Rather than trying to change the goals pursued by these stakeholders, we suggest that appraisal systems be designed to fit (to the extent possible) these goals.

The process described here starts with an assessment of stakeholder goals. The technology for assessing these goals is still in its infancy and at this point borrows heavily from techniques developed by decision researchers (e.g., multiattribute utility technologies). Next, potential conflicts among goals must be assessed, and where goals come into conflict, priorities must be set. If a consensus can be reached around a core set of important and compatible goals, it is then possible to design a goal-based performance appraisal system.

Appraisal system design involves assessments of the possible conflicts between performance appraisal system features and key stakeholder goals. For example, if the principal purpose of appraisal is validly to rank-order employees, it makes little sense to evaluate job performance in terms of improvements over past performance (the person who improves the most is not likely also to be the person who is performing the best).

Goals not only provide a basis for designing appraisal systems, they also provide a basis for evaluating those systems. In the past, performance appraisal systems have been evaluated in terms of context-free criteria such as leniency, halo, or accuracy. The systems described here will be evaluated in terms of their contribution to accomplishing important goals. If a performance appraisal system yields inflated ratings that are plagued with halo and hopelessly inaccurate, but it also motivates employees, guides their future development, provides useful feedback, and so forth, that system should be termed a success, not a failure.

Directions for Research
and Practice

In this chapter we will identify what we regard as promising directions for future research and practice in performance appraisal (PA). In our previous book (Murphy & Cleveland, 1991) we treated research and practice as separate topics, devoting a chapter to each. Here, we focus on the integration between research and practice (Dunnette, 1990; Murphy & Saal, 1990). In many areas, behavioral science research forms the basis for practice, and practical applications provide the testing ground for research-based innovations. This is certainly the case for performance appraisal; this chapter discusses 53 specific questions and suggestions for future research and practice in performance appraisal.

This chapter is organized in terms of the four-component model of appraisal presented in Chapter 1 and articulated in Chapters 2 through 14.

First, we discuss directions for research and practice as they relate to contextual influences on appraisal. Second, we suggest a number of ideas for future research and practice in relation to evaluative judgments of job performance. Third, we discuss the types of research and practice likely to advance our understanding of as well as the quality of performance ratings. Finally, we suggest directions for enhancing the validity, accuracy, and usefulness of a performance appraisal system.

CONTEXT

The effects of context variables on appraisal processes and outcomes have been the object of speculation but have not been empirically examined in the detail that these effects warrant. We believe that context is the key to understanding appraisal in organizations, and believe that several specific questions can be posed that will advance our understanding of this critical variable. Contextual variables also provide a promising avenue for improving the practice of appraisal in organizations.

Levels of Context

The first set of issues that require attention revolves around defining the various levels of context that may affect appraisal. *Context* refers to a complex set of variables that exist in the immediate and distal environment; we need to know more about the way in which people respond to different levels of context.

1. How many levels of context do people respond to? Are there some individuals who are sensitive to the immediate context only and others who focus on more distal levels? Do some individuals attend to many levels of context simultaneously?

2. Distal context variables, by definition, do not affect behavior directly. What are the intervening variables between distal context and rater and ratee behavior? What comes between distal factors such as the national economy or the current legal climate and rater/ratee behavior?

The Technological Context

Changes in the technology of work are likely to have a significant impact on performance appraisal. In particular, computer-based technologies often allow employees to work with minimal supervision, perhaps even working at home and communicating with the office via modem. In other cases, supervision is still required, but supervisors may be less familiar with the technology than are the individuals they are asked to evaluate. Three questions could be posed regarding the effects of technological changes on appraisal processes and outcomes:

3. Does advanced technology undermine the role of the supervisor in performance appraisal? This is particularly likely to happen if the technology is one that the employees understand, but the supervisor does not. In this case the supervisor might lose "expert power" and may not be perceived as a competent judge of the subordinates' performance. This may also occur if the new technology allows or requires the employee to work with little or no direct supervision.

4. How do technologies that allow the automatic monitoring of employee behavior affect appraisals? For example, it is possible to collect a minute-by-minute analysis of the work of a person who works at a computer terminal. How does this type of record influence the appraisal process? One possibility is that supervisors will feel compelled to bring their evaluations in line with the objective counts, even if they know that the workers who spend the most time at their desks may not be the best performers.

5. Is it possible to develop training programs to increase supervisors' understanding of and ability to evaluate performance in technologically complex jobs? This should be an integral part of the organization's program to update workers (Kozlowski & Farr, 1988). That is, supervisors will need to keep up to date in their own jobs and also in the jobs of the individuals they supervise.

The Changing Workforce and Organizational Context

6. Demographic changes in the workforce may substantially affect the dynamics of performance appraisal. In the near term, raters are likely to be white males, whereas ratees are increasingly likely to be members of some other demographic group. In the long term, more members of currently underrepresented groups are likely to serve as raters. The increasing diversity of the pool of raters and ratees poses a number of research questions (e.g., how demographic differences might affect perceptions of fairness and

accuracy in appraisal), as well as several opportunities and demands for practical applications (e.g., diversity awareness training).

7. As organizations move toward more decentralized and flatter structures, how should performance appraisal systems change? We see this as part of a broader question of how human resource systems should change as organizations evolve. For example, changes in the structure of organizations (e.g., fewer levels of management, more use of semi-autonomous teams) also change the career paths, the ratio of supervisors to subordinates, the likelihood that peer input will be considered in appraisal, and more. There is little theory, research, or systematic accumulation of practical experience at this point to guide the development of appraisal and other human resource systems as organizational forms evolve.

Context Effects

The next set of issues to be examined concerns the effects of several specific context factors on appraisal processes and outcomes. In particular, the appraisal literature has mentioned two distal variables that are thought to be highly relevant to appraisal: (a) the perceived performance of the organization, and (b) the culture and values of the organization.

8. How does the performance of the organization affect performance appraisal? Do raters and ratees behave differently if they think the organization is doing well or poorly? What defines organizational success or failure in their eyes? If they believe that the organization is doing poorly, do they focus on different goals than if they think it is doing well?

9. How do organizational cultures and values affect the definition of job performance? How do they affect the perceived difference between good and poor performance and perceptions of the causes of good or poor performance?

10. Can we determine ways of modifying the climate of the organization to: (a) ensure uniform rater goals and (b) ensure that raters' goals are consistent with those of the organization? It may be useful to design socialization programs to develop rater goals that are consistent with those of the organization.

Measuring the Context

We have two suggestions for developing methods of measuring key contextual variables:

11. Develop measures for assessing distal context variables (e.g., sociopolitical or technological context) that are likely to affect appraisal. It is useful here to note that distal variables, by definition, do not affect behavior directly. Rather, rater and ratee *perceptions* regarding these variables are likely to be the important determinant of rating behavior. One implication is that self-report measures might be appropriate for measuring perceptions of these distal variables and their effects.

12. Develop measures for assessing proximal context variables (e.g., timing and purpose of appraisal) that are likely to affect appraisal. There may be more latitude in measuring proximal than distal context factors. Self-reports will still be useful, but a variety of objective measures may also be available for assessing these factors. For example, one set of context factors deals with the administration of appraisals (e.g., annual or more often? supervisor only or multiple sources?); it may be possible to classify these facets of context objectively.

Purpose of Rating

One contextual variable that has been examined in depth is the effect of the purpose of appraisal on appraisal outcomes. This research is useful but is limited in two important ways. First, it has focused on only a small number of purposes that are explicitly defined by the organization. Second, it has generally considered the effects of only one purpose at a time. Appraisals in organizations often serve a number of purposes, some of which are explicitly defined by the organization and others that are implicitly defined by the rater. Furthermore, some purposes are incompatible with others. There are several opportunities for research and application in this key area:

13. In the minds of the major users of appraisal (e.g., raters, ratees), what are the purposes of performance appraisal? Is there consensus regarding these purposes or is there wide variation in the implicit purposes that different raters and ratees believe exist?

14. If raters differ in their perceptions of the purpose of rating, will systematic differences in ratings emerge? The research on the effects of purpose frequently shows that raters are more lenient or severe, depending on the perceived purpose of appraisal. However, this research has been

restricted to a consideration of the effects of a single, explicit purpose (typically contrasting appraisal for research purposes with appraisal that is linked to administrative decisions) and has not considered implicit purposes. It is possible that much of what we dismiss as "rater error" is in fact the result of differences in the perceived purposes of appraisal.

15. It is important to determine the maximum number of purposes that can be adequately served by a single performance appraisal system. This figure will depend in part on the specific set of purposes that are being served. If several purposes are compatible or conceptually related, the system might be effective in serving a relatively large number of purposes. If different purposes require very different types of information, the system is likely to adequately serve a smaller number of purposes.

16. It is equally important to determine which purposes are mutually incompatible. We noted in Chapter 4 that uses of appraisal that concentrate on between-person differences (e.g., using PA to determine promotions) may be incompatible with uses that concentrate on within-person differences (e.g., using PA to give feedback regarding strengths and weaknesses). In Chapter 14 we discussed general principles for determining whether goals of appraisal are likely to come into conflict. Too little is known, however, about the potential conflicts among uses of appraisal. For example, rating a person's promotability may or may not interfere with giving valid feedback about strengths and weaknesses.

Rater and Ratee Reactions

Finally, raters' and ratees' reactions to the performance appraisal system are critical contextual determinants of appraisal processes and outcomes. To help guarantee a favorable or constructive reaction to appraisal practices, two avenues might be pursued:

17. Determine what appraisal practices are either accepted as legitimate or rejected by major constituencies in the organization. Practices that are not accepted as legitimate are unlikely to work well, no matter how sophisticated the technology or theory involved.

18. Develop training programs or strategies for communicating the organization's rationale for following appraisal practices that are not viewed favorably by raters or ratees. The rationale here is that organizations will

not want to retain policies that do little more than anger employees. There is thus likely to be a well-defined rationale for adopting and retaining appraisal practices that are not received well. This rationale is not always communicated well to the users of the appraisal system.

JUDGMENT

Papers by Feldman (1981), Landy and Farr (1980), and DeNisi et al. (1984) stimulated a significant body of research dealing with cognitive processes involved in evaluative judgments about job performance. This cognitive research is useful and contributes to our overall understanding of appraisal, but we should not ignore aspects of judgment that fall outside of the traditional realm of cognitive psychologists. We believe that significant progress could be made by exploring issues such as the nature and communication of performance standards, the nature of the comparison processes involved in evaluation, the sources of information considered in appraisal, and the way in which raters use descriptive versus evaluative information about their subordinates' performance. The suggested directions listed below include some research questions that are clearly within the cognitive domain and others that have not been considered by cognitively oriented researchers.

Cognitively oriented research has been criticized on the grounds that it provides few solutions to practical problems in organizations (Banks & Murphy, 1985; Ilgen, 1986), although some practical suggestions have been put forth (Feldman, 1986). We believe that the key to increasing the practical relevance of research on judgment and cognition is to broaden the scope of our inquiry. We should continue to pursue questions that emerge when applying theories of encoding, storage, retrieval, and so on, to performance judgments, but should also pursue several lines of research that are somewhat outside of the traditional domain of cognitive psychology. For example, we need to know how supervisors obtain the information they need to make judgments and how we might facilitate the process. We also need to know how raters and ratees define good and poor performance and how to increase the congruence of these definitions. We need to know how to train raters to make good judgments. Finally, we need to know whether and when cognitive research provides information that is useful for understanding appraisal in organizations.

Cognitive Processes

The first set of issues that we believe requires attention concerns cognitive processes in appraisal, and in particular the generalizability of laboratory research to evaluative judgment in organizations.

19. Can theories from cognitive psychology and social cognition be used to make valid predictions about important phenomena in performance appraisal? If so, what are the important boundary conditions? For example, Hartel (1988) used the two-process theory of attention to make a number of specific predictions about behavior rating and behavior recognition in a simulated appraisal task. Her study carefully controlled for many of the potential confounds and involved the careful development of scales and procedures specifically defined to test hypotheses derived from two-process theory. Virtually none of the predictions held up; observed results were virtually the opposite of what would be predicted by the theory. Does this indicate a weakness in the study or a weakness in the theory? We suspect that even more serious problems will be encountered when attempting to apply more modern theories (e.g., parallel distributive processing models of cognitions) whose key constructs are still being defined.

20. When information is obtained for multiple purposes, which cognitive processes are affected by: (a) the purpose of observation and (b) the purpose of rating? The issue that needs to be considered here is one of external validity. We know that purpose of observation and purpose of rating *can* affect ratings, but we don't know if they *do*. That is, there is little basis, at this point, for claiming that the effects of these variables are either strong or trivially weak; we simply do not know how variables of this sort affect judgments in complex, real-world tasks.

21. What aspects of evaluation are totally context-free, partially context-bound, or fully context-bound? In other words, which aspects of evaluation are universal and which are tied to the particular context? We suspect that different processes might be involved in context-free versus context-bound evaluations. For example, attractive people are evaluated more favorably in virtually all contexts than are equally deserving but unattractive people. The cognitive and affective processes that are responsible for attractiveness biases may be quite different from those that allow raters to distinguish successful from unsuccessful behavior in a specific context.

22. Much of the research on cognitive processes in appraisal has examined issues relating to the encoding/categorization process. It would be useful to assess the categories raters actually use when assessing their subordinates. Thus, it might be worthwhile to develop methods for assessing raters' "theories of the job." Raters may differ in their conceptions of what is important on the job and in terms of their conceptions of good and poor performance.

23. It would be very useful to determine the types of memory aids that will be most helpful in increasing appraisal reliability, validity, and accuracy. These might include diaries or other methods of recording observations shortly after they are made.

24. It would also be helpful to develop training programs that aid raters in adopting consistent category systems (and consistent definitions of each category) for classifying what they observe. This recommendation is consistent with recommendations made more than 35 years ago by researchers who were studying the selection interview (Webster, 1982). These researchers noted that interview decisions are often based on stereotypes. Because it is very hard to change basic decision processes, they suggested that interviewers should be trained to develop valid, consistent stereotypes of good, average, and poor performance, and use those.

Acquiring Information

The first set of suggestions deals with the type of information that is available to the rater at the time he or she does appraisals. Two main issues arise. First, we need to know what type of information is or should be obtained directly by the supervisor. Second, when information is obtained from some source other than direct observation, we need to know how to evaluate and effectively use that information.

25. It is important to determine what sorts of information are collected via direct versus indirect observation. What is needed here is an analysis of the "job" of rater. How does the rater collect information about performance? Good descriptive research in this area would contribute to both science and practice.

26. It is clear that input from people other than the direct supervisor could contribute to the quality of appraisals. We need to develop strategies to increase the acceptability of using sources such as peers, subordinates,

or the ratee himself or herself as sources of information in performance appraisal. Organizations are losing a great deal of potentially relevant information by not attending to these sources. What steps can be taken to make the use of these sources more acceptable? One possibility, mentioned earlier, is to identify what each source does well or poorly. One way to do that is to ask what sorts of information are available to different sources. If information that is critical for making important decisions is unavailable to the supervisor, this provides some incentive to use sources other than the direct supervisor in performance appraisal.

Norms and Performance Standards

The standards that define good versus poor performance and the processes by which individual ratees are compared to those standards have received little attention in research on evaluative judgments of performance. This may be an extremely fruitful area for research: The question of developing, communicating, and using performance standards pervades many of the issues that are considered daily by practitioners in organizations. These range from the acceptance of feedback (negative feedback is more likely to be accepted if the standards for evaluating performance are clear) to the minimization of stress on the job (ambiguous standards may be a source of stress).

27. How do raters reconcile inconsistencies between internal and external standards? If their own standards are different from those of the organization, department, or workgroup, how do they reconcile these differences? Under what circumstances do raters use their own versus someone else's standards?

28. Some standards refer to procedures and others refer to results. How do raters deal with inconsistencies between these (e.g., worker follows the correct procedures and fails; worker fails to follow procedures and succeeds)?

29. Will supervisors who have risen through the ranks have more rigid standards or more tolerant standards than those who have not? Attribution theory suggests that raters who have risen through the ranks will have a distorted perception of how well they performed in the job (they will readily recall good performance and will discount poor performance), which may lead to unrealistically high standards.

30. Organizations should develop programs to facilitate the communication of performance norms from: (a) top management to supervisors, (b) peers to supervisors, and (c) supervisors to subordinates. Different methods may be required for each of these. One issue that will need to be addressed here is to define the content of performance norms. Different methods of communicating norms might be best if they represent implicit distributions than if they represent thresholds between ordered categories of performance (e.g., good, average, and poor performer).

31. Organizations should also develop programs to help new managers quickly identify the appropriate reference groups for defining performance standards. New managers may not know who sets the standards; socialization activities for new managers should include explicit attention to standard setting.

External Validity

The last issue to be considered here is one that was mentioned earlier in this chapter, that is, the external validity of research on evaluative judgment of performance. We need to know whether, and under what circumstances, this research will yield generalizable and useful results. Two suggestions for determining whether this research generalizes to the field are:

32. Determine the critical variables that determine the extent to which a laboratory study generalizes to the field. Locke (1986) argues that the obvious differences between the lab and the field are not always the important ones, and that some laboratory studies will generalize better to the field than a study conducted in one organization will generalize to another organization.

33. Some of the more interesting laboratory research on appraisal has examined the ways in which rating scale formats affect judgment processes. Assuming that different psychological processes are evoked by different formats, it is important to determine whether (and under what circumstances) these differences are sufficiently large to have any effect on the outcomes of appraisal. There is good reason to believe that different scale formats do indeed evoke different psychological processes. At present, we know virtually nothing about the size or even the direction of this effect. It is entirely possible that there is a systematic effect but that it is too small to be important in the field.

RATING

The failure to distinguish clearly between judgment and rating represents the most significant barrier to the successful application of much of the recent research on performance appraisal. This distinction is not unique to our model; Banks & Murphy (1985) make a similar distinction between the rater's capacity to evaluate employees and his or her willingness to record accurate ratings (see also Mohrman & Lawler, 1983). Nevertheless, we think that the single most important contribution our model makes to clarifying research on PA is to distinguish between the rater's own judgment and the ratings he or she records. Previous researchers, to the extent that they considered this distinction at all, have regarded differences between judgments and ratings as a nuisance variable and a source of error variance. We disagree, and believe that potential discrepancies between judgment and ratings represent a unique opportunity to study a wide variety of psychological processes in organizations. We believe that comparisons between judgments and ratings may shed light on issues ranging from the level of trust in the appraisal system to the importance of good interpersonal relations between supervisors and subordinates.

Rater Goals

Our analysis of rating behavior focuses on the goal-directed behavior of the supervisor and treats performance rating as a communication process rather than as a measurement process. From this perspective, our task as psychologists is to decipher the message that raters are trying to send, and to understand the individual and contextual forces that shape that message. The first set of issues to be considered here are those dealing with the nature of rater goals and the integration of multiple goals.

34. There is a critical need to determine the best way (and the optimum frequency) to assess rater goals. Here, self-reports may be somewhat useful, but their validity will be limited by the extent to which raters are able and willing to state their goals. We may be able to use characteristics of the ratings themselves to infer goals. For example, a rater who inflates all of his or her ratings is probably attempting to use ratings to either: (a) motivate employees or (b) avoid negative ratee reactions. Another possibility is to compare ratings to the feedback the ratee receives. If there are discrepancies

between ratings given to the organization and the feedback given to employees, this may give some insight into the rater's goals. If feedback is given in written form, these discrepancies may be easy to assess. If not, ratee's self-reports will be informative but not definitive; discrepancies could result from differences between what the rater tells the ratee and what the rater tells the organization or they could reflect distortions and misunderstandings on the part of the ratee.

35. Are raters aware of the goals they are pursuing in appraisal? If not, would they embrace these goals if they could be made aware of them? Although we regard performance rating as an instance of goal-directed behavior, it is not necessary to assume that raters are fully aware of any or all of the goals they are pursuing when filling out rating scales and other appraisal forms. For example, the rater who has experienced a dramatic decline in the quality of interpersonal relations in the workgroup as the result of giving unfavorable ratings might adopt a goal of avoiding these problems in the future, without ever being fully conscious of the goal itself.

Goals and Ratee Performance Level

A second set of issues emerges when the rater's goals are considered in the light of the ratee's true performance level. The same rater may be pursuing very different goals for good performers (e.g., using appraisal as a developmental tool) than for poor performers (e.g., using appraisal to improve performance in the present job). Three questions should be considered:

36. If the ratee's performance is truly good, what will the rater attempt to communicate to the organization? If the ratee's performance is truly bad, what will the rater attempt to communicate to the organization? If the ratee's performance is neither good nor bad, what will the rater attempt to communicate to the organization?

37. Raters who treat all employees the same are probably conforming to the personnel handbook but are probably not using performance appraisal as an effective management tool. Raters should develop different goals and strategies in rating good, average, and poor performers. Training programs to help raters tailor their use of appraisal to the needs of the individual subordinate might be a worthwhile investment.

Rating Inflation

It is well known that ratings are skewed in a positive direction, and that many ratees receive higher ratings than they deserve. Traditionally, this phenomenon has been treated as just another rater error, and attempts to reduce this problem have focused on developing scales or rater training programs that would combat inflation. It is probably more useful to examine rating inflation from a motivational standpoint. In most rating contexts, strong incentives exist to inflate ratings, and few incentives exist to report accurate ratings. There are several promising areas for research and application in the area of rating inflation.

38. Earlier, we noted that the decision to turn in ratings that are either inflated or that more accurately reflect performance levels is a function of the costs and benefits (to the rater) of inflating ratings. We need to identify the outcomes that are valued (positively or negatively) by raters and assess the value and perceived probability attached to each outcome. Some outcomes are relevant to all raters, whereas others are important to some raters and not to others. Some outcomes are viewed as highly likely (e.g., giving low ratings is very likely to lead to strained interpersonal relations), whereas others may be viewed as very uncertain. Expectancy theories of motivation suggest that both outcome value and outcome probability must be assessed to understand the motivation to pursue a specific course of action.

39. One outcome that is likely to be highly salient to raters is their own discomfort with giving negative feedback. It would therefore be useful to develop methods of delivering negative feedback that are less stressful for the *rater.* Training represents one approach to the problem, but others might include changes in the nature and structure of performance feedback. For example, negative feedback may be easier to give and receive if there are multiple raters who all agree in their evaluations.

Reducing Inflation

It is not always clear whether rating inflations *should* be reduced. For example, raters might use inflation as a highly effective motivational tool. Both costs and benefits must be carefully considered before attempting to reduce rating inflation. If it is determined that reducing inflation is worthwhile, several steps could be taken to reduce the negative outcomes associated with reduced inflation. Two suggestions for dealing with rating inflation are:

40. Determine the circumstances under which raters *should* be trained to use distortion in ratings as a motivational tool. As noted above, this will entail a careful comparison of costs and benefits of accurate ratings versus higher levels of motivation. This will therefore require research in at least two areas. First, it will be necessary to determine whether and when rating inflation works as a motivational tool. Second, it will be necessary to determine what benefits the organization receives if accurate ratings are given. For example, if it is concluded that rating inflation is a moderately effective motivator, and that the organization would not do anything different with accurate ratings than it now does with inflated ratings, it would *not* be worthwhile to reduce rating inflation.

41. Develop methods to increase raters' and ratees' trust in the appraisal system; high levels of trust in the system are likely to increase the match between judgments and ratings. One way to increase trust in the system is to communicate clearly and honestly to raters and ratees what is done with performance evaluations and what the consequences of high versus low ratings really are. Trust is likely to be higher if the system is developmental in its orientation (e.g., ratings are used to help improve performance) than if it is punitive in orientation (e.g., ratings are used to weed out poor performers).

Ratings as Communication Tools

The next set of suggestions involves determining precisely what the rater is trying to communicate when giving ratings. Four suggestions relevant to this issue are:

42. Develop ways of clearly separating evaluations of present performance from recommendations concerning outcomes (e.g., salary increases, promotions, etc.). One possibility is to develop and articulate policies that make it clear that present performance is not the sole determinant of outcomes such as raises and promotions.

43. Determine the best way to elicit and communicate information about the absolute and relative performance levels of ratees. For some

purposes (e.g., promotion), the organization needs to know who are the best performers. For others (e.g., manpower planning), the organization needs to know how well workers perform their jobs. It is important to determine what the organization needs to know about the ratee's performance. Presumably, some of the potential uses of appraisal are unimportant and some of the information provided in a typical appraisal is of little value to the organization. Appraisals that focus on truly important purposes would be preferable to those that do not.

44. Help make raters aware of the goals they are now pursuing and of the goals the organization is trying to achieve with appraisal. Communication is likely to be clearer if the rater is aware of both his or her goals and the goals of the organization.

45. Train managers to recognize and deal effectively with political factors in performance appraisal. Researchers often note, with apparent disapproval, the political nature of appraisals in organizations (see, for example, Longenecker et al., 1987). The fact that appraisal is partly political is, however, neither good nor bad. What is bad is the fact that some managers are *ineffective* politicians who do not know what they should do to achieve their goals in appraisal. Training all raters to be effective politicians in organizations might be strongly preferable to leaving this critical but maligned managerial skill to chance.

Rater and Ratee Expectations

A related set of questions concerns rater and ratee expectations regarding PA. Suppose, for example, that workers have received inflated ratings in the past. Giving honest ratings now may lead to very negative reactions; workers may come to regard high ratings as an entitlement and may regard low ratings as a breach of the unwritten agreement between raters and ratees. Two questions related to rater and ratee expectations are:

46. How do norms regarding procedural justice in appraisal develop, and how can they be modified? Is it possible to give low ratings without suffering negative consequences if the procedures involved in evaluating performance are accepted by ratees as fair and accurate? How do norms regarding distributive justice in appraisal develop, and how can they be modified? We suspect that ratees will be more concerned with outcomes than with procedures, and that appraisal procedures that are regarded as fair

but that produce results that are regarded as unfair will not be easily accepted by ratees.

47. What leads ratees to expect either inflated ratings or ratings that accurately reflect their level of performance? Are there aspects of the context that either create or discourage ratees' expectations that ratings will be inflated? Should we attempt to change the rater, or should we attempt to change the context?

EVALUATION

The last component of our four-component model represents the complex set of issues that arise when one attempts to evaluate a performance appraisal system. In our judgment, researchers' inability sensibly to evaluate PA systems represents the single greatest barrier to the application of the results of psychological research on performance appraisal. There are two main issues that need to be addressed before performance appraisal systems can be evaluated in any systematic fashion: (a) the choice of criteria for evaluating the system and (b) the operationalization of measures of these criteria.

Choice of Criteria

In choosing criteria for evaluating appraisal systems, several questions need to be addressed:

48. Can a theory of job performance be developed that describes what a valid measure of performance *should* look like? This is a prerequisite for the use of criteria such as adequacy in covering the domain of construct validity in evaluating rating systems. Murphy and Kroeker (1988) suggested one approach to developing such a theory (i.e., using position goals to define performance dimensions), but little progress has been made in mapping the performance domain for most jobs in the workforce. In the absence of such a theory, little can be said about whether the appraisal system is measuring the right dimensions or whether it will produce valid measures of the construct "performance." Most evaluations of construct validity depend exclusively on the multitrait-multimethod approach to assessing convergent and discriminant validity (see, for example, Vance, McCallum, Coovert, & Hedge, 1988), but this may not be enough. If you

cannot specify in advance how measures of different aspects of performance *should* be related, there is no meaningful way to assess construct validity (Murphy & Davidshofer, 1988).

49. Develop methods for measuring the accuracy of ratings in organizations. The most formidable problem here is that although most organizations designate the supervisor as the sole rater, accuracy measurement in organizations will require the use of multiple raters (see Chapter 10). Murphy (1982b) suggested that only a small number of raters (e.g., 3-6) would be necessary to combat halo errors; this same number might also be sufficient for assessing accuracy.

50. Determine the conditions under which so-called rater errors are beneficial versus harmful. For example, we know that halo *facilitates* between-person comparisons (Murphy & Balzer, 1986; Nathan & Tippins, 1990); it is reasonable to assume that halo also interferes with some of the potential uses of rating data (e.g., using ratings to make placement decisions). Similarly, it is likely that leniency sometimes serves a valid purpose (e.g., increasing motivation); in other cases, it might interfere with the organization's ability to make important decisions (e.g., promotion decisions are more difficult if large numbers of ratees receive near-perfect appraisals).

Utility Estimation

The next set of issues to be considered are those related to the credibility and completeness of utility estimates that are computed for appraisal systems. Two problems should be considered: (a) Have all of the relevant criteria been considered? (b) Are the estimates derived from utility equations credible? Two specific suggestions for dealing with these questions are:

51. Determine whether reaction criteria are important, and if so, how these criteria should be integrated with quantitative evaluations of ratings. We believe that these criteria are important, and that they are typically ignored in utility estimates. Utility estimates that focus on short-term results of appraisal systems without considering reactions to the system are likely, in the long run, to be inaccurate. For example, the introduction of an electronic system for recording a ratee's behavior (e.g., number of minutes per day spent at the keyboard) may lead to an immediate rise in the class of behaviors recorded, but may also increase negative reactions to the

appraisal system and the organization. In the long run, these reactions might have a significant negative effect on performance.

52. Determine whether utility estimates provide useful and credible information to organizational decision makers. If not, determine what is missing and whether it can reasonably be obtained. For example, we suspect that many organizations do not regard utility estimates as useful. In some cases this is because procedures that are normally followed by the organization (e.g., accounting procedures) have not been applied to the estimates. In other cases, managers may not accept the data (e.g., validity estimates) that underlie these estimates. The solution to the problem of credibility will be quite different in these two cases.

Balancing the Pain and Gain

Our final suggestion deals with the question of whether the costs of performance appraisal outweigh the gain.

53. Consider doing away with performance appraisal. One way to determine whether this is a good idea is to imagine the organization without appraisal. Although performance appraisal systems are often the target for criticism and complaint, the possibility of doing without appraisal entirely is not always an appealing one. One way to identify the concrete benefits of an appraisal system is to consider what would be different if there were no appraisal system at all (e.g., how would employees get feedback? how would career decisions be made? would this lead to *more* concern about fairness?).

INTEGRATING SCIENCE AND PRACTICE

The relationship between science and practice is often a difficult one, particularly when we attempt to apply research to organizations (Dunnette, 1990; Murphy & Saal, 1990). Performance appraisal is a case in point. There seems to be a significant gap between research and practice in PA (Banks & Murphy, 1985); many published studies seem irrelevant to practice, and many appraisal practices seem to fly in the face of research findings.

Despite the problems noted above, we are optimistic that scientific theory and research can make a worthwhile contribution to performance appraisal practice. We also believe that real-world experiences with performance appraisal help to provide a springboard for guiding research and theory. For example, the goal-oriented approach to performance appraisal described in chapters 8 and 14 (and in Cleveland & Murphy, 1992) grew out of our experiences with the performance appraisal systems used in the U.S. Navy.

This final section considers two questions. First, do laboratory studies of PA (often involving college sophomores doing an appraisal-like task for an hour or so) tell us anything about the complex dynamics of performance appraisal in organizations? We think they can, but that there are real limits to the contributions of this type of study. Second, we pursue the broader question of what it takes to meaningfully integrate science and practice in applying behavioral science in organizations. Once again, we recognize significant barriers but are optimistic that science can inform practice and that practice can inform science in the area of performance appraisal.

Can Laboratory Studies Tell Us Anything About Appraisal in Organizations?

The debate over the usefulness and external validity of appraisal research has usually been framed in terms of comparisons between laboratory and field studies. One inference we draw from this debate is that laboratory studies are thought by many appraisal researchers to have little external validity, and that field studies are thought to have substantial external validity. In other words, if the objective is to understand appraisal in organizations, many researchers feel that research should be conducted in the field, not in the lab.

A book edited by Locke (1986) examined in detail the question of whether lab research in industrial and organizational (I/O) psychology generalizes to the field. It is clear from the material reviewed in Locke's book that the issue of external validity is more complex than the simple lab-versus-field dichotomy. Indeed, several authors argue that the lab-versus-field debate is pointless, and that it only serves to distract us from the more important question of whether our research tells us anything about the phenomena we are trying to understand (Campbell, 1986; Ilgen, 1986). Empirical examinations of lab studies versus field studies strongly support this argument. For example, Locke (1986) compared the outcomes of lab and field studies in 14 separate areas of I/O psychology to determine whether the direction of the effects and the size of the effects were similar or different. In more than 92% of the comparisons made, Locke (1986) concluded that the size and/or the direction of the effects found was either highly similar or virtually identical in lab and field studies. Murphy, Herr et al. (1986) compared the outcomes of laboratory studies of performance appraisal using a method that should minimize internal and external validity (i.e., studies in which hypothetical ratees were described in written vignettes) with the outcomes of studies, usually conducted in organizations, using a method that should have much more fidelity (i.e., studies in which direct observations of ratee behavior served as the basis for appraisals). They found only small differences in the sizes of the effects (mean d values of .42 and .30, respectively) and almost perfect consistency in the direction of the effects.

If the choice of method (i.e., lab vs. field) does not govern external validity, what does? Several researchers suggest that boundary conditions must be set that describe the potential limits to the generalizability of research results (Fromkin & Streufert, 1976; Locke, 1986; Ilgen, 1986). These boundary conditions reflect critical variables that may affect the direction or magnitude of research findings (Fromkin & Streufert, 1976). For example, if we wanted to study the effects of raters' expectations regarding the outcomes of appraisal on rating behavior, it would be important to structure a study in which the type and the importance of the outcomes were similar to those encountered in the field. In this case, a laboratory study in which there were no real rewards or punishments for giving high versus low ratings would probably not provide generalizable information.

Some researchers have attempted to solve external validity problems through cosmetic changes in their methods. For example, Ilgen (1986) notes that studies involving business students as subjects are incorrectly thought by some to be more generalizable than studies using college sophomores. Bernardin and Villanova (1986) attempted to apply a more systematic approach to outlining the variables that characterize appraisal in organizations and were able to identify 15 variables that described the modal setting for collecting appraisals in organizations. These variables are listed in Table 15.1. Some of these characteristics would be relatively easy to capture in a lab or field experiment (e.g., Items 1, 7, 10, & 14), whereas others would be very difficult to capture in a study and would be present only in real rating situations (e.g., Item 5). Bernardin and Villanova (1986) suggest that external validity is most likely to be high when most or all of the characteristics listed in Table 15.1 are present in a study, and that studies that do not include these characteristics are less likely to generalize.

TABLE 15.1   Characteristics of a Typical Performance Appraisal

---

1. More than six ratees
2. Ratees see the ratings
3. The rater's supervisor sees the ratings
4. Ratees are aware of the evaluations their peers receive
5. Ratings are done on an annual basis
6. Ratings are used to make important administrative decisions
7. Raters do not have adequate time to appraise ratees
8. The performance of the ratees affects the evaluation the rater receives
9. Raters have experience performing major components of the ratees' jobs
10. Countable results are unavailable
11. Raters feel that they are above average in the accuracy of their ratings
12. Raters dislike giving appraisals
13. Supervisors do not use formal appraisals to determine the feedback they give to ratees
14. Raters evaluate ratee traits
15. Ratings, rather than rankings, are done

SOURCE: From H. J. Bernardin & P. Villanova, "Performance Appraisal," in E. Locke (Ed.), *Generalizing From Laboratory to Field Settings* (Lexington, MA: Lexington Books, 1986).

Although we applaud Bernardin and Villanova's (1986) efforts to identify boundary conditions for external validity, we disagree with some of their conclusions. First, we are not sure whether the question of external validity can be asked in the abstract: The critical boundary conditions for generalizing the results of a study must surely depend in part on the phenomenon being studied. Thus, a single list of boundary conditions will probably set conditions that are irrelevant in some studies and omit conditions that are critical in others. Second, the list in Table 15.1 is descriptive but not evaluative. We could probably add many other modal features to this list. For example, most ratings are done by white males. Is this a critical characteristic? The answer probably depends on the purpose of the study: It may be necessary to consider such characteristics when researching certain questions (e.g., effects of rater and ratee race).

The key to specifying boundary conditions for establishing external validity is to clearly understand (a) the phenomenon being studied, (b) the context in which it will be studied, and (c) the context in which the results will be applied. The key variable, in our opinion, is the investigator's (and the field's) understanding of the phenomenon being studied. Boundary conditions are essentially moderator variables; it is hard to see how we can correctly identify moderators if the effects of the variables we are studying are not well understood. One implication is that it may not always be possible to identify nonarbitrary boundary conditions. For example, if you don't know what processes are involved in relating rating scale formats to rating behavior, it is hard to see how you can identify variables that will moderate those processes.

I/O psychologists, by virtue of their training, should have some general knowledge of both the context of research and the context in which that research is applied. That is, most Ph.D.s in psychology will receive extensive training in research methods, which hopefully gives them some insight into the context of their own research. These same individuals also are likely to engage in a number of activities that are designed in part to increase their understanding of the organizational context. These include internships, consulting projects, and field research projects. One way to translate this general knowledge into specific knowledge about the similarities and differences between the research context and the organizational context may be to engage in role-playing. Bernardin and Villanova's (1986) list of modal characteristics is useful for describing what typically happens in appraisal. You could go beyond this descriptive level by asking what psychological processes are likely to be triggered by each of these characteristics. Putting yourself into the role of a manager in this modal situation may help highlight the psychological effects of the 15 variables in Table 15.1.

A second application of role-playing techniques is to put yourself in the role of a subject in your own study. Are the psychological processes evoked in your study comparable to those that are likely to be found in the organizational context? The answer to this question is clearly a matter of more than the cosmetic similarity of the two contexts. For example, laboratory research in performance appraisal tends to follow one of two strategies: (a) having the subjects play the role of managers, doing a task that is similar to that done by managers, or (b) having the subjects do a familiar task that is in some way comparable to a task done by managers. We would argue that either strategy could yield generalizable results, and that the choice of a strategy should depend primarily on the researcher's comparison between the psychological processes that are likely to occur in the research context and those that are likely to occur in the organization.

Many reviews have expressed doubt about the generalizability of psychological research (particularly laboratory research) on performance appraisal (e.g., Latham, 1986). Like Locke (1986), we are more optimistic.

In the final analysis, the generalizability of different types of research is an empirical issue; analyses such as those presented by Locke (1986) suggest that generalizability is more often the rule than the exception.

Can We Integrate Science and Practice in Organizations?

The successful application of psychological research in organizations depends on a careful (or fortuitous) match between the characteristics of psychologists and the characteristics of the settings in which they do and apply research. Three essential prerequisites can be identified. First, psychologists (and students of psychology) must have values that are compatible with the dual roles of scientist and practitioner. Second, they must have the skills to do and to apply scientific research. Third, and perhaps most important, the settings in which they work must allow them opportunity to do relevant research and/or to apply the results of research.

Values. The role of applied psychologist requires the integration of two distinct value systems, one that emphasizes precision and scientific caution and another that emphasizes action and the solution of practical problems (Spence, 1987). This integration is especially difficult for clinical and other health-service areas of psychology, because the humanistic value system that often characterizes practice is fundamentally different from the scientific value system that usually characterizes research (Kimble, 1984). This integration, however, is probably difficult in *any* applied area of psychology. As Spence (1987) notes, few psychologists have the inclination or the flexibility to be comfortable in both scientist and practitioner roles.

It is easier to describe value systems that would *prevent* one from effectively integrating the roles of scientist and practitioner than to describe the value system that would allow this integration. First, there is the belief, sometimes expressed by psychologists in nonapplied fields, that applied psychology is not real psychology. There is some merit to this point of view; virtually all applications of psychology involve activities, interventions, and so on, that are not solely psychological in nature. For example, a psychologist who designs a performance appraisal system strictly on the basis of the most recent research on cognition and judgment will not be successful. A successful application of psychology in this instance will require the psychologist to be aware of and to take into account organizational realities; it is unlikely that the system that is best for use in the real world will be the same as the system that is best for scientific research.

Value systems that are sometimes associated with practice can also prevent the successful integration of science and practice. In particular, the belief that the *process* of doing research is irrelevant to one's activities as a practitioner appears to be widespread and will clearly hinder the integration of science and practice. One's beliefs about the fundamental causes of behavior might also have direct implications for the value that is attached to research. The belief that the causes of behavior are completely idiosyncratic, and that they can be understood only from the subjective perspective of the actor, will make it impossible for one to do psychological research or to use the results of other peoples' research. Being an effective applied psychologist requires believing that research is possible and that research can help solve practical problems.

A related value system is common among managers, and to a lesser extent, among practitioners. Personal experience is often viewed as a necessary and sufficient prerequisite for solving practical problems. This value system has two components: (a) that knowledge, results, and so forth, from other settings do not apply in your setting and (b) people learn to solve problems simply by being repeatedly exposed to them. Both components will lead you to distrust research as a process for addressing real-world problems and will greatly hinder the integration of science and practice.

Skills. The second requirement for the effective integration of science and practice is that psychologists have the skills necessary to perform successfully in both roles. Research skills would include skills in (a) problem definition, (b) operationalization, (c) design of experiments and studies, (d) data collection, and (e) data analysis and interpretation. Most graduate students in psychology receive some training in all five areas, although the amount of coursework involved and the centrality of these skills to the student's training vary considerably across different areas of psychology. Even in graduate programs that offer a professional degree rather than a Ph.D. (e.g., programs that offer a Psy.D.), students are likely to receive some exposure to these topics. It is thus safe to assume that most psychologists will have *some* skills as researchers, although many may lose seldom-used skills over time.

The set of skills that is needed to apply psychology will depend greatly on the context in which the psychologist works. The skills needed to work effectively in a large organization may be different from those needed to function in a small one. An I/O psychologist working as an external consultant to a large organization may need different skills than one who is working as an internal consultant in the same organization. Because of the diversity of skills required in different settings, we will focus on one type of psychologist and on one setting, and will discuss skills required of psychologists employed either as members of an organization's human resources department or as an external consultant to that department.

Howard (1984) describes the role of the psychologist in industry and notes that several skills that are not taught in graduate school are highly relevant to success in organizations. First, psychologists must "sell their services," or convince other organizational members or units that their services will be useful in solving practical problems. As psychologists in organizations quickly learn, there is usually little spontaneous demand for their services nor is there clear recognition of the types of problems psychologists might be able to solve. Second, psychologists in organizations usually function as managers rather than as autonomous professionals. They must therefore be skilled in supervising others, delegating authority and tasks, planning, and other typical managerial functions. Third, they must be able to communicate the results and implications of their work to a nonprofessional audience and must be able to translate jargon into understandable prose. Fourth, and perhaps most important, they must understand the context. That is, they must learn or know how the organization functions and why, and must understand the goals, the culture, and the climate of the organization. Understanding the context is essential to recognizing and avoiding constraints on one's ability to address problems effectively in the organization.

Skills in problem definition and diagnosis are especially critical for external consultants. It is common for consultants to find that the *real* problem is substantially different from the problem that is presented to them when they are contacted by the organization. For example, what managers describe as a problem with their PA scales may in fact reflect problems with rater motivation or with communication between different levels of the organization. External consultants are less likely to know, in any detail, the context of the organization (although they may know the contexts of organizations in general) and thus cannot draw upon their knowledge of the particular situation to diagnose organizational problems.

Opportunities. No matter what your values or skills, you cannot effectively integrate science and practice if the setting in which you work does not allow this. For example, many psychologists working in organizations have few, if any, opportunities to do research and must devote all of their time to solving practical problems. Similarly, a clinician in private practice may not have access to the data needed to test his or her hypotheses. Many academics have limited opportunities to apply their knowledge of psychology (or are discouraged from devoting time and energy to application).

Although opportunities to do both research and practice may be rare, we should not overemphasize the limitations this places on one's ability to integrate science and practice. Psychologists working in an organization may not have the opportunity to do research, but there is nothing to prevent them from basing their practice as a psychologist on others' research findings. Similarly, some academics and employees of research units may have few opportunities actually to practice psychology in organizations. This does not prevent them, however, from doing research on problems that are relevant to the practice of I/O psychology. Although doing both research and practice is desirable, it is not essential for the effective integration of science and practice. Thus, limitations on one's ability to do research or to practice are barriers to their integration, but these barriers are not insurmountable. Recognition of the constraints that are often placed on a psychologist's ability to do research *and* apply this research in organizations may help us to develop more realistic expectations about applying psychological research in organizations and may also point toward recommendations for minimizing those constraints.

Appendix

![shaded bar]

Rating Scale Formats

If the number of studies devoted to various topics in performance appraisal (PA) since 1950 were counted, one would probably conclude that the format of the rating scale was one of the most important issues in appraisal. Although there is still some interest in the psychological processes that are engaged by different formats (Murphy & Constans, 1987, 1988), current PA research pays little attention to the question of which format is best. This is a direct result of Landy and Farr's (1980) review, in which they concluded that formats have only a minimal effect on the quality of ratings and that no one format is consistently better than the others. Their call for a moratorium on rating scale format research was heeded by most researchers; as a result, the topic that accounted for the majority of studies from 1950 to 1980 now receives little attention. Nevertheless, it is useful to examine some of the features of widely used scale formats.

In this Appendix we discuss several scale formats, including graphic scales, Behaviorally Anchored Rating Scales (BARS), Mixed Standard Scales (MSS), and Behavior Observation Scales (BOS), as well as methods of defining performance criteria (e.g., Performance Distribution Assessment, Management by Objectives, and employee comparison methods). We will not go into the question of which format or method is best overall but we will comment on factors that might lead a person to adopt one format rather than another. In addition, we will briefly discuss several methods for comparing or ranking employees. Although these are not rating scales per se, they are frequently included in performance appraisals and form the basis for some personnel decisions.

GRAPHIC RATING SCALES

The simplest scale format asks the rater to record his or her judgment about some specific aspect of the ratee's performance on a scale that can be used to obtain numeric values that correspond with the rater's evaluation of the ratee. Several examples of a graphic scale that might be used to record ratings of a performance dimension are presented in Figure A.1.

This type of scale format provides little structure for the rater in recording his or her judgment. Graphic scales can range from those like our Example 1, which contains no definitions of what is meant by *very poor, very good,* or *intermediate* levels of performance, to those that define each level in terms of some label (e.g., our Example 3), or even in terms of a brief description of what is meant by each level of performance.

The principal advantage of this scale type is simplicity. The disadvantage of this format, which led to efforts to develop alternative formats, is the lack of clarity and definition. First, the scale does not define what is meant by *Time Management.* Different supervisors might include very different behaviors under this general heading. Second, the scale does not define what is meant by such categories as *Poor* or *Average.* Supervisors might apply very different standards in evaluating the same behaviors. Behaviorally Anchored Rating Scales and Mixed Standard Scales attempt to solve these problems by defining performance dimensions and performance levels in behavioral terms.

BEHAVIORALLY ANCHORED RATING SCALES

The development and use of Behaviorally Anchored Rating Scales (BARS) accounted for much of the research on performance appraisal in the late 1960s and the 1970s. These scales use behavioral examples of different levels of performance to define both the dimension being rated and the performance levels on the scale in clear, behavioral terms. The process of scale development can be long and complex but it will usually result in scales that are clearly defined and well accepted

1.

✓
Very				Very
Poor				Good

2.

1	2	3	4	5
Very				Very
Poor				Good

3.

1	2	3	4	5
Very	Poor	Average	Good	Very
Poor				Good

Figure A.1. Time Management

by both raters and ratees. An example of a BARS used by Murphy and Constans (1987) in one of their studies of teacher rating is presented in Figure A.2.

Much of the rating format research of the 1970s seemed to reflect the assumption that BARS were more objective than graphic scales and that defining performance in behavioral terms would result in more accurate ratings. This assumption was not supported in subsequent research, which has led many researchers and practitioners to question the utility of BARS. This question is especially relevant because the process of developing BARS can be time-consuming and expensive. BARS, however, appear to have one advantage that was not fully anticipated by early BARS researchers—they are accepted by the users. The reason for this is that most BARS development procedures incorporate feedback from large numbers of raters (and sometimes ratees) in the process of constructing scales. As a result, many of the raters and ratees are likely to feel that they have some personal investment in the scales. Even those raters and ratees who do not participate in scale development may view the scales favorably because of their heavy reliance on their colleagues' feedback.

MIXED STANDARD SCALES

Mixed Standard Scales (MSS) also incorporate behavioral examples, but they employ a different response format from that used in BARS. An example of a MSS will help illustrate the similarities and differences. A MSS designed to measure two performance dimensions (Response to Questions and Speaking Style), again taken from Murphy and Constans's (1987) research, is shown in Figure A.3. Here, Items 1, 4, and 5 refer to behaviors that represent "Response to Questions." Items 2, 3, and 6 refer to behaviors that represent "Speaking Style."

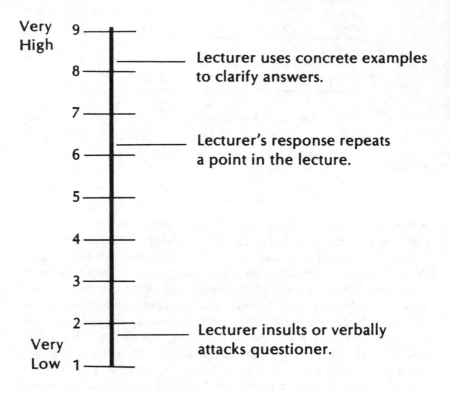

Figure A.2. Response to Questions

By carefully examining the examples, it can be seen that for each dimension there is one item describing good performance, one item describing average performance, and one item describing poor performance. The rater responds to a MSS by noting, for each item, whether the ratee's performance is better than, about equal to, or worse than the behavior described in each item. Several algorithms exist for translating these ratings into an overall numeric score for each dimension.

One apparent advantage of MSS is that it may simplify the rater's task. Rather than evaluating each lecturer's performance by using vague, undefined terms (e.g., good), raters have only to compare the ratee with the example. It is important to note, however, that research on MSS does not strongly support this claim. The complexity of the MSS scoring system is the source of one of its greatest disadvantages. Raters typically do not know which items measure which dimensions

1._____Lecturer's response repeats a point in the lecture.
2._____Lecturer stands behind the podium.
3._____Lecturer misses words when reading from notes.
4._____Lecturer insults or verbally attacks questioner.
5._____Lecturer uses concrete examples to clarify answers.
6._____Lecturer varies pitch and tone of voice to emphasize points.

Figure A.3.

(they may not know what dimensions are measured) or how their ratings are translated into numeric scores. As a result, the rater using MSS will find it very difficult to give meaningful feedback. If a subordinate asks why he or she received a low rating on "Speaking Style," the rater may not be able to answer.

BEHAVIOR OBSERVATION SCALES

A final variation on the use of behavioral examples in evaluating performance is the Behavior Observation Scale (BOS). This type of scale uses the same class of items as the MSS but it asks for a different sort of judgment. Rather than asking for evaluations of each ratee, the BOS asks the rater to describe how frequently each behavior occurred over the period covered by appraisal. Proponents of BOS suggest that this method removes much of the subjectivity that is usually present in evaluative judgments. Unfortunately, research into the cognitive processes involved in responding to BOS (Murphy & Constans, 1988; Murphy, Martin, & Garcia, 1982) suggests that the process of judging behavior frequency is every bit as subjective as the process of forming evaluative judgments. In fact, behavior frequency ratings may be *more* subjective than trait ratings or overall judgments; overall evaluations of the ratee's performance appear to serve as a critical cue for estimating behavior frequencies. Thus, the use of BOS probably does not allow the rater to avoid the subjectivity of overall impressions or judgments.

We cited potential advantages for graphic scales, BARS, and even MSS; however, we are not as enthusiastic about BOS. The behavioral orientation of these scales appears on the surface to be a decided advantage, but there are several reasons to believe that raters do not respond to these scales in terms of behaviors. Rather, they use their overall, subjective evaluations to guide their behavior ratings. This type of scale might actually disguise the inherent subjectivity of evaluative judgment by phrasing judgments in an apparently objective behavioral language. Our rather negative evaluation of this type of scale may reflect our biases as much as it reflects shortcomings in BOS. One of the authors of this book (Murphy) has been involved in much of the research questioning BOS, and it is possible that this evaluation of BOS is not shared by other researchers.

PERFORMANCE DISTRIBUTION ASSESSMENT

Performance distribution assessment (PDA) represents a more sophisticated version of the basic approach exemplified by BOS. In PDA, raters must indicate the frequency of different outcomes (e.g., behaviors, results) that indicate specific *levels* of performance on a given dimension. For example, the scale might describe the most effective outcome and the least effective outcome that could reasonably be expected in a particular job function, as well as several intermediate outcomes. The rater is asked to estimate the frequency of each outcome level for each ratee. One of the potential advantages of this format is that it allows the rater to consider the distribution or the variability of performance as well as the average level of performance in forming an evaluation. PDA involves some fairly complex scoring rules and results in measures of the relative effectiveness of performance, the consistency of performance, and the frequency with which especially positive or negative outcomes is observed. (A concise description of PDA is presented in Bernardin & Beatty [1984]. Also, software now exists for PDA scoring.)

Our evaluation of PDA is similar to our evaluation of BOS. Both depend on the rater's ability to indicate accurately the frequency of specific behaviors or outcomes. In our view, cognitive research suggests that raters are simply incapable of performing this task in an objective way. It is very likely that raters infer the frequency of different behaviors or outcomes from their global evaluations of individuals, and that when one asks for data on the frequency of effective or ineffective behaviors, what one actually gets is a restatement of the rater's overall evaluation. Thus we do not believe that assessments obtained using PDA or BOS will be more specific, objective, or behavior-based than assessments obtained with much simpler scales.

MANAGEMENT BY OBJECTIVES

Management by Objectives (MBO) is not a performance appraisal system per se; rather, it represents a method for defining goals, objectives, and priorities. However, MBO includes an appraisal component in the sense that a person working under an MBO system is evaluated in terms of the goals and objectives he or she (together with the supervisor) has previously defined. Thus the MBO process defines objectives for a given period of time and defines the relevant dimensions and criteria for evaluating performance at the end of that period. MBO represents the most common format for evaluating managerial performance.

One danger of MBO is that goals and objectives will be set that are (a) easily quantified, (b) easily achieved, and (c) not really central to the job. This simplifies the process of performance appraisal but also implies that appraisals will be virtually worthless. It is important, however, to note that goals do not always have these characteristics and that MBO *can* work. The effectiveness of MBO depends on the skills of both the supervisor and the subordinate in defining appropriate goals and objectives. For this reason it is somewhat difficult to evaluate MBO as a system. The same MBO program might work very well for some supervisor-subordinate dyads and poorly for others.

EMPLOYEE COMPARISON METHODS

There is a useful distinction between rating and ranking (i.e., employee comparison). *Rating* involves comparing a person to a standard. This standard might be undefined or subjective (e.g., a scale in which the anchors of *good, average,* and *poor* are undefined) or it might be defined in exact behavioral terms. *Ranking* involves comparing a person to another person. We believe that the psychological processes involved in rating versus ranking may be different (Murphy & Constans, 1988). Even if this is true, however, ratings and rankings often lead to similar conclusions about the performance of a group of ratees.

To illustrate ranking procedures, consider the example of a supervisor who evaluates eight subordinates. One possibility is simply to rank-order those eight individuals, from the best performer to the worst. With small numbers of ratees, this should not be difficult. As the supervisor's span of control increases, however, ranking of all subordinates can become tedious and sometimes arbitrary. Although it might be easy to pick out the best and the worst performers out of a group of 30 workers, it can be very difficult to distinguish the 15th best from the 16th, 17th, or 18th. The forced-distribution ranking procedure provides a partial solution to this problem.

A forced-distribution scale requires supervisors to sort subordinates into ordered categories. An example of such a scale is given in Figure A.4. A supervisor using this scale to evaluate eight subordinates would have to decide who his or her two best and two worst performers are; the remaining subordinates will fall in the middle category. This procedure is particularly useful if administrative rewards correspond to the categories. For example, the supervisor who must designate two subordinates out of eight for promotion does not need to rank all eight subordinates. The forced-distribution scale illustrated in Figure A.4 would be sufficient.

Figure A.4. Sort Subordinates Into These Three Categories

The principal distinction between a forced-distribution scale and a scale that requires all subordinates to be ranked is that in a full ranking, the number of categories is equal to the number of persons being evaluated. In a forced-distribution scale, the number of categories is less than the number of persons. The choice between these two methods depends in part on the specificity of the information required. If there are different outcomes for each individual (e.g., the sixth best performer will get a larger raise than the seventh best), full ranking is worthwhile. Otherwise, a forced-distribution scale might be easier to use.

There is one more procedure that should be considered, especially if the rater or the organization requires precise information about the rank-order of employees as well as the size of the differences in performance among employees. The pair-comparison method allows the rater to scale subordinates with some precision on a ratio-level scale of overall performance. An example of a pair-comparison scale for a supervisor with four subordinates (A, B, C, and D) is shown in Figure A.5.

If the number of comparisons is sufficiently large, scaling procedures can be applied that transform these comparisons into a ratio scale that establishes both the ranking and the extent to which subordinates differ in their performance. The principal drawback of this method is that the number of comparisons expands geometrically as the number of subordinates increases. In the example shown in Figure A.5, six comparisons were needed to evaluate four subordinates. If there

Circle the better performer in each pair:
A or B   B or C
A or C   B or D
A or D   C or D

Figure A.5.

were 10 subordinates, 45 comparisons would be needed. With 20 subordinates, 190 comparisons are needed.

There is a real dilemma for users of a pair-comparison scale. The accuracy of the scaling is a direct function of the number of comparisons that are made. Thus if the number of comparisons is sufficiently small to be easily carried out, the scaling may not be precise. If the number of comparisons is sufficiently large to yield accurate measurement, the pair-comparison procedure may be extremely time-consuming. For this reason, pair-comparison procedures seem to have attracted more attention in the basic research literature than in the field.

References

Abelson, R. P. (1976). Script processing in attitude formation and decision making. In J. Carroll & J. Payne (Eds.), *Cognition and social behavior.* Hillsdale, NJ: Lawrence Erlbaum.

Adams, J. S. (1965). Inequity in social exchange. In L. Berkowitz (Ed.), *Advances in experimental social psychology* (Vol. 2). New York: Academic Press.

Adams, J. S. (1976). The structure and dynamics of behavior in organizational boundary roles. In M. Dunnette (Ed.), *Handbook of industrial and organizational psychology.* Chicago: Rand McNally.

Agervold, M. (1975). Swedish experiments in industrial democracy. In L. Davis & A. Cherns (Eds.), *The quality of working life* (Vol. 2). New York: Free Press.

Aiello, J. R. (1993). Computer-based work monitoring: Electronic surveillance and its effects. *Journal of Applied Social Psychology, 23,* 499-507.

Aiello, J. R., & Svec, C. M. (1993). Computer monitoring of work performance: Extending the social facilitation framework to electronic presence. *Journal of Applied Social Psychology, 23,* 537-548.

Alba, J. W., & Hasher, L. (1983). Is memory schematic? *Psychological Bulletin, 93,* 203-231.

Albemarle Paper Co. v. Moody, 10 FEP 1181 (1975).

442

Allport, G. W. (1937). *Personality: A psychological interpretation.* New York: Holt.

Alluisi, E., & Morgan, B. (1976). Engineering psychology and human performance. *Annual Review of Psychology, 27,* 320-365.

Amaya, T. (1990). *Recent trends in human resource development.* Tokyo: Japan Institute of Labor.

Ancona, D. G., & Caldwell, D. F. (1988). Beyond task maintenance: Defining external functions in groups. *Group and Organizational Studies, 13,* 468-494.

Anderson, N. (1971). Integration theory and attitude change. *Psychological Review, 77,* 153-170.

Anderson, N., & Alexander, G. (1971). Choice test of the averaging hypothesis for information integration. *Cognitive Psychology, 2,* 313-324.

Argyle, M. (1981). The experimental study of the basic features of situations. In D. Magnusson (Ed.), *Toward a psychology of situations: An interactional perspective.* Hillsdale, NJ: Lawrence Erlbaum.

Argyris, C. (1980). *Inner contradictions of rigorous research.* New York: Academic Press.

Arvey, R. D., & Faley, R. (1988). *Fairness in selecting employees.* Menlo Park, CA: Addison-Wesley.

Arvey, R. D., & Jones, A. P. (1985). The use of discipline in organizations: A framework for future research. In L. Cummings & B. Staw (Eds.), *Research in organizational behavior* (Vol. 7). Greenwich, CT: JAI Press.

Ashford, S. J. (1986). Feedback-seeking in individual adaptation: A resource perspective. *Academy of Management Journal, 29,* 465-487.

Ashford, S. J. (1989). Self-assessments in organizations: A literature review and integrative model. In L. L. Cummings & B. M. Staw (Eds.), *Research in organizational behavior* (Vol. 11). Greenwich, CT: JAI Press.

Ashford, S. J., & Cummings, L. L. (1983). Feedback as an individual resource: Personal strategies of creating information. *Organizational Behavior and Human Performance, 32,* 370-398.

Astin, A. (1964). Criterion-centered research. *Educational and Psychological Measurement, 24,* 807-822.

Austin, J. T., & Villanova, P. (1992). The criterion problem: 1917-1992. *Journal of Applied Psychology, 77,* 836-874.

Austin, J. T., Villanova, P., Kane, J. S., & Bernardin, H. J. (1991). Construct validation of performance measures: Issues, development, and evaluation of indicators. In G. Ferris & K. Rowland (Eds.), *Research in personnel and human resource management* (Vol. 9, pp. 159-233). Greenwich, CT: JAI Press.

Austrin, T. (1991). Flexibility, surveillance and hype in New Zealand financial retailing. *Work, Employment and Society, 5,* 201-221.

Backburn, R. (1981). Lower participant power: Toward a conceptual integration. *Academy of Management Review, 6,* 127-131.

Balzer, W. K. (1986). Biases in the recording of performance-related information: The effects of initial impression and centrality of the appraisal task. *Organizational Behavior and Human Decision Processes, 37,* 329-347.

Balzer, W. K., & Sulsky, L. M. (1990). Performance appraisal effectiveness and productivity. In K. Murphy & F. Saal (Eds.), *Psychology in organizations: Integrating science and practice.* Hillsdale, NJ: Lawrence Erlbaum.

Balzer, W. K., & Sulsky, L. M. (1992). Halo and performance appraisal research: A critical examination. *Journal of Applied Psychology, 77,* 975-985.

Bandura, A. (1982). Self-efficacy mechanisms in human agency. *American Psychologist, 37*, 122-147.

Bandura, A. (1986). *Social foundations of thought and action: A social cognitive theory.* Englewood Cliffs, NJ: Prentice Hall.

Bandura, A., & Walters, R. H. (1963). *Social learning and personality theory.* New York: Holt, Rinehart & Winston.

Banks, C. G., & Murphy, K. R. (1985). Toward or narrowing the research-practice gap in performance appraisal. *Personnel Psychology, 38*, 335-345.

Bannister, B. D., & Balkin, D. B. (1990). Performance evaluation and compensation feedback messages: An integrated model. *Journal of Occupational Psychology, 63*, 97-111.

Bargh, J. A. (1984). Automatic and conscious processing of social information. In R. Wyer & T. Srull (Eds.), *Handbook of social cognition* (Vol. 2). Hillsdale, NJ: Lawrence Erlbaum.

Barley, S. R. (1986). Technology as an occasion for structuring: Evidence from observations of CT scanners and the social order of radiology departments. *Administrative Science Quarterly, 31*, 78-108.

Barnes, J. L., & Landy, F. J. (1979). Scaling behavioral anchors. *Applied Psychological Measurement, 3*, 193-200.

Baron, J., & Hershey, J. C. (1988). Outcome bias in decision evaluation. *Journal of Personality and Social Psychology, 54*, 569-579.

Barrett, G. V., & Kernan, M. C. (1987). Performance appraisal and termination: A review of court decisions since *Brito v. Zia* with implications for personnel practices. *Personnel Psychology, 40*, 489-503.

Barrett, R. S., Taylor, E. K., Parker, J. W., & Martens, L. (1958). Rating scale content: I. Scale information and supervisory ratings. *Personnel Psychology, 11*, 333-346.

Bass, A. R., & Turner, J. N. (1973). Ethnic group differences in relationships among criteria of job performance. *Journal of Applied Psychology, 57*, 101-109.

Bassett, G. A. (1979). PAIR records and information systems. In D. Yoder & H. G. Heneman (Eds.), *ASPA handbook of personnel and industrial relations.* Washington, DC: Bureau of National Affairs.

Bazerman, M., Beekum, R., & Schoorman, F. (1982). Performance evaluation in a dynamic context: A laboratory study of the impact of a prior commitment to the ratee. *Journal of Applied Psychology, 67*, 873-876.

Beach, L. R. (1985). Action: Decision-implementation strategies and tactics. In M. Frese & J. Sabini (Eds.), *Goal directed behavior: The concept of action in psychology.* Hillsdale, NJ: Lawrence Erlbaum.

Beach, L. R. (1990). *Image theory: Decision making in personal and organizational contexts.* Chichester, UK: John Wiley.

Beach, L. R., & Mitchell, T. R. (1987). Image theory: Principles, plans and goals in decision making. *Acta Psychologica, 66*, 201-220.

Beatty, R. W., Schneier, C. E., & Beatty, J. R. (1978). An empirical investigation of perceptions of ratee behavior frequency and ratee behavior change using behaviorally anchored rating scales (BARS). *Personnel Psychology, 30*, 647-658.

Becker, B. E., & Cardy, R. L. (1986). Influence of halo error on appraisal effectiveness: A conceptual and empirical reconsideration. *Journal of Applied Psychology, 71*, 662-671.

Bellows, R. M., & Estep, M. F. (1954). *Employment psychology: The interview.* New York: Rinehart.

Belous, R. S. (1987). High technology labor markets: Projections and policy implications. In C. Anderson & A. Kleingartner (Eds.), *Human resource management practices in high technology firms* (pp. 25-46). Lexington, MA: Lexington Books.

Bem, D. J. (1981). Assessing situations by assessing persons. In D. Magnusson (Ed.), *Toward a psychology of situations: An interactional perspective.* Hillsdale, NJ: Lawrence Erlbaum.

Bem, D. J., & Funder, D. C. (1978). Predicting more of the people more of the time: Assessing the personality of situations. *Psychological Review, 85,* 485-501.

Bendig, A. W. (1952a). A statistical report on a revision of the Miami instructor rating sheet. *Journal of Educational Psychology, 43,* 423-429.

Bendig, A. W. (1952b). The use of student rating scales in the evaluation of instructors in introductory psychology. *Journal of Educational Psychology, 43,* 167-175.

Bendig, A. W. (1953). The reliability of self-ratings as a function of the amount of verbal anchoring and the number of categories on the scale. *Journal of Applied Psychology, 37,* 38-41.

Bendig, A. W. (1954a). Reliability and number of rating scale categories. *Journal of Applied Psychology, 38,* 38-40.

Bendig, A. W. (1954b). Reliability of short rating scales and the heterogeneity of the rated stimuli. *Journal of Applied Psychology, 38,* 167-170.

Berger, C. J., & Cummings, L. L. (1979). Organizational structure, attitudes and behaviors. In B. Staw (Ed.), *Research in organizational behavior* (Vol. 1, pp. 169-208). Greenwich, CT: JAI Press.

Berkshire, H., & Highland, R. (1953). Forced-choice performance rating: A methodological study. *Personnel Psychology, 6,* 355-378.

Bernardin, H. J. (1977). Behavioral expectation scales versus summated rating scales: A fairer comparison. *Journal of Applied Psychology, 62,* 422-427.

Bernardin, H. J. (1979). *A study to identify feasible appraisal systems for employees of the U.S. Geological Survey* (Final Technical Report to the U.S. Geological Survey). Washington, DC: Government Printing Office.

Bernardin, H. J., Alvares, K. M., & Cranny, C. J. (1976). A recomparison of behavioral expectation scales to summated scales. *Journal of Applied Psychology, 61,* 564-570.

Bernardin, H. J., & Beatty, R. W. (1984). *Performance appraisal: Assessing human behavior at work.* Boston: Kent.

Bernardin, H. J., & Buckley, M. R. (1981). Strategies in rater training. *Academy of Management Review, 6,* 205-212.

Bernardin, H. J., Cardy, R. L., & Carlyle, J. J. (1982). Cognitive complexity and appraisal effectiveness: Back to the drawing board? *Journal of Applied Psychology, 67,* 151-160.

Bernardin, H. J., Dahmus, S. A., & Redmon, G. (1993). Attitudes of first-line supervisors toward subordinate appraisals. *Human Resource Management Journal, 32,* 315-324.

Bernardin, H. J., & Klatt, L. A. (1985, November). Managerial appraisal systems: Has practice caught up with the state of the art? *Public Personnel Administrator,* pp. 79-86.

Bernardin, H. J., LaShells, M. B., Smith, P. C., & Alvares, K. M. (1976). Behavioral expectation scales: Effects of developmental procedures and formats. *Journal of Applied Psychology, 61,* 75-79.

Bernardin, H. J., Orban, J., & Carlyle, J. (1981). Performance ratings as a function of trust in appraisal and rater individual differences. *Proceedings of the 41st annual meeting of the Academy of Management,* pp. 311-315.

Bernardin, H. J., & Pence, E. C. (1980). Effects of rater error training: Creating new response sets and decreasing accuracy. *Journal of Applied Psychology, 65,* 60-66.

Bernardin, H. J., & Smith, P. C. (1981). A clarification of some issues regarding the development and use of behaviorally anchored rating scales. *Journal of Applied Psychology, 66,* 458-463.

Bernardin, H. J., & Villanova, P. (1986). Performance appraisal. In E. Locke (Ed.), *Generalizing from laboratory to field settings.* Lexington, MA: Lexington Books.

Bernardin, H. J., & Walter, C. S. (1977). Effects of rater training and diary keeping on psychometric error in ratings. *Journal of Applied Psychology, 62,* 64-69.

Bettenhausen, K. L. (1991). Five years of group research: What we have learned and what needs to be addressed. *Journal of Management, 17,* 345-381.

Bialek, H., Zapf, D., & McGuire, W. (1977, June). *Personnel turbulence and time utilization in an infantry division* (HumRRO FR-WD-CA 77-11). Alexandria, VA: Human Resources Research Organization.

Bingham, W. V. (1939). Halo, valid and invalid. *Journal of Applied Psychology, 23,* 221-228.

Bjerke, D. G., Cleveland, J. N., Morrison, R. F., & Wilson, W. C. (1987). *Officer fitness report evaluation study* (Navy Personnel Research and Development Center Report, TR 88-4). San Diego, CA: NPRDC.

Blanz, F., & Ghiselli, E. E. (1972). The mixed standard scale: A new rating system. *Personnel Psychology, 25,* 185-199.

Blau, F. D., & Ferber, M. A. (1985). Women in the labor market: The last 20 years. In L. Larwood, A. H. Stromberg, & B. A. Gutek (Eds.), *Women and work: An annual review* (Vol. 1, pp. 19-49). Beverly Hills, CA: Sage.

Blencoe, A. G. (1984). *An examination of raters' cognitive processes in performance appraisal: A laboratory investigation.* Unpublished doctoral dissertation, University of South Carolina.

Block, J., & Block, J. H. (1981). Studying situational dimensions: A grand perspective and some limited empiricism. In D. Magnusson (Ed.), *Toward a psychology of situations: An interactional perspective.* Hillsdale, NJ: Lawrence Erlbaum.

Blum, M. L., & Naylor, J. C. (1968). *Industrial psychology.* New York: Harper & Row.

Bobko, P., & Colella, A. (1994). Employee reactions to performance standards: A review of related literatures and identification of future research needs. *Personnel Psychology, 47,* 1-30.

Bobko, P., Karren, R., & Kerkar, S. (1987). Systematic research needs for understanding supervisory-based estimates of SDY in utility analysis. *Organizational Behavior and Human Decision Processes, 40,* 69-95.

Boice, R. (1983). Observational skills. *Psychological Bulletin, 90,* 218-244.

Borman, W. C. (1974). The rating of individuals in organizations: An alternative approach. *Organizational Behavior and Human Performance, 12,* 105-124.

Borman, W. C. (1977). Consistency of rating accuracy and rater errors in the judgment of human performance. *Organizational Behavior and Human Performance, 20,* 238-252.

Borman, W. C. (1978). Exploring the upper limits of reliability and validity in job performance ratings. *Journal of Applied Psychology, 63,* 135-144.

Borman, W. C. (1979). Format and training effects on rating accuracy and rater errors. *Journal of Applied Psychology, 64,* 410-421.

Borman, W. C. (1983). Implication of personality theory and research for the rating of work performance in organizations. In F. Landy, S. Zedeck, & J. Cleveland (Eds.), *Performance measurement and theory.* Hillsdale, NJ: Lawrence Erlbaum.

Borman, W. C. (1987). Personal constructs, performance schemata, and "folk theories" of subordinate effectiveness: Exploration in an army officer sample. *Organizational Behavior and Human Decision Processes, 40,* 307-322.

Borman, W. C., & Brush, D. H. (1993). More progress toward a taxonomy of managerial performance requirements. *Human Performance, 6,* 1-21.

Borman, W. C., & Dunnette, M. D. (1975). Behavior-based versus trait-oriented performance ratings: An empirical study. *Journal of Applied Psychology, 60,* 561-565.

Borman, W. C., & Motowidlo, S. J. (1993). Expanding the criterion domain to include elements of contextual performance. In N. Schmitt & W. Borman (Eds.), *Personnel selection in organizations.* San Francisco: Jossey-Bass.

Borman, W. C., & Vallon, W. R. (1974). A review of what can happen when behavioral expectation scales are developed in one setting and used in another. *Journal of Applied Psychology, 59,* 197-201.

Borreson, H. (1967). The effects of instructions and item content on three types of ratings. *Educational and Psychological Measurement, 27,* 855-862.

Boudreau, J. W. (1991). Utility analysis for decisions in human resource management. In M. Dunnette & L. Hough (Eds.), *Handbook of industrial and organizational psychology* (2nd ed.) (Vol. 2, pp. 621-745). Palo Alto, CA: Consulting Psychologists Press.

Boudreau, J. W., & Berger, C. J. (1985). Decision-theoretic utility analysis applied to employee separations and acquisitions. *Journal of Applied Psychology, 70,* 581-612.

Bower, G. (1981). Mood and memory. *American Psychologist, 36,* 129-148.

Bowers, K. S. (1973). Situationism in interaction psychology. Analysis and critique. *Psychological Review, 80,* 307-336.

Brannick, M. T., Prince, A., Salas, E., & Prince, C. (1993, April). *Impact of raters and events on team performance measurement.* Paper presented at the annual convention of the Society for Industrial and Organizational Psychology, San Francisco.

Brannick, M. T., Roach, R. M., & Salas, E. (1991, April). *Understanding team performance: A multi-method study.* Paper presented at the annual convention of the Society for Industrial and Organizational Psychology, St. Louis.

Bretz, R. D., & Milkovich, G. T. (1989). *Performance appraisal in large organizations: Practice and research implications* (Working paper #89-17). Center for Advances in Human Resource Studies, School of Industrial and Labor Relations, Cornell University.

Brewer, M. B. (1979). In-group bias in the minimal intergroup situations: A cognitive-motivational analysis. *Psychological Bulletin, 86,* 307-324.

Brief, A. P., & Motowidlo, S. J. (1986). Prosocial organizational behaviors. *Academy of Management Review, 11,* 710-725.

Brito v. Zia Company (428 F.2d 12001 [10th cir. 1973]).

Broadbent, D. E. (1985). Multiple goals and flexible procedures in the design of work. In M. Frese & J. Sabini (Eds.), *Goal directed behavior: The concept of action in psychology.* Hillsdale, NJ: Lawrence Erlbaum.

Brogden, H. (1949). When testing pays off. *Personnel Psychology, 2,* 171-183.

Brown, J. D. (1986). Evaluations of self and others: Self-enhancement biases in social judgments. *Social Cognition, 4,* 353-376.

Brown, R., & Herrnstein, R. J. (1975). *Psychology.* Boston: Little, Brown.

Brunswick, E. E. (1952). *The conceptual framework of psychology.* Chicago: University of Chicago Press.

Buchanan, B. (1974). Building organizational commitment: The socialization of managers in work organizations. *Administrative Science Quarterly, 19,* 533-546.

Buchholz, R. (1978). An empirical study of contemporary beliefs about work in American Society. *Journal of Applied Psychology, 63,* 219-227.

Burchett, S. R., & DeMeuse, K. P. (1985). Performance appraisal and the law. *Personnel, 62,* 29-37.

Bureau of National Affairs. (1974). Management performance appraisal programs. *Personnel Policies Forum Survey, 104.*

Burger, J. M. (1986). Temporal effects on attributions: Actor and observer differences. *Social Cognition, 4,* 377-387.

Burnaska, R. F., & Hollmann, T. D. (1974). An empirical comparison of the relative effects of rater response biases on three rating scale formats. *Journal of Applied Psychology, 59,* 307-312.

Burrell, G. (1992). Back to the future: Time and organization. In M. Reed & H. Hughes (Eds.), *Rethinking organization: New directions in organization theory and analysis.* London: Sage.

Cafferty, T. P., DeNisi, A. S., & Williams, K. J. (1986). Search and retrieval patterns for performance information: Effects on evaluations of multiple targets. *Journal of Personality and Social Psychology, 71,* 672-678.

Campbell, D. J., & Lee, C. (1988). Self-appraisal in performance evaluation: Development versus education. *Academy of Management Review, 13,* 302-314.

Campbell, D. T., & Stanley, J. C. (1966). *Experimental and quasi-experimental design for research.* Chicago: Rand McNally.

Campbell, J. P. (1982). Some remarks from an outgoing editor [Editorial]. *Journal of Applied Psychology, 67,* 691-700.

Campbell, J. P. (1983). Some possible implications of "modeling" for the conceptualization of measurement. In F. Landy, S. Zedeck, & J. Cleveland (Eds.), *Performance measurement and theory.* Hillsdale, NJ: Lawrence Erlbaum.

Campbell, J. P. (1986). Labs, fields, and straw issues. In E. Locke (Ed.), *Generalizing from laboratory to field settings.* Lexington, MA: Lexington Books.

Campbell, J. P. (1990). An overview of the army selection and classification project (Project A). *Personnel Psychology, 43,* 231-239.

Campbell, J. P., Crooks, L. A., Mahoney, M. H., & Rock, D. A. (1973). *An investigation of sources of bias in the prediction of job performance: A six-year study* (Final Project Report No. PR-73-37). Princeton, NJ: Educational Testing Service.

Campbell, J. P., Dunnette, M., Lawler, E., & Weick, K. (1970). *Managerial behavior, performance and effectiveness.* New York: McGraw-Hill.

Campbell, J. P., Ford, P., Rumsey, M. C., Pulakos, E. D., Borman, W. C., Felker, D. B., deVera, M. V., & Riegelhaupt, B. J. (1990). Development of multiple job performance measures in a representative sample of jobs. *Personnel Psychology, 43,* 277-300.

Campbell, J. P., McCloy, R. A., Oppler, S. H., & Sager, C. E. (1992). A theory of performance. In N. Schmitt & W. Borman (Eds.), *Personnel selection in organizations.* San Francisco: Jossey-Bass.

Cantor, N. (1981). Perception of situations: Situation prototypes and person-situation prototype. In D. Magnusson (Ed.), *Toward a psychology of situations: An interactional perspective.* Hillsdale, NJ: Lawrence Erlbaum.

Cantor, N., & Mischel, W. (1977). Traits as prototypes: Effects on recognition memory. *Journal of Personality and Social Psychology, 35,* 38-48.

Cantor, N., & Mischel, W. (1979). Prototypes in person perception. In L. Berkowitz (Ed.), *Advances in experimental social psychology.* New York: Academic Press.

Cantor, N., Mischel, W., & Schwartz, J. (1982). A prototype analysis of psychological situation. *Cognitive Psychology, 14,* 45-77.

Cardy, R. L., Bernardin, H. J., Abbott, J. G., Senderak, M. P., & Taylor, K. (1987). The effects of individual performance schemata and dimension familiarization on rating accuracy. *Journal of Occupational Psychology, 60,* 197-205.

Cardy, R. L., & Dobbins, G. H. (1986). Affect and appraisal accuracy: Liking as an integral dimension in evaluating performance. *Journal of Applied Psychology, 71,* 672-678.

Cardy, R. L., & Dobbins, G. H. (1994). *Performance appraisal: Alternative perspectives.* Cincinnati, OH: South-Western Publishing.

Cardy, R. L., & Krzystofiak, F. J. (1988, April). *Observation and rating accuracy: WYSI-WYG?* Paper presented at the annual convention of the Society for Industrial/Organizational Psychology, Dallas.

Carroll, S. J., & Schneier, C. E. (1982). *Performance appraisal and review systems: The identification, measurement and development of performance in organizations.* Glenview, IL: Scott, Foresman.

Carson, K. P., Cardy, R. L., & Dobbins, G. H. (1991). Performance appraisal as effective management or deadly management disease: Two initial empirical investigations. *Group and Organizational Studies, 16,* 143-159.

Carson, K. P., Cardy, R. L., & Dobbins, G. H. (1992). *Traditional performance appraisal v. Total Quality management: Avoiding the collision.* Unpublished manuscript, State University of New York, Buffalo.

Cartwright, D., & Zander, A. (1968). *Group dynamics: Research and theory* (3rd ed.). New York: Harper & Row.

Carver, C. S., & Scheier, M. F. (1981). *Attention and self-regulation: A control theory approach to human behavior.* New York: Springer.

Cascio, W. F. (1982). *Costing human resources: The financial input of behavior in organizations.* Boston: Kent.

Cascio, W. F. (1987). *Applied psychology in personnel management* (3rd ed.). Englewood Cliffs, NJ: Prentice Hall.

Cascio, W. F., & Bernardin, H. J. (1980). *An annotated bibliography of court cases relevant to employment decisions* [Mimeo]. Tampa, FL. (Available from University of Colorado, Denver.)

Cascio, W. F., & Bernardin, H. J. (1981). Implications of performance appraisal litigation for personnel decisions. *Personnel Psychology, 34,* 211-226.

Cascio, W. F., & Ramos, R. A. (1986). Development and applications of a new method for assessing job performance in behavioral/economic terms. *Journal of Applied Psychology, 71,* 20-28.

Cascio, W. F., & Silbey, V. (1979). Utility of the assessment center as a selection device. *Journal of Applied Psychology, 64,* 107-118.

Cawley, B. D., & Levy, P. E. (1993, April). *A meta-analysis of participation and satisfaction in the performance appraisal process.* Paper presented at the annual convention of the Society for Industrial and Organizational Psychology, San Francisco.

Chadwick-Jones, J. K., Brown, C., Nicholson, N., & Sheppard, A. (1971). Absence measures: Their reliability and stability in an industrial setting. *Personnel Psychology, 24,* 463-470.

Chadwick-Jones, J. K., Nicholson, N., & Brown, C. (1982). *The social psychology of absenteeism.* New York: Praeger.

Chalykoff, J., & Kochan, T. A. (1989). Computer-aided monitoring: Its influence on employee job satisfaction and turnover. *Personnel Psychology, 42,* 808-834.

Chao, G. T. (1988, April). *Organizational socialization and role design features on job and career outcomes.* Paper presented at the annual conference of the Society for Industrial/Organizational Psychology, Dallas.

Christal, R. E. (1974). *The United States Air Force occupational research project* (AFHRL-TR-73-75). Lackland AFB, TX: USAF, AFHRL, Occupation Research Division.

Clark, C. L., & Primoff, E. J. (1979). Job elements and performance appraisal. *Management: A Magazine for Government Managers, 1,* 3-5.

Clark, M. S., & Isen, A. M. (1982). Toward understanding the relationship between feeling states and social behavior. In A. Hastorf & A. Isen (Eds.), *Cognitive social psychology.* New York: Elsevier.

Cleveland, J. N., Festa, R. M., & Montgomery, L. (1988). Applicant pool composition and job perceptions: Impact on decisions regarding an older applicant. *Journal of Vocational Behavior, 32,* 112-125.

Cleveland, J. N., & Hollmann, G. (1991). Context and discrimination in personnel decisions: Direct and mediated approaches. In J. R. Meindl, R. L. Cardy, & S. Puffer (Eds.), *Advances in information processing in organizations* (Vol. 4, pp. 223-238). Greenwich, CT: JAI Press.

Cleveland, J. N., & Landy, F. J. (1983). The effects of person and job stereotypes on two personnel decisions. *Journal of Applied Psychology, 68,* 609-619.

Cleveland, J. N., Morrison, R., & Bjerke, D. (1986, April). *Rater intentions in appraisal ratings: Malevolent manipulation or functional fudging.* Paper presented at the First Annual Conference of the Society for Industrial and Organizational Psychology, Chicago.

Cleveland, J. N., & Murphy, K. R. (1992). Analyzing performance appraisal as goal-directed behavior. In G. Ferris & K. Rowland (Eds.), *Research in personnel and human resources management* (Vol. 10, pp. 121-185). Greenwich, CT: JAI Press.

Cleveland, J. N., Murphy, K. R., Barnes-Farrell, J. L., & Banks, C. G. (1988). *Analyzing appraisal as goal-directed behavior: An alternative approach to performance appraisal research and practice.* Unpublished manuscript, Department of Psychology, Colorado State University, Ft. Collins.

Cleveland, J. N., Murphy, K. R., & Williams, R. E. (1989). Multiple uses of performance appraisal: Prevalence and correlates. *Journal of Applied Psychology, 74,* 130-135.

Cocheu, T. (1986). Performance appraisal: A case in point. *Personal Journal, 65,* 48-55.

Cohen, C., & Ebbeson, E. B. (1979). Observational goals and schema activation: A theoretical framework for behavior perception. *Journal of Experimental Social Psychology, 15,* 305-329.

Connolly, T., Conlon, E. J., & Deutsch, S. J. (1980). Organizational effectiveness: A multiple constituency approach. *Academy of Management Review, 5,* 211-217.

Constans, J. I. (1987). *Scale and weight bias in behaviorally anchored rating scales.* Unpublished master's thesis, Colorado State University.

Cook, T. D., Campbell, D. T., & Peracchio, L. (1990). Quasi experimentation. In M. Dunnette & L. Hough (Eds.), *Handbook of industrial and organizational psychology* (2nd ed.) (Vol. 1, pp. 492-576). Palo Alto, CA: Consulting Psychologists Press.

Cooper, W. (1981a). Conceptual similarity as a source of illusory halo in job performance ratings. *Journal of Applied Psychology, 66,* 302-307.

Cooper, W. (1981b). Ubiquitous halo. *Psychological Bulletin, 90,* 218-244.

Cornelius, E. T., Hakel, M. D., & Sackett, P. R. (1979). A methodological approach to job classification for performance appraisal purposes. *Personnel Psychology, 2,* 283-297.

Craik, F. M., & Lockhart, R. S. (1972). Levels of processing: A framework for memory research. *Journal of Verbal Learning and Verbal Behavior, 11,* 671-684.

Cronbach, L. J. (1955). Processes affecting scores on "understanding of others" and "assumed similarity." *Psychological Bulletin, 52,* 177-193.

Cronbach, L. J. (1970). *Essentials of psychological testing* (3rd ed.). New York: Harper & Row.

Cronbach, L. J. (1990). *Essentials of psychological testing* (5th Ed). New York: Harper & Row.

Cronbach, L. J., & Gleser, G. C. (1965). *Psychological tests and personnel decisions* (2nd ed.). Urbana: University of Illinois Press.

Cronbach, L. J., Gleser, G. C., Nanda, H., & Rajaratnam, N. (1972). *The dependability of behavioral measurements: Theory of generalizability for scores and profiles.* New York: John Wiley.

Cronbach, L. J., & Snow, R. E. (1977). *Aptitudes and instructional methods: A handbook for research on interactions.* New York: Halstead.

Cronshaw, S. F., & Alexander, R. A. (1985). One answer to the demand for accountability: Selection utility as an investment decision. *Organizational Behavior and Human Decision Processes, 35,* 102-118.

Crowder, R. G. (1976). *Principles of learning and memory.* Hillsdale, NJ: Lawrence Erlbaum.

Crown, D. F. (1992, April). *Maximizing group level performance for nonsummative interdependent tasks: Integrating individual and group goals.* Paper presented at the annual convention of the Society for Industrial and Organizational Psychology, San Francisco.

Cummings, L. L., & Schwab, D. P. (1973). *Performance in organizations: Determinants and appraisal.* Glenview, IL: Scott, Foresman.

Daft, R. L. (1986). *Organizational theory and design.* St. Paul, MN: West.

Daniels, R. L., & Keller, L. R. (1992). Choice-based assessment of utility functions. *Organizational Behavior and Human Decision Processes, 52,* 524-543.

Dansereau, F., Cashman, J., & Graen, G. (1973). Instrumentality theory and equity theory as complementary approaches in predicting the relationship of leadership and turnover among managers. *Organizational Behavior and Human Performance, 10,* 184-200.

Dansereau, F., Jr., Graen, G., & Haga, W. J. (1975). A vertical dyad linkage approach to leadership within formal organizations: A longitudinal investigation of role-making processes. *Organizational Behavior and Human Performance, 13,* 46-78.

Darley, J., & Fazio, R. (1980). Expectancy confirmation processes in the social interaction sequence. *American Psychologist, 35,* 867-881.

Davis, B. L., & Mount, M. K. (1984, March). Design and use of performance appraisal feedback systems. *Personnel Administrator,* pp. 91-107.

Davis, D. D., & Dickinson, T. L. (1987, August). *Organizational and contextual determinants of perceived utility of performance appraisals.* Paper presented at the annual conference of the American Psychological Association, New York.

Davis, J. H. (1992). Some compelling intuitions about group consensus decisions, theoretical and empirical research, and interpersonal aggregation phenomena: Selected examples, 1950-1990. *Organizational Behavior and Human Decision Processes, 52,* 3-38.

Dawes, R. M., & Corrigan, B. (1974). Linear models in decision making. *Psychological Bulletin, 81,* 95-106.

DeCotiis, T., & Petit, A. (1978). The performance appraisal process: A model and some testable propositions. *Academy of Management Review, 3,* 635-646.

DeGregorio, M., & Fisher, C. D. (1988). Providing performance feedback: Reactions to alternate methods. *Journal of Management, 14,* 605-616.

Delbridge, R., & Turnbull, P. (1992). Human resource maximization: The management of labour under just-in-time management systems. In P. Blyton & P. Turnbull (Eds.), *Reassessing human resource management* (pp. 56-73). London: Sage.

Deming, W. E. (1986). *Out of the crisis.* Cambridge: MIT Institute for Advanced Engineering Study.

Demuse, K. P. (1987). A review of the effects of non-verbal cues on the performance appraisal process. *Journal of Occupational Psychology, 60,* 207-226.

DeNisi, A. S., Cafferty, T., & Meglino, B. (1984). A cognitive view of the performance appraisal process: A model and research propositions. *Organizational Behavior and Human Performance, 33,* 360-396.

DeNisi, A. S., Robbins, T., & Cafferty, T. P. (1989). Organization of information used for performance appraisals: Role of diary keeping. *Journal of Applied Psychology, 74,* 124-129.

DeNisi, A. S., & Stevens, G. E. (1981). Profiles of performance evaluations and personnel decisions. *Academy of Management Journal, 24,* 592-602.

DeNisi, A. S., & Williams, K. J. (1988). Cognitive approaches to performance appraisal. In G. Ferris & K. Rowland (Eds.), *Research in personnel and human resource management* (Vol. 6). Greenwich, CT: JAI Press.

Department of the Air Force. (1988). *USAF officer's guide to the officer evaluation system* (AF Pamphlet 36-6). Washington, DC: Department of the Air Force.

DeVries, D. L. (1983, August). *Viewing performance appraisal with a wide angle lens.* Paper presented at the annual conference of the American Psychological Association, Anaheim, CA.

DeVries, D. L., Morrison, A. M., Shullman, S. L., & Gerlach, M. L. (1986). *Performance appraisal on the line.* Greensboro, NC: Center for Creative Leadership.

Dickinson, T. L. (1987). Designs for evaluating the validity and accuracy of performance ratings. *Organizational Behavior and Human Decision Processes, 40,* 1-21.

Dickson, J., & Buchholz, R. (1977). Managerial beliefs about work in Scotland and the U.S.A. *Journal of Management Studies, 12,* 80-101.

Dipboye, R. L. (1985). Some neglected variables in research on discrimination in appraisals. *Academy of Management Review, 10,* 116-127.

Dipboye, R. L., & dePontbriand, R. (1981). Correlates of employee reactions to performance appraisals and appraisal systems. *Journal of Applied Psychology, 66,* 248-251.

Dipboye, R. L., Stramler, C. S., & Fontenelle, G. A. (1984). The effects of the application on recall of information from an interview. *Academy of Management Journal, 27,* 261-275.

Dobbins, G. H., Cardy, R. L., & Platz, S. J. (1988). *The moderating effects of organizational characteristics on the relationships between appraisal characteristics and appraisal satisfaction.* Unpublished manuscript, University of Tennessee.

Dobbins, G. H., Cardy, R. L., & Platz-Vieno, S. J. (1990). A contingency approach to appraisal satisfaction: An initial investigation of the joint effects of organizational variables and appraisal characteristics. *Journal of Management, 16,* 619-632.

Dobbins, G. H., Cardy, R. L., & Truxillo, D. M. (1988). The effects of individual differences in stereotypes of women and purpose of appraisal on sex differences in performance ratings: A laboratory and field study. *Journal of Applied Psychology, 73,* 551-558.

Dobbins, G. H., & Russell, J. M. (1986). The biasing effect of subordinate likeableness on leaders' reactions to poor performers: A laboratory and a field study. *Personnel Psychology, 39,* 759-777.

Dorfman, P. W., Stephan, W. G., & Loveland, J. (1986). Performance appraisal behaviors: Supervisor perceptions and subordinate reactions. *Personnel Psychology, 39,* 579-597.

Dornbusch, S. M., & Scott, W. R. (1975). *Evaluation and the exercise of authority.* San Francisco: Jossey-Bass.

Drucker, P. F. (1954). *The practice of management.* New York: Harper.

DuBois, C.L.Z., Sackett, P. R., Zedeck, S., & Fogli, L. (1993). Further exploration of typical and maximum performance criteria: Definitional issues, prediction, and white-black differences. *Journal of Applied Psychology, 78,* 205-211.

Dudycha, L. W., & Naylor, J. C. (1966). Characteristics of the human inference process in complex choice behavior situations. *Organizational Behavior and Human Performance, 1,* 110-128.

Duncan, R. (1972). Characteristics of organizational environments and perceived environmental uncertainty. *Administrative Science Quarterly, 17,* 313-327.

Duncan, R., & Weiss, A. (1979). Organizational learning: Implications for organizational design. In B. Staw (Ed.), *Research in organizational behavior* (Vol. 1, pp. 75-124). Greenwich, CT: JAI Press.

Dunnette, M. D. (1990). Blending the science and practice in industrial and organizational psychology: Where are we and where are we going? In M. Dunnette & L. Hough (Eds.), *Handbook of industrial and organizational psychology* (2nd ed.) (Vol. 1, pp. 1-27). Palo Alto, CA: Consulting Psychologists Press.

Edwards, A. L. (1957). *Techniques of attitude scale construction.* New York: Appleton-Century-Crofts.

Edwards, J. E., & Morrison, R. F. (1992). Selecting and classifying future naval officers: The paradox of greater specialization in broader arenas. In M. Rumsey, C. Walker, & J. Harris (Eds.), *Research on personnel measurement: New directions.* Hillsdale, NJ: Lawrence Erlbaum.

Edwards, W. (1968). Conservatism in human information processing. In B. Kleinmuntz (Ed.), *Formal representation of human judgments.* New York: John Wiley.

Edwards, W. (1980). Multiattribute utility for evaluation: Structures, uses, and problems. In M. Klein & K. Teilmann (Eds.), *Handbook of criminal justice evaluation.* Beverly Hills: Sage.

Edwards, W., & Newman, J. (1982). *Multiattribute evaluation.* Beverly Hills: Sage.

Ekehammar, B. (1974). Interactionism personality from a historical perspective. *Psychological Bulletin, 81,* 1026-1048.

Ekvall, E. (1980). Industrial psychology in Sweden. In X. Zamek-Gliszezynska (Ed.), *Work psychology in Europe.* Warsaw: Polish Scientific Publishers.

Endler, N. S. (1982). Interactionism comes of age. In M. P. Zanna, E. T. Higgins, & C. P. Herman (Eds.), *Consistency in social behavior: The Ontario Symposium* (Vol. 2, pp. 209-250). Hillsdale, NJ: Lawrence Erlbaum.

Endler, N. S., & Magnusson, D. (1976). Toward an interactional psychology of personality. *Psychological Bulletin, 83,* 956-974.

Englehard, G. (1994). Examining rater errors in the assessment of written composition with a many-facet Rasch model. *Journal of Educational Measurement, 31,* 93-112.

Etzioni, A. (1975). *A comparative analysis of complex organizations* (rev. ed.). New York: Free Press.

Eulberg, J. R., O'Connor, E. J., Peters, L. H., & Watson, T. W. (1984). *Performance constraints: A selective review of relevant literature* (AFHRL-TP-83-48). Brooks AFB, TX: Air Force Human Resources Laboratory, Manpower and Personnel Division.

Exter, T. G. (1992). In and out of work. *American Demographics, 14,* 63.

Famularo, J. F. (1972). *Handbook of modern personnel administration.* New York: McGraw-Hill.

Farh, J. L., Dobbins, G. H., & Cheng, B. S. (1991). Cultural relativity in action: A comparison of self-ratings made by Chinese and U.S. workers. *Personnel Psychology, 44,* 129-147.

Farh, J. L., & Werbel, J. D. (1986). Effects of purpose of the appraisal and expectation of validation on self-appraisal leniency. *Journal of Applied Psychology, 71,* 527-529.

454   UNDERSTANDING PERFORMANCE APPRAISAL

Farr, J. L., O'Leary, B. S., & Bartlett, C. J. (1971-1977). Ethnic group membership as a moderator of the prediction of job performance. *Personnel Psychology, 24,* 609-636.

Feild, H. S., & Holley, W. H. (1982). The relationship of performance appraisal system characteristics to verdicts in selected employment discrimination cases. *Academy of Management Journal, 25,* 392-406.

Feldman, D. C. (1976). A contingency theory of socialization. *Administrative Science Quarterly, 21,* 443-452.

Feldman, J. M. (1981). Beyond attribution theory: Cognitive processes in performance appraisal. *Journal of Applied Psychology, 66,* 127-148.

Feldman, J. M. (1986). Instrumentation and training for performance appraisal: A perceptual cognitive viewpoint. In K. Rowland & J. Ferris (Eds.), *Research in personnel and human resources management* (Vol. 4). Greenwich, CT: JAI Press.

Feldman, K. A. (1989). Instructional effectiveness of college teachers as judged by teachers themselves, current and former students, colleagues, administrators, and external (neutral) observers. *Research in Higher Education, 32*(2), 137-194.

Ferris, G. R., Fedor, D. B., Chachere, J. G., & Pondy, L. R. (1989). Myths and politics in organizational contexts. *Group and Organization Studies, 14*(1), 83-103.

Ferris, G. R., & Judge, T. A. (1991). Personnel/human resource management: A political influence perspective. *Journal of Management, 17,* 447-488.

Finn, R. H. (1972). Effects of some variations in rating scale characteristics on the means and reliabilities of ratings. *Educational and Psychological Measurement, 32,* 255-265.

Fischoff, B. (1975). Hindsight (does not equal) foresight: The effect of outcome knowledge on judgment under uncertainty. *Journal of Experimental Psychology: Human Perception and Performance, 1,* 288-299.

Fisher, B. A. (1974). *Small group decision making: Communication and the group process.* New York: McGraw-Hill.

Fisher, C. D. (1974). Transmission of positive and negative feedback to subordinates: A laboratory investigation. *Journal of Applied Psychology, 64,* 533-540.

Fisher, C. D. (1986). Organizational socialization: An integrative review. In K. Rowland & G. Ferris (Eds.), *Research in personnel and human resources management* (Vol. 4). Greenwich, CT: JAI Press.

Fisher, C. D. (1989). *Self and superior assessment: Unraveling the causes of disagreement.* Unpublished manuscript, University of Baltimore.

Fisher, C. D., & Taylor, M. S. (1979). Consequences of individual feedback on behavior in organizations. *Journal of Applied Psychology, 64,* 349-371.

Fisicaro, S. A. (1988). A reexamination of the relationship between halo error and accuracy. *Journal of Applied Psychology, 73,* 239-244.

Fitzgibbons, J., & Moch, A. (1980). *Employee absenteeism: A summary of research.* Washington, DC: Educational Research Service.

Flanagan, J. C. (1949). Critical requirements: A new approach to evaluation. *Personnel Psychology, 2,* 419-425.

Flanagan, J. C. (1954). The critical incidents technique. *Psychological Bulletin, 51,* 327-358.

Fleishman, E., & Quaintance, M. (1984). *Taxonomies of human performance: The description of human tasks.* New York: Academic Press.

Fleishman, E. A., & Zaccaro, S. J. (1992). Toward a taxonomic classification of team performance functions: Initial considerations, subsequent evaluations, and current formulations. In R. Swezey & E. Salas (Eds.), *Teams: Their training and performance.* Norwood, NJ: Ablex.

Fletcher, C. A. (1978). Manager-subordinate communication and leadership style. *Personnel Review, 7,* 59-62.

Fodor, E. M. (1974). Disparagement by a subordinate as an influence on the use of power. *Journal of Applied Psychology, 59,* 652-655.

Folger, R., & Greenberg, J. (1985). Procedural justice: An interpretive analysis of personnel systems. In K. Rowland & G. Ferris (Eds.), *Research in personnel and human resources management* (Vol. 3). Greenwich, CT: JAI Press.

Folger, R., Konovsky, M., & Cropanzano, R. (1992). A due process metaphor for performance appraisal. In B. Staw & L. Cummings (Eds.), *Research in organizational behavior* (Vol. 14, pp. 127-148). Greenwich, CT: JAI Press.

Forehand, G. A. (1968). On the interaction of persons and organizations. In R. Taguire & G. Litwin (Eds.). *Organizational climate: Explorations of a concept.* Boston: Harvard Business School.

Form, W. (1987). On the degradation of skills. *Annual Review of Sociology, 13,* 29-47.

Foster, S. L., & Cone, J. D. (1980). Current issues in direct observation. *Behavioral Assessment, 2,* 313-338.

Foti, R. (1988). *Differences in performance schemata as a function of subordinate and superior rank.* Paper presented at the annual convention of the Academy of Management, Anaheim, CA.

Foti, R. J., & Lord, R. G. (1987). Prototypes and scripts: The effects of alternative methods of processing information on rating accuracy. *Organizational Behavior and Human Decision Processes, 39,* 318-340.

Fox, S., & Thornton, G. C., III. (1987). *Implicit distribution theory: The influence of schematic perception of differentiation on actual ratings.* Unpublished manuscript, Bar-Ilan University, Israel.

Fredericksen, N. (1962). Factors in in-basket performance. *Psychological Monographs, 76* (22, Whole No. 541).

Fredericksen, N. (1972). Toward a taxonomy of situations. *American Psychologist, 27,* 114-123.

Fredericksen, N., Jensen, C., & Beatrin, A. (1972). *Prediction of organizational behavior.* Elmsford, NY: Pergamon.

Freeberg, N. F. (1969). Relevance of rater-ratee acquaintance in the validity and reliability of ratings. *Journal of Applied Psychology, 53,* 518-524.

Freedom, J. L., Sears, D. O., & Carlsmith, J. M. (1981). *Social psychology* (4th ed.). Englewood Cliffs, NJ: Prentice Hall.

French, J., & Caplan, R. (1973). Organizational stress and individual strain. In A. Morrow (Ed.), *The failure of success.* New York: Amacon.

French, J., & Raven, B. (1959). The bases of social power. In D. Cartwight (Ed.), *Studies in social power.* Ann Arbor: University of Michigan, Institute for Social Research.

Frese, M., & Sabini, J. (1985). Action theory: An introduction. In M. Frese & J. Sabini (Eds.), *Goal directed behavior: The concept of action in psychology.* Hillsdale, NJ: Lawrence Erlbaum.

Friedlander, F., & Pickle, H. (1968). Components of effectiveness in small organizations. *Administrative Science Quarterly, 13,* 289-304.

Friedman, B. A., & Cornelius, E. T. (1976). Effects of rater participation in scale construction on the psychometric characteristics of two rating scale formats. *Journal of Applied Psychology, 61,* 210-216.

Friedman, M. (1986). 10 steps to objective appraisals. *Personal Journal, 65,* 66-71.

Fromkin, H. L., & Streufert, S. (1976). Laboratory experimentation. In M. Dunnette (Ed.), *Handbook of industrial and organizational psychology*. Chicago: Rand McNally.

Fry, L. (1982). Technology-structure research: Three critical issues. *Academy of Management Journal, 25*, 532-552.

Fuller, J. L. (1950). Situation analysis: A classification of organism-field interactions. *Psychological Review, 7*, 3-18.

Fuller, L., & Smith, V. (1991). Consumers' reports: Management by customers in a changing economy. *Work, Employment and Society, 5*, 1-16.

Funder, D. C. (1987). Errors and mistakes: Evaluating the accuracy of social judgment. *Psychological Bulletin, 101*, 75-90.

Gabor, A. (1990). *The man who discovered quality: How W. Edwards Deming brought the quality revolution to America—The stories of Ford, Xerox and G. M.* New York: Times Books.

Garber, B. D., & Miller, M. L. (1986). On beasties and butterflies: Evidence for the stability and domain-specificity of individual differences in categorization. *Journal of Personality, 54*, 647-658.

Garson, B. (1988). *The electronic sweatshop: How computers are transforming the office of the future into the factory of the past.* New York: Simon & Schuster.

George, J. (1986). Appraisal in the public sector: Dispensing with the big stick. *Personnel Management, 18*(4), 32-35.

Gerhart, B., & Milkovich, G. T. (1992). Employee compensation: Research and practice. In M. Dunnette & L. Hough (Eds.), *Handbook of industrial and organizational psychology* (2nd ed.) (Vol. 3, pp. 481-570). Palo Alto, CA: Consulting Psychologists Press.

Ghiselli, E. E. (1964). *Theory of psychological measurement*. New York: McGraw-Hill.

Gioia, D. A., & Longenecker, C. O. (1994). Delving into the dark side: The politics of executive appraisal. *Organizational Dynamics, 22*(3), 47-58.

Gioia, D. A., & Sims, H. P. (1985). Self-serving bias and actor-observer differences in organizations: An empirical analysis. *Journal of Applied Social Psychology, 15*, 547-563.

Goldman, P. (1983). A sociohistorical perspective on performance assessment. In F. Landy, S. Zedeck, & J. Cleveland (Eds.), *Performance measurement and theory*. Hillsdale, NJ: Lawrence Erlbaum.

Goldstein, I. L. (1986). *Training in organizations. Needs assessment, development, and evaluation* (2nd ed.). Pacific Grove, CA: Brooks/Cole.

Goldstein, I. L., & Mobley, W. H. (1971). Error and variability in the visual processing of dental radiographs. *Journal of Applied Psychology, 55*, 549-553.

Gordon, G. E., & Kelly, M. M. (1986). *Telecommuting: How to make it work for you and your company*. Englewood Cliffs, NJ: Prentice Hall.

Gorman, C. D., Clover, W. H., & Doherty, M. E. (1978). Can we learn anything about interviewing real people from "interviews" of paper people? Two studies on the external validity of a paradigm. *Organizational Behavior and Human Performance, 22*, 165-192.

Gosselin, A., Werner, J., & Halle, N. (1994). *So why don't we just ask them? A survey of ratee preferences concerning performance appraisal and management*. Unpublished paper, University of Montreal.

Graen, G. (1976). Role-making processes within complex organizations. In M. Dunnette (Ed.), *Handbook of industrial and organizational psychology*. Chicago: Rand McNally.

Grant, R. A., & Higgins, C. A. (1991). The impact of computerized performance monitoring on service work: Testing a causal model. *Information Systems Research, 2*, 116-142.

Green, B. F. (1980). Note on Bem and Funder's scheme for scoring Q-sorts. *Psychological Review, 87*, 212-214.

Green, B. F., & Wigdor, A. K. (1988). *Measuring job competency: Report of the Committee on Performance of Military Personnel, National Research Council.* Washington, DC: National Academy Press.

Greenberg, J. (1986). Determinants of perceived fairness of performance evaluations. *Journal of Applied Psychology, 71,* 340-342.

Greenberg, J. (1987). Using diaries to promote procedural justice in performance appraisal. *Social Justice Research, 1,* 219-234.

Greenberg, J., & Folger, R. (1983). Procedural justice, participation, and fair process effects in groups and organizations. In P. Paulus (Ed.), *Basic group processes.* New York: Springer.

Gregson, R. A. (1975). *Psychometrics of similarity.* New York: Academic Press.

Greller, M. M. (1975). Subordinate participation and reactions to the appraisal interview. *Journal of Applied Psychology, 60,* 554-559.

Greller, M. M. (1978). The nature of subordinate participation in the appraisal interview. *Academy of Management Journal, 21,* 646-658.

Grey, R. J., & Kipnis, D. (1976). Untangling the performance appraisal dilemma. The influence of perceived organizational context on evaluative processes. *Journal of Applied Psychology, 61,* 329-335.

Guilford, J. P. (1954). *Psychometric methods* (2nd ed.). New York: McGraw-Hill.

Guion, R. M. (1961). Criterion measurement and personnel judgments. *Personnel Psychology, 14,* 141-149.

Guion, R. M. (1965). *Personnel testing.* New York: McGraw-Hill.

Guzzo, R. A., & Bondy, J. S. (1983). *A guide to worker productivity experiments in the United States 1976-1981.* Elmsford, NY: Pergamon.

Guzzo, R. A., Jette, R. D., & Katzell, R. A. (1985). The effects of psychologically-based intervention programs on worker productivity. *Personnel Psychology, 38,* 275-293.

Haberstroh, C. J. (1965). Organization design and systems analysis. In M. March (Ed.), *Handbook of organizations.* Chicago: Rand McNally.

Hackett, J. D. (1928). Rating legislators. *Personnel, 7*(2), 130-131.

Hackman, J. R. (1976). Group influences on individuals. In M. Dunnette (Ed.), *Handbook of industrial and organizational psychology.* Chicago: Rand McNally.

Hackman, J. R. (1990). *Groups that work (and those that don't): Creating conditions for effective teamwork.* San Francisco: Jossey-Bass.

Hackman, J. R. (1992). Group influences on individuals in organizations. In M. Dunnette & L. Hough (Eds.), *Handbook of industrial and organizational psychology* (2nd ed.; Vol. 3, pp. 199-267). Palo Alto, CA: Consulting Psychologists Press.

Hackman, J. R., & Morris, G. G. (1975). Group task, group interaction processes, and group performance effectiveness. In L. Berkowitz (Ed.), *Advances in experimental social psychology* (Vol. 7). New York: Academic Press.

Hackman, J. R., & Oldham, G. R. (1980). *Work redesign.* Reading, MA: Addison-Wesley.

Hackman, J. R., & Porter, L. W. (1968). Expectancy predictions of work effectiveness. *Organizational Behavior and Human Performance, 3,* 417-426.

Hakel, M. D. (1986). Personnel selection and placement. *Annual Review of Psychology, 37,* 351-380.

Hakmiller, K. L. (1966). Threat as a determinant of downward comparison. *Journal of Experimental Social Psychology, 2*(Suppl. 1), 32-39.

Hale, M. (1982). History of employment testing. In A. Wigdor & W. Garner (Eds.), *Ability testing: Uses, consequences, and controversies: Part II.* Washington, DC: National Academy Press.

Hammond, K. R., McClelland, G. H., & Mumpower, J. (1980). *Human judgment and decision making: Theories, methods, and procedures.* New York: Praeger.

Harrington, J. M. (1978). *Shiftwork and health: A critical review of the literature.* London: HMSO.

Harris, M. H., & Sackett, P. R. (1988, April). *Interpersonal affect and performance rating level: An individual differences analysis.* Paper presented at the annual convention of the Society for Industrial and Organizational Psychology, Dallas.

Harris, M. H., & Schaubroeck, J. (1988). A meta-analysis of self-supervisory, self-peer, and peer-supervisor ratings. *Personnel Psychology, 41,* 43-62.

Hartel, C. E. J. (1988). *The effects of cognitive availability of behavioral exemplars on performance ratings.* Unpublished master's thesis, Colorado State University.

Hartigan, J. A., & Wigdor, A. K. (1989). *Fairness in employment testing: Validity generalization, minority issues and the General Aptitude Test Battery.* Washington, DC: National Academy Press.

Harvey, R. J. (1982). The future of partial correlation as a means to reduce halo in performance ratings. *Journal of Applied Psychology, 67,* 171-176.

Hastie, R. (1980). Memory for behavioral information that confirms or contradicts a personality impression. In R. Hastie et al. (Eds.), *Person memory: The cognitive basis of social perception.* Hillsdale, NJ: Lawrence Erlbaum.

Hastie, R., & Kumar, P. (1979). Person memory: Personality traits as organizing principles in memory for behaviors. *Journal of Personality and Social Psychology, 37,* 25-38.

Hastie, R., & Park, B. (1986). The relationship between memory and judgment depends on whether the judgment task is memory-based or on-line. *Psychological Review, 93,* 256-268.

Hauenstein, N. M. (1992). An information-processing approach to leniency in performance judgments. *Journal of Applied Psychology, 77,* 485-493.

Hautaluoma, J., Jobe, L., Visser, S., & Donkersgoed, W. (1993). *Employee reactions to different upward feedback methods.* Unpublished manuscript, Colorado State University.

Haynes, M. E. (1986). Partnerships in management: Employee involvement gets results. *Personnel Journal, 65,* 46-55.

Heilbroner, R. L. (1953). *The worldly philosophers.* New York: Simon & Schuster.

Heilman, M. E. (1983). Sex bias in the work setting: The lack of fit model. *Research in organizational behavior* (Vol. 5, pp. 269-298). Greenwich, CT: JAI Press.

Heneman, R. L. (1986). The relationship between supervisory ratings and results-oriented measures of performance: A meta-analysis. *Personnel Psychology, 39,* 811-826.

Heneman, R. L. (1990). Merit pay research. In *Research in personnel and human resource management* (Vol. 8, pp. 203-263). Greenwich, CT: JAI Press.

Heneman, R. L., & Wexley, K. N. (1983). The effects of delay in rating and amount of information observed on performance rating accuracy. *Academy of Management Journal, 26,* 677-686.

Heneman, R. L., Wexley, K. N., & Moore, M. L. (1987). Performance-rating accuracy: A critical review. *Journal of Business Research, 15,* 431-448.

Heron, A. (1956). The effects of real-life motivation on questionnaire response. *Journal of Applied Psychology, 40,* 65-68.

Higgins, E. T., & King, G. (1981). Accessibility of social constructs: Information processing consequences of individual and contextual variability. In N. Cantor & J. Kihlstrom (Eds.), *Personality, cognition, and social interaction.* Hillsdale, NJ: Lawrence Erlbaum.

Higgins, E. T., King, G., & Mavin, G. H. (1982). Individual construct accessibility and subjective impressions and recall. *Journal of Personality and Social Psychology, 43,* 35-47.

Higgins, E. T., & Stangor, C. (1988). A "change-of-standard" perspective on relations among context, judgment, and memory. *Journal of Personality and Social Psychology, 54*, 181-192.

Hobson, C. J., & Gibson, F. W. (1983). Policy capturing as an approach to understanding and improving performance appraisal: A review of the literature. *Academy of Management Review, 8*, 640-649.

Hogan, E. A. (1987). Effects of prior expectations on performance ratings: A longitudinal study. *Academy of Management Journal, 30*, 354-368.

Hogan, J., Hogan, R. T., & Busch, C. M. (1984). How to measure service orientation. *Journal of Applied Psychology, 69*, 167-173.

Hogarth, R. M. (1980). *Judgment and choice: The psychology of decision.* Chichester, UK: John Wiley.

Hom, P. W., Caranikas-Walker, F., Prussia, G. E., & Griffeth, R. W. (1992). A meta-analytical structural equations analysis of a model of employee turnover. *Journal of Applied Psychology, 77*, 890-909.

House, R. J. (1971). A path goal theory of leader effectiveness. *Administrative Science Quarterly, 16*, 321-338.

Howard, A. (1984). I/O careers in industry. *The Industrial-Organizational Psychologist, 21*, 46-54.

Hoxworth, T. L. (1988). *The impact of feedback sign and type on perceived feedback accuracy, self-ratings, and performance.* Unpublished doctoral dissertation, Colorado State University.

Hulin, C. L. (1982). Some reflections on general performance dimensions and halo rating error. *Journal of Applied Psychology, 67*, 165-170.

Hunter, J. E., & Hunter, R. F. (1984). Validity and utility of alternate predictors of job performance. *Psychological Bulletin, 96*, 72-98.

Hunter, J. E., Schmidt, F. L., & Judiesch, M. K. (1990). Individual differences in output variability as a function of job complexity. *Journal of Applied Psychology, 75*, 28-42.

Ilgen, D. R. (1983). Gender issues in performance appraisal: A discussion of O'Leary and Hansen. In F. Landy, S. Zedeck, & J. Cleveland (Eds.), *Performance measurement and theory.* Hillsdale, NJ: Lawrence Erlbaum.

Ilgen, D. R. (1986). Laboratory research: A question of when, not if. In E. Locke (Ed.), *Generalizing from laboratory to field settings.* Lexington, MA: Lexington Books.

Ilgen, D. R. (1993). Performance appraisal accuracy: An illusive and sometimes misguided goal. In H. Schuler, J. L. Farr, M. Smith (Eds.), *Personnel selection and assessment: Individual and organizational perspectives* (pp. 235-252). Hillsdale, NJ: Lawrence Erlbaum.

Ilgen, D. R., Barnes-Farrell, J. L., & McKellin, D. B. (1993). Performance appraisal process research in the 1980s: What has it contributed to appraisals in use? *Organizational Behavior and Human Decision Processes, 54*, 321-368.

Ilgen, D. R., & Favero, J. L. (1985). Limits in generalization from psychological research to performance appraisal processes. *Academy of Management Review, 10*, 311-321.

Ilgen, D. R., & Feldman, J. M. (1983). Performance appraisal: A process focus. In L. Cummings & B. Staw (Eds.), *Research in organizational behavior* (Vol. 5). Greenwich, CT: JAI Press.

Ilgen, D. R., Fisher, C. D., & Taylor, S. M. (1979). Consequences of individual feedback on behavior in organization. *Journal of Applied Psychology, 64*, 347-371.

Ilgen, D. R., & Hollenbeck, J. H. (1977). The role of job satisfaction in absence behavior. *Organizational Behavior and Human Performance, 19*, 148-161.

Ilgen, D. R., & Hollenbeck, J. R. (1991). The structure of work: Jobs and roles. In M. Dunnette & L. Hough (Eds.), *Handbook of industrial and organizational psychology* (2nd ed.). Palo Alto, CA: Consulting Psychologists Press.

Ilgen, D. R., Mitchell, T. R., & Frederickson, J. W. (1981). Poor performers: Supervisors' and subordinates' responses. *Organizational Behavior and Human Performance, 27,* 386-410.

Imada, A. S. (1982). Social interaction, observation and stereotypes as determinants of differentiation in peer ratings. *Organizational Behavior and Human Performance, 29,* 397-415.

Imada, A. S., & Hakel, M. D. (1977). The effects of nonverbal communication and rater proximity on impressions and decisions in simulated employment interviews. *Journal of Applied Psychology, 62,* 295-300.

Isen, A. M. (1984). Toward understanding the role of affect in cognition. In R. Wyer & T. Srull (Eds.), *Handbook of social cognition* (Vol. 3). Hillsdale, NJ: Lawrence Erlbaum.

Isen, A. M., & Daubman, K. A. (1984). The influence of affect on categorization. *Journal of Personality and Social Psychology, 47,* 1207-1217.

Isen, A. M., Shalker, T. E., Clark, M. S., & Karp, L. (1978). Positive affect, accessibility of material in memory, and behavior. A cognitive loop? *Journal of Personality and Social Psychology, 36,* 1-12.

Jackson, J. (1965). Structural characteristics of norms. In I. Steiner & M. Fishbein (Eds.), *Current studies in social psychology.* New York: Holt, Rinehart & Winston.

Jacobs, M., Jacobs, A., Feldman, D., & Cavior, N. (1973). Feedback II—The "credibility gap": Delivery of positive and negative and emotional and behavioral feedback in groups. *Journal of Consulting and Clinical Psychology, 41,* 215-223.

Jacobs, R., & Campbell, D. T. (1961). The perpetuation of an arbitrary tradition through several generations of a laboratory microculture. *Journal of Abnormal and Social Psychology, 62,* 649-658.

Jacobs, R., Kafry, D., & Zedeck, S. (1980). Expectations of behaviorally anchored rating scales. *Personnel Psychology, 33,* 595-640.

Jako, R. A., & Murphy, K. (1990). Distributional ratings, judgment decomposition, and their impact on inter-rater agreement and rating accuracy. *Journal of Applied Psychology, 75,* 500-505.

James, L. (1973). Criterion models and construct validity for criteria. *Psychological Bulletin, 80,* 75-83.

Jeffrey, K. M., & Mischel, W. (1979). Effects of purpose on the organization and recall of information in person perception. *Journal of Personality, 47,* 397-419.

Johnston, W. B., & Packer, A. H. (1987). *Workforce 2000: Work and workers for the twenty-first century.* Indianapolis, IN: Hudson Institute.

Joiner, B. L. (1994). *Fourth generation management: The new business consciousness.* New York: McGraw-Hill.

Jones, A. P., Tait, M., & Butler, M. C. (1983). Perceived punishment and reward values of supervisory actions. *Motivation and Emotion, 1,* 313-329.

Jones, E., Kanhouse, D., Kelley, H., Nisbett, R., Valins, S., & Weiner, B. (1972). *Attribution: Perceiving the causes of behavior.* Morristown, NJ: General Learning Press.

Jones, E., & Nisbett, R. (1971). The actor and the observer: Divergent perceptions of the causes of behavior. In E. Jones, D. Kanhouse, H. Kelley, R. Nisbett, S. Valins, & B. Weiner (Eds.), *Attribution: Perceiving the causes of behavior.* Morristown, NJ: General Learning Press.

Jones, S. D., Buerkle, M., Hall, A., Rupp, L., & Roth, P. L. (1993, April). *Work group performance measurement and feedback: An integrated, comprehensive system for a manufacturing department.* Paper presented at the annual convention of the Society for Industrial and Organizational Psychology, San Francisco.

Judge, T. A., & Ferris, G. R. (1993). Social context of performance evaluation decisions. *Academy of Management Journal, 36,* 80-105.

Judiesch, M. K., Schmidt, F. L., & Mount, M. K. (1992). Estimates of the dollar value of employee output in utility analyses: An empirical test of two theories. *Journal of Applied Psychology, 77,* 234-250.

Kahn, R., & Katz, D. (1953). Leadership practices in relation to productivity and morale. In D. Cartwright & A. Zander (Eds.), *Group dynamics.* Evanston, IL: Row & Peterson.

Kahn, R., & Quinn, R. (1970). Role stress: A framework for analysis. In A. McLean (Ed.), *Mental health and work organizations.* Chicago: Rand McNally.

Kahn, R., Wolf, D., Quinn, R., Snoeck, J., & Rosenthal, R. (1964). *Organizational stress: Studies in role conflict and ambiguity.* New York: John Wiley.

Kahneman, D., & Tversky, A. (1979). Prospect theory: An analysis of decision under risk. *Econometrica, 47,* 263-291.

Kallejian, V., Brown, P., & Weschler, I. R. (1953, October). The impact of interpersonal relations on ratings of performance. *Public Performance Review,* pp. 166-170.

Kane, J. (1981, August). *Improving the measurement basis of performance appraisal.* Paper presented at the American Psychological Association Convention, Los Angeles.

Kane, J. S. (1986). Performance distribution assessment. In R. Berk (Ed.), *The state of art in performance assessment.* Baltimore, MD: Johns Hopkins University Press.

Kane, J. S. (1987). Measure for measure in performance appraisal. *Computers in Personnel, 2,* 31-39.

Kane, J. S., & Kane, K. F. (1992a). The analytic framework: The most promising approach for the advancement of performance appraisal. *Human Resource Management Review, 2,* 37-70.

Kane, J. S., & Kane, K. F. (1992b). TQM-compatible performance appraisal: An American cultural imperative. *Journal of Management Systems, 4*(2), 11-28.

Kane, J. S., & Lawler, E. E. (1979). Performance appraisal effectiveness: Its assessment and determinants. In B. Staw (Ed.), *Research in organizational behavior* (Vol. 1). Greenwich, CT: JAI Press.

Kane, J. S., & Lawler, E. E. (1980). In defense of peer assessment: A rebuttal to Brief's critique. *Psychological Bulletin, 88,* 80-81.

Kanter, R. M. (1977). *Men and women of the organization.* New York: Basic Books.

Katz, D., & Kahn, R. (1978). *The social psychology & organizations* (2nd ed.). New York: John Wiley.

Kaufman, H. (1960). *The forest ranger: A study in administrative behavior.* Baltimore, MD: Johns Hopkins University Press.

Kavanaugh, M. J. (1971). The content issue in performance appraisal: A review. *Personnel Psychology, 24,* 653-668.

Kavanaugh, M. J., MacKinney, A. C., & Wolins, L. (1971). Issues in managerial performance: Multitrait-multimethod analysis of ratings. *Psychological Bulletin, 75,* 34-49.

Kay, E., Meyer, H., & French, J. (1965). Effects of threat in a performance interview. *Journal of Applied Psychology, 49,* 311-317.

Keeney, R. L., & Raiffa, H. (1976). *Decisions with multiple objectives: Preferences and value tradeoffs.* New York: John Wiley.

Keller, R. T. (1983). Predicting absenteeism from prior absenteeism, attitudinal factors, and nonattitudinal factors. *Journal of Applied Psychology, 68,* 536-540.

Kelley, H. H. (1971). Attribution in social interaction. In E. Jones, D. Kanhouse, H. Kelley, R. Nisbett, S. Valins, & B. Weiner (Eds.), *Attribution: Perceiving the causes of behavior.* Morristown, NJ: General Learning Press.

Kenny, D. A., & Berman, J. S. (1980). Statistical approaches to the correction of bias. *Psychological Bulletin, 88,* 288-295.

Kidd, J. S., & Christy, R. T. (1961). Supervisory procedures and work-team productivity. *Journal of Applied Psychology, 45,* 388-392.

Kim, M., & Rosenberg, S. (1980). Comparison of two structural models of implicit personality theory. *Journal of Personality and Social Psychology, 38,* 375-389.

Kimble, G. A. (1984). Psychology's two cultures. *American Psychology, 39,* 833-839.

Kingsbury, F. A. (1922). Analyzing ratings and training raters. *Journal of Personnel Research, 1,* 377-382.

Kingsbury, F. A. (1933). Psychological tests for executives. *Personnel, 9,* 121-133.

Kingstrom, P. O., & Mainstone, L. E. (1985). An investigation of rater-ratee acquaintance and rater bias. *Academy of Management, 28,* 641-653.

Kipnis, D., Schmidt, S. M., Price, K., & Stitt, C. (1980). Why do I like thee? Is it your performance or my orders? *Journal of Applied Psychology, 66,* 324-328.

Kipnis, D., Schmidt, S. M., & Wilkinson, I. (1980). Intra-organizational influence tactics: Explorations of getting one's way. *Journal of Applied Psychology, 65,* 440-452.

Kipnis, D., & Vanderveer, R. (1971). Ingratiation and the use of power. *Journal of Personality and Social Psychology, 17,* 280-286.

Kirkpatrick, D. L. (1967). Evaluation of training. In R. L. Craig & L. R. Bittel (Eds.), *Training and development handbook.* New York: McGraw-Hill.

Kirkpatrick, I., Davies, A., & Oliver, N. (1992). Decentralization: Friend or foe of HRM. In P. Blyton & P. Turnbull (Eds.), *Reassessing human resource management* (pp. 131-147). London: Sage.

Kleiger, W. A., & Mosel, J. N. (1953). The effect of opportunity to observe and rater status on the reliability of performance ratings. *Personnel Psychology, 6,* 57-64.

Klein, H. J., & Snell, S. A. (1993). *The impact of contextual factors on performance appraisal interview effectiveness.* Unpublished paper, Ohio State University.

Klein, H. J., Snell, S. A., & Wexley, K. N. (1987). Systems model of the performance appraisal interview process. *Industrial Relations, 26,* 267-280.

Klimoski, R., & Inks, L. (1990). Accountability forces in performance appraisal. *Organizational Behavior and Human Decision Processes, 45,* 194-208.

Kohn, M. L., & Schooner, C. (1978). The reciprocal effects of the substantive complexity of work and intellectual flexibility. A longitudinal assessment. *American Journal of Sociology, 84,* 24-52.

Komaki, J., Collins, R. L., & Thoene, T. (1980). Behavioral measurement in business, industry, and government. *Behavioral Assessment, 2,* 103-123.

Kopelman, R. E. (1986). Objective feedback. In E. A. Locke (Ed.), *Generalizing from laboratory to field settings.* Lexington, MA: Lexington Books.

Koprowski, E. J. (1983). Cultural myths: Clues to effective management. *Organizational Dynamics, 12,* 39-51.

Kosslyn, S. M. (1980). *Image and mind.* Cambridge, MA: Harvard University Press.

Kozlowski, S. W., & Farr, J. (1988). An integrative model of updating and performance. *Human Performance, 1,* 5-29.

Kozlowski, S. W., & Hults, B. M. (1987). An exploration of climates for technical updating, and performance. *Personnel Psychology, 40,* 539-563.

Kozlowski, S. W., & Kirsch, M. (1986, April). *The systematic distortion hypothesis and halo error: An individual-level analysis.* Paper presented at the annual convention of the Society for Industrial and Organizational Psychology, Chicago.

Kozlowski, S. W., Kirsch, M. P., & Chao, G. T. (1986). Job knowledge, ratee familiarity, conceptual similarity, and halo error: An exploration. *Journal of Applied Psychology, 71,* 45-49.

Kraiger, K., & Ford, J. K. (1985). A meta-analysis of race effects in performance appraisal. *Journal of Applied Psychology, 70,* 56-65.

Krause, M. S. (1970). Use of social situations for research purposes. *American Psychology, 25,* 748-753.

Krystofiak, F., Cardy, R., & Newman, J. (1988). Implicit personality and performance appraisal: The influence of trait inferences on evaluations of behavior. *Journal of Applied Psychology, 73,* 515-521.

Lacho, K. J., Stearns, G. K., & Villere, M. F. (1979). A study of employee appraisal systems of major cities in the United States. *Public Personnel Management, 8,* 111-125.

Lahey, M. A., & Saal, F. E. (1981). Evidence incompatible with a cognitive complexity theory of rating behavior. *Journal of Applied Psychology, 66,* 706-715.

Landy, F. J. (1985). *Psychology of work behavior* (3rd ed.). Homewood, IL: Dorsey.

Landy, F. J. (1987). *Psychology: The science of people* (2nd ed.). Englewood Cliffs, NJ: Prentice Hall.

Landy, F. J., Barnes, J., & Murphy K. (1978). Correlates of perceived fairness and accuracy of performance appraisals. *Journal of Applied Psychology, 63,* 751-754.

Landy, F. J., Barnes-Farrell, J., & Cleveland, J. (1980). Perceived fairness and accuracy of performance appraisals: A follow-up. *Journal of Applied Psychology, 65,* 355-356.

Landy, F. J., & Farr, J. L. (1976). Police performance appraisal [M.S. No. 1315]. *JSAS Catalog of Selected Documents in Psychology, 6,* 83.

Landy, F. J., & Farr, J. L. (1980). Performance rating. *Psychological Bulletin, 87,* 72-107.

Landy, F. J., & Farr, J. L. (1983). *The measurement of work performance: Methods, theory, and applications.* New York: Academic Press.

Landy, F. J., Farr, J. L., & Jacobs, R. R. (1982). Utility concepts in performance measurement. *Organizational Behavior and Human Performance, 30,* 15-40.

Landy, F. J., & Guion, R. M. (1970). Development of scales for the measurement of work motivation. *Organizational Behavior and Human Performance, 5,* 93-103.

Landy, F. J., Vance, R. J., Barnes-Farrell, J. L., & Steele, J. W. (1980). Statistical control of halo error in performance ratings. *Journal of Applied Psychology, 65,* 177-180.

Lane, D. M., Murphy, K. R., & Marques, T. (1982). Measuring the importance of cues in policy capturing. *Organizational Behavior and Human Performance, 30,* 231-240.

Langer, E. J., Taylor, S. E., Fiske, S. T., & Chantowitz, B. (1976). Stigma, staring and discomfort: A novel-stimulus hypothesis. *Journal of Experimental Social Psychology, 12,* 451-463.

Latham, G. (1986). Job performance and appraisal. In C. Cooper & I. Robertson (Eds.), *International review of industrial and organizational psychology.* Chichester, UK: John Wiley.

Latham, G., & Whyte, G. (1994). The futility of utility analysis. *Personnel Psychology, 47,* 31-46.

Latham, G. P., Fay, C. H., & Saari, L. M. (1979). The development of behavioral observation scales for appraising the performance of foremen. *Personnel Psychology, 32,* 299-311.

Latham, G. P., & Pursell, E. D. (1975). Measuring absenteeism from the opposite side of the coin. *Journal of Applied Psychology, 60,* 369-371.

Latham, G. P., Skarlick, D., Irvine, D., & Siegel, J. P. (1993). The increasing importance of performance appraisals to employee effectiveness in organizational settings in North America. In C. Cooper (Ed.), *International review of industrial and organizational psychology* (Vol. 8, pp. 87-132). Chichester, UK: John Wiley.

Latham, G. P., & Wexley, K. N. (1977). Behavioral observation scales. *Personnel Psychology, 30,* 255-268.

Lawler, E. E. (1967). The multitrait-multirate approach to measuring managerial job performance. *Journal of Applied Psychology, 51,* 369-381.

Lawler, E. E. (1971). *Pay and organizational effectiveness: A psychological view.* New York: McGraw-Hill.

Lawler, E. E. (1972). Secrecy and the need to know. In M. Dunnette, R. House, & H. Tosi (Eds.), *Readings in managerial motivation and compensation.* East Lansing: Michigan State University Press.

Lawler, E. E. (1976). Control systems in organizations. In M. Dunnette (Ed.), *Handbook of industrial/organizational psychology.* Chicago: Rand McNally.

Lawler, E. E., & Jenkins, G. D. (1992). Strategic reward systems. In M. Dunnette & L. Hough (Eds.), *Handbook of industrial and organizational psychology* (2nd ed.) (Vol. 3, pp. 1009-1055). Palo Alto, CA: Consulting Psychologists Press.

Lay, C. H., & Jackson, D. N. (1969). Analysis of the generality of trait-inferential relationships. *Journal of Personality and Social Psychology, 12,* 12-21.

Lazer, R. I., & Wikstrom, W. S. (1977). *Appraising managerial performance: Current practices and future directions* (Conference Board Rep. No. 723). New York: Conference Board.

Lee, C. (1985). Increasing performance appraisal effectiveness. Matching task types, appraisal processes, and rater training. *Academy of Management Review, 10,* 322-331.

Lee, S. L. (1993). *The moderating effects of leader-member exchange theory on performance appraisal agreement.* Unpublished master's thesis, Colorado State University.

Lerner, B. (1983). Reality, utopia, and performance appraisal: Another view. In F. Landy, S. Zedeck, & J. Cleveland (Eds.), *Performance measurement and theory.* Hillsdale, NJ: Lawrence Erlbaum.

Lewin, K., Dembo, T., Festinger, L., & Sears, P. (1944). Level of aspiration. In J. McV. Hunt (Ed.), *Personality and behavioral disorders.* New York: Ronald Press.

Lichtenstein, S., Slovic, P., Fischoff, B., Layman, M., & Combs, B. (1978). Judged frequency of lethal events. *Journal of Experimental Psychology: Human Learning and Memory, 4,* 551-578.

Liden, R. C., & Graen, G. (1980). Generalizability of the vertical dyadic linkage model of leadership. *Academy of Management Journal, 23,* 451-465.

Liden, R. C., & Mitchell, T. R. (1983). The effects of group interdependence on supervisor performance evaluations. *Personnel Psychology, 36,* 289-300.

Liden, R. C., & Mitchell, T. R. (1985). Reactions to feedback: The role of attributions. *Academy of Management Journal, 28,* 291-308.

Lind, E. A., Kanfer, R., & Earley, P. C. (1990). Voice, control, and procedural justice: Instrumental and noninstrumental concerns in fairness judgments. *Journal of Personality and Social Psychology, 59,* 952-959.

Linville, P. W., & Jones, E. J. (1980). Polarized appraisals of out-group members. *Journal of Personality and Social Psychology, 38,* 689-703.

Lissitz, R. W., & Green, S. B. (1975). Effect of the number of scale points on reliability: A Monte Carlo approach. *Journal of Applied Psychology, 60,* 10-13.

Lloyd, C., & Rawlinson, M. (1992). New technology and human resource management. In P. Blyton & P. Turnbull (Eds.), *Reassessing human resource management* (pp. 184-199). London: Sage.

Locke, E. A. (1983). Performance appraisal under capitalism, socialism, and the mixed economy. In F. Landy, S. Zedeck, & J. Cleveland (Eds.), *Performance measurement and theory.* Hillsdale, NJ: Lawrence Erlbaum.

Locke, E. A. (1986). *Generalizing from laboratory to field settings.* Lexington, MA: Lexington Books.

Locke, E., & Latham, G. (1990). *A theory of goal setting and task feedback.* Englewood Cliffs, NJ: Prentice Hall.

Locke, E. A., Shaw, K. N., Saari, L. M., & Latham, G. P. (1981). Goal setting and task performance: 1969-1980. *Psychological Bulletin, 90,* 125-152.

Lodge, G., & Vogel, E. (1987). *Ideology and national competitiveness: An analysis of nine countries.* Cambridge, MA: Harvard University Press.

Long, P. (1986). *Performance appraisal revisited.* London: Institute of Personnel Management.

Longenecker, C. O. (1994, April). *The paradoxes of political appraisals: Tales from the dark side.* Paper presented at the annual convention of the Society for Industrial and Organizational Psychology, Nashville.

Longenecker, C. O., & Gioia, D. A. (1988, Winter). Neglected at the top: Executives talk about executive appraisal. *Sloan Management Review,* pp. 41-47.

Longenecker, C. O., & Gioia, D. A. (1992). The executive appraisal paradox. *Academy of Management Executive, 6*(2), 18-28.

Longenecker, C. O., & Goff, S. J. (1992). Performance appraisal effectiveness: A matter of perspective. *Advanced Management Journal, 57*(2), 18-23.

Longenecker, C. O., Sims, H. P., & Gioia, D. A. (1987). Behind the mask: The politics of employee appraisal. *Academy of Management Executive, 1,* 183-193.

Lopez, F. M. (1968). *Evaluating employee performance.* Chicago: Public Personnel Association.

Lord, C. O. (1982). Predicting behavioral consistency from an individual's perception of situational similarities. *Journal of Personality and Social Psychology, 42,* 1076-1088.

Lord, F. M., & Novick, M. R. (1968). *Statistical theories of mental test scores.* Reading, MA: Addison-Wesley.

Lord, R. G. (1985a). Accuracy in behavioral measurement: An alternative definition based on raters' cognitive schema and signal detection. *Journal of Applied Psychology, 70,* 66-71.

Lord, R. G. (1985b). An information processing approach to social perception, leadership and behavioral measurement in organizations. In B. Staw & L. Cummings (Eds.), *Research in organizational behavior* (Vol. 7). Greenwich, CT: JAI Press.

Lord, R. G., Foti, R. J., & DeVader, C. (1984). A test of leadership categorization theory: Internal structure, information processing, and leadership perceptions. *Organizational Behavior and Human Performance, 34,* 343-378.

Lord, R. G., & Maher, K. J. (1991). Cognitive theory in industrial and organizational psychology. In M. Dunnette & L. Hough (Eds.), *Handbook of industrial and organizational psychology* (2nd ed.) (Vol. 2, pp. 1-62). Palo Alto, CA: Consulting Psychologists Press.

Lorenzo, R. V. (1984). Effect of assessorship on managers' proficiency in acquiring, evaluating, and communicating information about people. *Personnel Psychology, 37,* 617-636.

Luthans, F., & Kreitner, R. (1985). *Organizational behavior modification and beyond: An operant and social learning approach.* Glenview, IL: Scott, Foresman.

MacKenzie, S. B., Podsakoff, P. M., & Fetter, R. (1991). Organizational citizenship behavior and objective productivity as determinants of managerial evaluations of salespersons' performance. *Organizational Behavior and Human Decision Processes, 50,* 123-150.

Magnusson, D. (1971). An analysis of situational dimensions. *Perceptual and Motor Skills, 32,* 851-867.

Magnusson, D. (1976). The person and the situation in an interactional model of behavior. *Scandinavian Journal of Psychology, 17,* 253-271.

Magnusson, D. (1981). Wanted: A psychology of situations. In D. Magnusson (Ed.), *Toward a psychology of situations.* Hillsdale, NJ: Lawrence Erlbaum.

Magnusson, D., & Endler, N. S. (1977). *Personality at the crossroads: Current issues in interactional psychology.* Hillsdale, NJ: Lawrence Erlbaum.

Mahew, B. H. (1983). Hierarchical differentiation in imperatively coordinated associations. In S. Bacharach (Ed.), *Research in the sociology of organizations* (Vol. 2). Greenwich, CT: JAI Press.

Mahfood, P. E. (1992). *How to hire, manage, and monitor employees who work at home.* Chicago: Probus.

Maier, N. F., & Thurber, J. A. (1968). Accuracy of judgments of deception when an interview is watched, heard, or read. *Personnel Psychology, 21,* 23-30.

March, J. C., & March, J. G. (1978). Performance sampling in social matches. *Administrative Science Quarterly, 23,* 434-453.

March, J. G., & Simon, H. A. (1958). *Organizations.* New York: John Wiley.

Martell, R. F., & Guzzo, R. A. (1991). The dynamics of implicit theories of group performance: When and how do they operate? *Organizational Behavior and Human Decision Processes, 50,* 51-74.

Martell, R. F., & Willis, C. E. (1993). Effects of observers' performance expectations on behavior ratings of work groups: Memory or response bias? *Organizational Behavior and Human Decision Processes, 56,* 91-109.

Martin, D. C. (1986). Performance appraisal 2: Improving the rater's effectiveness. *Personnel, 63,* 28-33.

Martin, J., & Siehl, C. (1983). Organizational culture and counter culture: An uneasy symbiosis. *Organizational Dynamics, 12,* 52-64.

Martinko, M. J., & Gardner, W. L. (1985). Beyond structural observation: Methodological issues and new directions. *Academy of Management Review, 10,* 676-695.

Martocchio, J. J., & Ferris, G. R. (1991). Performance evaluation in high technology firms. *Journal of High Technology Management Research, 2,* 83-97.

Maslow, A. H. (1970). *Motivation and personality* (2nd ed.). New York: Harper & Row.

Massey, D. J. (1975). Narrowing the gap between intended and existing results of appraisal systems. *Personnel Journal, 54,* 522-524.

McArthur, L. (1980). What grabs you? The role of attention in impression formation causal attribution. In E. Higgins, C. Herman, & M. Zanna (Eds.), *Social cognition: The Ontario Symposium on Personality and Social Psychology.* Hillsdale, NJ: Lawrence Erlbaum.

McCall, M. W., & DeVries, D. L. (1977). *Appraisal in context: Clashing with organizational realities* (Tech. Rep. No. 4). Greensboro, NC: Center for Creative Leadership.

McCormick, E. J. (1976). Job and task analysis. In M. Dunnette (Ed.), *Handbook of industrial and organizational psychology.* Chicago: Rand McNally.

McCormick, E. J. (1979). *Job analysis: Methods and applications.* New York: Amacon.

McCormick, E. J., Jeanneret, P. R., & Mecham, R. C. (1972). A study of job characteristics and job dimensions as based on the position analysis questionnaire (PAQ). *Journal of Applied Psychology, 56,* 247-267.

McDougall, W. (1908). *An introduction to social psychology.* London: Methuen.

McDougall, W. (1932). *The energies of men: A study of the fundamentals of dynamic psychology.* London: Methuen.

McGregor, D. (1957). An uneasy look at performance appraisal. *Harvard Business Review, 35*(3), 89-94.

McGregor, D. (1960). *The human side of enterprise.* New York: McGraw-Hill.

McIntyre, R. M. (1986, August). *The use of cognitive modeling as a method for training behavioral observation.* Paper presented at the annual convention of the American Psychological Association, Toronto.

McIntyre, R. M., Smith, D., & Hassett, C. E. (1984). Accuracy of performance ratings as affected by rater training and perceived purpose of rating. *Journal of Applied Psychology, 69,* 147-156.

Mechanic, D. (1962). Sources of power of lower participants in complex organizations. *Administrative Science Quarterly, 7,* 349-364.

Medin, E. L., & Schaffer, M. M. (1978). Context theory of classification learning. *Psychological Review, 85,* 207-238.

Meier, R. A., & Feldhusen, J. F. (1979). Another look at Dr. Fox: Effect of stated purpose of evaluation, lecturer's expressiveness and density of lecture content on student ratings. *Journal of Educational Psychology, 71,* 339-345.

Merton, R. K. (1957). *Social theory and social structure.* New York: Free Press.

Meyer, H. H. (1980). Self appraisal of job performance. *Personnel Psychology, 33,* 291-295.

Meyer, H. H. (1991). A solution to the performance appraisal feedback enigma. *Academy of Management Executive, 5,* 68-76.

Meyer, H. H., Kay, E., & French, J. (1965). Split roles in performance appraisal. *Harvard Business Review, 43,* 123-129.

Miceli, M. P., Jung, I., Near, J. P., & Greenberg, D. B. (1991). Predictors and outcomes of reactions to pay-for-performance plans. *Journal of Applied Psychology, 76,* 508-521.

Milkovich, G. T., & Wigdor, A. K. (1991). *Pay for performance.* Washington, DC: National Academy Press.

Miller, D. T., & Ross, M. (1975). Self-serving biases in the attribution of causality: Fact or fiction? *Psychological Bulletin, 82,* 213-225.

Miller, G. A., Galanter, E., & Pribram, K. H. (1960). *Plans and the structure of behavior.* New York: Holt, Rinehart & Winston.

Mintzberg, H. (1971). Managerial work: Analysis from observation. *Management Science, 18,* (No. 2).

Mintzberg, H. (1977, July-August). The manager's job: Folklore and fact. *Harvard Business Review,* pp. 49-61.

Mintzberg, H. (1980). *The nature of managerial work.* Englewood Cliffs, NJ: Prentice Hall.

Mintzberg, H. (1989). *Mintzberg on management: Inside our strange world of organizations.* New York: Free Press.

Mischel, W. (1977). The interaction of person and situation. In D. Magnusson & N. S. Endler (Eds.), *Personality at the crossroads: Current issues in interactional psychology.* Hillsdale, NJ: Lawrence Erlbaum.

Mitchell, T. D., Green, S. G., & Wood, R. E. (1981). An attributional model of leadership and the poor performing subordinate: Development and validation. In B. Staw & L. Cummings (Eds.), *Research in organizational behavior* (Vol. 3). Greenwich, CT: JAI Press.

Mitchell, T. R., & Beach, L. R. (1990). Do I love thee? Let me count: Toward an understanding of intuitive and automatic decision making. *Organizational Behavior and Human Decision Processes, 47,* 1-20.

Mitchell, T. R., & Liden, R. C. (1982). The effects of the social context on performance evaluations. *Organizational Behavior and Human Performance, 29,* 241-256.

Mitchell, T. R., & O'Reilly, C. A. (1983). Managing poor performance and productivity in organizations. In K. Rowland & G. Ferris (Eds.), *Research in personnel and human resources management* (Vol. 1). Greenwich, CT: JAI Press.

Mitroff, I. (1983). Archetypal social systems analysis: On the deeper structure of human systems. *Academy of Management Review, 8,* 387-397.

Mobley, W. H. (1982). *Employee turnover: Causes, consequences, and control.* Reading, MA: Addison-Wesley.

Mohr, L. B. (1973). The concept of organizational goal. *American Political Science Review, 67,* 470-481.

Mohrman, A. M. (1986, April). *Multiple purposes in appraisal events.* Paper presented at the annual convention of the Society for Industrial Organizational Psychology, Chicago.

Mohrman, A. M., & Lawler, E. E. (1983). Motivation and performance appraisal behavior. In F. Landy, S. Zedeck, & J. Cleveland (Eds.), *Performance measurement and theory.* Hillsdale, NJ: Lawrence Erlbaum.

Moos, R. (1973). Conceptualizations of human environments. *American Psychologist, 28,* 652-665.

Mora, N. D. (1985). *Work belief systems: An extension of Kanungo's model of job involvement.* Unpublished doctoral dissertation, New York University.

Morgan, B. B., Glickman, A. S., Woodward, E. A., Blaines, A. S., & Salas, E. (1986). *Measurement of team behaviors in a navy environment* (THERAPY-86-014). Orlando, FL: Naval Training Systems Center, Human Factors Division.

Morrison, R. F., & Brantner, T. M. (1992). What enhances or inhibits learning a new job? A basic career issue. *Journal of Applied Psychology, 77,* 926-940.

Motowidlo, S. J. (1986). Information processing in organizations. In K. Rowland & G. Ferris (Eds.), *Research in personnel and human resources management* (Vol. 4). Greenwich, CT: JAI Press.

Mount, M. K. (1983). Comparison of managerial and employee satisfaction with a performance appraisal system. *Personnel Psychology, 36,* 99-110.

Mount, M. K. (1984a). Psychometric properties of subordinate ratings of managerial performance. *Personnel Psychology, 37,* 687-702.

Mount, M. K. (1984b). Satisfaction with a performance appraisal system and appraisal discussion. *Journal of Occupational Behavior, 5,* 271-279.

Mowday, R. T., Porter, L. W., & Steers, R. M. (1981). *Employee-organization linkages: The psychology of commitment, absenteeism, and turnover.* New York: Academic Press.

Muchinsky, P. (1977). Employee absenteeism: A review of the literature. *Journal of Vocational Behavior, 10,* 316-340.

Mullins, C. S., & Ratliff, F. R. (1979). Criterion problems. In C. J. Mullins (Ed.), *Criterion development for job performance evaluations* (Proceedings from symposium) (AFHRL-TR78-85). Brooks AFB, TX: Air Force Human Resource Laboratory.

Murphy, K. R. (1979). *Convergent and discriminant validity of subjectively weighted models and regression models of decision making processes.* Unpublished doctoral dissertation, Pennsylvania State University.

Murphy, K. R. (1982a). Assessing the discriminant validity of regression models and subjectively weighted models of judgments. *Multivariate Behavioral Research, 17*, 354-370.

Murphy, K. R. (1982b). Difficulties in the statistical control of halo. *Journal of Applied Psychology, 67*, 161-164.

Murphy, K. R. (1986). When your top choice turns you down: Effects of rejected offers on the utility of selection tests. *Psychological Bulletin, 99*, 133-138.

Murphy, K. R. (1989a). Dimensions of job performance. In R. Dillon & J. Pelligrino (Eds.), *Testing: Applied and theoretical perspectives* (pp. 218-247). New York: Praeger.

Murphy, K. R. (1989b). Is the relationship between cognitive ability and job performance stable over time? *Human Performance, 2*, 183-200.

Murphy, K. R. (1991). Criterion issues in performance appraisal research. *Organizational Behavior and Human Decision Processes, 50*, 45-50.

Murphy, K. R. (1993). *Honesty in the workplace*. Pacific Grove, CA: Brooks/Cole.

Murphy, K. R. (in press). Toward a broader conception of jobs and job performance: Impact of changes in the military environment on the structure, assessment, and prediction of job performance. In M. Rumsey, C. Walker, & J. Harris (Eds.), *Research on personnel measurement: New directions*. Hillsdale, NJ: Lawrence Erlbaum.

Murphy, K. R., & Anhalt, R. L. (1992). Is halo error a property of the rater, ratees, or the specific behaviors observed? *Journal of Applied Psychology, 77*, 494-500.

Murphy, K. R., & Balzer, W. K. (1981, August). *Rater errors and rating accuracy*. Paper presented at the annual convention of the American Psychological Association, Los Angeles.

Murphy, K. R., & Balzer, W. K. (1986). Systematic distortions in memory-based behavior ratings and performance evaluations: Consequences for rating accuracy. *Journal of Applied Psychology, 71*, 39-44.

Murphy, K. R., & Balzer, W. K. (1989). Rater errors and rating accuracy. *Journal of Applied Psychology, 74*, 619-624.

Murphy, K. R., Balzer, W. K., Kellam, K. L., & Armstrong, J. (1984). Effect of purpose of rating on accuracy in observing teacher behavior and evaluating teaching performance. *Journal of Educational Psychology, 76*, 45-54.

Murphy, K. R., Balzer, W. K., Lockhart, M., & Eisenman, E. (1985). Effects of previous performance on evaluations of present performance. *Journal of Applied Psychology, 70*, 72-84.

Murphy, K. R., & Cleveland, J. N. (1991). *Performance appraisal: An organizational perspective*. Needham Heights, MA: Allyn & Bacon.

Murphy, K. R., & Constans, J. I. (1987). Behavioral anchors as a source of bias in rating. *Journal of Applied Psychology, 72*, 523-579.

Murphy, K. R., & Constans, J. I. (1988). Psychological issues in scale format research: Behavioral anchors as a source of bias in rating. In R. Cardy, S. Peiffer, & J. Newman (Eds.), *Advances in information processing in organizations* (Vol. 3). Greenwich, CT: JAI Press.

Murphy, K. R., & Davidshofer, C. O. (1988). *Psychological testing: Principles and applications*. Englewood Cliffs, NJ: Prentice Hall.

Murphy, K. R., Gannett, B. A., Herr, B. M., & Chen, J. A. (1986). Effects of subsequent performance on evaluations of previous performance. *Journal of Applied Psychology, 71*, 427-431.

Murphy, K. R., Garcia, M., Kerkar, S., Martin, C., & Balzer, W. K. (1982). Relationship between observational accuracy and accuracy in evaluating performance. *Journal of Applied Psychology, 67,* 320-325.

Murphy, K. R., Herr, B. M., Lockhart, M. C., & Maguire, E. (1986). Evaluating the performance of paper people. *Journal of Applied Psychology, 71,* 654-661.

Murphy, K. R., & Jako, B. (1989). Under what conditions are observed intercorrelations greater than or smaller than true intercorrelations? *Journal of Applied Psychology, 74,* 827-830.

Murphy, K. R., Jako, R. A., & Anhalt, R. L. (1993). The nature and consequences of halo error: A critical analysis. *Journal of Applied Psychology, 78,* 218-225.

Murphy, K. R., & Kroeker, L. P. (1988). *Dimensions of job performance* (NPRDC TN 88-39). San Diego, CA: Navy Personnel Research and Development Center.

Murphy, K. R., Martin, C., & Garcia, M. (1982). Do behavioral observation scales measure observation? *Journal of Applied Psychology, 67,* 562-567.

Murphy, K. R., & Pardaffy, V. (1989). Bias in behaviorally anchored rating scales: Global or scale-specific? *Journal of Applied Psychology, 74,* 343-346.

Murphy, K. R., Philbin, T. A., & Adams, S. R. (1989). Effect of purpose of observation on accuracy of immediate and delayed performance ratings. *Organizational Behavior and Human Decision Processes, 43,* 336-354.

Murphy, K. R., & Reynolds, D. H. (1988a). Does true halo affect observed halo? *Journal of Applied Psychology, 73,* 235-238.

Murphy, K. R., & Reynolds, D. H. (1988b). *Student attitudes toward employee drug testing.* Unpublished manuscript, Colorado State University.

Murphy, K. R., & Saal, F. E. (1990). *Psychology in organizations: Integrating science and practice.* Boston: Allyn & Bacon.

Nagle, B. F. (1953). Criterion development. *Personnel Psychology, 6,* 271-289.

Nagy, M. S. (1993, April). *Integrating goal setting and performance appraisal into total quality management.* Paper presented at the annual convention of the Society for Industrial and Organizational Psychology, San Francisco.

Naiper, B. J., & Ferris, G. R. (in press). Distance in organizations. *Human Resource Management Review.*

Naiper, N., & Latham, G. (1986). Outcome expectancies of people who conduct performance appraisals. *Personnel Psychology, 39,* 827-837.

Nathan, B., & Alexander, R. A. (1988). A comparison of criteria for test validation: A meta-analytic investigation. *Personnel Psychology, 41,* 517-535.

Nathan, B., & Lord, R. G. (1983). Cognitive categorization and dimensional schemata: A process approach to the study of halo in performance ratings. *Journal of Applied Psychology, 68,* 102-114.

Nathan, B. R., & Tippins, N. (1990). The consequences of halo "error" in performance ratings: A field study of the moderating effects of halo on test validation results. *Journal of Applied Psychology, 75,* 290-296.

Naylor, J. C., Pritchard, R. D., & Ilgen, D. R. (1980). *A theory of behavior in organizations.* New York: Academic Press.

Newcomb, T. (1931). A design to test the validity of a rating technique. *Journal of Educational Psychology, 22,* 279-289.

Newtson, D. (1976). Foundations of attribution: The perception of ongoing behavior. In J. Harvey, W. Ikes, & R. Kidd (Eds.), *New directions in attribution research* (Vol. 1). Hillsdale, NJ: Lawrence Erlbaum.

Nirenberg, J. (1993). *The living organization: Transforming teams into workplace communities.* Homewood, IL: Business One Irwin.

Norman, C. A., & Zawacki, R. A. (1991). Team appraisals—Team approach. *Personnel Journal, 70,* 101-104.

O'Connor, E. J., Peters, L. H., Pooyang, A., Weekly, J., Frank, B., & Erenkrantz, B. (1984). Situational constraint effects on performance, affective reactions, and turnover: A field replication and extension. *Journal of Applied Psychology, 69,* 663-672.

Odiorne, G. S. (1965). *Management by objectives. A system of managerial leadership.* New York: Pitman.

Office of Technology Assessment. (1987). *The electronic supervisor: New technology, new tensions.* Washington, DC: Government Printing Office.

Office of Technology Assessment. (1991). *Biological rhythms: Implications for the worker.* Washington, DC: Government Printing Office.

Oldham, G. R., Kulik, C. T., Stepina, L. P., & Ambrose, M. L. (1986). Relations between situational factors and the comparative referents used by employees. *Academy of Management Journal, 29,* 599-608.

Olsen, L. O., & Bennett, A. C. (1975). Performance appraisal: Management technique or social process. Part I: Management technique. *Management Review, 64,* 18-23.

Organ, D. W. (1988). *Organizational citizenship behavior: The good soldier syndrome.* Lexington, MA: Lexington Books.

Osburn, J. D., Moran, L., Musselwhite, E., Zenger, J. H., & Perrin, C. (1990). *Self-directed work teams: The new American challenge.* Homewood, IL: Business One Irwin.

Osgood, C. E. (1962). Studies of the generality of affective meaning systems. *American Psychologist, 17,* 10-28.

Ostroff, C. (1993). Rater perceptions, satisfaction and performance ratings. *Journal of Occupational and Organizational Psychology, 66,* 345-356.

Ostroff, C., & Ilgen, D. R. (1986, April). *The relationship between cognitive categories of raters and rating accuracy.* Paper presented at the annual meeting of the Society for Industrial and Organizational Psychology, Chicago.

Padgett, M. Y. (1989, August). *Performance appraisal in context: Motivational influences on performance ratings.* Paper presented at the annual conference of the Academy of Management, Washington, DC.

Paese, P. W., & Switzer, F. S. (1988). Validity generalization and hypothetical reliability distributions: A test of the Schmidt-Hunter procedure. *Journal of Applied Psychology, 73,* 267-274.

Palermo, D. S. (1983). Cognition, concepts, and an employee's theory of the world. In F. Landy, S. Zedeck, & J. Cleveland (Eds.), *Performance measurement and theory.* Hillsdale, NJ: Lawrence Erlbaum.

Park, B., & Rothbart, M. (1982). Perception of out-group homogeneity and levels of social categorization: Memory for subordinate attributes of in-group members. *Journal of Personality and Social Psychology, 42,* 1051-1068.

Pascale, R., & Athos, A. (1981). *The art of Japanese management: Applications for American executives.* New York: Simon & Schuster.

Patten, T. H., Jr. (1977). *Pay: Employee compensation and incentive plans.* London: Free Press.

Patz, A. L. (1975). Performance appraisal: Useful but still resisted. *Harvard Business Review, 53,* 74-80.

Pearn, M. (1993). Fairness in selection and assessment: A European perspective. In H. Schuler, J. L. Farr, & M. Smith (Eds.), *Personnel selection and assessment: Individual and organizational perspectives* (pp. 205-220). Hillsdale, NJ: Lawrence Erlbaum.

Perrow, C. (1973, Summer). The short and glorious history of organizational theory. *Organizational Dynamics*, pp. 192-202.

Pervin, L. A. (1968). Performance and satisfaction as a function of individual environment fit. *Psychological Bulletin, 69*, 56-68.

Pervin, L. A. (1981). The relation of situations to behavior. In D. Magnusson (Ed.), *Toward a psychology of situations*. Hillsdale, NJ: Lawrence Erlbaum.

Pervin, L. A. (1983). The stasis and flow of behavior: Toward a theory of goals. In M. Page (Ed.), *Personality: Current theory and research* (pp. 1-53). Lincoln: University of Nebraska Press.

Pervin, L. A. (1989). Persons, situations, interactions: The history of a controversy and a discussion of theoretical models. *Academy of Management Review, 14*, 350-360.

Peters, L. H., Fisher, C. D., & O'Connor, E. J. (1982). The moderating effect of situational control of performance variance on the relationship between individual differences and performance. *Personnel Psychology, 35*, 609-621.

Peters, L. H., & O'Connor, E. J. (1980). Situational constraints and work outcomes: The influences of a frequently overlooked construct. *Academy of Management Review, 5*, 391-397.

Peters, L. H., O'Connor, E. J., & Eulberg, J. R. (1985). Situational constraints: Sources, consequences, and future considerations. In K. Rowland & G. Ferris (Eds.), *Research in personnel and human resource management* (Vol. 3). Greenwich, CT: JAI Press.

Peters, L. H., O'Connor, E. J., & Rudolph, C. J. (1980). The behavioral and affective consequences of performance-relevant situational variables. *Organizational Behavior and Human Performance, 25*, 79-96.

Peterson, C. R., & Beach, L. R. (1967). Man as an intuitive statistician. *Psychological Bulletin, 68*, 29-46.

Petrie, F. A. (1950). Is there something new in efficiency rating? *Personnel Administrator, 13*, 24.

Pfeffer, J. (1981). *Power in organizations*. Belmont, CA: Pitman.

Pfeffer, J., & Salancik, G. (1978). *The external control of organizations: A resource dependence perspective*. New York: Harper & Row.

Philbin, T. A. (1988). *Conceptual and behavioral factors associated with expertise*. Unpublished doctoral dissertation, Colorado State University.

Phillips, J. S., & Freedman, S. M. (1982, August). *Situational constraints, task characteristics, and affective task reactions*. Paper presented at the annual meeting of the Academy of Management, New York.

Phillips, J. S., & Lord, R. G. (1982). Schematic information processing and perceptions of leadership in problem-solving groups. *Journal of Applied Psychology, 67*, 486-492.

Podsakoff, P. M., & Farh, J. (1989). Effects of feedback sign and credibility on goal setting and task performance: A preliminary test of some control theory propositions. *Organizational Behavior and Human Decision Processes, 44*, 45-67.

Porras, J. L., & Robertson, P. J. (1992). Organizational development: Theory, practice and research. In M. Dunnette & L. Hough (Eds.), *Handbook of industrial and organizational psychology* (2nd ed.) (Vol. 3, pp. 719-822). Palo Alto, CA: Consulting Psychologists Press.

Porter, L. W., Allen, R. W., & Angle, L. L. (1981). The politics of upward influence in organizations. *Research in Organizational Behavior, 3*, 109-149.

Porter, L. W., & Lawler, E. E. (1968). *Managerial attitudes and performance.* Homewood, IL: Dorsey Press.

Posner, M. I. (1978). *Chronometric explorations of the mind.* Hillsdale, NJ: Lawrence Erlbaum.

Poulton, E. C. (1968). Range effects in experiments with people. *American Psychologist, 88,* 3-32.

Prieto, J. M. (1993). The team perspective in selection and assessment. In H. Schuler, J. L. Farr, & M. Smith (Eds.), *Personnel selection and assessment: Individual and organizational perspectives* (pp. 221-234). Hillsdale, NJ: Lawrence Erlbaum.

Prince, C., Salas, E., & Franz, T. M. (1990, May). *Aircrew coordination performance and skill development.* Presented at the 1990 Symposium on Independent Research/Independent Exploratory Development, Baltimore, MD.

Pritchard, R. D. (1990). *Measuring and improving organizational productivity: A practical guide.* New York: Praeger.

Pritchard, R. D., Jones, S. D., Roth, P. L., Stuebing, K. K., & Ekeberg, S. E. (1989). The evaluation of an integrated approach to measuring organizational productivity. *Personnel Psychology, 42,* 69-115.

Pritchard, R. D., & Karasick, B. W. (1973). The effect of organizational climate on managerial job perceptions and job satisfaction. *Organizational Behavior and Human Performance, 9,* 126-146.

Pulakos, E. D. (1984). A comparison of rater training programs: Error training and accuracy training. *Journal of Applied Psychology, 69,* 581-588.

Pulakos, E. D. (1986). The development of training programs to increase accuracy in different rating tasks. *Organizational Behavior and Human Decision Processes, 38,* 76-91.

Pulakos, E. D., Schmitt, N., & Ostroff, C. (1986). A warning about the use of a standard deviation across dimensions to measure halo. *Journal of Applied Psychology, 71,* 29-32.

Quattrone, G. A., & Jones, E. E. (1980). The perception of variability within in-groups and out-groups: Implications for the law of small numbers. *Journal of Personality and Social Psychology, 38,* 141-152.

Raiffa, H. (1968). *Decision analysis: Introductory lectures on choices under uncertainty.* Reading, MA: Addison-Wesley.

Ralston, D. A., Gustafson, D. J., Chueng, F., & Terpstra, R. H. (1992). Eastern values: A comparison of U.S., Hong Kong, and PRC managers. *Journal of Applied Psychology, 77,* 664-671.

Rambo, W. W., Chomiak, A. M., & Price, J. M. (1983). Consistency of performance under stable conditions of work. *Journal of Applied Psychology, 68,* 78-87.

Ramsover, R. M. N. (1983). *Telecommuting: The organizational and behavioral effects of working at home.* Ann Arbor: University of Michigan Press.

Rand, T. M., & Wexley, K. N. (1975). A demonstration of the Byrnes similarity hypothesis in simulated employment interviews. *Psychological Reports, 36,* 535-544.

Reilly, C. E., & Balzer, W. K. (1988). *Effect of purpose on observation and evaluation of teaching performance.* Unpublished manuscript, Bowling Green State University.

Reither, F., & Staudel, T. (1985). Thinking and action. In M. Frese & J. Sabini (Eds.), *Goal directed behavior: The concept of action in psychology.* Hillsdale, NJ: Lawrence Erlbaum.

Ritti, R. R. (1964). Control of "halo" in factor analysis of a supervisory behavior inventory. *Personnel Psychology, 17,* 305-318.

Roach, D. E., & Wherry, R. J. (1970). Performance dimensions of multi-line insurance agents, *Personnel Psychology, 23*, 239-250.

Robbins, T. L., & DeNisi, A. S. (1994). A closer look at interpersonal affect as a distinct influence on cognitive processing in performance evaluations. *Journal of Applied Psychology, 79*, 341-353.

Roethlisberger, F. I., & Dickson, W. J. (1939). *Management and the worker.* Cambridge, MA: Harvard University Press.

Rogers, R., & Hunter, J. (1991). The impact of management by objectives on organizational productivity. *Journal of Applied Psychology, 76*, 322-336.

Rommetveit, R. (1981). On meanings of situations and social control of such meaning in human communication. In D. Magnusson (Ed.), *Toward a psychology of situations.* Hillsdale, NJ: Lawrence Erlbaum.

Rosch, E. (1977). Human categorization. In N. Warren (Ed.), *Studies in cross-cultural psychology* (Vol. 1). New York: Academic Press.

Rosch, E. (1978). Principles of categorization. In E. Rosch & B. Lloyd (Eds.), *Cognition and categorization.* Hillsdale, NJ: Lawrence Erlbaum.

Rosch, E., & Lloyd, B. B. (1978). *Cognition and categorization.* Hillsdale, NJ: Lawrence Erlbaum.

Rosch, E., Mervis, C. G., Gray, W. D., Johnson, D. M., & Boyes-Braem, P. (1976). Basic objects in natural categories. *Cognitive Psychology, 8*, 382-439.

Rosen, N. (1989). *Teamwork and the bottom line.* Hillsdale, NJ: Lawrence Erlbaum.

Rothe, H. F. (1946a). Output rates among butter wrappers: I. Work curves and their stability. *Journal of Applied Psychology, 30*, 199-211.

Rothe, H. F. (1946b). Output rates among butter wrappers: II. Frequency distributions and hypotheses regarding the "restriction of output." *Journal of Applied Psychology, 30*, 320-327.

Rothe, H. F. (1947). Output rates among machine operators: I. Distributions and their reliability. *Journal of Applied Psychology, 31*, 384-389.

Rothe, H. F. (1949). The relation of merit ratings to length of service. *Personnel Psychology, 2*, 237-242.

Rothe, H. F. (1951). Output rates among chocolate dippers. *Journal of Applied Psychology, 35*, 94-97.

Rothe, H. F., & Nye, C. T. (1958). Output rates among coil workers. *Journal of Applied Psychology, 42*, 182-186.

Rothe, H. F., & Nye, C. T. (1959). Output rates among machine operators: II. Consistency-related methods of pay. *Journal of Applied Psychology, 43*, 417-420.

Rothe, H. F., & Nye, C. T. (1961). Output rates among machine operators: III. A nonincentive situation in two levels of business activity. *Journal of Applied Psychology, 45*, 50-54.

Rotter, J. B. (1955). The role of the psychological situation in determining the direction of human behavior. In M. R. Jones (Ed.), *Nebraska Symposium on Motivation.* Lincoln: University of Nebraska Press.

Rotter, J. B. (1982). *The development and application of social learning theory.* New York: Praeger.

Rousseau, D. M. (1988). The construction of climate in organizational research. In C. Cooper & I. Robertson (Eds.), *International review of industrial and organizational psychology* (Vol. 3). Chichester, UK: John Wiley.

Rozelle, R. M., & Baxter, J. C. (1981). The influence of role pressures on the perceiver: Judgment of videotaped interviews varying judge accountability and responsibility. *Journal of Applied Psychology, 66,* 437-441.

Rudd, H. (1921). Is the rating of human character practicable? *Journal of Educational Psychology, 12,* 425-438.

Russell, J. S., Terborg, J. R., Jr., & Powers, M. L. (1985). Organizational performance and organizational level training and support. *Personnel Psychology, 38,* 849-863.

Russo, A., & Hartman, E. A. (1987, August). *Comparison of four career stage theories using data from self and significant others.* Paper presented at the annual conference of the Academy of Management, New Orleans.

Saal, F. E., Downey, R. G., & Lahey, M. A. (1980). Rating the ratings: Assessing the quality of rating data. *Psychological Bulletin, 88,* 413-428.

Saal, F. E., & Knight, P. A. (1988). *Industrial/organizational psychology: Science and practice.* Pacific Grove, CA: Brooks/Cole.

Saavedra, R., Earley, P. C., & Van Dyne, L. (1993). Complex interdependence in task-performing groups. *Journal of Applied Psychology, 78,* 61-72.

Saavedra, R., & Kwun, S. K. (1993). Peer evaluation in self-managing work groups. *Journal of Applied Psychology, 78,* 450-462.

Sackett, P. R., Zedeck, S., & Fogli, L. (1988). Relations between measures of typical and maximum job performance. *Journal of Applied Psychology, 73,* 482-486.

Salas, E., Dickinson, T. L., Converse, S. A., & Tannenbaum, S. I. (in press). Toward understanding of team performance and training. In R. W. Swezey & E. Salas (Eds.), *Teams: Their training and performance.* Norwood, NJ: Ablex.

Salvendy, G., & Seymour, W. (1973). *Prediction and development of industrial work performance.* New York: John Wiley.

Sandlands, L. E., & Calder, B. J. (1987). Perceptual organization in task performance. *Organizational Behavior and Human Decision Processes, 40,* 287-306.

Schall, M. S. (1983). A communication-rules approach to organizational culture. *Administrative Science Quarterly, 28,* 557-581.

Schank, R. C., & Abelson, R. P. (1977). *Scripts, plans, goals, and understanding.* Hillsdale, NJ: Lawrence Erlbaum.

Schein, E. H. (1971). The individual, the organization, and the career: A conceptual scheme. *Journal of Applied Behavioral Science, 1,* 401-426.

Schein, E. H. (1985). *Organizational culture and leadership.* San Francisco: Jossey-Bass.

Schein, E. H., & Ott, J. (1962). The legitimacy of organizational influence. *American Journal of Sociology, 67,* 682-689.

Schlenker, B. R. (1980). *Impression management: The self-concept, social identity, and interpersonal relations.* Monterey, CA: Brooks/Cole.

Schmidt, F. L., & Hunter, J. E. (1977). Development of a general solution to the problem of validity generalization. *Journal of Applied Psychology, 62,* 529-540.

Schmidt, F. L., & Hunter, J. E. (1981). Employment testing: Old theories and new research findings. *American Psychologist, 36,* 1128-1137.

Schmidt, F. L., & Hunter, J. E. (1983). Individual differences in productivity: An empirical test of estimates derived from studies of selection procedure utility. *Journal of Applied Psychology, 68,* 407-414.

Schmidt, F. L., Hunter, J. E., & Caplan, J. R. (1981). Validity generalization results for two jobs in the petroleum industry. *Journal of Applied Psychology, 66,* 261-273.

Schmidt, F. L., Hunter, J. E., McKenzie, R. C., & Muldrow, T. (1979). The impact of valid selection procedures on work force productivity. *Journal of Applied Psychology, 64,* 609-626.

Schmidt, F. L., Hunter, J. E., & Outerbridge, A. N. (1986). Impact of job experience and ability on job knowledge, work sample performance, and supervisory ratings of job performance. *Journal of Applied Psychology, 71,* 432-439.

Schmidt, F. L., & Kaplan, L. B. (1971). Composite versus multiple criteria: A review and resolution of the controversy. *Personnel Psychology, 24,* 419-434.

Schmitt, N., Gooding, R. Z., Noe, R. A., & Kirsch, M. (1984). Meta-analysis of validity studies published between 1964 and 1982 and the investigation of study characteristics. *Personnel Psychology, 37,* 407-422.

Schmitt, N., & Schneider, B. (1983). Current issues in personnel selection. In K. Rowland & R. Ferris (Eds.), *Research in personnel and human resources management* (Vol. 1). Greenwich, CT: JAI Press.

Schneider, B. (1975). Organizational climates: An essay. *Personnel Psychology, 28,* 447-479.

Schneider, B. (1978). Person-situation selection: A review of some ability situation interaction research. *Personnel Psychology, 31,* 281-304.

Schneider, B. (1983a). Interactional psychology and organizational behavior. In H. Cummings & B. M. Staw (Eds.), *Research in organizational behavior* (Vol. 5). Greenwich, CT: JAI Press.

Schneider, B. (1983b). Organizational effectiveness: An interactional perspective. In D. Whetten & K. S. Cameron (Eds.), *Organizational effectiveness: A comparison of multiple models* (pp. 27-54). New York: Academic Press.

Schneider, B. (1985). Organizational behavior. *Annual Review of Psychology, 36,* 573-611.

Schneider, B. (1987). The people make the place. *Personnel Psychology, 40,* 437-454.

Schneider, B., & Reichers, A. E. (1983). On the etiology of climates. *Personnel Psychology, 36,* 19-40.

Schneier, C. E. (1977). Operational utility and psychometric characteristics of behavioral expectation scales. *Journal of Applied Psychology, 62,* 541-548.

Schneier, C. E., & Beatty, R. W. (1978). The influence of role prescriptions on the performance appraisal processes. *Academy of Management Journal, 21,* 129-134.

Schroeder, H. M., Driver, M. J., & Streufert, S. (1967). *Human information processing:* New York: Holt, Rinehart & Winston.

Schuler, H., Farr, J. L., & Smith, M. (1993). *Personnel selection and assessment: Individual and organizational perspectives.* Hillsdale, NJ: Lawrence Erlbaum.

Schuler, R. S. (1987). *Personnel and human resource management.* New York: West Publishing.

Schwab, D. P., Olian-Gottlieb, J., & Heneman, H. (1979). Between subjects expectancy theory research: A statistical review of studies predicting effort and performance. *Psychological Bulletin, 86,* 139-147.

Schwab, D. P., Rynes, S. L., & Aldag, R. J. (1987). Theories and research on job search and choice. In K. Rowland & G. Ferris (Eds.), *Research in personnel and human resource management* (Vol. 5). Greenwich, CT: JAI Press.

Scott, W. D., Clothier, R. C., & Spriegel, W. R. (1941). *Personnel management.* New York: McGraw-Hill.

Sewell, G., & Wilkinson, B. (1992). Empowerment or emasculation? Shopfloor surveillance in a total quality organization. In P. Blyton & P. Turnbull (Eds.), *Reassessing human resource management* (pp. 97-115). London: Sage.

Shamir, B., & Salomon, I. (1985). Work-at-home and the quality of working life. *Academy of Management Review, 10,* 455-464.

Shannon, C., & Weaver, W. (1948). *The mathematical theory of communication.* Champaign: University of Illinois Press.

Shapira, Z., & Shirom, A. (1980). New issues in the use of behaviorally anchored rating scales: Level of analysis, the effects of incident frequency and external validation. *Journal of Applied Psychology, 65,* 517-523.

Sharon, A. (1970). Eliminating bias from student rating of college instructors. *Journal of Applied Psychology, 54,* 278-281.

Sharon, A., & Bartlett, C. (1969). Effect of instructional conditions in producing leniency on two types of rating scales. *Personnel Psychology, 22,* 252-263.

Sherif, M., & Sherif, C. W. (1964). *Reference groups: Exploration into the conformity and deviation of adolescents.* New York: Harper & Row.

Sherif, M., & Sherif, C. W. (1969). *Social psychology.* New York: Harper & Row.

Shimmin, S. (1989). Selection in a European context. In P. Herriot (Ed.), *Assessment and selection in organizations.* Chichester, UK: John Wiley.

Shweder, R. A. (1975). How relevant is an individual difference theory of personality? *Journal of Personality, 43,* 455-483.

Shweder, R. A., & D'Andrade, R. G. (1980). The systematic distortion hypothesis. In R. A. Shweder (Ed.), *Fallible judgment in behavioral research: New directions for methodology of social and behavioral science* (Vol. 4). San Francisco: Jossey-Bass.

Silverman, S. B., & Wexley, K. N. (1984). Reactions of employees to performance appraisal interviews as a function of their participation in rating scale development. *Personnel Psychology, 37,* 703-710.

Sinclair, R. C. (1988). Mood, categorization, breadth, and performance appraisal: The effects of order of information acquisition and affective state on halo, accuracy, information retrieval, and evaluations. *Organizational Behavior and Human Decision Processes, 42,* 22-46.

Sisson, E. D. (1948). Forced-choice: The new army rating. *Personnel Psychology, 1,* 365-381.

Sjoeberg, L. (1981). Life situations and episodes as a basis for situational influence on action. In D. Magnusson (Ed.), *Toward a psychology of situations.* Hillsdale, NJ: Lawrence Erlbaum.

Slovic, P. (1966). Cue consistency and cue utilization in judgment. *American Journal of Psychology, 79,* 427-434.

Slovic, P., & Lichtenstein, S. (1971). Comparison of Bayesian and regression approaches to the study of information processing in judgment. *Organizational Behavior and Human Performance, 6,* 649-744.

Smith, C. A., Organ, D. W., & Near, J. P. (1983). Organizational citizenship behavior: Its nature and antecedents. *Journal of Applied Psychology, 68,* 653-663.

Smith, P. C. (1976). Behaviors, results, and organizational effectiveness. In M. Dunnette (Ed.), *Handbook of industrial and organizational psychology.* Chicago: Rand McNally.

Smith, P. C., & Kendall, L. M. (1963). Retranslation of expectations: An approach to the construction of unambiguous anchors for rating scales. *Journal of Applied Psychology, 47,* 149-155.

Smither, R. D. (1994). *The psychology of work and human performance.* New York: HarperCollins.

Sonnenfeld, J. (1982). Clarifying critical confusion in the Hawthorne hysteria. *American Psychologist, 37,* 1397-1399.

Spence, J. T. (1987). Centrifugal versus centripetal tendencies in psychology: Will the center hold? *American Psychologist, 42,* 1052-1054.

Spool, M. D. (1978). Training programs for observers of behavior: A review. *Personnel Psychology, 31,* 853-888.

Spriegel, W. R. (1962). Company practices in appraisal of managerial performance. *Personnel, 39,* 77.

Srull, T. K., & Brand, J. F. (1983). Memory for information about persons: The effect of encoding operations on subsequent retrieval. *Journal of Verbal Learning and Verbal Behavior, 22,* 219-230.

Srull, T. K., & Wyer, R. S. (1980). Category accessibility and social perception: Some implications for the study of person memory and interpersonal judgment. *Journal of Personality and Social Psychology, 38,* 841-856.

Starbuck, W. H. (1976). Organizations and their environments. In M. Dunnette (Ed.), *Handbook of industrial and organizational psychology.* Chicago: Rand McNally.

Steel, R. P., & Mento, A. J. (1986). Impact of situational constraints on subjective and objective criteria of managerial performance. *Organizational Behavior and Human Decision Processes, 37,* 254-265.

Steel, R. P., & Ovalle, N. K. (1984). Self-appraisal based on supervisory feedback. *Personnel Psychology, 37,* 667-685.

Steers, R. M., & Rhodes, S. R. (1978). Major influences on employee attendance: A process model. *Journal of Applied Psychology, 63,* 391-407.

Steiner, D., & Raine, J. (1989). Immediate and delayed primacy and recency effects in performance evaluation. *Journal of Applied Psychology, 74,* 136-142.

Sternberg, R. J., & Wagner, R. K. (1986). *Practical intelligence: Nature and origins of competence in the everyday world.* New York: Cambridge University Press.

Stokols, D. (1981). Group × place transactions: Some neglected issues in psychological research on settings. In D. Magnusson (Ed.), *Toward a psychology of situations.* Hillsdale, NJ: Lawrence Erlbaum.

Stone, D. L., & Stone, E. F. (1985). Effects of feedback consistency and feedback favorability on self-perceived task competence and perceived feedback accuracy. *Organizational Behavior and Human Decision Processes, 36,* 167-185.

Stricker, L. J., Jacobs, P. I., & Kogan, N. (1974). Trait interrelations in implicit personality theories and questionnaire data. *Journal of Personality and Social Psychology, 30,* 198-207.

Sulsky, L. M., & Balzer, W. K. (1988). The meaning and measurement of performance rating accuracy: Some methodological concerns. *Journal of Applied Psychology, 73,* 497-506.

Szilagyi, A. D., & Wallace, M. J. (1983). *Organizational behavior and performance* (3rd ed.). Glenview, IL: Scott, Foresman.

Tagiuri, R., & Litwin, G. H. (1968). *Organizational climate: Exploration of a concept.* Cambridge, MA: Harvard University Press.

Tajfel, H. (1969). Social and cultural factors in perception. In G. Lindzey & E. Aronson (Eds.), *Handbook of social psychology* (2nd ed.) (pp. 315-394). Reading, MA: Addison-Wesley.

Tannenbaum, S. I., Beard, R. L., & Salas, E. (1992). Team building and its influence on team effectiveness: An examination of conceptual and empirical developments. In K. Kelley (Ed.), *Issues, theory and research in industrial/organizational psychology.* Amsterdam: Elsevier.

Taylor, E., & Wherry, R. (1951). A study of leniency of two rating systems. *Personnel Psychology, 4,* 39-47.

Taylor, M. S., Fisher, C. D., & Ilgen, D. R. (1984). Individual reactions to performance feedback in organizations: A control theory perspective. In K. Rowland & G. Ferris (Eds.), *Research in personnel and human resources management* (Vol. 2). Greenwich, CT: JAI Press.

Taylor, S. E., & Fiske, S. T. (1978). Salience, attention, and attributions: Top of the head phenomena. In L. Berkowitz (Ed.), *Advances in experimental social psychology* (Vol. 11). New York: Academic Press.

Teasdale, J. D., & Fogarty, S. J. (1979). Differential effects of induced mood on retrieval of pleasant and unpleasant events from episodic memory. *Journal of Abnormal Psychology, 88,* 248-257.

Telecommuting. (1992, July 29). *Hearing before the subcommittee on telecommunications and finance. Committee on Energy and Commerce, House of Representatives.* Serial No. 102-149.

Terborg, J. R. (1981). Interactional psychology and research on human behavior in organizations. *Academy of Management Review, 6,* 569-576.

Tetlock, P. E. (1985a). Accountability: The neglected social context of judgment and choice. In B. Staw & L. Cummings (Eds.), *Research in organizational behavior* (Vol. 7, pp. 297-332). Greenwich, CT: JAI Press.

Tetlock, P. E. (1985b). Accountability: A social check on the fundamental attribution error. *Social Psychology Quarterly, 48,* 227-236.

Tetlock, P. E., & Boetteger, R. (1989). Accountability: A social magnifier of the dilution effect. *Journal of Personality and Social Psychology, 45,* 74-83.

Tetlock, P. E., & Kim, J. I. (1987). Accountability and judgment processes in a personality prediction task. *Journal of Personality and Social Psychology, 52,* 700-709.

Thibaut, J. W., & Kelly, H. H. (1959). *The social psychology of groups.* New York: John Wiley.

Thibaut, J., & Walker, L. (1975). *Procedural justice: A psychological analysis.* Hillsdale, NJ: Lawrence Erlbaum.

Thomas, R. (1991). *Beyond race and gender.* New York: Amacom.

Thompson, J. D. (1967). *Organizations in action.* New York: McGraw-Hill.

Thorndike, E. L. (1920). A constant error in psychological ratings. *Journal of Applied Psychology, 4,* 25-29.

Thorndike, R. L. (1949). *Personnel selection.* New York: John Wiley.

Thornton, G. C., III. (1980). Psychometric properties of self-appraisals of job performance. *Personnel Psychology, 33,* 263-271.

Thornton, G. C., III, & Zorich, S. (1980). Training to improve observer accuracy. *Journal of Applied Psychology, 65,* 351-354.

Tiffin, J., & McCormick, E. J. (1958). *Industrial psychology.* Englewood Cliffs, NJ: Prentice Hall.

Tjosvold, D. (1992). *Team organization: An enduring competitive edge.* New York: John Wiley.

Toffler, A. (1980). *The third wave.* New York: William Morrow.

Tolman, E. C. (1932). *Purposive behavior in men and animals.* New York: Appleton-Century-Crofts.

Tornow, W. W. (1993). Perceptions or reality: Is multiple-perspective measurement a means or an end? *Human Resource Management, 32,* 221-230.

Tsui, A. S., & Barry, B. (1986). Interpersonal affect and rating errors. *Academy of Management Journal, 29,* 586-599.

Tulving, E. (1974). Recall and recognition of semantically encoded words. *Journal of Experimental Psychology, 102,* 778-787.

Tulving, E. (1983). *Essentials of episodic memory.* New York: Oxford University Press.

Tulving, E., & Thompson, D. (1973). Encoding specificity and retrieval processes in episodic memory. *Psychological Review, 80,* 352-373.

Tversky, A. (1977). Features of similarity. *Psychological Review, 84,* 327-352.

Tversky, A., & Gati, I. (1978). Studies of similarity. In E. Rosch & B. Lloyd (Eds.), *Cognition and categorization.* Hillsdale, NJ: Lawrence Erlbaum.

Tversky, A., & Kahneman, D. (1974). Judgment under uncertainty: Heuristics and biases. *Science, 185,* 1124-1131.

Tziner, A., Latham, G. P., Prince, B. S., & Haccoun, R. (1994). *Development and validation of a questionnaire for measuring political considerations in performance appraisal.* Unpublished paper, University of Montreal.

Uniform Guidelines on Employee Selection Procedures. (1978). *Federal Register, 43*(166), 38209-38309.

Vance, R. J., Kuhnert, K. W., & Farr, J. L. (1978). Interview judgments: Using external criteria to compare behavioral and graphic scale ratings. *Organizational Behavior and Human Performance, 22,* 279-294.

Vance, R. J., MacCallum, R. C., Coovert, M. D., & Hedge, J. W. (1988). Construct validity of multiple job performance measures using conformatory factor analysis. *Journal of Applied Psychology, 73,* 74-80.

Vance, R. J., Winne, P. S., & Wright, E. S. (1983). A longitudinal examination of rater and ratee effects in performance ratings. *Personnel Psychology, 36,* 609-620.

Van Maanen, J. (1975). Police socialization. *Administrative Science Quarterly, 20,* 207-228.

Van Maanen, J. (1976). Breaking in: Socialization to work. In R. Dubin (Ed.), *Handbook of work, organization, and society.* Chicago: Rand McNally.

Van Maanen, J., & Schein, E. H. (1979). Toward a theory of organizational socialization. In B. Staw (Ed.), *Research in organizational behavior* (Vol. 1). Greenwich, CT: JAI Press.

Vecchio, R. P., & Gobdel, B. C. (1984). The vertical dyadic linkage mode of leadership: Problems and prospects. *Organizational Behavior and Human Performance, 34,* 5-20.

Villanova, P., & Bernardin, H. J. (1989). Impression management in the context of performance appraisal. In R. A. Giacalone & P. Rosenfeld (Eds.), *Impression management in the organization* (pp. 299-314). Hillsdale, NJ: Lawrence Erlbaum.

Vroom, V. (1964). *Work and motivation.* New York: John Wiley.

Vroom, V. (1969). Industrial social psychology. In G. Lindzey & E. Aronson (Eds.), *The handbook of social psychology* (2nd ed.). Reading, MA: Addison-Wesley.

Wachtel, P. L. (1973). Psychodynamics, behavior therapy, and the implacable experimenter: An inquiry into the consistency of personality. *Journal of Abnormal Psychology, 82,* 324-334.

Wagner, R. K. (1986). Tacit knowledge in everyday-intelligent behavior. *Journal of Personality and Social Psychology, 52,* 1236-1247.

Wainer, H. (1976). Estimating coefficients in linear models: It don't make no never mind. *Psychological Bulletin, 83,* 213-217.

Waldman, D. A., & Avolio, B. J. (1986). A meta analysis of age differences in job performance. *Journal of Applied Psychology, 71,* 33-38.

Waldman, D. A., & Avolio, B. J. (1991). Race effects in performance evaluations: Controlling for ability, education, and experience. *Journal of Applied Psychology, 76,* 897-901.

Waldman, D. A., Bass, B. M., & Einstein, W. O. (1987). Leadership and outcomes of performance appraisal process. *Journal of Occupational Psychology, 60,* 177-186.

Waldman, D. A., & Thornton, G. C., III. (1988). A field study of rating conditions and leniency in performance appraisal. *Psychological Reports, 63,* 835-840.

Wanous, J. P. (1980). *Organizational entry: Recruitment, selection, and socialization of newcomers.* Reading, MA: Addison-Wesley.

Ward, W. D., & Jenkins, J. (1965). The display of information and the judgment of contingency. *Canadian Journal of Psychology, 19,* 231-241.

Wardell, M. (1992). Changing organizational forms: From the bottom up. In M. Reed & H. Hughes (Eds.), *Rethinking organization: New directions in organization theory and analysis.* London: Sage.

Washington v. Davis, 12 FEP 1415 (1976).

Waterhouse, J. M., Folkard, S., & Minors, D. S. (1992). *Shiftwork, health and safety: An overview of the scientific literature 1978-1990.* London: HMSO.

Wayne, S. J., & Ferris, G. R. (1990). Influence tactic, affect, and exchange quality in supervisor-subordinate interactions: A laboratory experiment and field study. *Journal of Applied Psychology, 75,* 487-499.

Wayne, S. J., & Kacmar, K. M. (1991). The effects of impression management on the performance appraisal process. *Organizational Behavior and Human Decision Processes, 48,* 70-88.

Wayne, S. J., & Rubinstein, D. (1987, August). *The influence of subordinate impression management behaviors on supervisor performance appraisal and exchange quality.* Paper presented at the 47th annual meeting of the Academy of Management, New Orleans.

Webster, E. C. (1964). *Decision making in the employment interview.* Montreal: McGill University, Industrial Relations Center.

Webster, E. C. (1982). *The employment interview: A social judgment process.* Schomberg, Ontario: SIP Publications.

Wegner, D., & Vallecher, R. (1977). *Implicit psychology.* New York: Oxford University Press.

Weick, K. (1977). Enactment processes in organizations. In B. Staw & G. Salancik (Eds.), *New directions in organizational behavior.* Chicago: St. Claire Press.

Weiss, H. M. (1978). Social learning of work values in organizations. *Journal of Applied Psychology, 63,* 711-718.

Wellins, R. S., Byham, W. C., & Wilson, J. M. (1991). *Empowered teams.* San Francisco: Jossey-Bass.

Wendelken, D., & Inn, A. (1981). Nonperformance influences on performance evaluations: A laboratory phenomenon? *Journal of Applied Psychology, 66,* 752-758.

Wexley, K. N. (1987). Discussant remarks in symposium chaired by K. R. Murphy. *Cognitive research in performance appraisal: Prospects for application.* New York: American Psychological Association.

Wexley, K. N., & Klimoski, R. (1984). Performance appraisal: An update. In K. Rowland & G. Ferris (Eds.), *Research in personnel and human resources* (Vol. 2). Greenwich, CT: JAI Press.

Wexley, K. N., & Youtz, M. A. (1985). Rater beliefs about others: Their effects on rating errors and rater accuracy. *Journal of Occupational Psychology, 58,* 265-275.

Wherry, R. J., & Bartlett, C. J. (1982). The control of bias in ratings: A theory of rating. *Personnel Psychology, 35,* 521-555.

Whetten, D. A. (1987). Organizational growth and decline processes. *Annual Review of Sociology, 13,* 335-358.

Whetten, D. A., & Cameron, K. S. (1983). *Organizational effectiveness: A comparison of multiple models.* New York: Academic Press.

Whipp, R. (1992). Human resource management, competition and strategy: Some productive tensions. In P. Blyton & P. Turnbull (Eds.), *Reassessing human resource management* (pp. 33-55). London: Sage.

Whisler, T. L. (1958). Performance appraisal and the organizational man. *Journal of Business, 31,* 19-27.

Whisler, T. L., & Harper, S. F. (Eds.). (1962). *Performance appraisal: Research and practice.* New York: Holt, Rinehart & Winston.

Whitaker, A. (1992). The transformation in work: Post-Fordism revisited. In M. Reed & H. Hughes (Eds.), *Rethinking organization: New directions in organization theory and analysis.* London: Sage.

Whitley, R. (1992). The social construction of organizations and markets: The constructive analysis of business recipes. In M. Reed & H. Hughes (Eds.), *Rethinking organization: New directions in organization theory and analysis.* London: Sage.

Whyte, W. (1955). *Money and motivation.* New York: Harper & Row.

Wigdor, A., & Garner, W. (1982). *Ability testing: Uses, consequences, and controversies: Part I.* Washington, DC: National Academy Press.

Wigdor, A. K., & Green, B. F. (1991). *Performance assessment in the workplace.* Washington, DC: National Academy Press.

Wiggins, J. S. (1973). *Personality and prediction: Principles of personality measurement.* Reading, MA: Addison-Wesley.

Williams, J. R., & Levy, P. E. (1992). The effects of perceived system knowledge on the agreement between self-ratings and supervisor ratings. *Personnel Psychology, 45,* 835-847.

Williams, K. J., Allinger, G. M., & Pulliam, R. (1988, April). *Rater affect and performance ratings: Evidence for the moderating effects of rater perceptions.* Paper presented at the annual convention of the Society for Industrial and Organizational Psychology, Dallas.

Williams, K. J., DeNisi, A. S., Blencoe, A. G., & Cafferty, T. P. (1985). The role of appraisal purpose: Effects of purpose on information acquisition and utilization. *Organizational Behavior and Human Performance, 35,* 314-339.

Williams, K. J., DeNisi, A. S., Meglino, B. M., & Cafferty, T. P. (1986). Initial decisions and subsequent performance ratings. *Journal of Applied Psychology, 71,* 189-195.

Williams, K. J., & Keating, C. W. (1987, April). *Affect and the processing of performance appraisal.* Paper presented at the annual convention of the Society for Industrial and Organizational Psychology, Atlanta.

Woodward, J. (1965). *Industrial organization: Theory and practice.* London: Oxford University Press.

Wright, P. (1974). The harassed decision-maker: Time pressures, distraction and use of evidence. *Journal of Applied Psychology, 59,* 555-561.

Wyer, J. C. (1988). A stochastic, psychometric valuation model for personnel selection systems. *Decision Sciences, 19,* 700-707.

Wyer, R. S. (1976). An investigation of the relations among probability estimates. *Organizational Behavior and Human Performance, 15,* 1-8.

Wyer, R. S., Jr., & Srull, T. K. (1986). Category accessibility: Some theoretical and empirical issues concerning the processing of social stimulus information. In E. T. Higgins, C. P. Herman, & M. P. Zanna (Eds.), *Social cognition: The Ontario Symposium on Personality and Social Psychology.* Hillsdale, NJ: Lawrence Erlbaum.

Yammarino, F. J., & Atwater, L. E. (1993). Understanding self-perception accuracy: Implications for human resource management. *Human Resource Management, 32,* 231-248.

Yammarino, F. J., Dubinsky, A. J., & Hartley, S. W. (1987). An approach for assessing individual versus group effects in performance evaluations. *Journal of Occupational Psychology, 60,* 157-167.

Yasai-Adekani, M. (1986). Structural adaptations to environments. *Academy of Management Review, 11,* 9-21.

Yu, J., & Murphy, K. (1993). Modesty bias in self ratings of performance: A test of the cultural relativity hypothesis. *Personnel Psychology, 46,* 357-363.

Yukl, G. (1982, April). *Innovations in research on leader behavior.* Paper presented at the annual meeting of the Eastern Academy of Management, Baltimore.

Yukl, G. A., & Latham, G. P. (1975). Consequences of reinforcement schedules and incentive magnitudes for employee performance: Problems encountered in an industrial setting. *Journal of Applied Psychology, 60,* 294-298.

Zajonc, R. B. (1980). Feeling and thinking: Preferences need no inferences. *American Psychologist, 35,* 151-175.

Zald, M. N. (1962). Power balance and stall conflict in correctional institutions. *Administrative Science Quarterly, 7,* 22-49.

Zaleznik, A., Christensen, C. R., & Roethlisberger, F. J. (1958). *The motivation, productivity, and satisfaction of workers: A production study.* Cambridge, MA: Harvard University Press.

Zand, D. E. (1981). *Information, organization and power: Effective management in the knowledge society.* New York: McGraw-Hill.

Zavala, A. (1965). Development of the forced-choice rating scale technique. *Psychological Bulletin, 63,* 117-124.

Zedeck, S., & Cascio, W. F. (1982). Performance appraisal decisions as a function of rater training and purpose of the appraisal. *Journal of Applied Psychology, 67,* 752-758.

Zohar, D. (1980). Safety climate in industrial organizations: Theoretical and applied implications. *Journal of Applied Psychology, 65,* 96-102.

Author Index

Subject Index

Absenteeism, 6-7
Accidents, 7
Accuracy. *See* Rating accuracy
Action theory, 217
Affect:
    and cognition, 212-213
    role in appraisal, 211-213
Anchoring and adjustment, 179-180
Assimilation effects, 202-203
Attribution theory, 130-131, 237-238,
    250
Automatic vs. controlled processing, 188,
    192-193

Behavior diaries, 126, 199-200
Business strategy, 354-355

Categorization, 189-191, 193-194
Climate. *See* Organizational climate
Cognitive complexity, 207
Cognitive processes, 14-15, 183-186,
    412-415
Computerized monitoring, 51-52
Construct validity, 273-275
Context, 19-22, 31-31
    assessment of, 65-66, 410
    classification, 62-65
    defined, 58-62, 407
    effects on performance appraisal, 409
    distal, 20, 230-231, 410
    group characteristics, 68-70
    perceived, 60
    proximal, 20, 228-230, 410
    technological, 407-408

About the Authors

Kevin R. Murphy is Professor of Psychology at Colorado State University. He received his B.A. (1974) from Siena College, his M.S. (1976) from Rensselaer Polytechnic University, and his Ph.D. (1979) from the Pennsylvania State University, all in psychology. Murphy serves as Associate Editor of the *Journal of Applied Psychology* and serves as a member of the editorial boards of *Personnel Psychology, Human Performance,* and *International Journal of Selection and Assessment.* He is the author of more than 50 articles and book chapters, and author or editor of four books, *Psychological Testing: Principles and Applications* (with C. Davidshofer), *Psychology in Organizations: Integrating Science and Practice* (with F. Saal), *Performance Appraisal: An Organizational Perspective* (with J. Cleveland), and *Honesty in the Workplace.* In addition to performance appraisal, his area of research includes personnel selection and assessment and honesty in the workplace.

Jeanette N. Cleveland is Professor of Psychology at Colorado State University. She received her B.A. (1977) from Occidental College and her M.S. (1979) and Ph.D. (1982) from the Pennsylvania State University, all in psychology. Cleveland serves on the editorial boards of *Academy of Management Journal* and *Journal of Vocational Behavior*. She is the author of more than 30 articles and book chapters, and is author or editor of three books, *Performance Measurement and Theory* (with F. Landy & S. Zedeck), *Performance Appraisal: An Organizational Perspective* (with K. Murphy), and *Women and Men in Organizations: Sex and Gender Issues* (with M. Stockdale & F. Saal). In addition to performance appraisal, her areas of research include the roles of age and gender in the workplace.